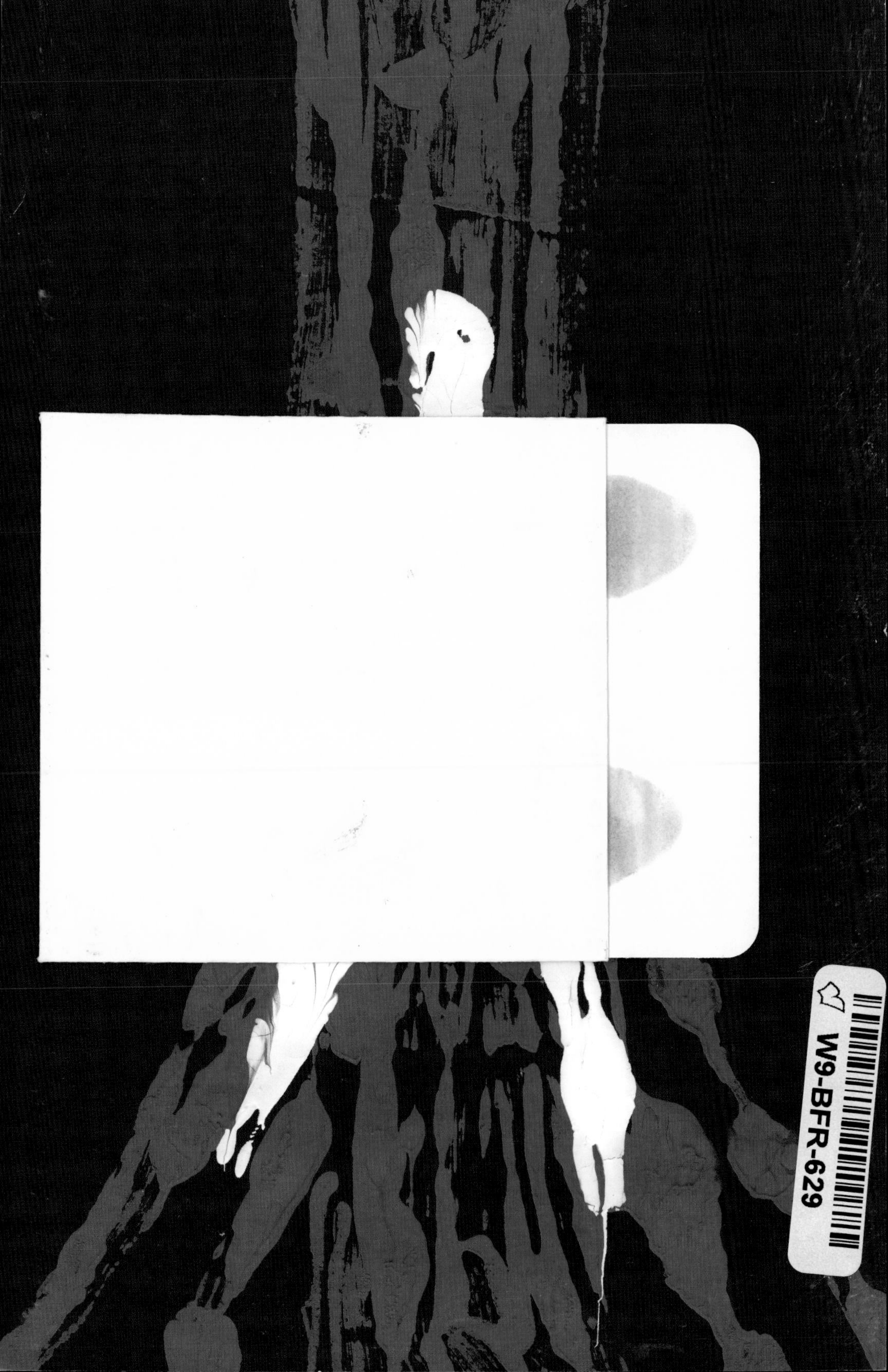

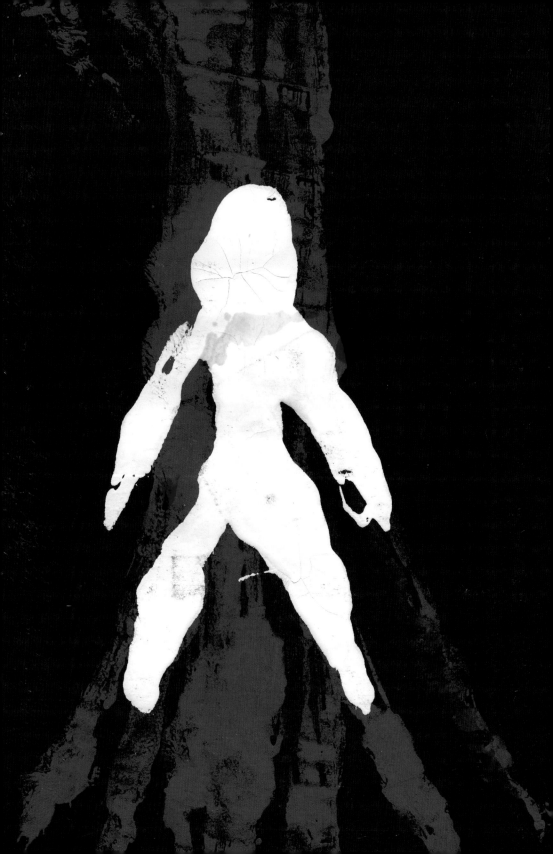

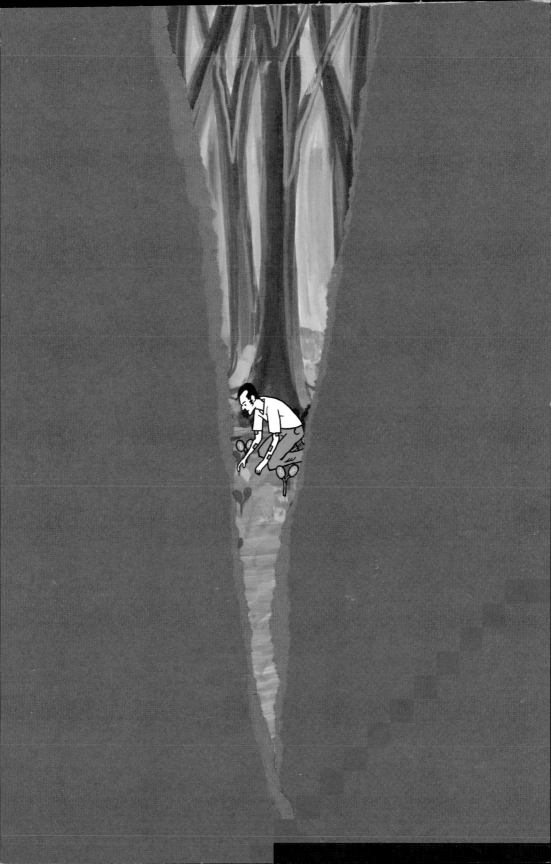

DARTH SHAW
DRAWN
MID 2007→ MID 2009
RICHMOND, VA → BROOKLYN, NY
WEBCOMIC → DEAD TREE COMIC
PANTHEON BOOKS, NY
PANTHEON COMIX HOUSE STYLE

THIS IS A WORK OF FICTION. NAMES, CHARACTERS, PLACES AND INCIDENTS EITHER ARE THE PRODUCT OF THE AUTHOR'S IMAGINATION OR ARE USED FICTITIOUSLY. ANY RESEMBLANCE TO ACTUAL PERSONS, LIVING OR DEAD, EVENTS OR LOCALES IS ENTIRELY COINCIDENTAL.

 PUBLISHED IN THE UNITED STATES BY PANTHEON BOOKS, A DIVISION OF RANDOM HOUSE, INC., NEW YORK, AND IN CANADA BY RANDOM HOUSE OF CANADA LIMITED, TORONTO. PANTHEON BOOKS AND COLOPHON ARE REGISTERED TRADEMARKS OF RANDOM HOUSE, INC. THIS BOOK IS FOR "IDEAL READERS" ONLY!!!

PORTIONS OF THIS WORK ORIGINALLY APPEARED, IN SLIGHTLY DIFFERENT FORM, ON WWW.DASHSHAW.COM. TWELVE CHAPTERS. PLEASE READ IN BED NAKED.

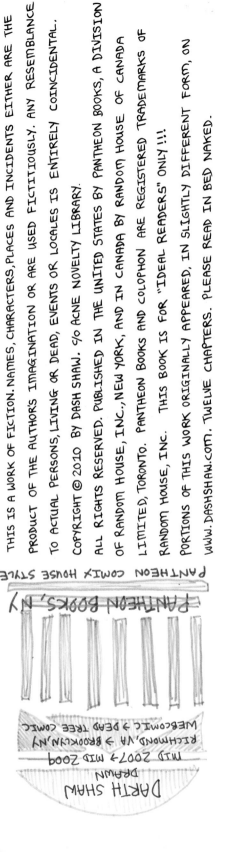

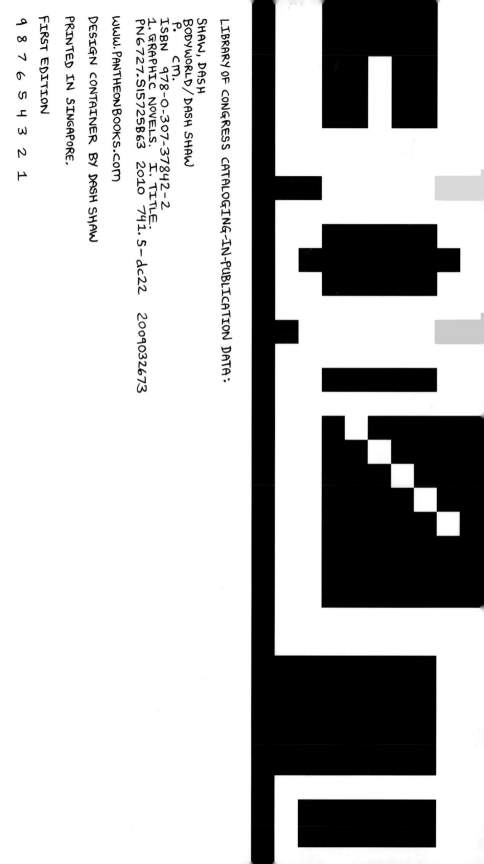

LIBRARY OF CONGRESS CATALOGING-IN-PUBLICATION DATA:

SHAW, DASH
BODYWORLD / DASH SHAW
P. CM.
ISBN 978-0-307-37842-2
1. GRAPHIC NOVELS. I. TITLE.
PN6727.S15725B63 2010 741.5—dc22 2009032673

WWW.PANTHEONBOOKS.COM

DESIGN CONTAINER BY DASH SHAW

PRINTED IN SINGAPORE.

FIRST EDITION

9 8 7 6 5 4 3 2 1

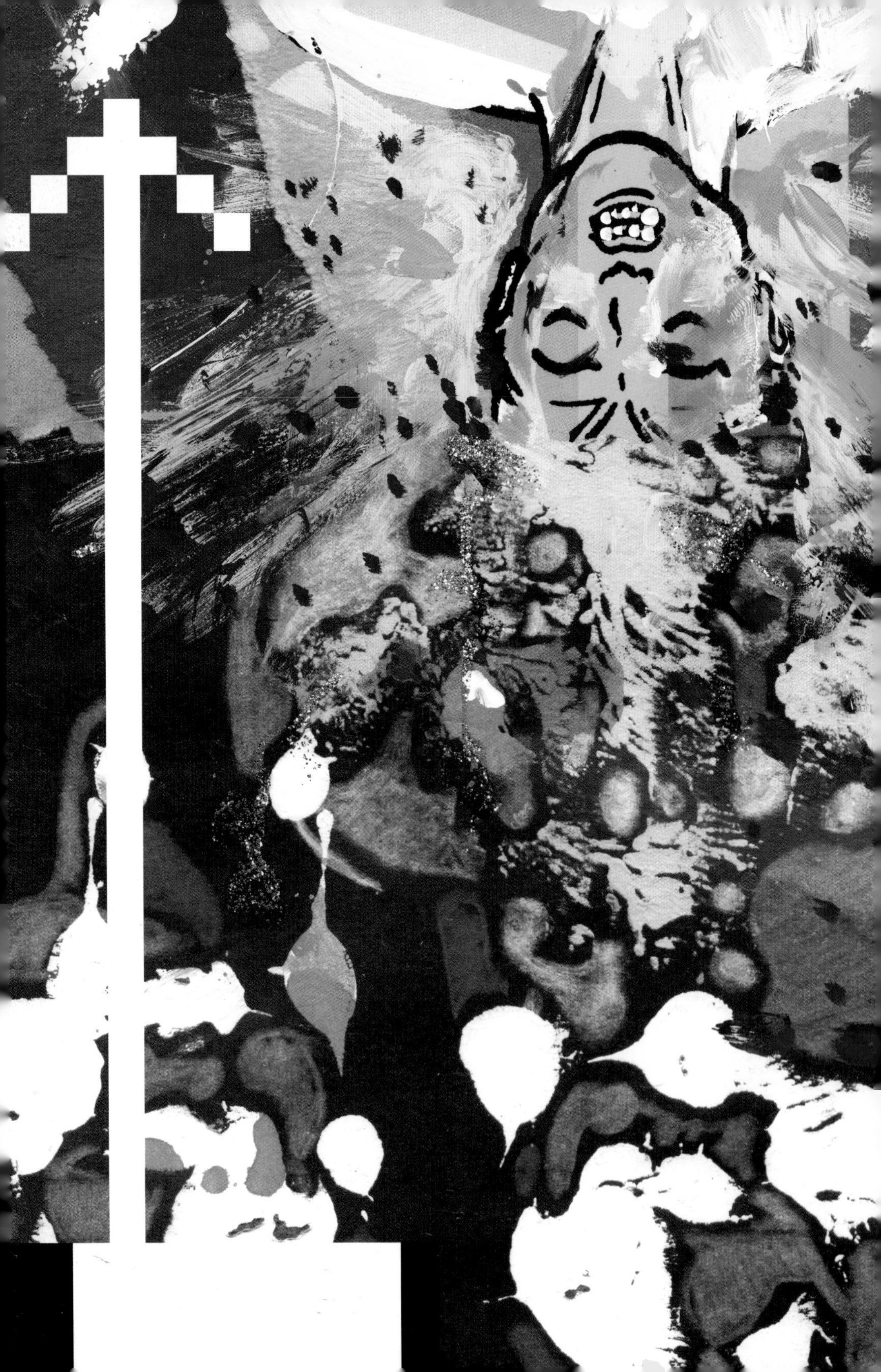

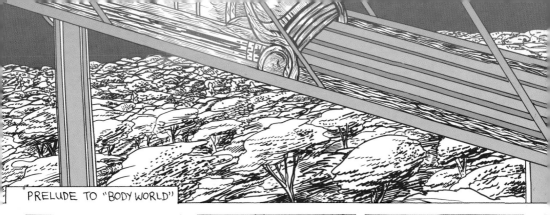

PRELUDE TO "BODY WORLD"

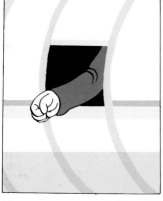

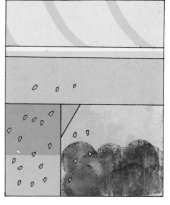

MAY I HAVE THIS SEAT?

WHATEVER.

THANK YOU.

I'VE NEVER DETECTED YOU IN BONEY BOROUGH. ARE YOU GOING HOME?

I'M HERE ON BUSINESS.

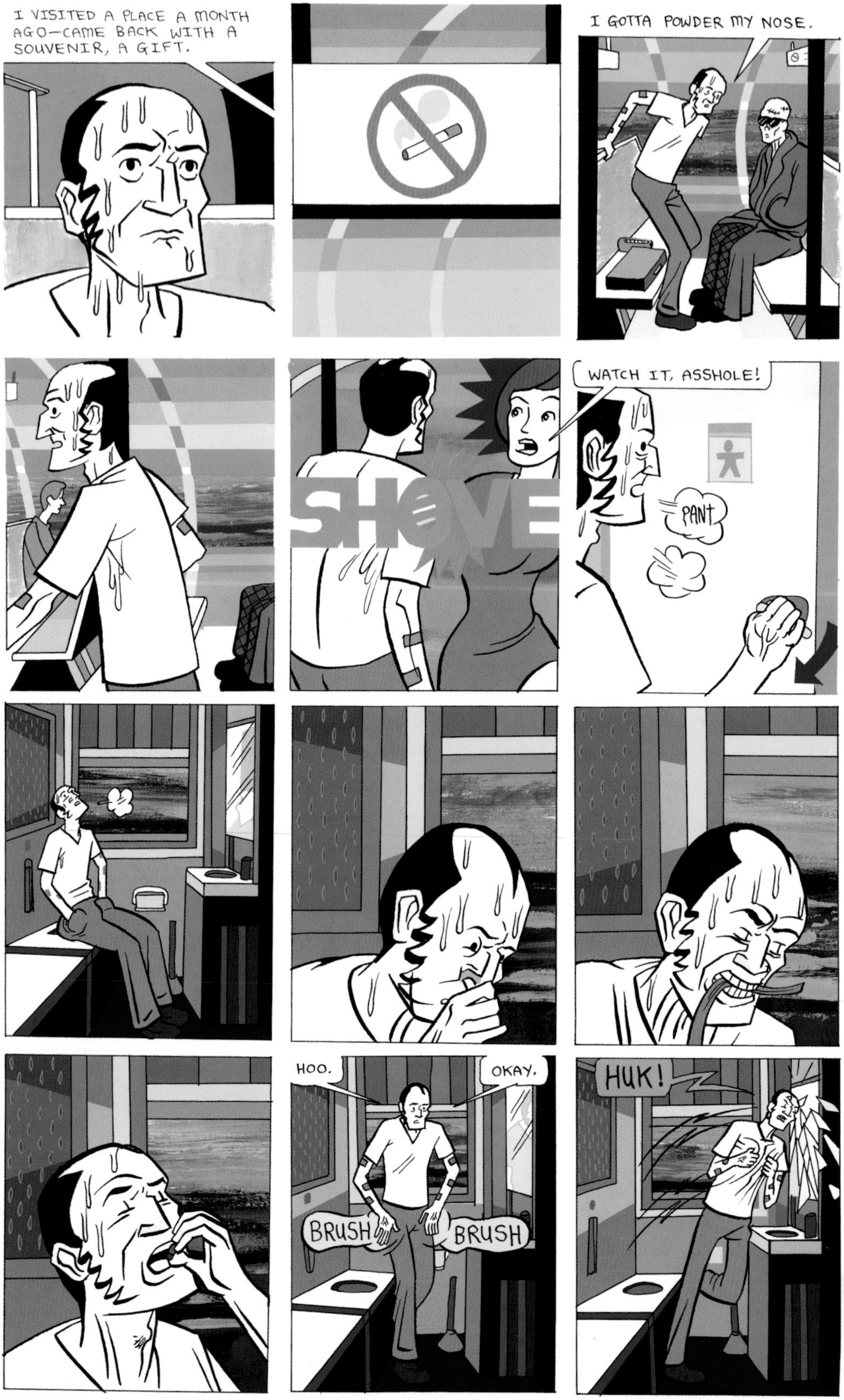
I VISITED A PLACE A MONTH AGO—CAME BACK WITH A SOUVENIR, A GIFT.
I GOTTA POWDER MY NOSE.
SHOVE
WATCH IT, ASSHOLE!
PANT
HOO.
OKAY.
BRUSH
BRUSH
HUK!

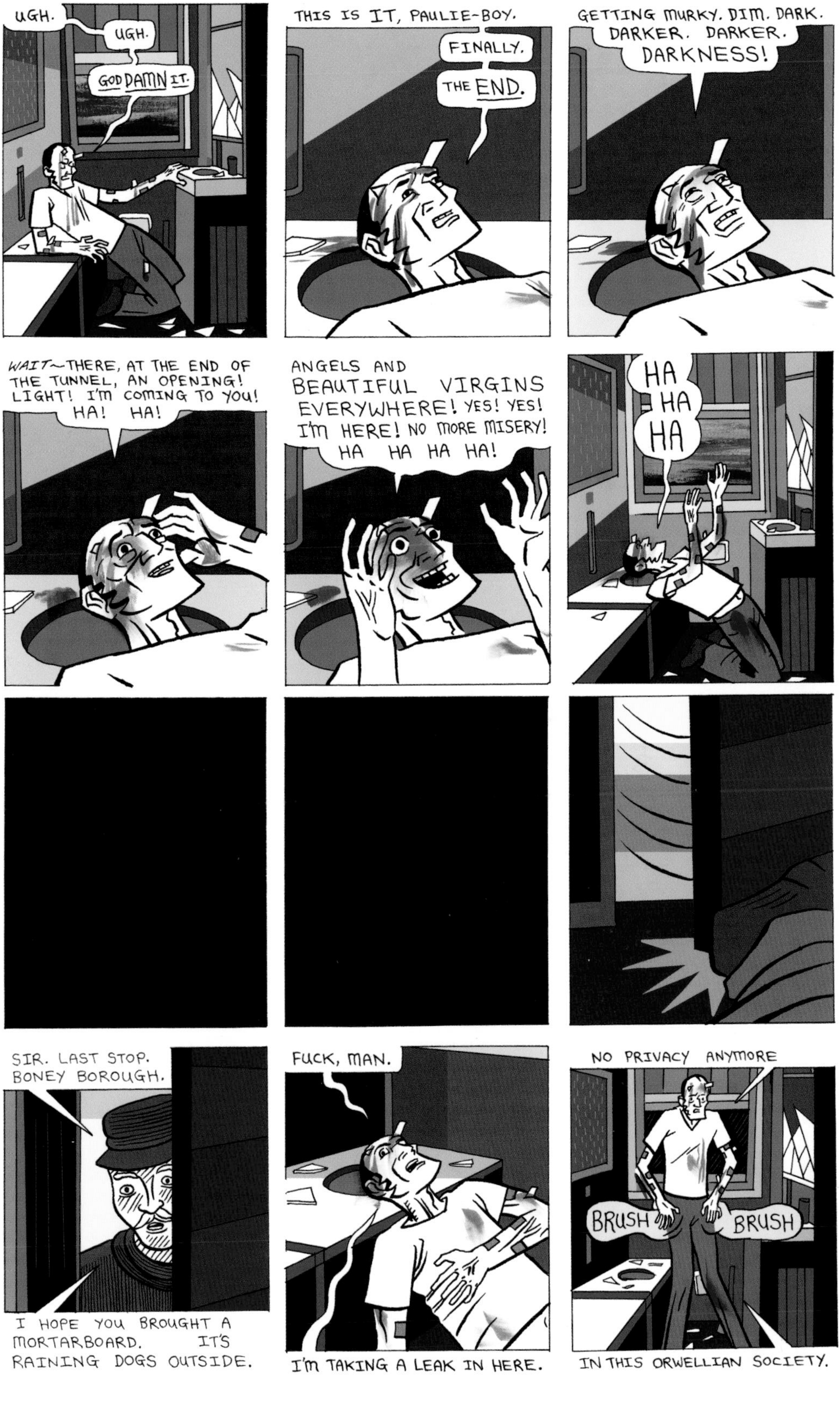
UGH.
UGH.
GOD DAMN IT.
THIS IS IT, PAULIE-BOY.
FINALLY.
THE END.
GETTING MURKY. DIM. DARK. DARKER. DARKER. DARKNESS!
WAIT~THERE, AT THE END OF THE TUNNEL, AN OPENING! LIGHT! I'M COMING TO YOU! HA! HA!
ANGELS AND BEAUTIFUL VIRGINS EVERYWHERE! YES! YES! I'M HERE! NO MORE MISERY! HA HA HA HA!
HA HA HA
SIR. LAST STOP. BONEY BOROUGH.
I HOPE YOU BROUGHT A MORTARBOARD. IT'S RAINING DOGS OUTSIDE.
FUCK, MAN.
I'M TAKING A LEAK IN HERE.
NO PRIVACY ANYMORE
BRUSH
BRUSH
IN THIS ORWELLIAN SOCIETY.

29 R

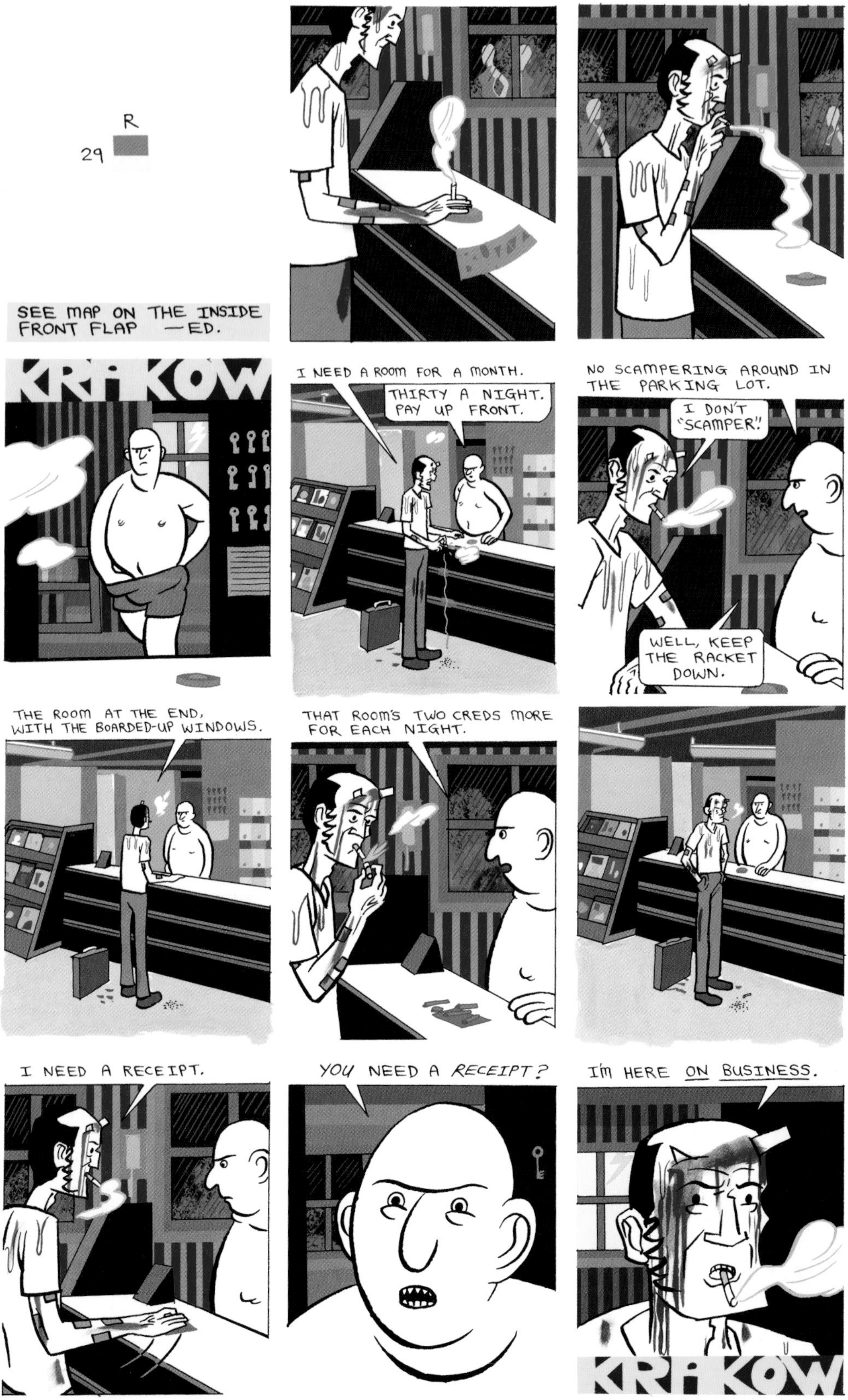
SEE MAP ON THE INSIDE FRONT FLAP —ED.
KRAKOW
I NEED A ROOM FOR A MONTH.
THIRTY A NIGHT. PAY UP FRONT.
NO SCAMPERING AROUND IN THE PARKING LOT.
I DON'T "SCAMPER."
WELL, KEEP THE RACKET DOWN.
THE ROOM AT THE END, WITH THE BOARDED-UP WINDOWS.
THAT ROOM'S TWO CREDS MORE FOR EACH NIGHT.
I NEED A RECEIPT.
YOU NEED A RECEIPT?
I'M HERE ON BUSINESS.
KRAKOW

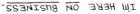

PARKING'S FIVE CREDS. WE HAVE CONDOMS AT THE FRONT DESK.

RAIN HITTING PAVEMENT

ALL KINDS.

CLEAN SHEETS'R AT THE FRONT DESK. IF YOU LOSE THE KEY, YOU PAY FOR IT.

KRAKOW

BOOB TUBE DOESN'T WORK.

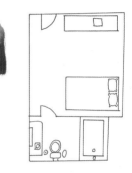

DOES THIS WORK?

UH-HUH.

SO THIS WORKS TOO?

TAP

YEAH.

PERFECT.

REMEMBER WHAT I SAID ABOUT THE KEY.

CONTENTS OF BRIEFCASE:
TOILETRIES
ELECTRIC TOOTHBRUSH (UNUSED)
TOOTHPICKS
FACIAL TISSUES
OXY PADS
DEODORANT
TOOTH PASTE
BOTTLES OF MISC. PILLS
SHAVING KIT
THREE STIGMATA OF PALMER ELDRITCH P.K.D.
ALAN MOORE'S THE COURT YARD
AVATAR
BOOKS ON CRYSTAL
"THE PSYCHEDELIC EXPERIENCE" DR. TIMOTHY LEARY
"SELECTED GUIDELINES FOR ETHNOBOTANICAL RESEARCH" DR. MIGUEL ALEXIADES
"PLANT TAXONOMY AND BIOSYSTEMATICS" CLIVE STACE
"GOLDEN GUIDE TO HALLUCINOGENIC PLANTS" RICHARD SHULTES
ALSO: PRINT POSTERS, BOOKS
WORK STATION
LAPTOP
PORTABLE HARD DRIVE
3-D SCANNER
DEHYDRATOR
GRINDER
MICROSCOPE, SLIDES
MOLECULAR SCANNER
BRAIN ACTIVITY PLUGS
2060 POT SMOKER
CALENDER
"POT SMOKER" 2060 MONTHLY
"DILBERT" 2058 DAILY
COUGH
COUGH COUGH
COUGH-
NNN~
PANT PANT

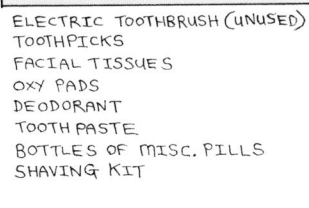

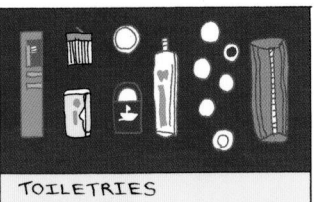

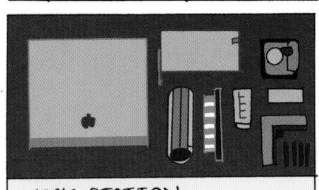

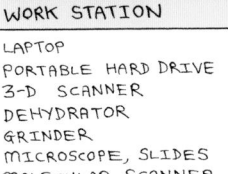

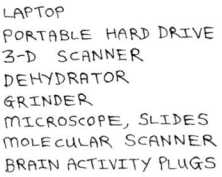

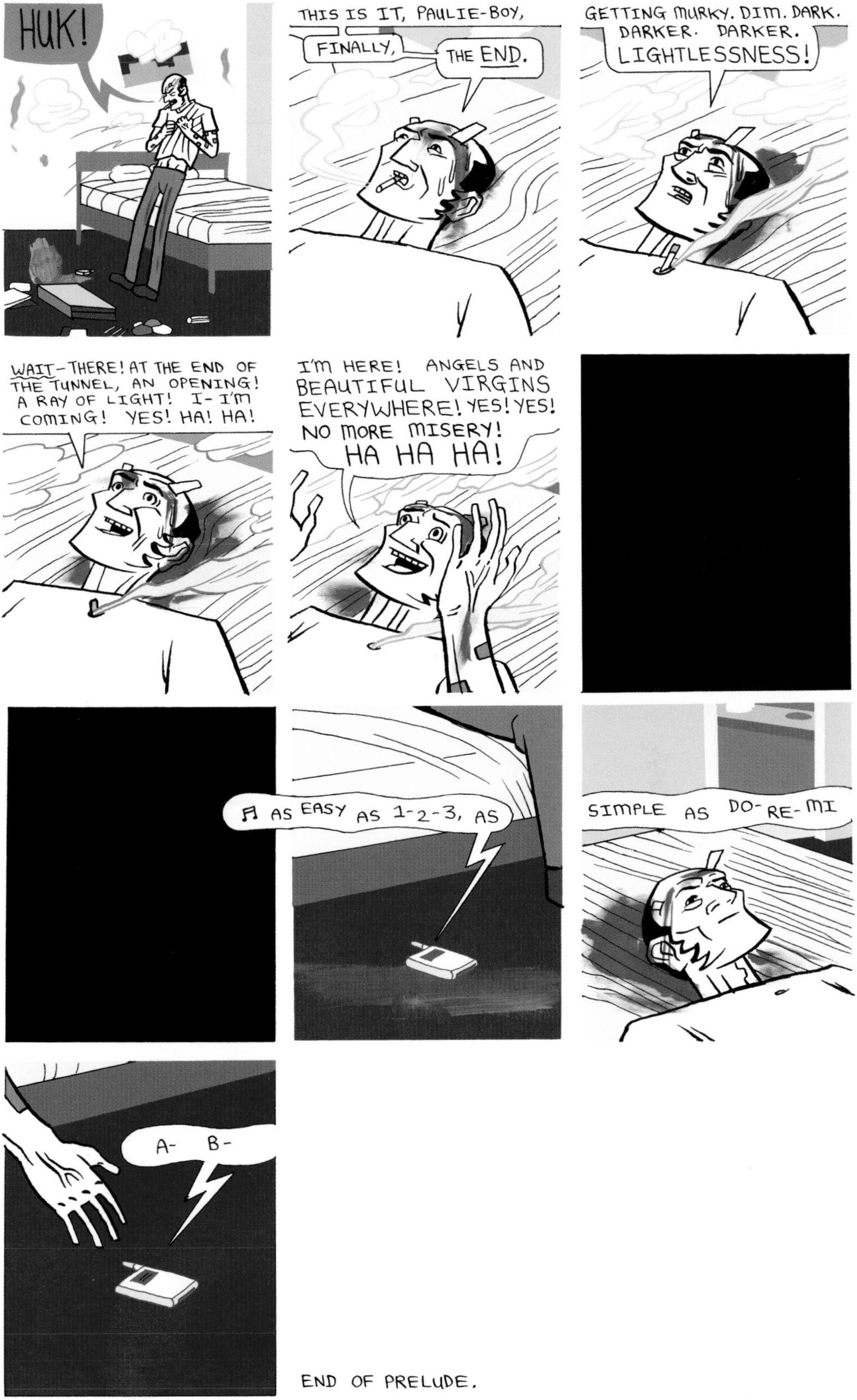
HUK!
THIS IS IT, PAULIE-BOY,
FINALLY,
THE END.
GETTING MURKY. DIM. DARK. DARKER. DARKER. LIGHTLESSNESS!
WAIT- THERE! AT THE END OF THE TUNNEL, AN OPENING! A RAY OF LIGHT! I- I'M COMING! YES! HA! HA!
I'M HERE! ANGELS AND BEAUTIFUL VIRGINS EVERYWHERE! YES! YES! NO MORE MISERY! HA HA HA!
♬ AS EASY AS 1-2-3, AS
SIMPLE AS DO-RE-MI
A- B-

END OF PRELUDE.

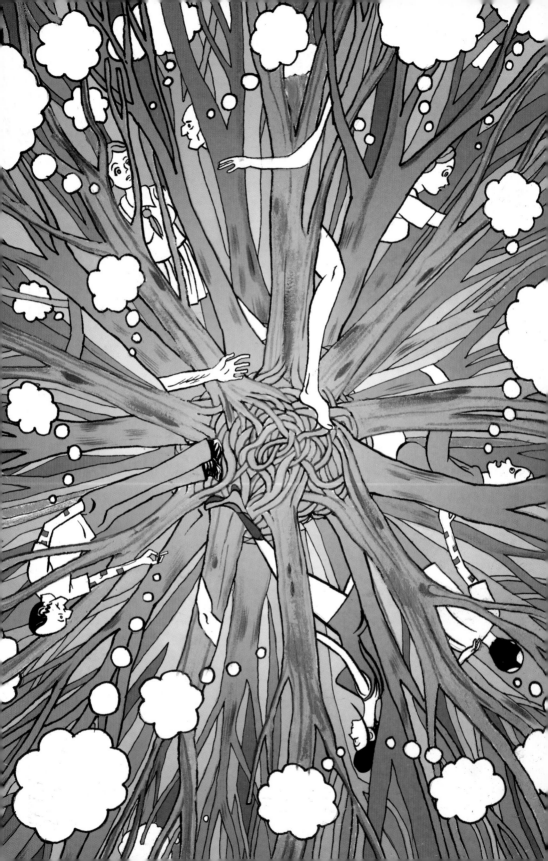

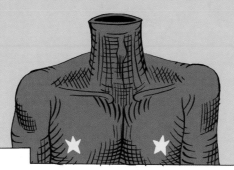

CHAPTER ONE

X
25

I'M EIGHTEEN, MOM! EIGHT—TEEN! AN ADULT.

IF I DON'T WANT TO GO TO SCHOOL ONE DAY, I SHOULDN'T HAVE TO! ADULTS MAKE THEIR OWN DECISIONS!

I PACKED YOUR LUNCH.

AGGH! I HATE IT HERE!

EVERYONE AT SCHOOL IS SO IMMATURE! THEY THINK BONEY BOROUGH IS THE WHOLE WORLD!

THEY THINK SCHOOL IS THE ENTIRE UNIVERSE!

"PB & J" AND A JUICY JUICE.

KISS

I CAN'T WAIT TILL I HAVE KIDS! I'LL LET THEM DO WHATEVER THEY WANT! THEN YOU'LL SEE!!!

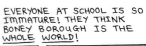

PROFESSOR PANTHER?

MISS JEWEL?

SHAKE

YOU CAN'T SMOKE ON SCHOOL PROPERTY.

ARE YOU SERIOUS? WHAT KIND OF SCHOOL IS THIS?

TAP

"K" THROUGH TWELVE.

aRRGG

WHAT ARE YOU LOOKING FOR?

PSSSS

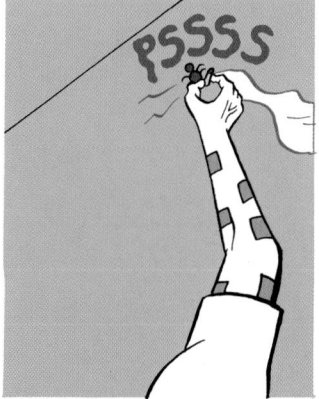

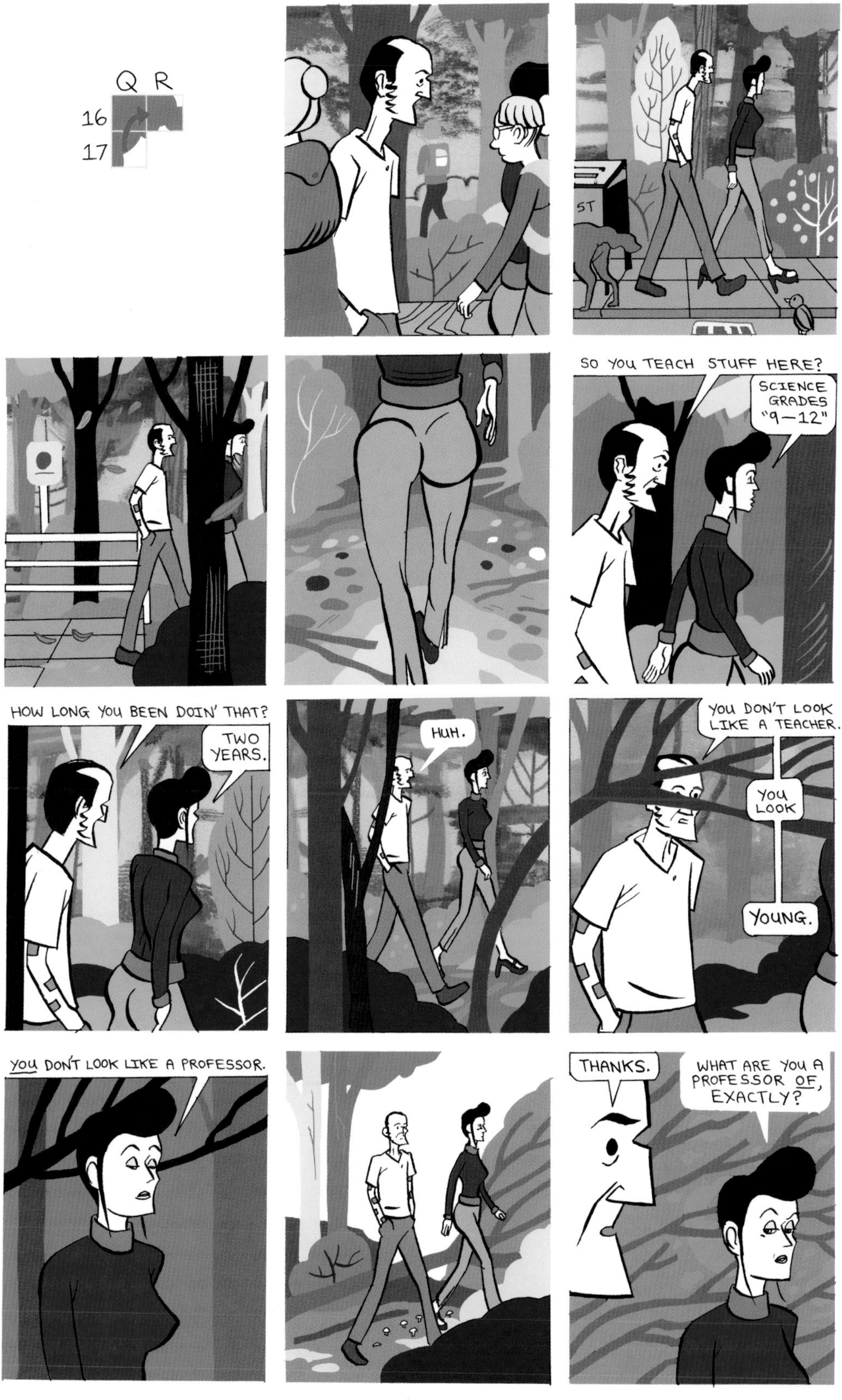
Q R
16
17
SO YOU TEACH STUFF HERE?
SCIENCE GRADES "9—12"
HOW LONG YOU BEEN DOIN' THAT?
TWO YEARS.
HUH.
YOU DON'T LOOK LIKE A TEACHER.
YOU LOOK
YOUNG.
YOU DON'T LOOK LIKE A PROFESSOR.
THANKS.
WHAT ARE YOU A PROFESSOR OF, EXACTLY?

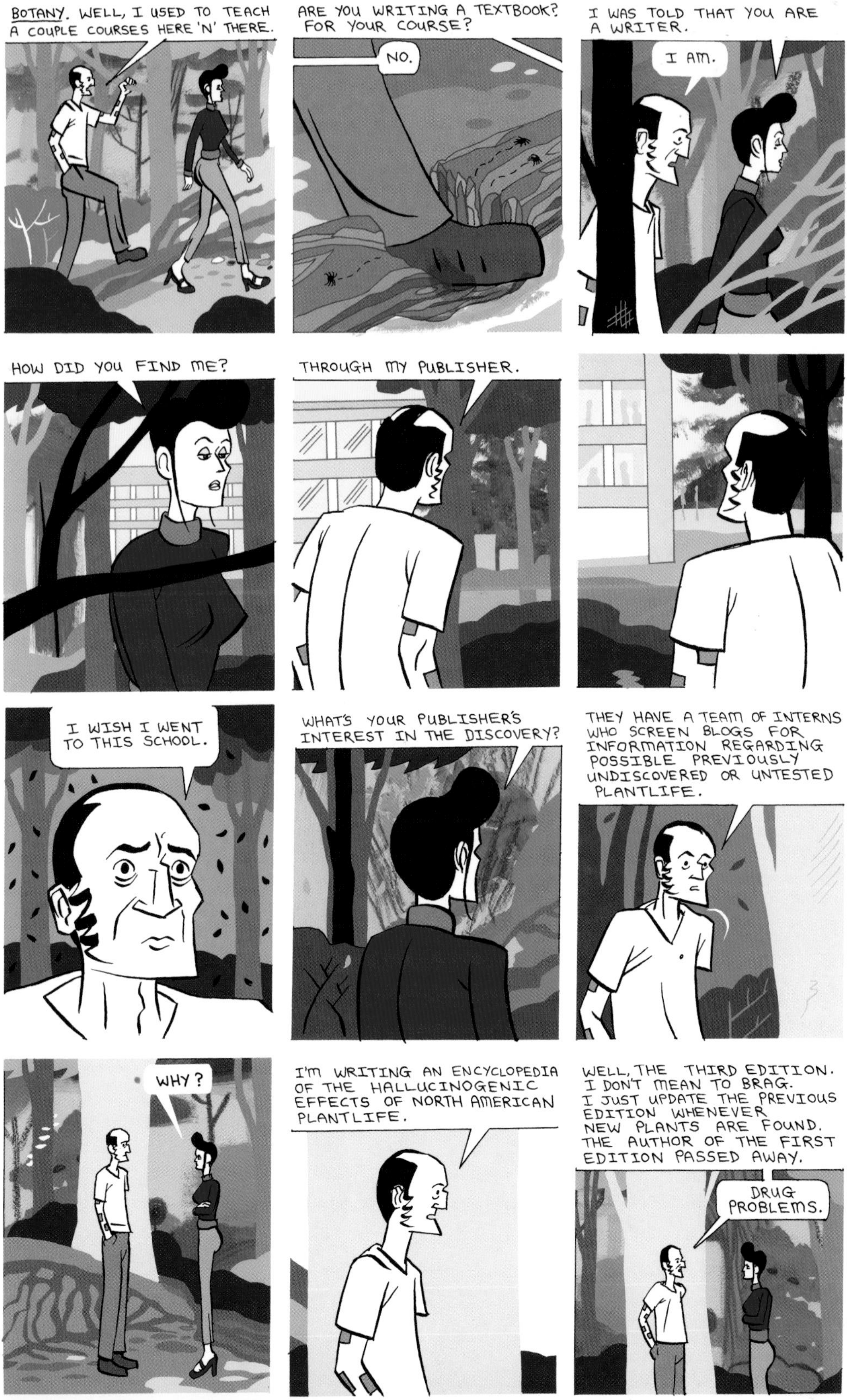
BOTANY. WELL, I USED TO TEACH A COUPLE COURSES HERE 'N' THERE.
ARE YOU WRITING A TEXTBOOK? FOR YOUR COURSE?
NO.
I WAS TOLD THAT YOU ARE A WRITER.
I AM.
HOW DID YOU FIND ME?
THROUGH MY PUBLISHER.
I WISH I WENT TO THIS SCHOOL.
WHAT'S YOUR PUBLISHER'S INTEREST IN THE DISCOVERY?
THEY HAVE A TEAM OF INTERNS WHO SCREEN BLOGS FOR INFORMATION REGARDING POSSIBLE PREVIOUSLY UNDISCOVERED OR UNTESTED PLANTLIFE.
WHY?
I'M WRITING AN ENCYCLOPEDIA OF THE HALLUCINOGENIC EFFECTS OF NORTH AMERICAN PLANTLIFE.
WELL, THE THIRD EDITION. I DON'T MEAN TO BRAG. I JUST UPDATE THE PREVIOUS EDITION WHENEVER NEW PLANTS ARE FOUND. THE AUTHOR OF THE FIRST EDITION PASSED AWAY.
DRUG PROBLEMS.

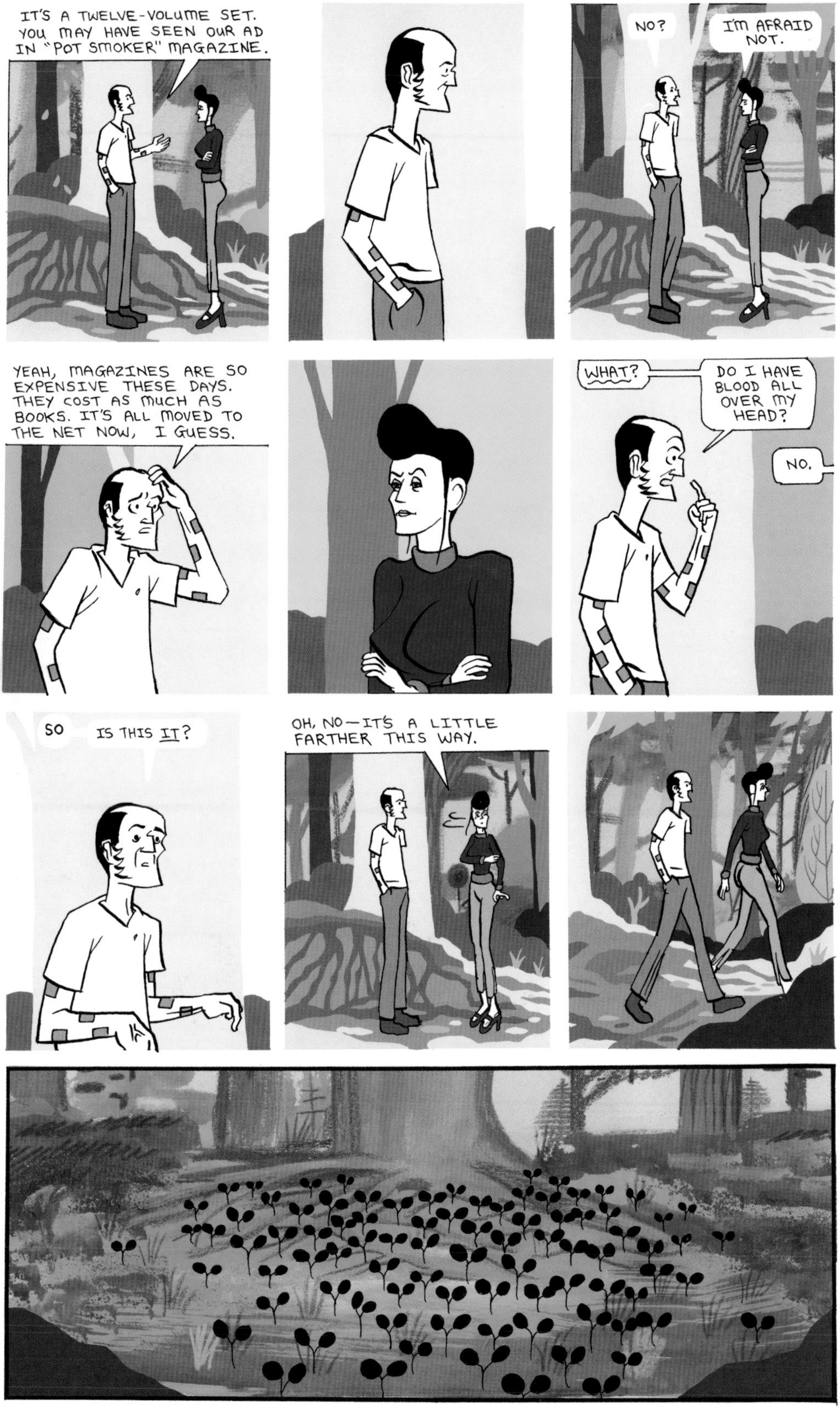

IT'S A TWELVE-VOLUME SET. YOU MAY HAVE SEEN OUR AD IN "POT SMOKER" MAGAZINE.
NO?
I'M AFRAID NOT.
YEAH, MAGAZINES ARE SO EXPENSIVE THESE DAYS. THEY COST AS MUCH AS BOOKS. IT'S ALL MOVED TO THE NET NOW, I GUESS.
WHAT?
DO I HAVE BLOOD ALL OVER MY HEAD?
NO.
SO
IS THIS IT?
OH, NO—IT'S A LITTLE FARTHER THIS WAY.

PLUCK
WHEN DID YOU FIND THIS?
A VISITING ARCOLOGY STUDENT CAME ACROSS IT A MONTH AGO.
HE NOTIFIED THE SCHOOL.
THE SCHOOL TOLD ME ABOUT TWO WEEKS AGO. I TOOK A CLASS OUT HERE TO TAKE SAMPLES. GET THEM OUT OF THE CLASSROOM.
ONE OF THE STUDENTS MUST HAVE BLOGGED ABOUT IT.
I DON'T HAVE A BLOG.
I LIKE TO KEEP MY SECRETS.
UH-HUH.

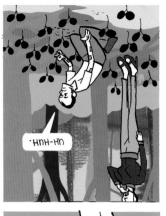

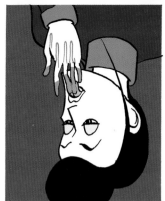

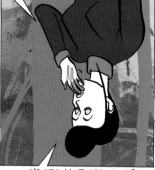

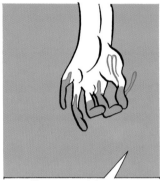

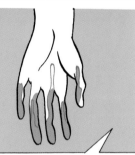

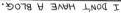

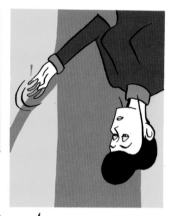

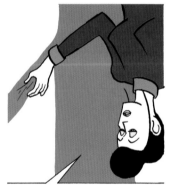

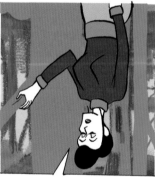

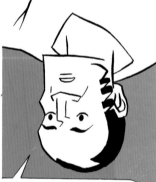

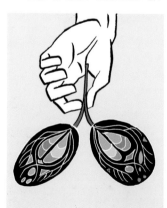

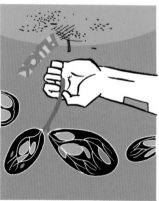

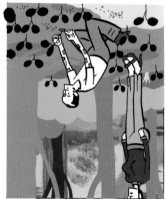

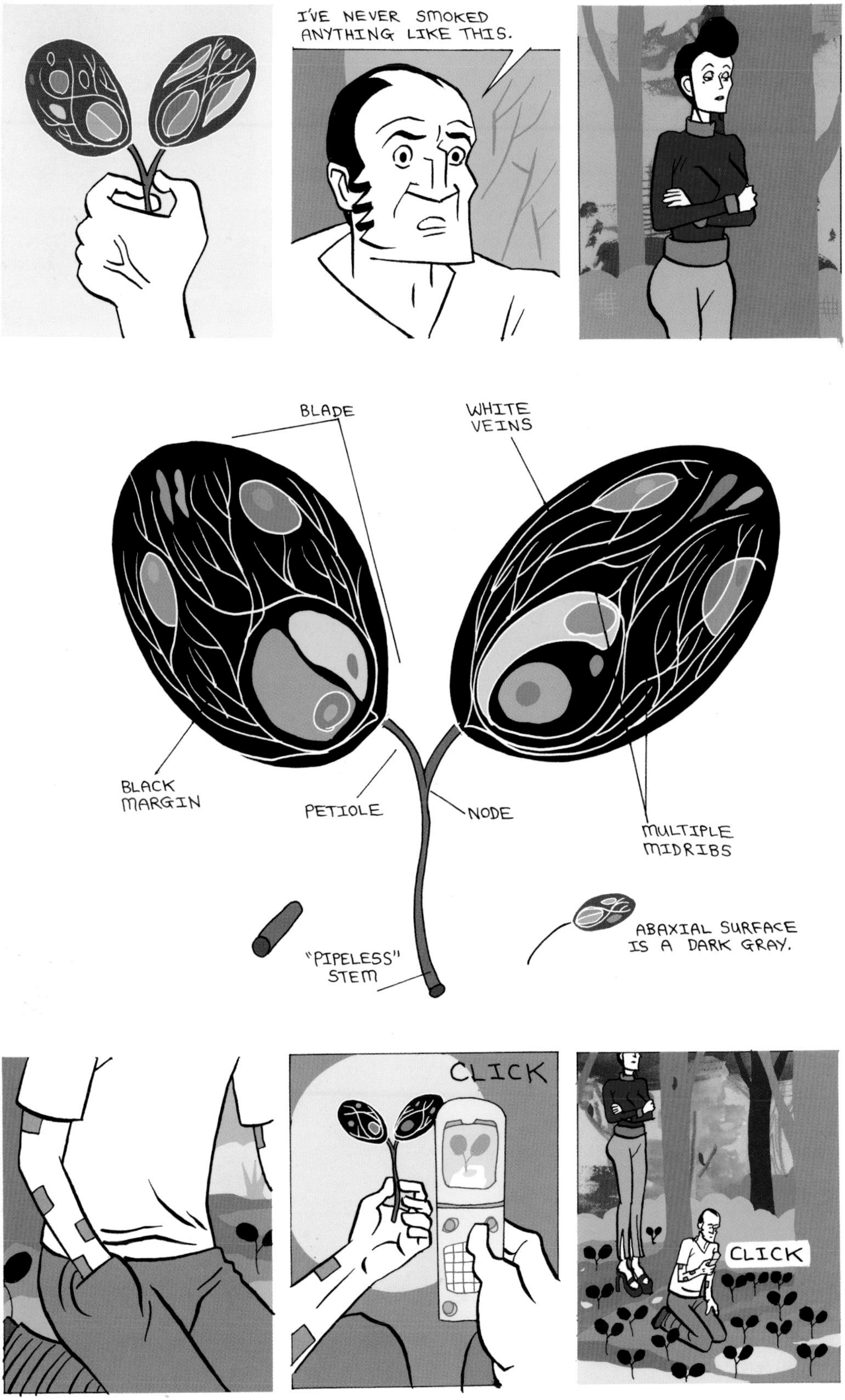
I'VE NEVER SMOKED ANYTHING LIKE THIS.
BLADE
WHITE VEINS
BLACK MARGIN
PETIOLE
NODE
MULTIPLE MIDRIBS
"PIPELESS" STEM
ABAXIAL SURFACE IS A DARK GRAY.
CLICK
CLICK

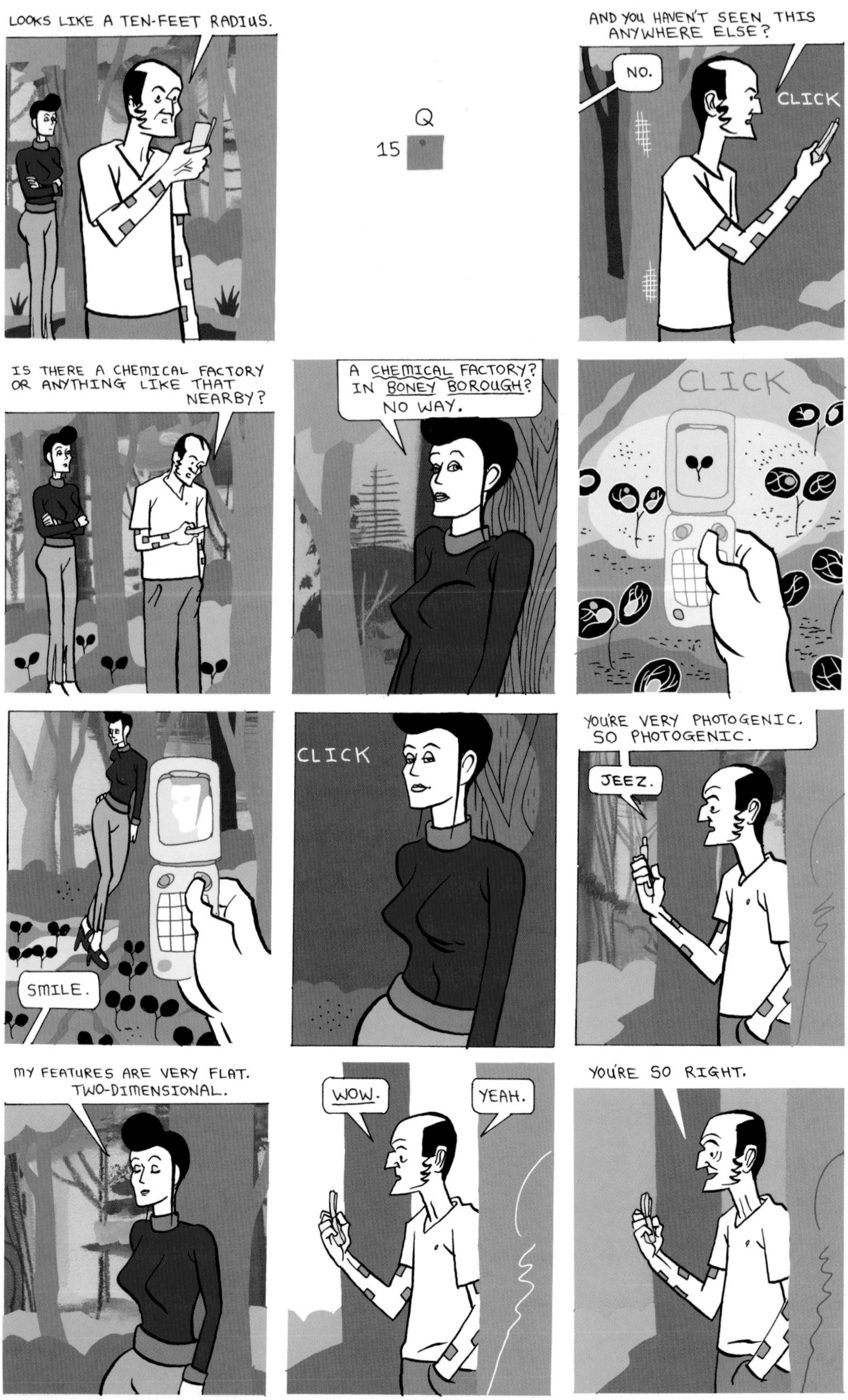
LOOKS LIKE A TEN-FEET RADIUS.
Q
15
AND YOU HAVEN'T SEEN THIS ANYWHERE ELSE?
NO.
CLICK
IS THERE A CHEMICAL FACTORY OR ANYTHING LIKE THAT NEARBY?
A CHEMICAL FACTORY? IN BONEY BOROUGH? NO WAY.
CLICK
SMILE.
CLICK
YOU'RE VERY PHOTOGENIC. SO PHOTOGENIC.
JEEZ.
MY FEATURES ARE VERY FLAT. TWO-DIMENSIONAL.
WOW.
YEAH.
YOU'RE SO RIGHT.

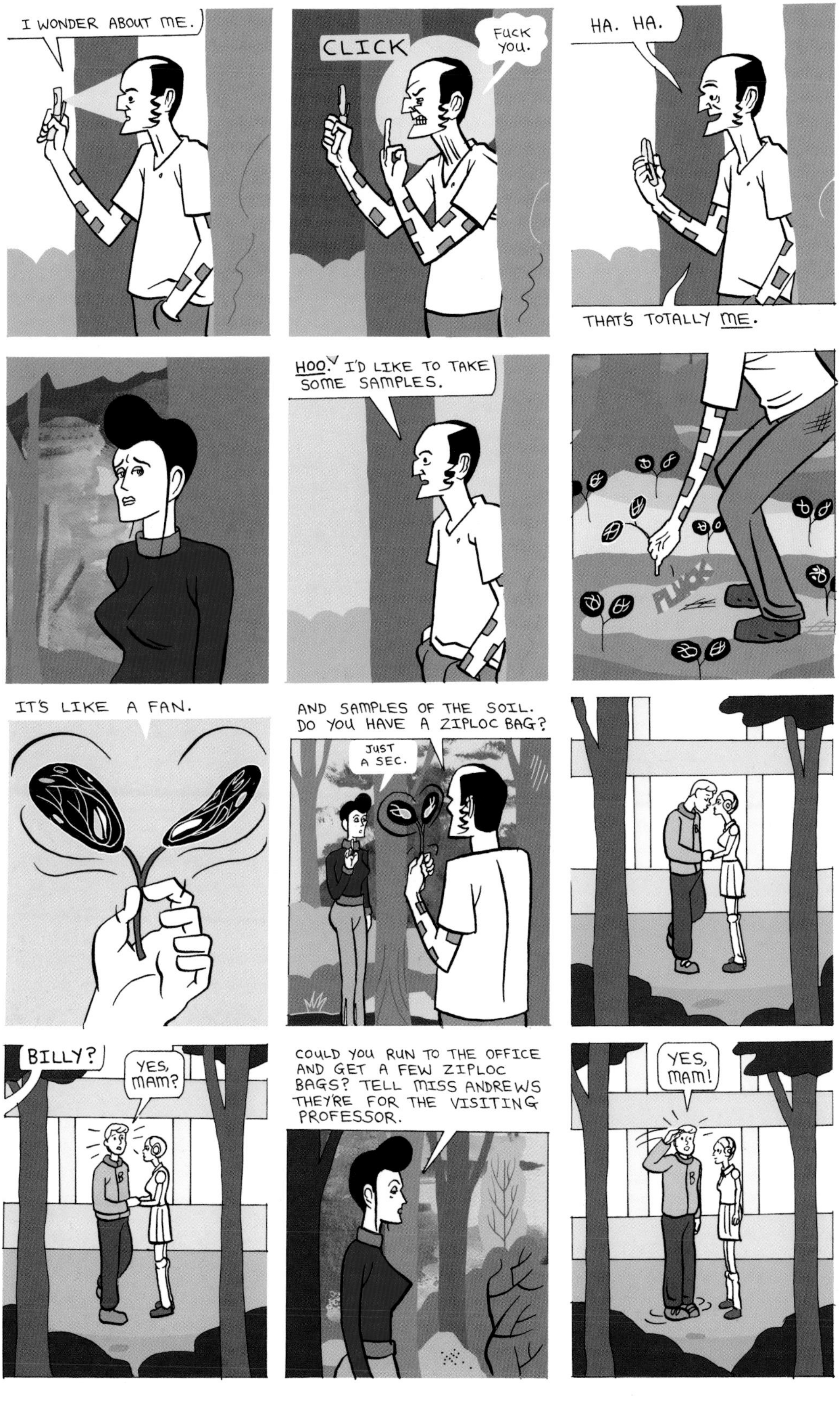

I WONDER ABOUT ME.
CLICK
FUCK YOU.
HA. HA.
THAT'S TOTALLY ME.
HOO. I'D LIKE TO TAKE SOME SAMPLES.
PLUCK
IT'S LIKE A FAN.
AND SAMPLES OF THE SOIL. DO YOU HAVE A ZIPLOC BAG?
JUST A SEC.
BILLY?
YES, MAM?
COULD YOU RUN TO THE OFFICE AND GET A FEW ZIPLOC BAGS? TELL MISS ANDREWS THEY'RE FOR THE VISITING PROFESSOR.
YES, MAM!

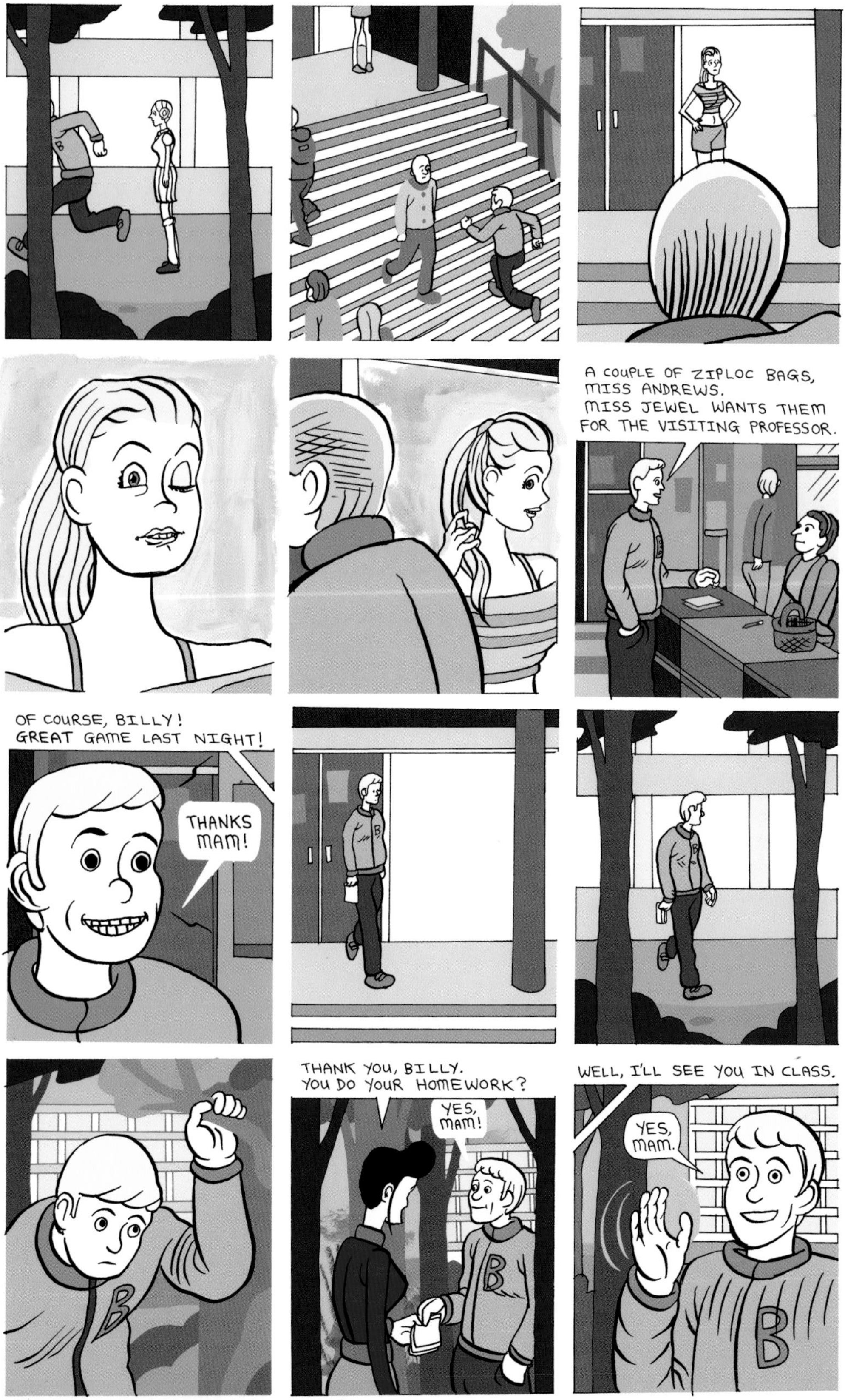
A COUPLE OF ZIPLOC BAGS, MISS ANDREWS. MISS JEWEL WANTS THEM FOR THE VISITING PROFESSOR.
OF COURSE, BILLY! GREAT GAME LAST NIGHT!
THANKS MAM!
THANK YOU, BILLY. YOU DO YOUR HOMEWORK?
YES, MAM!
WELL, I'LL SEE YOU IN CLASS.
YES, MAM.

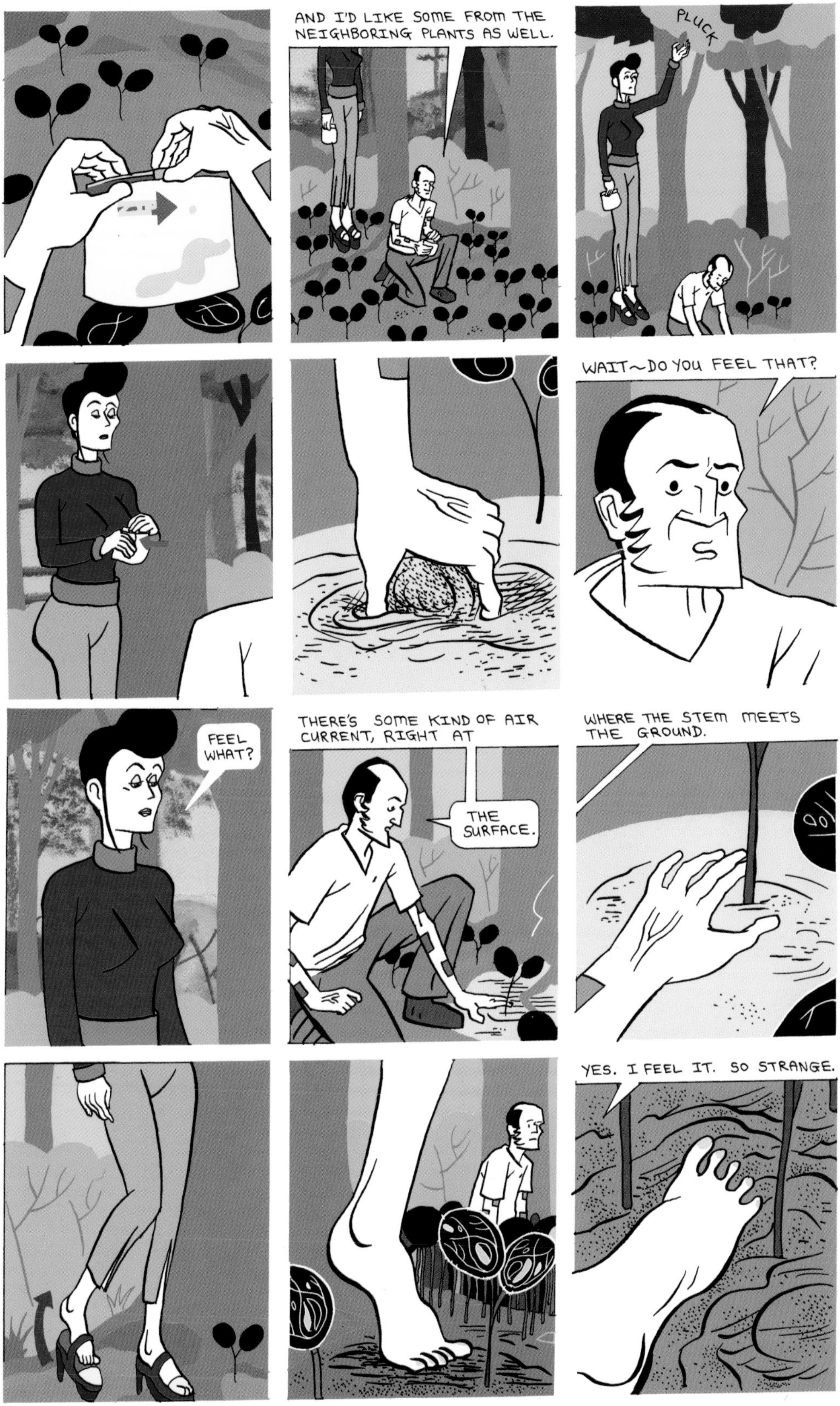
AND I'D LIKE SOME FROM THE NEIGHBORING PLANTS AS WELL.
PLUCK
WAIT~DO YOU FEEL THAT?
FEEL WHAT?
THERE'S SOME KIND OF AIR CURRENT, RIGHT AT
THE SURFACE.
WHERE THE STEM MEETS THE GROUND.
YES. I FEEL IT. SO STRANGE.

AND I KNOW A LOT...
ABOUT PLANTS.

I DON'T KNOW.

DO YOU THINK IT'S NEW?
I MEAN—A COMPLETELY NEW
SPECIES HERE?

WELL, THAT'LL DO FOR NOW.
I'LL PROBABLY BE BACK FOR
MORE SAMPLES LATER.

SURE.

THANKS.

UM.

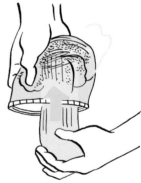

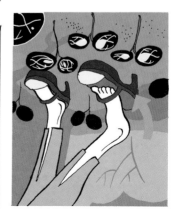

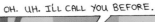

WHEN WILL YOU BE BACK?

OH. UH. I'LL CALL YOU BEFORE.

HOW LONG ARE YOU STAYING IN BONEY BOROUGH?

THREE WEEKS.

WHERE?

"THE SHADEY MOTEL"

IN THE OUTER RIM?

IT'S NEAR THE MONORAIL STATION, ACROSS A PARKING LOT FROM A GAS STATION.

YES.

I USED TO SPEND A LOT OF TIME IN THAT AREA. WHEN I WAS YOUNG.

WELL, IS THERE ANYTHING I SHOULD DO?

WHILE I'M HERE?

LIKE WHAT?

ANYTHING.

ARE YOU FAMILIAR WITH "DIEBALL"?

"DIE-BALL"?

MAYBE I'LL GO. I'M REAL BUSY.

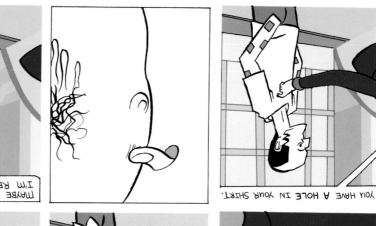

YOU HAVE A HOLE IN YOUR SHIRT.

SCRATCH

I MEAN, I'M A POPULAR GUY.

RUB

SCRATCH

THAT'S FUNNY CUZ I GO OUT ALL THE TIME.

YES—YOU LOOK LIKE YOU NEED TO GET OUT MORE.

I SHOULD GO, HUH?

PAT

YOU SHOULD GO.

THERE'S A GAME TOMORROW.

WELL, "DIEBALL" WAS INVENTED HERE, IT'S A LOCAL TREASURE.

NO.

I HATE SPORTS.

DO YOU LIKE SPORTS?

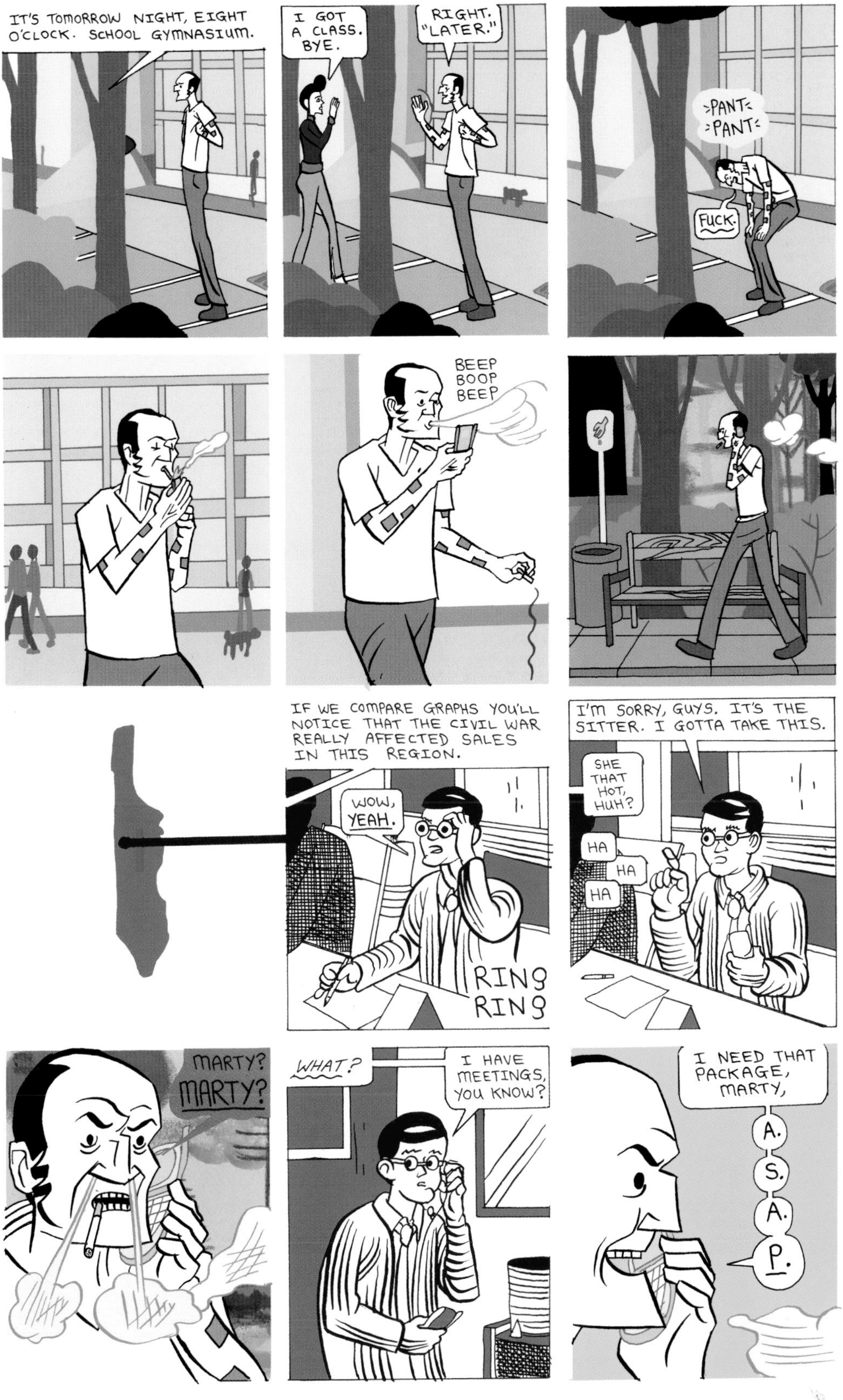
IT'S TOMORROW NIGHT, EIGHT O'CLOCK. SCHOOL GYMNASIUM.
I GOT A CLASS. BYE.
RIGHT. "LATER."
PANT PANT
FUCK.
BEEP BOOP BEEP
IF WE COMPARE GRAPHS YOU'LL NOTICE THAT THE CIVIL WAR REALLY AFFECTED SALES IN THIS REGION.
WOW, YEAH.
RING RING
I'M SORRY, GUYS. IT'S THE SITTER. I GOTTA TAKE THIS.
SHE THAT HOT, HUH?
HA
HA
HA
MARTY? MARTY?
WHAT?
I HAVE MEETINGS, YOU KNOW?
I NEED THAT PACKAGE, MARTY,
A. S. A. P.

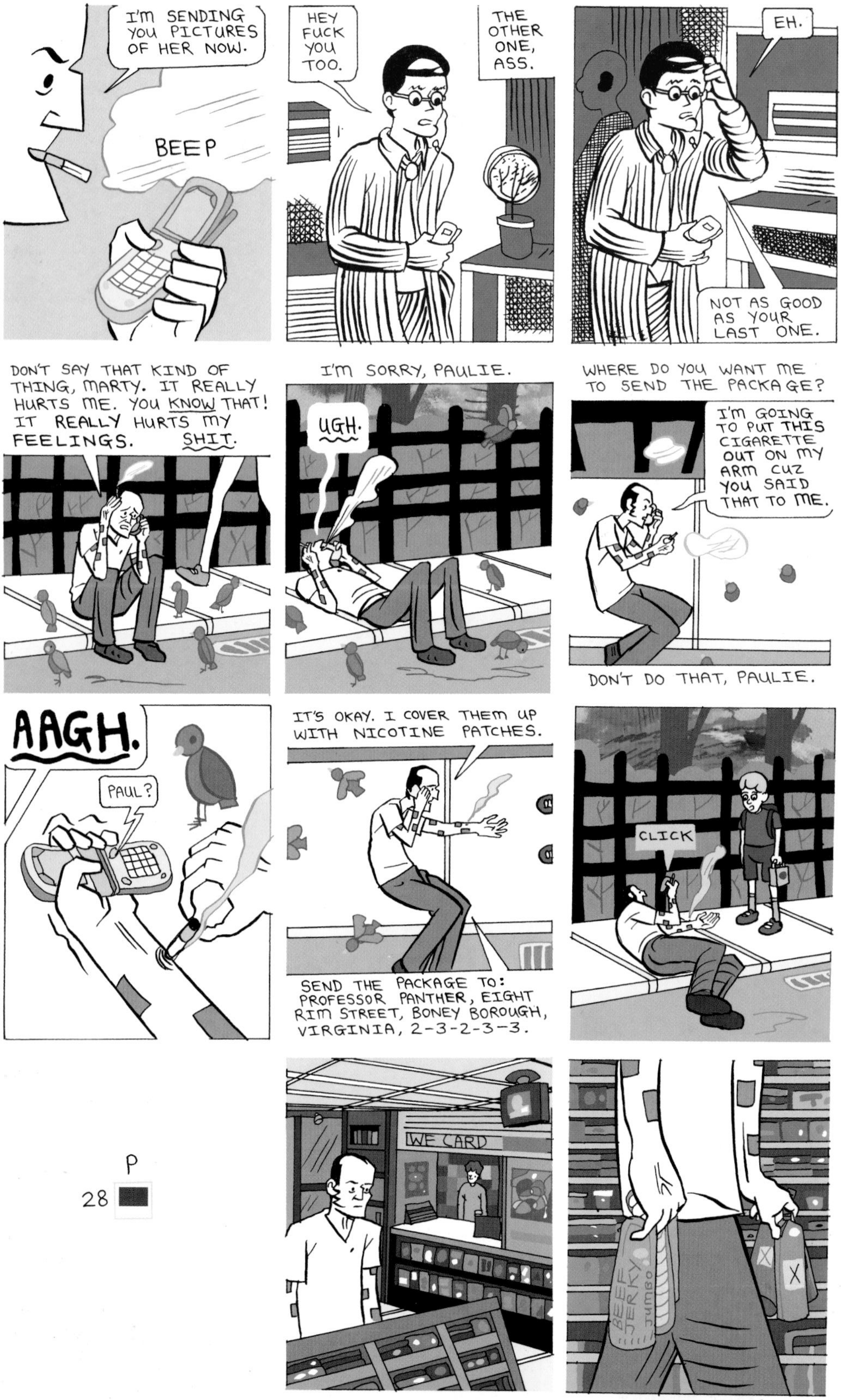
I'M SENDING YOU PICTURES OF HER NOW.
BEEP
HEY FUCK YOU TOO.
THE OTHER ONE, ASS.
EH.
NOT AS GOOD AS YOUR LAST ONE.
DON'T SAY THAT KIND OF THING, MARTY. IT REALLY HURTS ME. YOU KNOW THAT! IT REALLY HURTS MY FEELINGS. SHIT.
I'M SORRY, PAULIE.
UGH.
WHERE DO YOU WANT ME TO SEND THE PACKAGE?
I'M GOING TO PUT THIS CIGARETTE OUT ON MY ARM CUZ YOU SAID THAT TO ME.
DON'T DO THAT, PAULIE.
AAGH.
PAUL?
IT'S OKAY. I COVER THEM UP WITH NICOTINE PATCHES.
SEND THE PACKAGE TO: PROFESSOR PANTHER, EIGHT RIM STREET, BONEY BOROUGH, VIRGINIA, 2-3-2-3-3.
CLICK
WE CARD
BEEF JERKY JUMBO
X
X

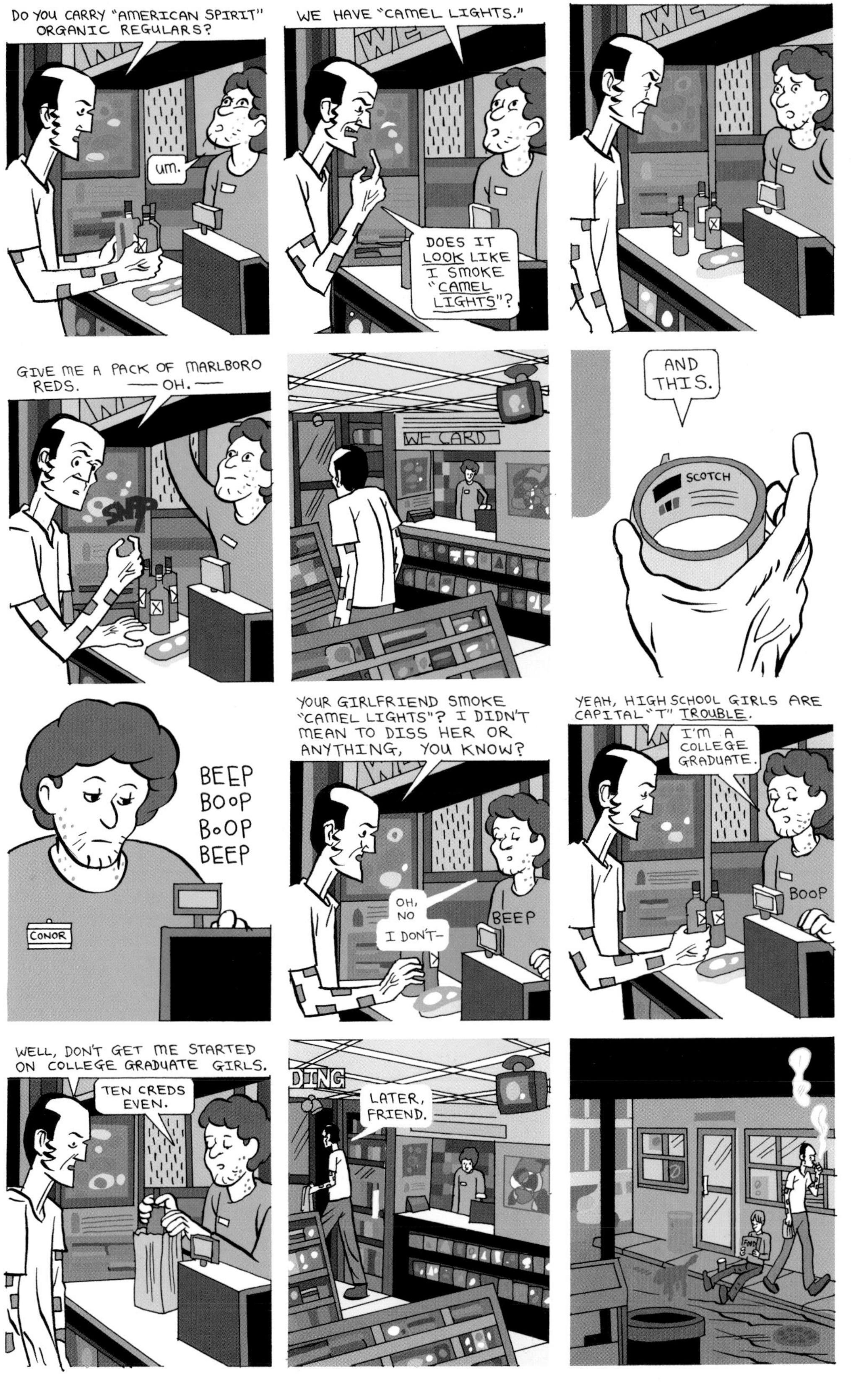

DO YOU CARRY "AMERICAN SPIRIT" ORGANIC REGULARS?
UM.
WE HAVE "CAMEL LIGHTS."
DOES IT LOOK LIKE I SMOKE "CAMEL LIGHTS"?
GIVE ME A PACK OF MARLBORO REDS. —OH.—
SNAP
WE CARD
AND THIS.
SCOTCH
BEEP BOOP BOOP BEEP
CONOR
YOUR GIRLFRIEND SMOKE "CAMEL LIGHTS"? I DIDN'T MEAN TO DISS HER OR ANYTHING, YOU KNOW?
OH, NO
I DON'T-
BEEP
YEAH, HIGH SCHOOL GIRLS ARE CAPITAL "T" TROUBLE.
I'M A COLLEGE GRADUATE.
BOOP
WELL, DON'T GET ME STARTED ON COLLEGE GRADUATE GIRLS.
TEN CREDS EVEN.
DING
LATER, FRIEND.

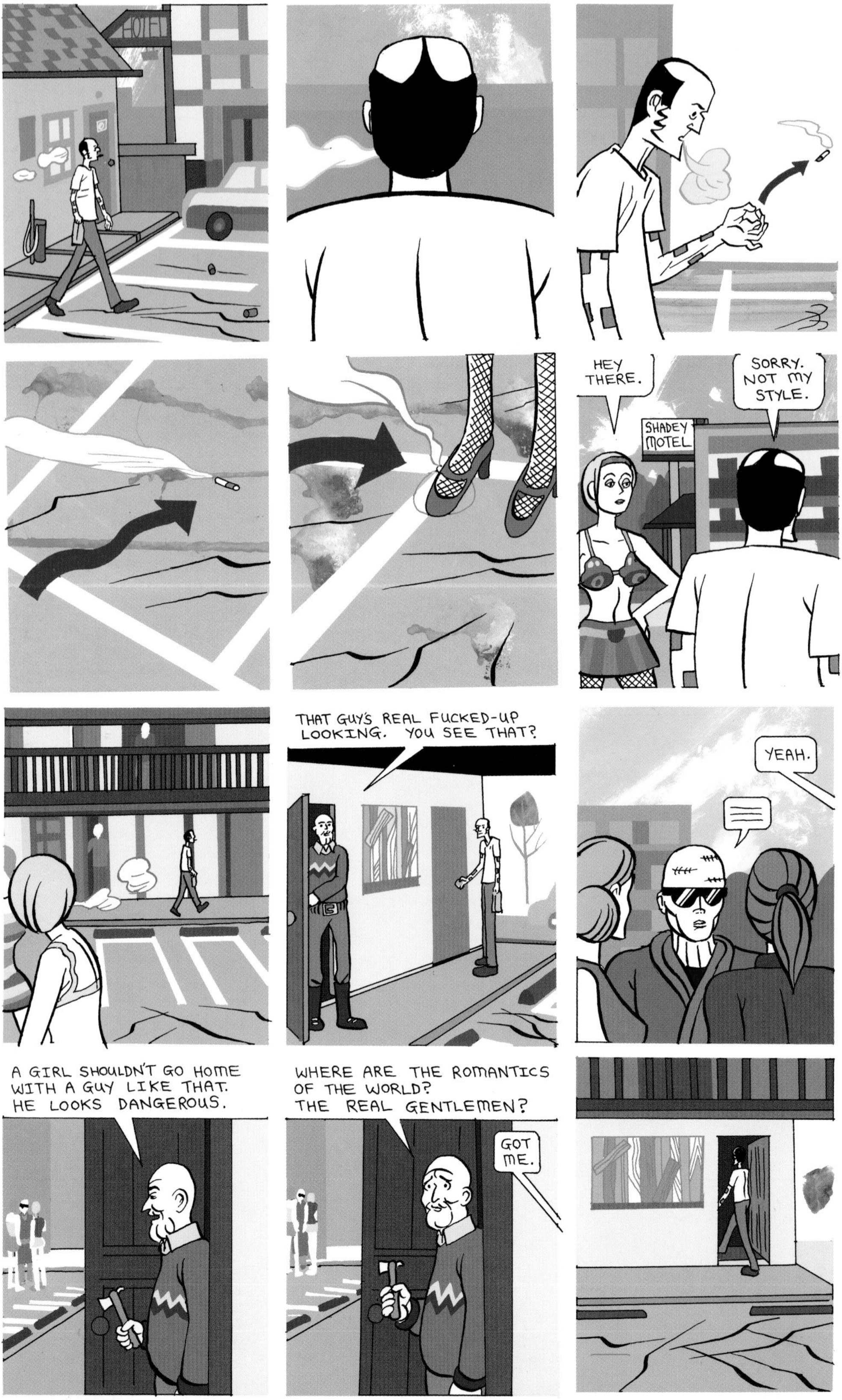
HOTEL
HEY THERE.
SHADEY MOTEL
SORRY. NOT MY STYLE.
THAT GUY'S REAL FUCKED-UP LOOKING. YOU SEE THAT?
YEAH.
A GIRL SHOULDN'T GO HOME WITH A GUY LIKE THAT. HE LOOKS DANGEROUS.
WHERE ARE THE ROMANTICS OF THE WORLD? THE REAL GENTLEMEN?
GOT ME.

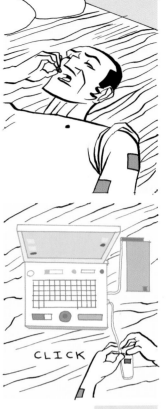

BONEY BOROUGH 4-6-60

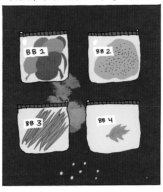

CLICK

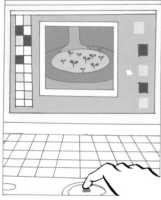

READING PROPERTIES

LOADING...

ESTIMATED TIME:
SIX DAYS, TEN HOURS

SIX DAYS?
SMACK!
READING PROPERTIES
LOADING...
ESTIMATED TIME: 45 SECONDS
READING PROPERTIES
LOADING...
ESTIMATED TIME: NINE DAYS, TWO HOURS
AGG.
CLICK
HUK!

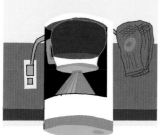

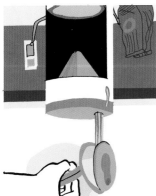

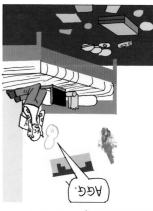

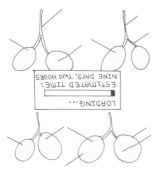

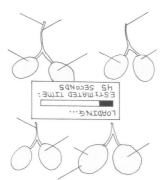

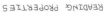

YES.

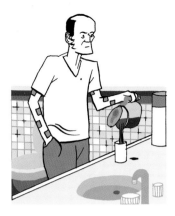

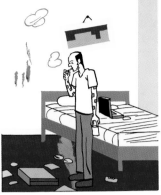

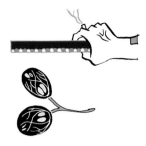

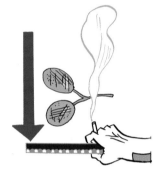

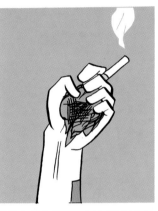

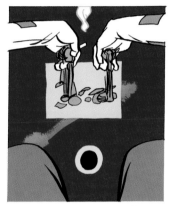

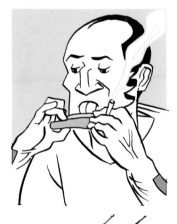

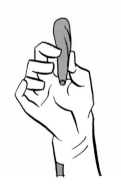

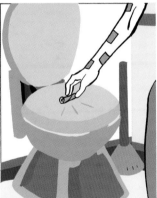

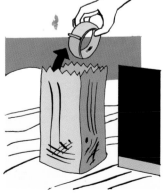

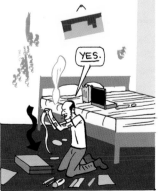

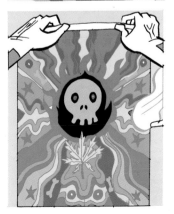

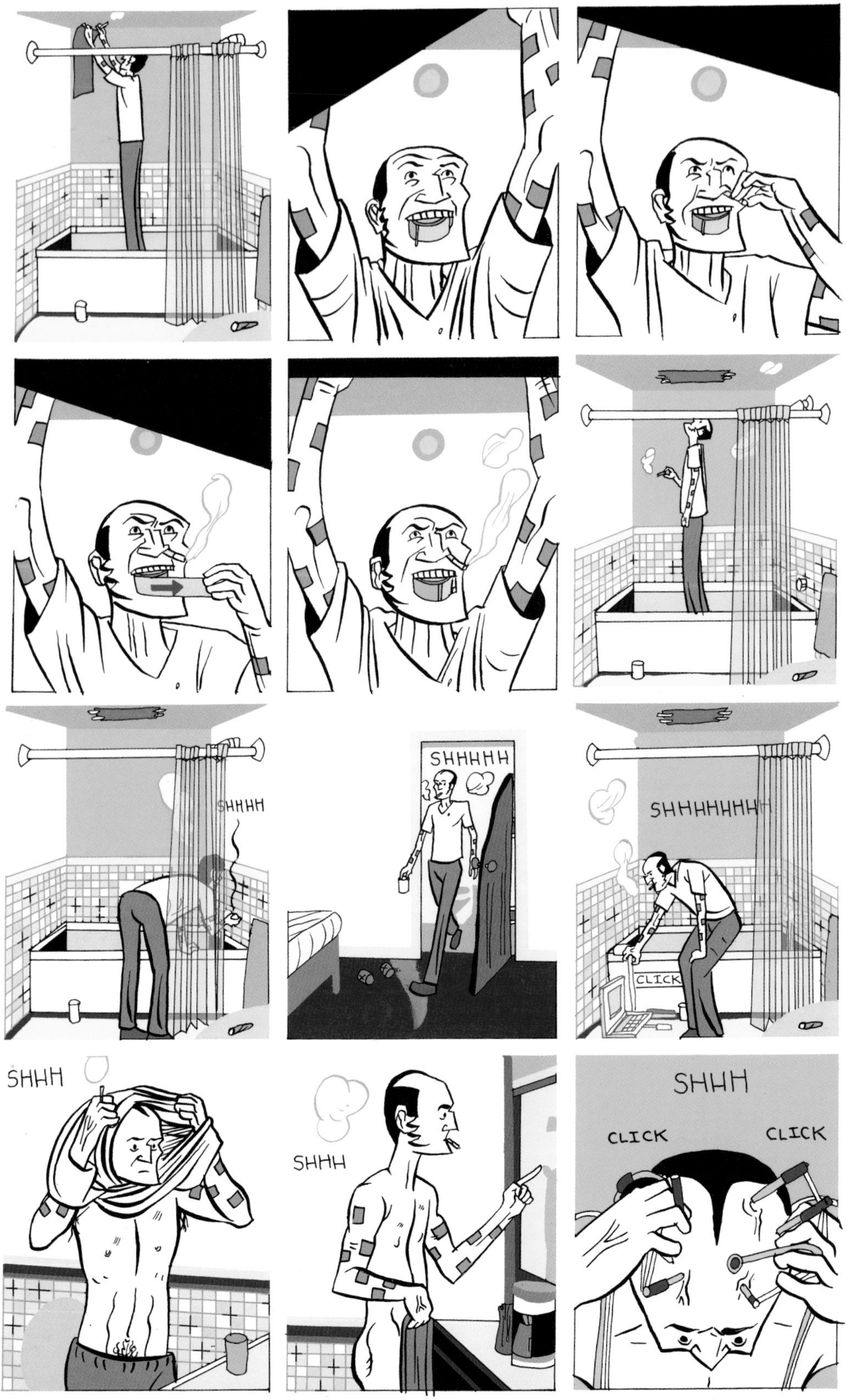
SHHHH
SHHHHH
SHHHHHHHH
CLICK
SHHH
SHHH
SHHH
CLICK
CLICK

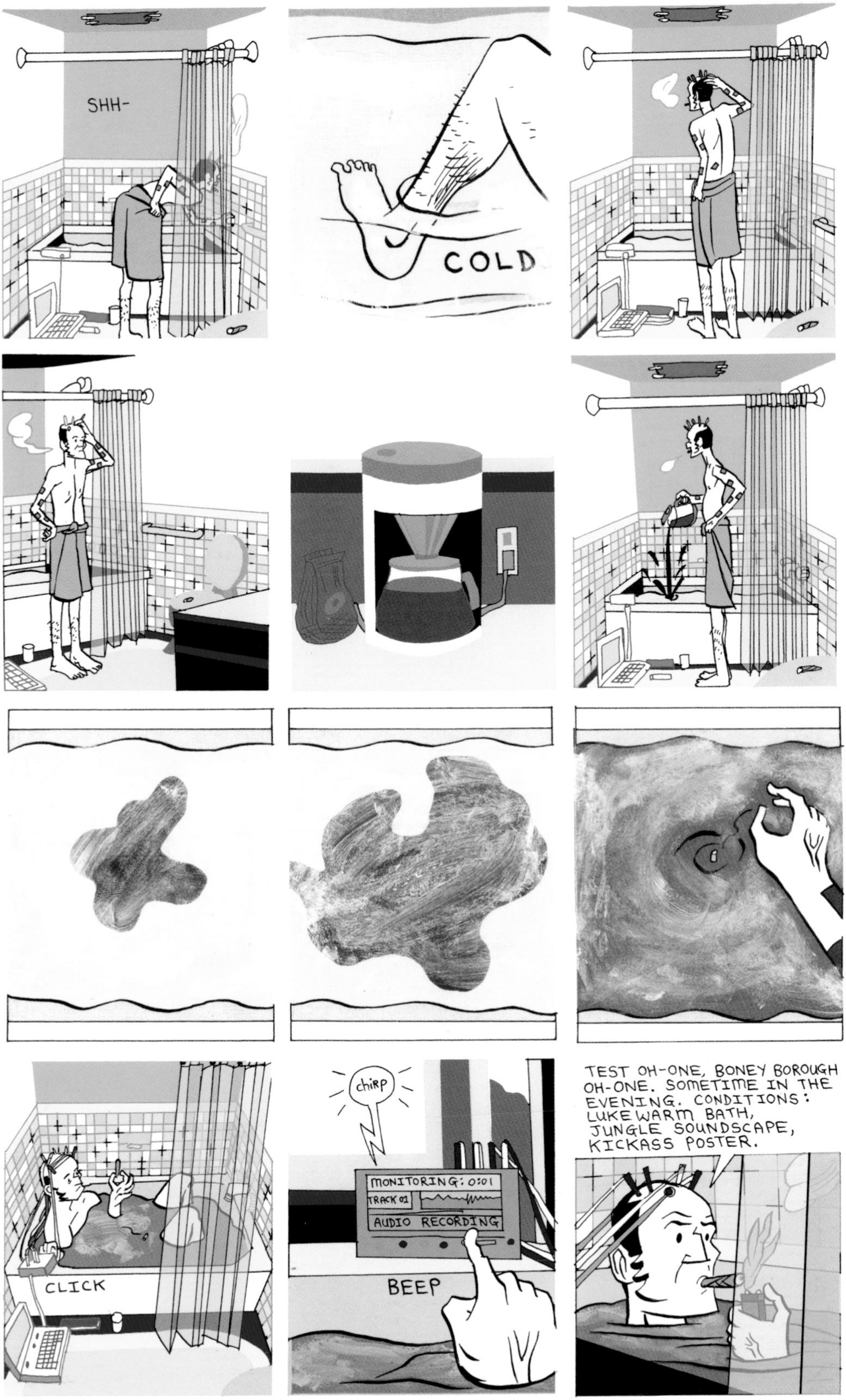
SHH-
COLD
CLICK
chirp
MONITORING: 0:01
TRACK 01
AUDIO RECORDING
BEEP
TEST OH-ONE, BONEY BOROUGH OH-ONE. SOMETIME IN THE EVENING. CONDITIONS: LUKEWARM BATH, JUNGLE SOUNDSCAPE, KICKASS POSTER.

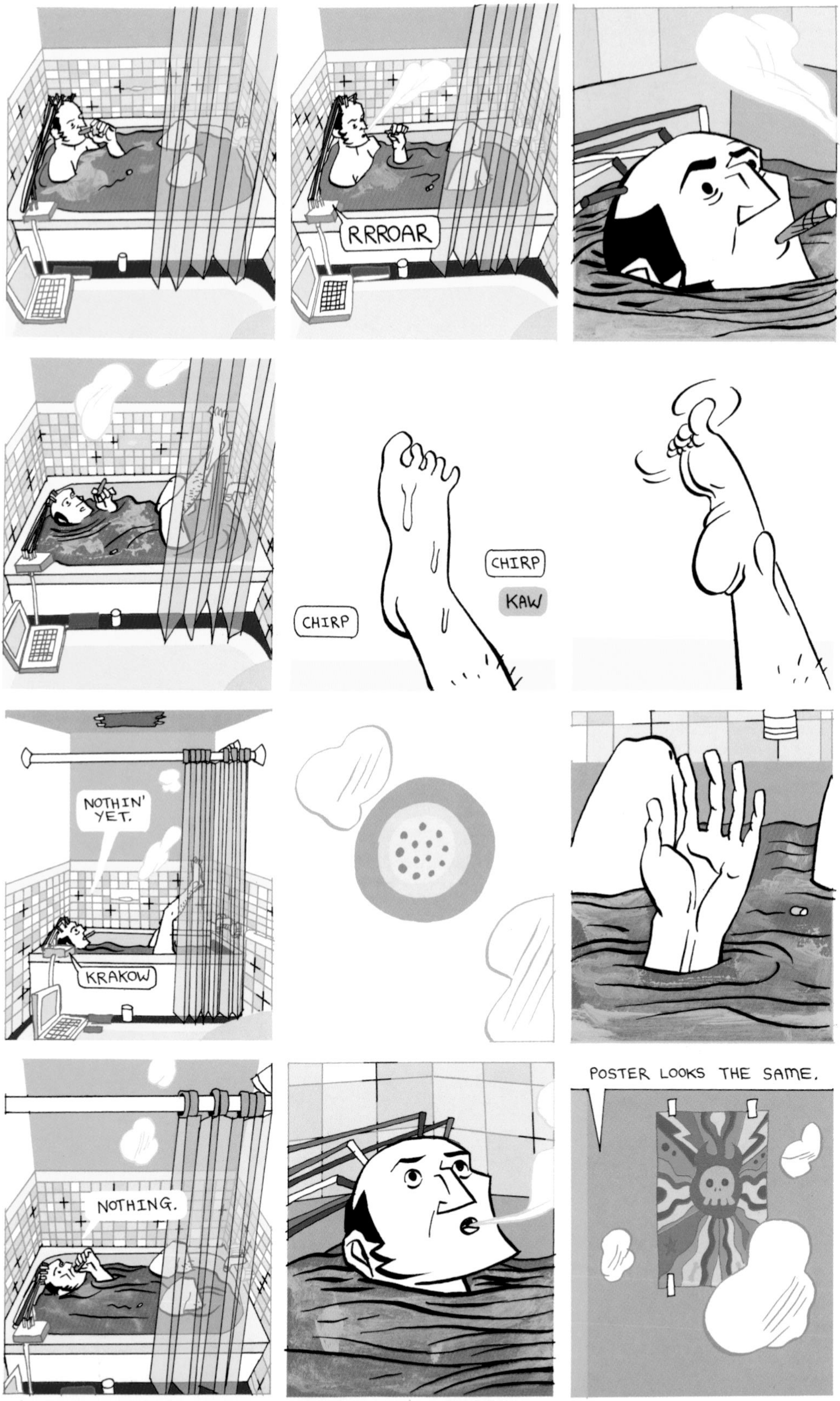
RRROAR
CHIRP
CHIRP
KAW
NOTHIN' YET.
KRAKOW
NOTHING.
POSTER LOOKS THE SAME.

NO BUZZ AT ALL.
HAND ALL WRINKLY NOW. THAT'S JUST THE WATER.
TEST ONE COMPLETE. FUCKING BULLSHIT.
CLICK

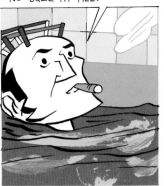

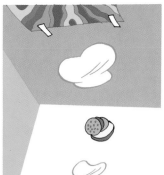

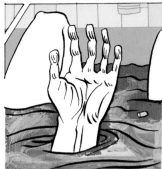

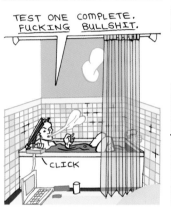

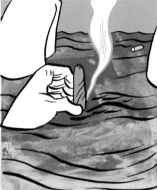

END OF CHAPTER ONE.

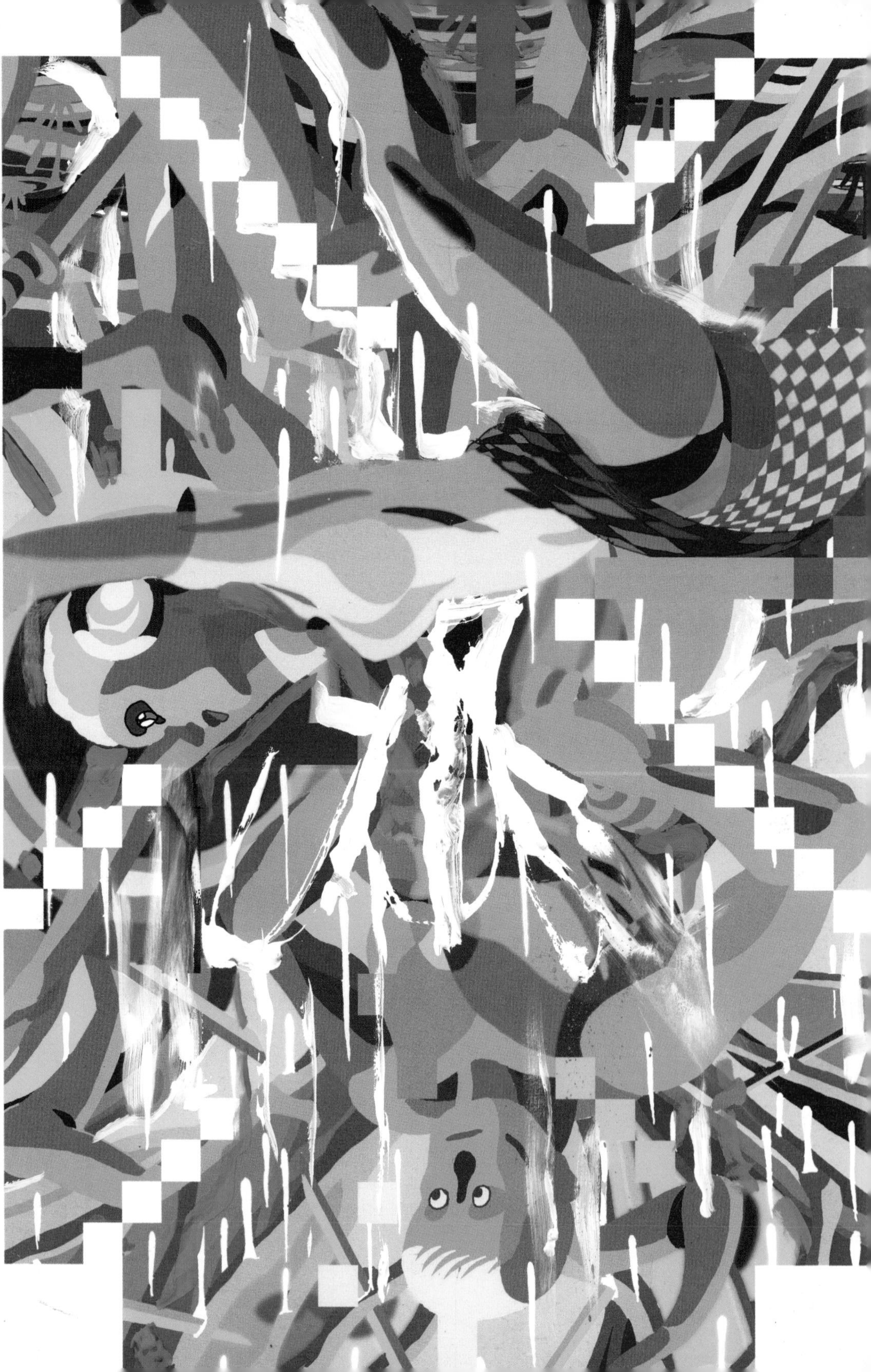

CHAPTER TWO

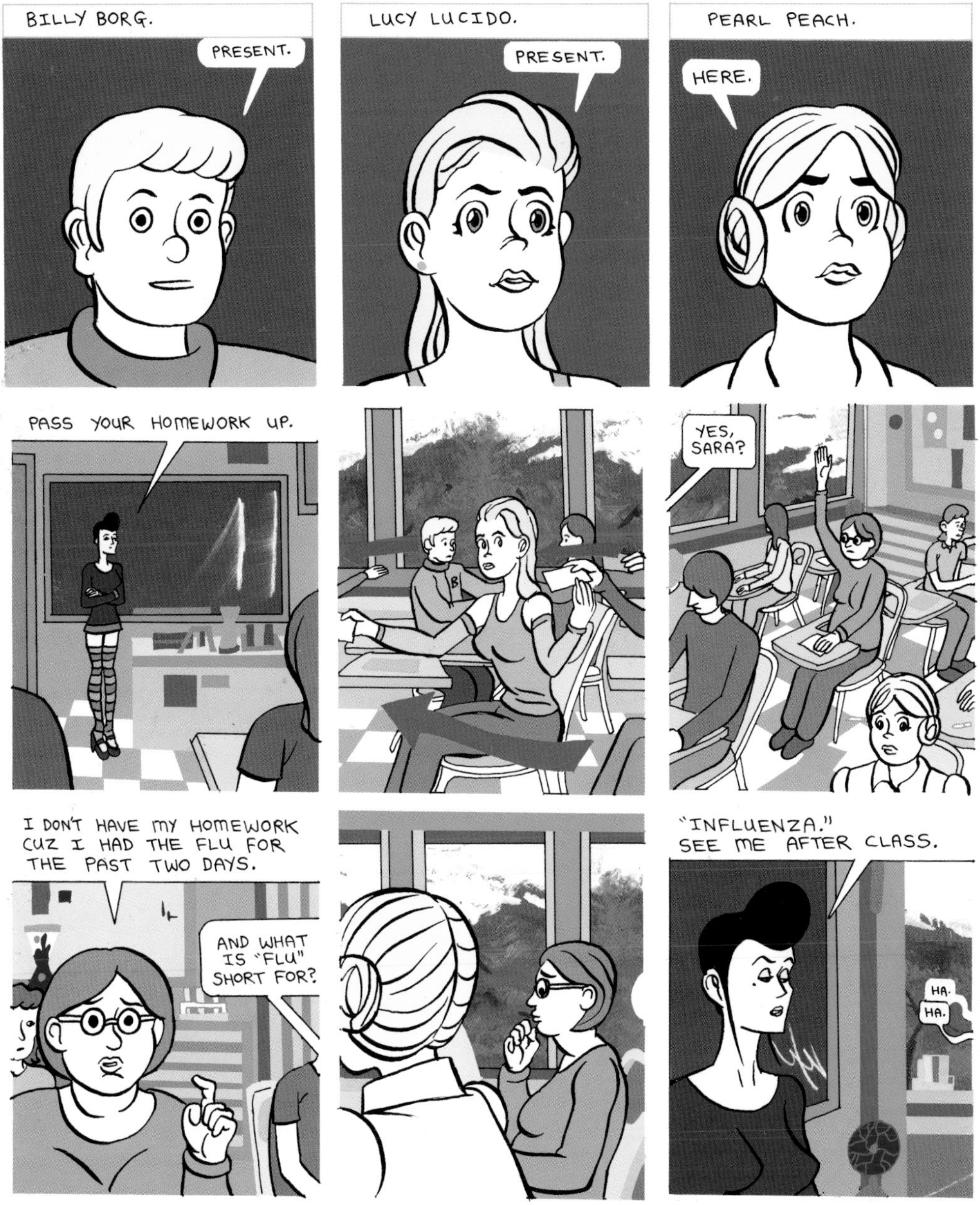

BILLY BORG.
PRESENT.
LUCY LUCIDO.
PRESENT.
PEARL PEACH.
HERE.
PASS YOUR HOMEWORK UP.
YES, SARA?
I DON'T HAVE MY HOMEWORK CUZ I HAD THE FLU FOR THE PAST TWO DAYS.
AND WHAT IS "FLU" SHORT FOR?
"INFLUENZA." SEE ME AFTER CLASS.
HA.
HA.

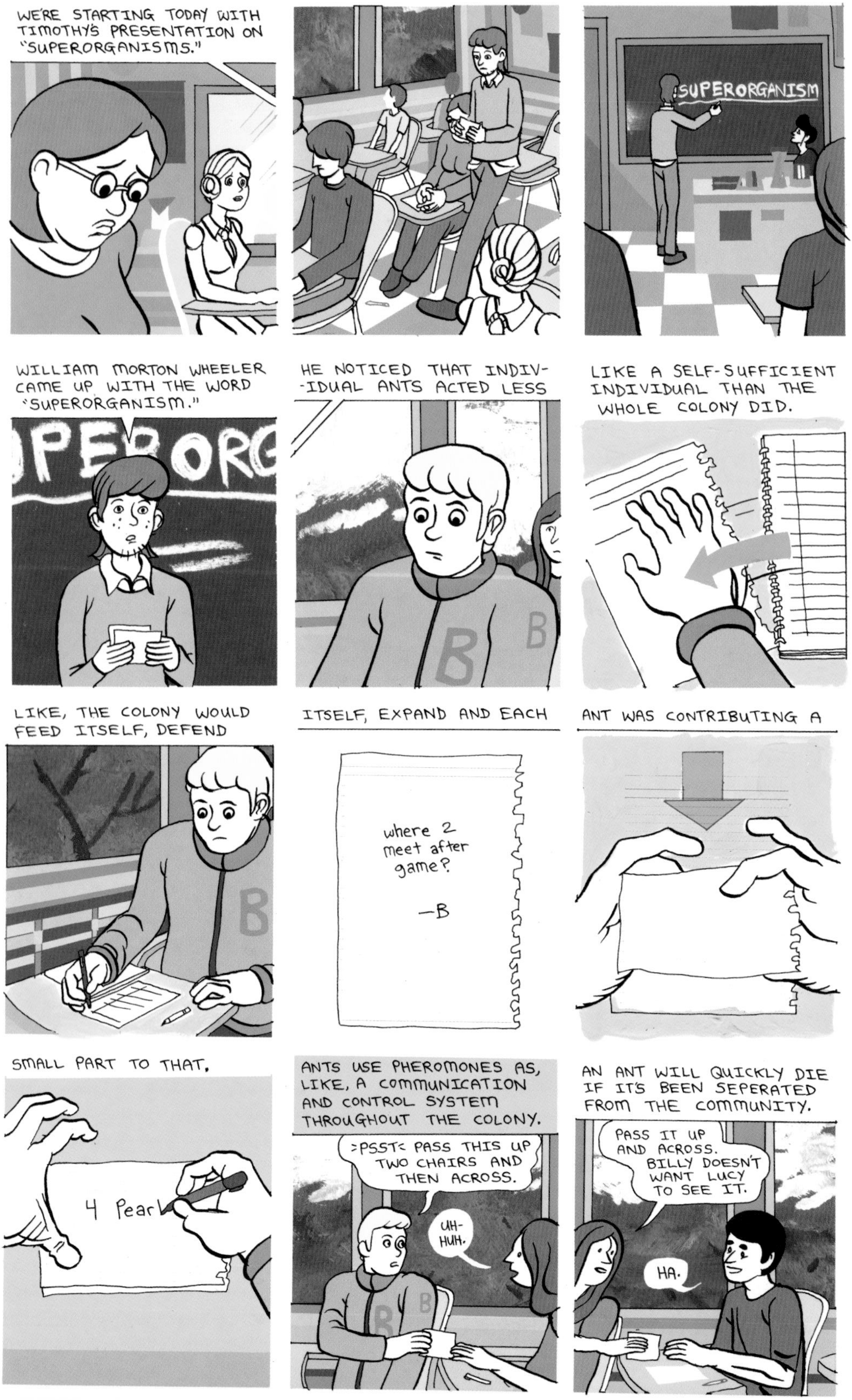
WE'RE STARTING TODAY WITH TIMOTHY'S PRESENTATION ON "SUPERORGANISMS."
SUPERORGANISM
WILLIAM MORTON WHEELER CAME UP WITH THE WORD "SUPERORGANISM."
HE NOTICED THAT INDIV-IDUAL ANTS ACTED LESS
LIKE A SELF-SUFFICIENT INDIVIDUAL THAN THE WHOLE COLONY DID.
LIKE, THE COLONY WOULD FEED ITSELF, DEFEND
ITSELF, EXPAND AND EACH
where 2 meet after game?
—B
ANT WAS CONTRIBUTING A
SMALL PART TO THAT.
4 Pear
ANTS USE PHEROMONES AS, LIKE, A COMMUNICATION AND CONTROL SYSTEM THROUGHOUT THE COLONY.
>PSST< PASS THIS UP TWO CHAIRS AND THEN ACROSS.
UH-HUH.
AN ANT WILL QUICKLY DIE IF IT'S BEEN SEPERATED FROM THE COMMUNITY.
PASS IT UP AND ACROSS. BILLY DOESN'T WANT LUCY TO SEE IT.
HA.

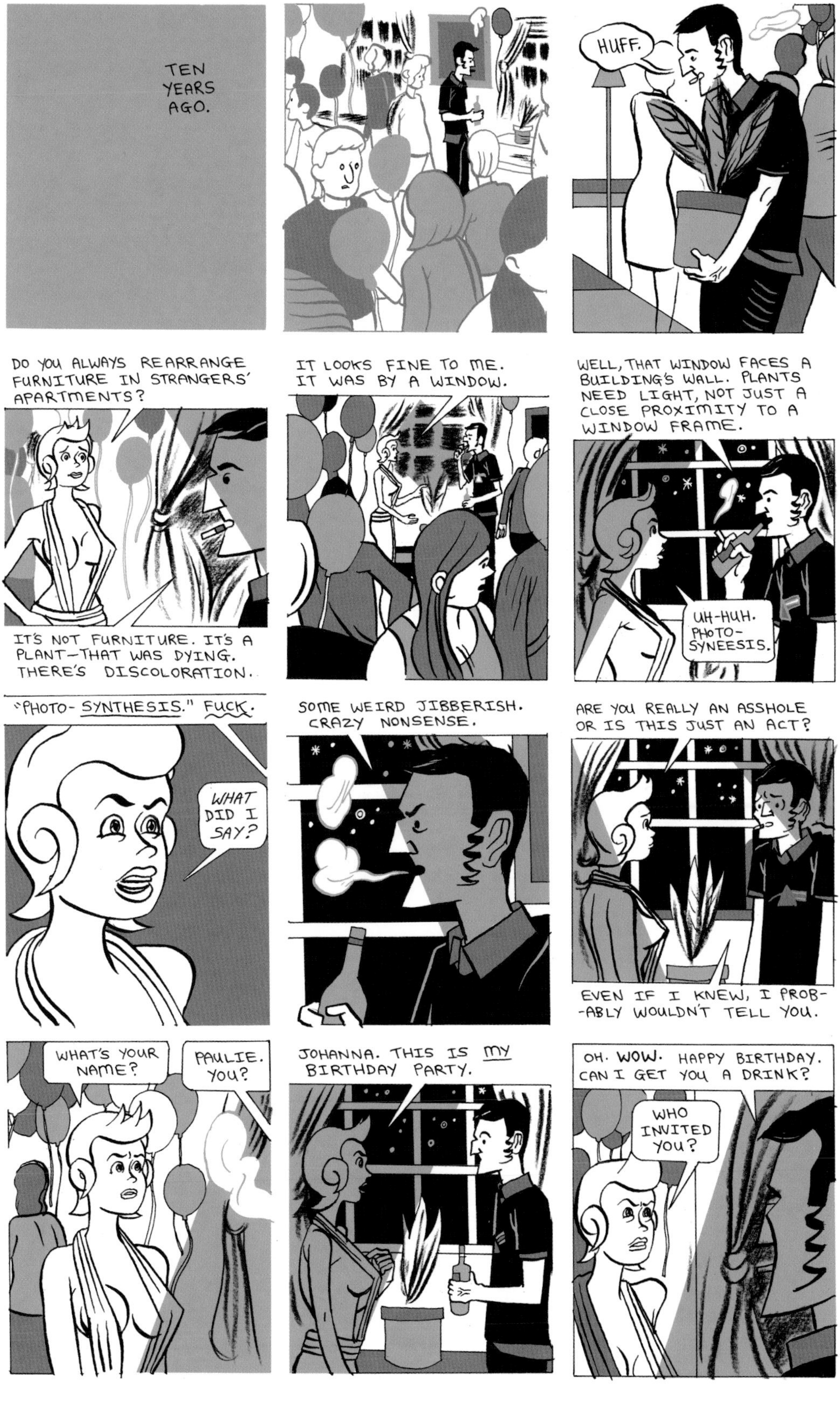
TEN YEARS AGO.
HUFF.
DO YOU ALWAYS REARRANGE FURNITURE IN STRANGERS' APARTMENTS?
IT'S NOT FURNITURE. IT'S A PLANT—THAT WAS DYING. THERE'S DISCOLORATION.
IT LOOKS FINE TO ME. IT WAS BY A WINDOW.
WELL, THAT WINDOW FACES A BUILDING'S WALL. PLANTS NEED LIGHT, NOT JUST A CLOSE PROXIMITY TO A WINDOW FRAME.
UH-HUH. PHOTO-SYNEESIS.
"PHOTO-SYNTHESIS." FUCK.
WHAT DID I SAY?
SOME WEIRD JIBBERISH. CRAZY NONSENSE.
ARE YOU REALLY AN ASSHOLE OR IS THIS JUST AN ACT?
EVEN IF I KNEW, I PROB-ABLY WOULDN'T TELL YOU.
WHAT'S YOUR NAME?
PAULIE. YOU?
JOHANNA. THIS IS MY BIRTHDAY PARTY.
OH. WOW. HAPPY BIRTHDAY. CAN I GET YOU A DRINK?
WHO INVITED YOU?

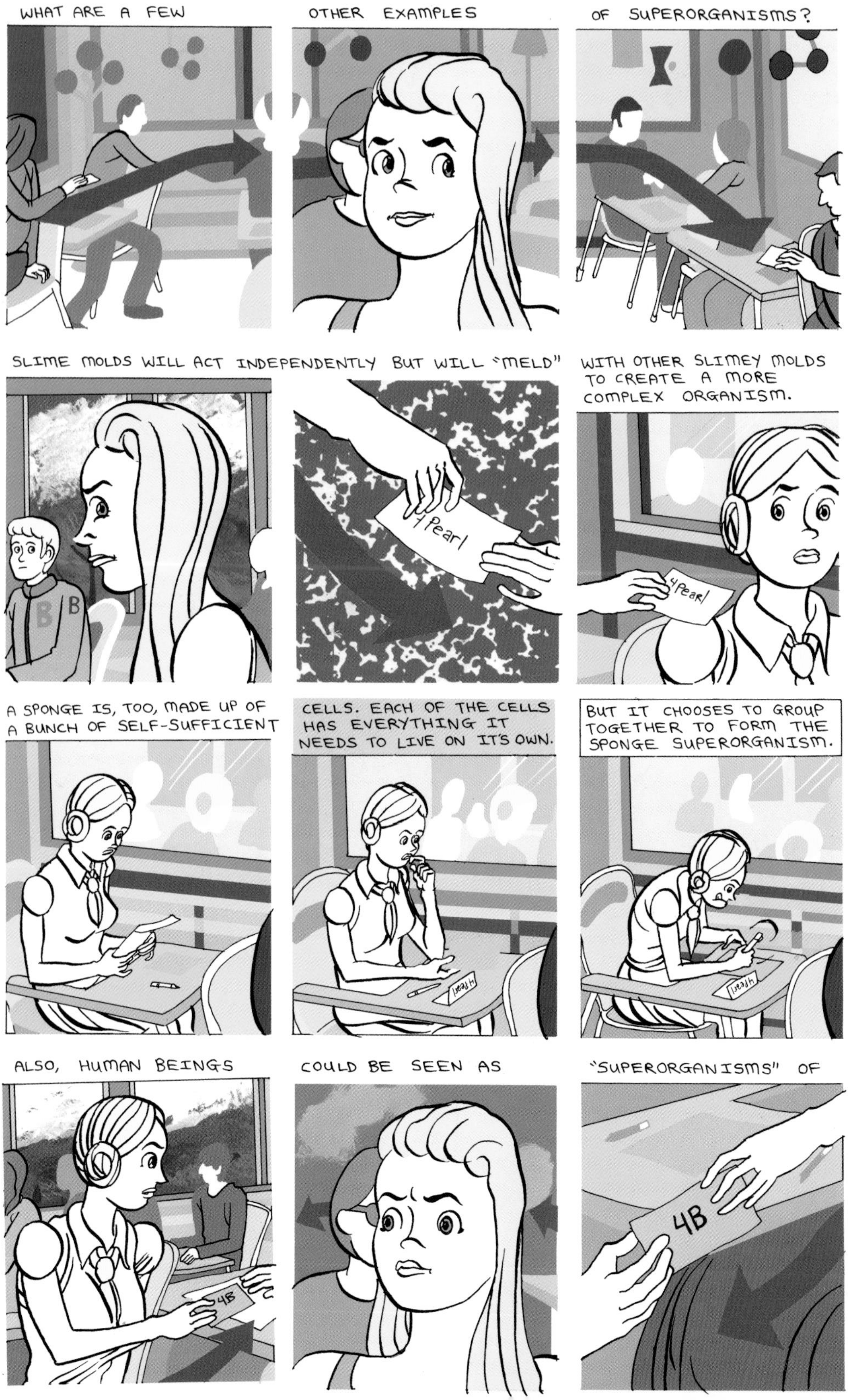
WHAT ARE A FEW
OTHER EXAMPLES
OF SUPERORGANISMS?
SLIME MOLDS WILL ACT INDEPENDENTLY BUT WILL "MELD"
4 Pearl
WITH OTHER SLIMEY MOLDS TO CREATE A MORE COMPLEX ORGANISM.
4 Pearl
A SPONGE IS, TOO, MADE UP OF A BUNCH OF SELF-SUFFICIENT
CELLS. EACH OF THE CELLS HAS EVERYTHING IT NEEDS TO LIVE ON IT'S OWN.
4 Pearl
BUT IT CHOOSES TO GROUP TOGETHER TO FORM THE SPONGE SUPERORGANISM.
4 Pearl
ALSO, HUMAN BEINGS
4B
COULD BE SEEN AS
"SUPERORGANISMS" OF
4B

SIX
YEARS
AGO.

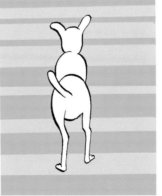

UM, NO—

HEY — DON'T — DON'T.

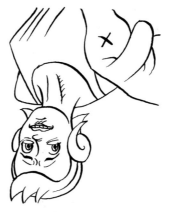
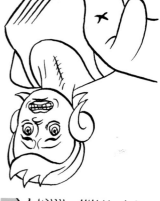

ARE YOU GONNA BE MAD AT ME?

I'M SORRY.

ALL THE SINGLE CELLS

AND OTHER STUFF

THAT MAKES UP OUR

ENTIRE

BODY.   OR

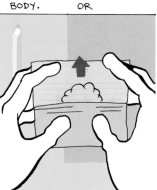

THE EARTH

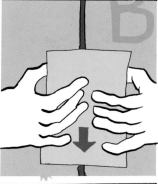

COULD BE SEEN AS ONE VAST SELF-SUPPORTING ORGANISM OF EVERYTHING

INSIDE IT, YOU KNOW?

YOU'RE REQUIRED TO HAVE A FEW VISUALS, TIMOTHY.

I HAVE SOME PHOTOS OF

ANTS   AND   SLIME MOLD

TO PASS OUT.

DIEBALL

"DIEBALL" IS A COMPETITIVE TEAM SPORT KNOWN FOR COMBINING CHANCE WITH INTENSE PHYSICAL PLAY.
IT WAS INVENTED BY MR. D.I. BAWL, A BONEY BOROUGH RESIDENT, IN 2010.
TODAY, DIEBALL EQUIPMENT, D10S AND DIEGUNK ARE BONEY BOROUGH'S CHIEF EXPORTS.

THE COURT

2 FEET SQUARE
60 FEET
120 FEET
BLUE TEAM SCORING SQUARES
PLAYER STARTING POSITIONS
RED
BLUE
DEFENSE
OFFENSE
D10 STARTING POSITION
RED TEAM SCORING SQUARES

4-FOOT TALL WALL SURROUNDS COURT. THE D10 BOUNCES OFF THE WALL. THERE IS NO "OUT OF BOUNDS" PLAY.

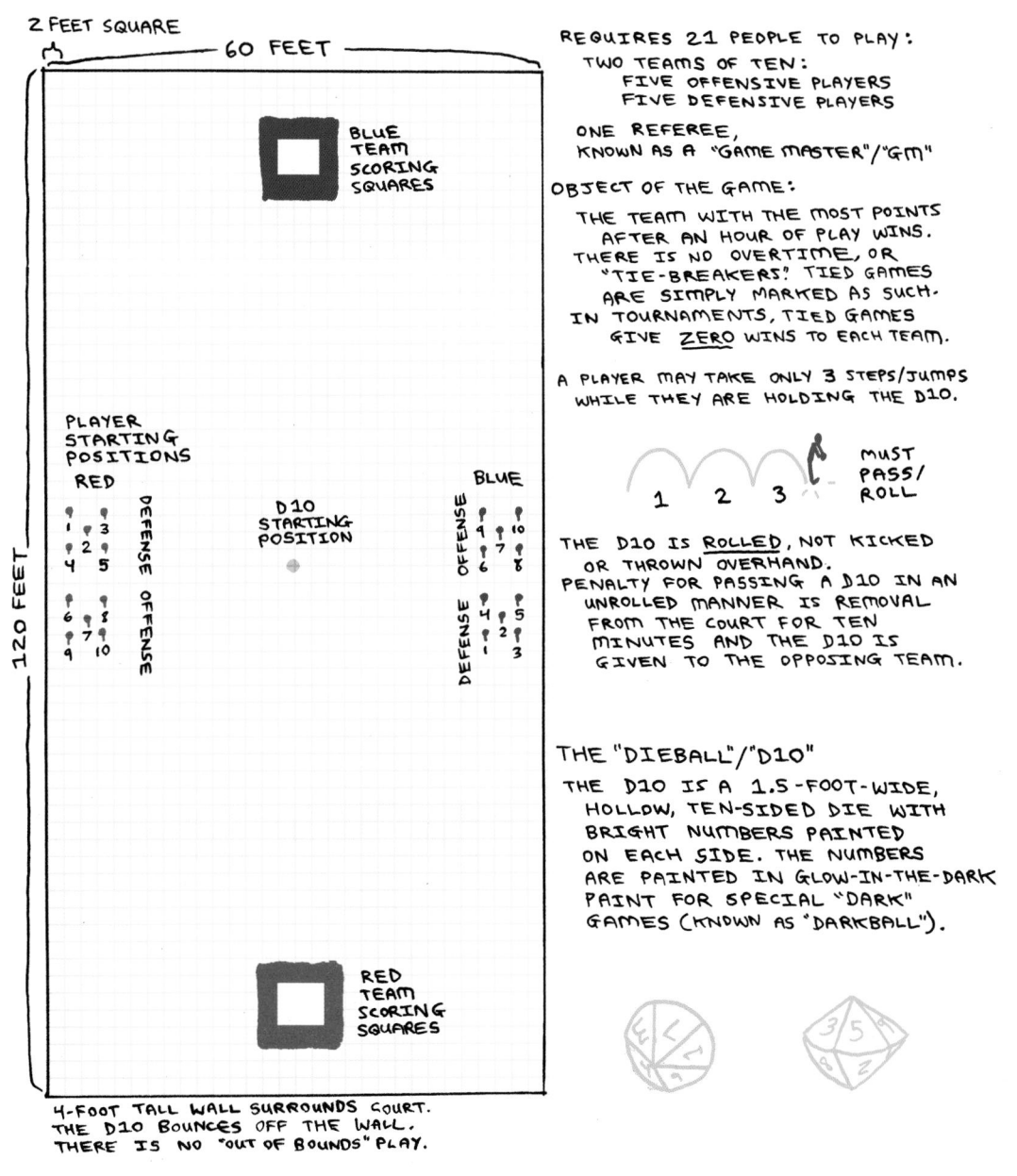

REQUIRES 21 PEOPLE TO PLAY:
- TWO TEAMS OF TEN:
  - FIVE OFFENSIVE PLAYERS
  - FIVE DEFENSIVE PLAYERS
- ONE REFEREE, KNOWN AS A "GAME MASTER"/"GM"

OBJECT OF THE GAME:

THE TEAM WITH THE MOST POINTS AFTER AN HOUR OF PLAY WINS.
THERE IS NO OVERTIME, OR "TIE-BREAKERS." TIED GAMES ARE SIMPLY MARKED AS SUCH.
IN TOURNAMENTS, TIED GAMES GIVE ZERO WINS TO EACH TEAM.

A PLAYER MAY TAKE ONLY 3 STEPS/JUMPS WHILE THEY ARE HOLDING THE D10.

1
2
3
MUST PASS/ ROLL

THE D10 IS ROLLED, NOT KICKED OR THROWN OVERHAND.
PENALTY FOR PASSING A D10 IN AN UNROLLED MANNER IS REMOVAL FROM THE COURT FOR TEN MINUTES AND THE D10 IS GIVEN TO THE OPPOSING TEAM.

THE "DIEBALL"/"D10"

THE D10 IS A 1.5-FOOT-WIDE, HOLLOW, TEN-SIDED DIE WITH BRIGHT NUMBERS PAINTED ON EACH SIDE. THE NUMBERS ARE PAINTED IN GLOW-IN-THE-DARK PAINT FOR SPECIAL "DARK" GAMES (KNOWN AS "DARKBALL").

SCORING:

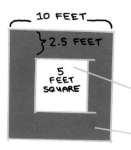

EACH TEAM HAS TWO SQUARES ON OPPOSITE SIDES OF THE COURT. PLAYERS ARE FORBIDDEN TO STEP IN THE SQUARES. THIS OFTEN CAUSES PLAYERS TO ATTEMPT TO FORCE AN OPPOSING TEAM MEMBER INTO A SQUARE.

PENALTY FOR ENTERING A SQUARE IS REMOVAL FROM THE GAME.

IF THE DIE LANDS IN THE CENTER SQUARE, THAT TEAM RECEIVES THE # OF POINTS FACING UP WHEN THE DIE HAS STOPPED.

IF THE DIE LANDS IN THE OUTSIDE SQUARE, OR HALF IN THE OUTSIDE SQUARE, THE NUMBER ROLLED'S CORRESPONDING TEAM MEMBER IS REMOVED FROM PLAY FOR TEN MINUTES.

EXAMPLE: A BLUE TEAM MEMBER ROLLS AN "8" ATTEMPTING TO SCORE, BUT IT LANDS IN THE OUTSIDE SQUARE. THE BLUE TEAM'S #8 IS REMOVED FOR TEN MINUTES.

DIE GUNK:

A CREAMY ADHESIVE SUBSTANCE KNOWN AS "DIEGUNK" IS USED BY PLAYERS TO KEEP HOLD OF A D10 DURING EXTREME PHYSICAL PLAY.

SMALL BAGS OF DIEGUNK WITH SQUIRTING TUBES ARE STRAPPED TO PLAYER'S UNIFORMS FOR EASY ACCESS.

NOTE: SOME BELIEVE THAT REPEATED EXPOSURE TO DIEGUNK MAY RESULT IN MENTAL ILLNESS/RETARDATION. THIS IS UNPROVEN.

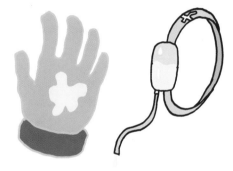

HELMETS/ UNIFORMS:

CLEARLY DISPLAY THE PLAYER'S # AND TEAM.

CULTURE:

PLAYERS OFTEN DEVELOP AN OBSESSION WITH RISK/CHANCE. SOME STAR PLAYERS HAVE FALLEN INTO GAMBLING AND SUBSTANCE ABUSE.

RITUALS:

PAINTING FACES WITH LUCKY NUMBERS OR WILD, INTIMIDATING MONSTERS TO SCARE PLAYERS OF THE OPPOSING TEAM.

RUBBING DIEGUNK OVER THEIR BODIES BEFORE A GAME.

DRINKING "PABST BLUE RIBBON" BEER AFTER A GAME. THIS IS UNKNOWN TO SCHOOL FACULTY.

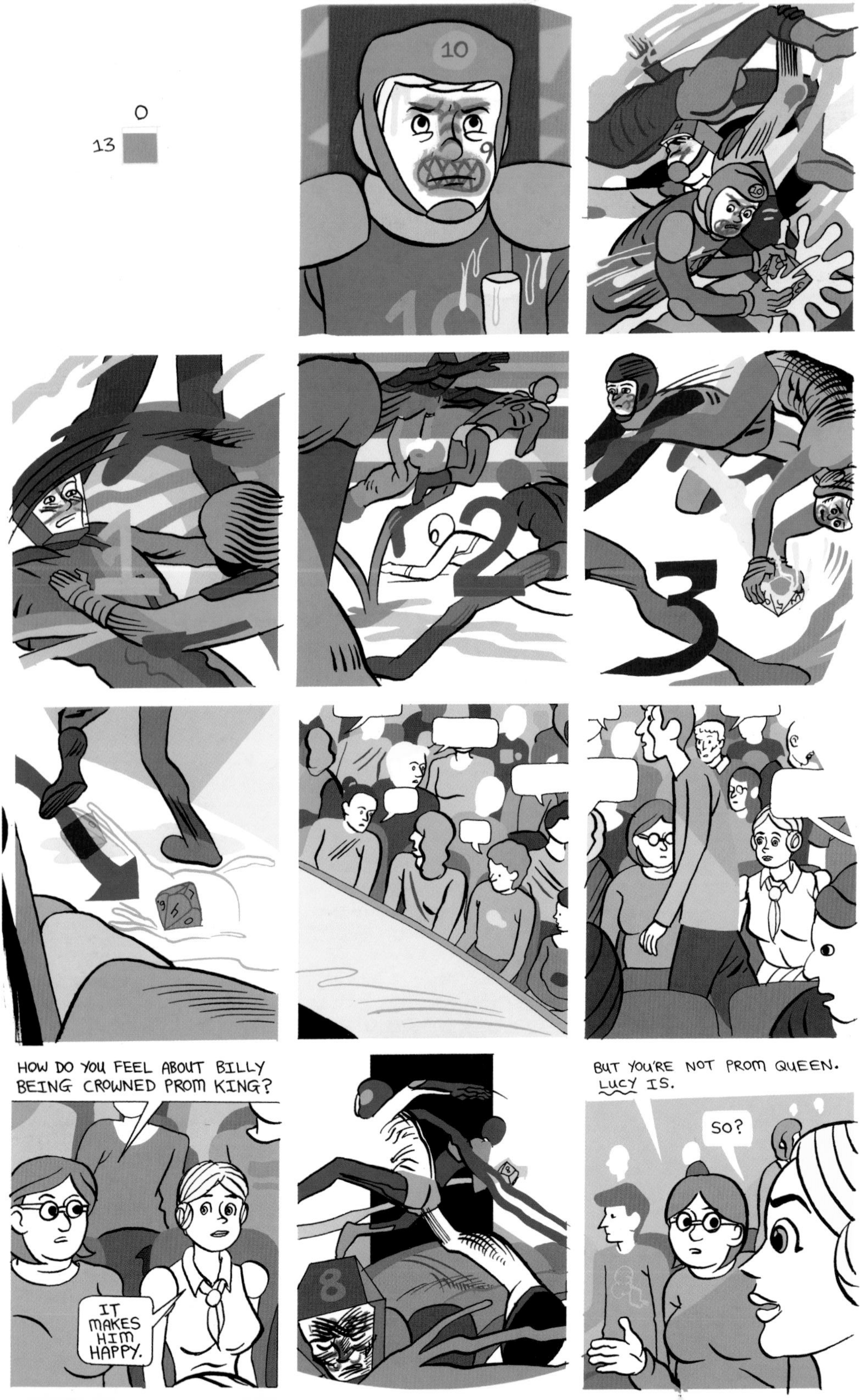
0
13
10
1
2
3
HOW DO YOU FEEL ABOUT BILLY BEING CROWNED PROM KING?
IT MAKES HIM HAPPY.
8
BUT YOU'RE NOT PROM QUEEN. LUCY IS.
SO?

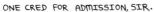

ONE CRED FOR ADMISSION, SIR.

I'M A VISITING TEACHER.

MISS JEWEL KNOWS ME.

EVEN FACULTY PAY ADMISSION. THE EARNINGS ARE DONATED—

AGH. WHATEVER.

I NEED A RECEIPT.

DON'T PLAY DUMB.

I'M NOT PLAYING DUMB! IT'S EVERYONE ELSE WHO'S DUMB. WHO'S PROM KING AND QUEEN DOESN'T MATTER AT ALL IN THE REAL WORLD.

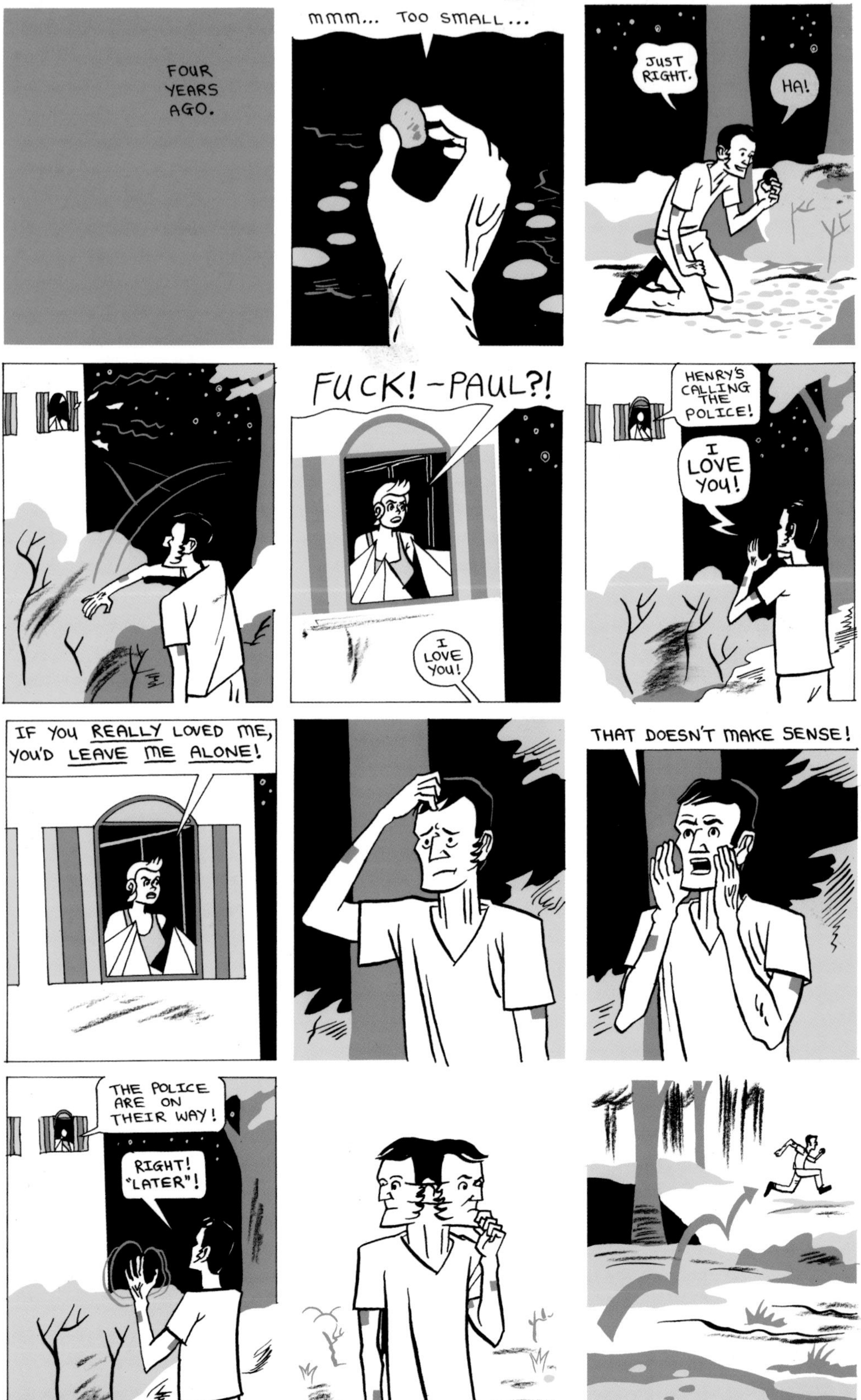
FOUR YEARS AGO.
MMM... TOO SMALL...
JUST RIGHT.
HA!
FUCK! -PAUL?!
I LOVE YOU!
HENRY'S CALLING THE POLICE!
I LOVE YOU!
IF YOU REALLY LOVED ME, YOU'D LEAVE ME ALONE!
THAT DOESN'T MAKE SENSE!
THE POLICE ARE ON THEIR WAY!
RIGHT! "LATER"!

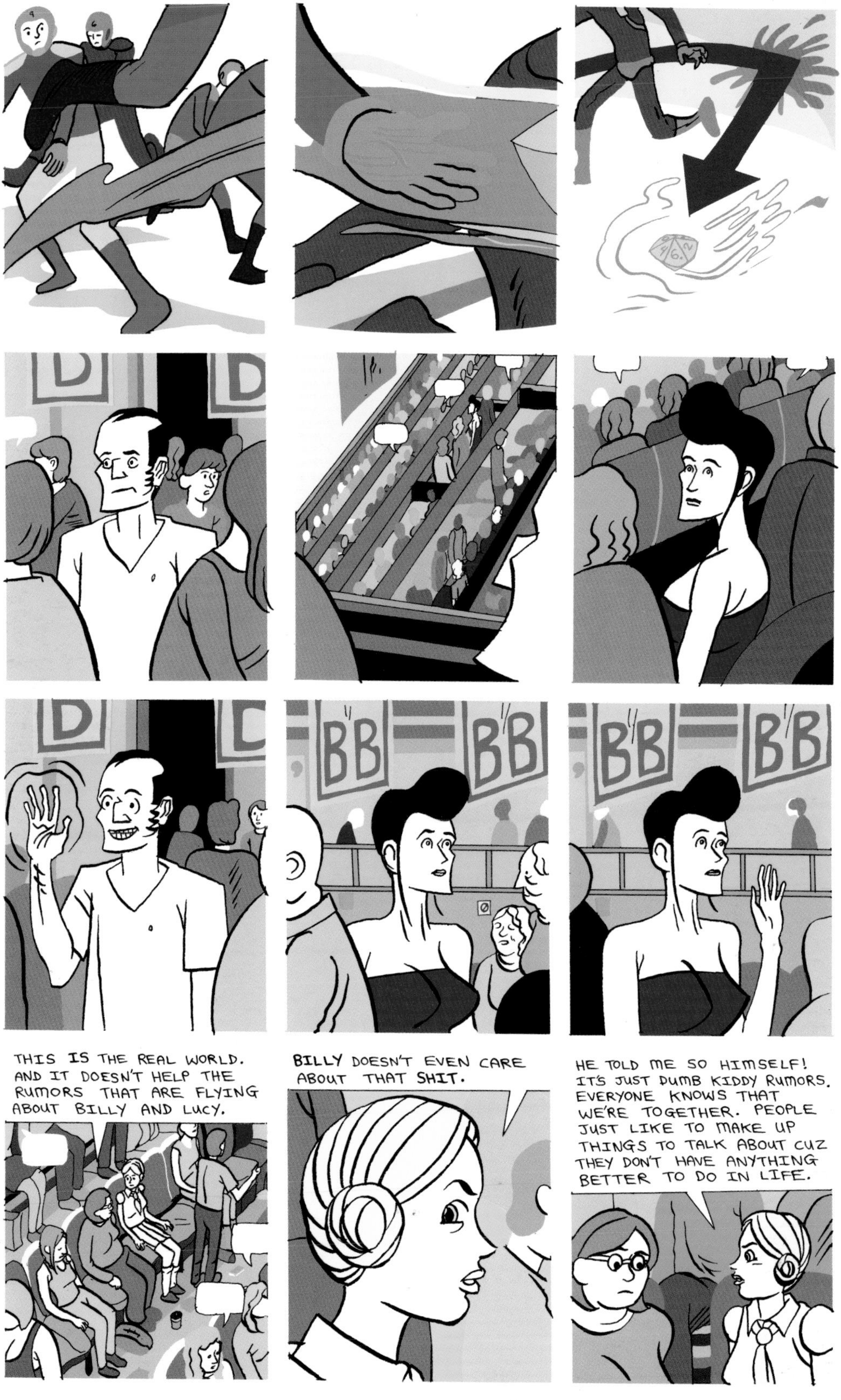
BB
BB
BB
BB
THIS IS THE REAL WORLD. AND IT DOESN'T HELP THE RUMORS THAT ARE FLYING ABOUT BILLY AND LUCY.
BILLY DOESN'T EVEN CARE ABOUT THAT SHIT.
HE TOLD ME SO HIMSELF! IT'S JUST DUMB KIDDY RUMORS. EVERYONE KNOWS THAT WE'RE TOGETHER. PEOPLE JUST LIKE TO MAKE UP THINGS TO TALK ABOUT CUZ THEY DON'T HAVE ANYTHING BETTER TO DO IN LIFE.

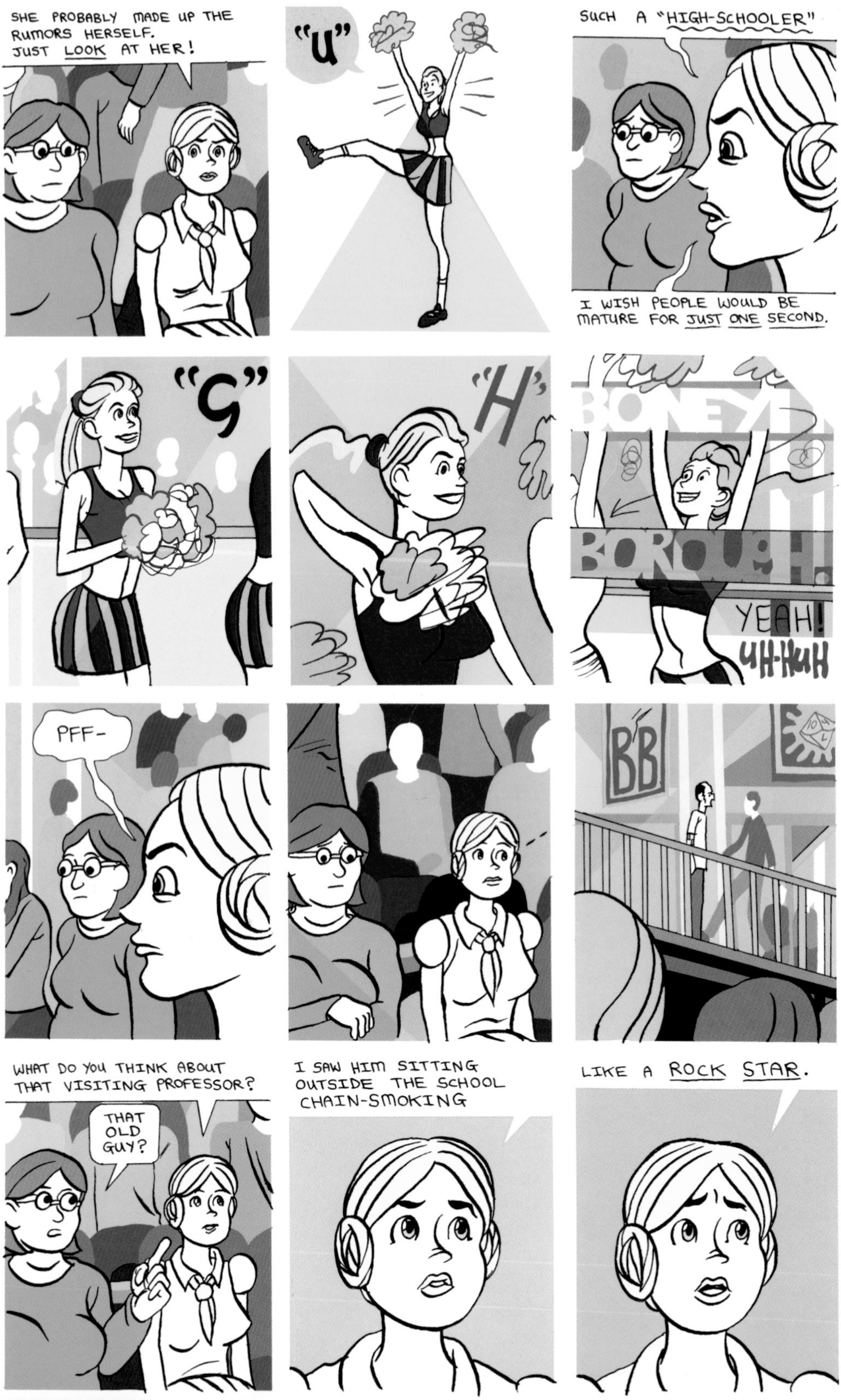
SHE PROBABLY MADE UP THE RUMORS HERSELF. JUST LOOK AT HER!
"U"
SUCH A "HIGH-SCHOOLER"
I WISH PEOPLE WOULD BE MATURE FOR JUST ONE SECOND.
"G"
"H"
BONEY
BOROUGH!
YEAH!
UH-HUH
PFF-
BB
WHAT DO YOU THINK ABOUT THAT VISITING PROFESSOR?
THAT OLD GUY?
I SAW HIM SITTING OUTSIDE THE SCHOOL CHAIN-SMOKING
LIKE A ROCK STAR.

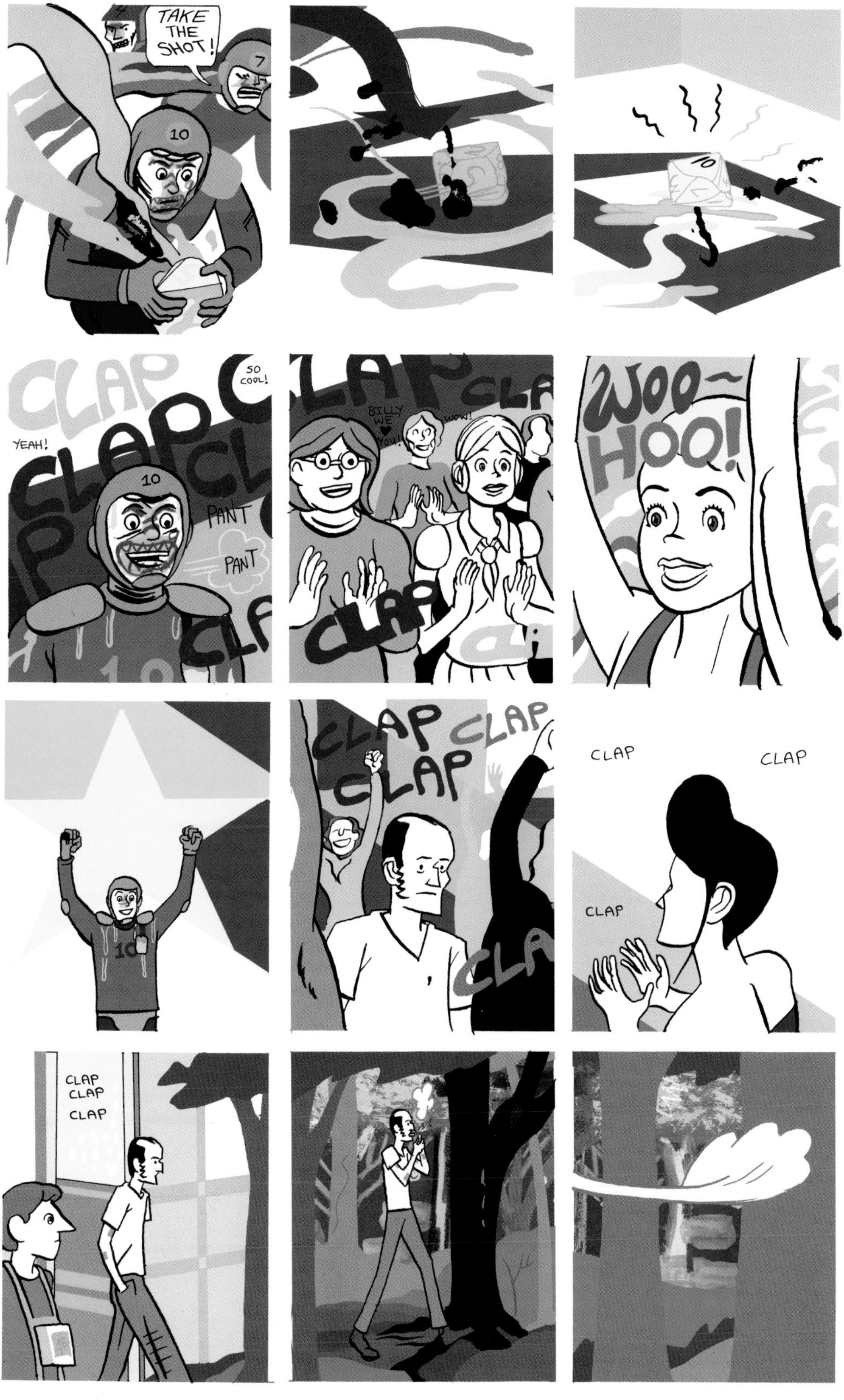
TAKE THE SHOT!
CLAP
SO COOL!
CLAP
YEAH!
PANT
PANT
CLAP
BILLY WE ♥ YOU!
WOW!
CLAP
WOO-HOO!
CLAP
CLAP
CLAP
CLAP
CLAP
CLAP
CLAP
CLAP
CLAP
CLAP

THREE YEARS AGO.
YOU ARE MY LAST CIGARETTE.
THIS IS IT, PAULIE-BOY, FINALLY, THE END.
TIGHT
TIGHT
FFF-
BEEP
YOU HAVE —ONE— NEW UNREAD MESSAGE.
N!
BEEP

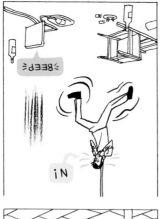

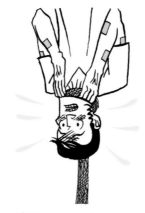

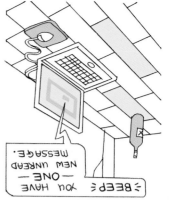

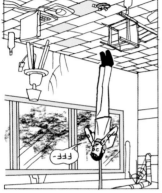

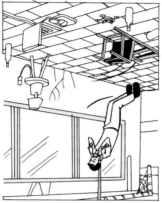

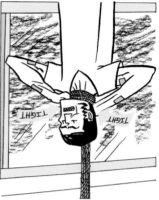

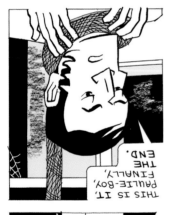

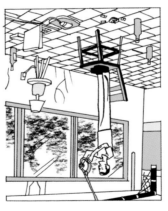

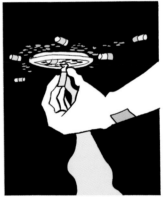

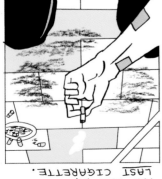

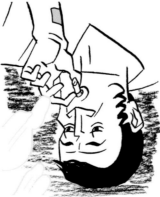

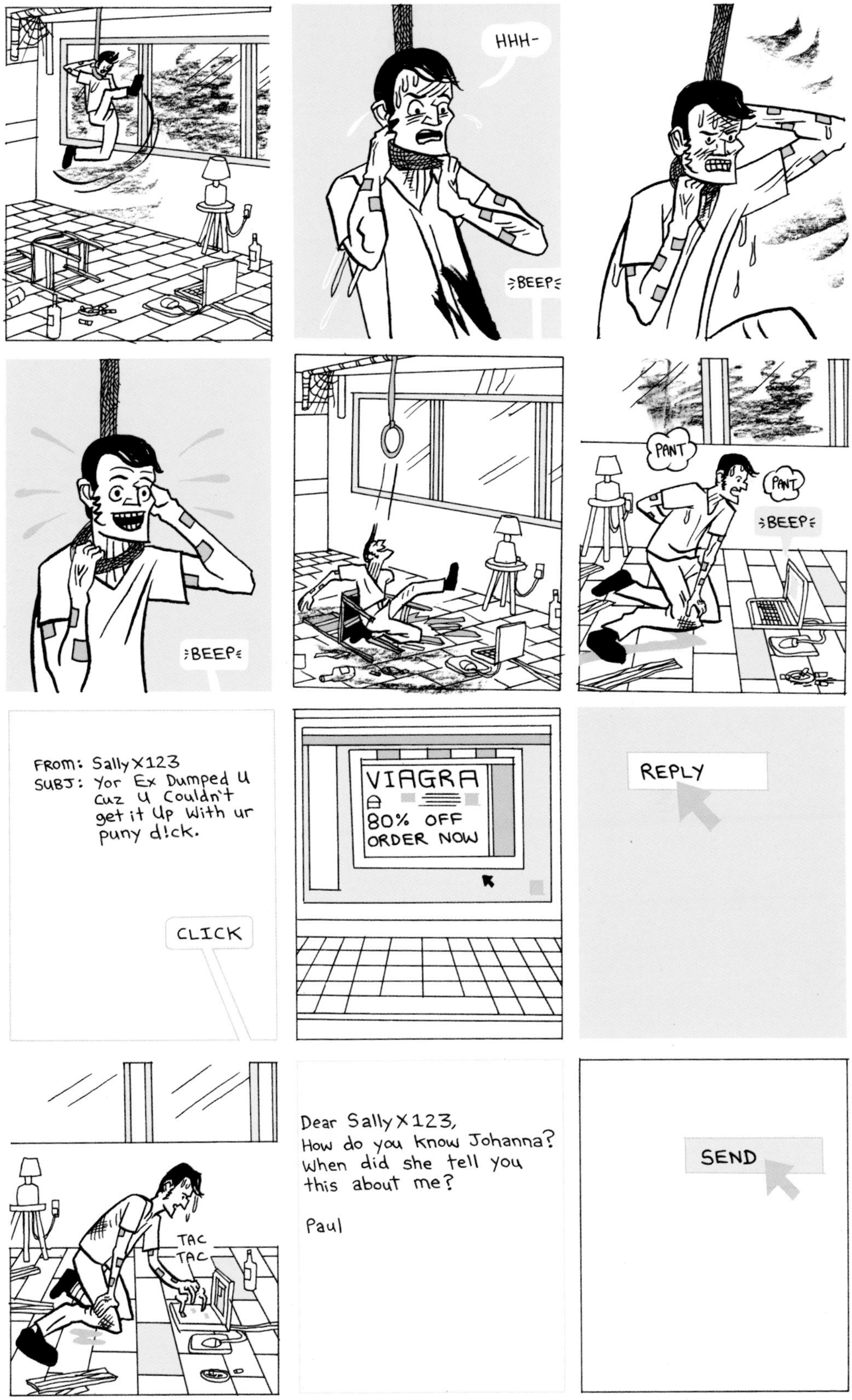
HHH-
BEEP
BEEP
PANT
PANT
BEEP
FROM: SallyX123
SUBJ: Yor Ex Dumped U Cuz U Couldn't get it Up With ur puny d!ck.
CLICK
VIAGRA
80% OFF
ORDER NOW
REPLY
TAC
TAC
Dear SallyX123,
How do you know Johanna? When did she tell you this about me?
Paul
SEND

24
R
P&B ∞
I CAN'T.
I'M ON MY PERIOD.

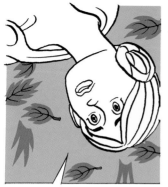

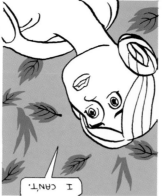

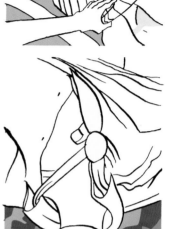

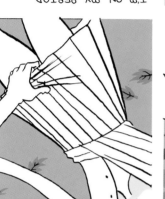

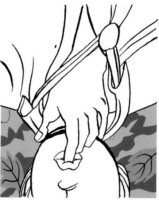

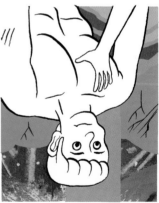

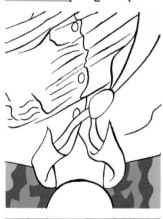

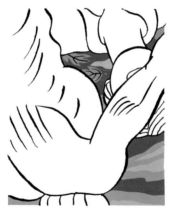

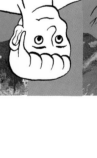

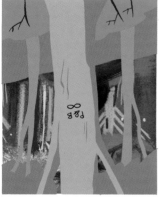

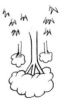

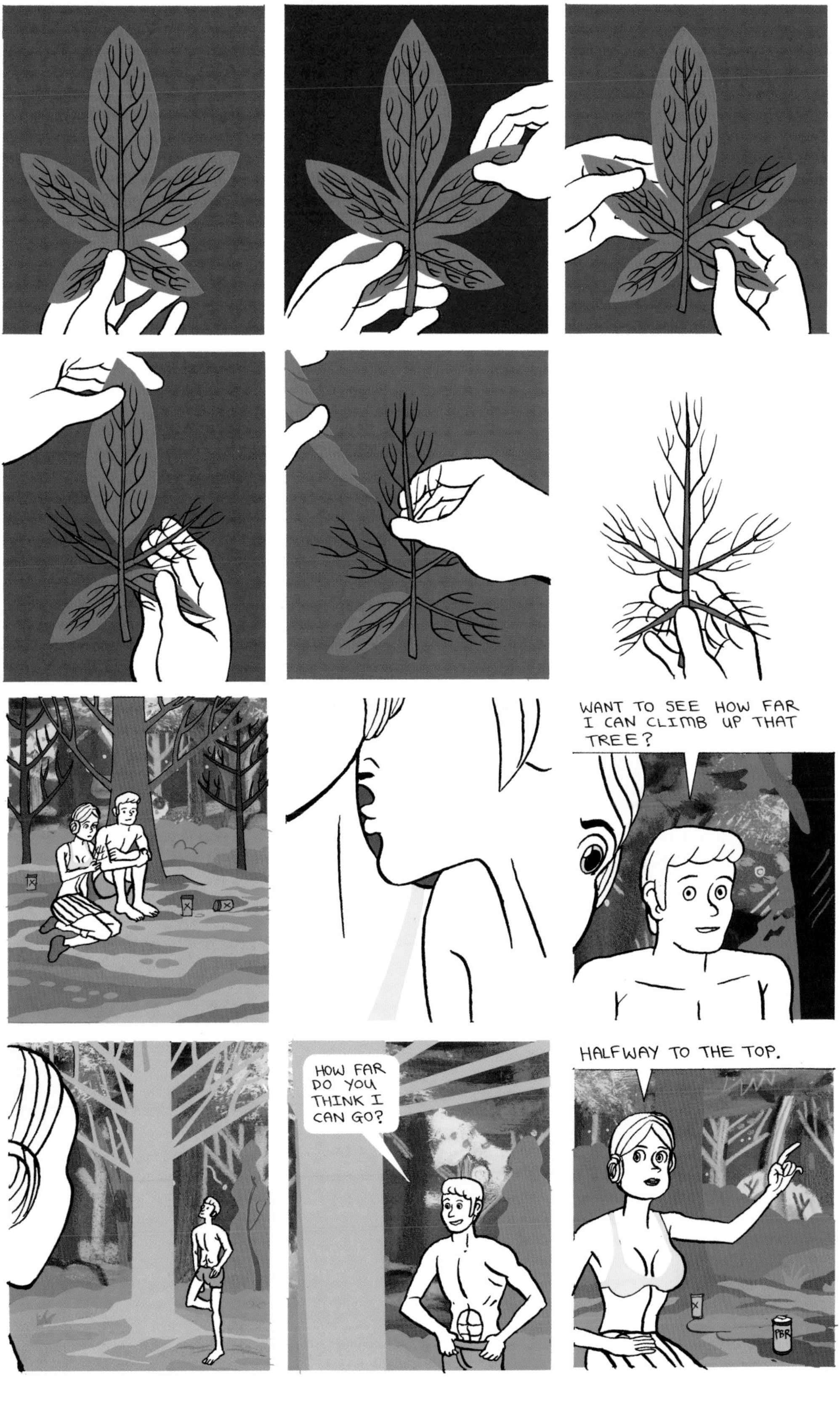
WANT TO SEE HOW FAR I CAN CLIMB UP THAT TREE?
HOW FAR DO YOU THINK I CAN GO?
HALFWAY TO THE TOP.
PBR

HA
SNAP

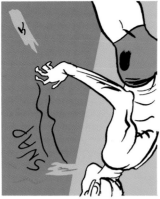

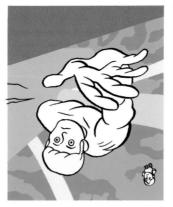

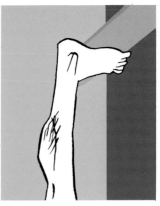

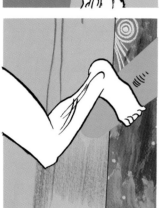

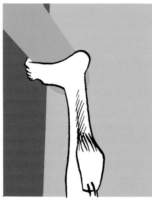

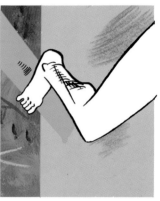

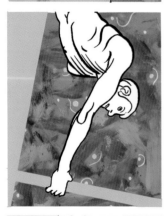

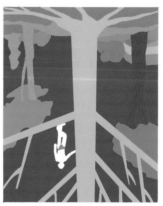

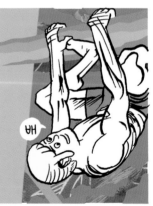

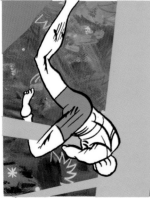

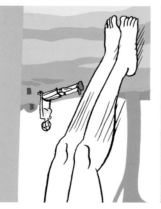

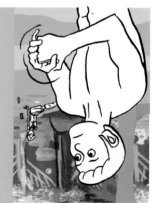

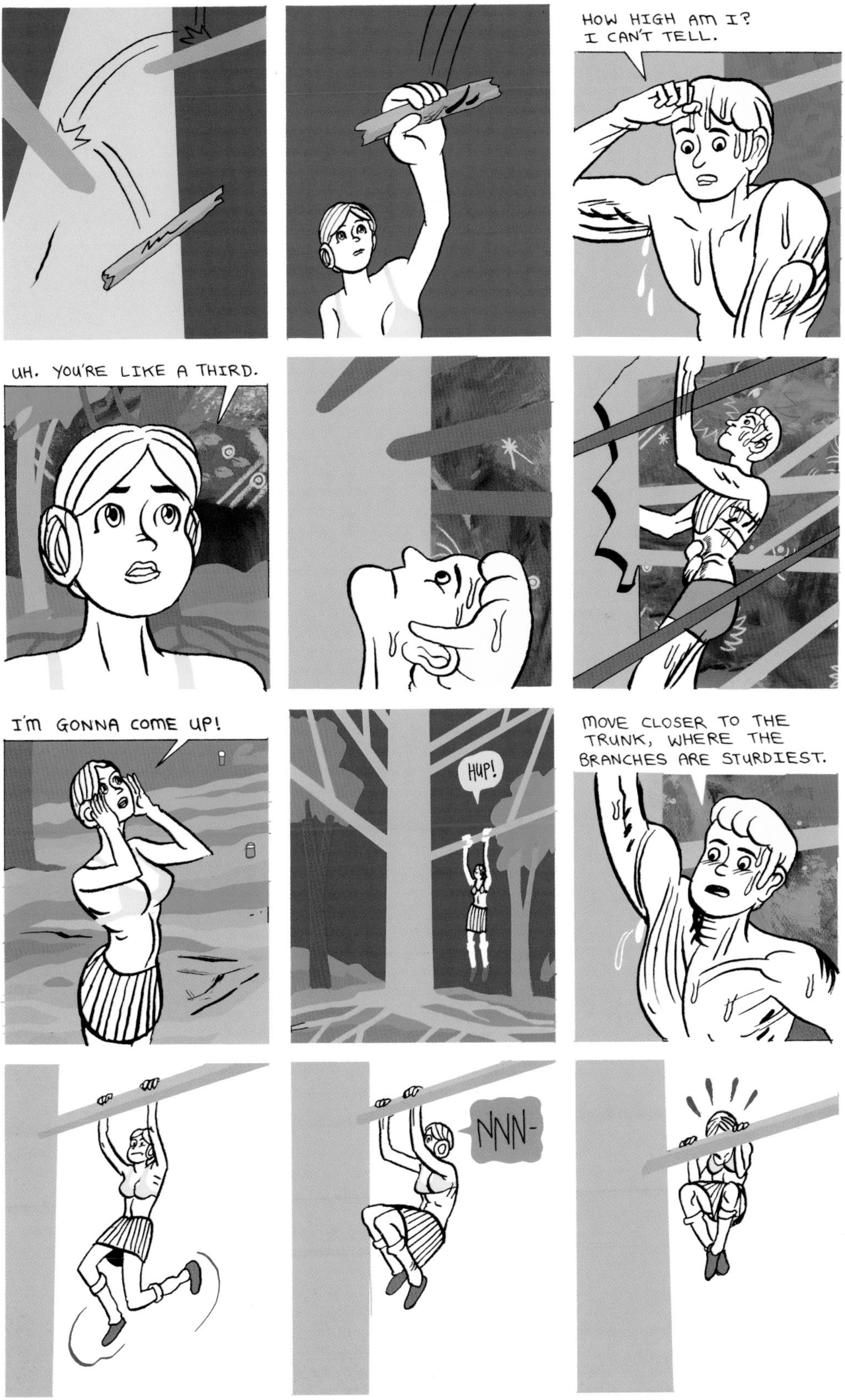
HOW HIGH AM I? I CAN'T TELL.
UH. YOU'RE LIKE A THIRD.
I'M GONNA COME UP!
HUP!
MOVE CLOSER TO THE TRUNK, WHERE THE BRANCHES ARE STURDIEST.
NNN-

YES!
WOW!
PANT PANT
TEST A BRANCH BEFORE YOU SUPPORT YOURSELF ON IT, YOU KNOW?
PANT
TEST
SUPPORT
I THINK I'M HALFWAY!
PANT
PANT

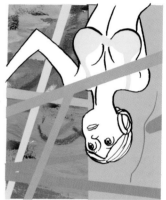

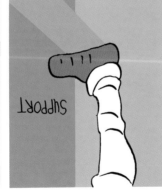

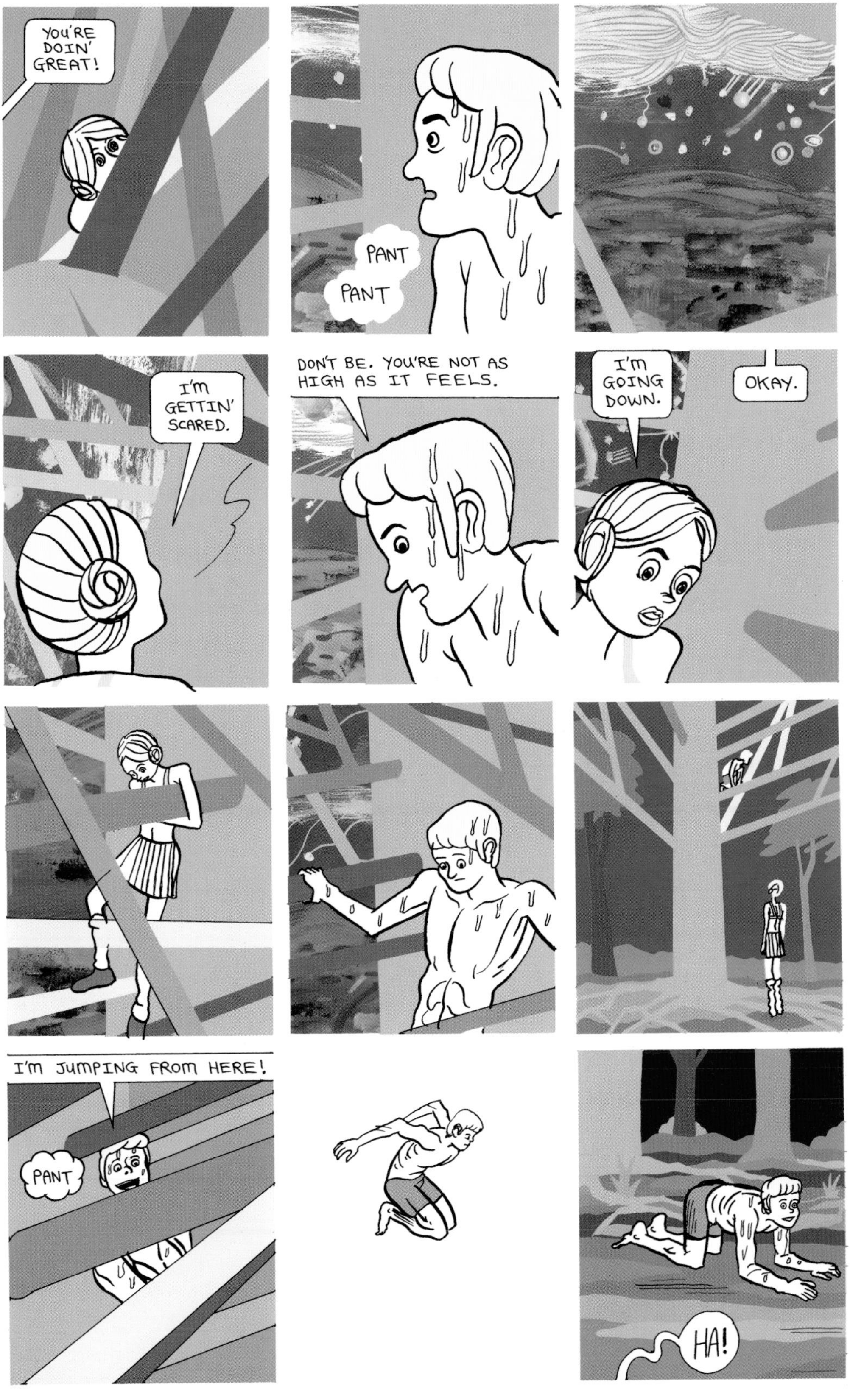

YOU'RE DOIN' GREAT!
PANT
PANT
I'M GETTIN' SCARED.
DON'T BE. YOU'RE NOT AS HIGH AS IT FEELS.
I'M GOING DOWN.
OKAY.
I'M JUMPING FROM HERE!
PANT
HA!

Ha.

HA HA

PANT

ROLL

LOOK AT YOU. YOU'RE ALL SWEATY.

PANT

YEAH. ALL THE GUYS ON THE TEAM DON'T SWEAT AS MUCH AS ME. IT'S KINDA EMBARASSING, YOU KNOW?

NO, NO, I LIKE IT.

HA. YEAH, RIGHT.

IT'S ALL GOOEY.

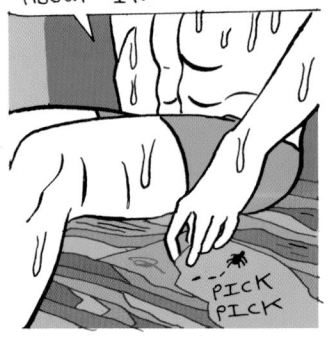

YEAH. I GET PIT STAINS. MOM ALWAYS BUGS ME ABOUT IT.

PICK PICK

I DON'T CARE. SWEAT IS ALWAYS INSIDE YOU—IN YOUR SKIN, RIGHT?

I GUESS SO.

BUT ONCE PEOPLE CAN SEE IT, THEY THINK IT'S SO DISGUSTING.

HA.

LIKE BLOOD. PEOPLE JUST DON'T WANT TO SEE WHAT'S GOING ON INSIDE.

SHRUG

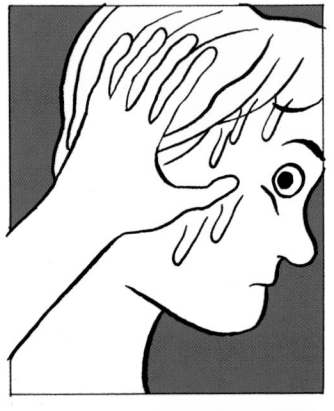

I WANT TO SEE WHAT'S INSIDE YOU. I WANT TO KNOW EVERYTHING ABOUT YOU.

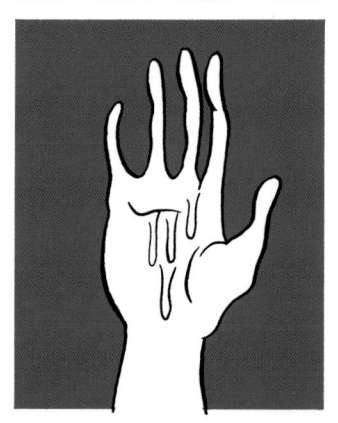

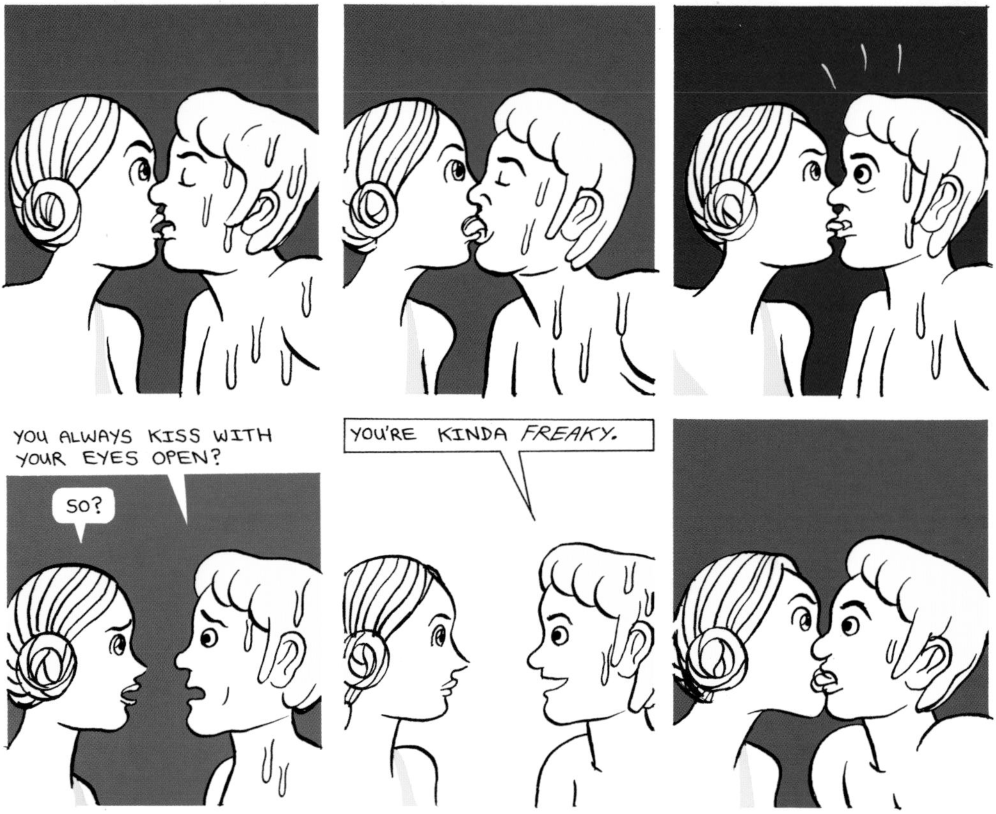
YOU ALWAYS KISS WITH YOUR EYES OPEN?
SO?
YOU'RE KINDA *FREAKY.*

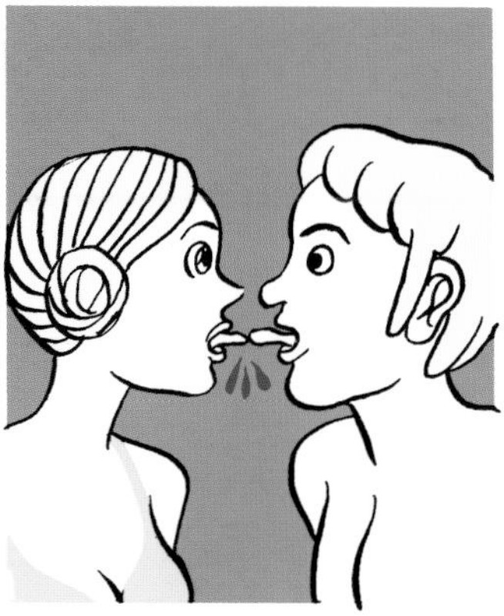

END OF CHAPTER TWO.

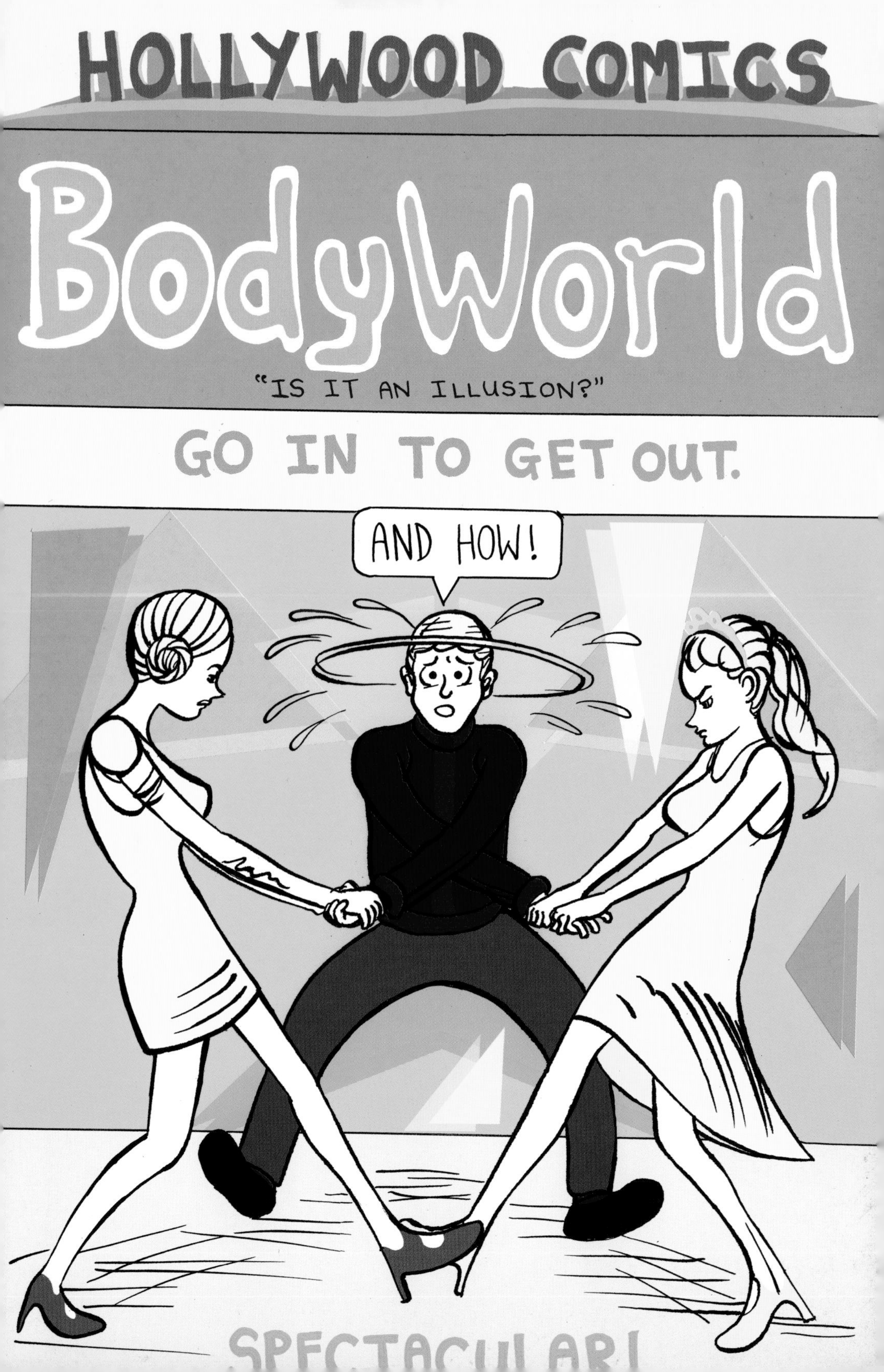
HOLLYWOOD COMICS
BodyWorld
"IS IT AN ILLUSION?"
GO IN TO GET OUT.
AND HOW!
SPECTACULAR!

CHAPTER THREE

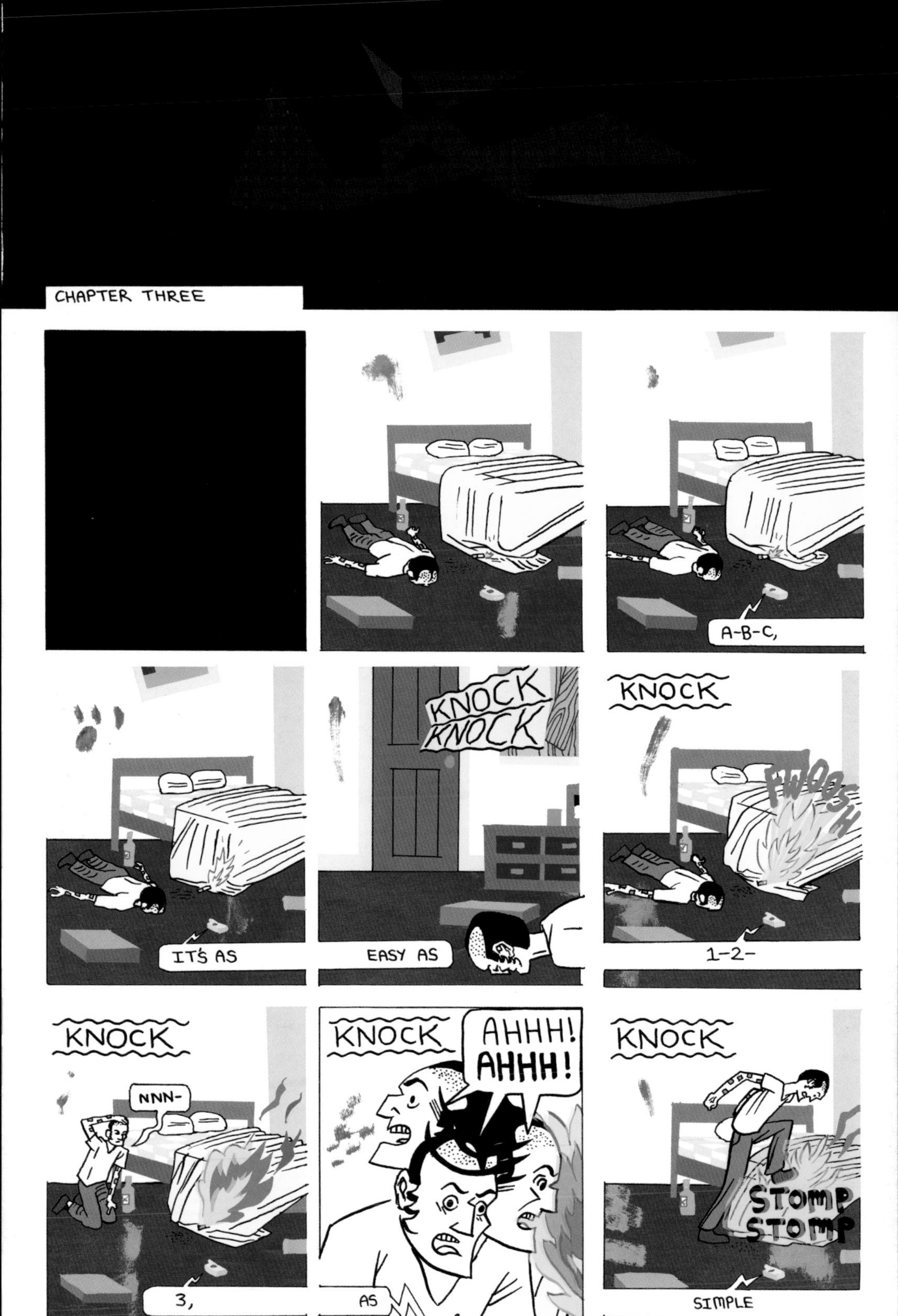
A-B-C,
IT'S AS
KNOCK KNOCK
EASY AS
KNOCK
FWOOSH
1-2-
KNOCK
NNN-
3,
KNOCK
AHHH! AHHH!
AS
KNOCK
STOMP STOMP
SIMPLE

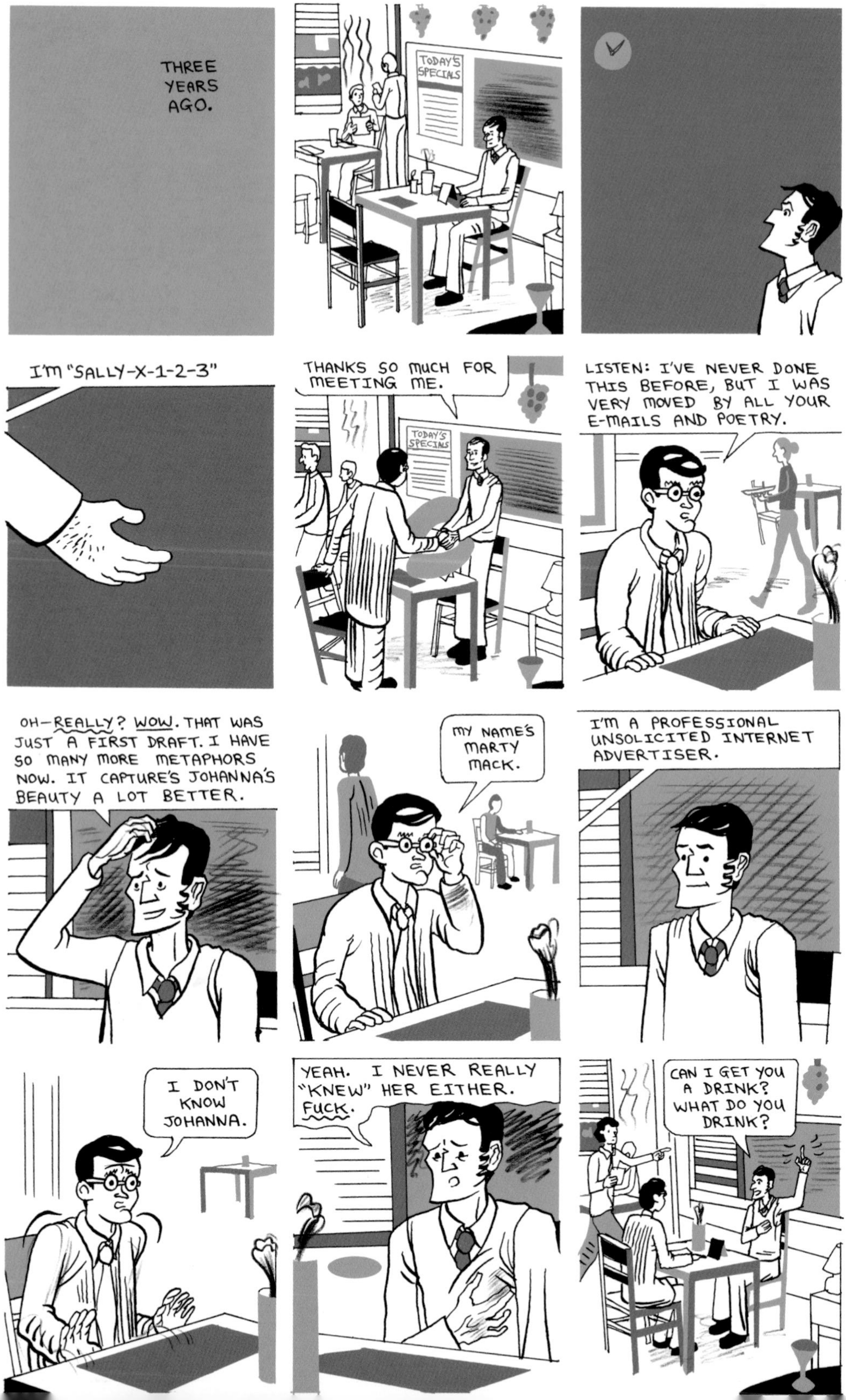
THREE YEARS AGO.
TODAY'S SPECIALS
I'M "SALLY-X-1-2-3"
THANKS SO MUCH FOR MEETING ME.
TODAY'S SPECIALS
LISTEN: I'VE NEVER DONE THIS BEFORE, BUT I WAS VERY MOVED BY ALL YOUR E-MAILS AND POETRY.
OH—REALLY? WOW. THAT WAS JUST A FIRST DRAFT. I HAVE SO MANY MORE METAPHORS NOW. IT CAPTURE'S JOHANNA'S BEAUTY A LOT BETTER.
MY NAME'S MARTY MACK.
I'M A PROFESSIONAL UNSOLICITED INTERNET ADVERTISER.
I DON'T KNOW JOHANNA.
YEAH. I NEVER REALLY "KNEW" HER EITHER. FUCK.
CAN I GET YOU A DRINK? WHAT DO YOU DRINK?

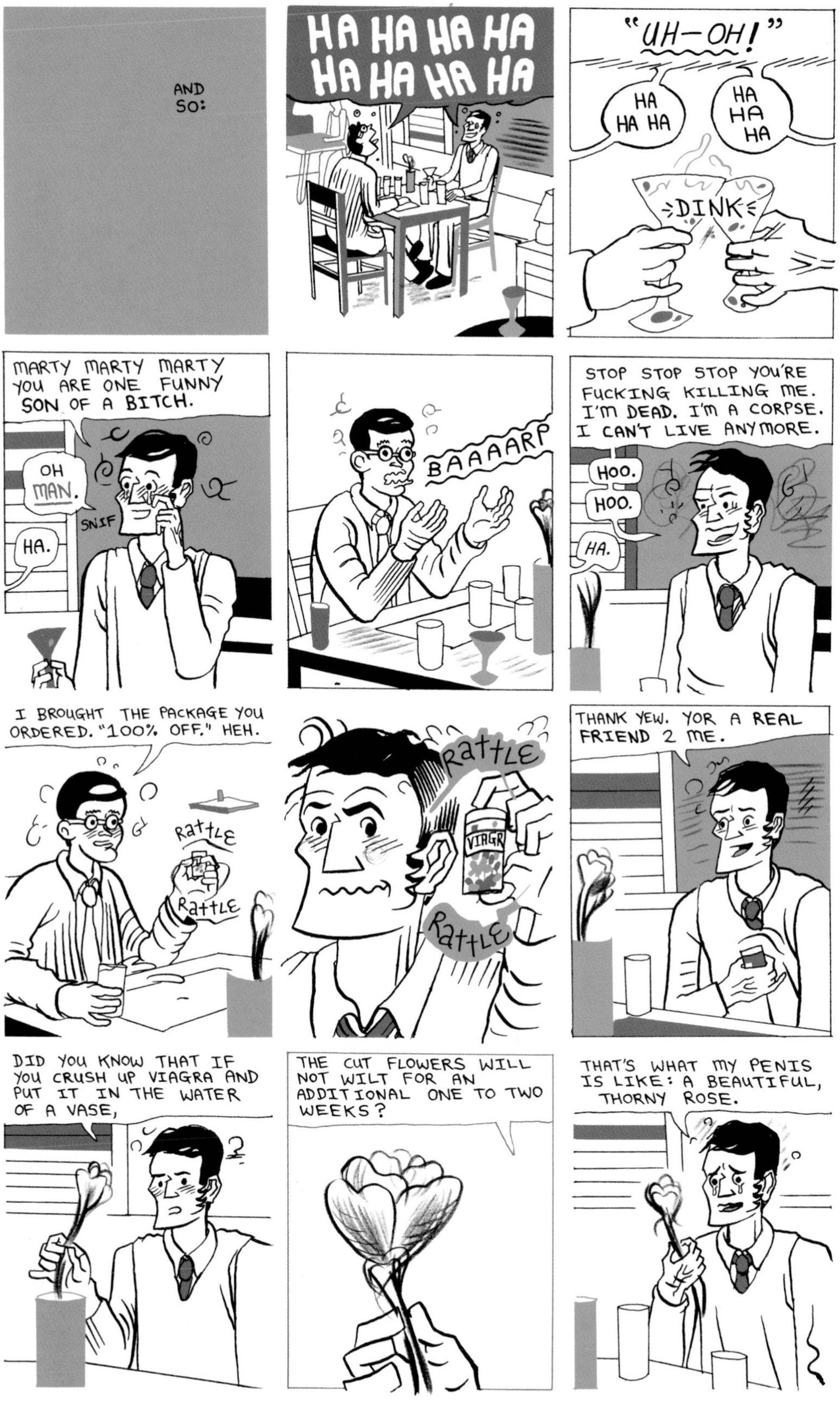
AND SO:
HA HA HA HA
HA HA HA HA
"UH-OH!"
HA HA HA
HA HA HA
DINK
MARTY MARTY MARTY YOU ARE ONE FUNNY SON OF A BITCH.
OH MAN.
SNIF
HA.
BAAAARP
STOP STOP STOP YOU'RE FUCKING KILLING ME. I'M DEAD. I'M A CORPSE. I CAN'T LIVE ANYMORE.
HOO.
HOO.
HA.
I BROUGHT THE PACKAGE YOU ORDERED. "100% OFF." HEH.
RATTLE
RATTLE
RATTLE
VIAGR
RATTLE
THANK YEW. YOR A REAL FRIEND 2 ME.
DID YOU KNOW THAT IF YOU CRUSH UP VIAGRA AND PUT IT IN THE WATER OF A VASE,
THE CUT FLOWERS WILL NOT WILT FOR AN ADDITIONAL ONE TO TWO WEEKS?
THAT'S WHAT MY PENIS IS LIKE: A BEAUTIFUL, THORNY ROSE.

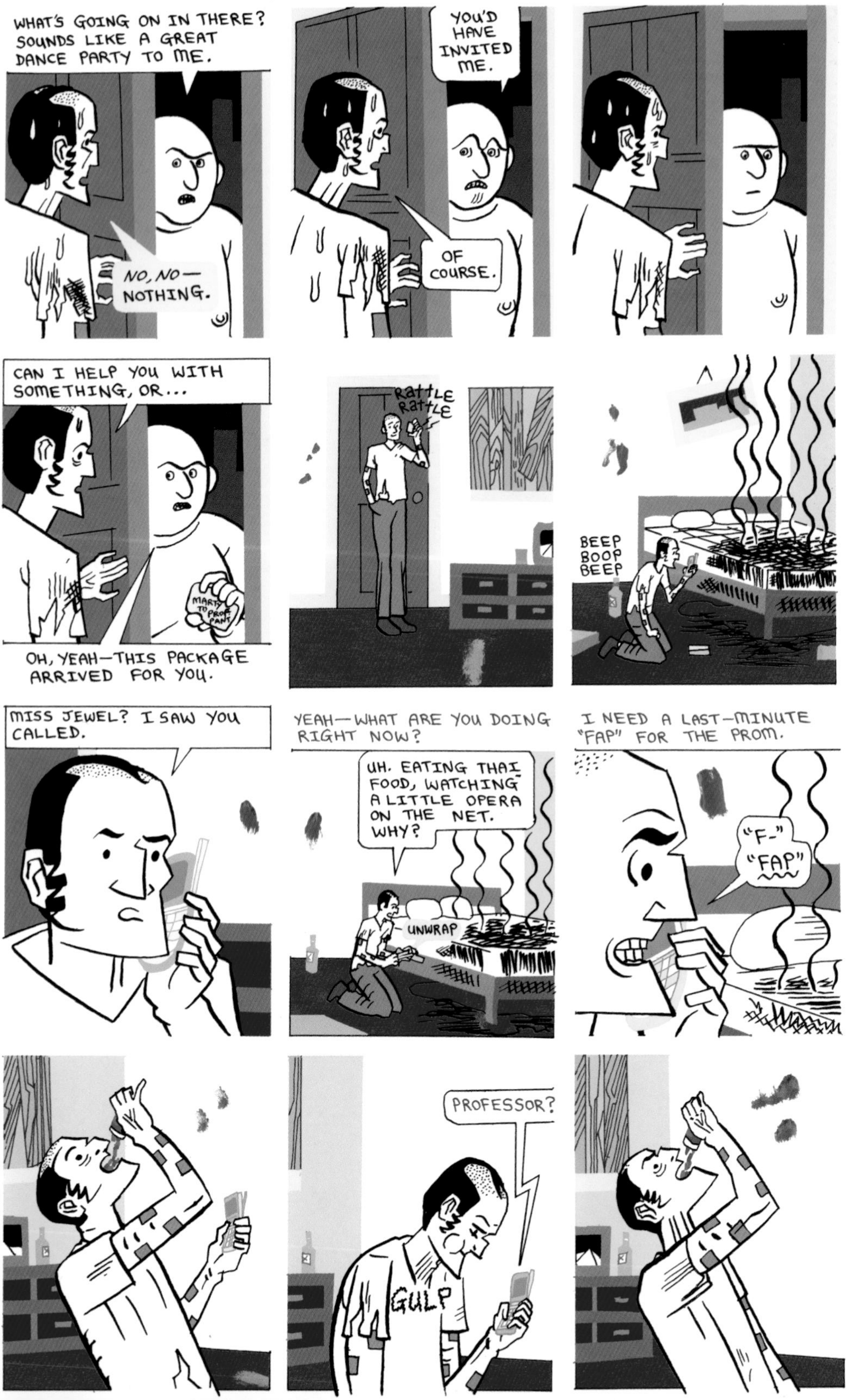

WHAT'S GOING ON IN THERE? SOUNDS LIKE A GREAT DANCE PARTY TO ME.
NO, NO— NOTHING.
YOU'D HAVE INVITED ME.
OF COURSE.
CAN I HELP YOU WITH SOMETHING, OR...
MARTY TO PROF PANT
OH, YEAH—THIS PACKAGE ARRIVED FOR YOU.
RATTLE RATTLE
BEEP BOOP BEEP
MISS JEWEL? I SAW YOU CALLED.
YEAH—WHAT ARE YOU DOING RIGHT NOW?
UH. EATING THAI FOOD, WATCHING A LITTLE OPERA ON THE NET. WHY?
UNWRAP
I NEED A LAST-MINUTE "FAP" FOR THE PROM.
"F-"
"FAP"
PROFESSOR?
GULP

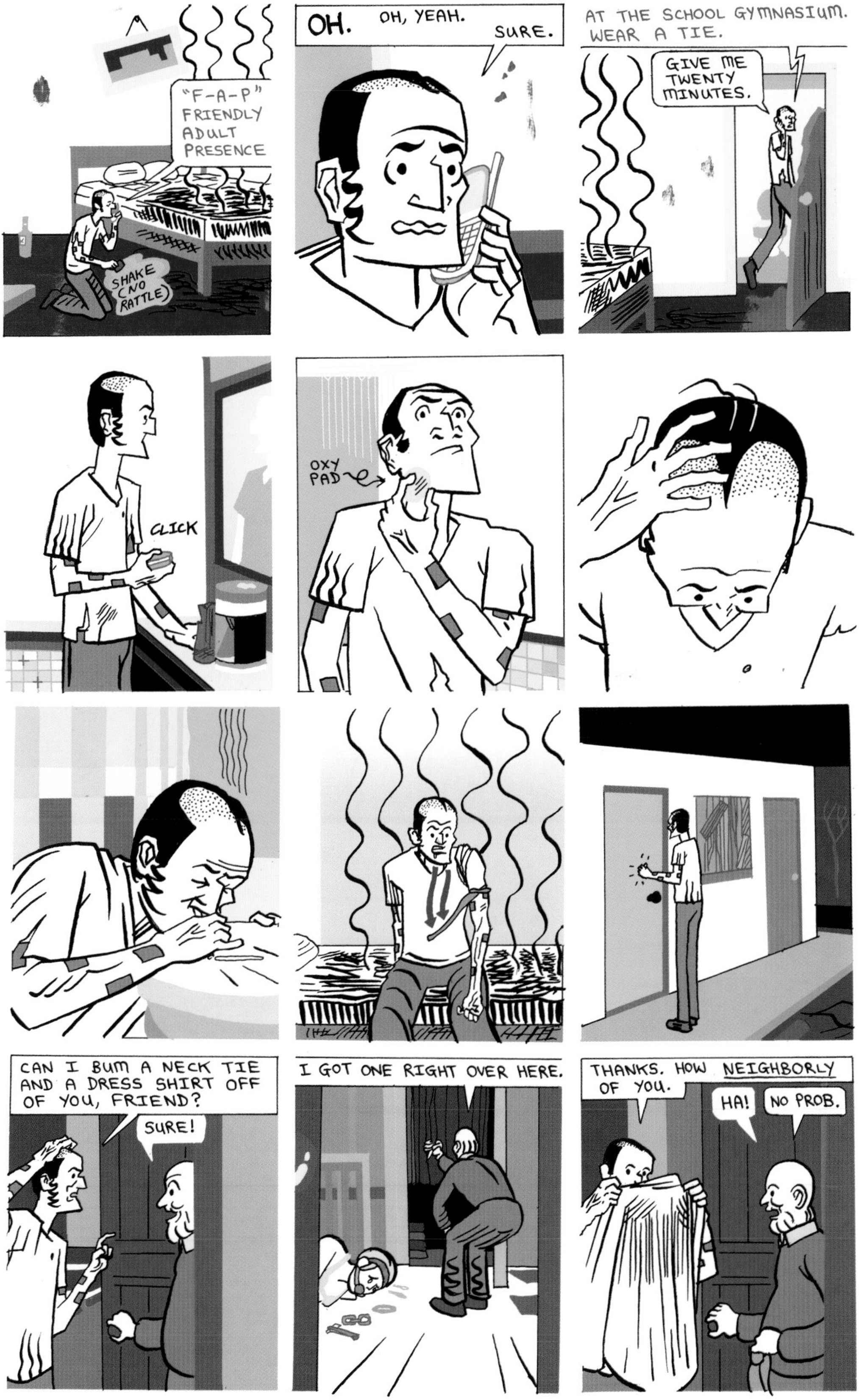
"F-A-P"
FRIENDLY ADULT PRESENCE
SHAKE (NO RATTLE)
OH.
OH, YEAH.
SURE.
AT THE SCHOOL GYMNASIUM. WEAR A TIE.
GIVE ME TWENTY MINUTES.
CLICK
OXY PAD
CAN I BUM A NECK TIE AND A DRESS SHIRT OFF OF YOU, FRIEND?
SURE!
I GOT ONE RIGHT OVER HERE.
THANKS. HOW NEIGHBORLY OF YOU.
HA!
NO PROB.

0

13

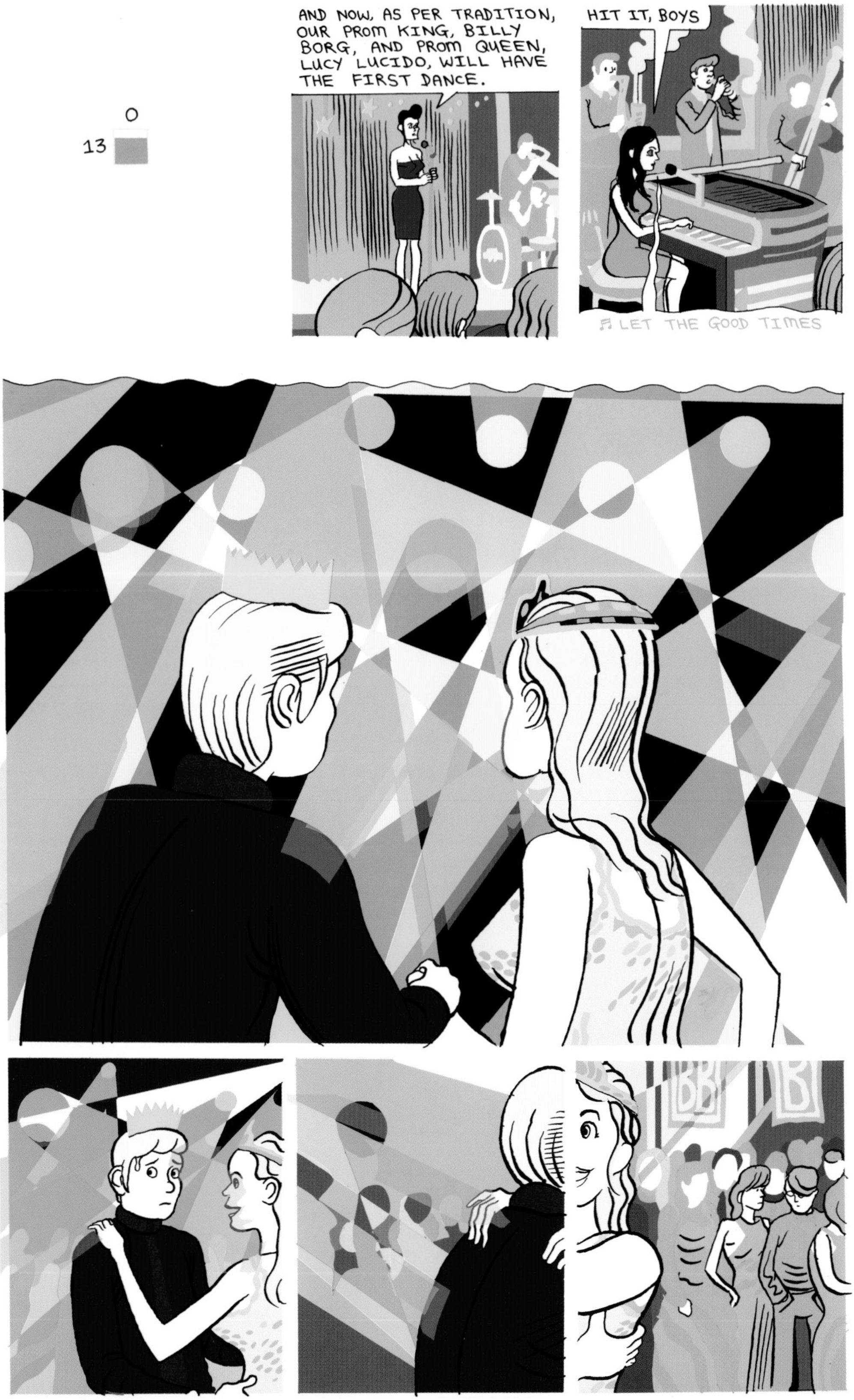
AND NOW, AS PER TRADITION, OUR PROM KING, BILLY BORG, AND PROM QUEEN, LUCY LUCIDO, WILL HAVE THE FIRST DANCE.
HIT IT, BOYS
♫ LET THE GOOD TIMES

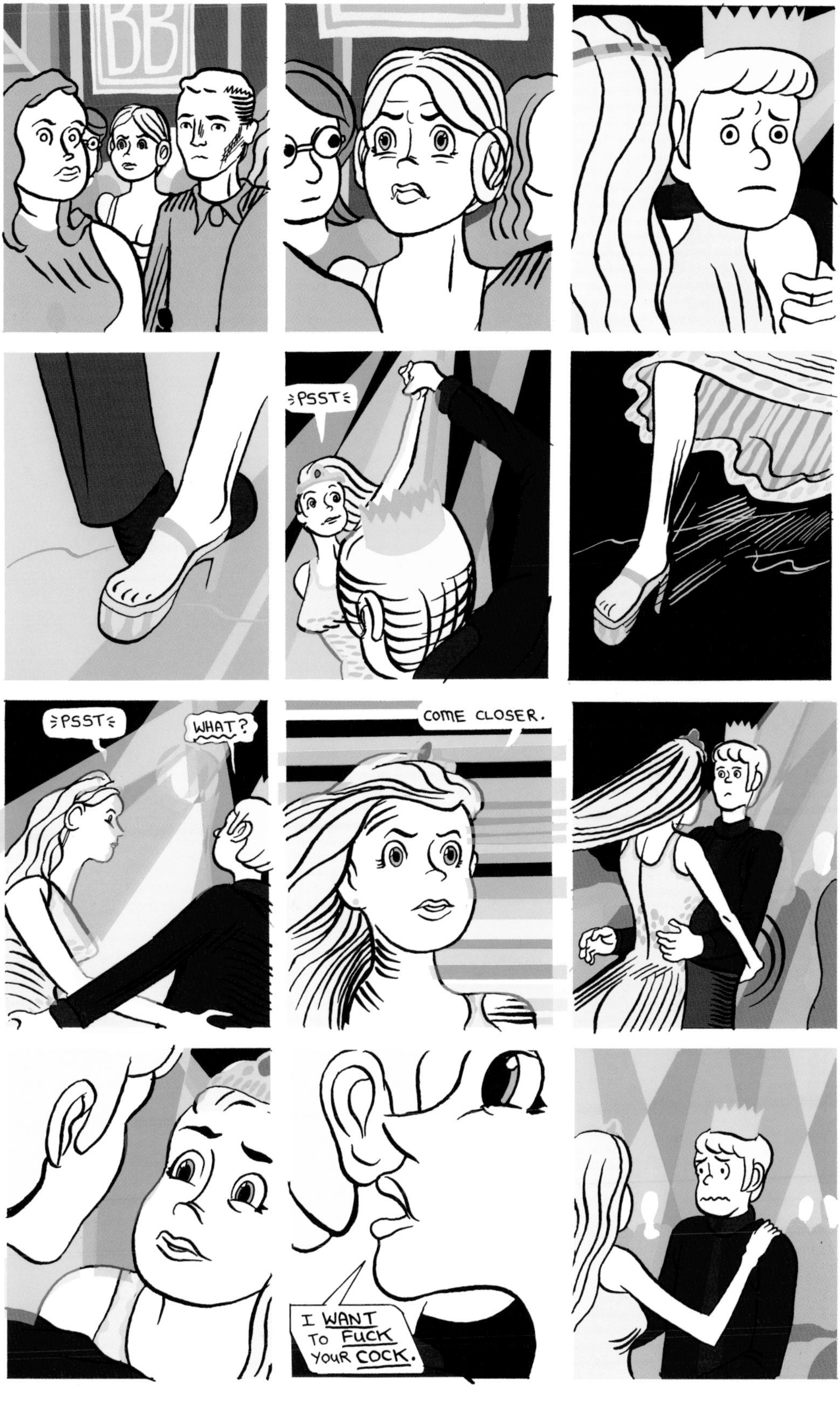
PSST
PSST
WHAT?
COME CLOSER.
I WANT TO FUCK YOUR COCK.

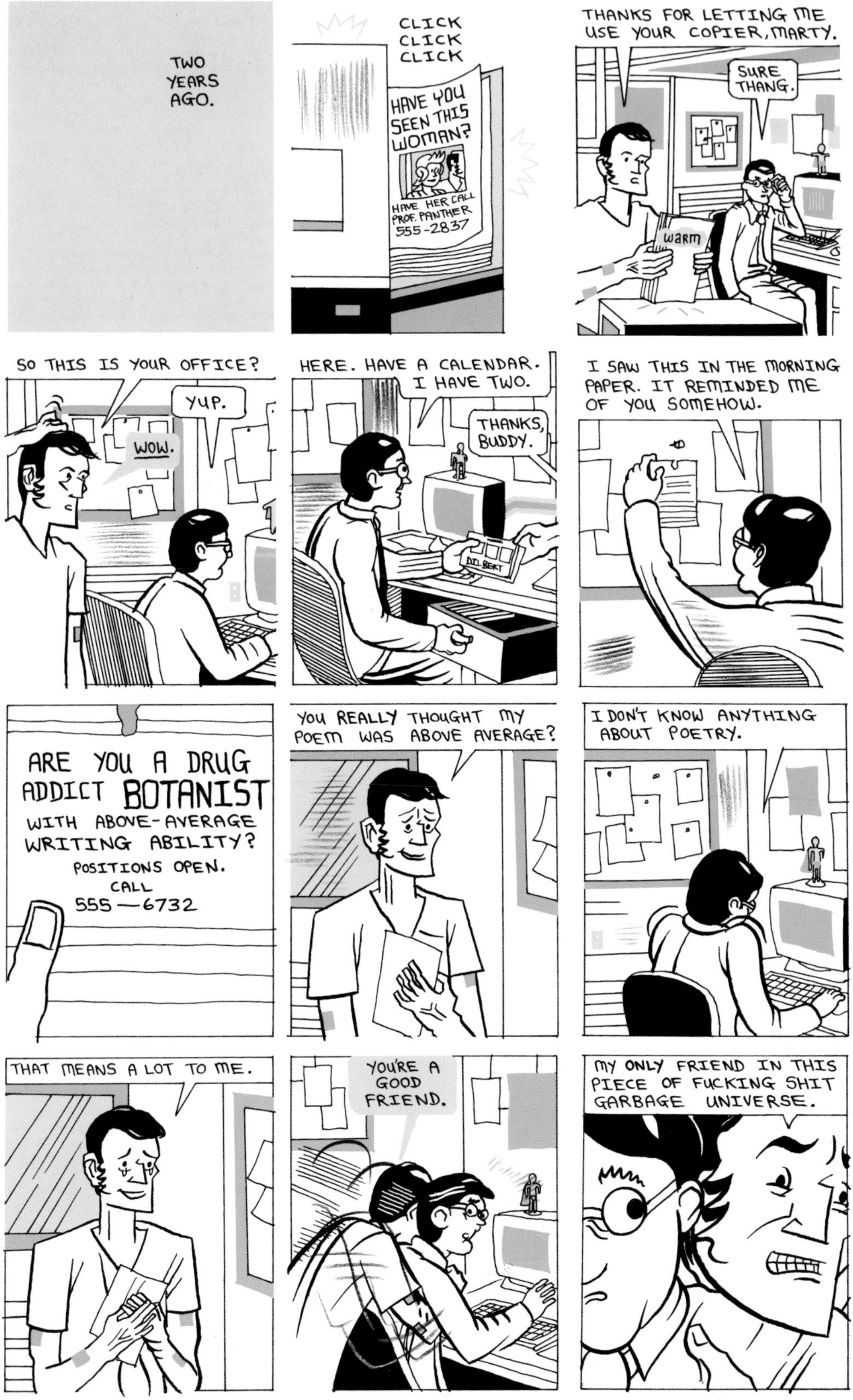
TWO YEARS AGO.
CLICK CLICK CLICK
HAVE YOU SEEN THIS WOMAN?
HAVE HER CALL PROF. PANTHER 555-2837
THANKS FOR LETTING ME USE YOUR COPIER, MARTY.
SURE THANG.
warm
SO THIS IS YOUR OFFICE?
YUP.
WOW.
HERE. HAVE A CALENDAR. I HAVE TWO.
THANKS, BUDDY.
I SAW THIS IN THE MORNING PAPER. IT REMINDED ME OF YOU SOMEHOW.
ARE YOU A DRUG ADDICT BOTANIST WITH ABOVE-AVERAGE WRITING ABILITY?
POSITIONS OPEN.
CALL 555—6732
YOU REALLY THOUGHT MY POEM WAS ABOVE AVERAGE?
I DON'T KNOW ANYTHING ABOUT POETRY.
THAT MEANS A LOT TO ME.
YOU'RE A GOOD FRIEND.
MY ONLY FRIEND IN THIS PIECE OF FUCKING SHIT GARBAGE UNIVERSE.

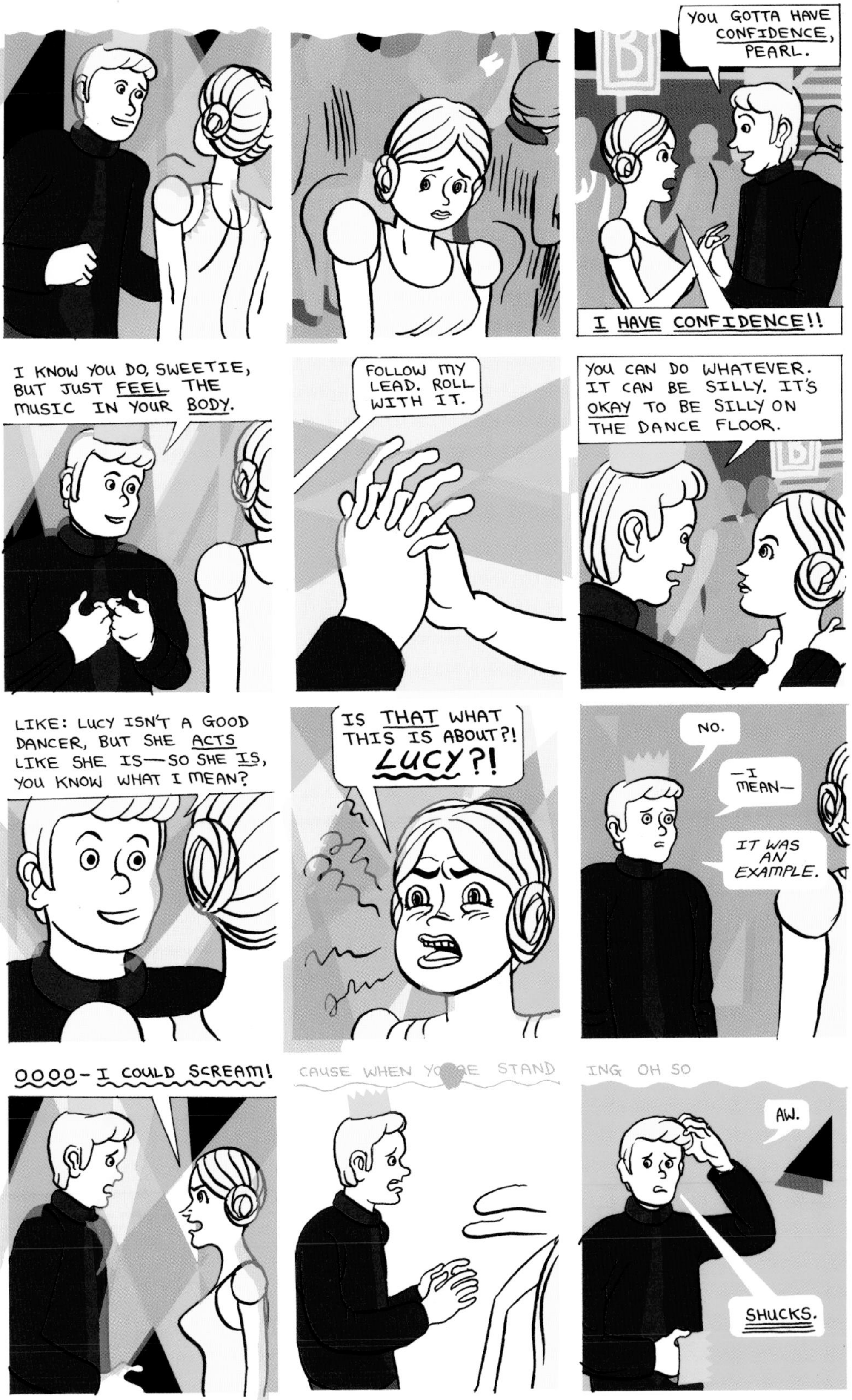

YOU GOTTA HAVE CONFIDENCE, PEARL.
I HAVE CONFIDENCE!!
I KNOW YOU DO, SWEETIE, BUT JUST FEEL THE MUSIC IN YOUR BODY.
FOLLOW MY LEAD. ROLL WITH IT.
YOU CAN DO WHATEVER. IT CAN BE SILLY. IT'S OKAY TO BE SILLY ON THE DANCE FLOOR.
LIKE: LUCY ISN'T A GOOD DANCER, BUT SHE ACTS LIKE SHE IS—SO SHE IS, YOU KNOW WHAT I MEAN?
IS THAT WHAT THIS IS ABOUT?! LUCY?!
NO.
—I MEAN—
IT WAS AN EXAMPLE.
OOOO-I COULD SCREAM!
CAUSE WHEN YO RE STAND
ING OH SO
AW.
SHUCKS.

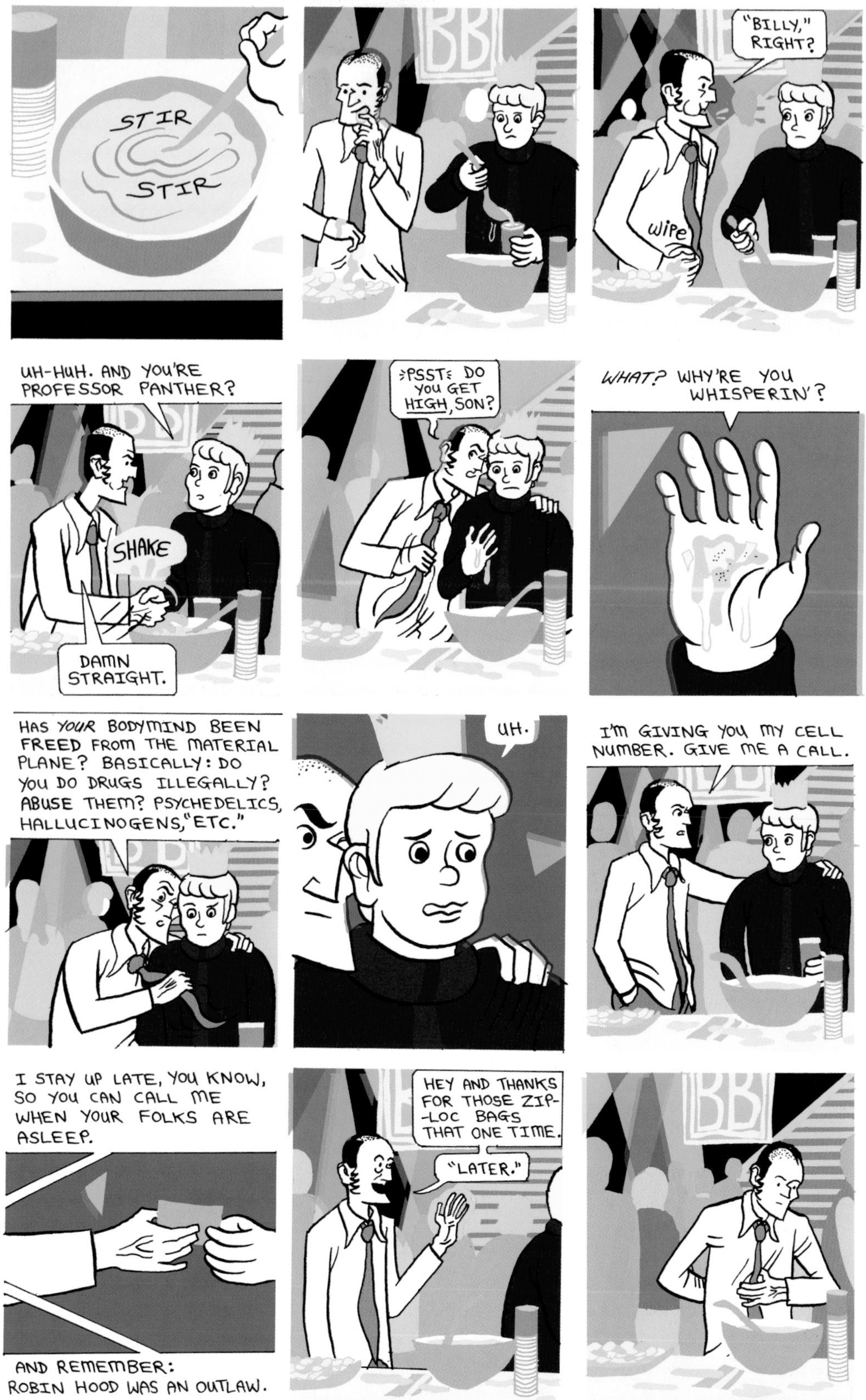
STIR
STIR
"BILLY," RIGHT?
wipe
UH-HUH. AND YOU'RE PROFESSOR PANTHER?
SHAKE
DAMN STRAIGHT.
=PSST= DO YOU GET HIGH, SON?
WHAT? WHY'RE YOU WHISPERIN'?
HAS YOUR BODYMIND BEEN FREED FROM THE MATERIAL PLANE? BASICALLY: DO YOU DO DRUGS ILLEGALLY? ABUSE THEM? PSYCHEDELICS, HALLUCINOGENS, "ETC."
UH.
I'M GIVING YOU MY CELL NUMBER. GIVE ME A CALL.
I STAY UP LATE, YOU KNOW, SO YOU CAN CALL ME WHEN YOUR FOLKS ARE ASLEEP.
AND REMEMBER: ROBIN HOOD WAS AN OUTLAW.
HEY AND THANKS FOR THOSE ZIP-LOC BAGS THAT ONE TIME.
"LATER."

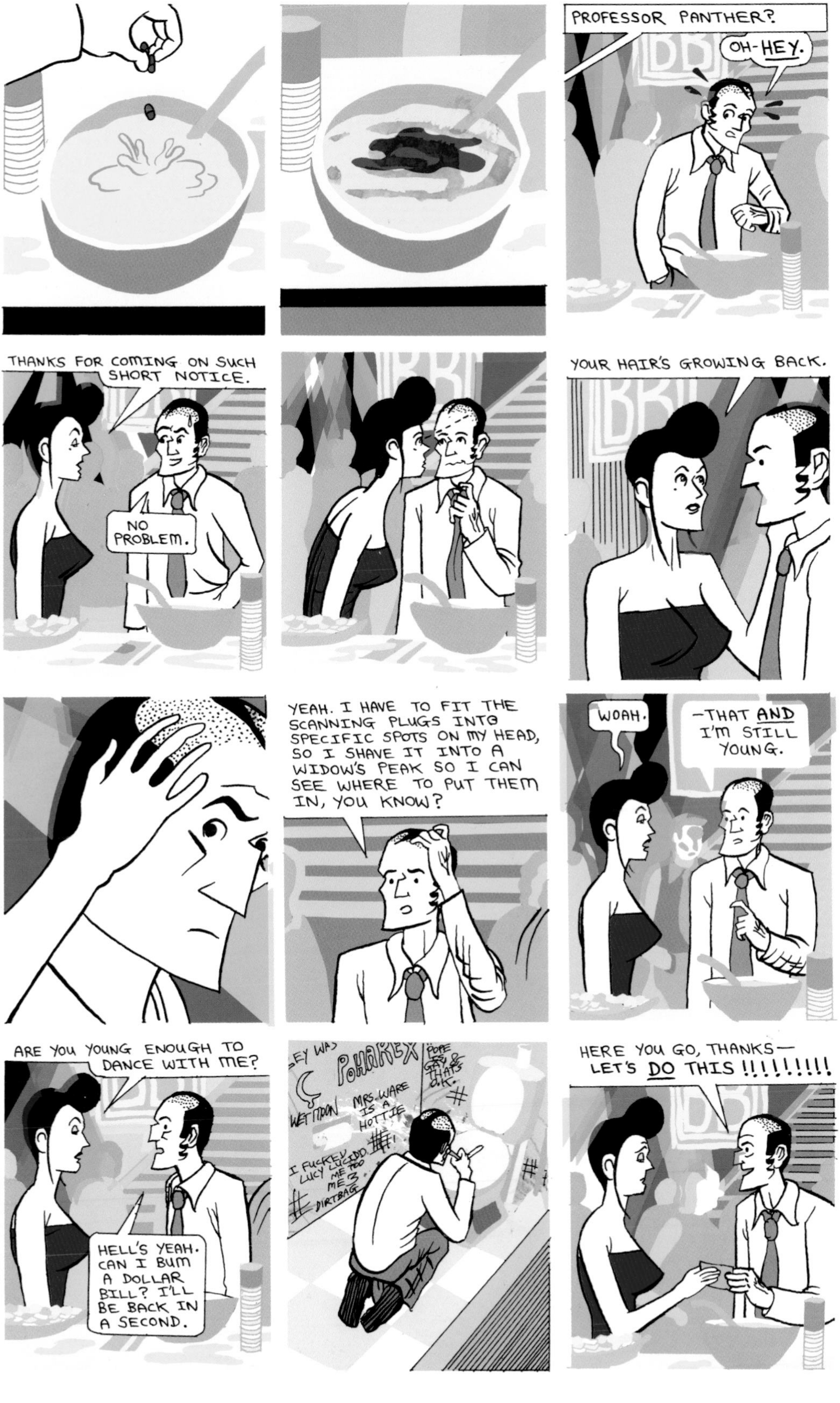
PROFESSOR PANTHER?
OH-HEY.
THANKS FOR COMING ON SUCH SHORT NOTICE.
NO PROBLEM.
YOUR HAIR'S GROWING BACK.
YEAH. I HAVE TO FIT THE SCANNING PLUGS INTO SPECIFIC SPOTS ON MY HEAD, SO I SHAVE IT INTO A WIDOW'S PEAK SO I CAN SEE WHERE TO PUT THEM IN, YOU KNOW?
WOAH.
-THAT AND I'M STILL YOUNG.
ARE YOU YOUNG ENOUGH TO DANCE WITH ME?
HELL'S YEAH. CAN I BUM A DOLLAR BILL? I'LL BE BACK IN A SECOND.
MRS. WARE IS A HOTTIE
DIRTBAG
HERE YOU GO, THANKS—LET'S DO THIS !!!!!!!!!

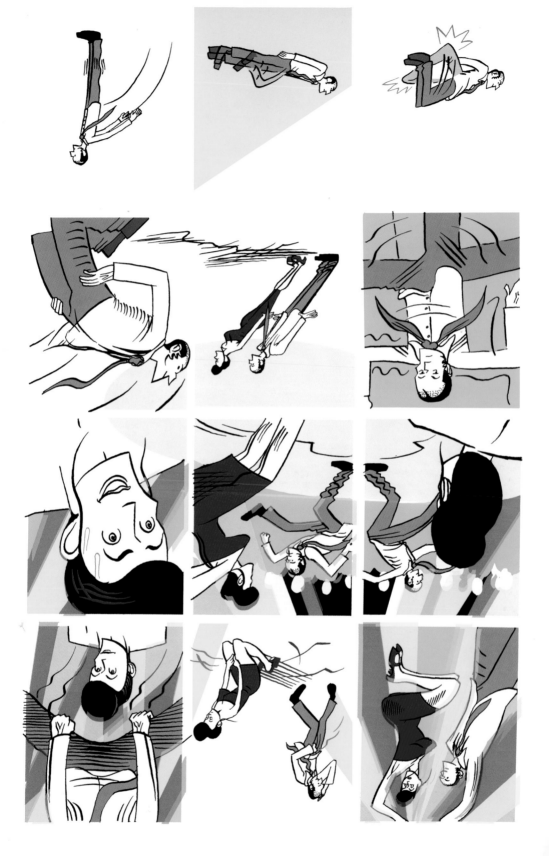

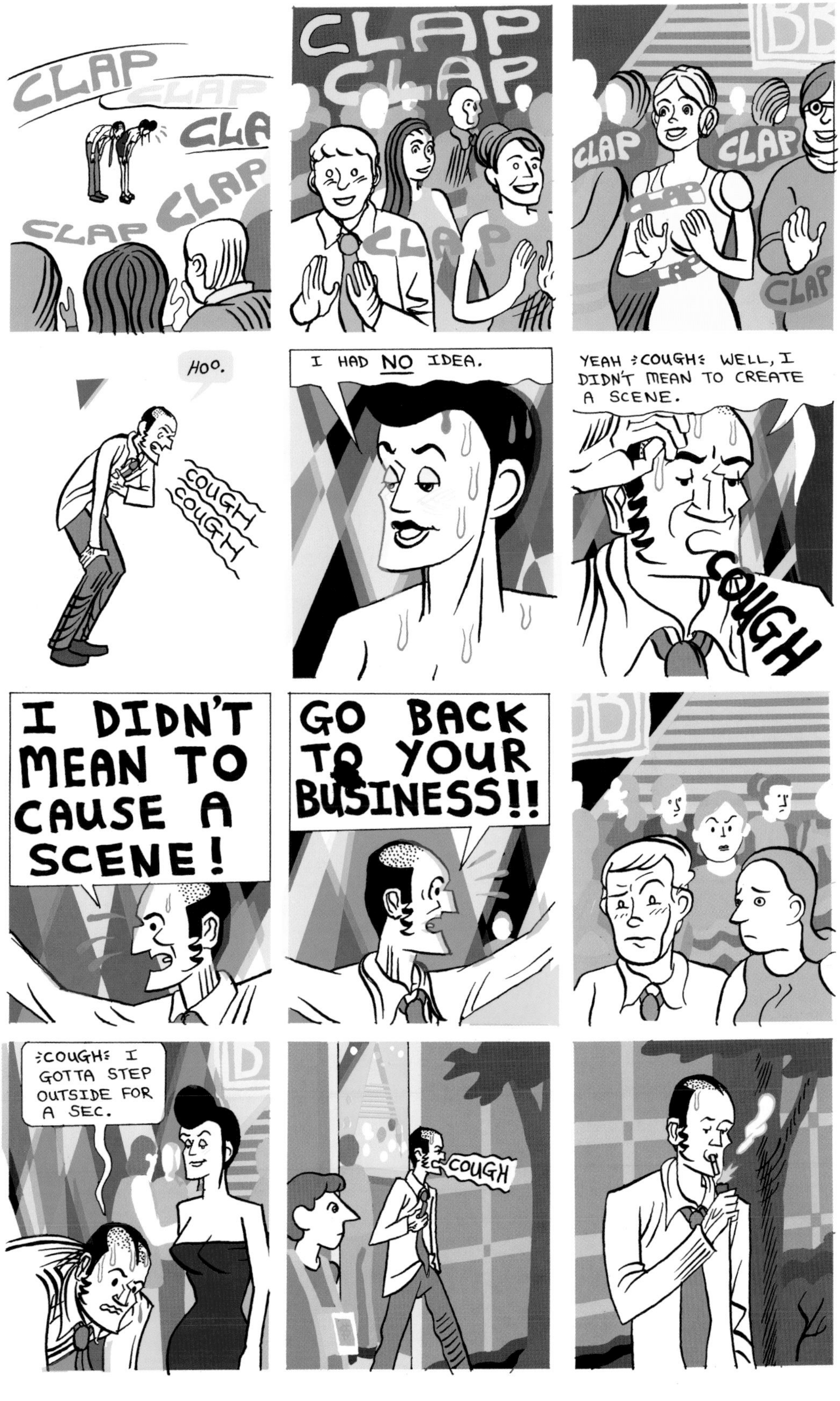
CLAP
CLAP
CLA
CLAP
CLAP
CLAP
CLAP
CLAP
CLAP
CLAP
CLAP
CLAP
CLAP
CLAP
HOO.
COUGH
COUGH
I HAD NO IDEA.
YEAH :COUGH: WELL, I DIDN'T MEAN TO CREATE A SCENE.
COUGH
I DIDN'T MEAN TO CAUSE A SCENE!
GO BACK TO YOUR BUSINESS!!
:COUGH: I GOTTA STEP OUTSIDE FOR A SEC.
COUGH

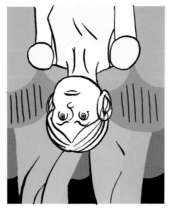

HA HA HA HA

I'LL DO THE GROSS FACE.

C'MON.

WILL YOU?

PEARLY, IT'S THE LAST DANCE. A SLOW ONE.

MOVING IN

LIFE'S THE SAME. I'M

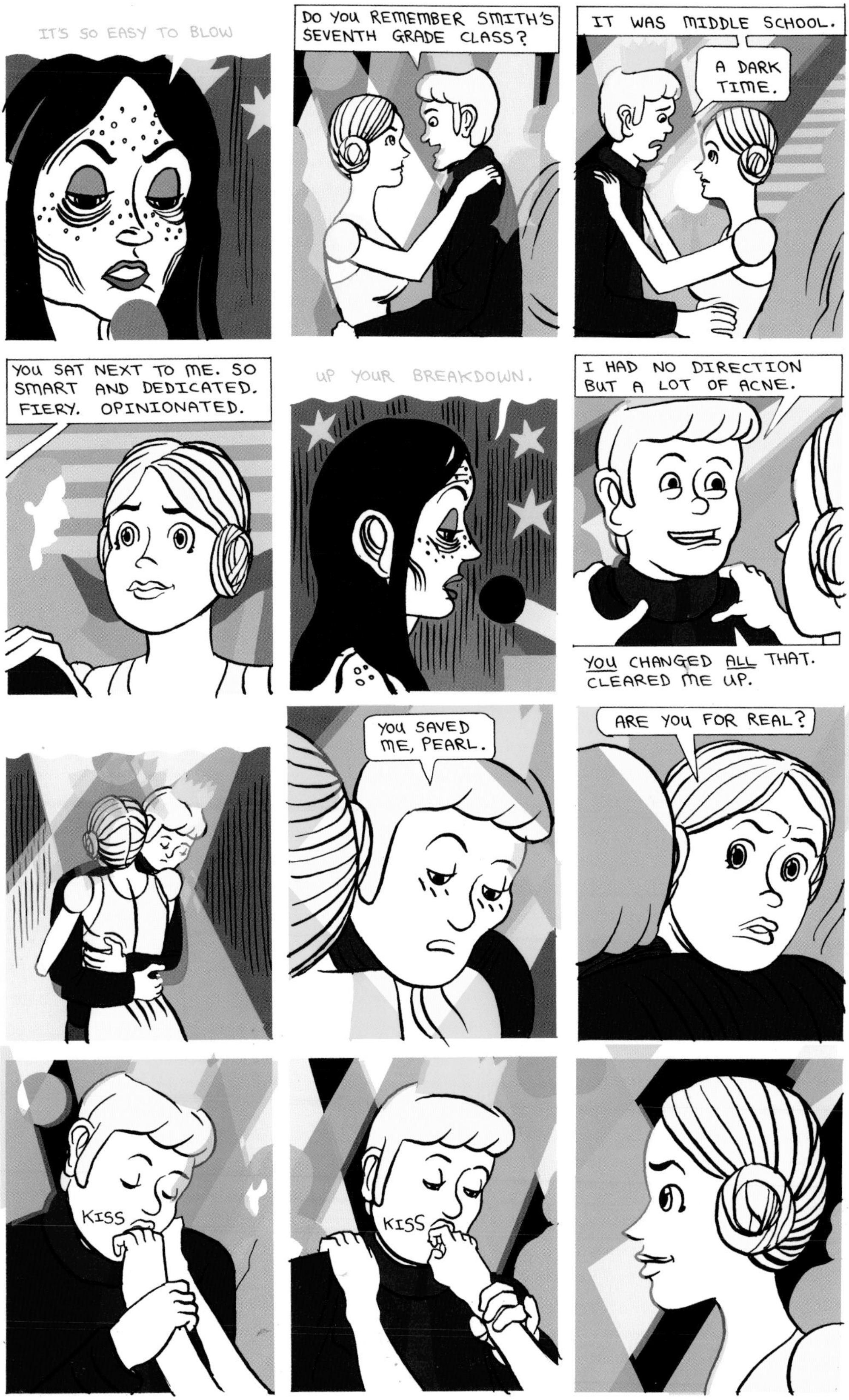
IT'S SO EASY TO BLOW
DO YOU REMEMBER SMITH'S SEVENTH GRADE CLASS?
IT WAS MIDDLE SCHOOL.
A DARK TIME.
YOU SAT NEXT TO ME. SO SMART AND DEDICATED. FIERY. OPINIONATED.
UP YOUR BREAKDOWN.
I HAD NO DIRECTION BUT A LOT OF ACNE.
YOU CHANGED ALL THAT. CLEARED ME UP.
YOU SAVED ME, PEARL.
ARE YOU FOR REAL?
KISS
KISS

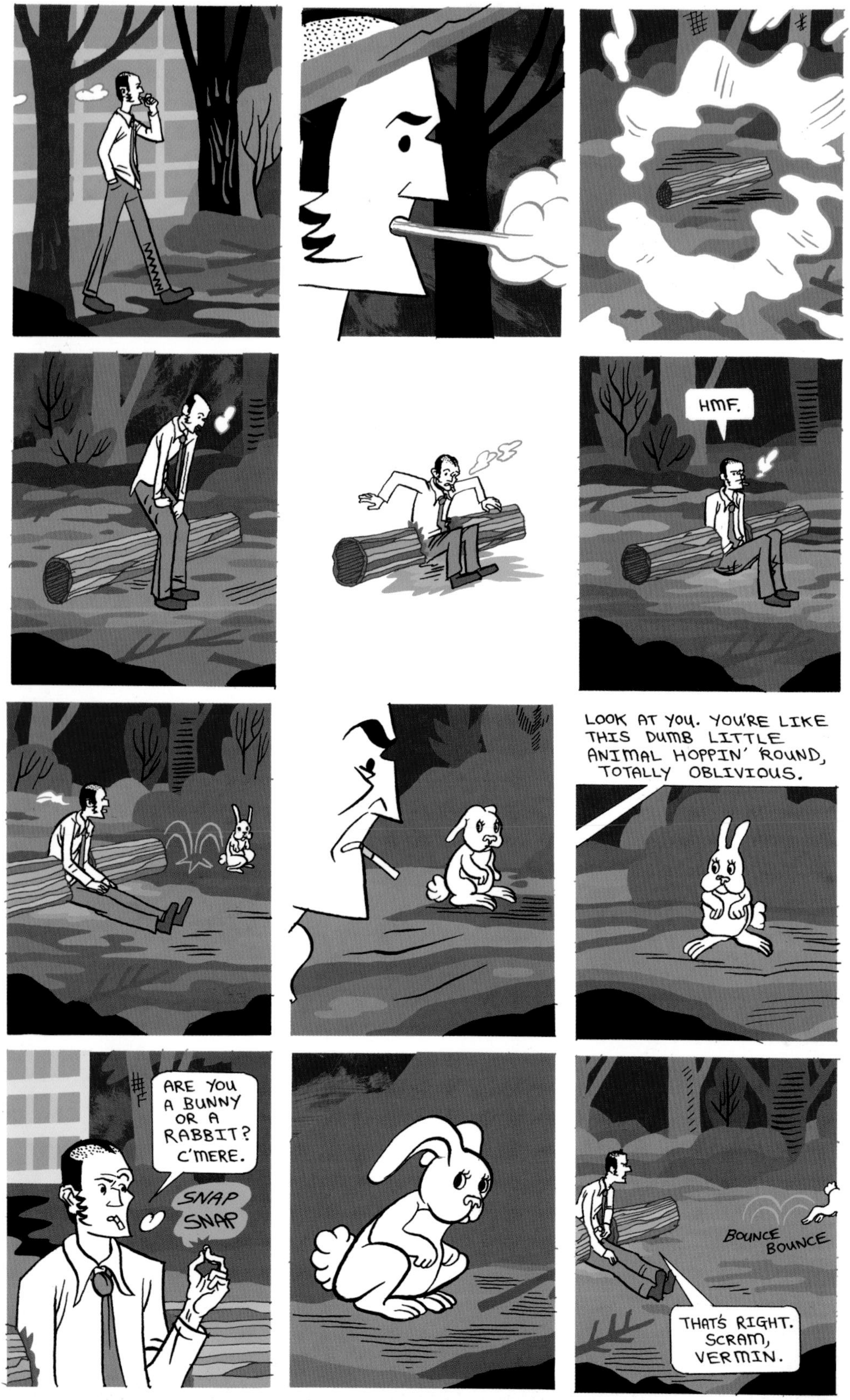
HMF.
LOOK AT YOU. YOU'RE LIKE THIS DUMB LITTLE ANIMAL HOPPIN' 'ROUND, TOTALLY OBLIVIOUS.
ARE YOU A BUNNY OR A RABBIT? C'MERE.
SNAP SNAP
BOUNCE BOUNCE
THAT'S RIGHT. SCRAM, VERMIN.

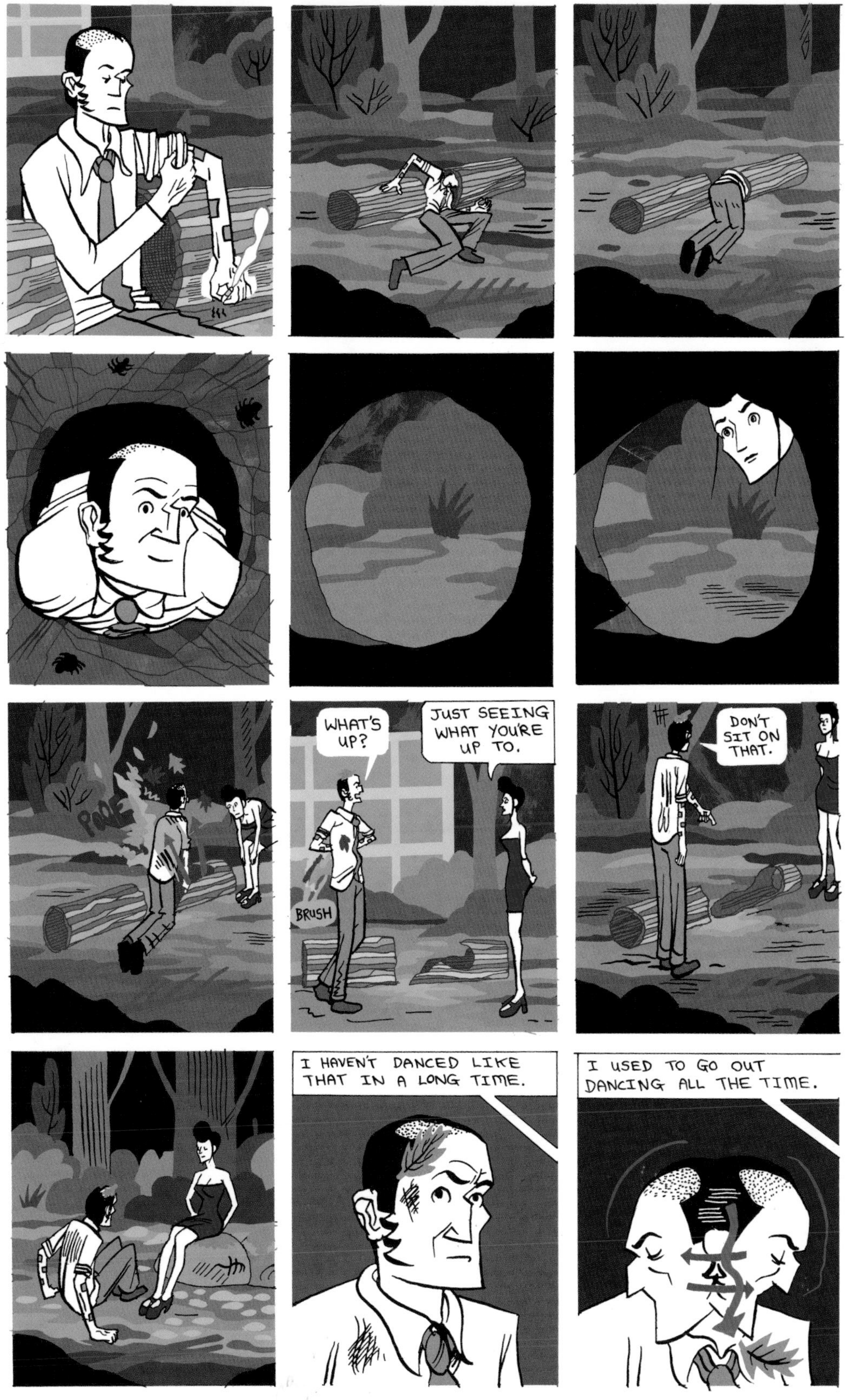

POKE
WHAT'S UP?
JUST SEEING WHAT YOU'RE UP TO.
BRUSH
DON'T SIT ON THAT.
I HAVEN'T DANCED LIKE THAT IN A LONG TIME.
I USED TO GO OUT DANCING ALL THE TIME.

WHAT'S THAT?
OH. IT'S JUST A SCAR.
I GOT IT WHEN I WAS FIVE. A DOG SCARED ME AND I FELL AND SCRAPED MY LEG. NO BIGGIE.
THIS WAS BEFORE MY MOM AND DAD MOVED TO THE AGE-RESTRICTED ZONE.
OBVIOUSLY.
I ALSO HAVE A SCAR HERE.
FELL AGAINST A DOOR FRAME OR SOMETHING. IN MY TEENS.
AND THIS:
MY BOYFRIEND IN HIGH SCHOOL WAS REALLY INTO "CUTTING."
I TRIED IT BUT DIDN'T GET TOO FAR. I DIDN'T LIKE IT. —HURTS.
RIGHT.
AND
THIS:

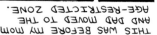

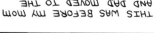

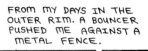
FROM MY DAYS IN THE OUTER RIM. A BOUNCER PUSHED ME AGAINST A METAL FENCE.

IN THE ARM PIT

Hmm.

TICKLE TICKLE

HAR HAR HAR!

OH MY GOD. YOU LAUGH LIKE A PIRATE.

YEAH, I KNOW. I TRY NOT TO LAUGH.

YOU HAVE A SCAR, TOO.

I FELL OFF MY TRICYCLE.

I HAVE A SCAR HERE.

I WAS, YOU KNOW, SCREWING IN A LIGHT BULB ON A CEILING AND FELL DOWN. SMASHED A CHAIR.

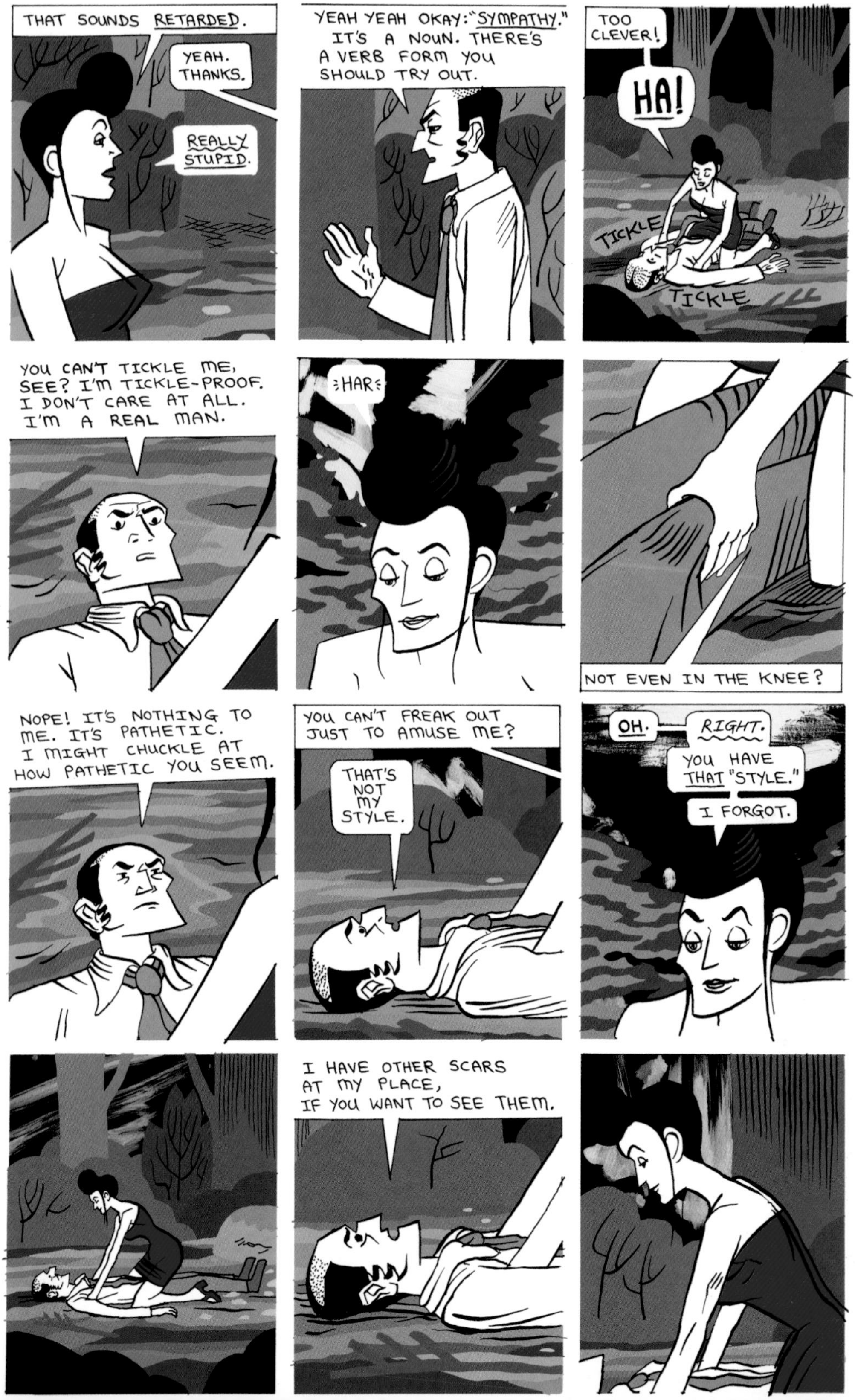
THAT SOUNDS RETARDED.
YEAH. THANKS.
REALLY STUPID.
YEAH YEAH OKAY: "SYMPATHY." IT'S A NOUN. THERE'S A VERB FORM YOU SHOULD TRY OUT.
TOO CLEVER!
HA!
TICKLE
TICKLE
YOU CAN'T TICKLE ME, SEE? I'M TICKLE-PROOF. I DON'T CARE AT ALL. I'M A REAL MAN.
HAR
NOT EVEN IN THE KNEE?
NOPE! IT'S NOTHING TO ME. IT'S PATHETIC. I MIGHT CHUCKLE AT HOW PATHETIC YOU SEEM.
YOU CAN'T FREAK OUT JUST TO AMUSE ME?
THAT'S NOT MY STYLE.
OH.
RIGHT.
YOU HAVE THAT "STYLE."
I FORGOT.
I HAVE OTHER SCARS AT MY PLACE, IF YOU WANT TO SEE THEM.

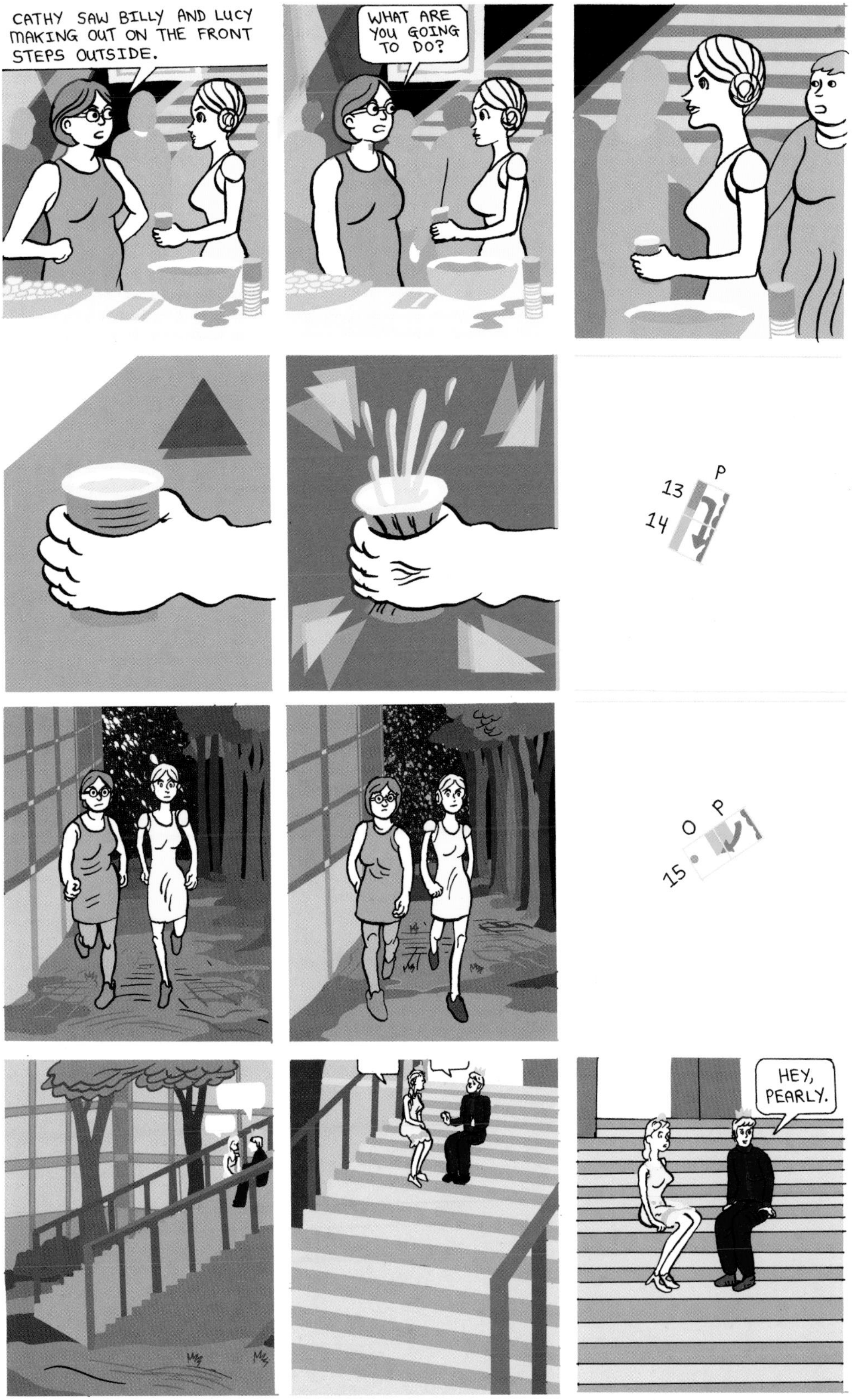
CATHY SAW BILLY AND LUCY MAKING OUT ON THE FRONT STEPS OUTSIDE.
WHAT ARE YOU GOING TO DO?
P
13
14
O P
15
HEY, PEARLY.

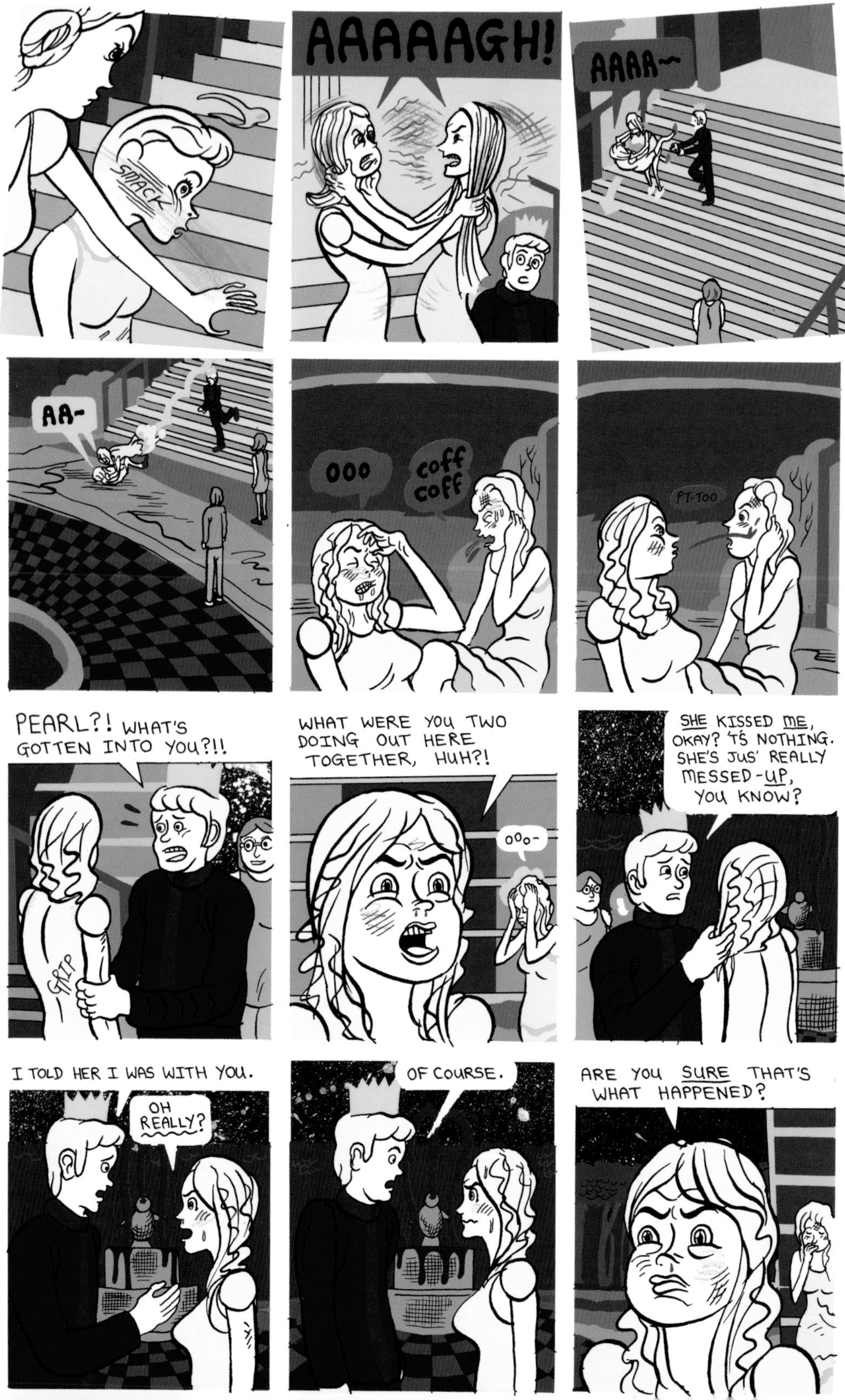
SMACK
AAAAAGH!
AAAA~
AA-
OOO
coff coff
PT-TOO
PEARL?! WHAT'S GOTTEN INTO YOU?!!
GRIP
WHAT WERE YOU TWO DOING OUT HERE TOGETHER, HUH?!
ooo-
SHE KISSED ME, OKAY? 'T'S NOTHING. SHE'S JUS' REALLY MESSED-UP, YOU KNOW?
I TOLD HER I WAS WITH YOU.
OH REALLY?
OF COURSE.
ARE YOU SURE THAT'S WHAT HAPPENED?

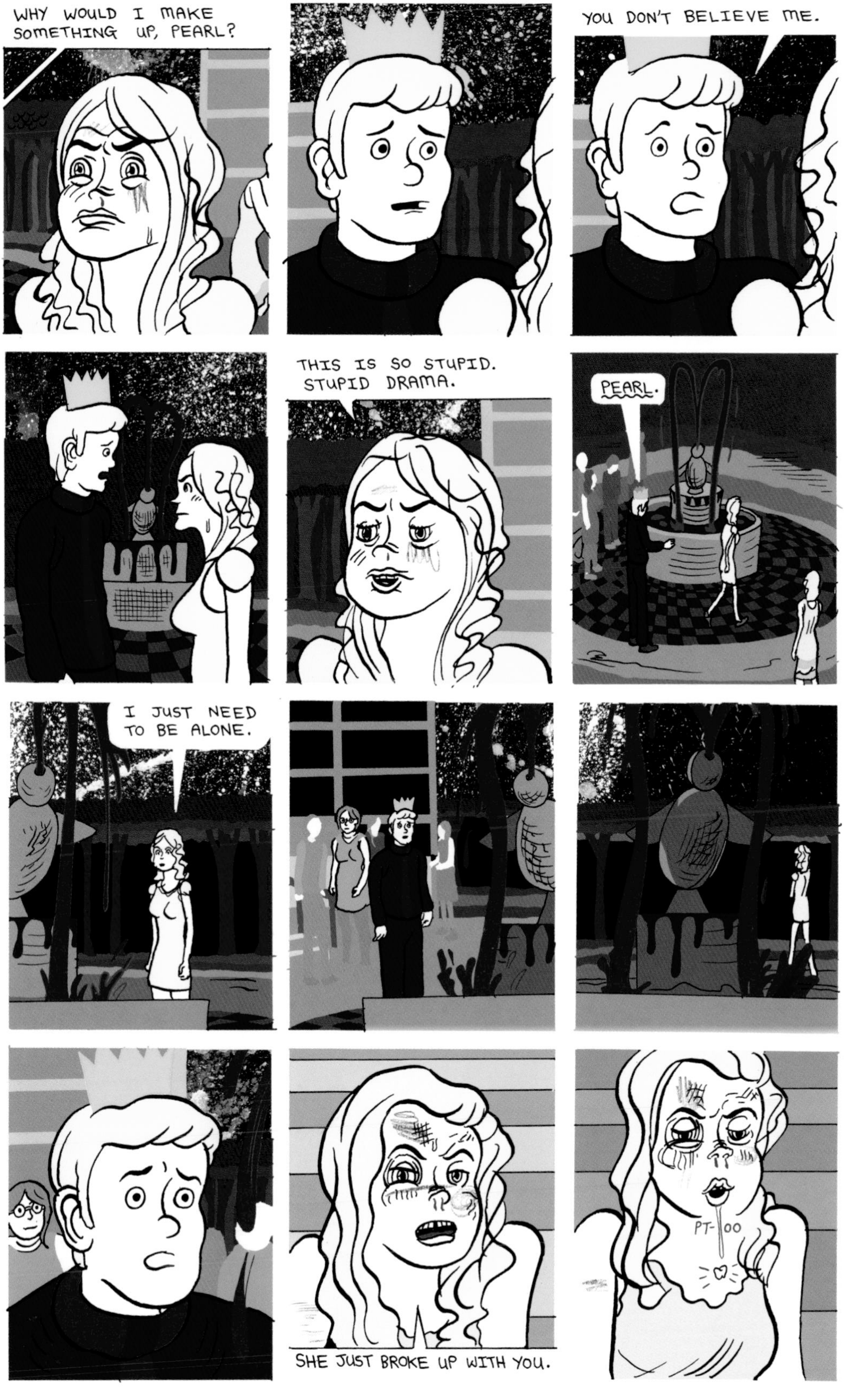

WHY WOULD I MAKE SOMETHING UP, PEARL?
YOU DON'T BELIEVE ME.
THIS IS SO STUPID. STUPID DRAMA.
PEARL.
I JUST NEED TO BE ALONE.
SHE JUST BROKE UP WITH YOU.
PT-OO

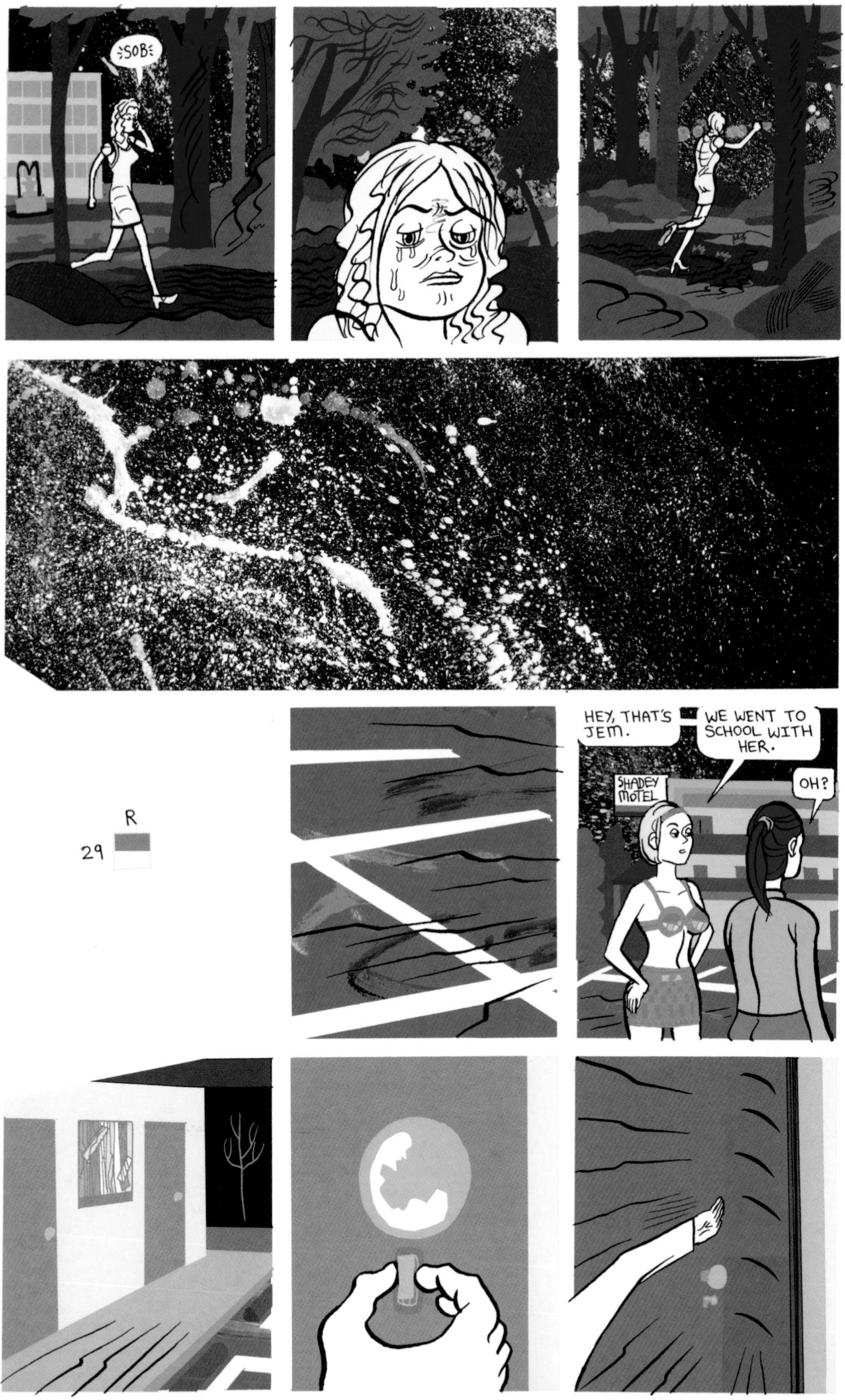
SOB
R
29
HEY, THAT'S JEM.
WE WENT TO SCHOOL WITH HER.
SHADEY MOTEL
OH?

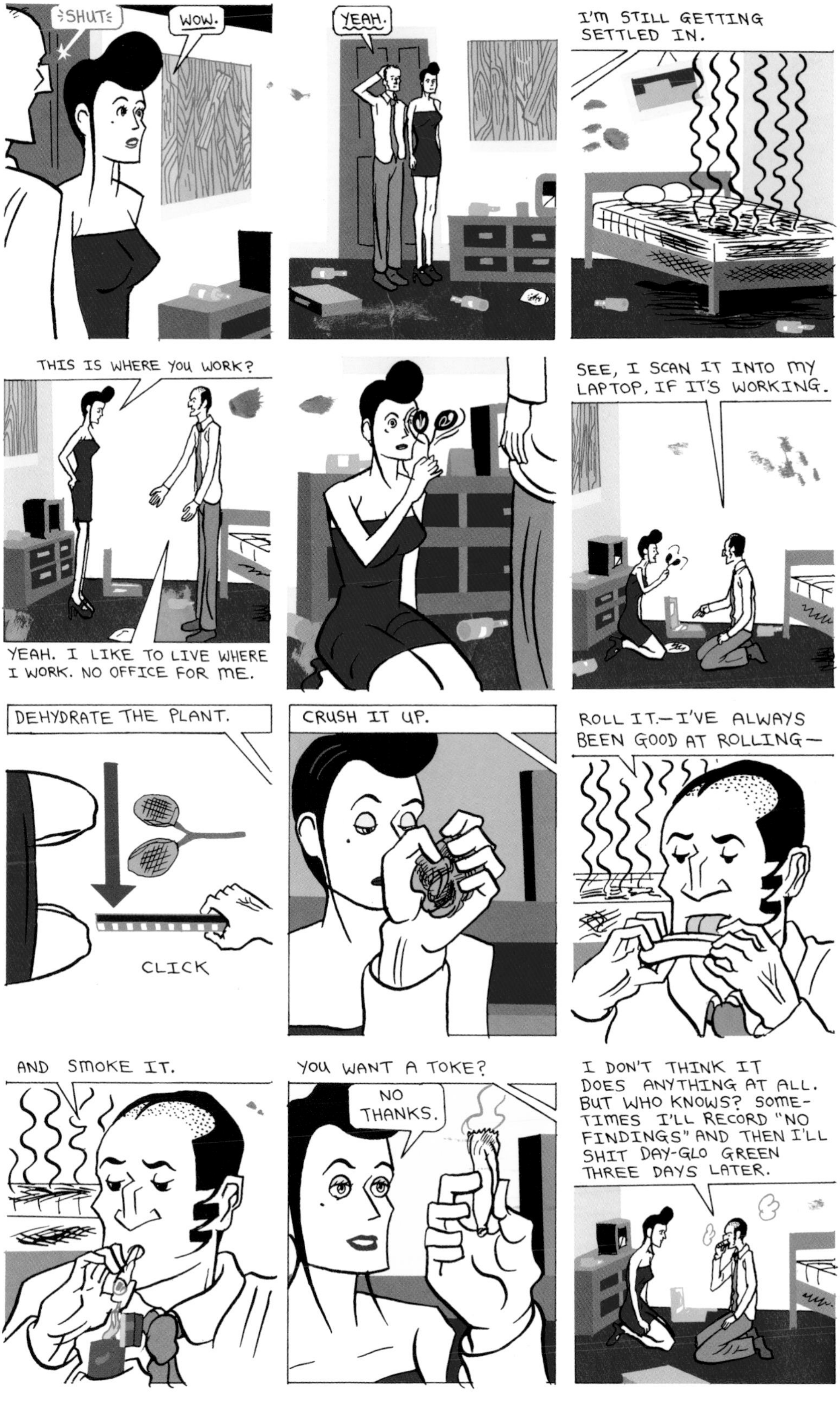
SHUT
WOW.
YEAH.
I'M STILL GETTING SETTLED IN.
THIS IS WHERE YOU WORK?
YEAH. I LIKE TO LIVE WHERE I WORK. NO OFFICE FOR ME.
SEE, I SCAN IT INTO MY LAPTOP, IF IT'S WORKING.
DEHYDRATE THE PLANT.
CLICK
CRUSH IT UP.
ROLL IT.—I'VE ALWAYS BEEN GOOD AT ROLLING—
AND SMOKE IT.
YOU WANT A TOKE?
NO THANKS.
I DON'T THINK IT DOES ANYTHING AT ALL. BUT WHO KNOWS? SOME-TIMES I'LL RECORD "NO FINDINGS" AND THEN I'LL SHIT DAY-GLO GREEN THREE DAYS LATER.

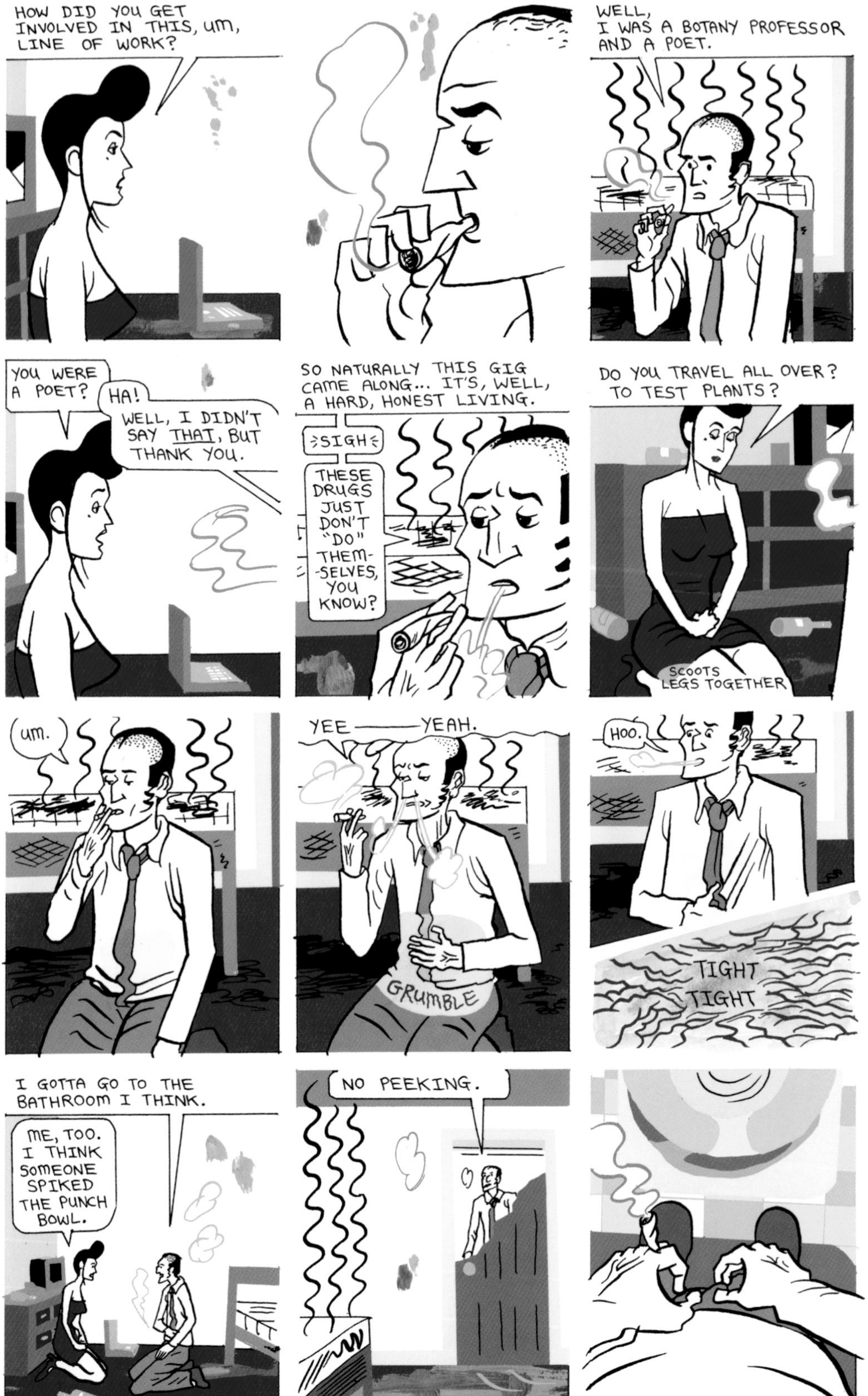

HOW DID YOU GET INVOLVED IN THIS, UM, LINE OF WORK?
WELL, I WAS A BOTANY PROFESSOR AND A POET.
YOU WERE A POET?
HA!
WELL, I DIDN'T SAY THAT, BUT THANK YOU.
SO NATURALLY THIS GIG CAME ALONG... IT'S, WELL, A HARD, HONEST LIVING.
SIGH
THESE DRUGS JUST DON'T "DO" THEM-SELVES, YOU KNOW?
DO YOU TRAVEL ALL OVER? TO TEST PLANTS?
SCOOTS LEGS TOGETHER
UM.
YEE——YEAH.
GRUMBLE
HOO.
TIGHT
TIGHT
I GOTTA GO TO THE BATHROOM I THINK.
ME, TOO. I THINK SOMEONE SPIKED THE PUNCH BOWL.
NO PEEKING.

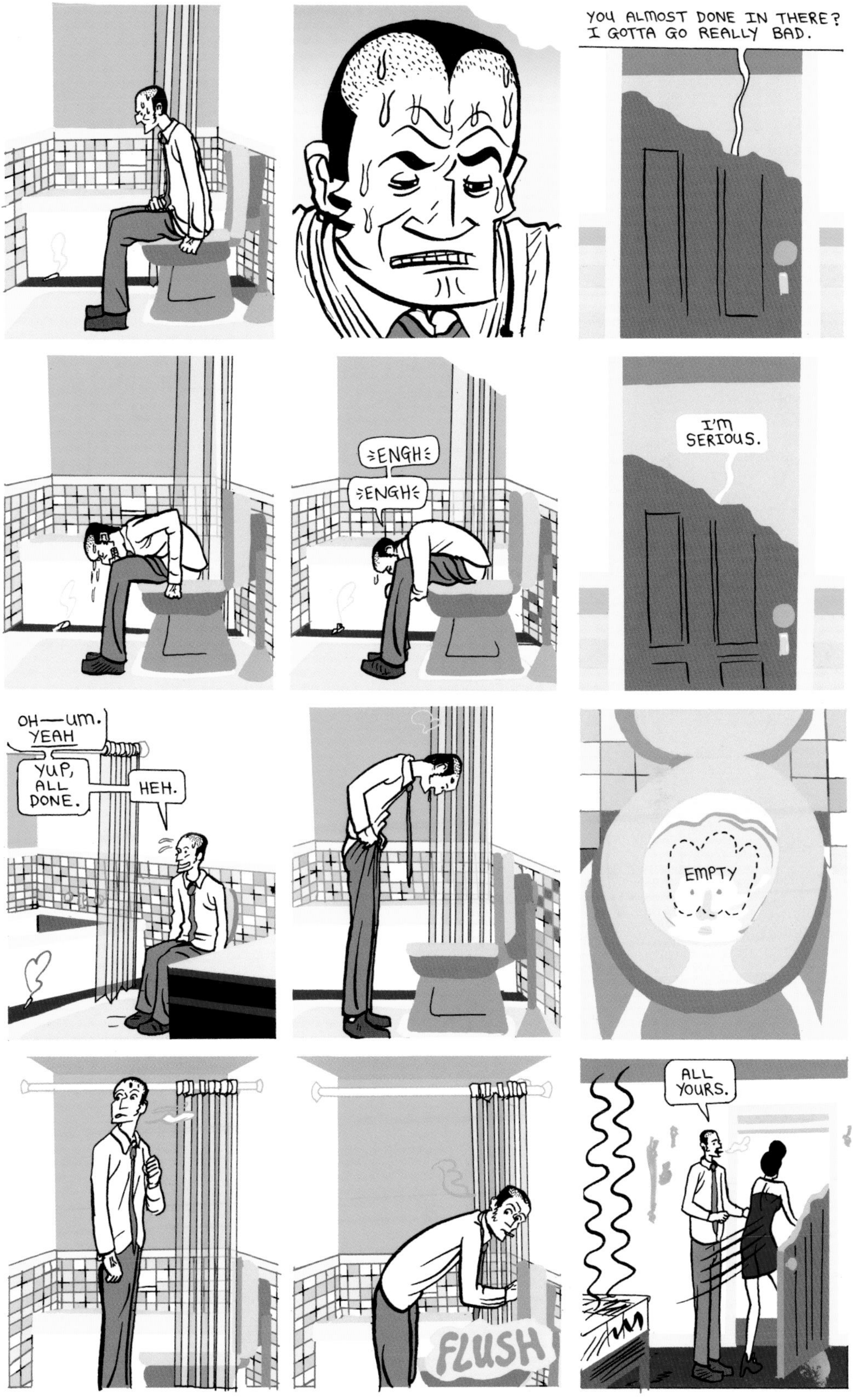

YOU ALMOST DONE IN THERE? I GOTTA GO REALLY BAD.
ENGH
ENGH
I'M SERIOUS.
OH—UM. YEAH
YUP, ALL DONE.
HEH.
EMPTY
FLUSH
ALL YOURS.

STOMACH
CLEARING
CLEARING
CLEAR
FLUSH
YOU WANT A CUP OF COFFEE?
I CAN BREW A CUP. I HAVE A COFFEE-MAKER HERE.
BED'S WARM.
OKAY.
SHAKEY
SHAKEY
WELL, IT SEEMS YOU LEAD QUITE AN EXCITING LIFE.
SHAKEY

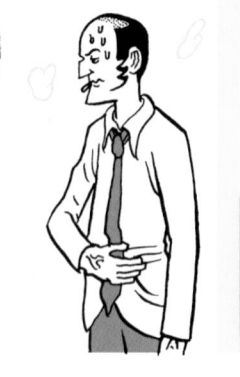

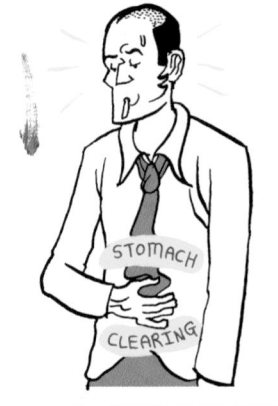

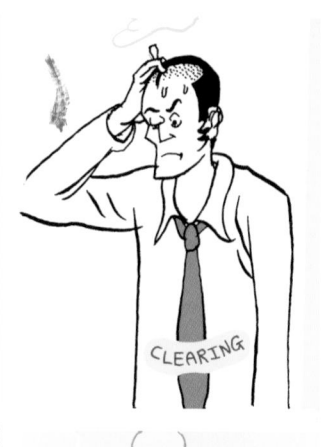

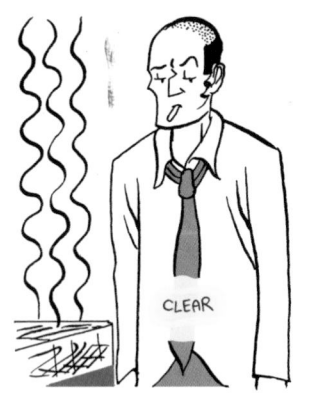

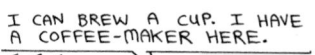

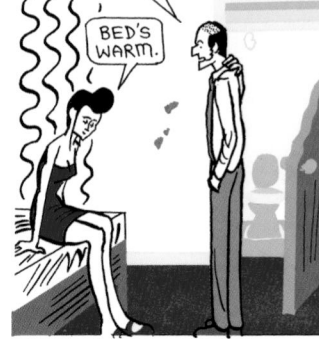

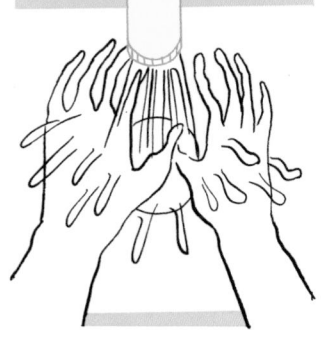

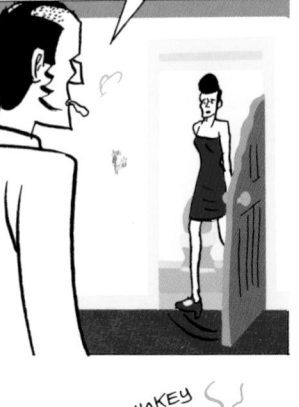

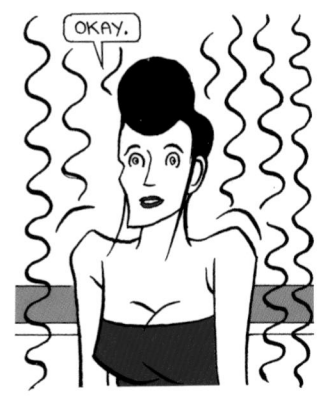

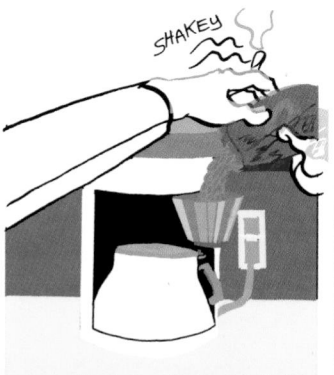

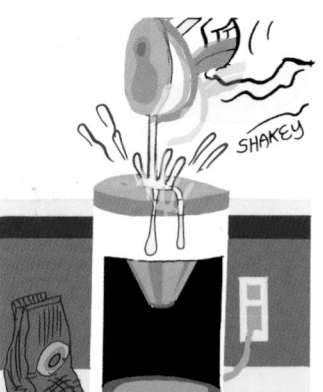

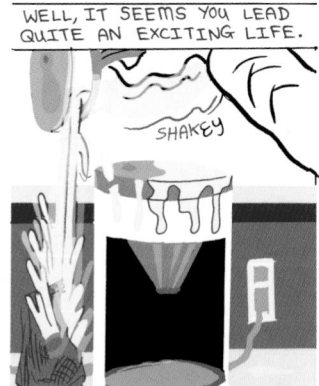

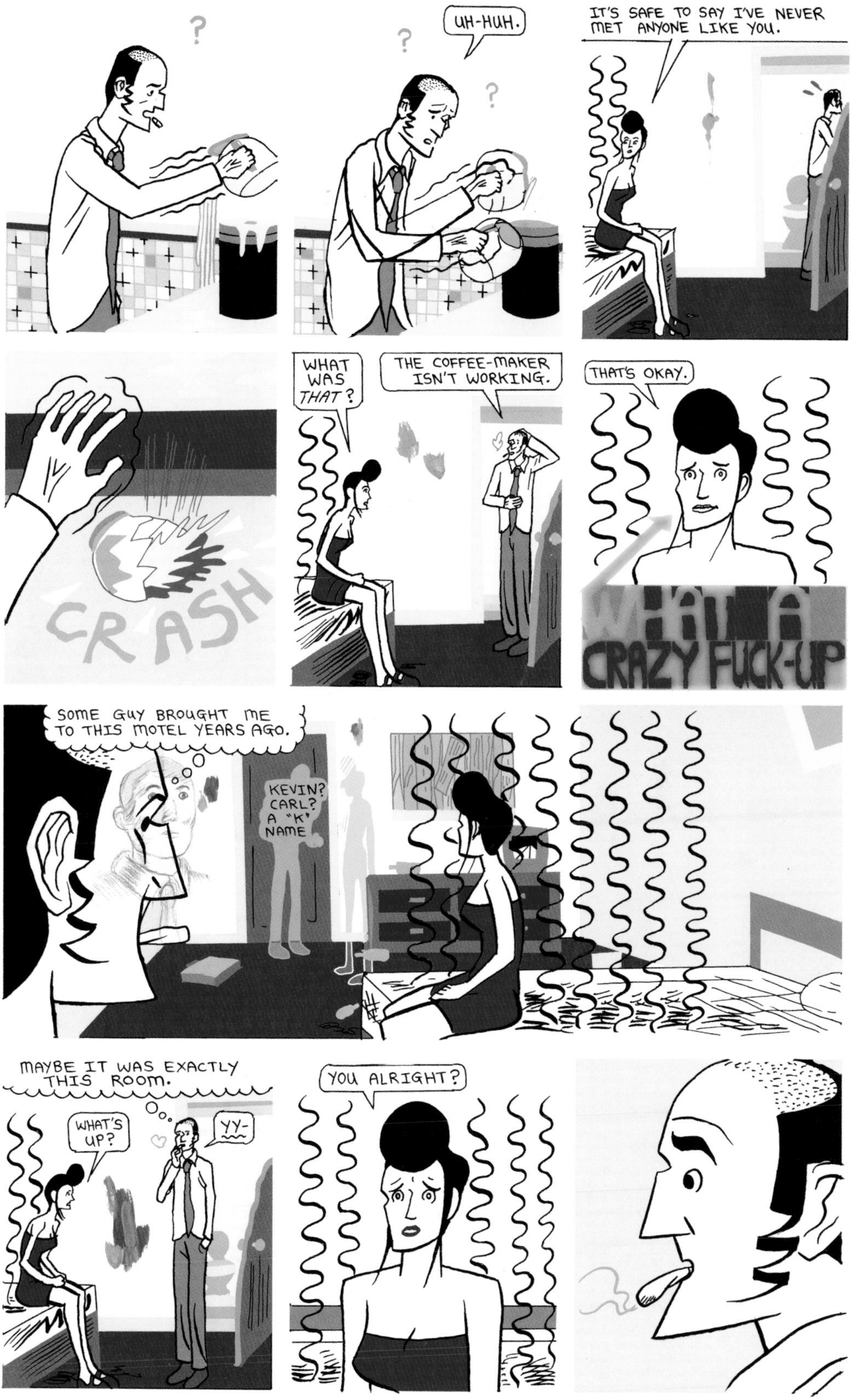
?
UH-HUH.
?
?
IT'S SAFE TO SAY I'VE NEVER MET ANYONE LIKE YOU.
CRASH
WHAT WAS THAT?
THE COFFEE-MAKER ISN'T WORKING.
THAT'S OKAY.
CRAZY FUCK-UP
SOME GUY BROUGHT ME TO THIS MOTEL YEARS AGO.
KEVIN? CARL? A "K" NAME
MAYBE IT WAS EXACTLY THIS ROOM.
WHAT'S UP?
YY-
YOU ALRIGHT?

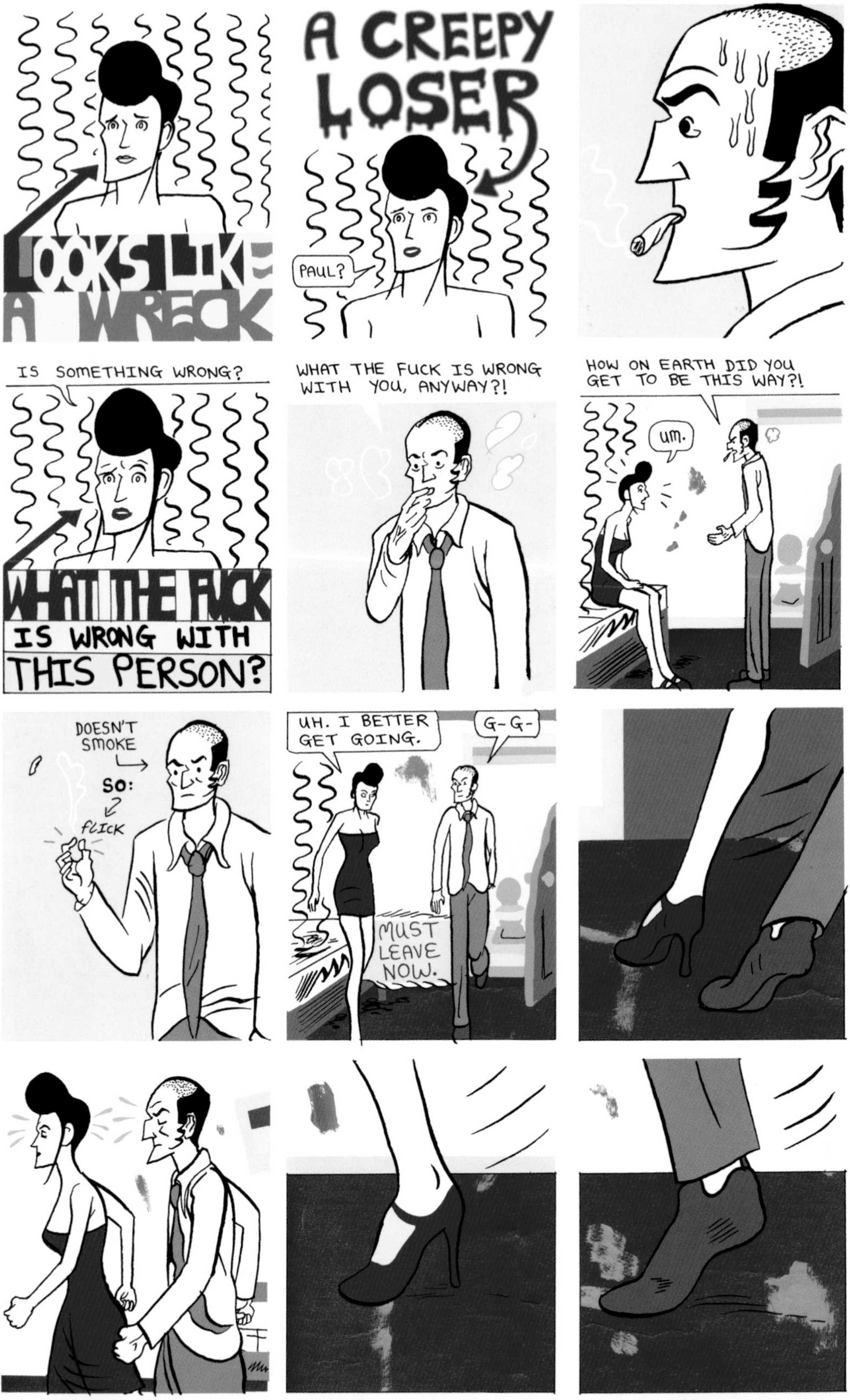
LOOKS LIKE
A WRECK
A CREEPY
LOSER
PAUL?
IS SOMETHING WRONG?
WHAT THE FUCK
IS WRONG WITH
THIS PERSON?
WHAT THE FUCK IS WRONG WITH YOU, ANYWAY?!
HOW ON EARTH DID YOU GET TO BE THIS WAY?!
UM.
DOESN'T SMOKE
SO:
FLICK
UH. I BETTER GET GOING.
G-G-
MUST LEAVE NOW.

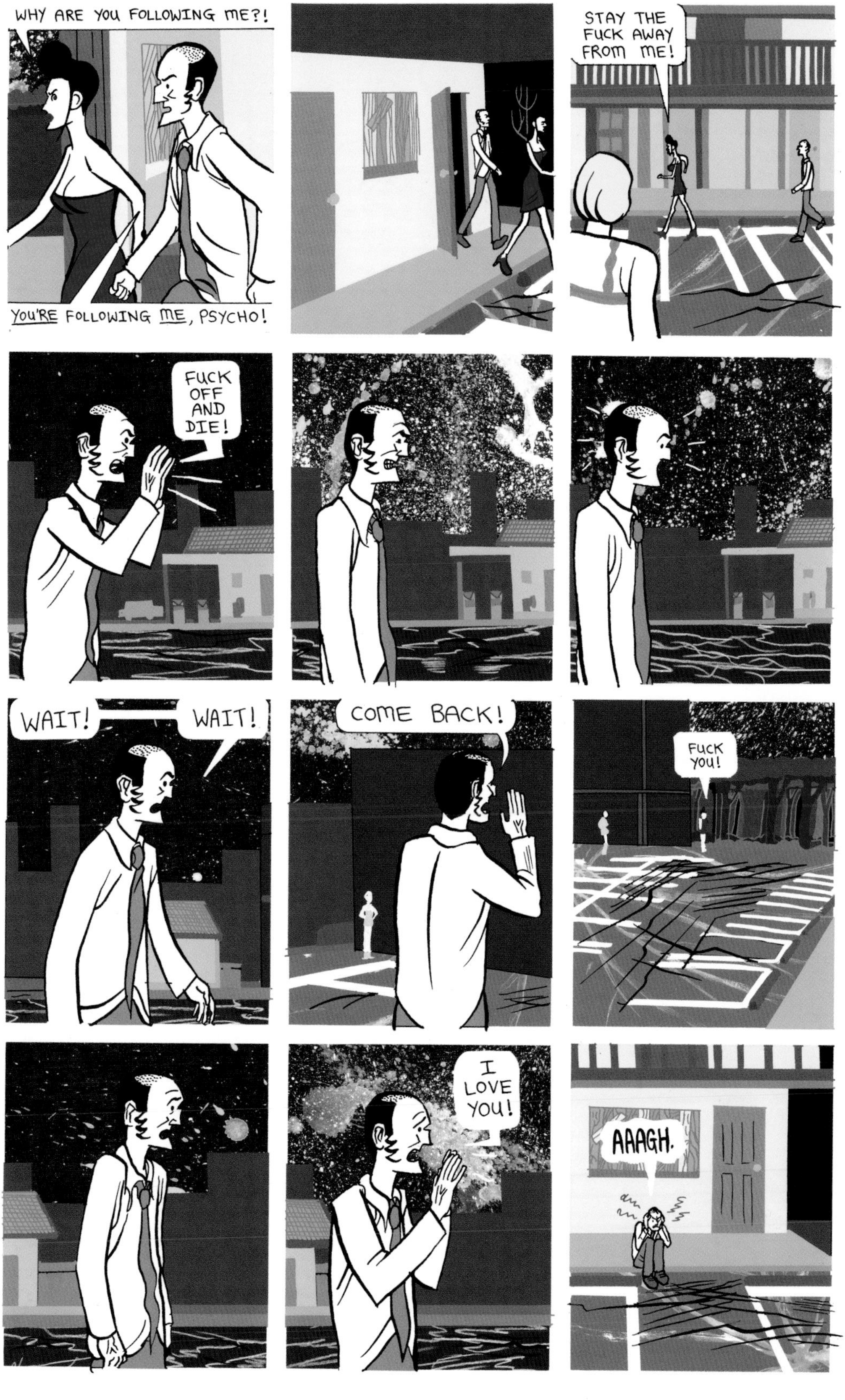
WHY ARE YOU FOLLOWING ME?!
YOU'RE FOLLOWING ME, PSYCHO!
STAY THE FUCK AWAY FROM ME!
FUCK OFF AND DIE!
WAIT!
WAIT!
COME BACK!
FUCK YOU!
I LOVE YOU!
AAAGH.

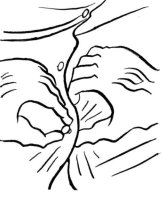

AND YOUR SHIRT.

YOU CAN HAVE IT BACK.

OH,
OH YEAH.

THAT'S
MY
TIE.

SNIF

STUPID
NOOSE!

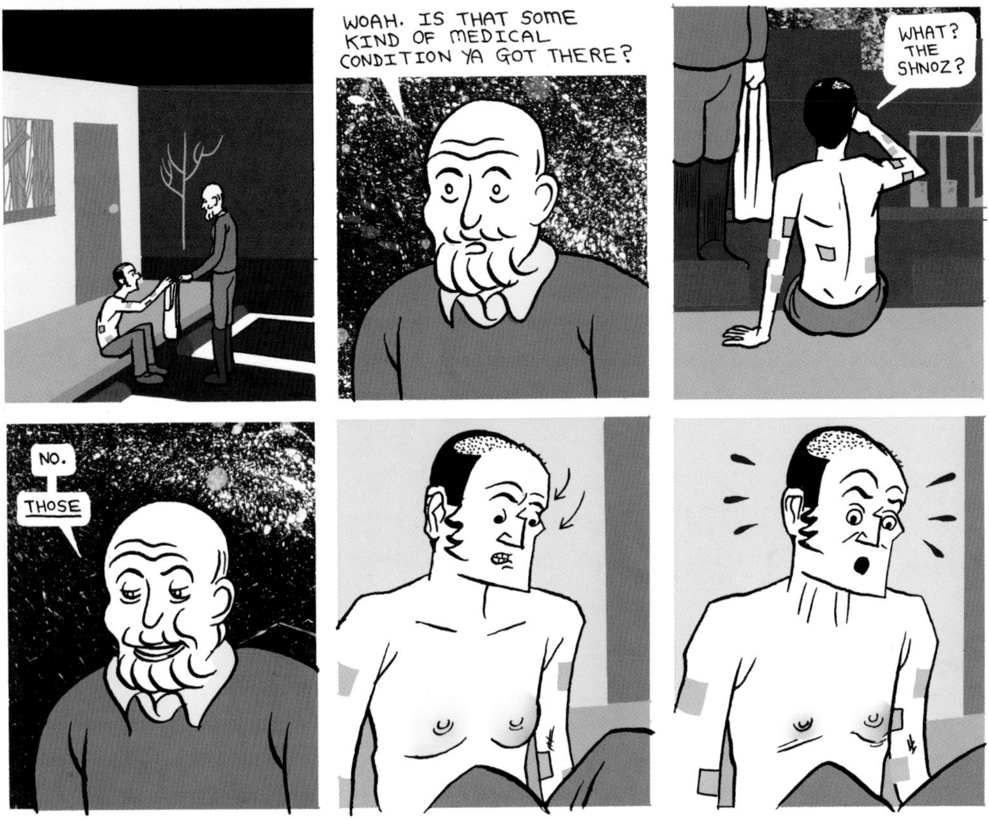
WOAH. IS THAT SOME KIND OF MEDICAL CONDITION YA GOT THERE?
WHAT? THE SHNOZ?
NO.
THOSE

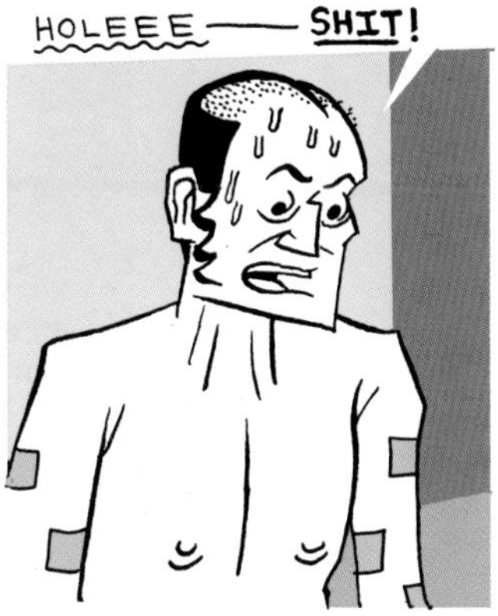
HOLEEE— SHIT!

END OF CHAPTER THREE.

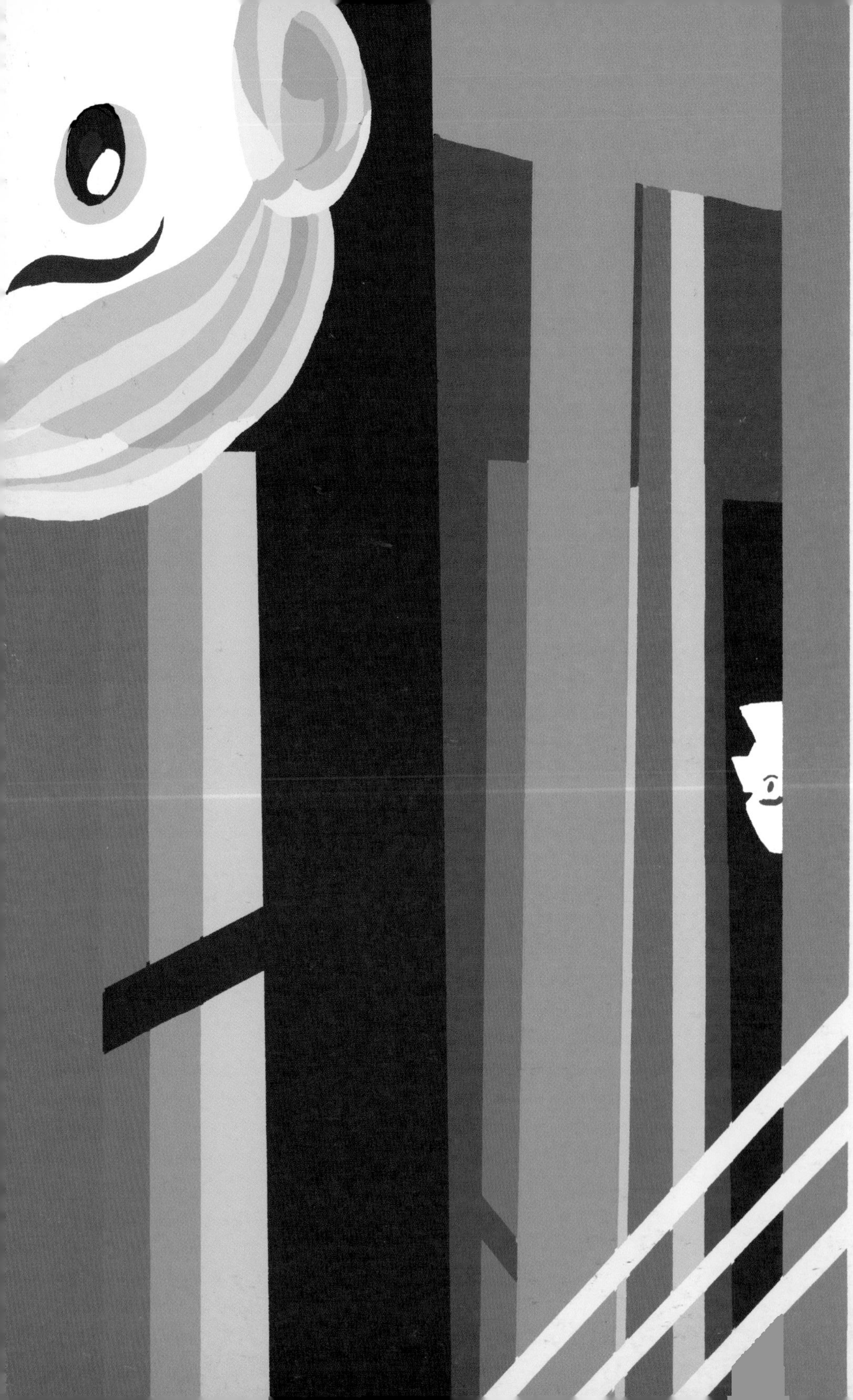

CHAPTER FOUR

G

18

YOU'RE ON

MY MIND, BABY,

WHY CAN'T

I HAVE YOU? YOU'RE BREAKING

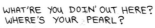

BILLY?

ER— MOMMA?

WHAT'RE YOU DOIN' OUT HERE? WHERE'S YOUR PEARL?

SHE DUMPED ME.

LIKE A TURD.

OH, BILLY.
SHE IS THE BEST GIRL.
SHE'S SMART AND PRETTY-LOOKING AND HAS AN AMAZING PERSONALITY.
ME, I'M A BIG DUMBO.
THAT'S NOT TRUE.
IT'S CUZ OF ALL THE DIEGUNK! MY BRAIN DOESN'T WORK STRAIGHT NO MORE!
NO, NO! YOU'RE A GOOD BOY. PEARL JUST MADE HER DECISION.
SHE THOUGHT I WAS WITH ANOTHER GIRL, AND I
OF COURSE YOU WEREN'T, BILLY.
WASN'T!
YOUR FATHER THOUGHT I WAS SEEING OTHER MEN. HE WAS ALWAYS FINDING CLOTHES UNDER THE BED, USED CONDOMS IN THE TOILET, I'D GET CALLS FROM MEN AT NIGHT...
WHEN HE LEFT US TEN YEARS AGO, YOU THINK I SPENT ALL NIGHT CRYING IN YOUR OLD TREE HOUSE?
UM. I DONNO.
NO, I DIDN'T. I DIDN'T CARE AT ALL.
YEAH, I GUESS YOU'RE RIGHT, MOMMA. IT HURTS THOUGH.
LIVING IS SUFFERING, BILLY. GIVE YOUR MOM A NICE BIG HUG.

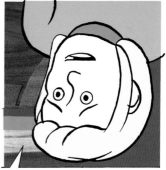

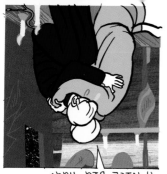

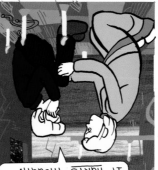

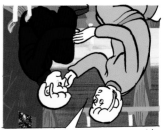

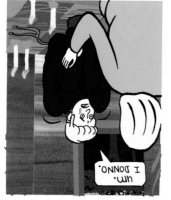

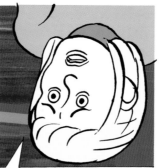

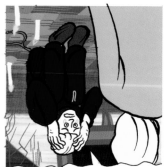

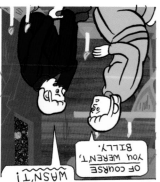

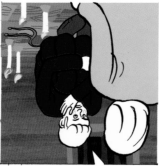

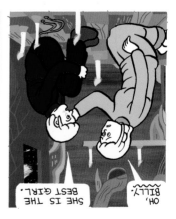

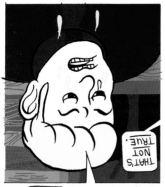

R

29

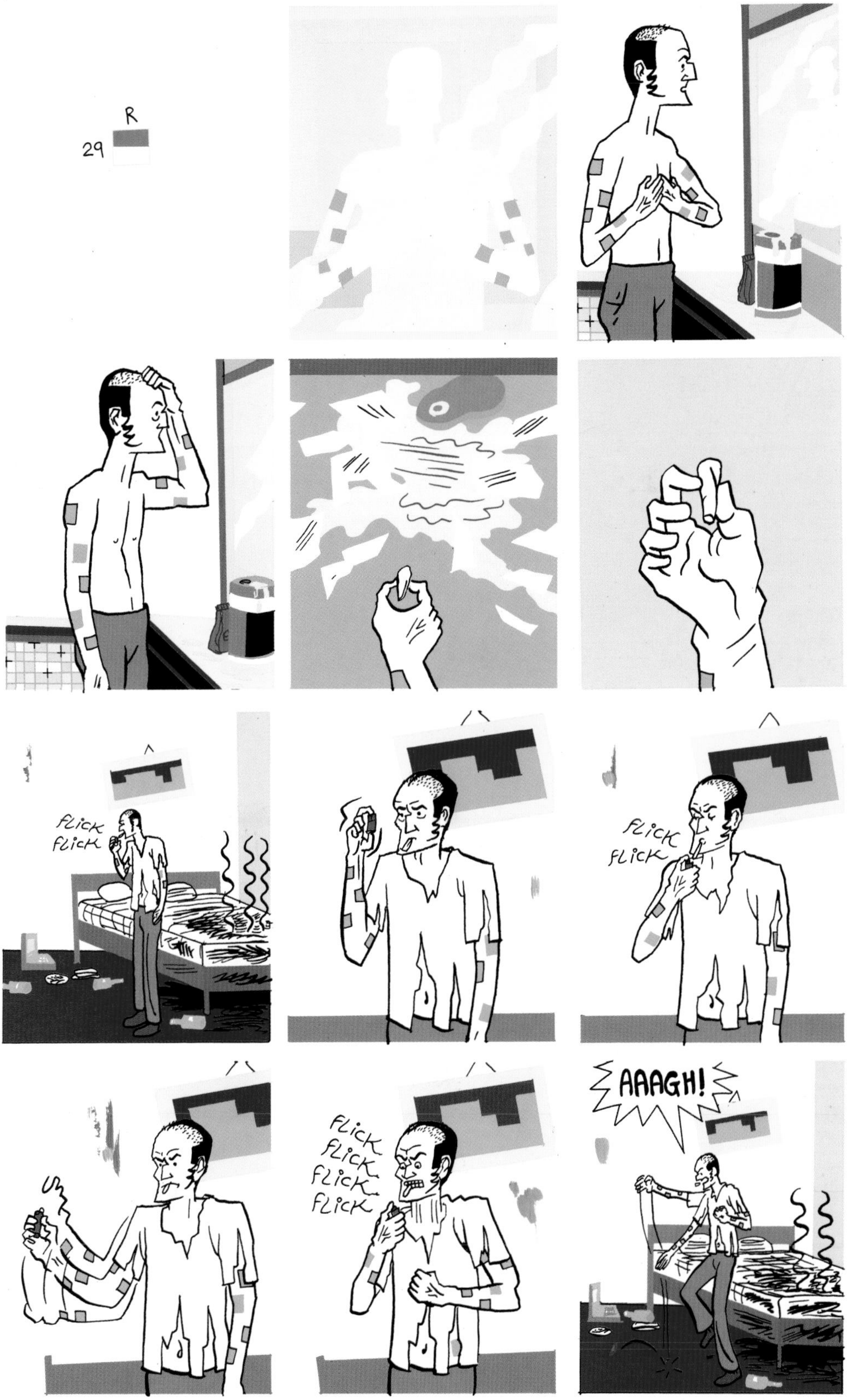
FLICK
FLICK
FLICK
FLICK
FLICK
FLICK
FLICK
FLICK
AAAGH!

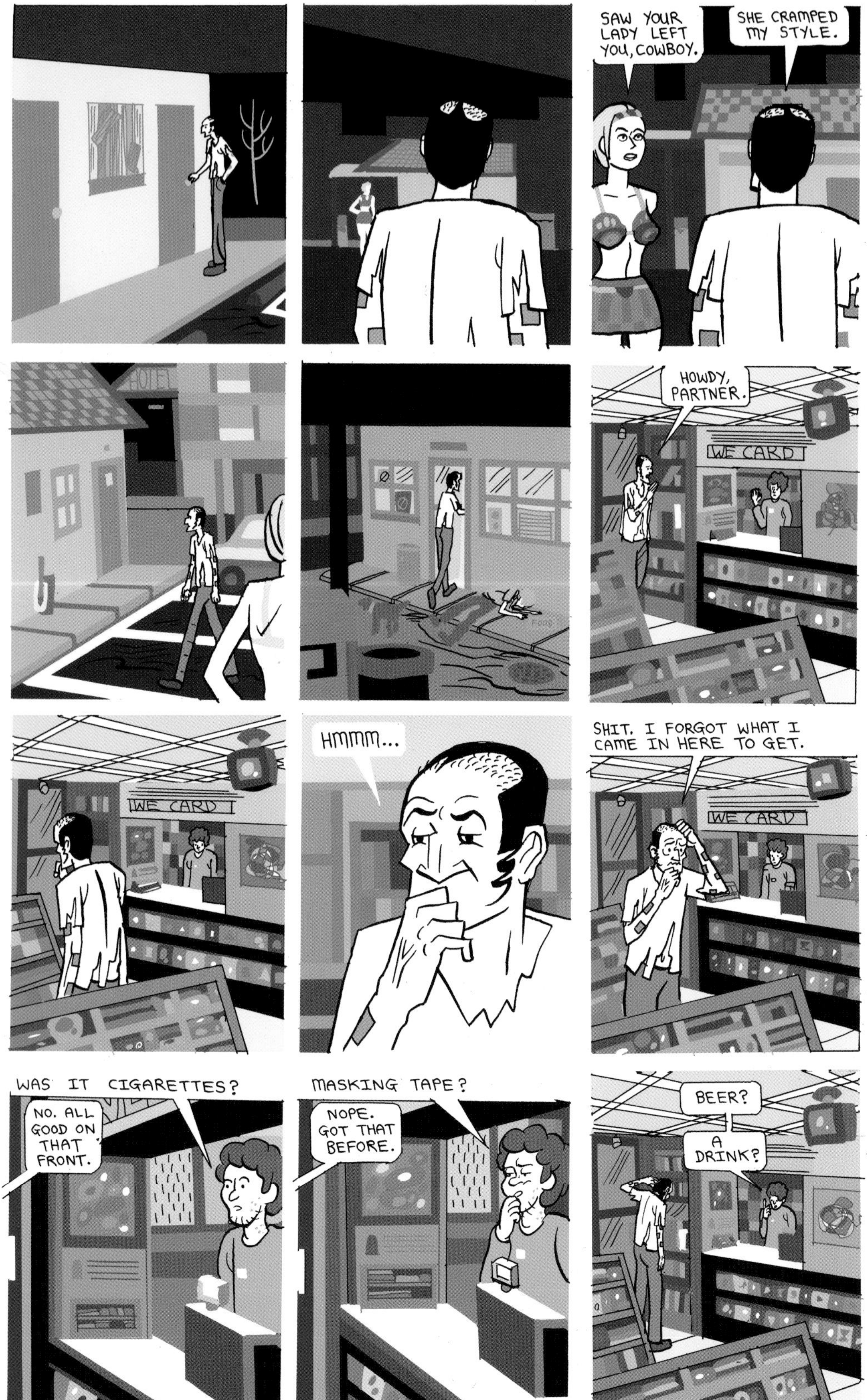
SAW YOUR LADY LEFT YOU, COWBOY.
SHE CRAMPED MY STYLE.
HOTEL
FOOD
HOWDY, PARTNER.
WE CARD
WE CARD
HMMM...
SHIT. I FORGOT WHAT I CAME IN HERE TO GET.
WE CARD
WAS IT CIGARETTES?
NO. ALL GOOD ON THAT FRONT.
MASKING TAPE?
NOPE. GOT THAT BEFORE.
BEER?
A DRINK?

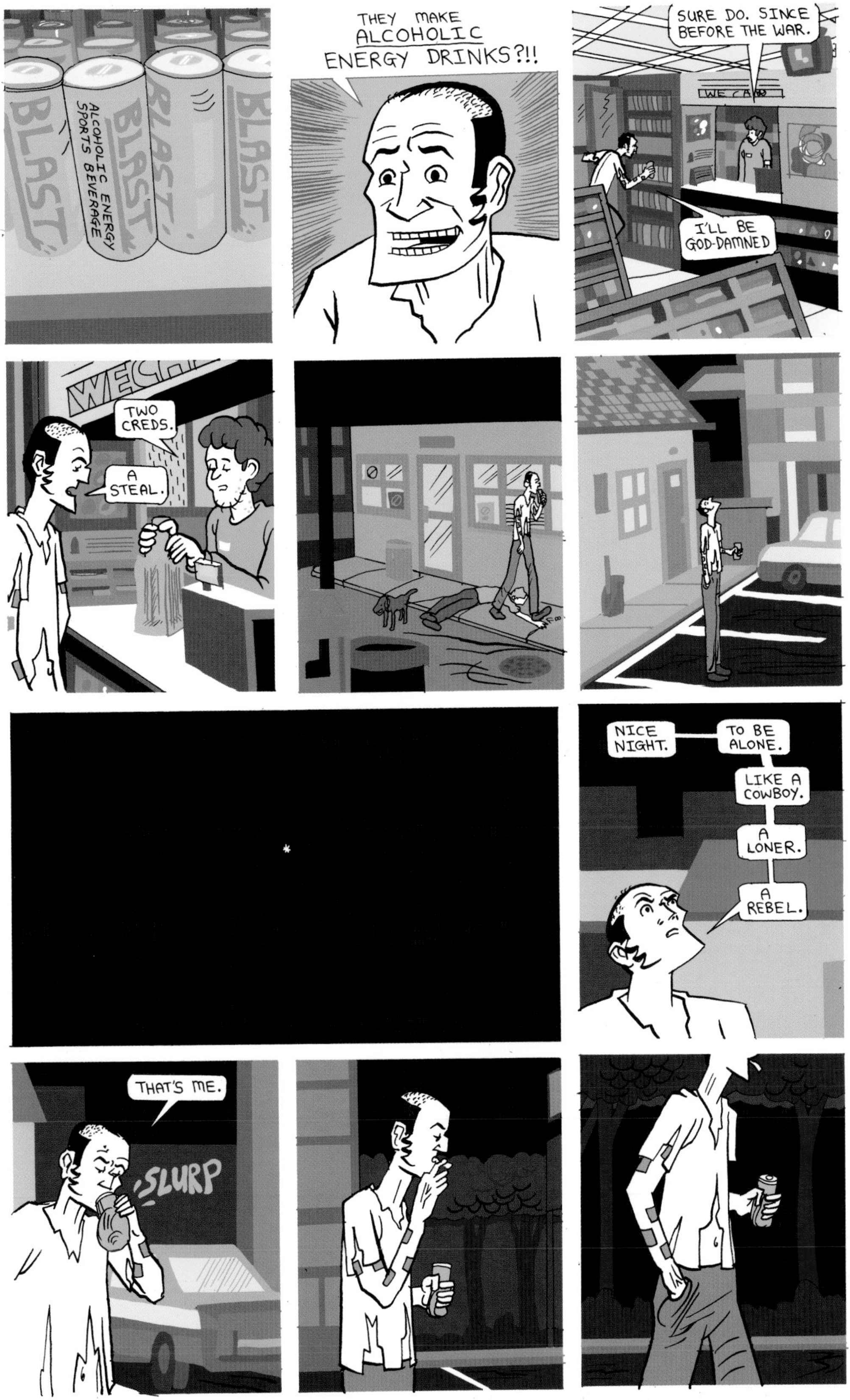

ALCOHOLIC ENERGY SPORTS BEVERAGE
BLAST
THEY MAKE ALCOHOLIC ENERGY DRINKS?!!
SURE DO. SINCE BEFORE THE WAR.
I'LL BE GOD-DAMNED
TWO CREDS.
A STEAL.
NICE NIGHT.
TO BE ALONE.
LIKE A COWBOY.
A LONER.
A REBEL.
THAT'S ME.
SLURP

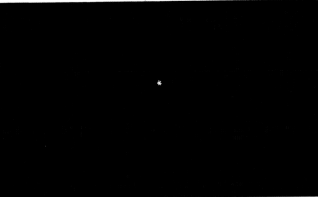

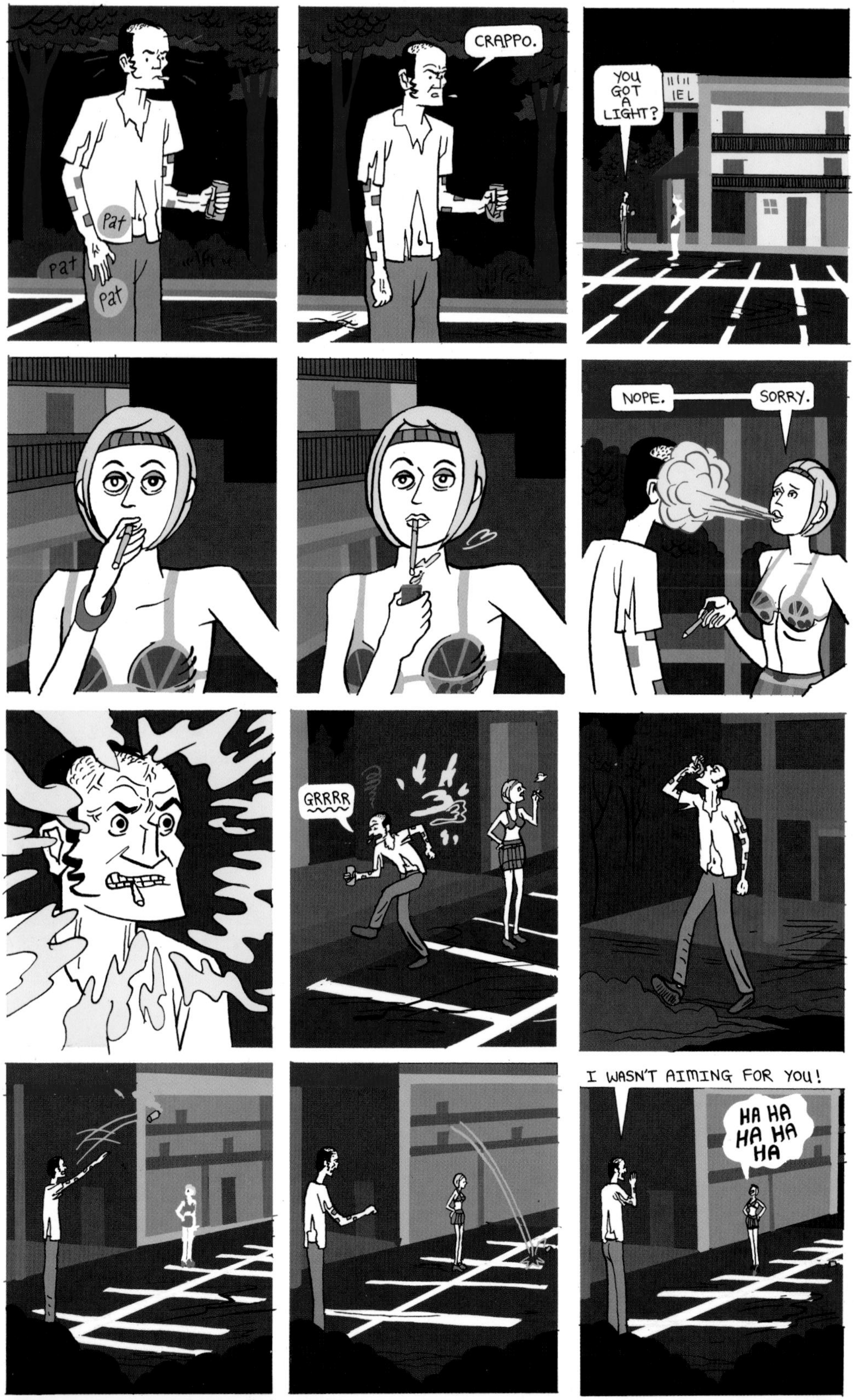
Pat
Pat
Pat
CRAPPO.
YOU GOT A LIGHT?
NOPE.
SORRY.
GRRRR
I WASN'T AIMING FOR YOU!
HA HA HA HA HA

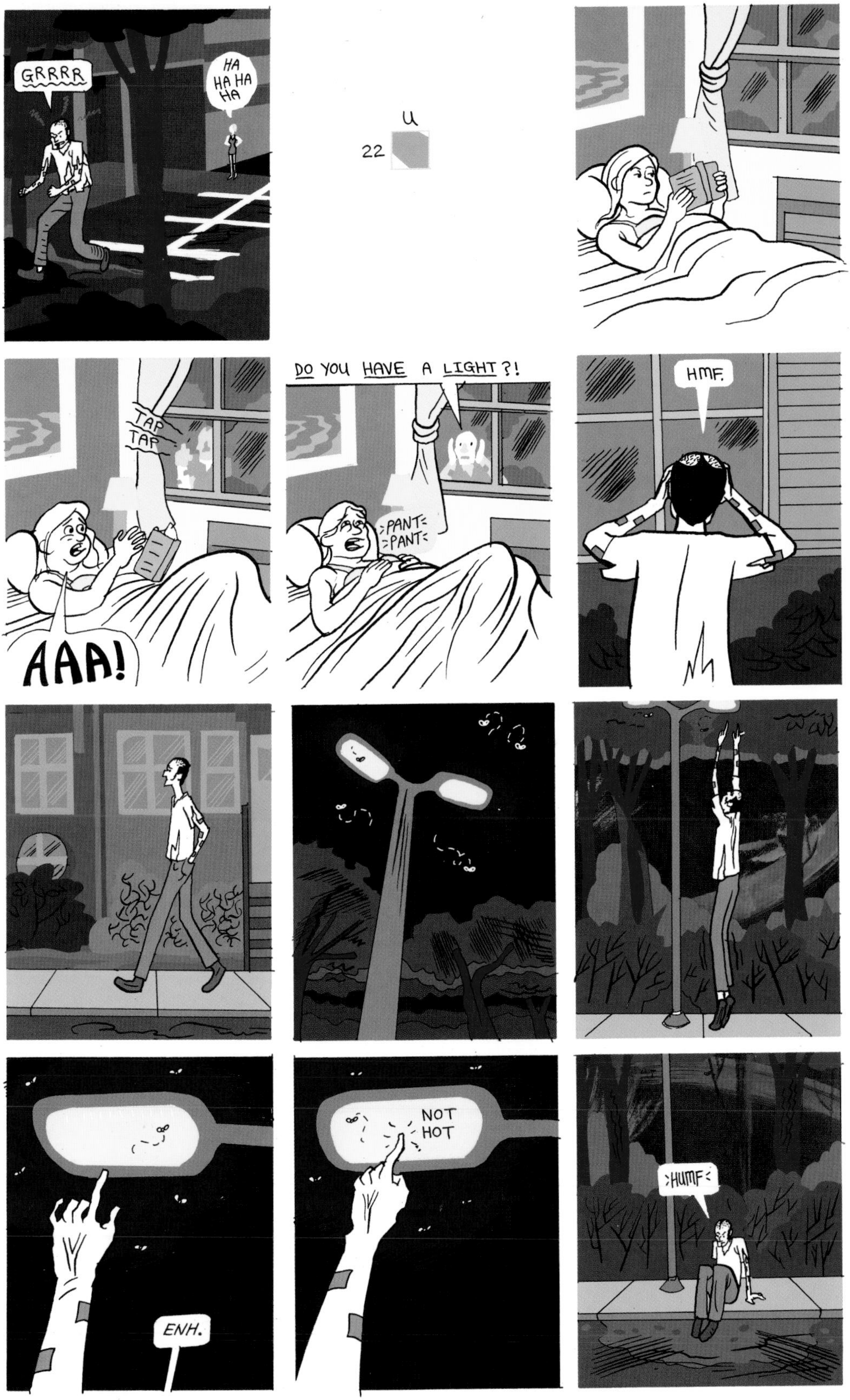
GRRRR
HA HA HA HA
TAP TAP
AAA!
DO YOU HAVE A LIGHT?!
PANT PANT
HMF.
ENH.
NOT HOT
HUMF

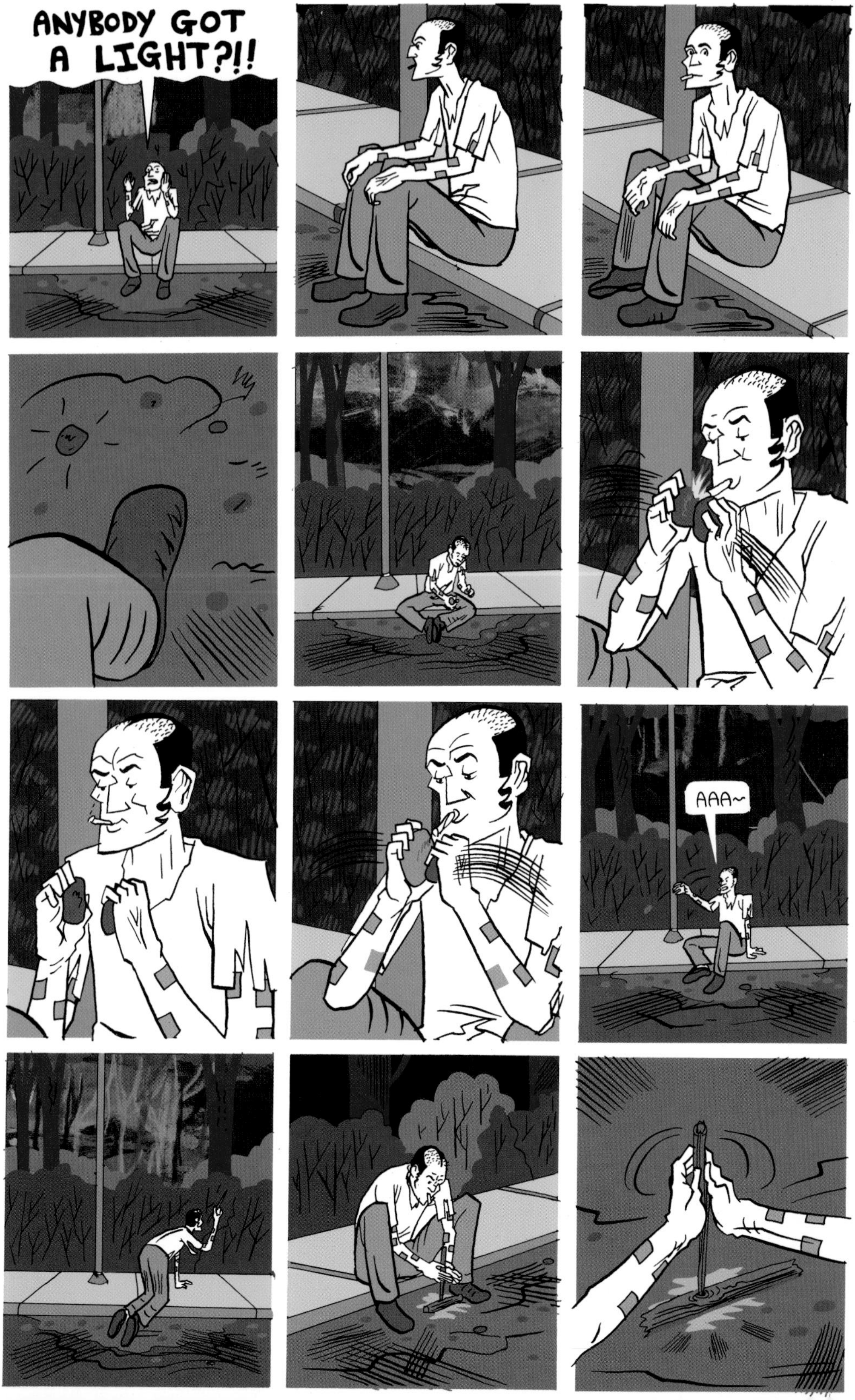
ANYBODY GOT A LIGHT?!!
AAA~

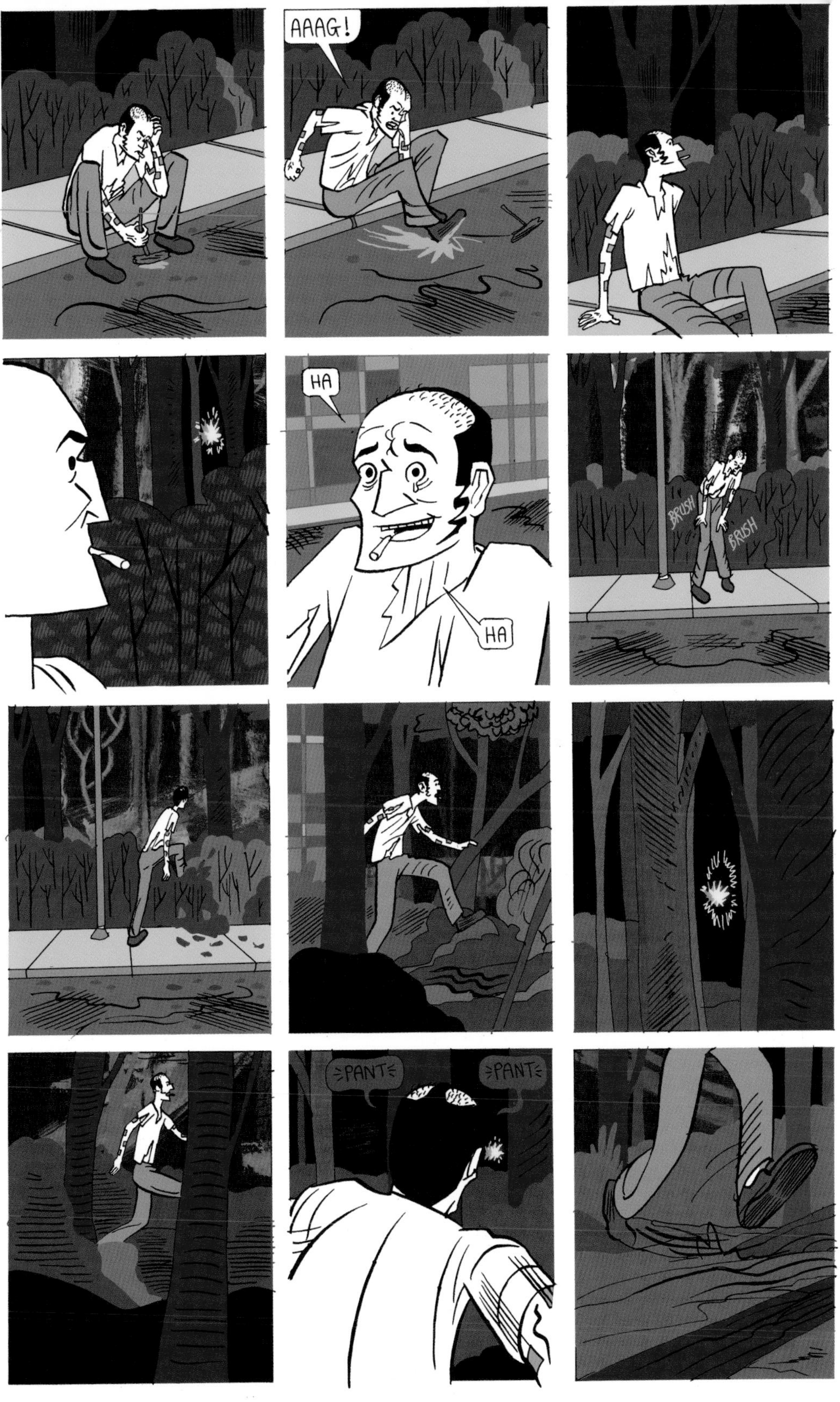
AAAG!
HA
HA
BRUSH
BRUSH
PANT
PANT

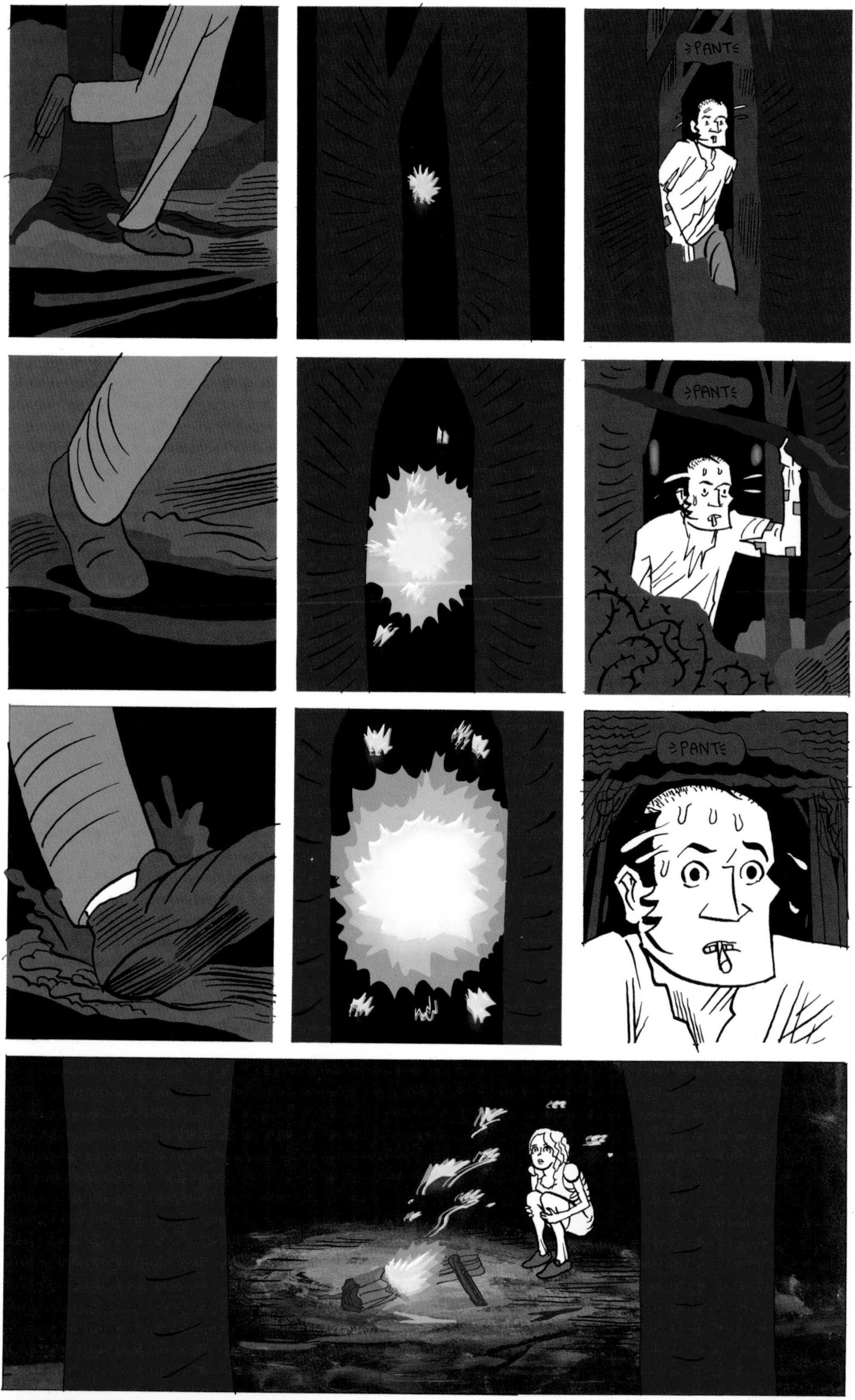
PANT
PANT
PANT

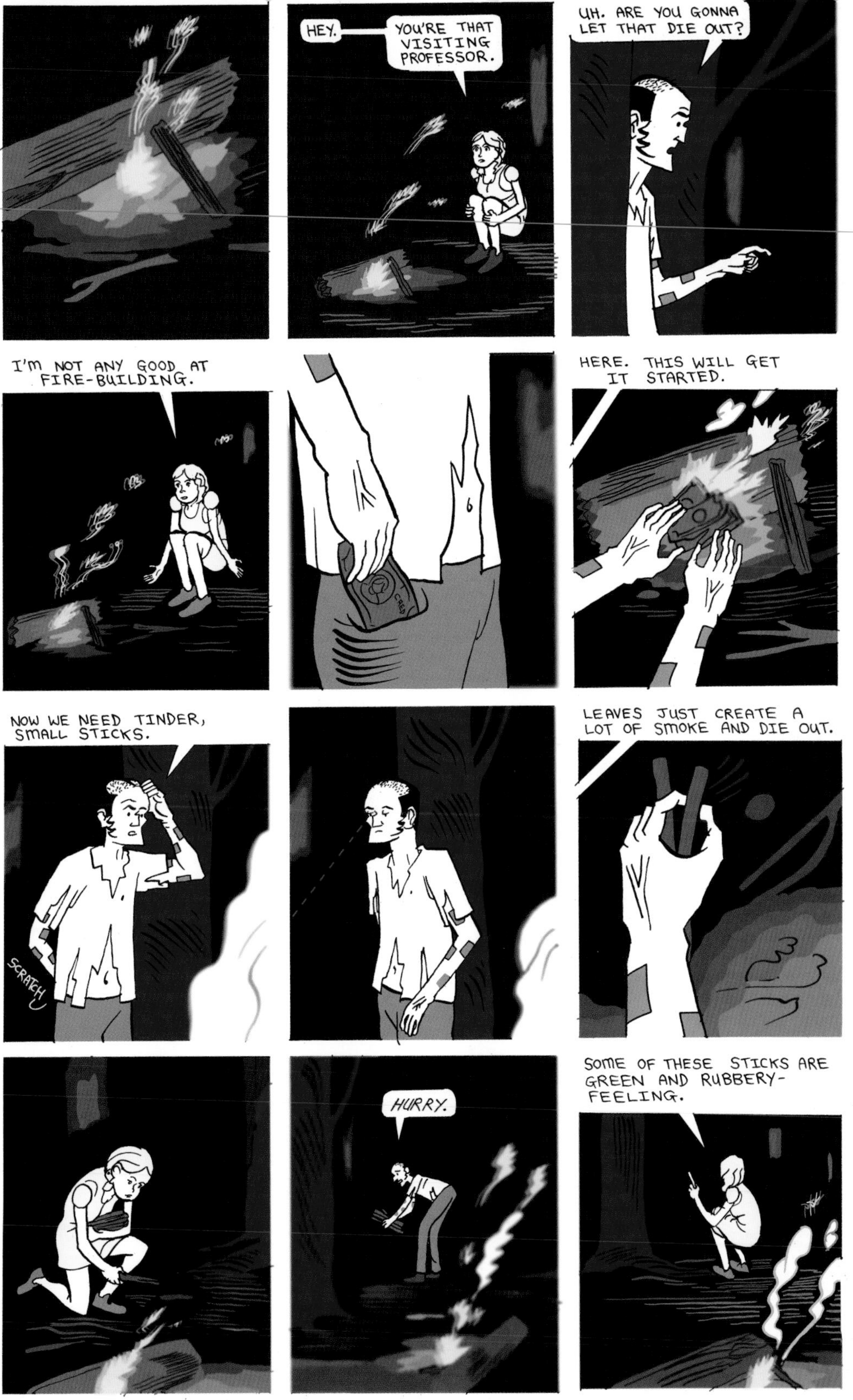
HEY.
YOU'RE THAT VISITING PROFESSOR.
UH. ARE YOU GONNA LET THAT DIE OUT?
I'M NOT ANY GOOD AT FIRE-BUILDING.
HERE. THIS WILL GET IT STARTED.
NOW WE NEED TINDER, SMALL STICKS.
SCRATCH
LEAVES JUST CREATE A LOT OF SMOKE AND DIE OUT.
HURRY.
SOME OF THESE STICKS ARE GREEN AND RUBBERY-FEELING.

YEAH, I'M PROFESSOR PANTHER.

SHIT.

MY NAME'S PEARL PEACH. I GO TO THE SCHOOL.

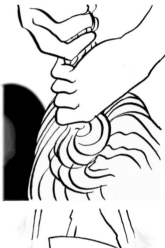

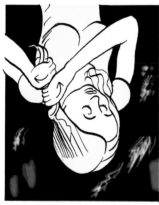

EVENTUALLY, YOU THROW LOGS ON THE FIRE.

THE STICKS GET BIGGER AND BIGGER UNTIL,

START WITH A SMALL STACK, LIKE A TEE-PEE, AND THEN ADD STICKS AS THE FIRE GROWS.

SEE?

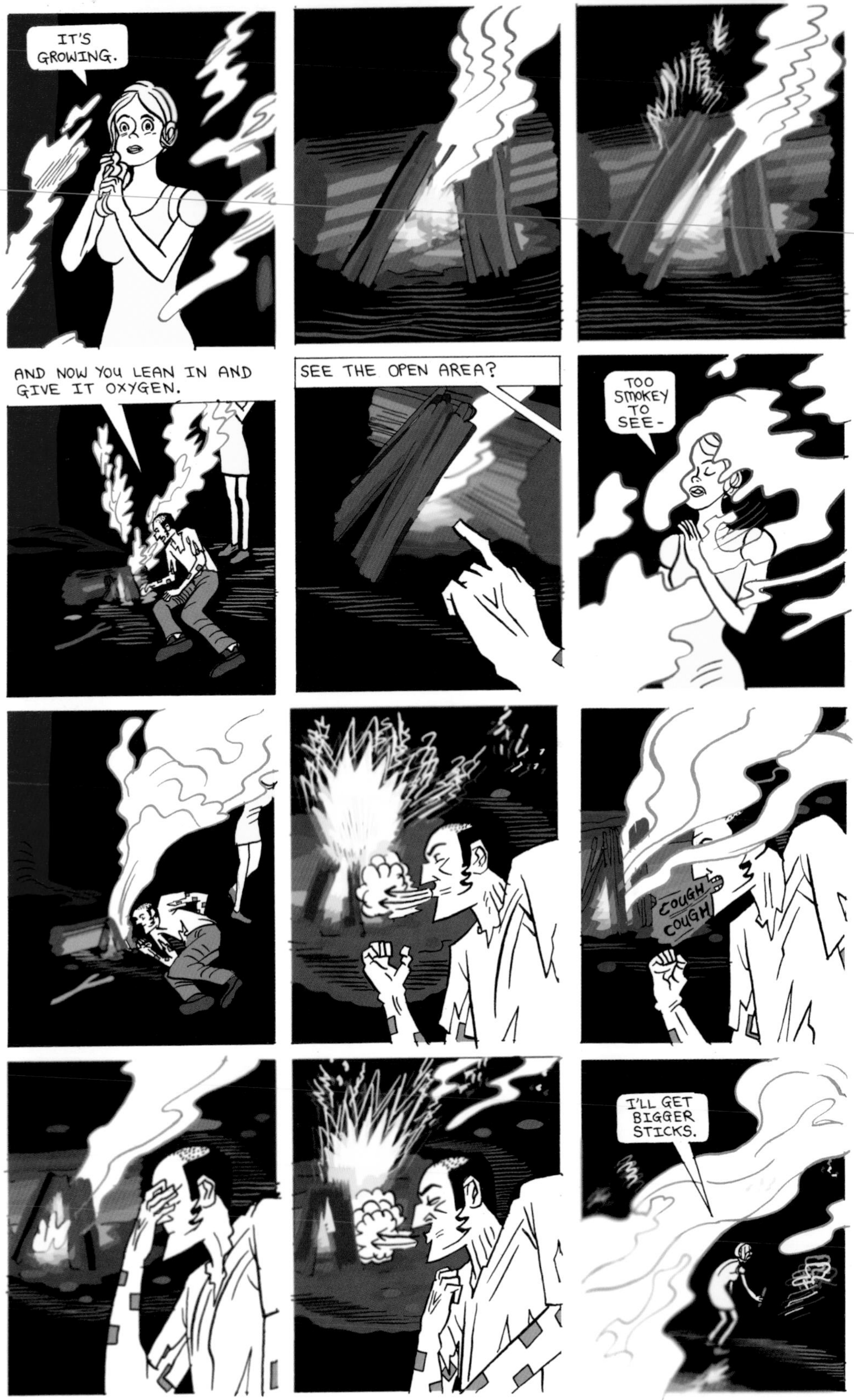
IT'S GROWING.
AND NOW YOU LEAN IN AND GIVE IT OXYGEN.
SEE THE OPEN AREA?
TOO SMOKEY TO SEE-
COUGH
COUGH
I'LL GET BIGGER STICKS.

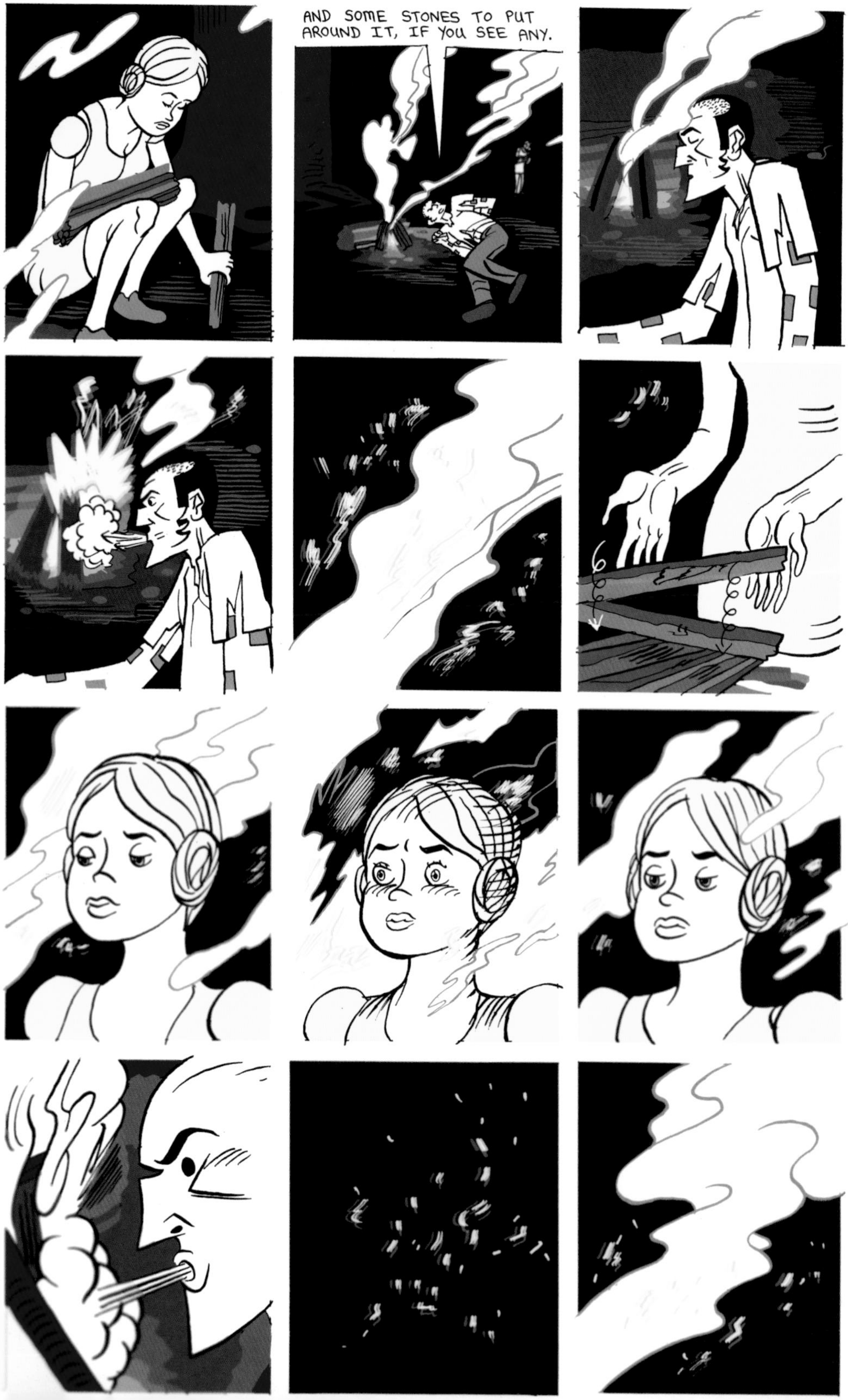
AND SOME STONES TO PUT AROUND IT, IF YOU SEE ANY.

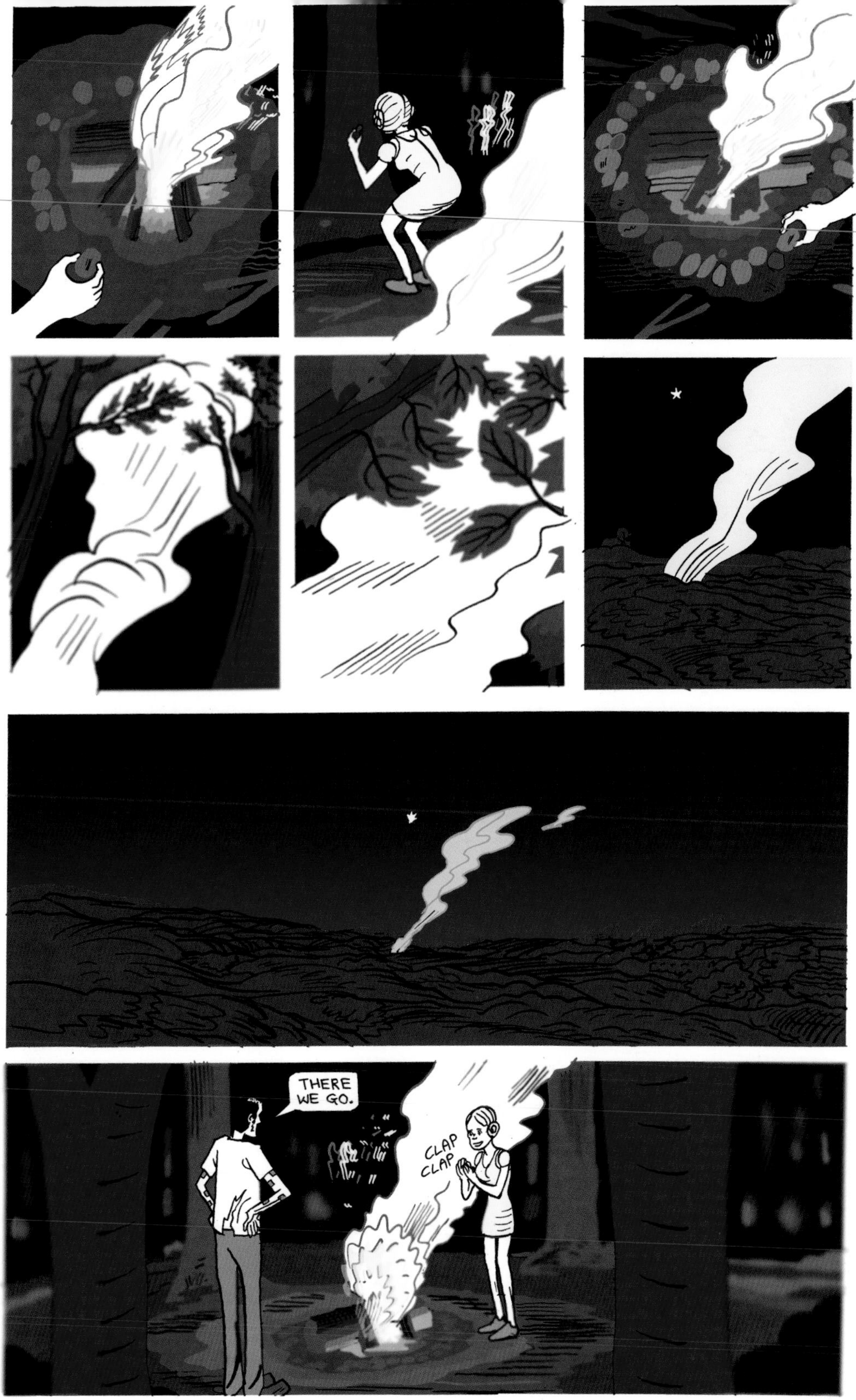
THERE WE GO.
CLAP CLAP

HA

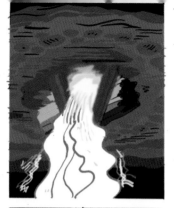

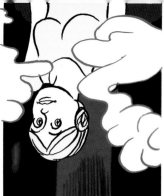

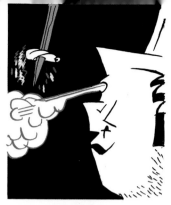

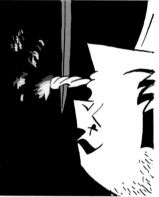

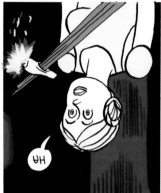

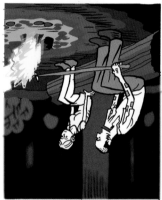

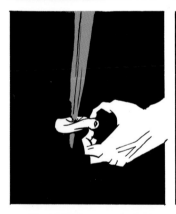

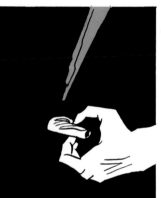

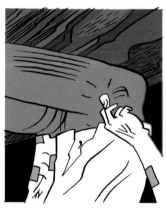

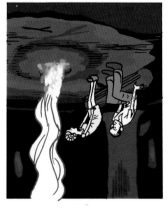

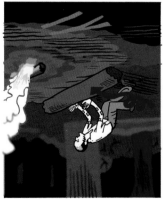

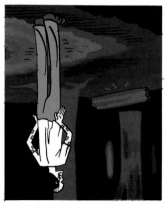

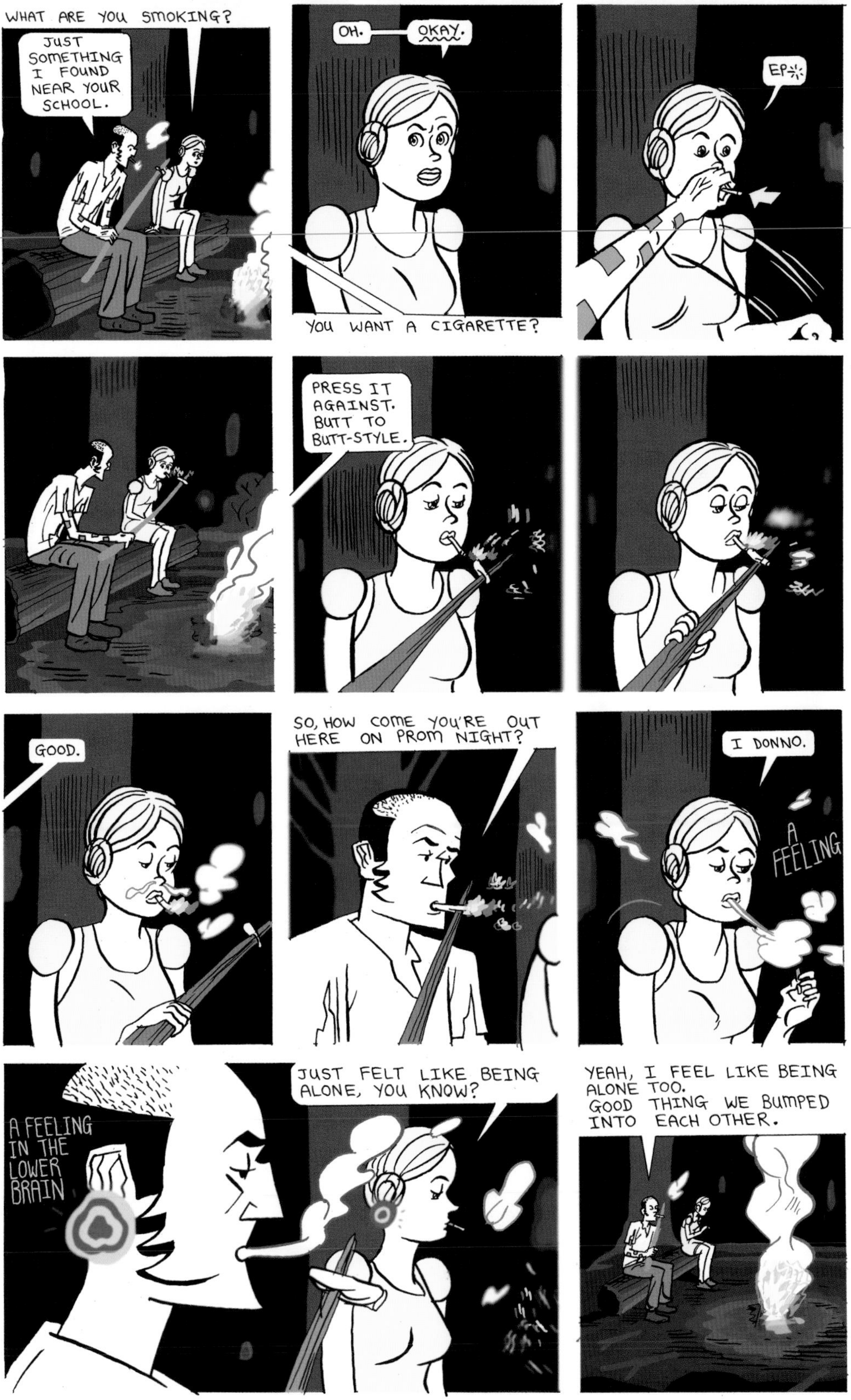
WHAT ARE YOU SMOKING?
JUST SOMETHING I FOUND NEAR YOUR SCHOOL.
OH.
OKAY.
YOU WANT A CIGARETTE?
EP
PRESS IT AGAINST. BUTT TO BUTT-STYLE.
GOOD.
SO, HOW COME YOU'RE OUT HERE ON PROM NIGHT?
I DONNO.
A FEELING
A FEELING IN THE LOWER BRAIN
JUST FELT LIKE BEING ALONE, YOU KNOW?
YEAH, I FEEL LIKE BEING ALONE TOO.
GOOD THING WE BUMPED INTO EACH OTHER.

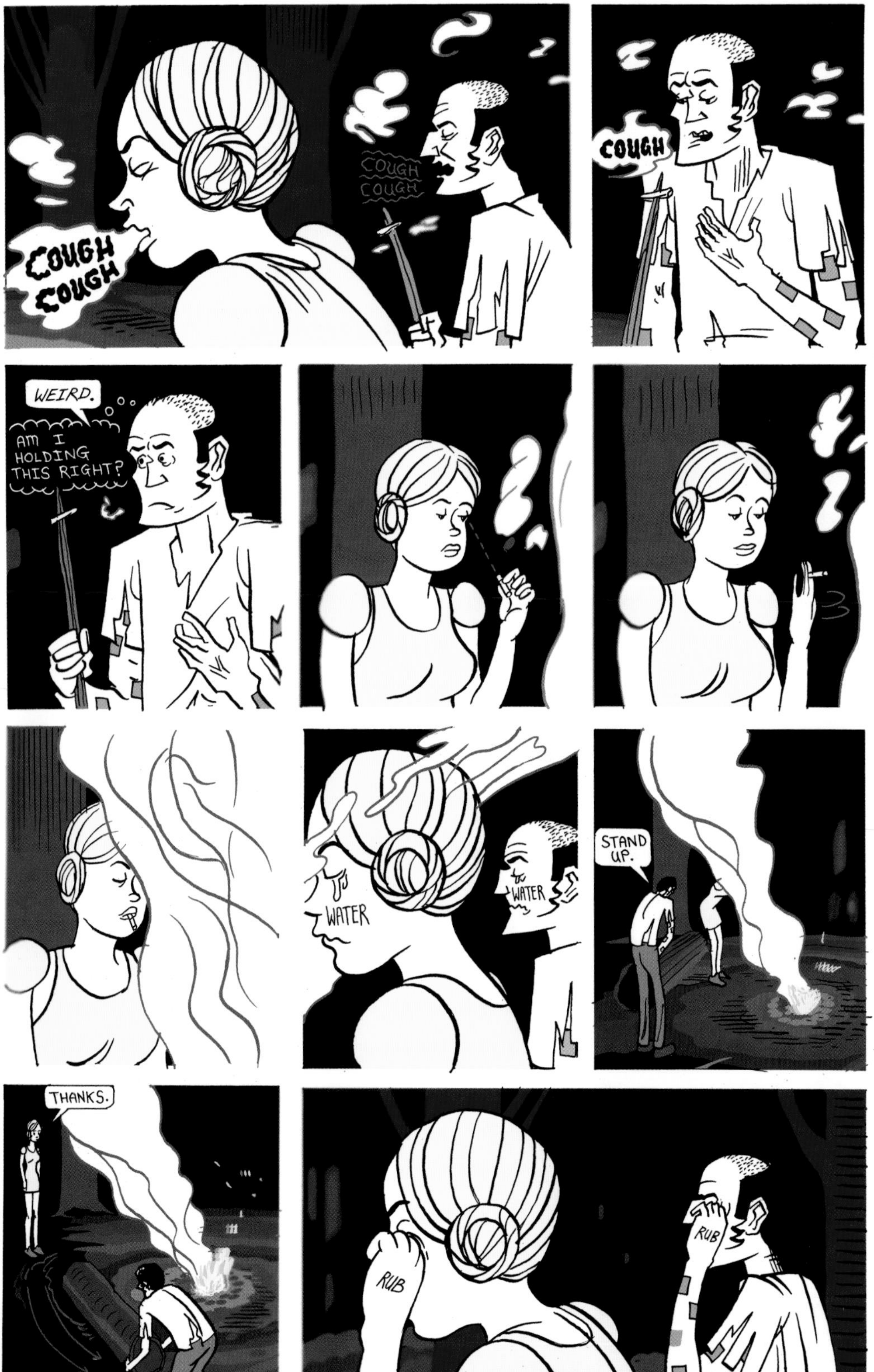
COUGH COUGH
COUGH COUGH
COUGH
WEIRD.
AM I HOLDING THIS RIGHT?
WATER
WATER
STAND UP.
THANKS.
RUB
RUB

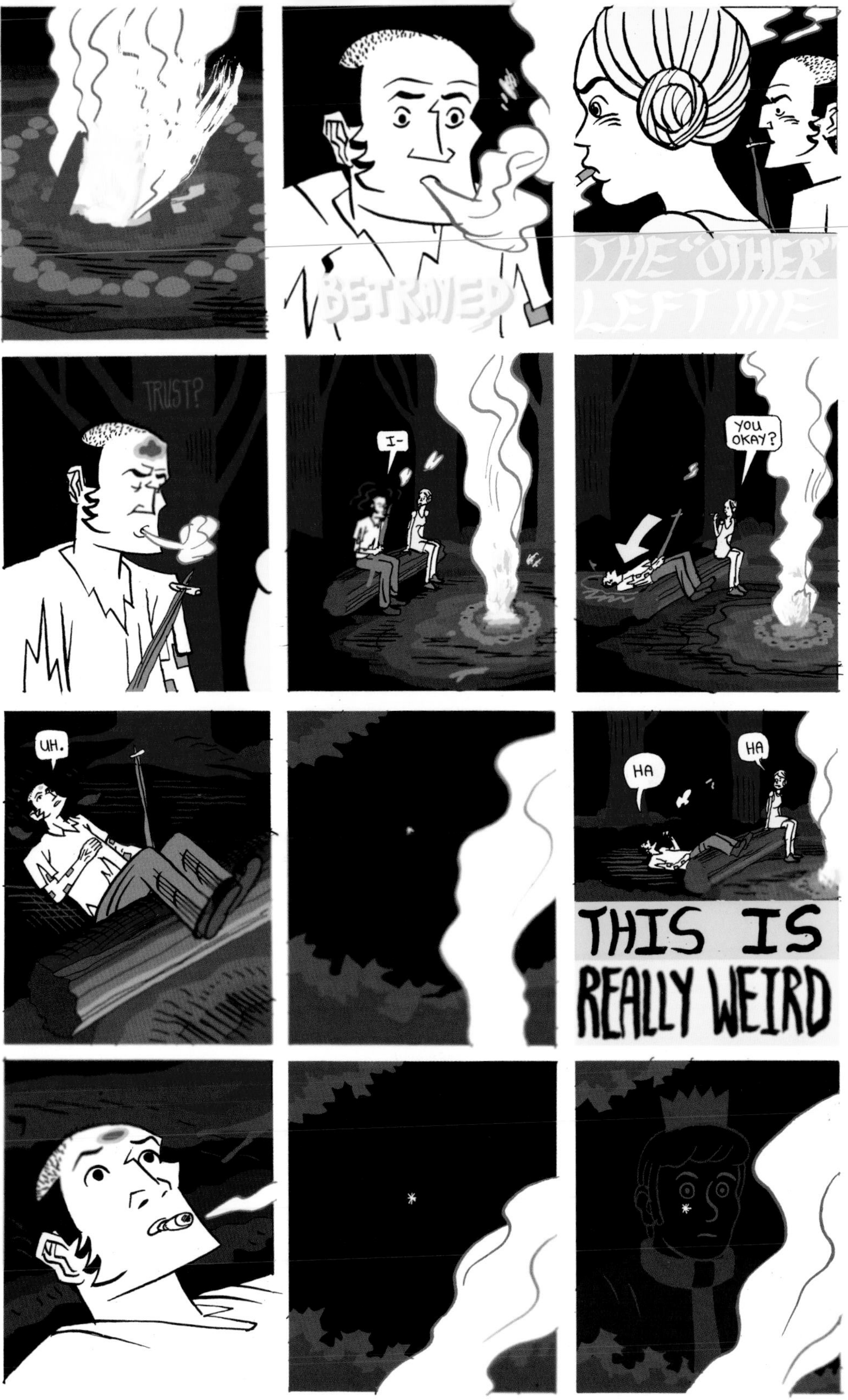
BETRAYED
THE "OTHER"
LEFT ME
TRUST?
I-
YOU OKAY?
UH.
HA
HA
THIS IS
REALLY WEIRD

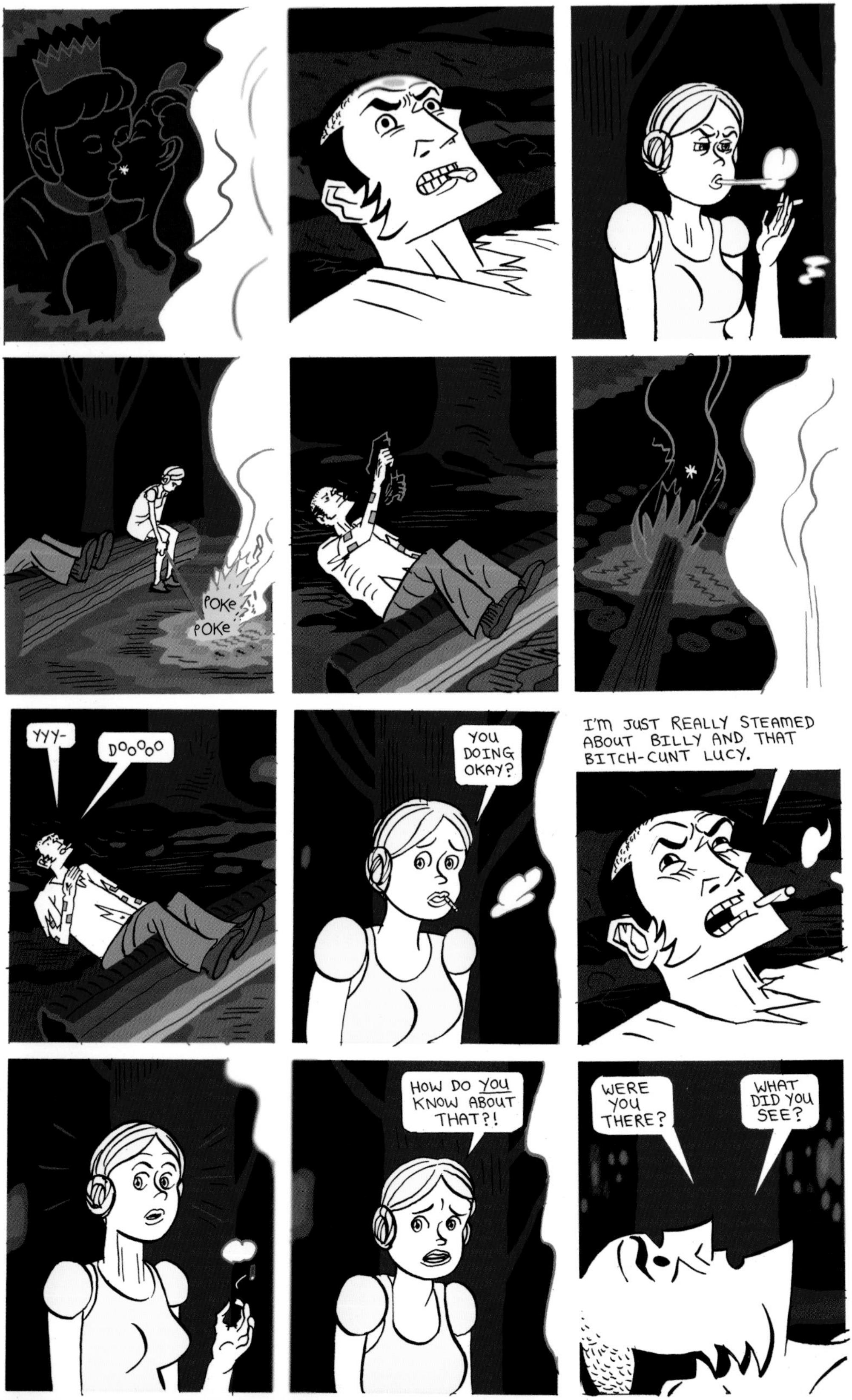
POKE
POKE
YYY-
DOOOOO
YOU DOING OKAY?
I'M JUST REALLY STEAMED ABOUT BILLY AND THAT BITCH-CUNT LUCY.
HOW DO YOU KNOW ABOUT THAT?!
WERE YOU THERE?
WHAT DID YOU SEE?

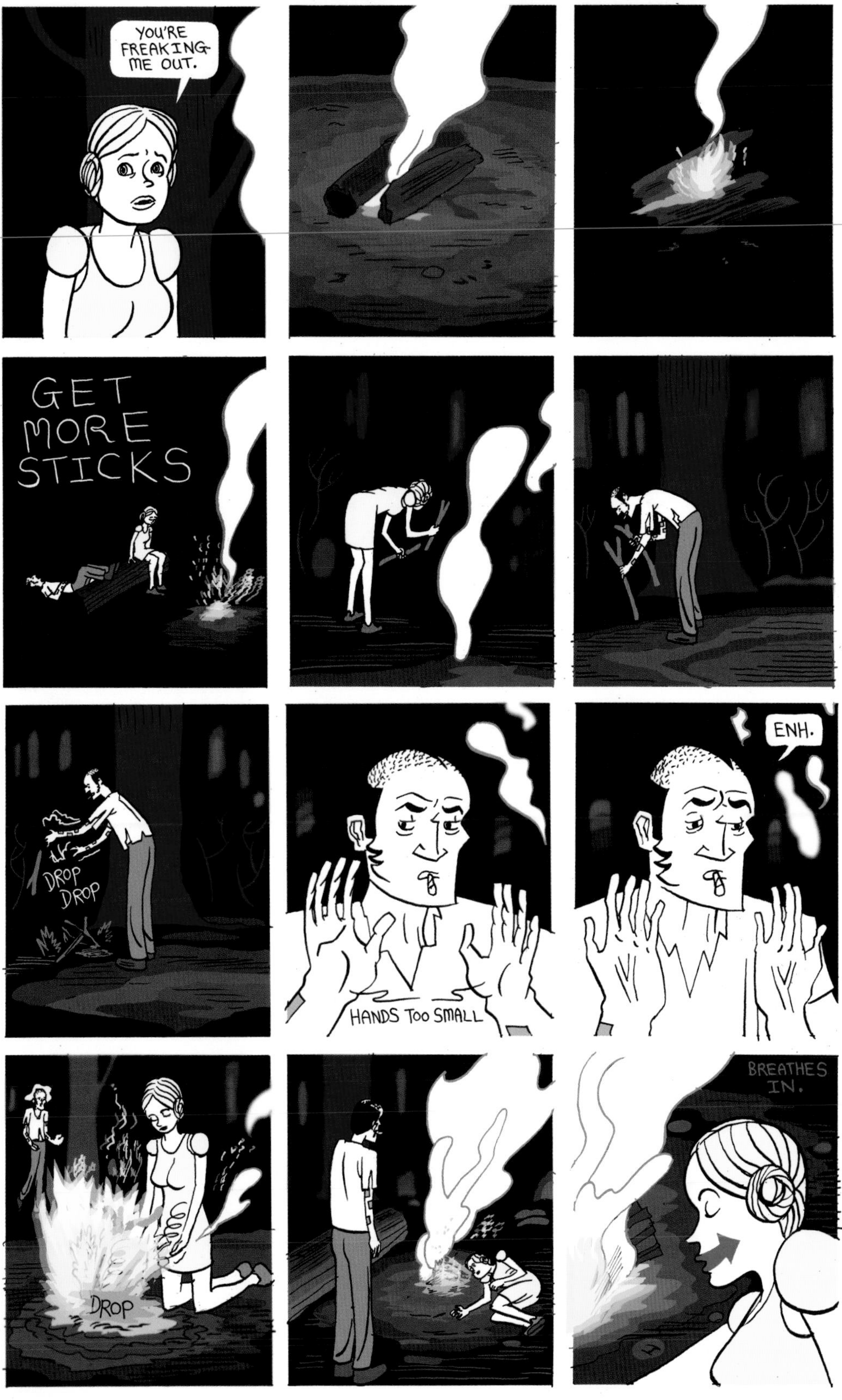
YOU'RE FREAKING ME OUT.
GET MORE STICKS
DROP DROP
HANDS TOO SMALL
ENH.
DROP
BREATHES IN.

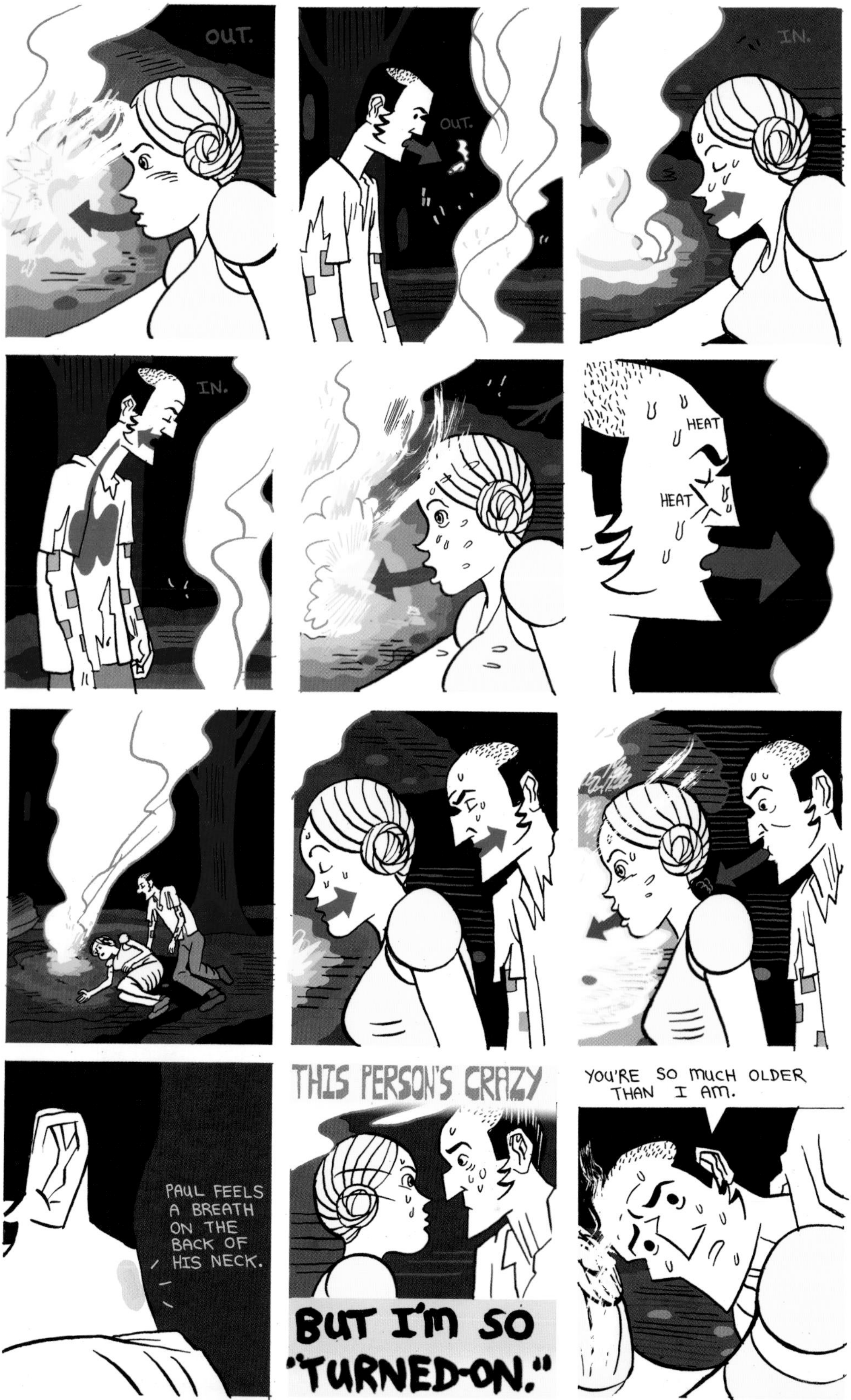
OUT.
OUT.
IN.
IN.
HEAT
HEAT
PAUL FEELS A BREATH ON THE BACK OF HIS NECK.
THIS PERSON'S CRAZY
BUT I'M SO "TURNED-ON."
YOU'RE SO MUCH OLDER THAN I AM.

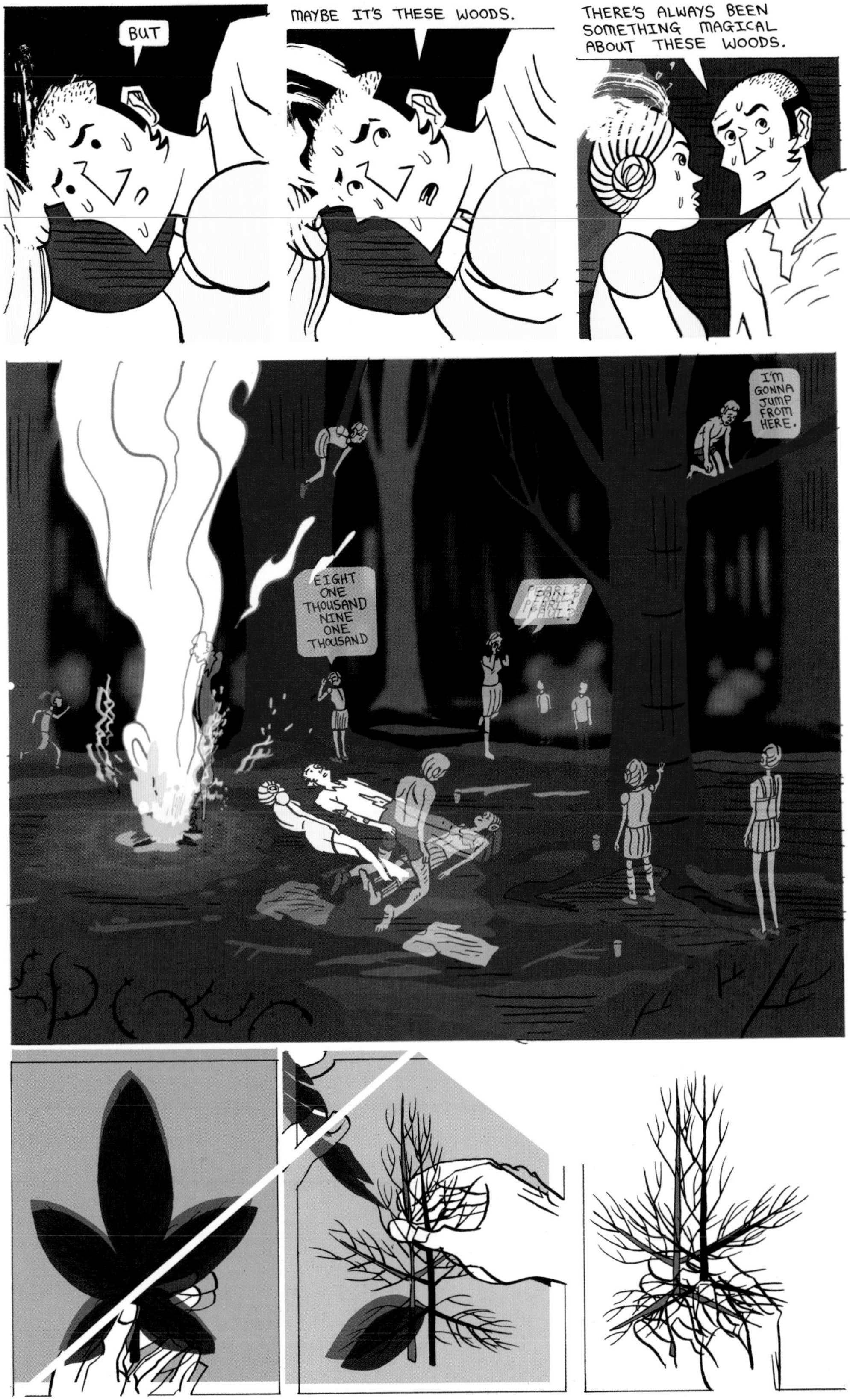
BUT
MAYBE IT'S THESE WOODS.
THERE'S ALWAYS BEEN SOMETHING MAGICAL ABOUT THESE WOODS.
I'M GONNA JUMP FROM HERE.
EIGHT ONE THOUSAND NINE ONE THOUSAND
PEARL? PAUL?

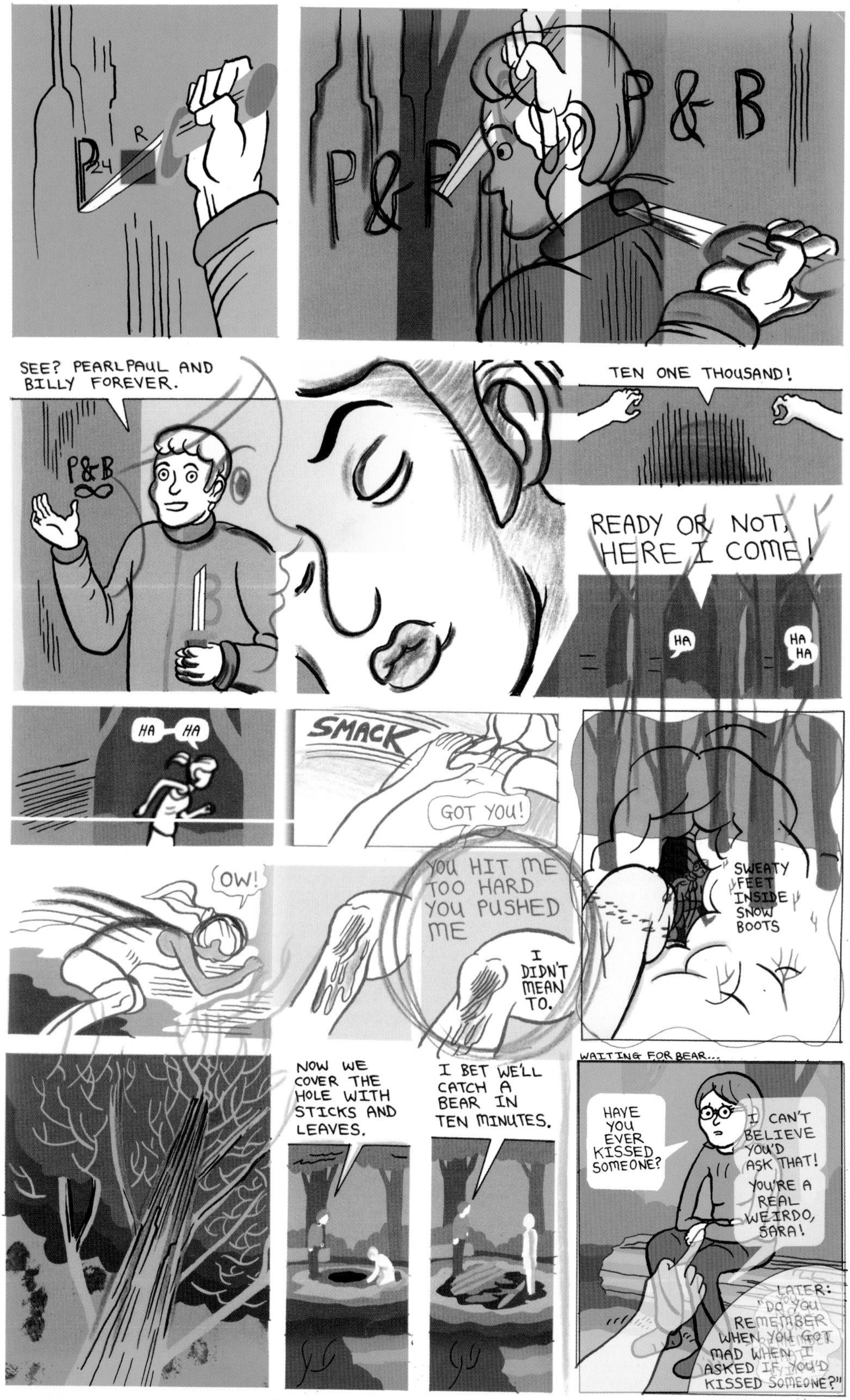
P&B
SEE? PEARLPAUL AND BILLY FOREVER.
P&B
TEN ONE THOUSAND!
READY OR NOT, HERE I COME!
HA
HA HA
HA HA
SMACK
GOT YOU!
OW!
YOU HIT ME TOO HARD YOU PUSHED ME
I DIDN'T MEAN TO.
SWEATY FEET INSIDE SNOW BOOTS
NOW WE COVER THE HOLE WITH STICKS AND LEAVES.
I BET WE'LL CATCH A BEAR IN TEN MINUTES.
WAITING FOR BEAR...
HAVE YOU EVER KISSED SOMEONE?
I CAN'T BELIEVE YOU'D ASK THAT!
YOU'RE A REAL WEIRDO, SARA!
LATER: "DO YOU REMEMBER WHEN YOU GOT MAD WHEN I ASKED IF YOU'D KISSED SOMEONE?"

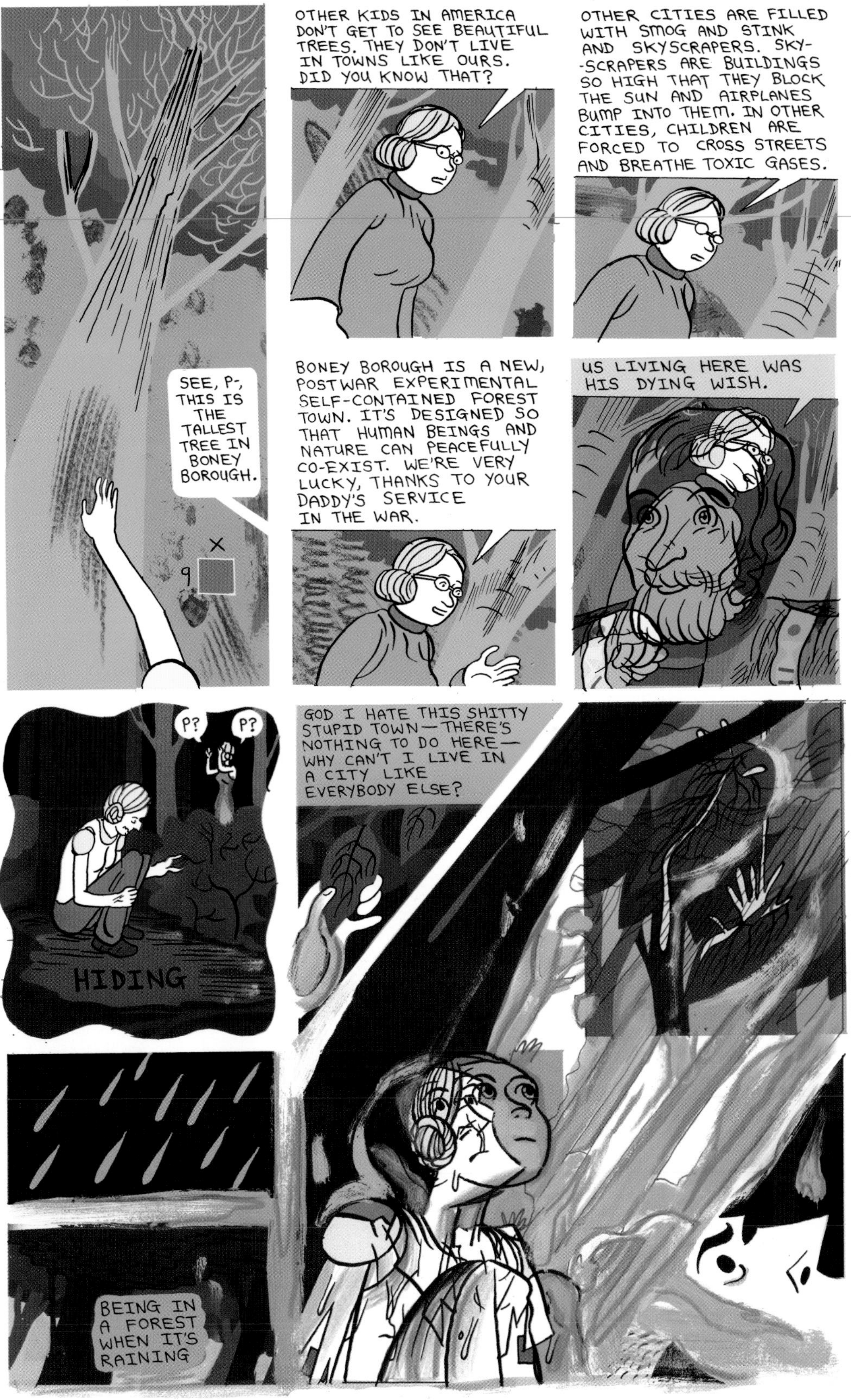
SEE, P-, THIS IS THE TALLEST TREE IN BONEY BOROUGH.
OTHER KIDS IN AMERICA DON'T GET TO SEE BEAUTIFUL TREES. THEY DON'T LIVE IN TOWNS LIKE OURS. DID YOU KNOW THAT?
OTHER CITIES ARE FILLED WITH SMOG AND STINK AND SKYSCRAPERS. SKY--SCRAPERS ARE BUILDINGS SO HIGH THAT THEY BLOCK THE SUN AND AIRPLANES BUMP INTO THEM. IN OTHER CITIES, CHILDREN ARE FORCED TO CROSS STREETS AND BREATHE TOXIC GASES.
BONEY BOROUGH IS A NEW, POSTWAR EXPERIMENTAL SELF-CONTAINED FOREST TOWN. IT'S DESIGNED SO THAT HUMAN BEINGS AND NATURE CAN PEACEFULLY CO-EXIST. WE'RE VERY LUCKY, THANKS TO YOUR DADDY'S SERVICE IN THE WAR.
US LIVING HERE WAS HIS DYING WISH.
P?
P?
HIDING
GOD I HATE THIS SHITTY STUPID TOWN—THERE'S NOTHING TO DO HERE—WHY CAN'T I LIVE IN A CITY LIKE EVERYBODY ELSE?
BEING IN A FOREST WHEN IT'S RAINING

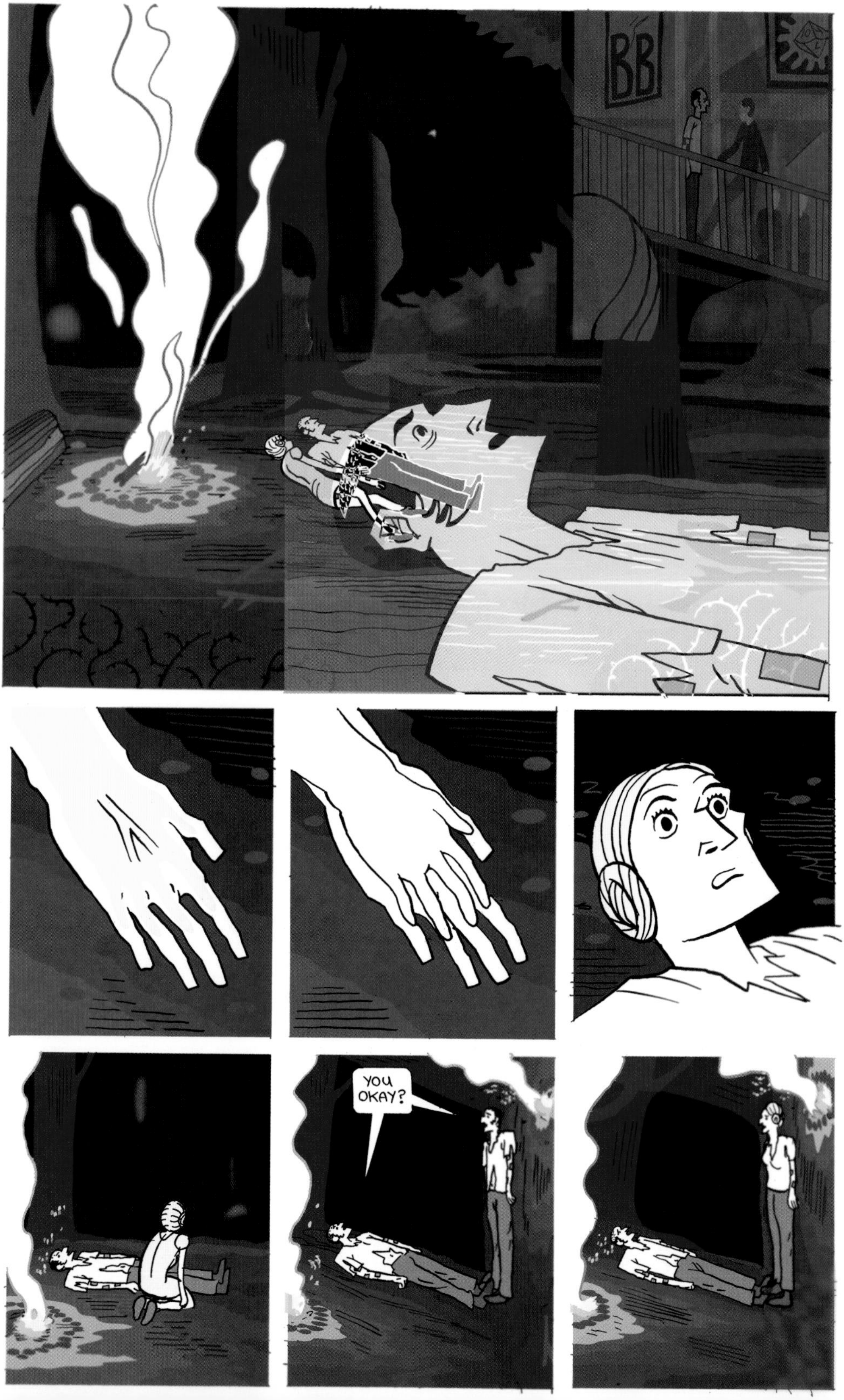
BB
YOU OKAY?

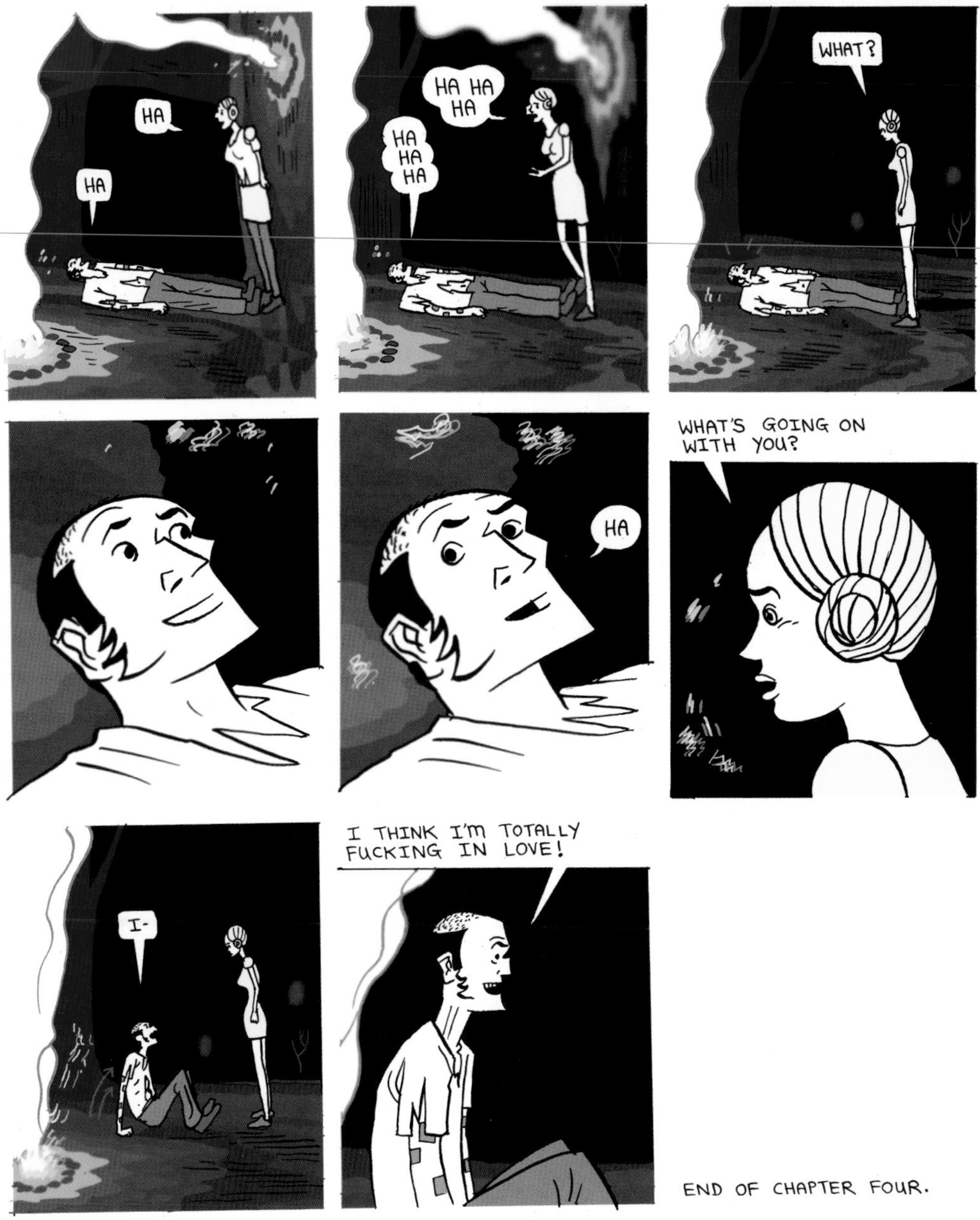
HA
HA
HA
HA
HA
HA HA
HA
WHAT?
HA
WHAT'S GOING ON WITH YOU?
I-
I THINK I'M TOTALLY FUCKING IN LOVE!

END OF CHAPTER FOUR.

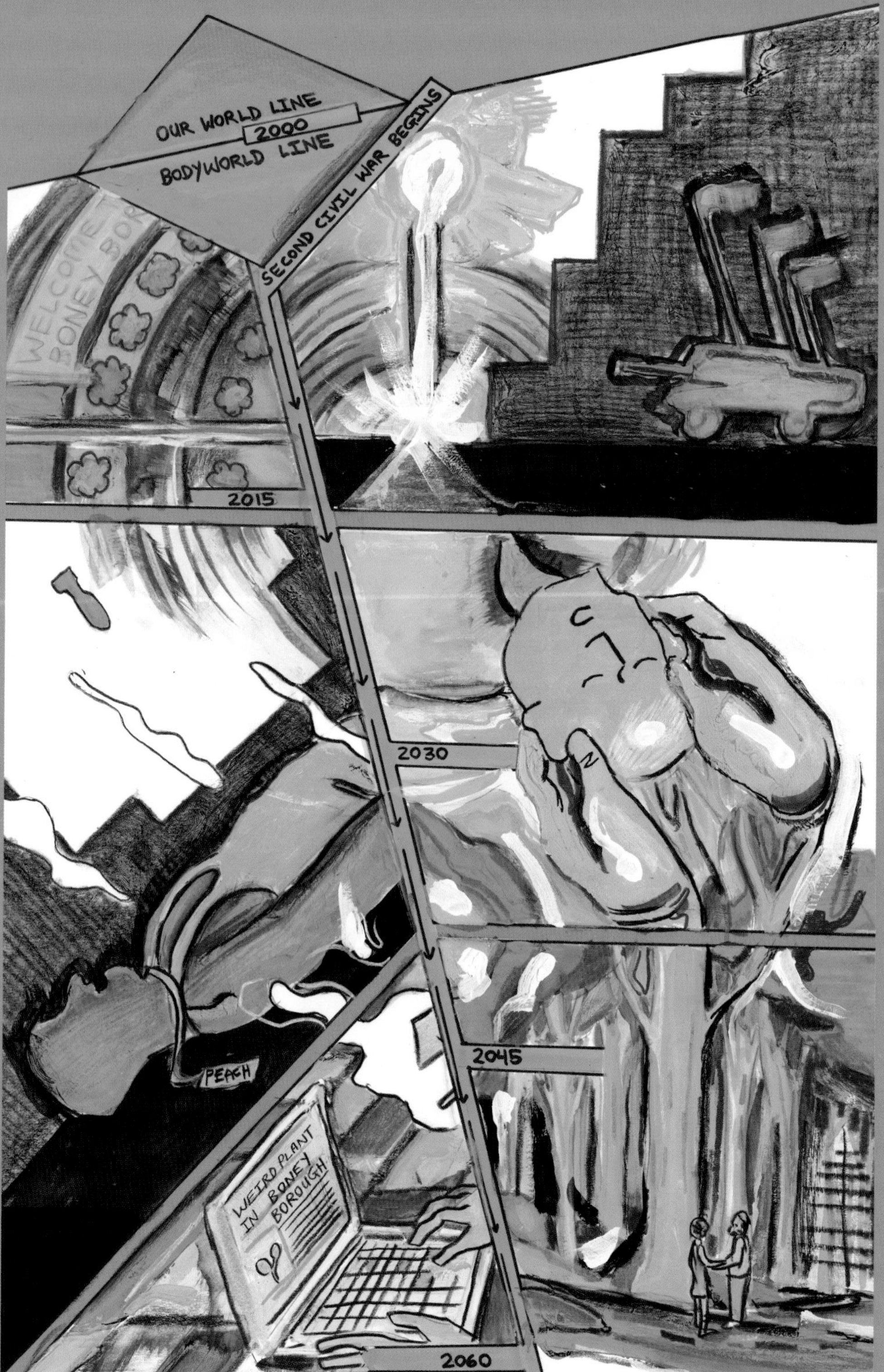
OUR WORLD LINE
2000
BODYWORLD LINE
SECOND CIVIL WAR BEGINS
WELCOME
BONEY BOR
2015
2030
PEACH
2045
WEIRD PLANT IN BONEY BOROUGH
2060

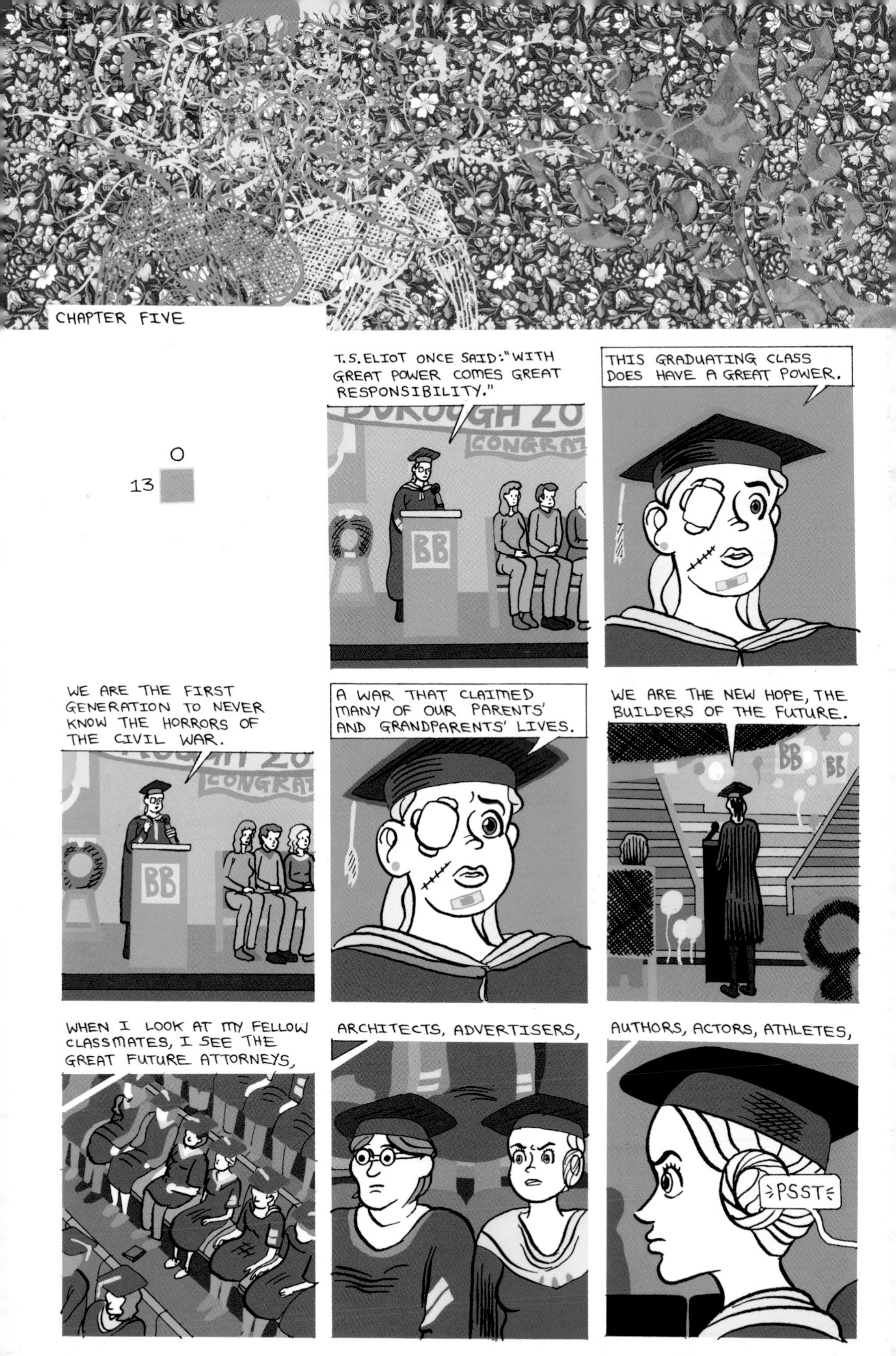
CHAPTER FIVE
O
13
T.S. ELIOT ONCE SAID: "WITH GREAT POWER COMES GREAT RESPONSIBILITY."
BB
THIS GRADUATING CLASS DOES HAVE A GREAT POWER.
WE ARE THE FIRST GENERATION TO NEVER KNOW THE HORRORS OF THE CIVIL WAR.
BB
A WAR THAT CLAIMED MANY OF OUR PARENTS' AND GRANDPARENTS' LIVES.
WE ARE THE NEW HOPE, THE BUILDERS OF THE FUTURE.
BB
BB
WHEN I LOOK AT MY FELLOW CLASSMATES, I SEE THE GREAT FUTURE ATTORNEYS,
ARCHITECTS, ADVERTISERS,
AUTHORS, ACTORS, ATHLETES,
PSST

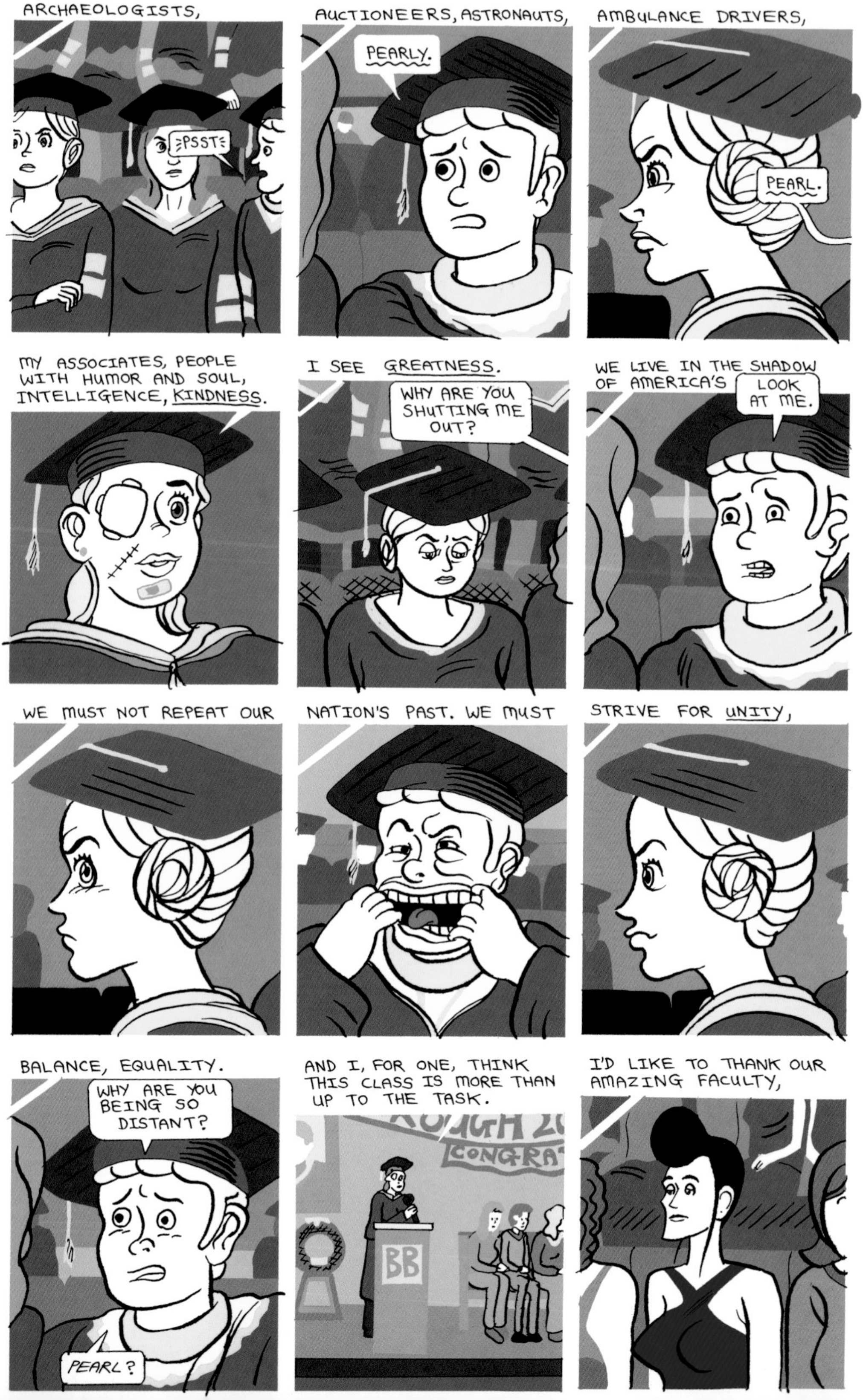
ARCHAEOLOGISTS,
PSST
AUCTIONEERS, ASTRONAUTS,
PEARLY.
AMBULANCE DRIVERS,
PEARL.
MY ASSOCIATES, PEOPLE WITH HUMOR AND SOUL, INTELLIGENCE, KINDNESS.
I SEE GREATNESS.
WHY ARE YOU SHUTTING ME OUT?
WE LIVE IN THE SHADOW OF AMERICA'S
LOOK AT ME.
WE MUST NOT REPEAT OUR
NATION'S PAST. WE MUST
STRIVE FOR UNITY,
BALANCE, EQUALITY.
WHY ARE YOU BEING SO DISTANT?
PEARL?
AND I, FOR ONE, THINK THIS CLASS IS MORE THAN UP TO THE TASK.
CONGRAT
BB
I'D LIKE TO THANK OUR AMAZING FACULTY,

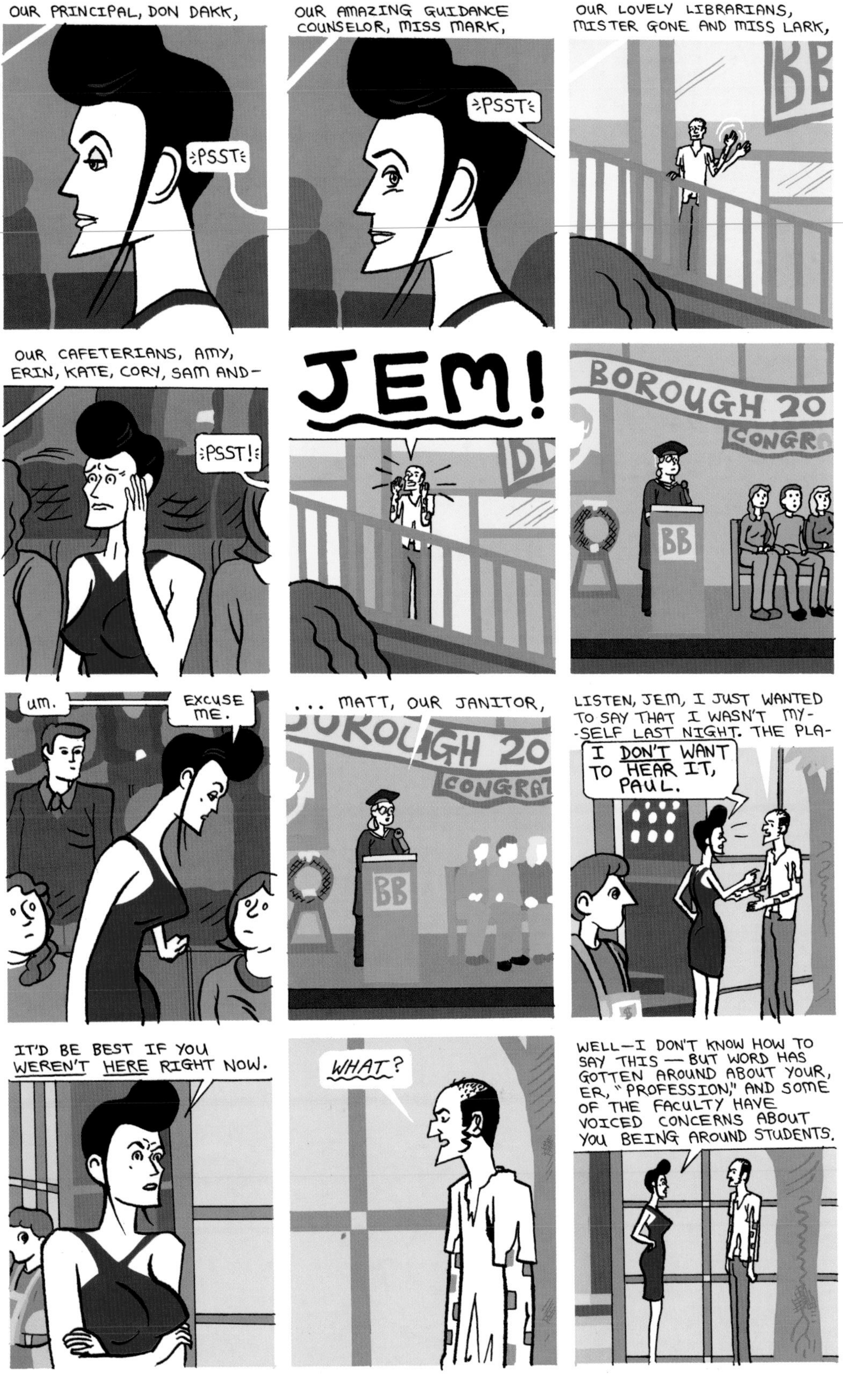

OUR PRINCIPAL, DON DAKK,
PSST
OUR AMAZING GUIDANCE COUNSELOR, MISS MARK,
PSST
OUR LOVELY LIBRARIANS, MISTER GONE AND MISS LARK,
BB
OUR CAFETERIANS, AMY, ERIN, KATE, CORY, SAM AND—
PSST!
JEM!
BOROUGH 20
CONGRA
BB
UM.
EXCUSE ME.
... MATT, OUR JANITOR,
CONGRAT
BB
LISTEN, JEM, I JUST WANTED TO SAY THAT I WASN'T MY-SELF LAST NIGHT. THE PLA-
I DON'T WANT TO HEAR IT, PAUL.
IT'D BE BEST IF YOU WEREN'T HERE RIGHT NOW.
WHAT?
WELL—I DON'T KNOW HOW TO SAY THIS — BUT WORD HAS GOTTEN AROUND ABOUT YOUR, ER, "PROFESSION," AND SOME OF THE FACULTY HAVE VOICED CONCERNS ABOUT YOU BEING AROUND STUDENTS.

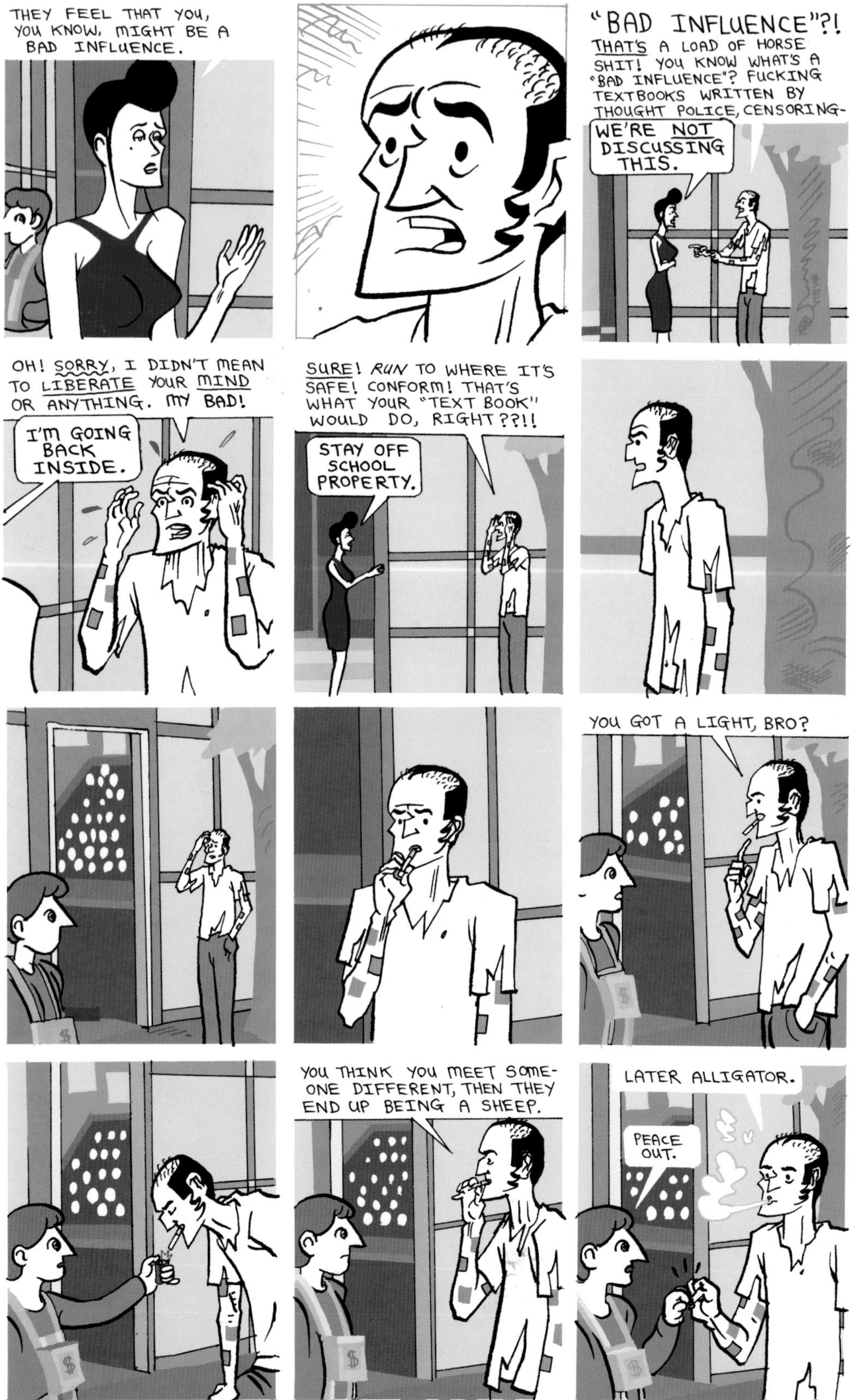
THEY FEEL THAT YOU, YOU KNOW, MIGHT BE A BAD INFLUENCE.
"BAD INFLUENCE"?! THAT'S A LOAD OF HORSE SHIT! YOU KNOW WHAT'S A "BAD INFLUENCE"? FUCKING TEXTBOOKS WRITTEN BY THOUGHT POLICE, CENSORING-
WE'RE NOT DISCUSSING THIS.
OH! SORRY, I DIDN'T MEAN TO LIBERATE YOUR MIND OR ANYTHING. MY BAD!
I'M GOING BACK INSIDE.
SURE! RUN TO WHERE IT'S SAFE! CONFORM! THAT'S WHAT YOUR "TEXT BOOK" WOULD DO, RIGHT??!!
STAY OFF SCHOOL PROPERTY.
YOU GOT A LIGHT, BRO?
YOU THINK YOU MEET SOME-ONE DIFFERENT, THEN THEY END UP BEING A SHEEP.
LATER ALLIGATOR.
PEACE OUT.

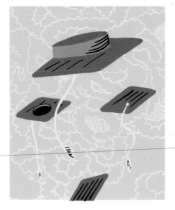

WHY'RE YOU SMOKING?

I LIKE THE FLAVOR.

TAP

TASTE'S GOOD, LIKE WINE.

ARE YOU GONNA GO TO TONY'S PLACE FOR THE AFTER-GRADUATION PARTY?

NO.

I'M TIRED OF LAME PARTIES FILLED WITH CHILDISH DOUCHEBAGS.

YOU JUST DON'T WANT TO BE AROUND BILLY.

"BILLY?" HA!

DON'T MAKE ME LAUGH! "BILLY!"

HA! HA! HA!

HA!

MY EYE'S ON SOMEONE ELSE NOW.

YEAH, SO? SO WHAT?

YOU TAKE BATHS? HA.

HERE'S WHAT I KNOW SO FAR: THE FIRST TIME I SMOKED THE PLANT, I WAS IN THE BATH, ALONE.

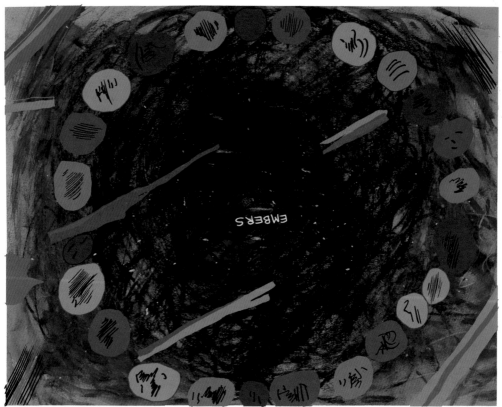

EMBERS

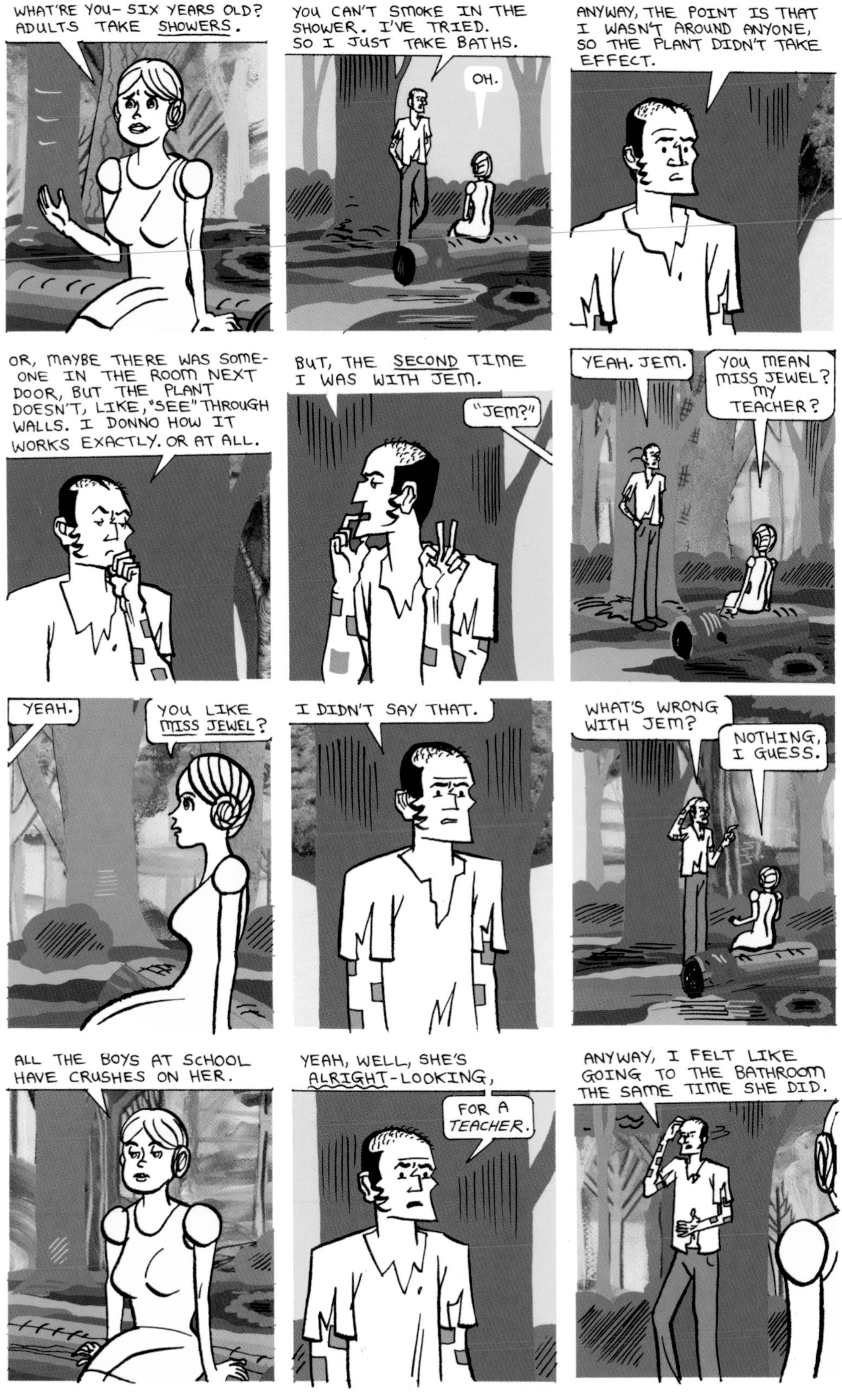

WHAT'RE YOU- SIX YEARS OLD? ADULTS TAKE SHOWERS.
YOU CAN'T SMOKE IN THE SHOWER. I'VE TRIED. SO I JUST TAKE BATHS.
OH.
ANYWAY, THE POINT IS THAT I WASN'T AROUND ANYONE, SO THE PLANT DIDN'T TAKE EFFECT.
OR, MAYBE THERE WAS SOME-ONE IN THE ROOM NEXT DOOR, BUT THE PLANT DOESN'T, LIKE, "SEE" THROUGH WALLS. I DONNO HOW IT WORKS EXACTLY. OR AT ALL.
BUT, THE SECOND TIME I WAS WITH JEM.
"JEM?"
YEAH. JEM.
YOU MEAN MISS JEWEL? MY TEACHER?
YEAH.
YOU LIKE MISS JEWEL?
I DIDN'T SAY THAT.
WHAT'S WRONG WITH JEM?
NOTHING, I GUESS.
ALL THE BOYS AT SCHOOL HAVE CRUSHES ON HER.
YEAH, WELL, SHE'S ALRIGHT-LOOKING,
FOR A TEACHER.
ANYWAY, I FELT LIKE GOING TO THE BATHROOM THE SAME TIME SHE DID.

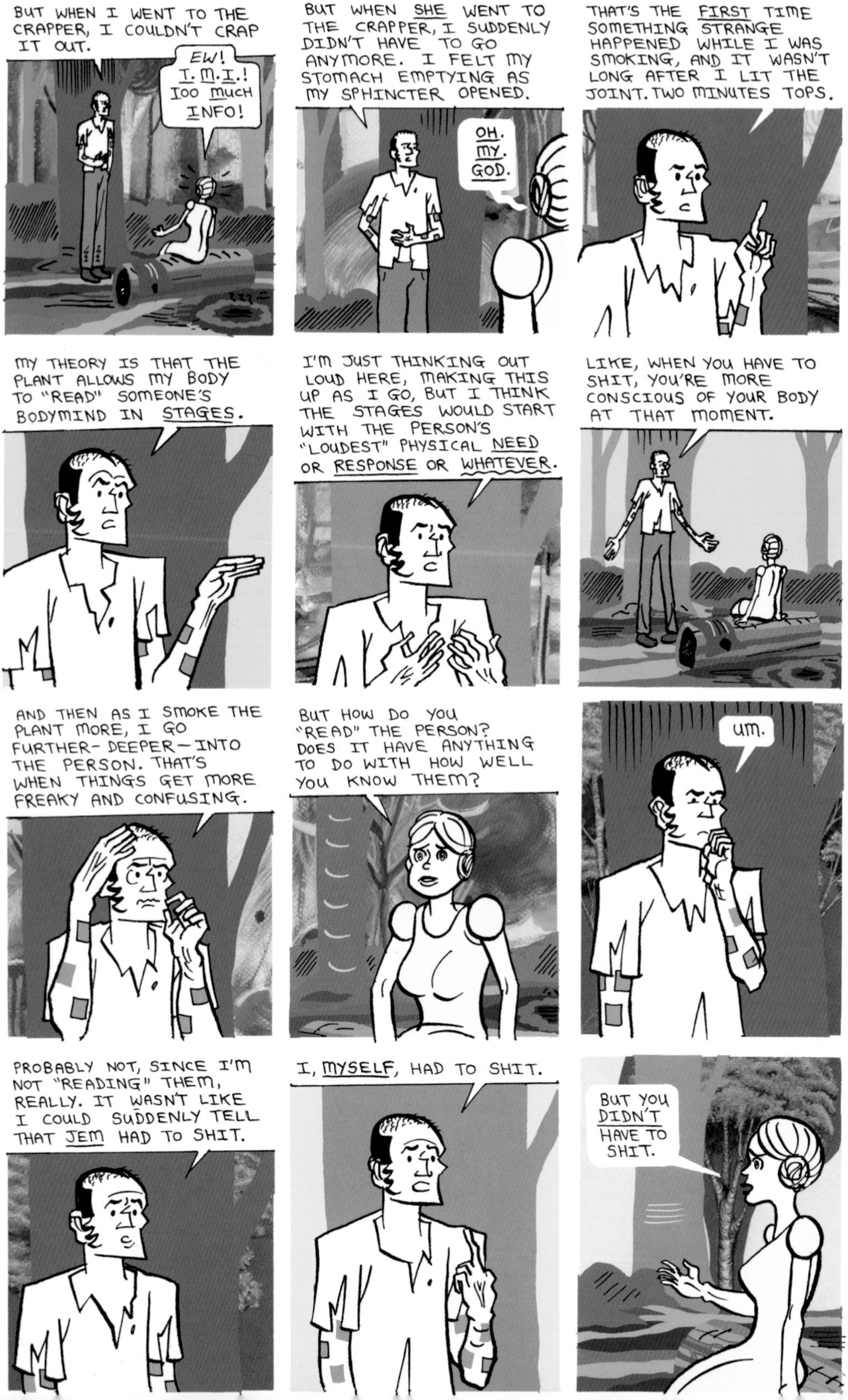

BUT WHEN I WENT TO THE CRAPPER, I COULDN'T CRAP IT OUT.
EW! I.M.I.! TOO MUCH INFO!
BUT WHEN SHE WENT TO THE CRAPPER, I SUDDENLY DIDN'T HAVE TO GO ANYMORE. I FELT MY STOMACH EMPTYING AS MY SPHINCTER OPENED.
OH. MY. GOD.
THAT'S THE FIRST TIME SOMETHING STRANGE HAPPENED WHILE I WAS SMOKING, AND IT WASN'T LONG AFTER I LIT THE JOINT. TWO MINUTES TOPS.
MY THEORY IS THAT THE PLANT ALLOWS MY BODY TO "READ" SOMEONE'S BODYMIND IN STAGES.
I'M JUST THINKING OUT LOUD HERE, MAKING THIS UP AS I GO, BUT I THINK THE STAGES WOULD START WITH THE PERSON'S "LOUDEST" PHYSICAL NEED OR RESPONSE OR WHATEVER.
LIKE, WHEN YOU HAVE TO SHIT, YOU'RE MORE CONSCIOUS OF YOUR BODY AT THAT MOMENT.
AND THEN AS I SMOKE THE PLANT MORE, I GO FURTHER- DEEPER—INTO THE PERSON. THAT'S WHEN THINGS GET MORE FREAKY AND CONFUSING.
BUT HOW DO YOU "READ" THE PERSON? DOES IT HAVE ANYTHING TO DO WITH HOW WELL YOU KNOW THEM?
UM.
PROBABLY NOT, SINCE I'M NOT "READING" THEM, REALLY. IT WASN'T LIKE I COULD SUDDENLY TELL THAT JEM HAD TO SHIT.
I, MYSELF, HAD TO SHIT.
BUT YOU DIDN'T HAVE TO SHIT.

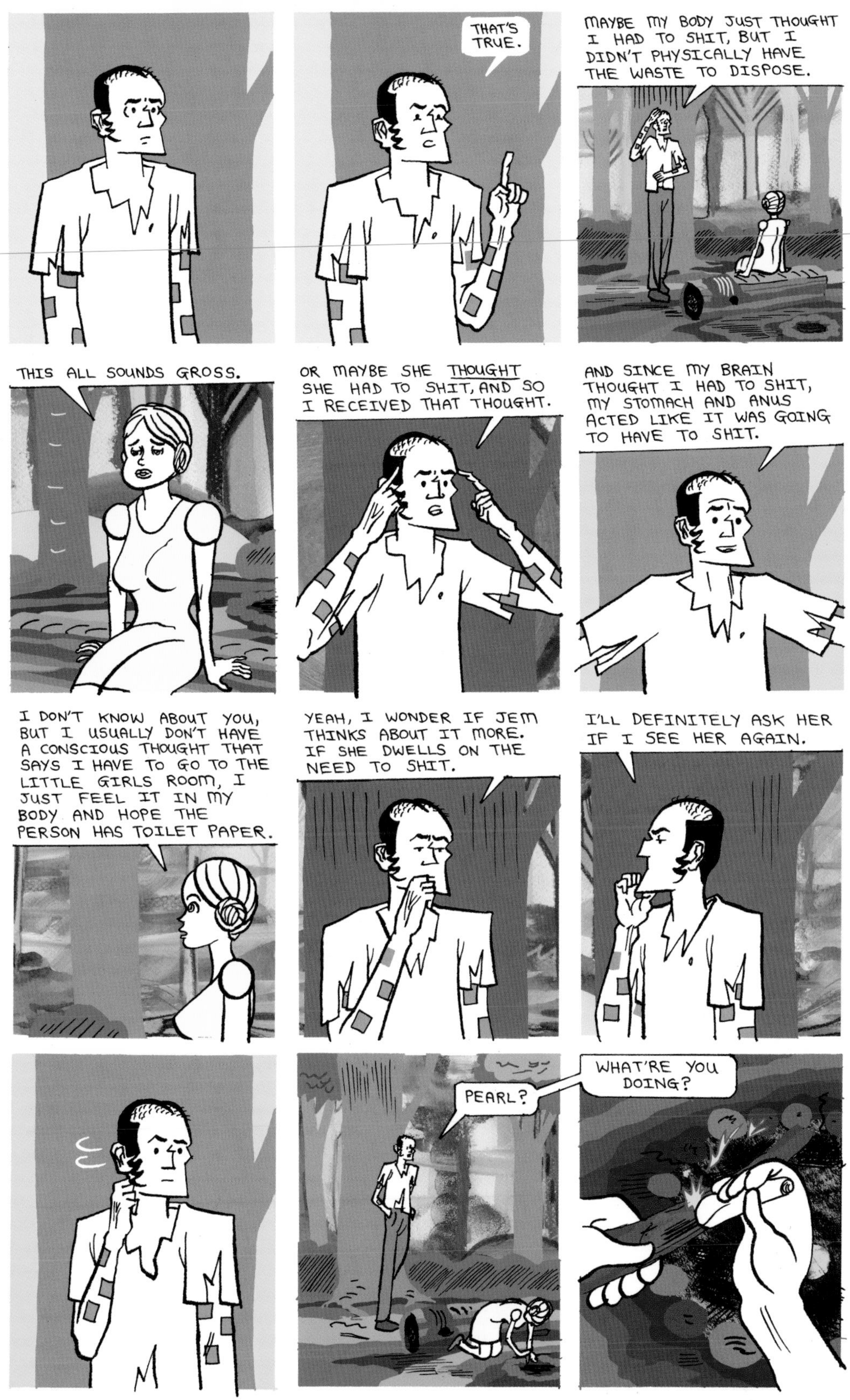
THAT'S TRUE.
MAYBE MY BODY JUST THOUGHT I HAD TO SHIT, BUT I DIDN'T PHYSICALLY HAVE THE WASTE TO DISPOSE.
THIS ALL SOUNDS GROSS.
OR MAYBE SHE THOUGHT SHE HAD TO SHIT, AND SO I RECEIVED THAT THOUGHT.
AND SINCE MY BRAIN THOUGHT I HAD TO SHIT, MY STOMACH AND ANUS ACTED LIKE IT WAS GOING TO HAVE TO SHIT.
I DON'T KNOW ABOUT YOU, BUT I USUALLY DON'T HAVE A CONSCIOUS THOUGHT THAT SAYS I HAVE TO GO TO THE LITTLE GIRLS ROOM, I JUST FEEL IT IN MY BODY AND HOPE THE PERSON HAS TOILET PAPER.
YEAH, I WONDER IF JEM THINKS ABOUT IT MORE. IF SHE DWELLS ON THE NEED TO SHIT.
I'LL DEFINITELY ASK HER IF I SEE HER AGAIN.
PEARL?
WHAT'RE YOU DOING?

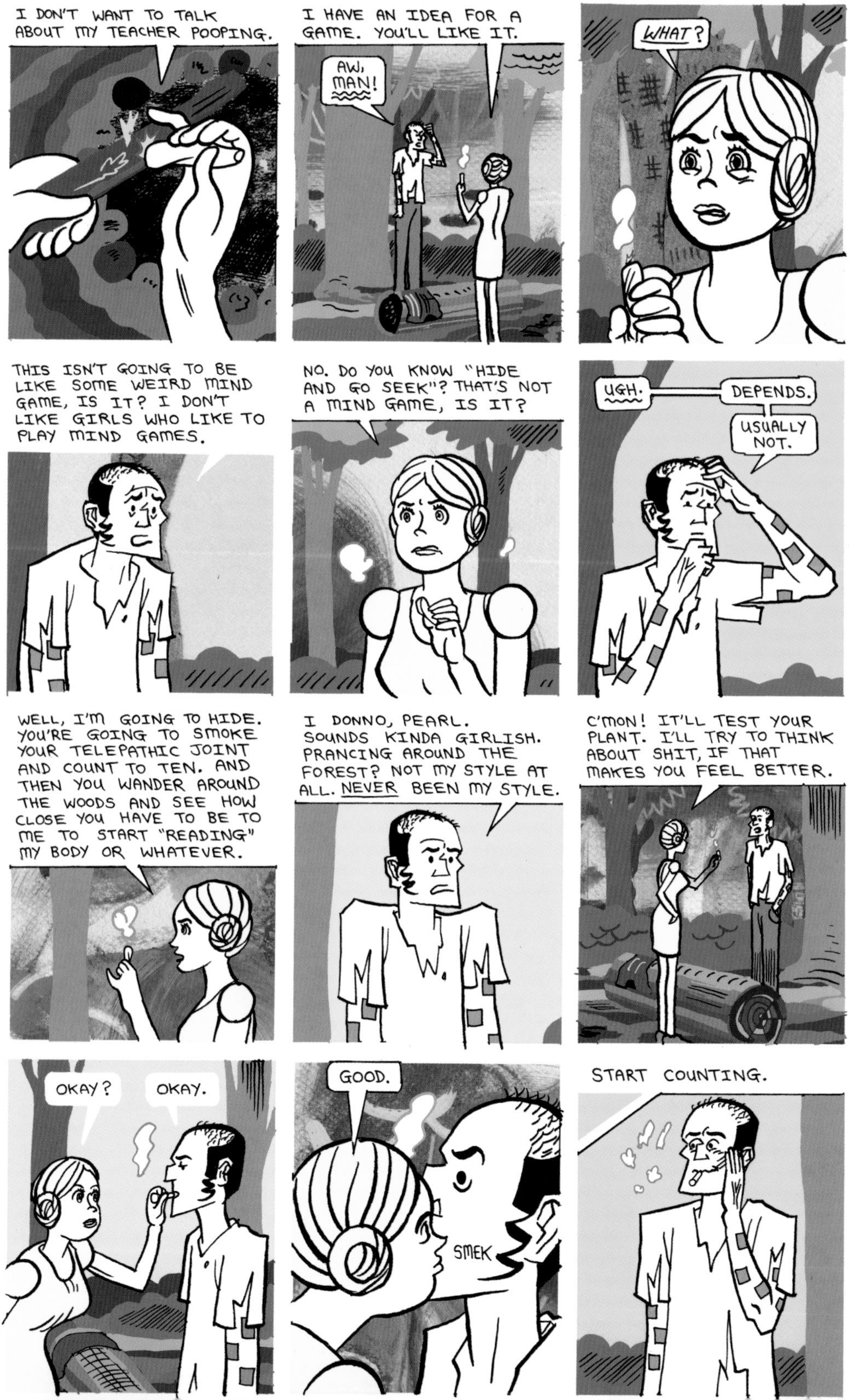
I DON'T WANT TO TALK ABOUT MY TEACHER POOPING.
I HAVE AN IDEA FOR A GAME. YOU'LL LIKE IT.
AW, MAN!
WHAT?
THIS ISN'T GOING TO BE LIKE SOME WEIRD MIND GAME, IS IT? I DON'T LIKE GIRLS WHO LIKE TO PLAY MIND GAMES.
NO. DO YOU KNOW "HIDE AND GO SEEK"? THAT'S NOT A MIND GAME, IS IT?
UGH.
DEPENDS.
USUALLY NOT.
WELL, I'M GOING TO HIDE. YOU'RE GOING TO SMOKE YOUR TELEPATHIC JOINT AND COUNT TO TEN. AND THEN YOU WANDER AROUND THE WOODS AND SEE HOW CLOSE YOU HAVE TO BE TO ME TO START "READING" MY BODY OR WHATEVER.
I DONNO, PEARL. SOUNDS KINDA GIRLISH. PRANCING AROUND THE FOREST? NOT MY STYLE AT ALL. NEVER BEEN MY STYLE.
C'MON! IT'LL TEST YOUR PLANT. I'LL TRY TO THINK ABOUT SHIT, IF THAT MAKES YOU FEEL BETTER.
OKAY?
OKAY.
GOOD.
SMEK
START COUNTING.

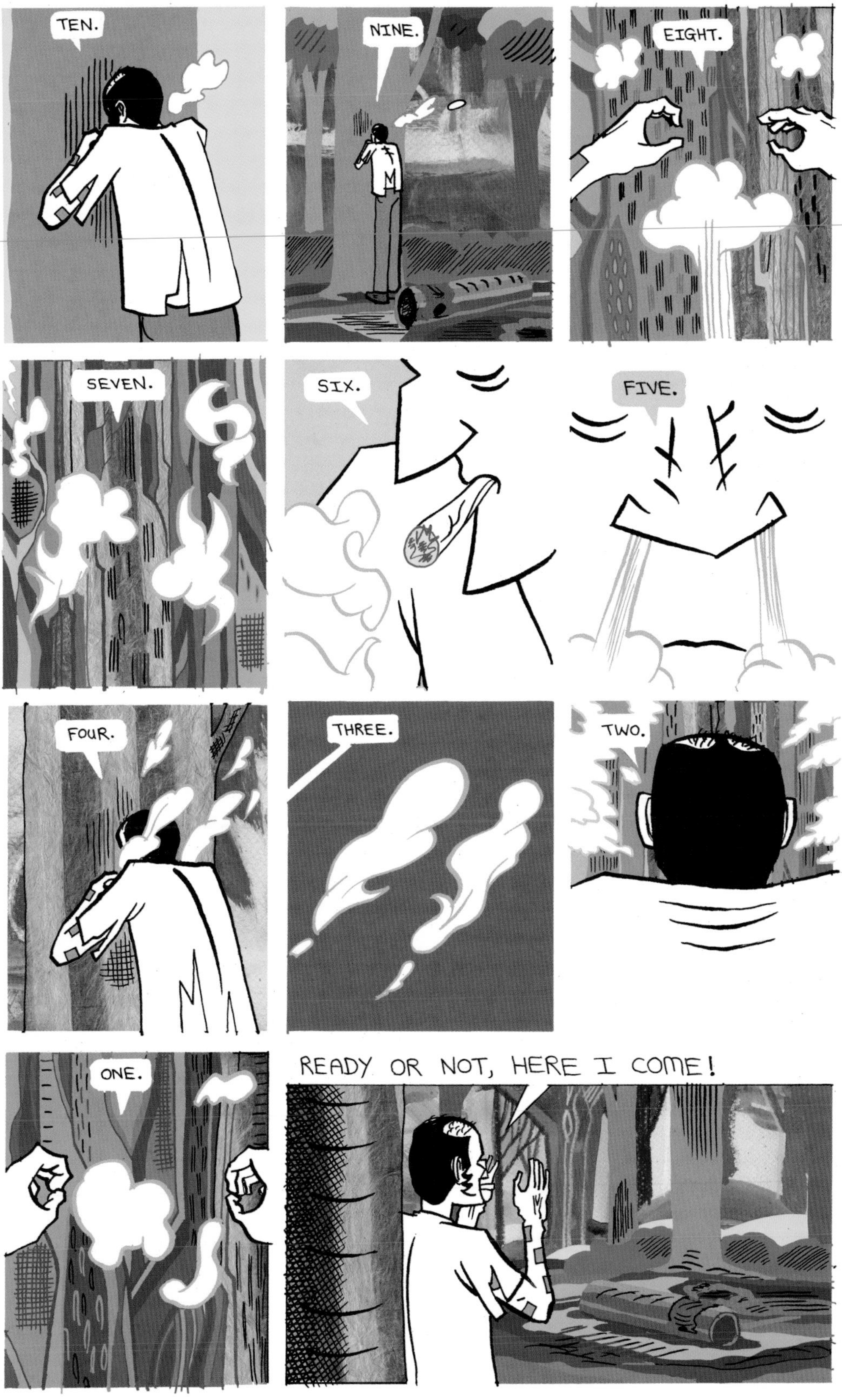
TEN.
NINE.
EIGHT.
SEVEN.
SIX.
FIVE.
FOUR.
THREE.
TWO.
ONE.
READY OR NOT, HERE I COME!

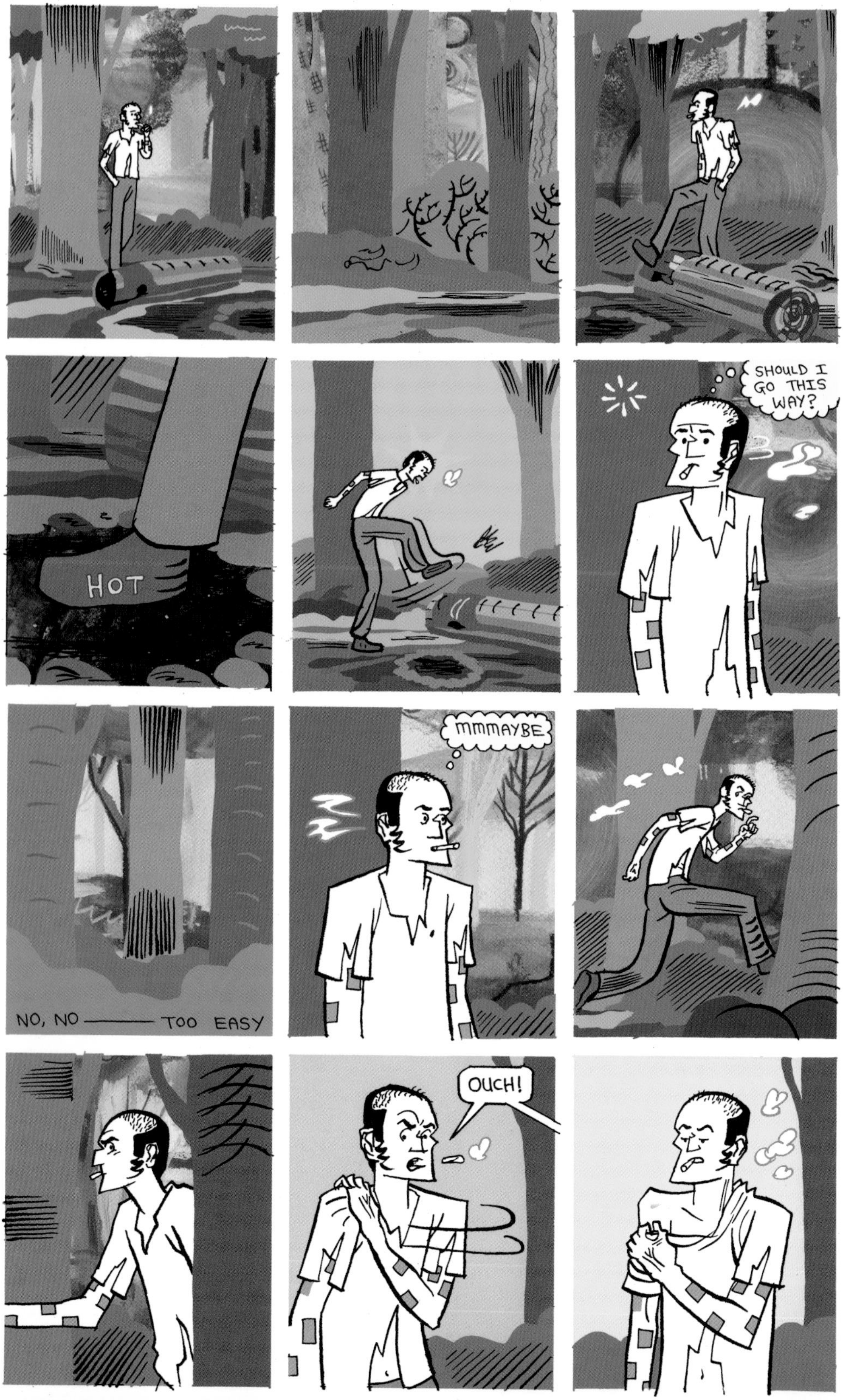
HOT
SHOULD I GO THIS WAY?
NO, NO —— TOO EASY
mmmAYBE
OUCH!

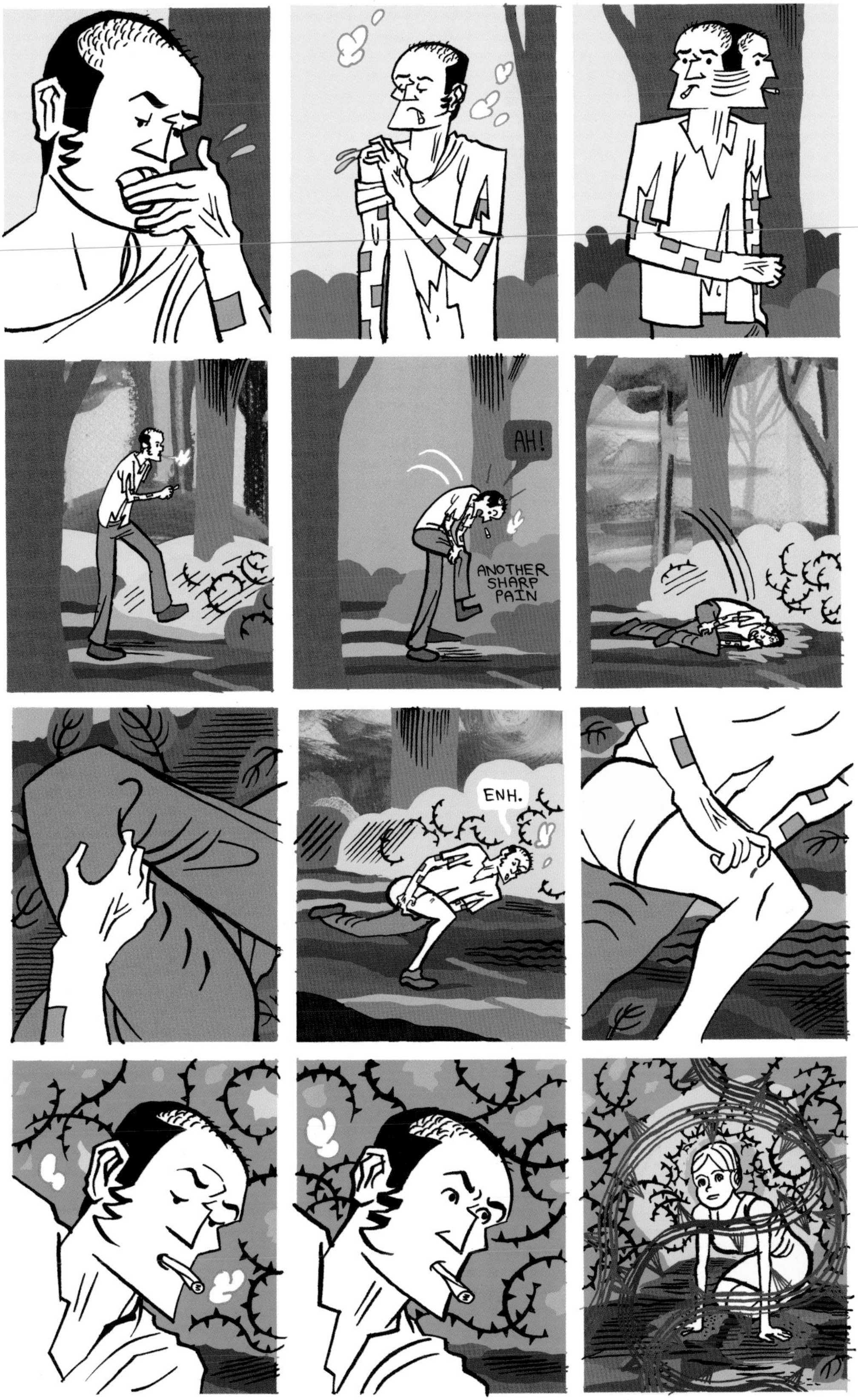
AH!
ANOTHER SHARP PAIN
ENH.

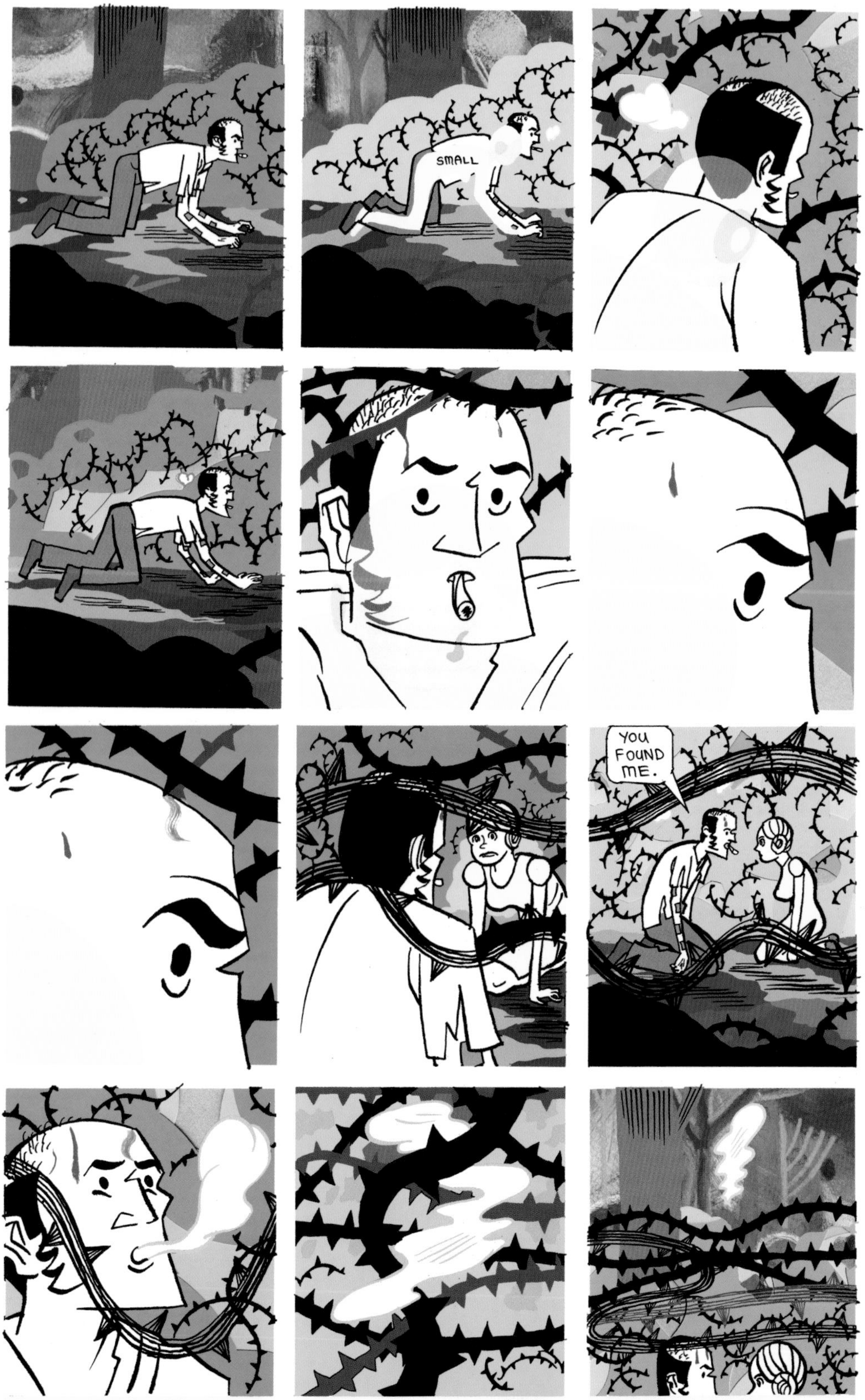
SMALL
YOU FOUND ME.
I WONDER IF
SOMEONE CAN SEE
US IN HERE.

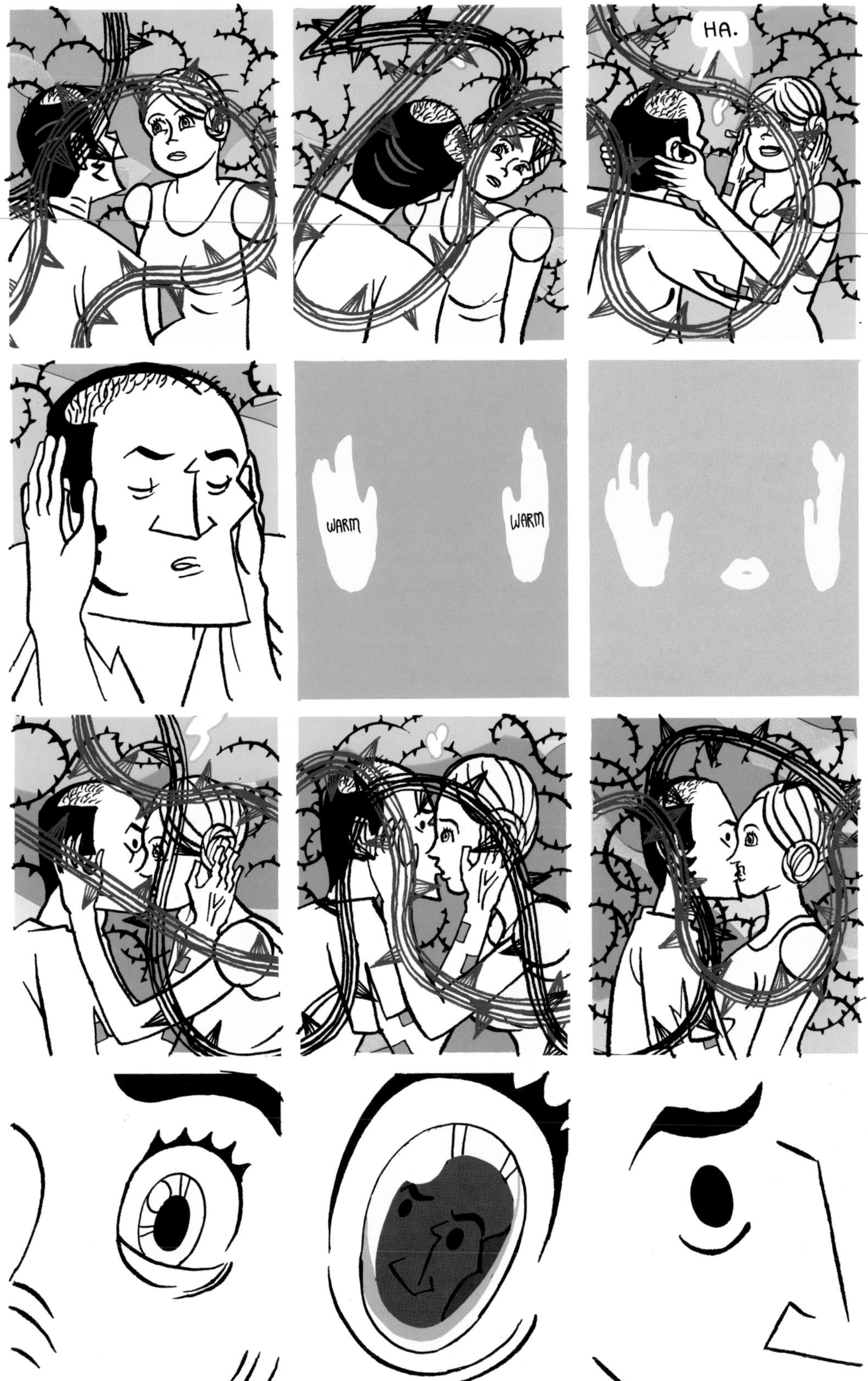
HA.
WARM
WARM

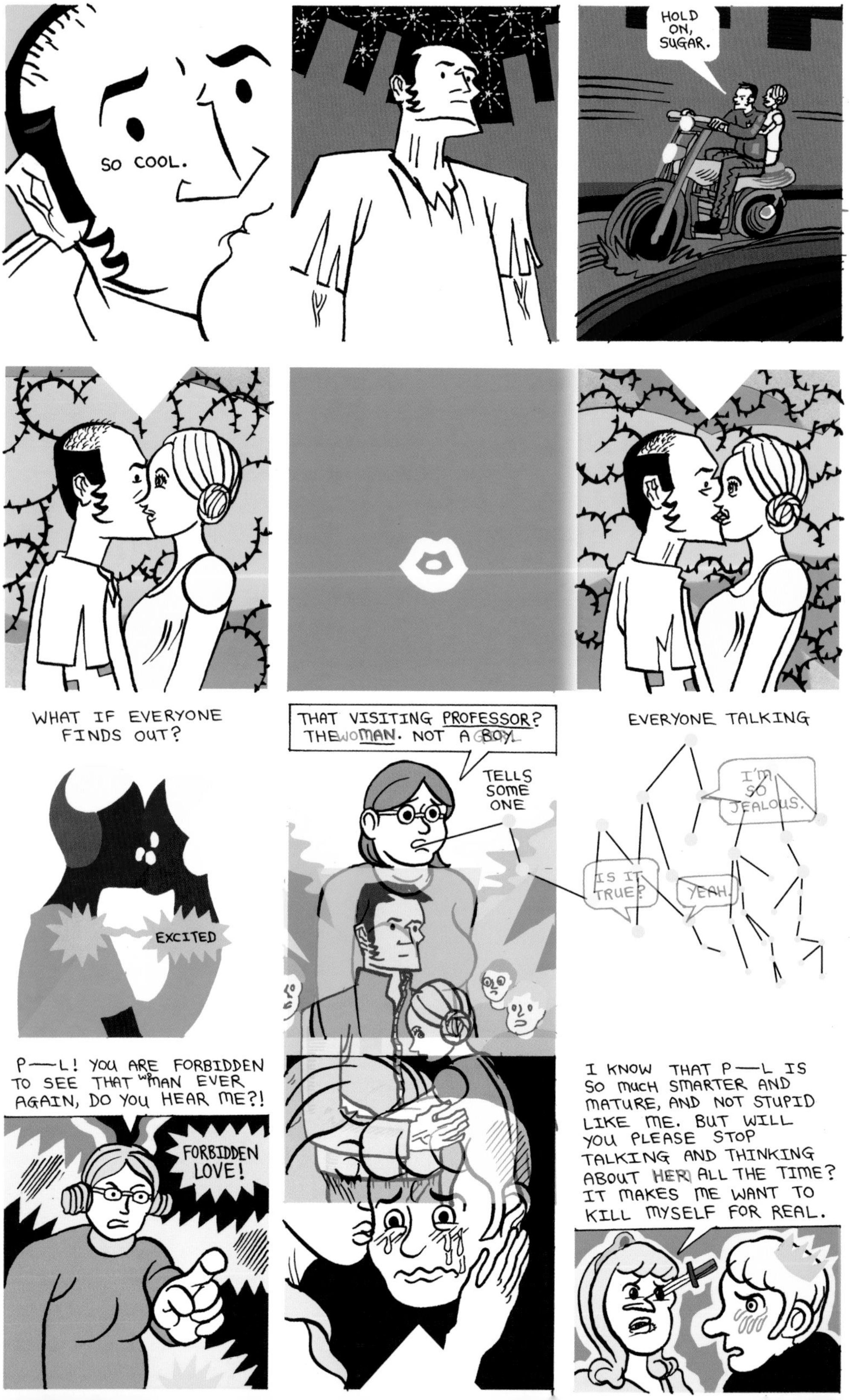
SO COOL.
HOLD ON, SUGAR.
WHAT IF EVERYONE FINDS OUT?
THAT VISITING PROFESSOR? THEwoMAN. NOT A BOY
TELLS SOME ONE
EVERYONE TALKING
I'M SO JEALOUS.
IS IT TRUE?
YEAH.
EXCITED
P—L! YOU ARE FORBIDDEN TO SEE THAT woMAN EVER AGAIN, DO YOU HEAR ME?!
FORBIDDEN LOVE!
I KNOW THAT P—L IS SO MUCH SMARTER AND MATURE, AND NOT STUPID LIKE ME. BUT WILL YOU PLEASE STOP TALKING AND THINKING ABOUT HER ALL THE TIME? IT MAKES ME WANT TO KILL MYSELF FOR REAL.

THERE'S DEFINITELY
SOMETHING GOING ON.
SOMETHING GOING ON.

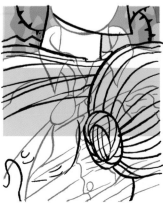

SHOULD I BE TAKING OFF YOUR CLOTHES FOR YOU?
AW, NO. 'S OKAY. I GOT IT.
A PENIS
WHY DON'T YOU CHANGE IN THE LOCKER ROOMS?
I LIKE CHANGING IN HERE.

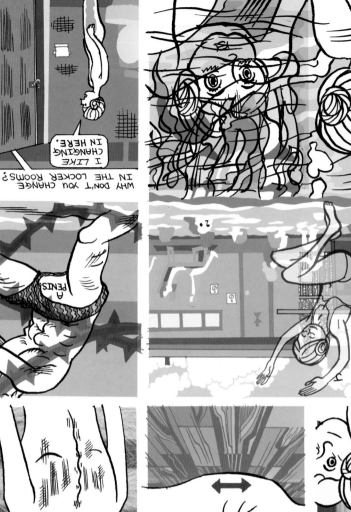

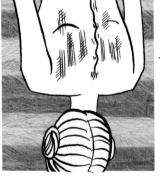

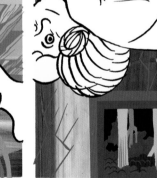

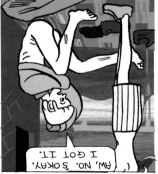

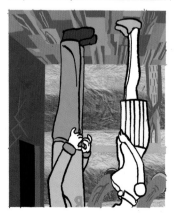

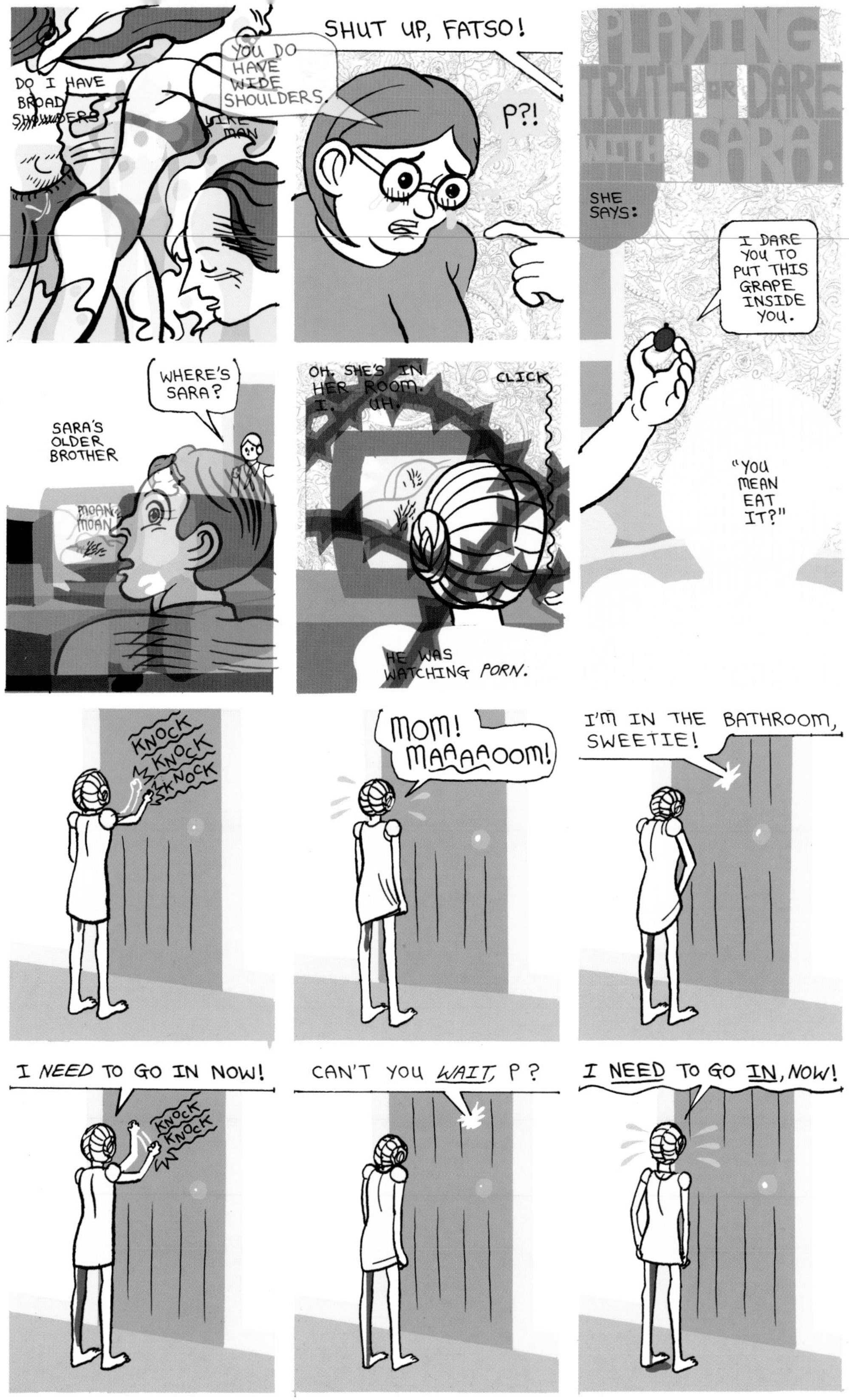
DO I HAVE BROAD SHOULDERS?
YOU DO HAVE WIDE SHOULDERS.
LIKE MAN
SHUT UP, FATSO!
P?!
PLAYING TRUTH OR DARE WITH SARA!
SHE SAYS:
I DARE YOU TO PUT THIS GRAPE INSIDE YOU.
"YOU MEAN EAT IT?"
SARA'S OLDER BROTHER
WHERE'S SARA?
MOAN MOAN
OH. SHE'S IN HER ROOM. I. UH.
CLICK
HE WAS WATCHING PORN.
KNOCK KNOCK KNOCK
MOM! MAAAAOOM!
I'M IN THE BATHROOM, SWEETIE!
I NEED TO GO IN NOW!
KNOCK KNOCK
CAN'T YOU WAIT, P?
I NEED TO GO IN, NOW!

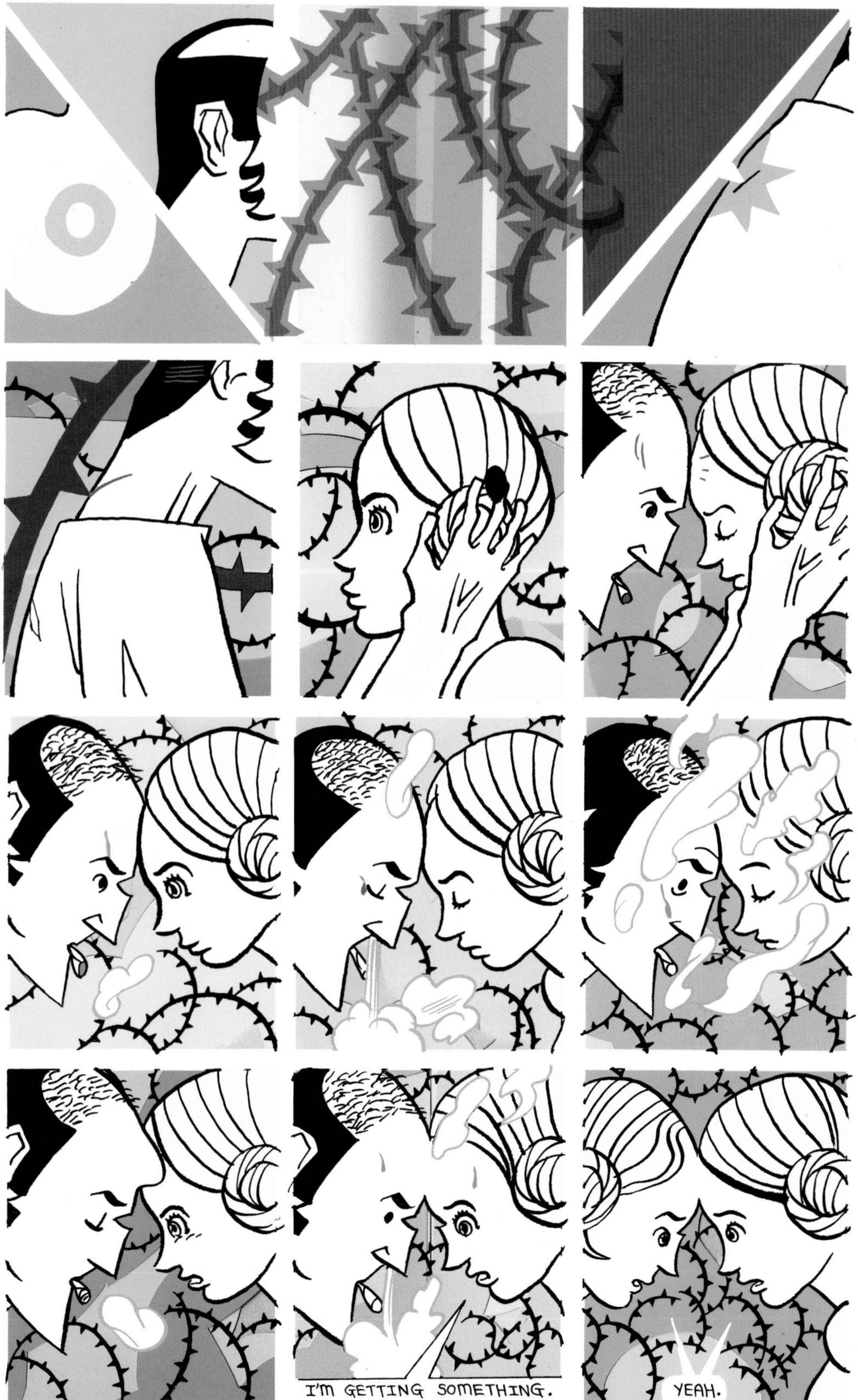
I'M GETTING SOMETHING.
YEAH.

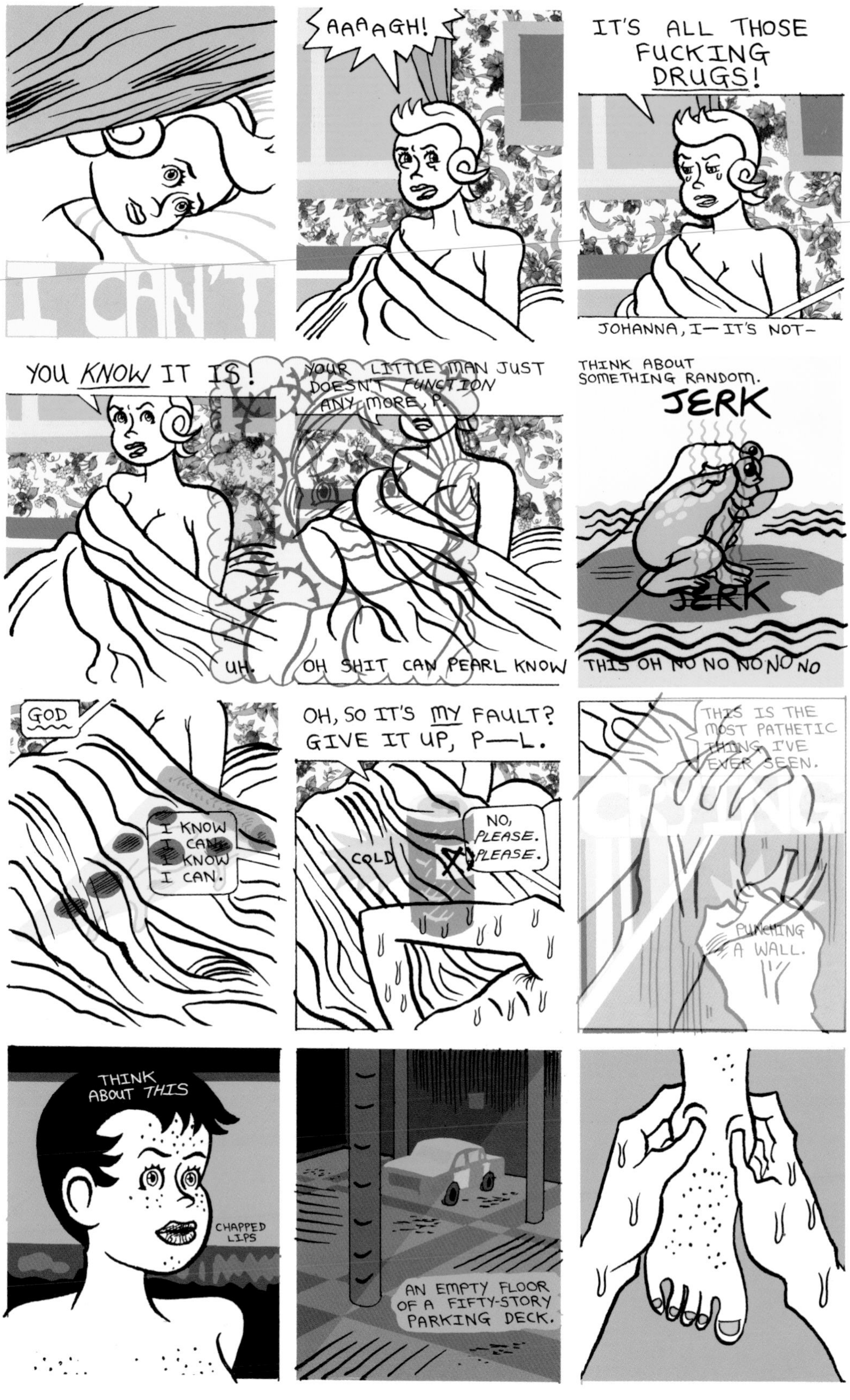

I CAN'T
AAAAGH!
IT'S ALL THOSE FUCKING DRUGS!
JOHANNA, I— IT'S NOT—
YOU KNOW IT IS!
UH.
YOUR LITTLE MAN JUST DOESN'T FUNCTION ANY MORE, P.
OH SHIT CAN PEARL KNOW
THINK ABOUT SOMETHING RANDOM.
JERK
JERK
THIS OH NO NO NO NO NO
GOD
I KNOW I CAN. I KNOW I CAN.
OH, SO IT'S MY FAULT? GIVE IT UP, P—L.
COLD
NO, PLEASE. PLEASE.
THIS IS THE MOST PATHETIC THING I'VE EVER SEEN.
PUNCHING A WALL.
THINK ABOUT THIS
CHAPPED LIPS
AN EMPTY FLOOR OF A FIFTY-STORY PARKING DECK.

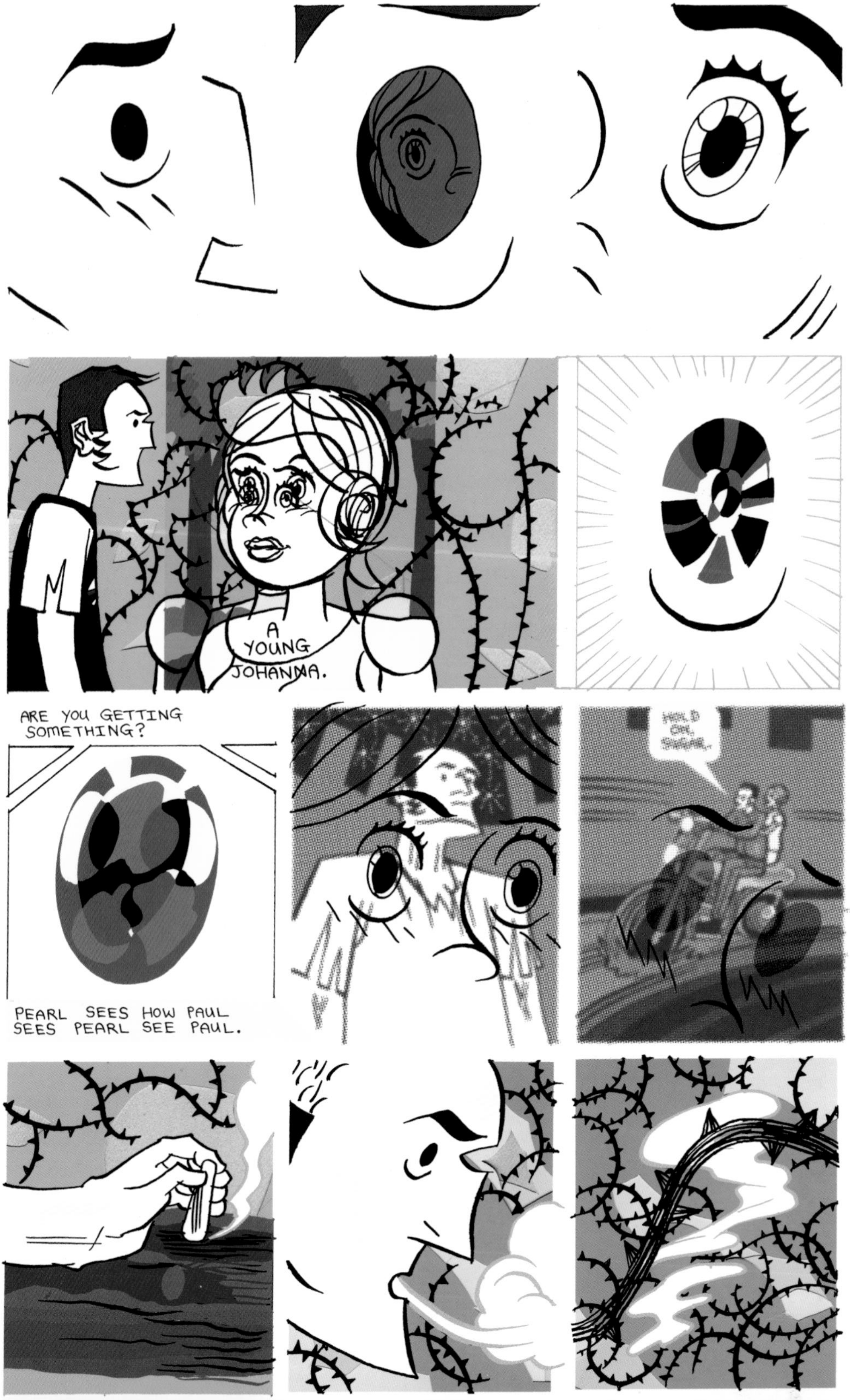
A YOUNG JOHANNA.
ARE YOU GETTING SOMETHING?
PEARL SEES HOW PAUL SEES PEARL SEE PAUL.

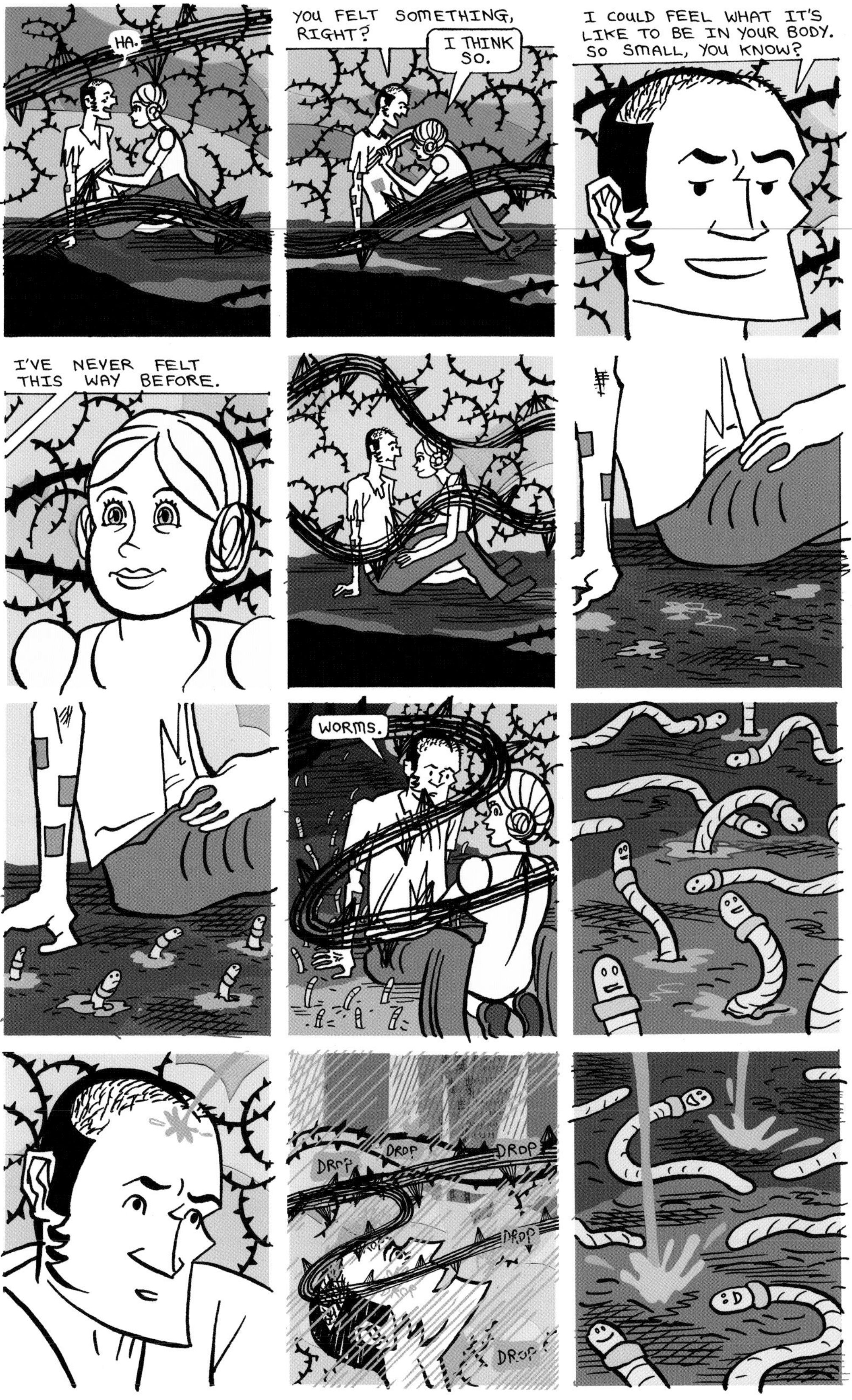
HA.
YOU FELT SOMETHING, RIGHT?
I THINK SO.
I COULD FEEL WHAT IT'S LIKE TO BE IN YOUR BODY. SO SMALL, YOU KNOW?
I'VE NEVER FELT THIS WAY BEFORE.
WORMS.
DROP
DROP
DROP
DROP
DROP

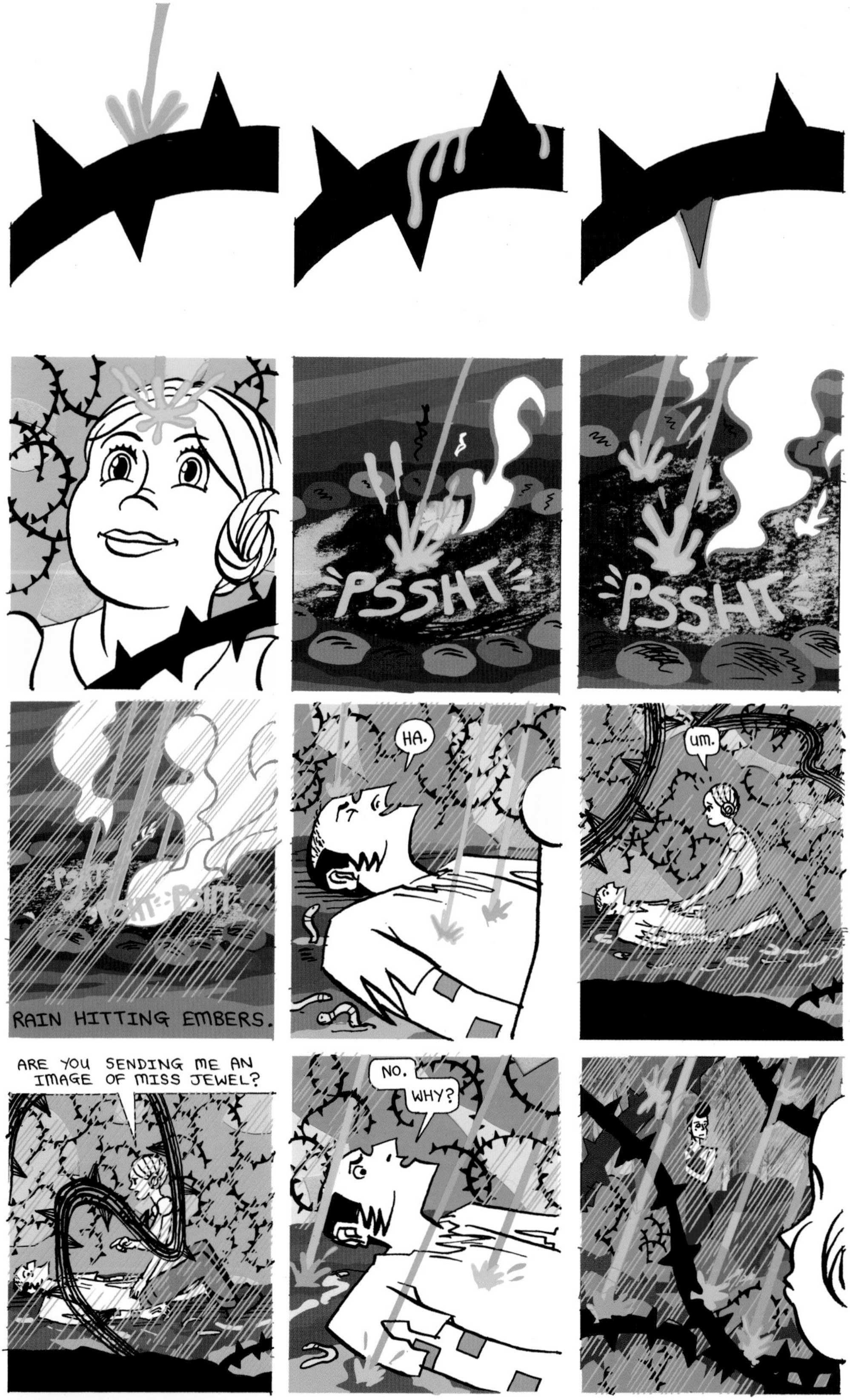
PSSHT
PSSHT
PSSHT
PSSHT::PSSHT
RAIN HITTING EMBERS.
HA.
UM.
ARE YOU SENDING ME AN IMAGE OF MISS JEWEL?
NO.
WHY?

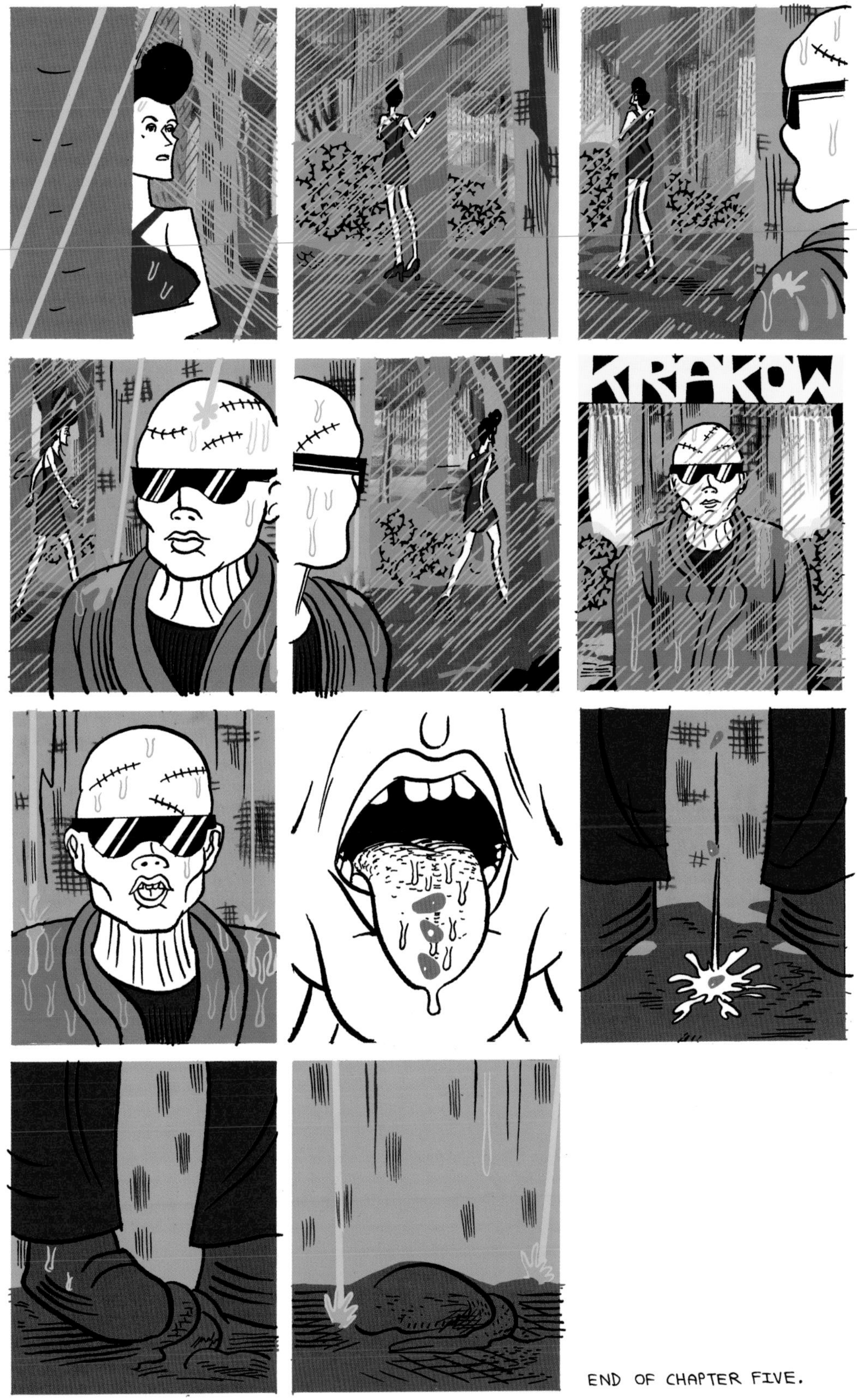
KRAKOW

END OF CHAPTER FIVE.

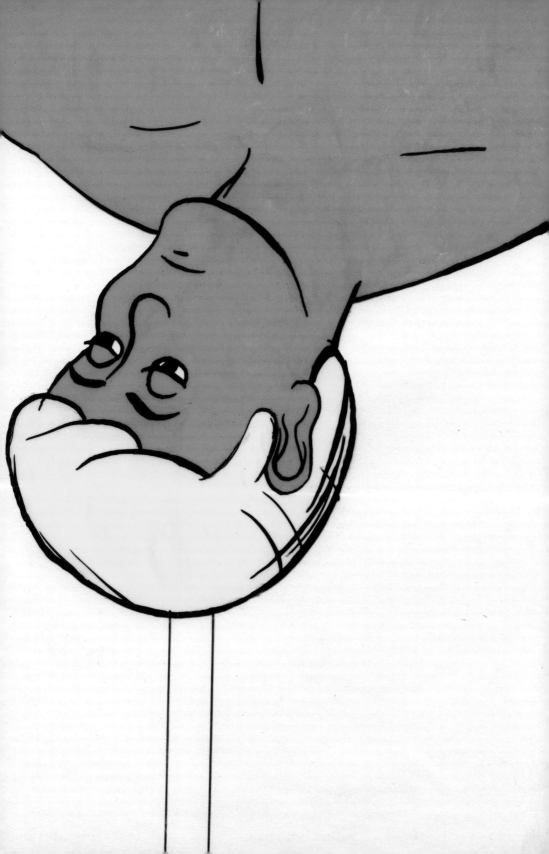

CHAPTER SIX

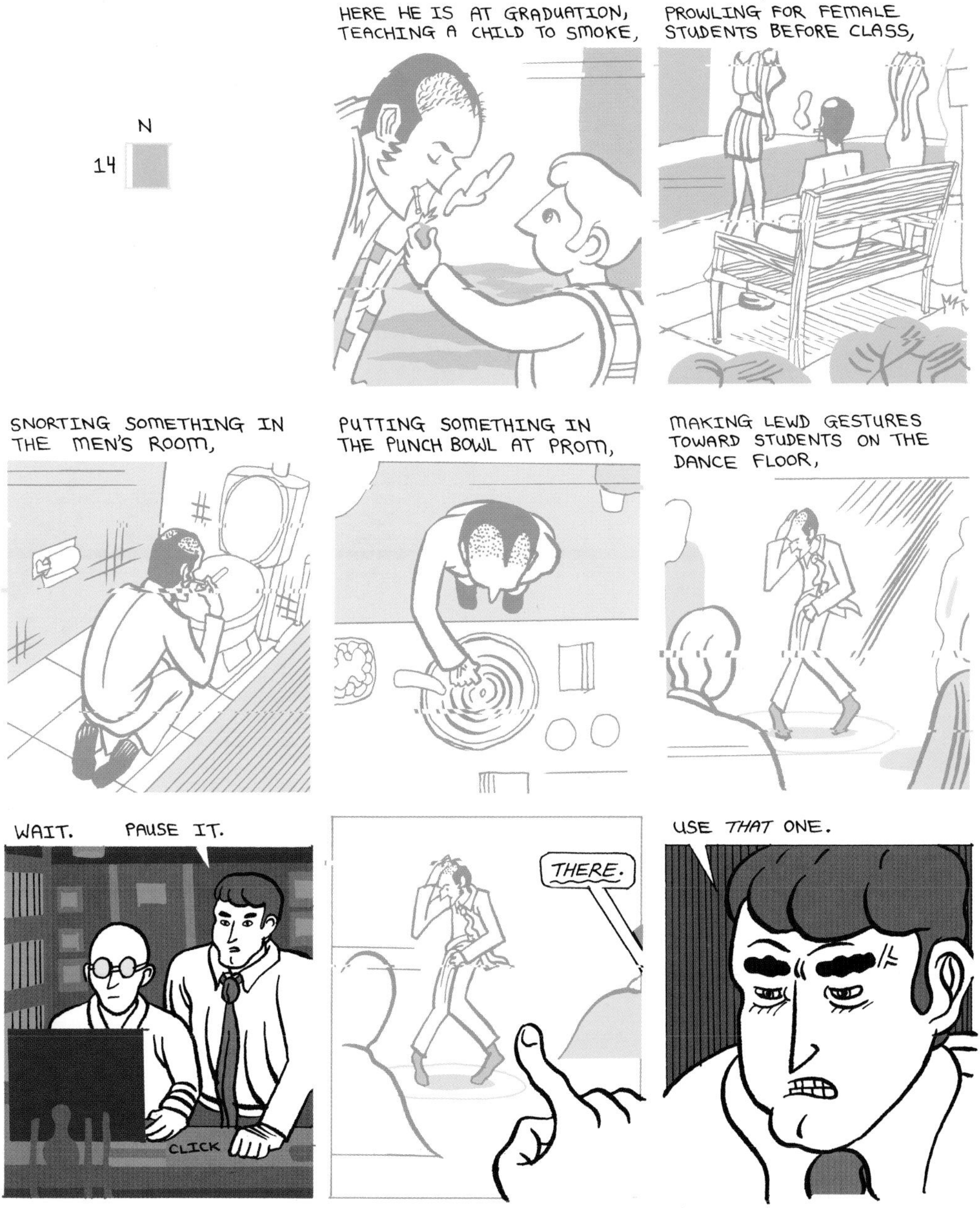
N
14
HERE HE IS AT GRADUATION, TEACHING A CHILD TO SMOKE,
PROWLING FOR FEMALE STUDENTS BEFORE CLASS,
SNORTING SOMETHING IN THE MEN'S ROOM,
PUTTING SOMETHING IN THE PUNCH BOWL AT PROM,
MAKING LEWD GESTURES TOWARD STUDENTS ON THE DANCE FLOOR,
WAIT. PAUSE IT.
CLICK
THERE.
USE *THAT* ONE.

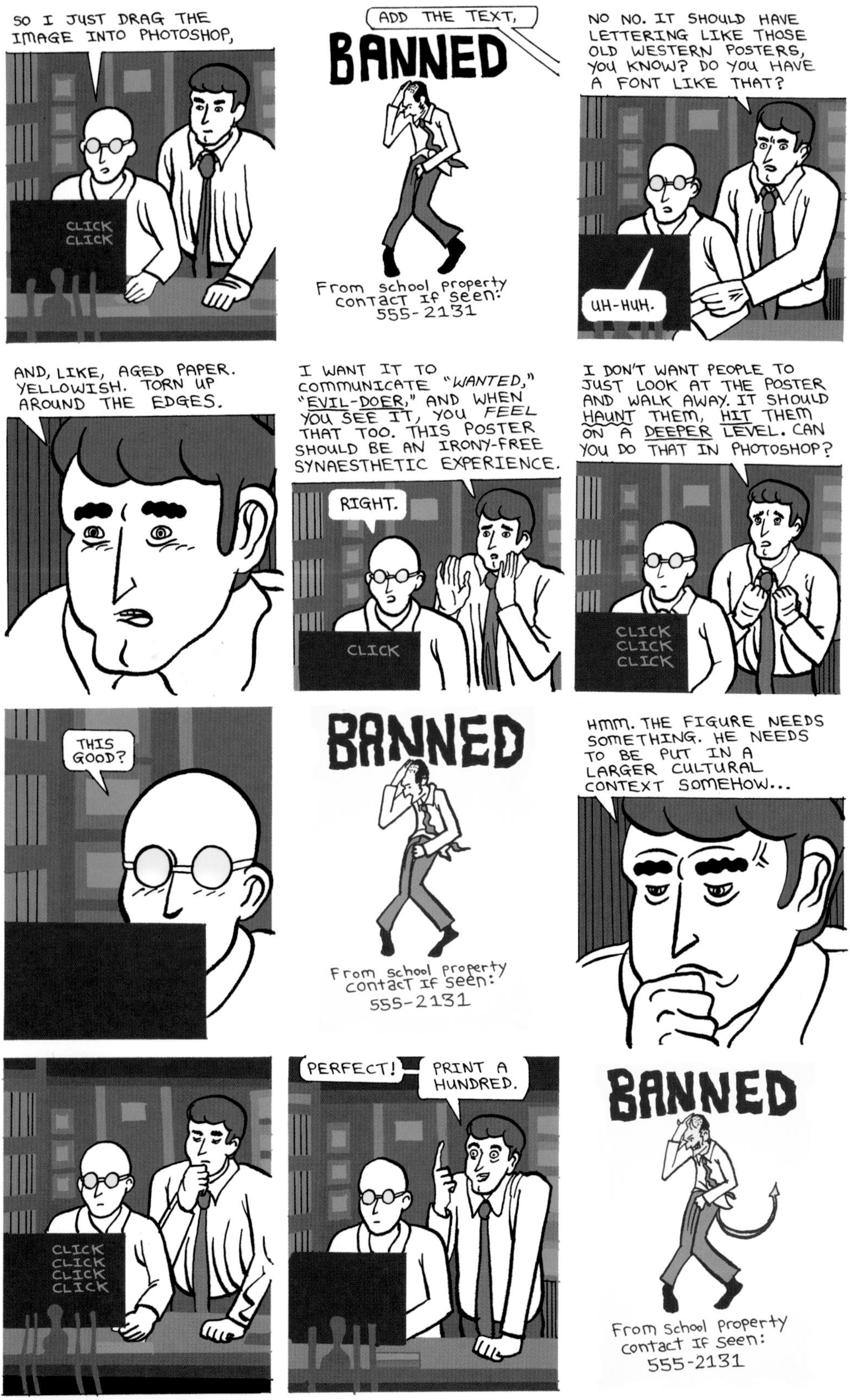
SO I JUST DRAG THE IMAGE INTO PHOTOSHOP,
CLICK CLICK
ADD THE TEXT,
BANNED
From school property contact If seen: 555-2131
NO NO. IT SHOULD HAVE LETTERING LIKE THOSE OLD WESTERN POSTERS, YOU KNOW? DO YOU HAVE A FONT LIKE THAT?
UH-HUH.
AND, LIKE, AGED PAPER. YELLOWISH. TORN UP AROUND THE EDGES.
I WANT IT TO COMMUNICATE "WANTED," "EVIL-DOER," AND WHEN YOU SEE IT, YOU FEEL THAT TOO. THIS POSTER SHOULD BE AN IRONY-FREE SYNAESTHETIC EXPERIENCE.
RIGHT.
CLICK
I DON'T WANT PEOPLE TO JUST LOOK AT THE POSTER AND WALK AWAY. IT SHOULD HAUNT THEM, HIT THEM ON A DEEPER LEVEL. CAN YOU DO THAT IN PHOTOSHOP?
CLICK CLICK CLICK
THIS GOOD?
BANNED
From school property contact If seen: 555-2131
HMM. THE FIGURE NEEDS SOMETHING. HE NEEDS TO BE PUT IN A LARGER CULTURAL CONTEXT SOMEHOW...
CLICK CLICK CLICK CLICK
PERFECT!
PRINT A HUNDRED.
BANNED
From School Property contact If Seen: 555-2131

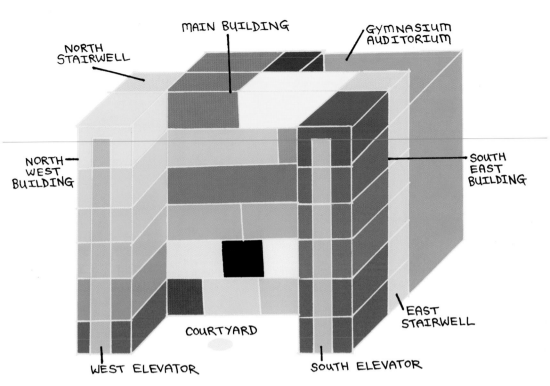

NORTH STAIRWELL

MAIN BUILDING

GYMNASIUM AUDITORIUM

NORTH WEST BUILDING

SOUTH EAST BUILDING

EAST STAIRWELL

COURTYARD

WEST ELEVATOR

SOUTH ELEVATOR

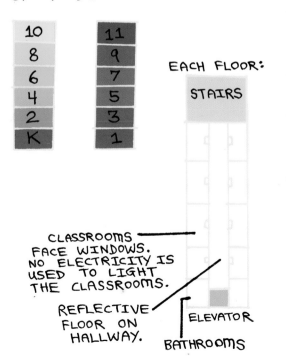

SIDE BUILDINGS'
FLOORS ARE DIVIDED
BY GRADE:

10		11
8		9
6		7
4		5
2		3
K		1

EACH FLOOR:

STAIRS

CLASSROOMS
FACE WINDOWS.
NO ELECTRICITY IS
USED TO LIGHT
THE CLASSROOMS.

REFLECTIVE
FLOOR ON
HALLWAY.

ELEVATOR

BATHROOMS

MAIN BUILDING:

- OBSERVATORY
- 12th GRADE CLASSROOMS
- STUDENT LOUNGE
- VISUAL ARTS STUDIO
- STUDENT GALLERY
- LIBRARY/STUDY ROOM
- CAFETERIA
- MUSIC HALL
- OFFICES
- MAIN ENTRANCE
- TEACHERS' LOUNGE
- LOCKER ROOMS
- AEROBIC STUDIO
- WEIGHT ROOM

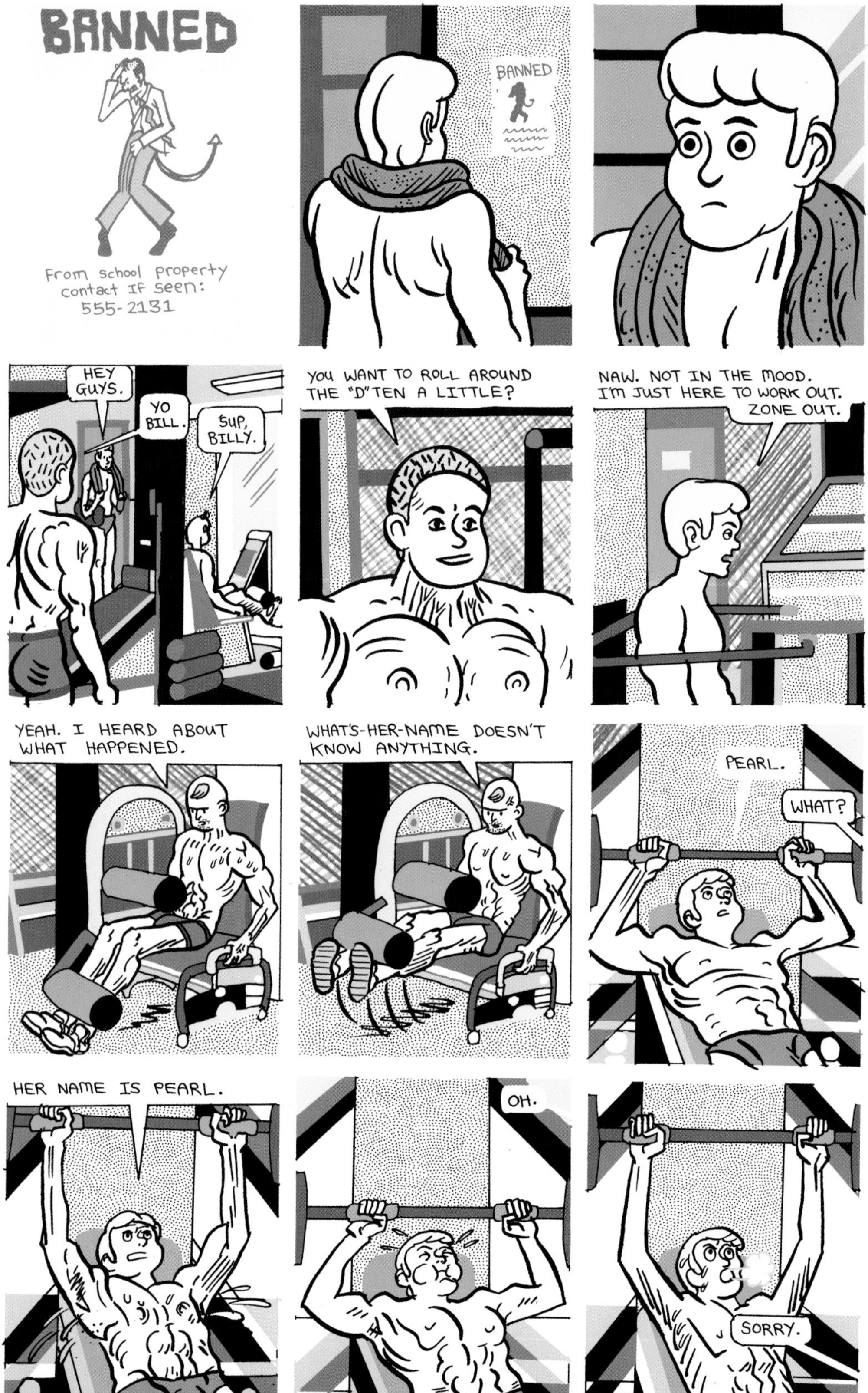
BANNED
From school property
contact if seen:
555-2131
BANNED
HEY GUYS.
YO BILL.
SUP, BILLY.
YOU WANT TO ROLL AROUND THE "D"TEN A LITTLE?
NAW. NOT IN THE MOOD. I'M JUST HERE TO WORK OUT. ZONE OUT.
YEAH. I HEARD ABOUT WHAT HAPPENED.
WHAT'S-HER-NAME DOESN'T KNOW ANYTHING.
PEARL.
WHAT?
HER NAME IS PEARL.
OH.
SORRY.

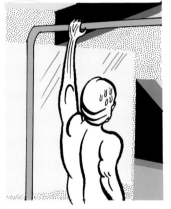
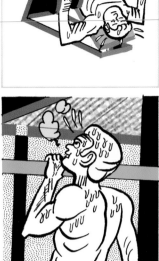

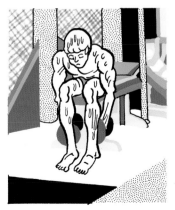

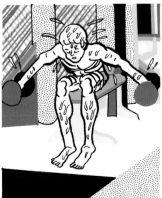

BOY! YOU SWEAT LIKE A PIG IN A SAUNA, BILL!

HA.

HA.

HA.

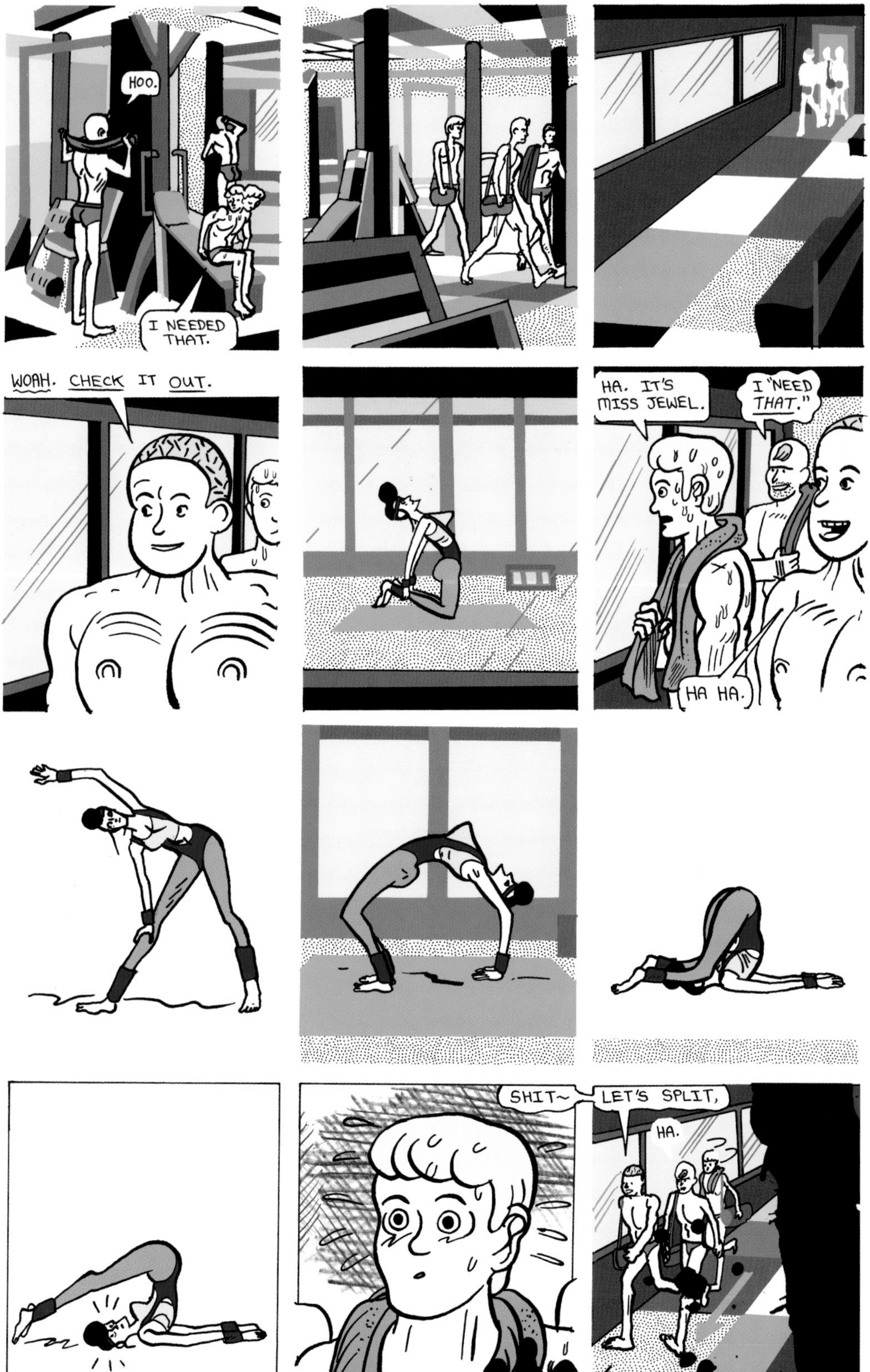
HOO.
I NEEDED THAT.
WOAH. CHECK IT OUT.
HA. IT'S MISS JEWEL.
I "NEED THAT."
HA HA.
SHIT~
LET'S SPLIT,
HA.

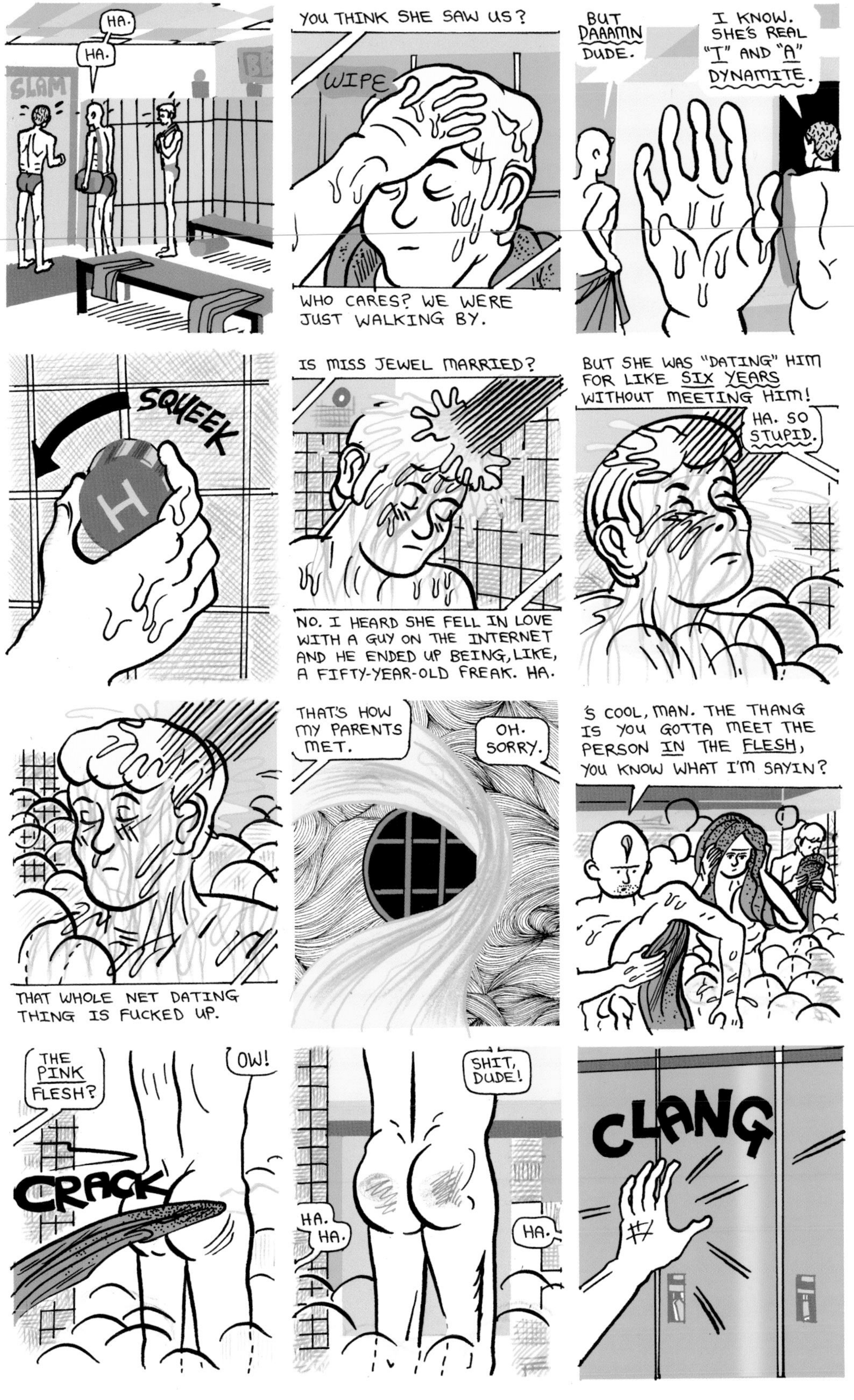

HA.
HA.
SLAM
YOU THINK SHE SAW US?
WIPE
WHO CARES? WE WERE JUST WALKING BY.
BUT DAAAMN DUDE.
I KNOW. SHE'S REAL "T" AND "A" DYNAMITE.
SQUEEK
H
IS MISS JEWEL MARRIED?
NO. I HEARD SHE FELL IN LOVE WITH A GUY ON THE INTERNET AND HE ENDED UP BEING, LIKE, A FIFTY-YEAR-OLD FREAK. HA.
BUT SHE WAS "DATING" HIM FOR LIKE SIX YEARS WITHOUT MEETING HIM!
HA. SO STUPID.
THAT WHOLE NET DATING THING IS FUCKED UP.
THAT'S HOW MY PARENTS MET.
OH. SORRY.
'S COOL, MAN. THE THANG IS YOU GOTTA MEET THE PERSON IN THE FLESH, YOU KNOW WHAT I'M SAYIN?
THE PINK FLESH?
OW!
CRACK
SHIT, DUDE!
HA. HA.
HA.
CLANG

WE GONNA SEE YOU 'ROUND THE COURT BILLY?
YEAH.
MAYBE.
SCRATCH
REMEMBER: BROS NOT HOES.
THAT SOUNDS GAY.
HA.
THANKS FELLAS.
'LATER.
SEE YA.
SHUT
TIP-TOE
SUPPLY ROOM

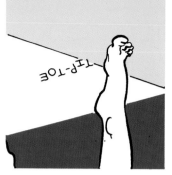

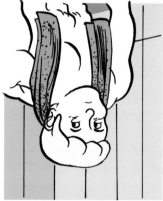

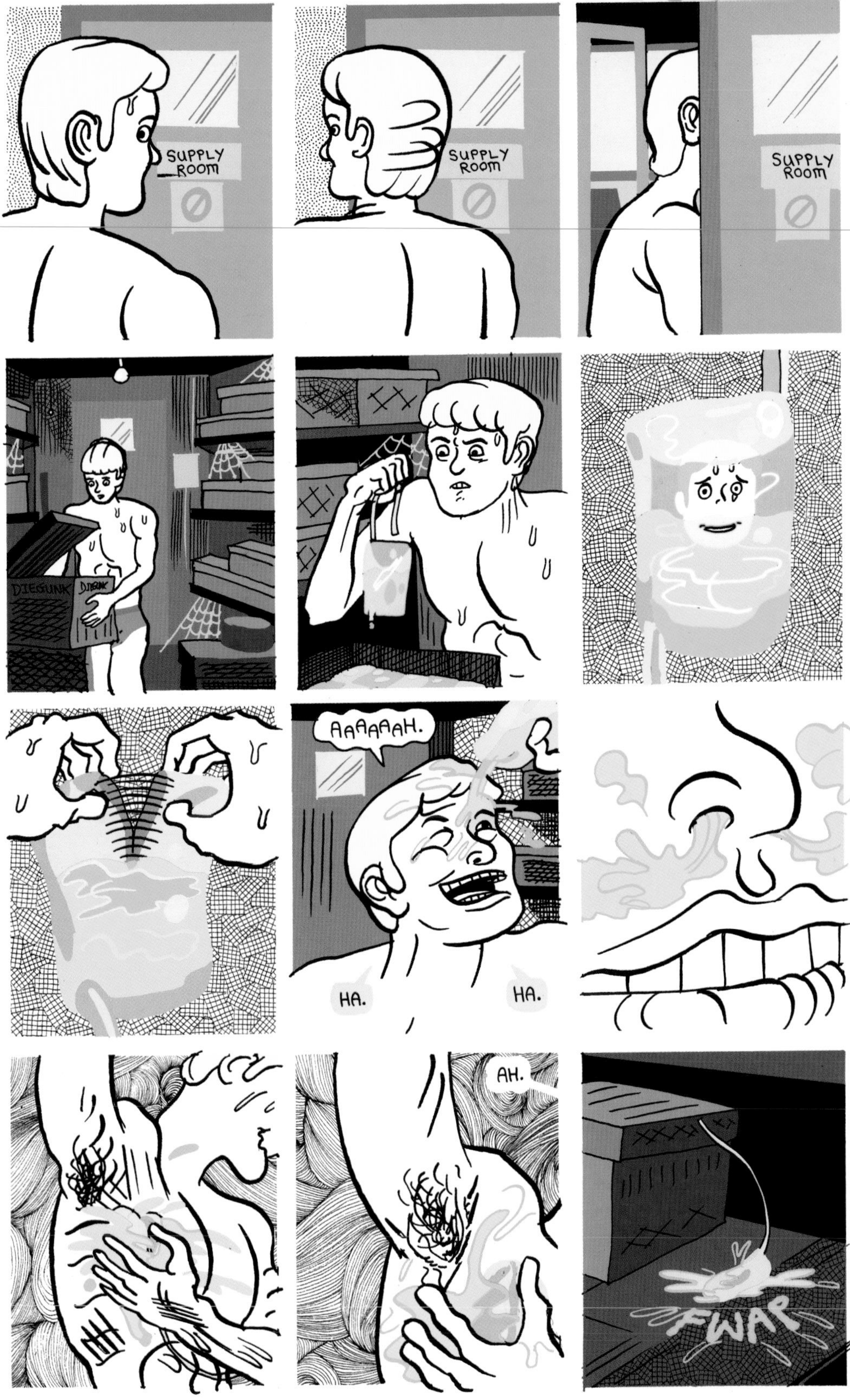
SUPPLY ROOM
SUPPLY ROOM
SUPPLY ROOM
DIEGUNK
AAAAAAH.
HA.
HA.
AH.
FWAP

WELL DIE FOREVER. YOU CAN'T ROLL THE

MOST PEOPLE NEED TO, BUT I DON'T.

YOU DON'T NEED TO USE YOUR BRAIN IN COLLEGE?

IT DOESN'T MATTER ANYMORE.

NO?

THAT STUFF DAMAGES YOUR BRAIN.

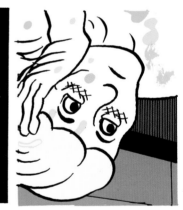

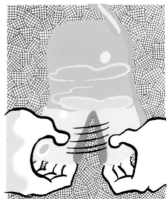

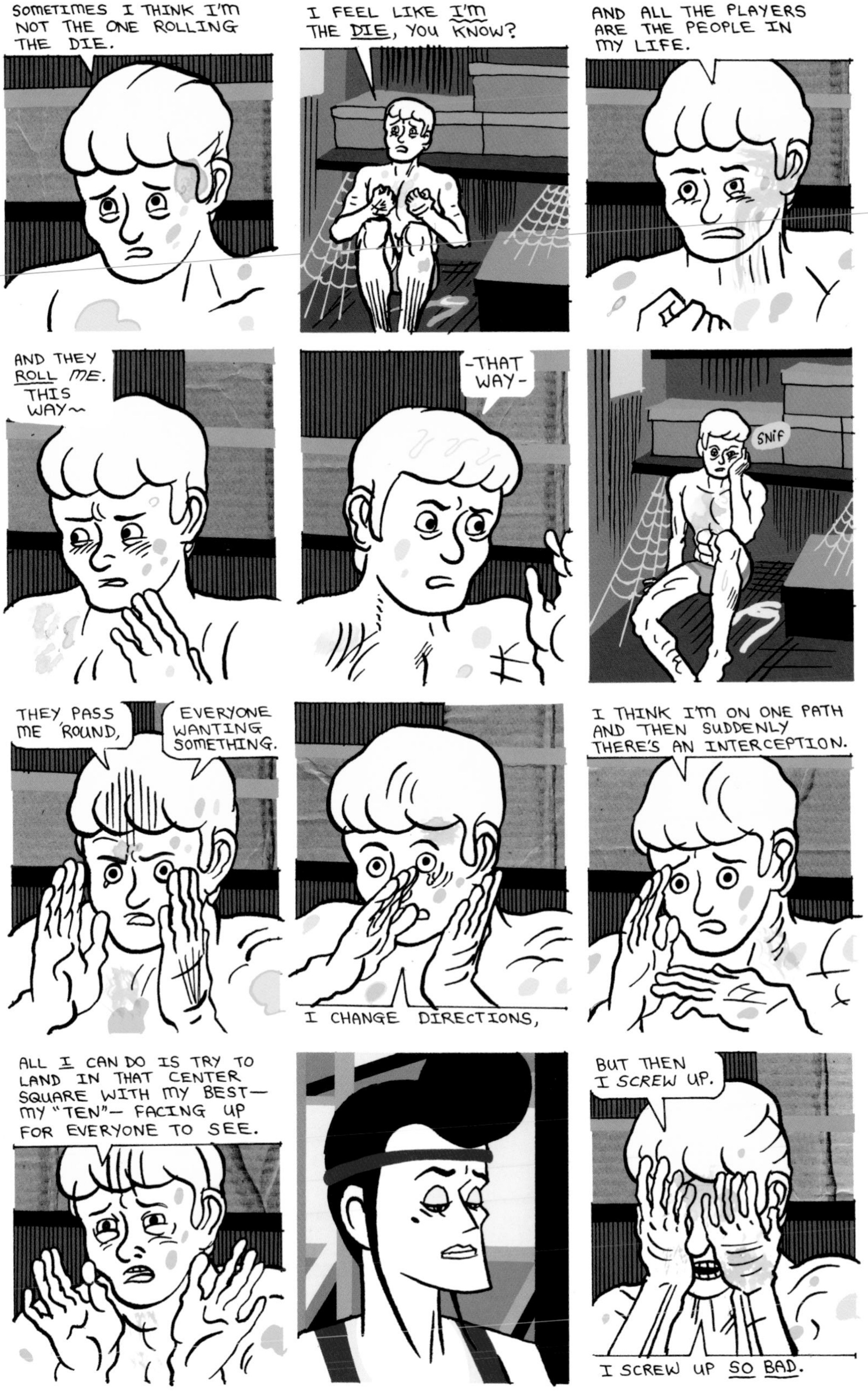
SOMETIMES I THINK I'M NOT THE ONE ROLLING THE DIE.
I FEEL LIKE I'M THE DIE, YOU KNOW?
AND ALL THE PLAYERS ARE THE PEOPLE IN MY LIFE.
AND THEY ROLL ME. THIS WAY~
-THAT WAY-
SNIF
THEY PASS ME 'ROUND,
EVERYONE WANTING SOMETHING.
I CHANGE DIRECTIONS,
I THINK I'M ON ONE PATH AND THEN SUDDENLY THERE'S AN INTERCEPTION.
ALL I CAN DO IS TRY TO LAND IN THAT CENTER SQUARE WITH MY BEST— MY "TEN"— FACING UP FOR EVERYONE TO SEE.
BUT THEN I SCREW UP.
I SCREW UP SO BAD.

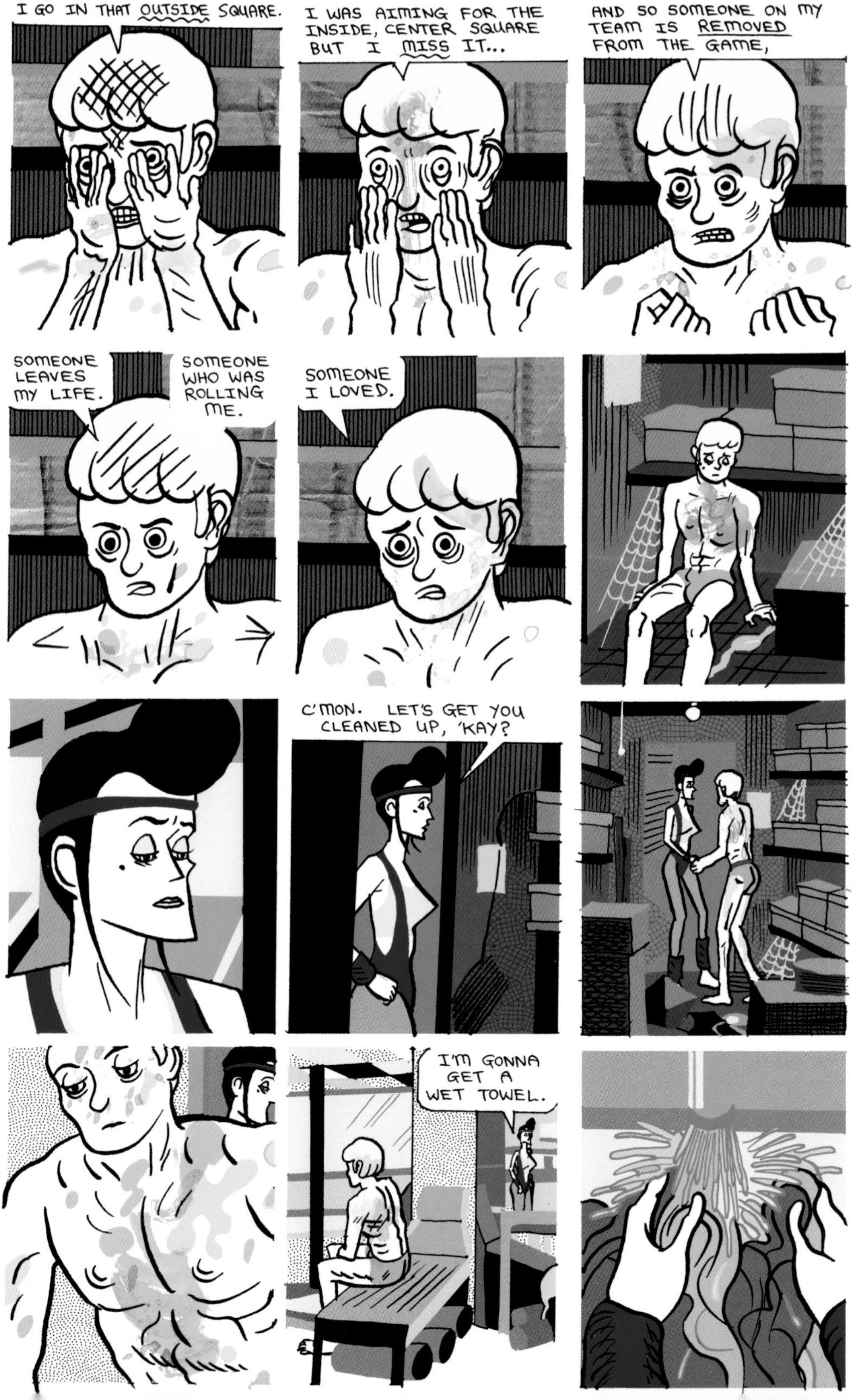
I GO IN THAT OUTSIDE SQUARE.
I WAS AIMING FOR THE INSIDE, CENTER SQUARE BUT I MISS IT...
AND SO SOMEONE ON MY TEAM IS REMOVED FROM THE GAME,
SOMEONE LEAVES MY LIFE.
SOMEONE WHO WAS ROLLING ME.
SOMEONE I LOVED.
C'MON. LET'S GET YOU CLEANED UP, 'KAY?
I'M GONNA GET A WET TOWEL.

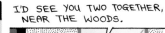

YOU WERE TALKING ABOUT PEARL, RIGHT? PEARL PEACH?

UH. HOW DID YOU KNOW?

I HEARD THINGS.

I'D SEE YOU TWO TOGETHER, NEAR THE WOODS.

YEAH. WE'D SPEND A LOT OF TIME IN THE WOODS.

SSSS SSSS

HOW WELL DO YOU KNOW... ... PROFESSOR PANTHER?

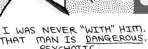
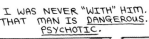

PANTHER? THE VISITING TEACHER? I SAW A POSTER BANNING HIM FROM SCHOOL PROPERTY.

WEREN'T YOU WITH HIM?

YOU TWO WOULD TALK.

I WAS NEVER "WITH" HIM. THAT MAN IS DANGEROUS. PSYCHOTIC.

DID YOU EVER SEE PEARL WITH HIM?

NO.

SHE EVER TALK TO YOU ABOUT HIM?

NO,

WHY?

I SAW THE TWO OF THEM.

-TOGETHER?

MOST DEFINITELY.

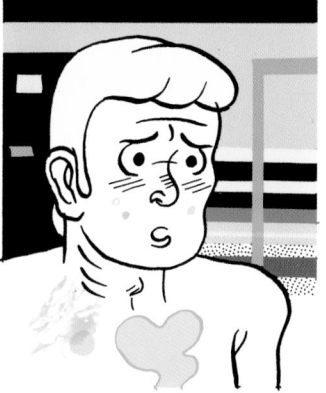

LEAN BACK.

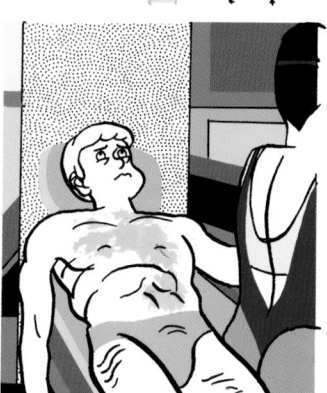

BUT— BUT ISN'T HE A LITTLE _OLD_?

WELL, BILLY, YOU'RE OUT OF SCHOOL.

YOU'RE AN ADULT, AND SO IS PEARL.

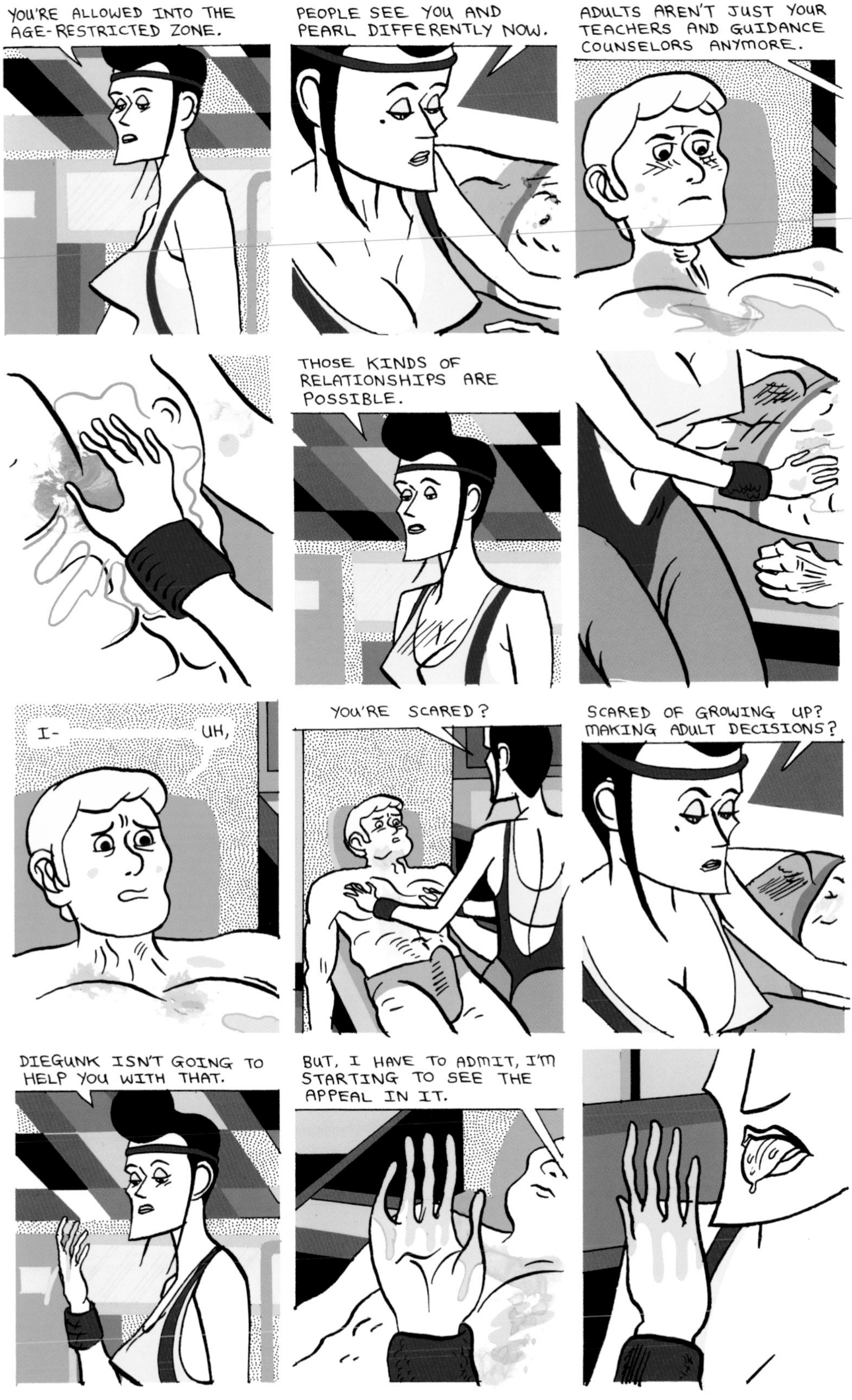
YOU'RE ALLOWED INTO THE AGE-RESTRICTED ZONE.
PEOPLE SEE YOU AND PEARL DIFFERENTLY NOW.
ADULTS AREN'T JUST YOUR TEACHERS AND GUIDANCE COUNSELORS ANYMORE.
THOSE KINDS OF RELATIONSHIPS ARE POSSIBLE.
I-
UH,
YOU'RE SCARED?
SCARED OF GROWING UP? MAKING ADULT DECISIONS?
DIEGUNK ISN'T GOING TO HELP YOU WITH THAT.
BUT, I HAVE TO ADMIT, I'M STARTING TO SEE THE APPEAL IN IT.

-DON'T!
IT'S NO GOOD DIRECTLY ON THE TONGUE. THAT'S REALLY BAD FOR YOU. EVERYONE JUST RUBS IT AGAINST THEIR SKIN.
LIKE THIS?
SPLAT
AM I DOING IT RIGHT?
NODS
WIPE

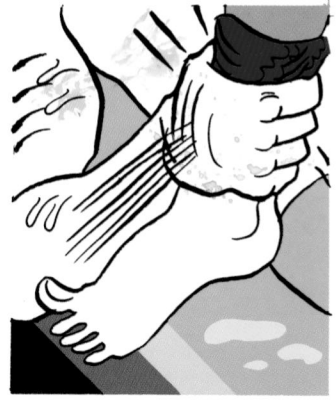

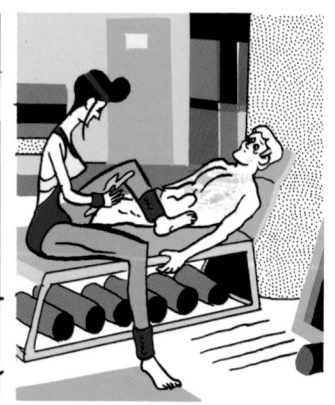

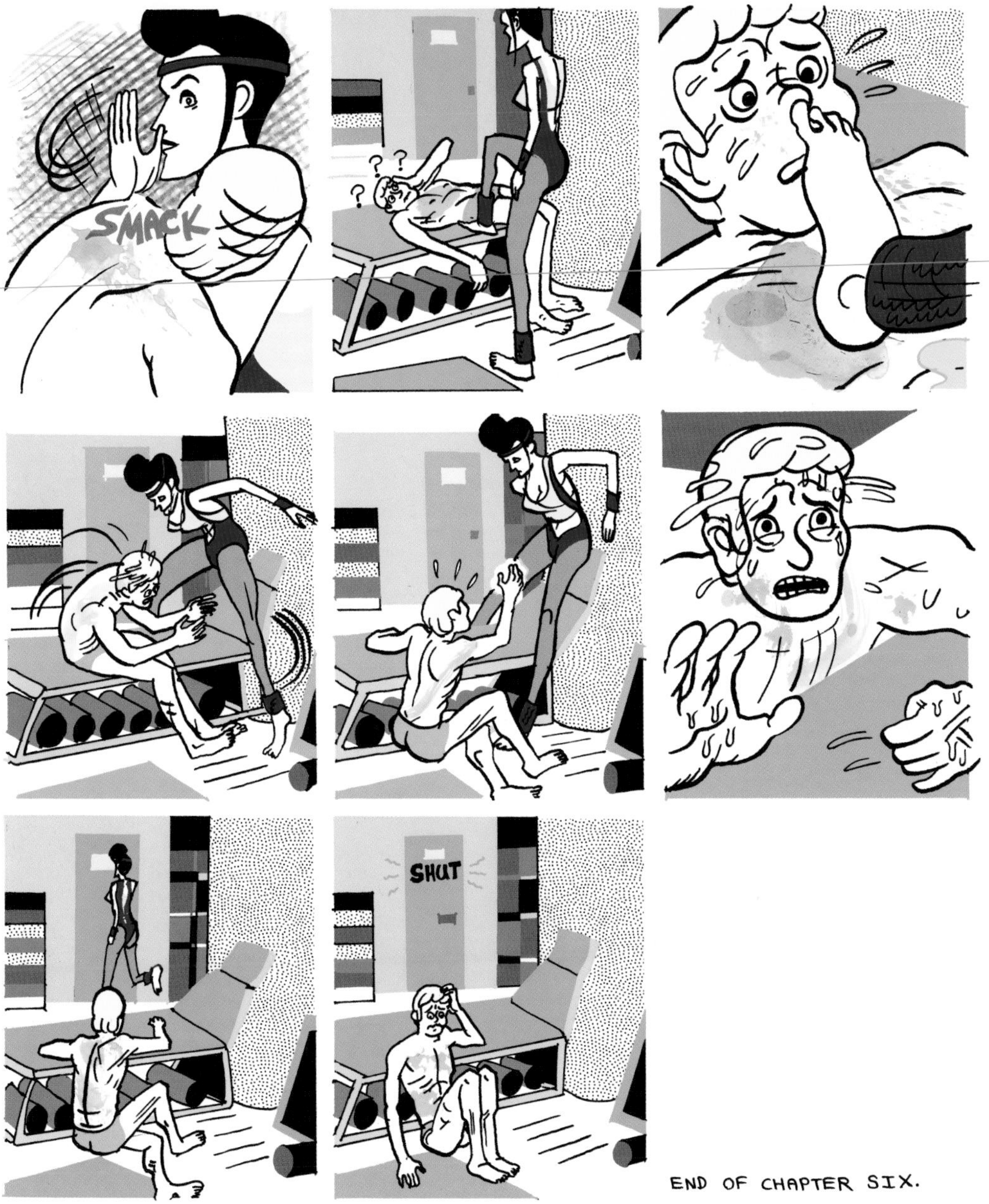
SMACK
SHUT

END OF CHAPTER SIX.

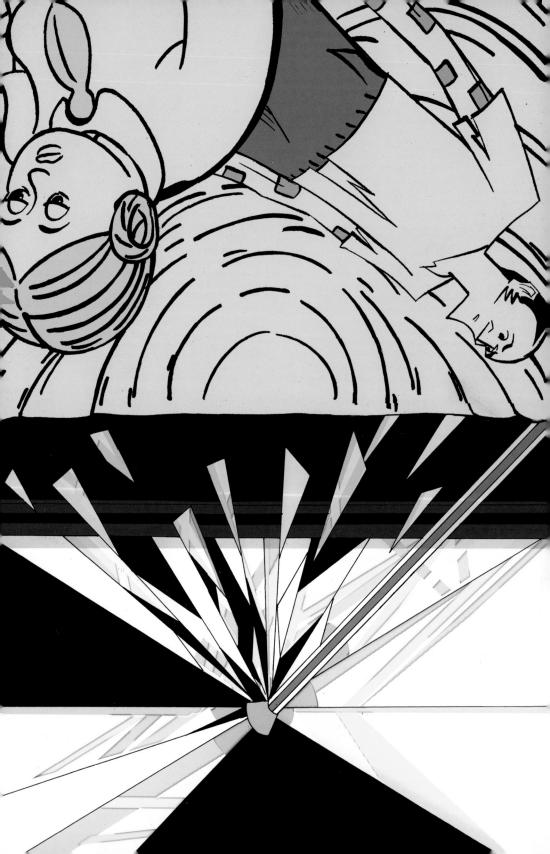

CHAPTER SEVEN
A-B-C, IT'S AS EASY AS 1-2-3, AS
MOSHI MOSHI.
PROFESSOR PANTHER?
PT-TOO
WHO'S THIS?
FOOD
THIS IS BILLY BORG. YOU GAVE ME YOUR NUMBER AT THE PROM.
PANT-
CARVE

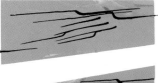

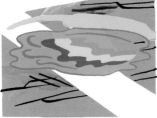

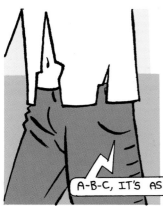

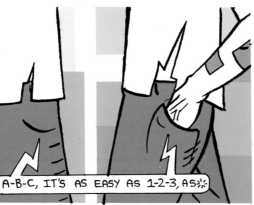

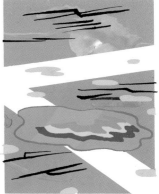

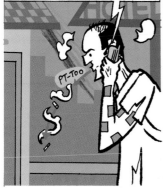

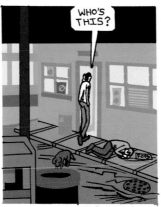

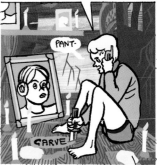

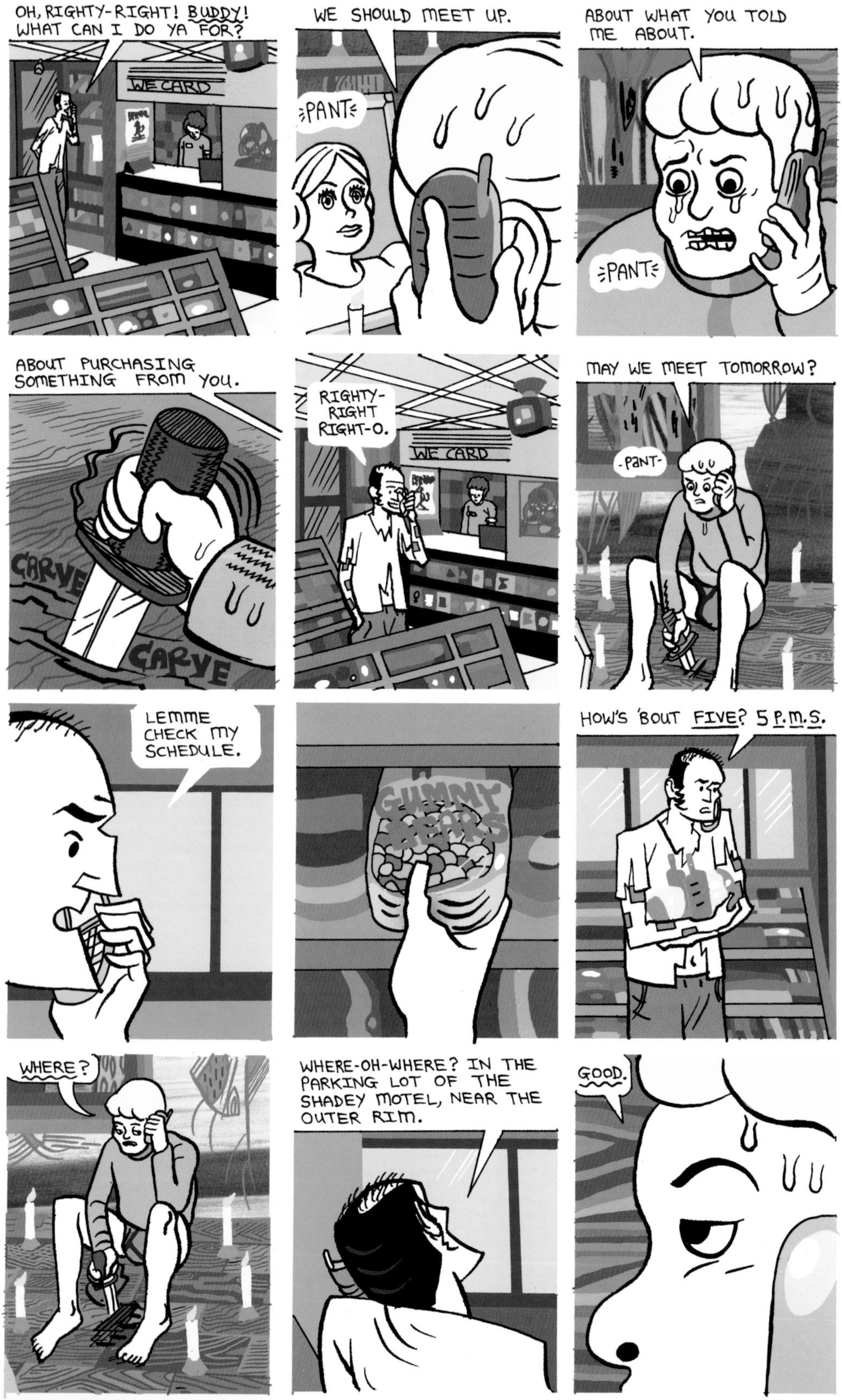
OH, RIGHTY-RIGHT! BUDDY! WHAT CAN I DO YA FOR?
WE CARD
WE SHOULD MEET UP.
PANT
ABOUT WHAT YOU TOLD ME ABOUT.
PANT
ABOUT PURCHASING SOMETHING FROM YOU.
CARVE
CARVE
RIGHTY-RIGHT RIGHT-O.
WE CARD
MAY WE MEET TOMORROW?
-PANT-
LEMME CHECK MY SCHEDULE.
GUMMY BEARS
HOW'S 'BOUT FIVE? 5 P.M.S.
WHERE?
WHERE-OH-WHERE? IN THE PARKING LOT OF THE SHADEY MOTEL, NEAR THE OUTER RIM.
GOOD.

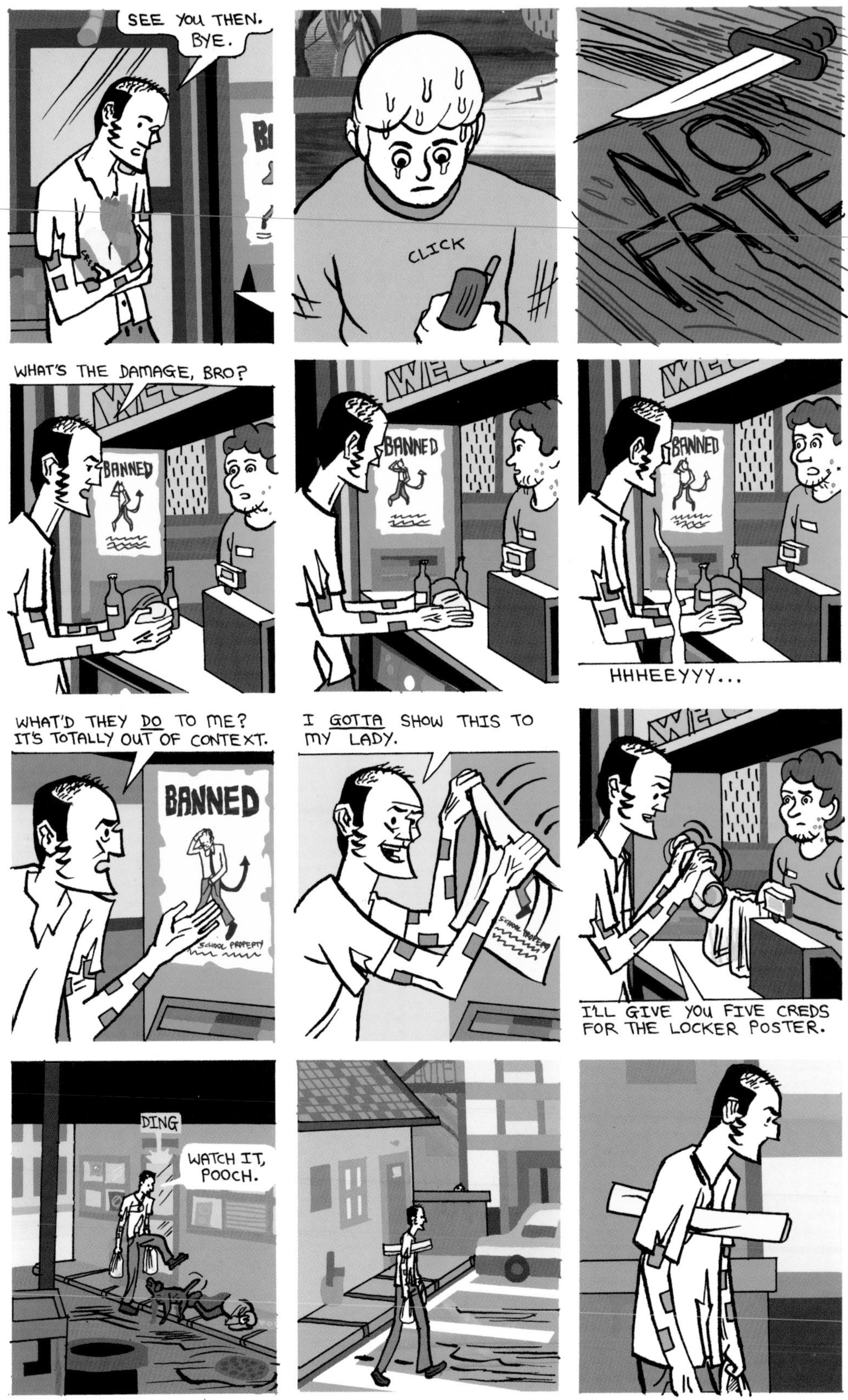
SEE YOU THEN. BYE.
CLICK
NO FATE
WHAT'S THE DAMAGE, BRO?
BANNED
HHHEEYYY...
WHAT'D THEY DO TO ME? IT'S TOTALLY OUT OF CONTEXT.
BANNED
SCHOOL PROPERTY
I GOTTA SHOW THIS TO MY LADY.
I'LL GIVE YOU FIVE CREDS FOR THE LOCKER POSTER.
DING
WATCH IT, POOCH.

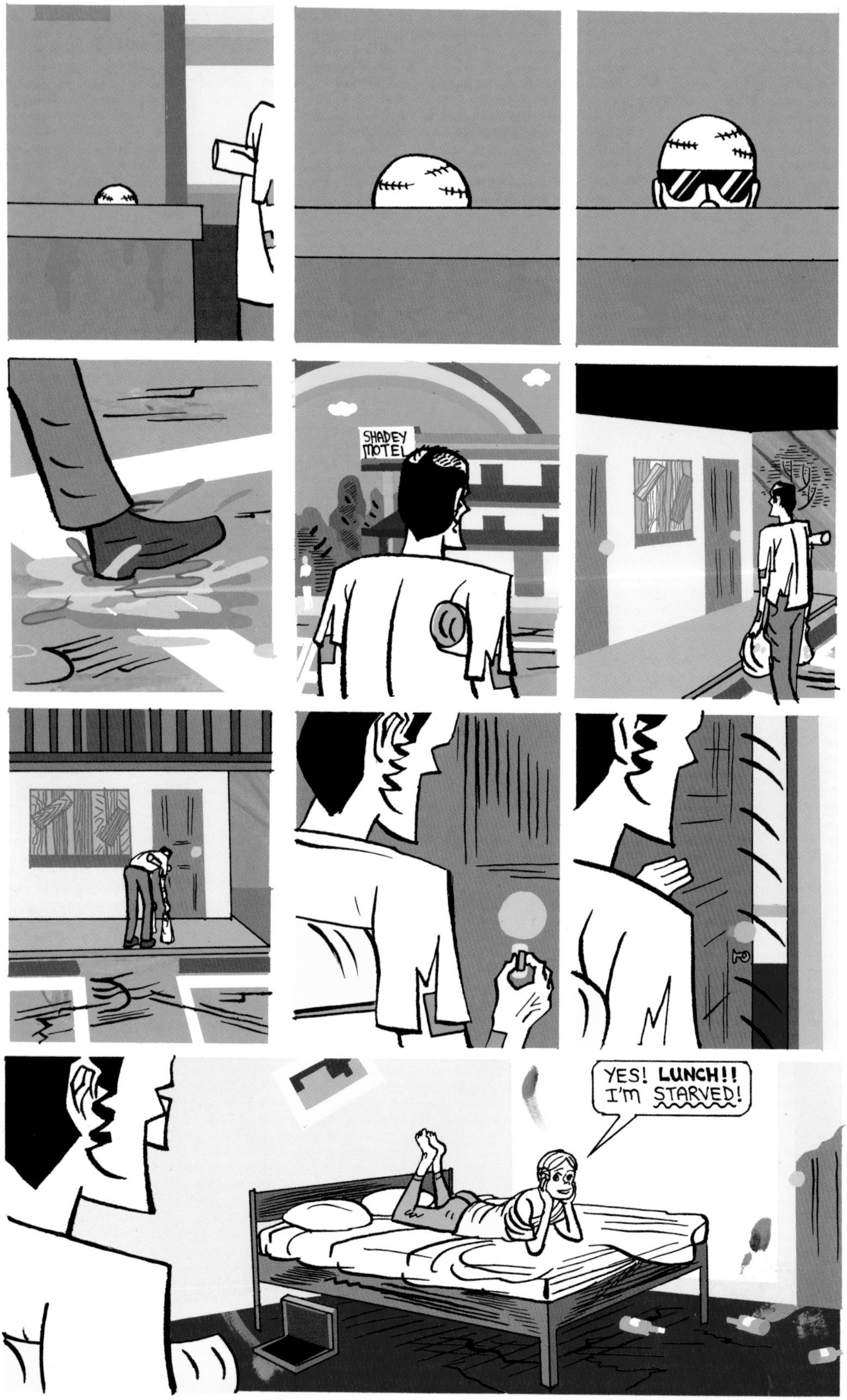
SHADEY MOTEL
YES! LUNCH!! I'M STARVED!

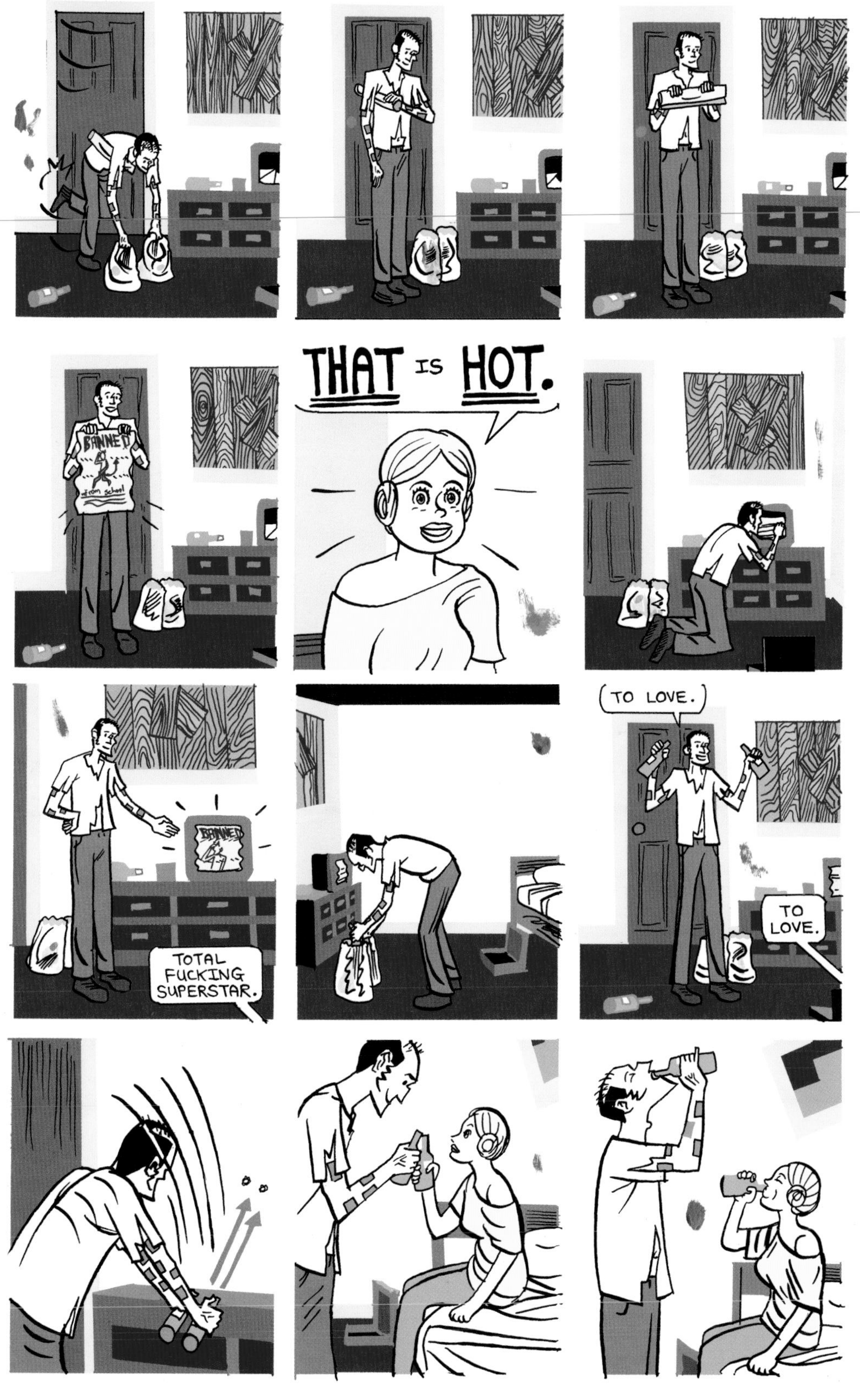

BANNED
from school
THAT IS HOT.
TOTAL FUCKING SUPERSTAR.
BANNED
TO LOVE.
TO LOVE.

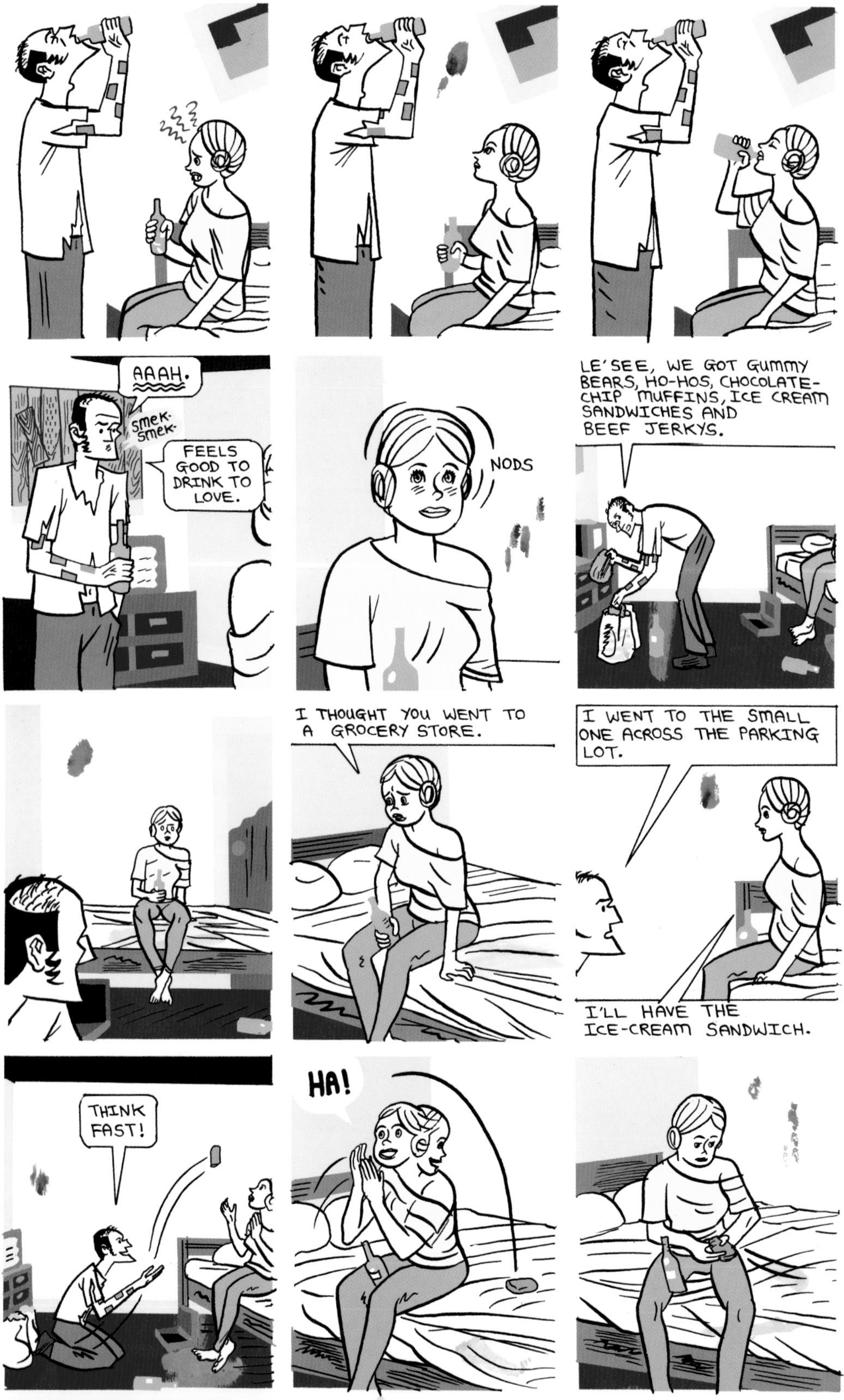
AAAH.
smek-smek-
FEELS GOOD TO DRINK TO LOVE.
NODS
LE'SEE, WE GOT GUMMY BEARS, HO-HOS, CHOCOLATE-CHIP MUFFINS, ICE CREAM SANDWICHES AND BEEF JERKYS.
I THOUGHT YOU WENT TO A GROCERY STORE.
I WENT TO THE SMALL ONE ACROSS THE PARKING LOT.
I'LL HAVE THE ICE-CREAM SANDWICH.
THINK FAST!
HA!

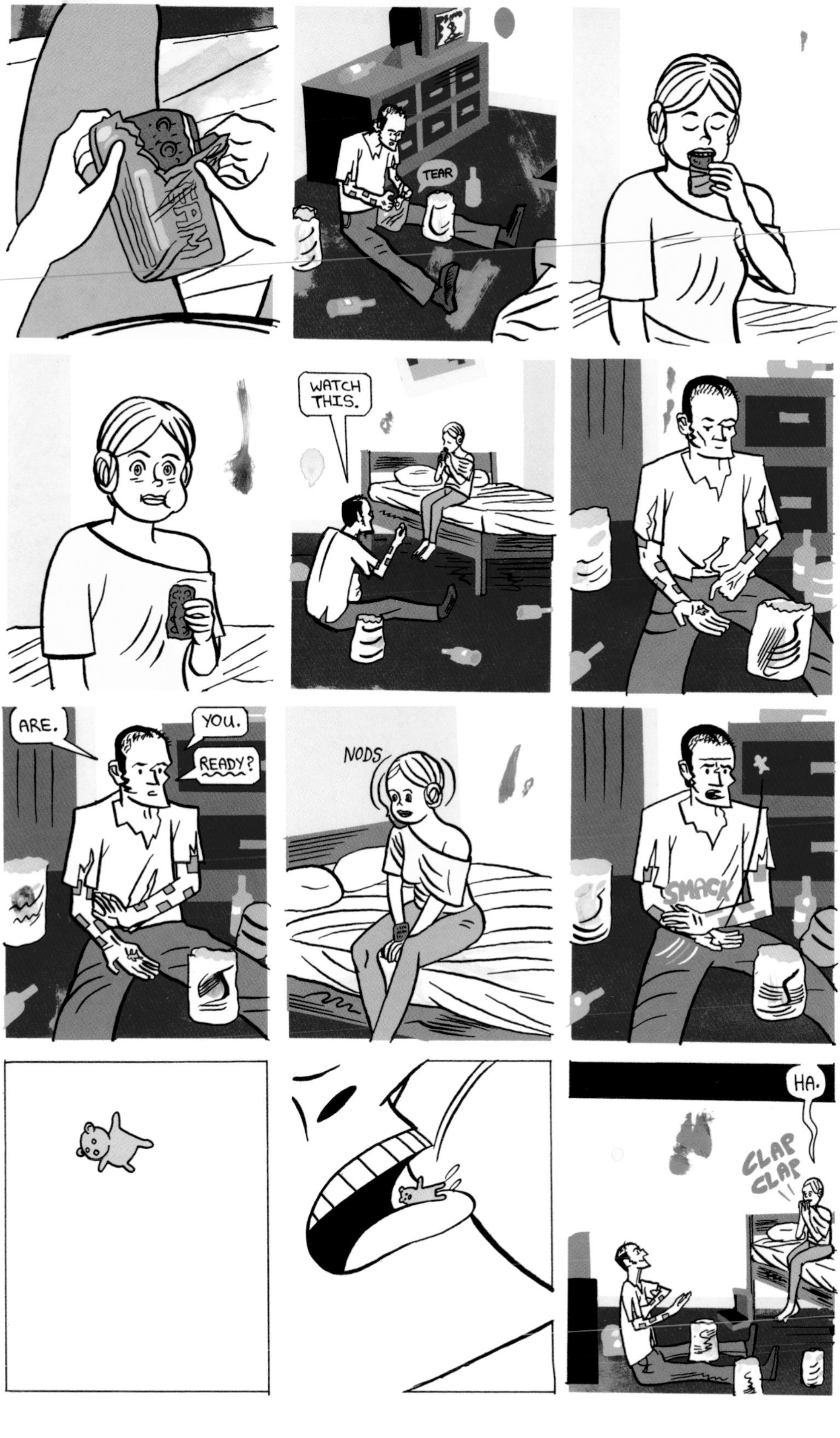

TEAR
WATCH THIS.
ARE.
YOU.
READY?
NODS
SMACK
HA.
CLAP CLAP

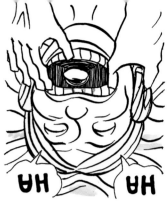

HA HA HA

THIS IS SCARY! PAUL!

I'M GONNA GET IT.

HA! PAUL!

LEAN BACK.

OPEN UP.

AAAA.

THIS STICKS TO THE TEETH.

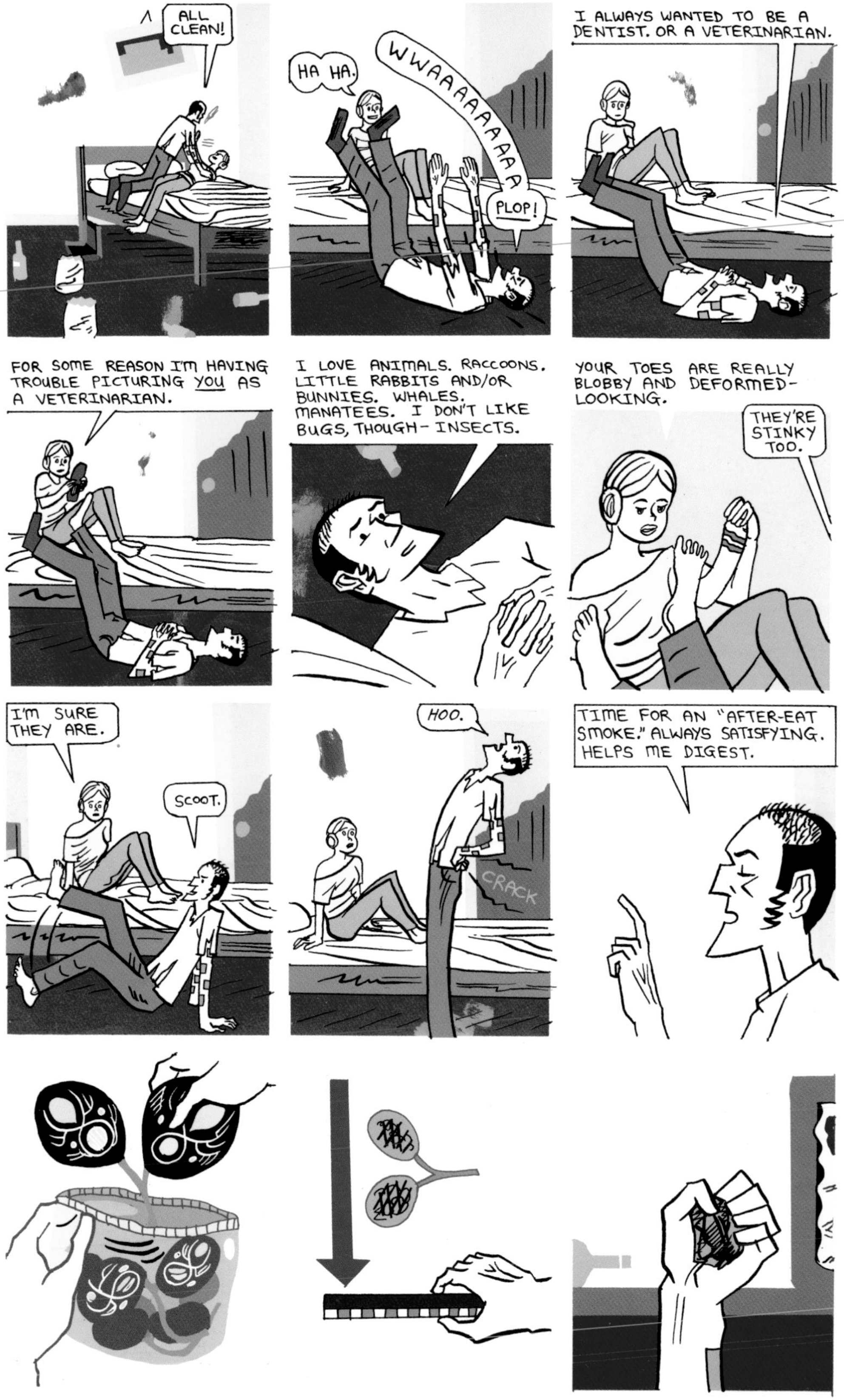
ALL CLEAN!
HA HA.
WWAAAAAAAAAA
PLOP!
I ALWAYS WANTED TO BE A DENTIST. OR A VETERINARIAN.
FOR SOME REASON I'M HAVING TROUBLE PICTURING YOU AS A VETERINARIAN.
I LOVE ANIMALS. RACCOONS. LITTLE RABBITS AND/OR BUNNIES. WHALES. MANATEES. I DON'T LIKE BUGS, THOUGH- INSECTS.
YOUR TOES ARE REALLY BLOBBY AND DEFORMED-LOOKING.
THEY'RE STINKY TOO.
I'M SURE THEY ARE.
SCOOT.
HOO.
CRACK
TIME FOR AN "AFTER-EAT SMOKE." ALWAYS SATISFYING. HELPS ME DIGEST.

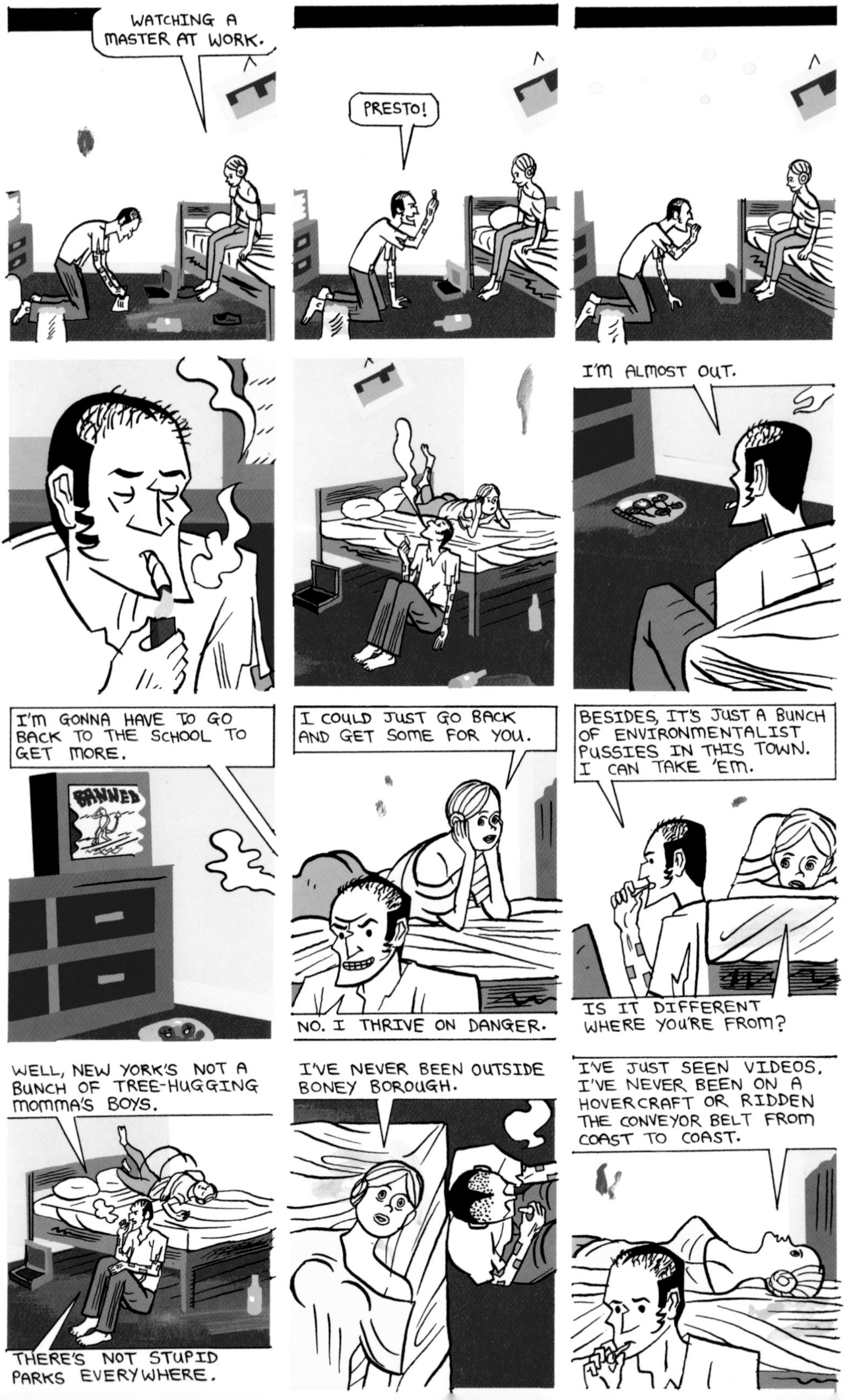
WATCHING A MASTER AT WORK.
PRESTO!
I'M ALMOST OUT.
I'M GONNA HAVE TO GO BACK TO THE SCHOOL TO GET MORE.
BANNED
I COULD JUST GO BACK AND GET SOME FOR YOU.
NO. I THRIVE ON DANGER.
BESIDES, IT'S JUST A BUNCH OF ENVIRONMENTALIST PUSSIES IN THIS TOWN. I CAN TAKE 'EM.
IS IT DIFFERENT WHERE YOU'RE FROM?
WELL, NEW YORK'S NOT A BUNCH OF TREE-HUGGING MOMMA'S BOYS.
THERE'S NOT STUPID PARKS EVERYWHERE.
I'VE NEVER BEEN OUTSIDE BONEY BOROUGH.
I'VE JUST SEEN VIDEOS. I'VE NEVER BEEN ON A HOVERCRAFT OR RIDDEN THE CONVEYOR BELT FROM COAST TO COAST.

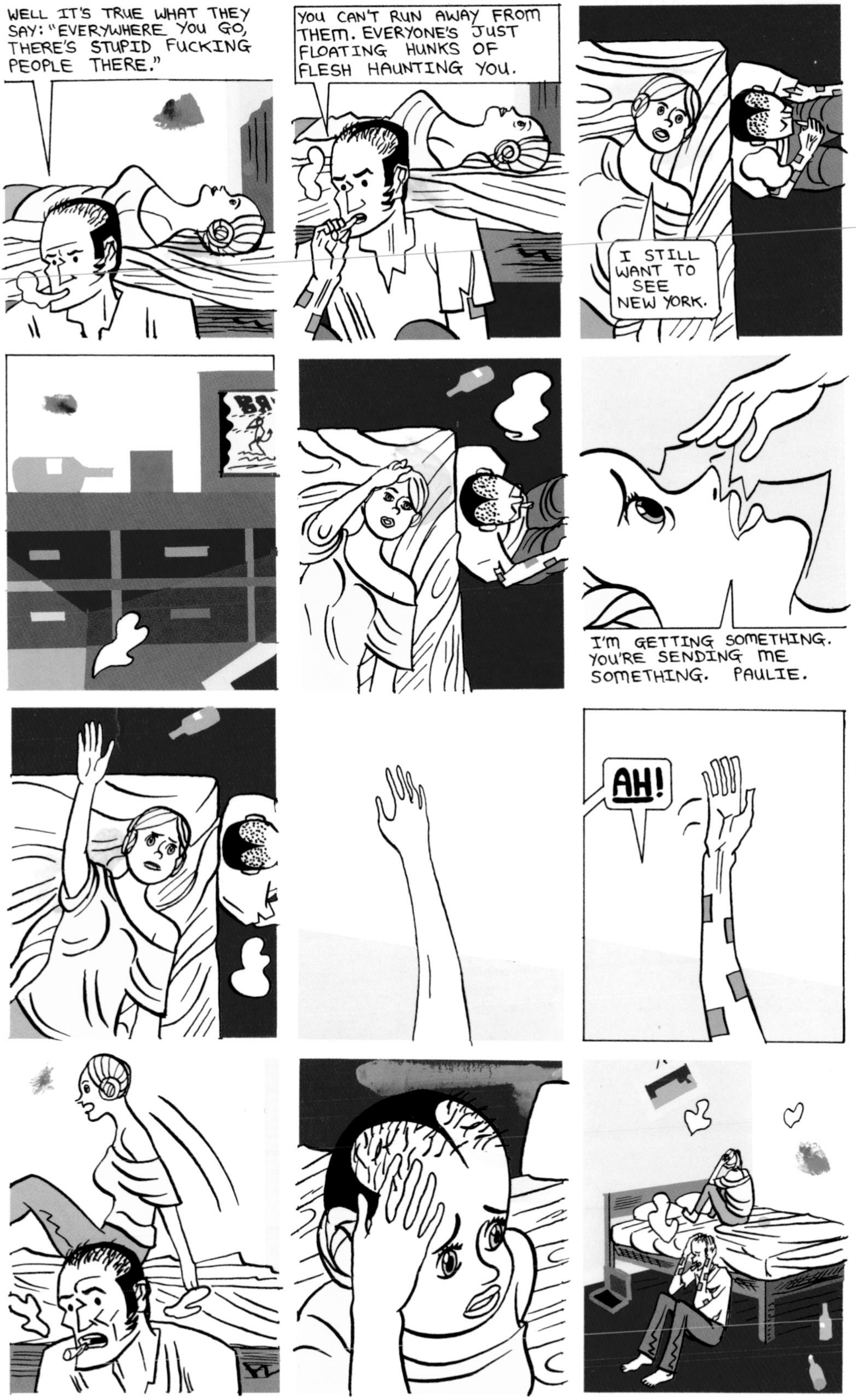
WELL IT'S TRUE WHAT THEY SAY: "EVERYWHERE YOU GO, THERE'S STUPID FUCKING PEOPLE THERE."
YOU CAN'T RUN AWAY FROM THEM. EVERYONE'S JUST FLOATING HUNKS OF FLESH HAUNTING YOU.
I STILL WANT TO SEE NEW YORK.
I'M GETTING SOMETHING. YOU'RE SENDING ME SOMETHING. PAULIE.
AH!

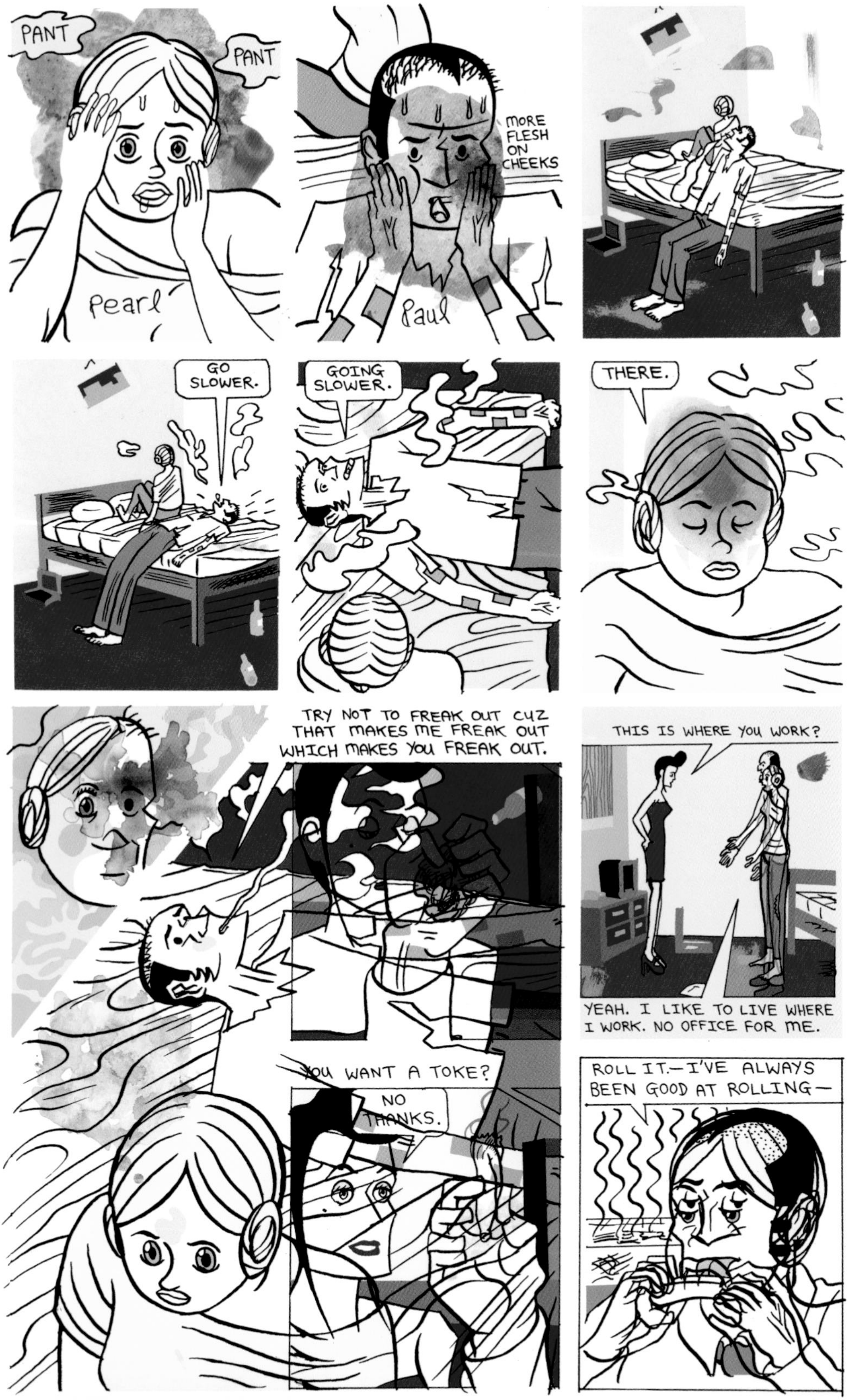
PANT
PANT
Pearl
MORE FLESH ON CHEEKS
Paul
GO SLOWER.
GOING SLOWER.
THERE.
TRY NOT TO FREAK OUT CUZ THAT MAKES ME FREAK OUT WHICH MAKES YOU FREAK OUT.
THIS IS WHERE YOU WORK?
YEAH. I LIKE TO LIVE WHERE I WORK. NO OFFICE FOR ME.
YOU WANT A TOKE?
NO THANKS.
ROLL IT.—I'VE ALWAYS BEEN GOOD AT ROLLING—

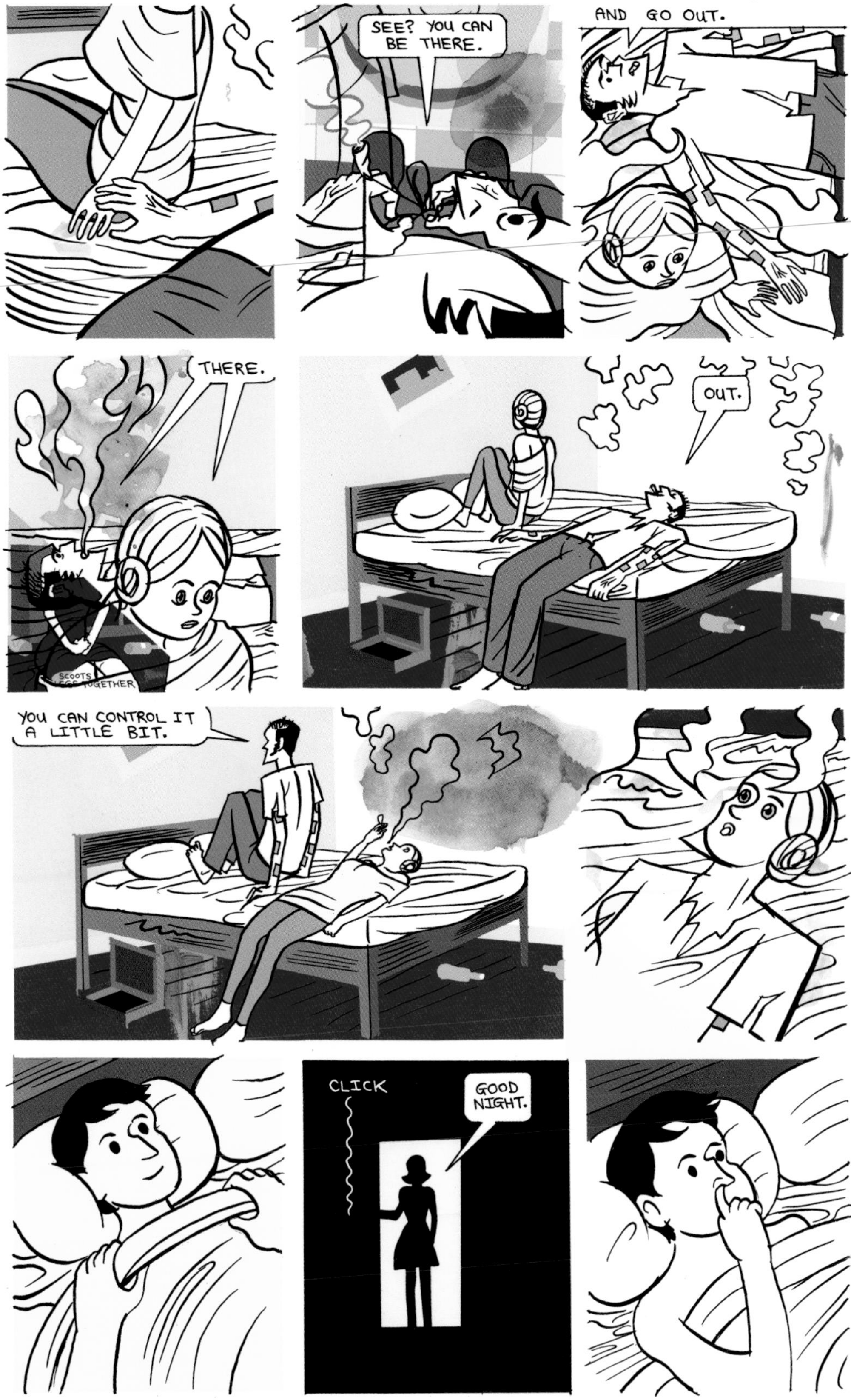

SEE? YOU CAN BE THERE.
AND GO OUT.
THERE.
SCOOTS LEGS TOGETHER
OUT.
YOU CAN CONTROL IT A LITTLE BIT.
CLICK
GOOD NIGHT.

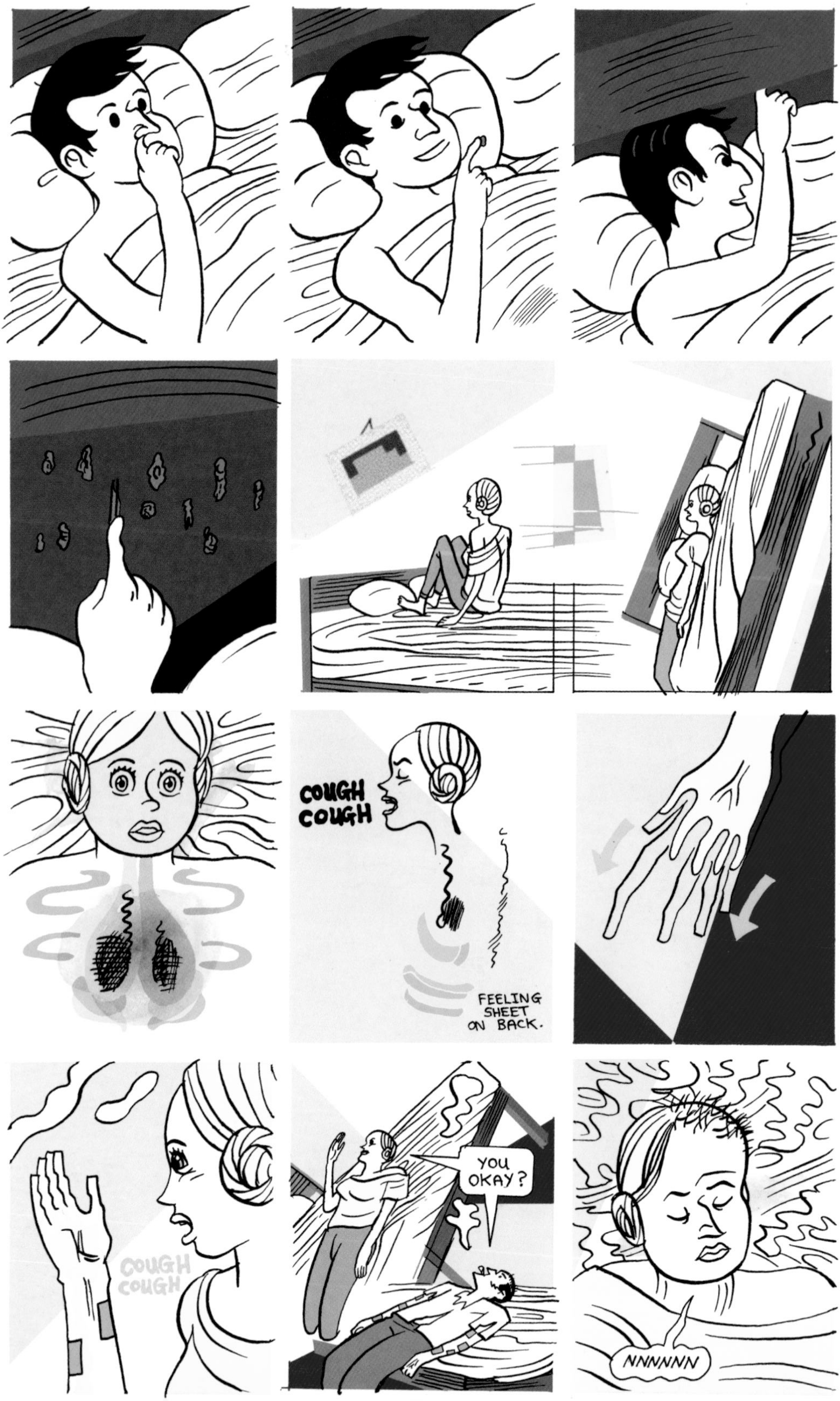
COUGH
COUGH
FEELING
SHEET
ON BACK.
COUGH
COUGH
YOU
OKAY?
NNNNNN

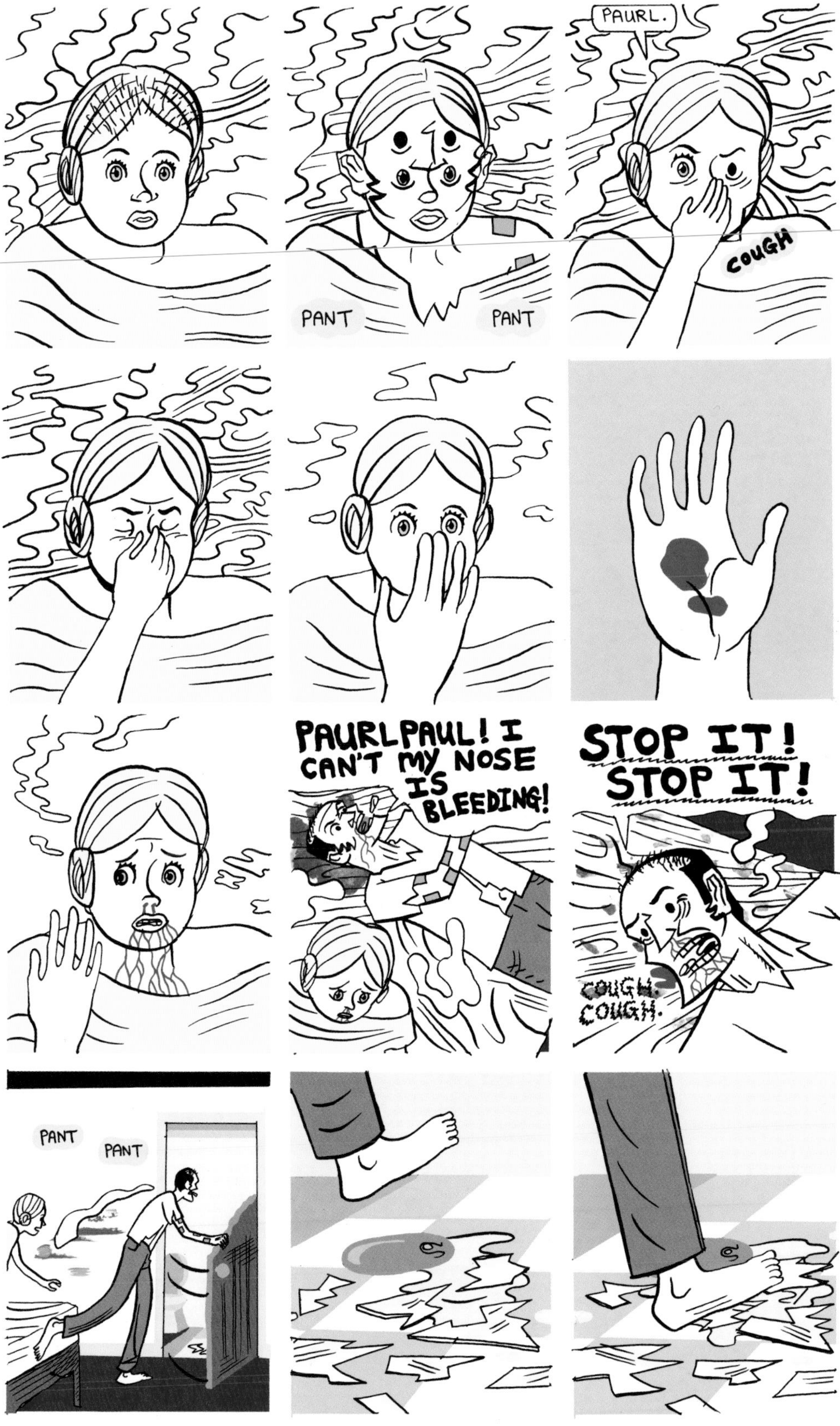
PANT
PANT
PAURL.
COUGH
PAURLPAUL! I CAN'T MY NOSE IS BLEEDING!
STOP IT!
STOP IT!
COUGH.
COUGH.
PANT
PANT

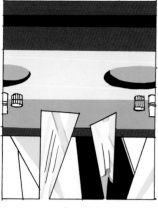

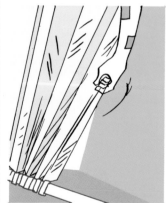

AAAA

AAAK!

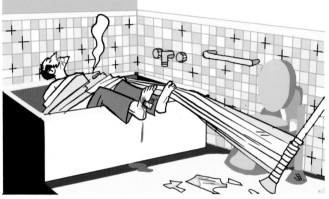

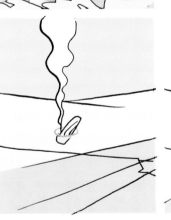

AAAA!

AAAA!

AAAAAAAA

'S COOL.
I GOT IT.

PEARL?
PEARL?
YOU OKAY? YOU WERE GOING TOO DEEP TOO FAST, I GUESS.
SHAKE
COUGH COUGH
PEARL?
HERE. I'M SENDING YOU SOMETHING.

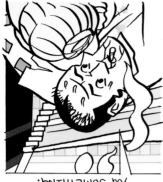

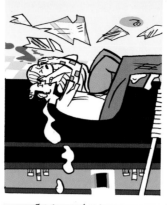

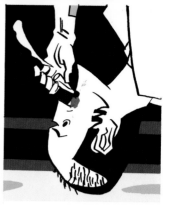

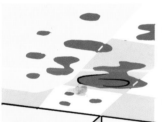

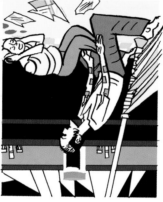

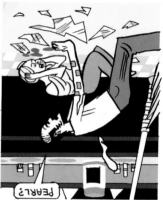

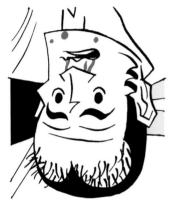

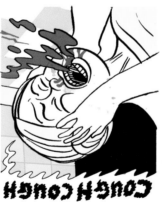

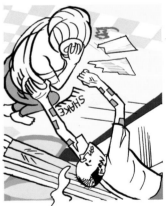

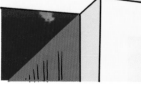

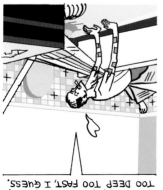

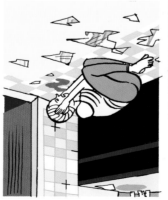

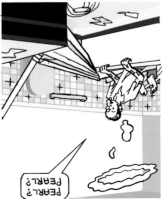

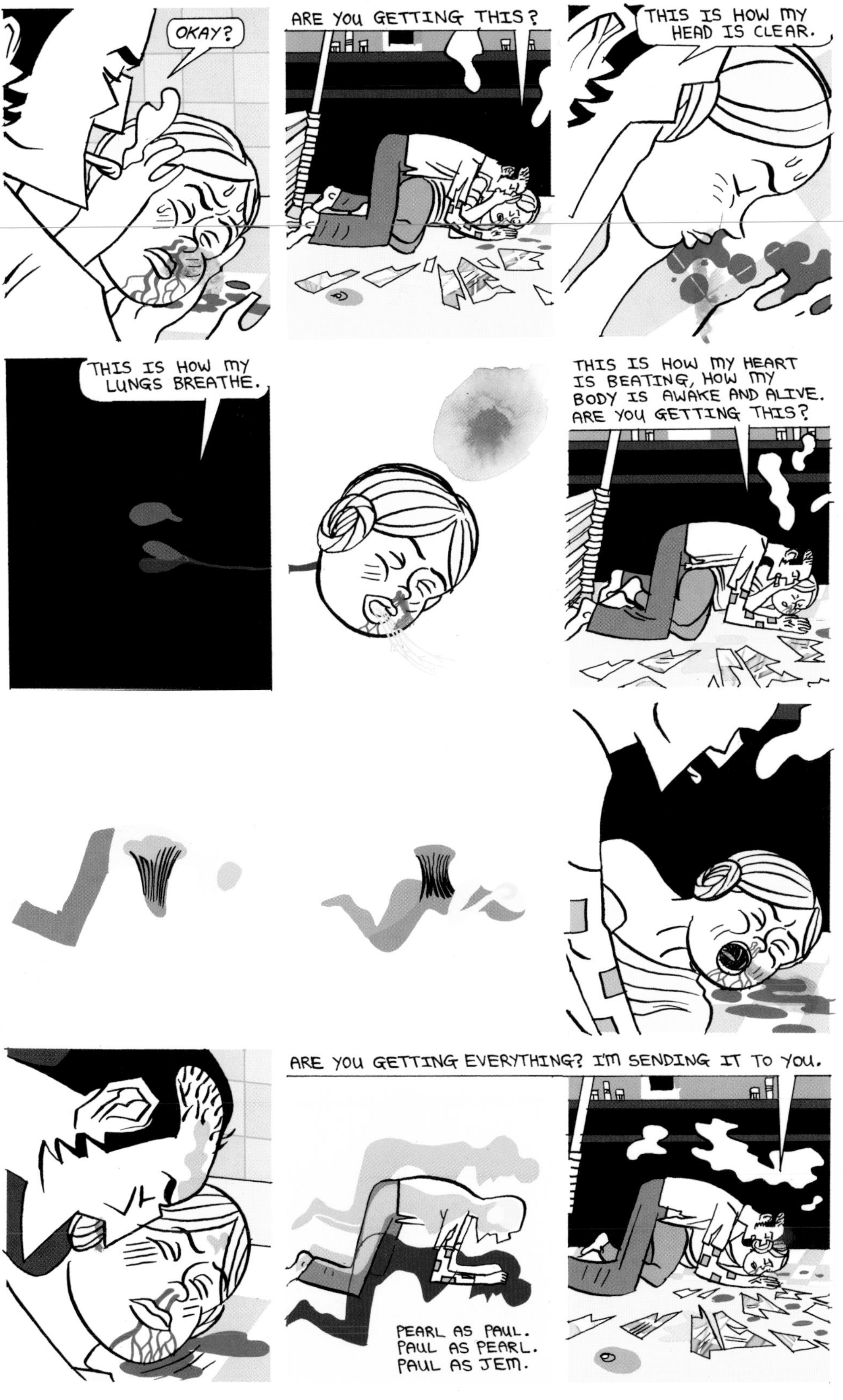
OKAY?
ARE YOU GETTING THIS?
THIS IS HOW MY HEAD IS CLEAR.
THIS IS HOW MY LUNGS BREATHE.
THIS IS HOW MY HEART IS BEATING, HOW MY BODY IS AWAKE AND ALIVE. ARE YOU GETTING THIS?
ARE YOU GETTING EVERYTHING? I'M SENDING IT TO YOU.
PEARL AS PAUL.
PAUL AS PEARL.
PAUL AS JEM.

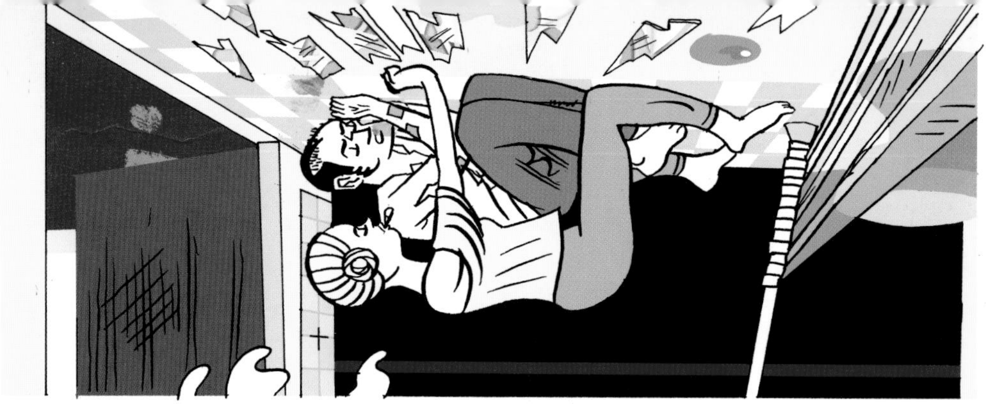

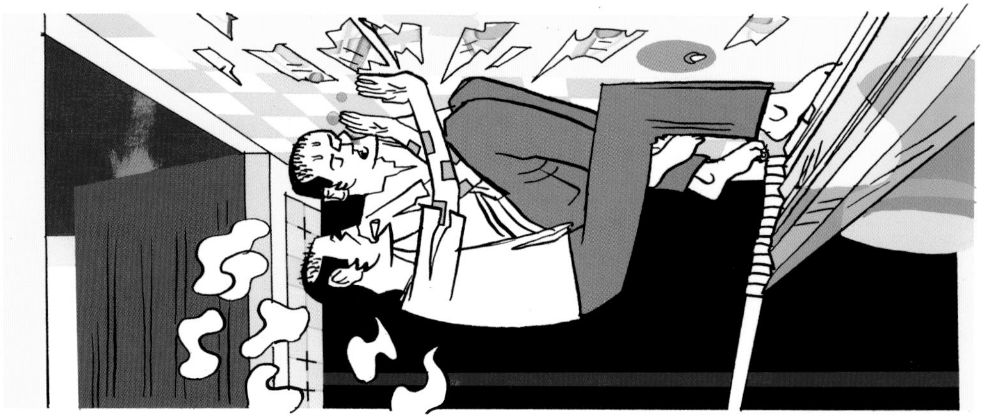

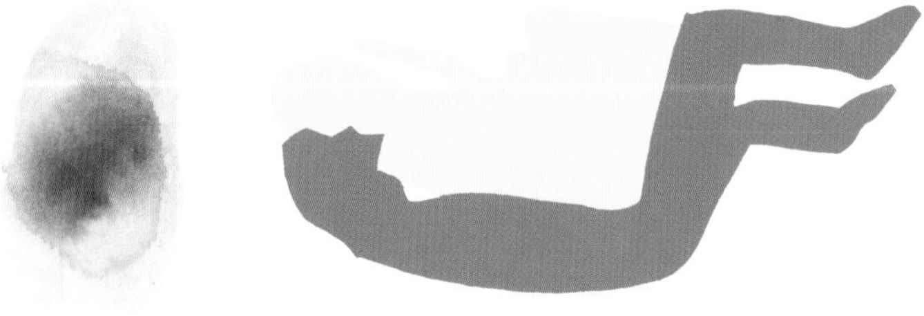

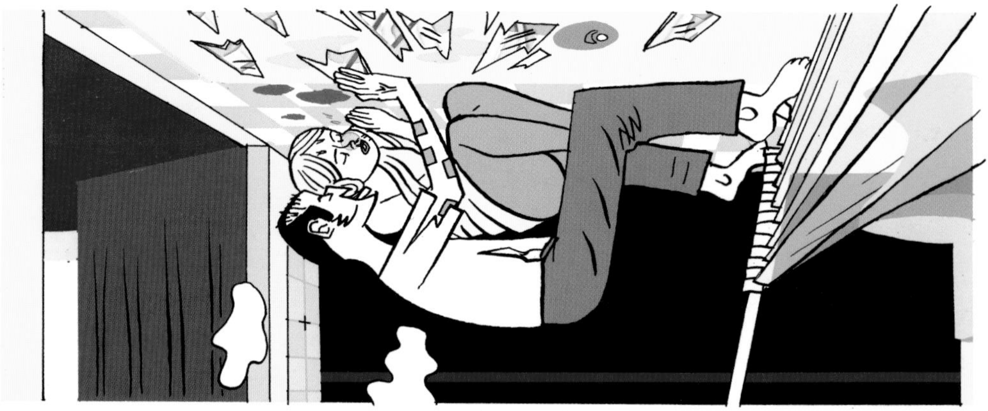

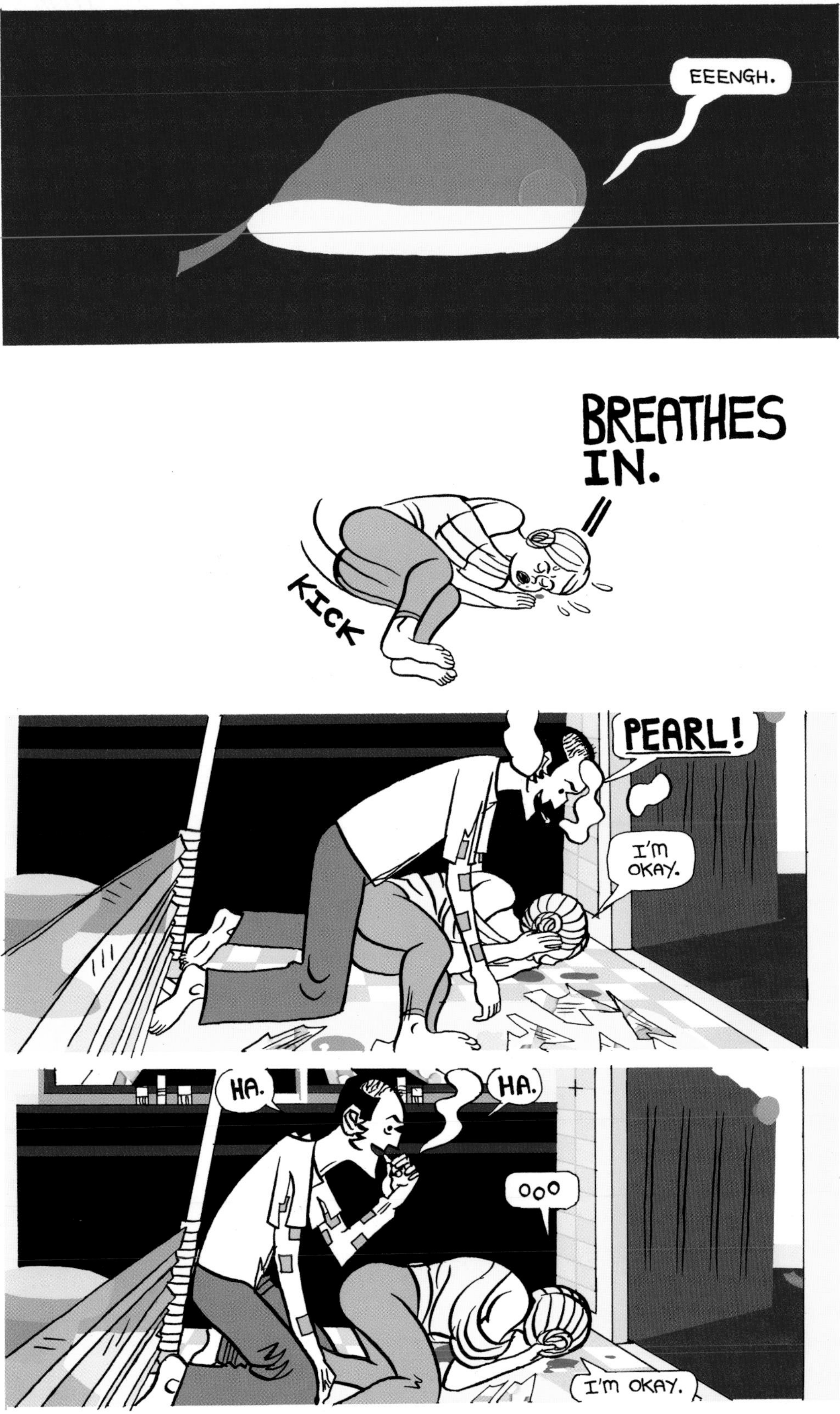
EEENGH.
BREATHES IN.
KICK
PEARL!
I'M OKAY.
HA.
HA.
OOO
I'M OKAY.

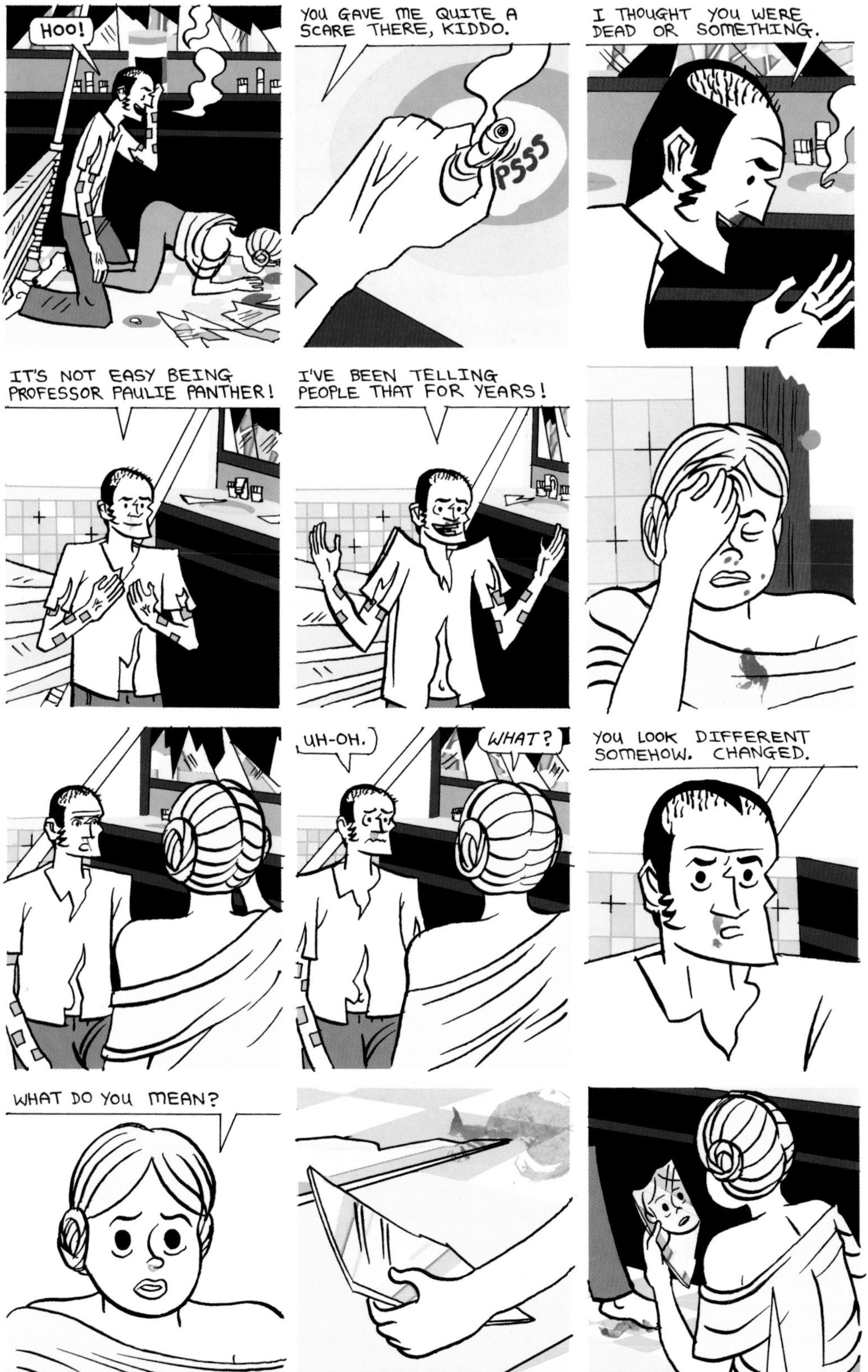
HOO!
YOU GAVE ME QUITE A SCARE THERE, KIDDO.
PSSS
I THOUGHT YOU WERE DEAD OR SOMETHING.
IT'S NOT EASY BEING PROFESSOR PAULIE PANTHER!
I'VE BEEN TELLING PEOPLE THAT FOR YEARS!
UH-OH.
WHAT?
YOU LOOK DIFFERENT SOMEHOW. CHANGED.
WHAT DO YOU MEAN?
I LOOK THE SAME TO ME, PAULIE.

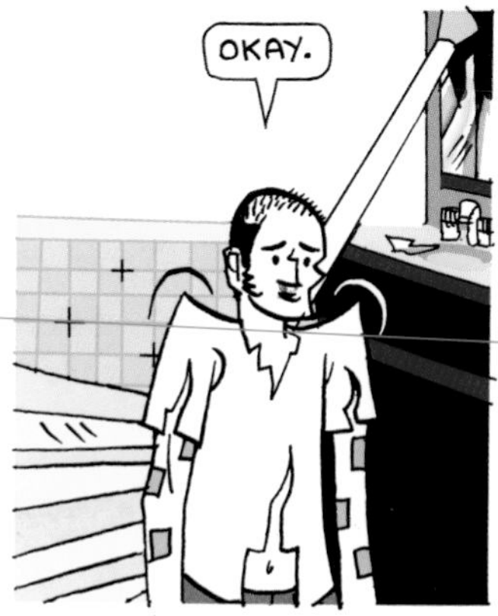
OKAY.

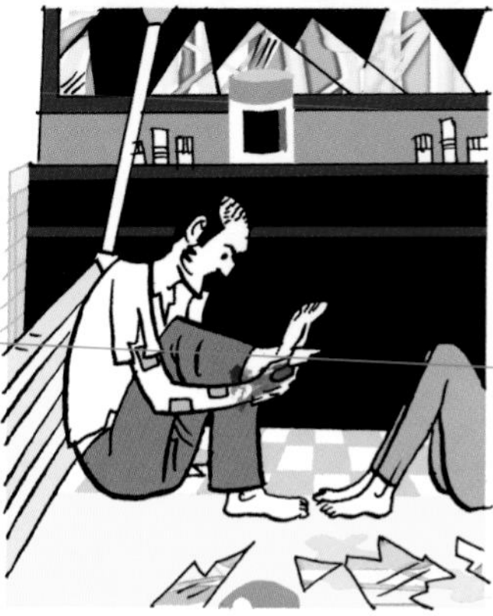

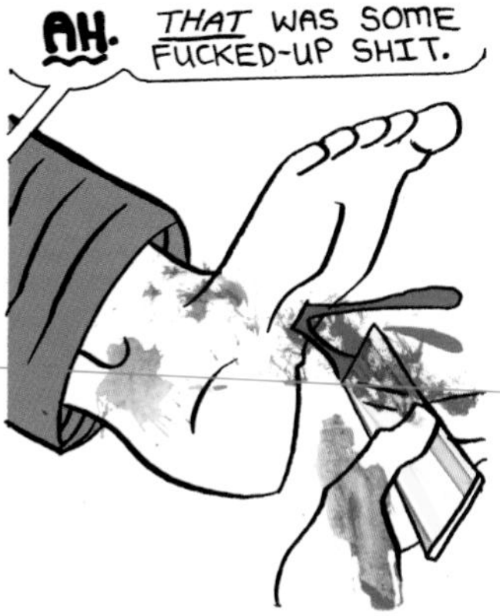
AH. THAT WAS SOME FUCKED-UP SHIT.

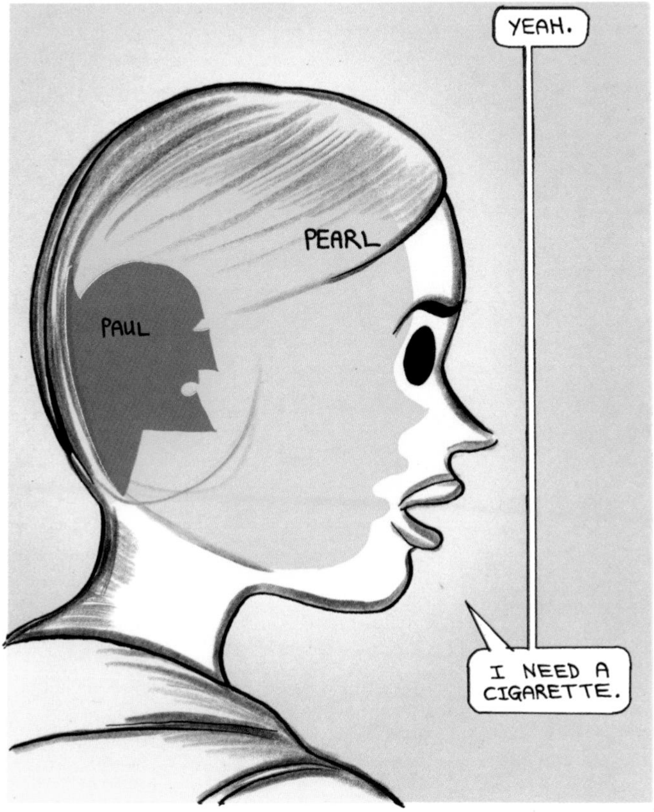
YEAH.
PEARL
PAUL
I NEED A CIGARETTE.

END OF CHAPTER SEVEN.

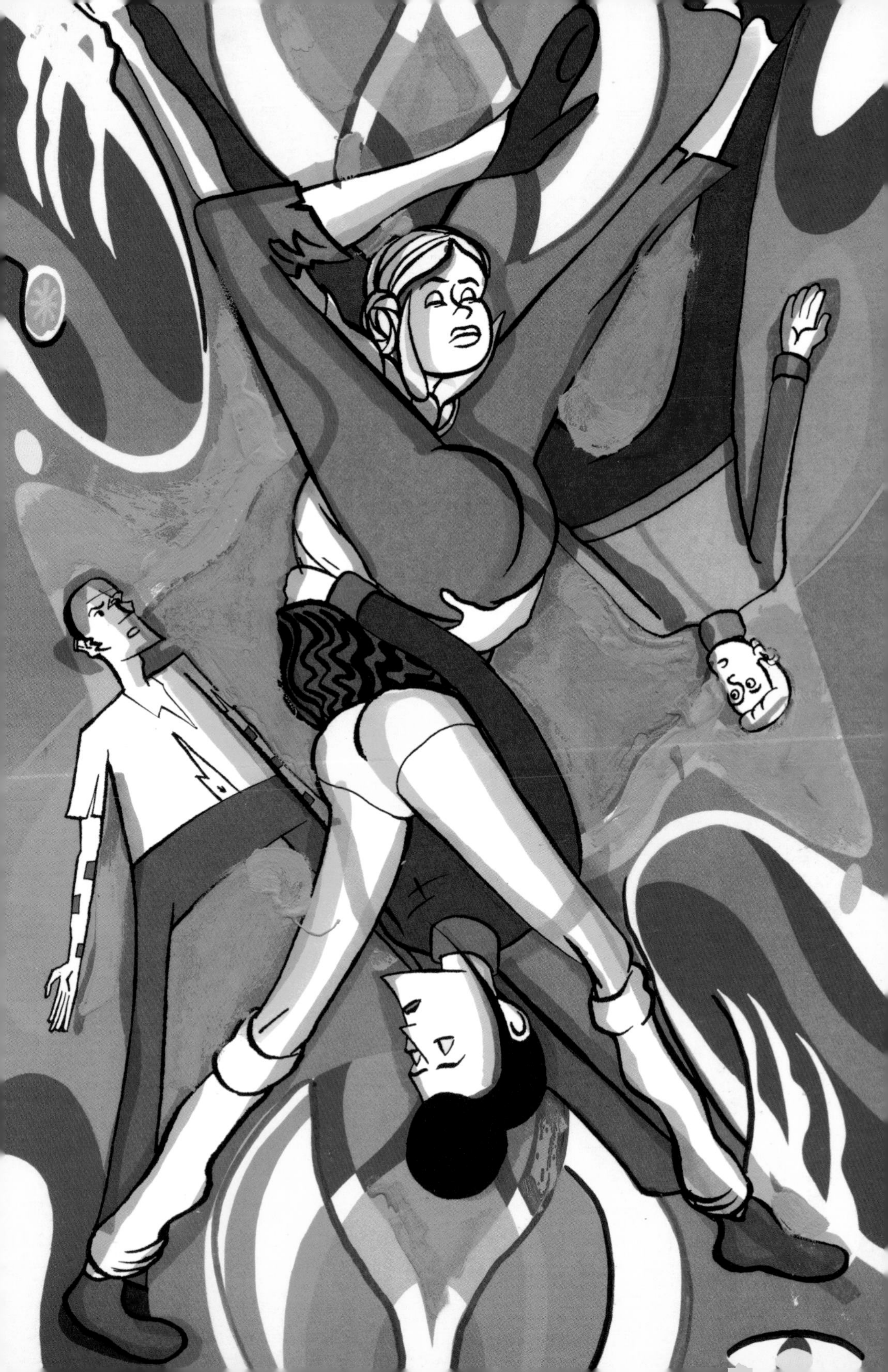

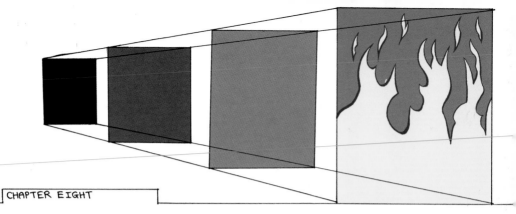

CHAPTER EIGHT

X
25

I'VE NOTICED YOU HAVEN'T DONE ANY OF YOUR COLLEGE APPLICATIONS.

COLLEGE? PFFT! I'VE HAD THIRTEEN YEARS OF FASCISTS TELLING ME HOW TO THINK—ISN'T IT TIME I THOUGHT FOR MYSELF?

YOU'VE BEEN ACTING STRANGE LATELY. IS THIS BECAUSE OF BILLY?

GAWD. A WOMAN CAN'T BEHAVE A CERTAIN WAY UNLESS THERE'S A MAN INVOLVED, HUH?

I-I DIDN'T MEAN,

YEAH, WELL, I GOTTA STEP OUTSIDE FOR A SEC, GET SOME AIR. IT SMELLS LIKE BULL SHIT IN HERE.

PSSS

29 R

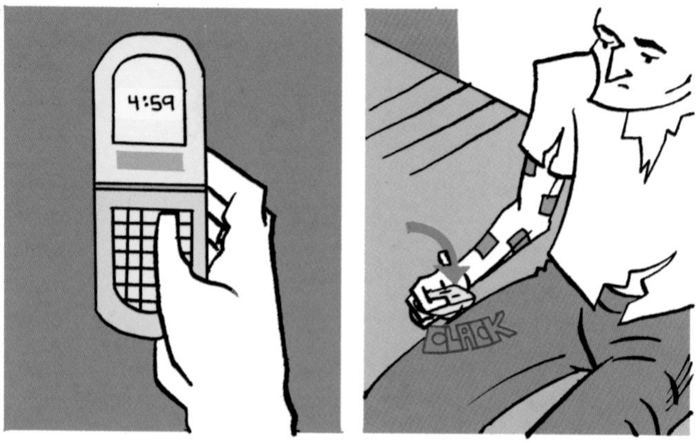
4:59
CLACK

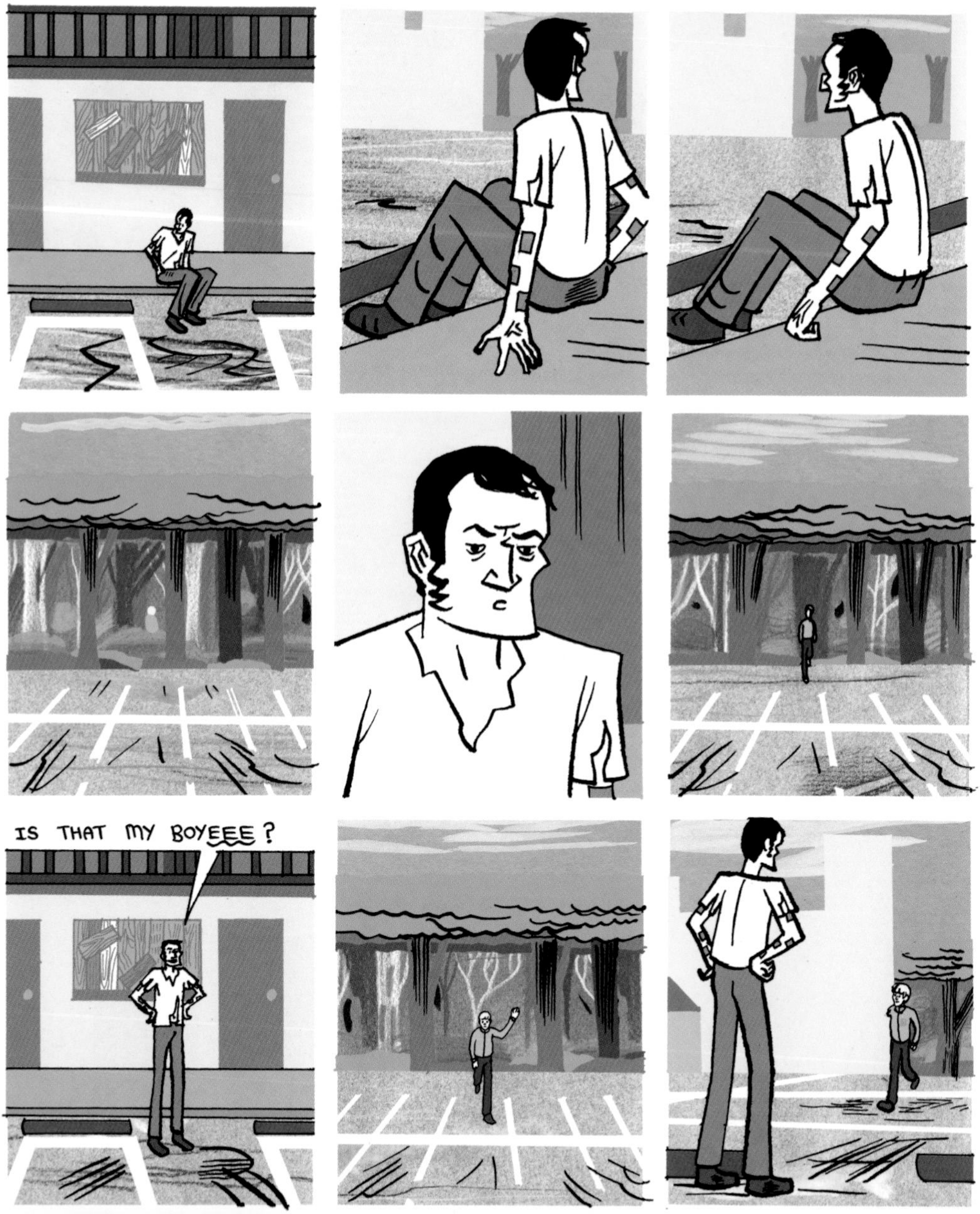
IS THAT MY BOYEEE?

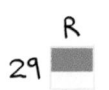

FROM FAR AWAY YOU LOOKED LIKE A CUTE LITTLE BLUE BERRY!

STEP IN STEP IN.

SHUT

THIS IS WHERE YOU *LIVE*?

IT'S TEMPORARY, MAN.

HERE'S THE DEAL-O: IF YOU WANT TO GET STONED, THAT'S COOL. THERE'S NOTHING WRONG WITH THAT. BUT THIS SHIT I PICKED UP AT YOUR SCHOOL IS <u>HOT</u>. A TOTAL EXTRA-SENSORY EXPERIENCE. "2001: A SPACE ODYSSEY."

THE PLANT YOU WERE COLLECTING WITH MISS JEWEL?

YUPPY.

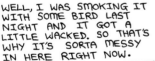
IT'S NOT LIKE A STRAIGHT HIGH OR ANYTHING. IT MORE FEEDS OFF OF THE ENVIRONMENT.

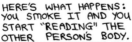

AND THIS IS A GOOD ENVIRONMENT?

WELL, I WAS SMOKING IT WITH SOME BIRD LAST NIGHT AND IT GOT A LITTLE WACKED. SO THAT'S WHY IT'S SORTA MESSY IN HERE RIGHT NOW.

..."SOME BIRD"?...

HERE'S WHAT HAPPENS: YOU SMOKE IT AND YOU START "READING" THE OTHER PERSON'S BODY.

YOUR ASSOCIATIONS WITH A PLACE OR WHATEVER WILL BECOME MY ASSOCIATIONS.

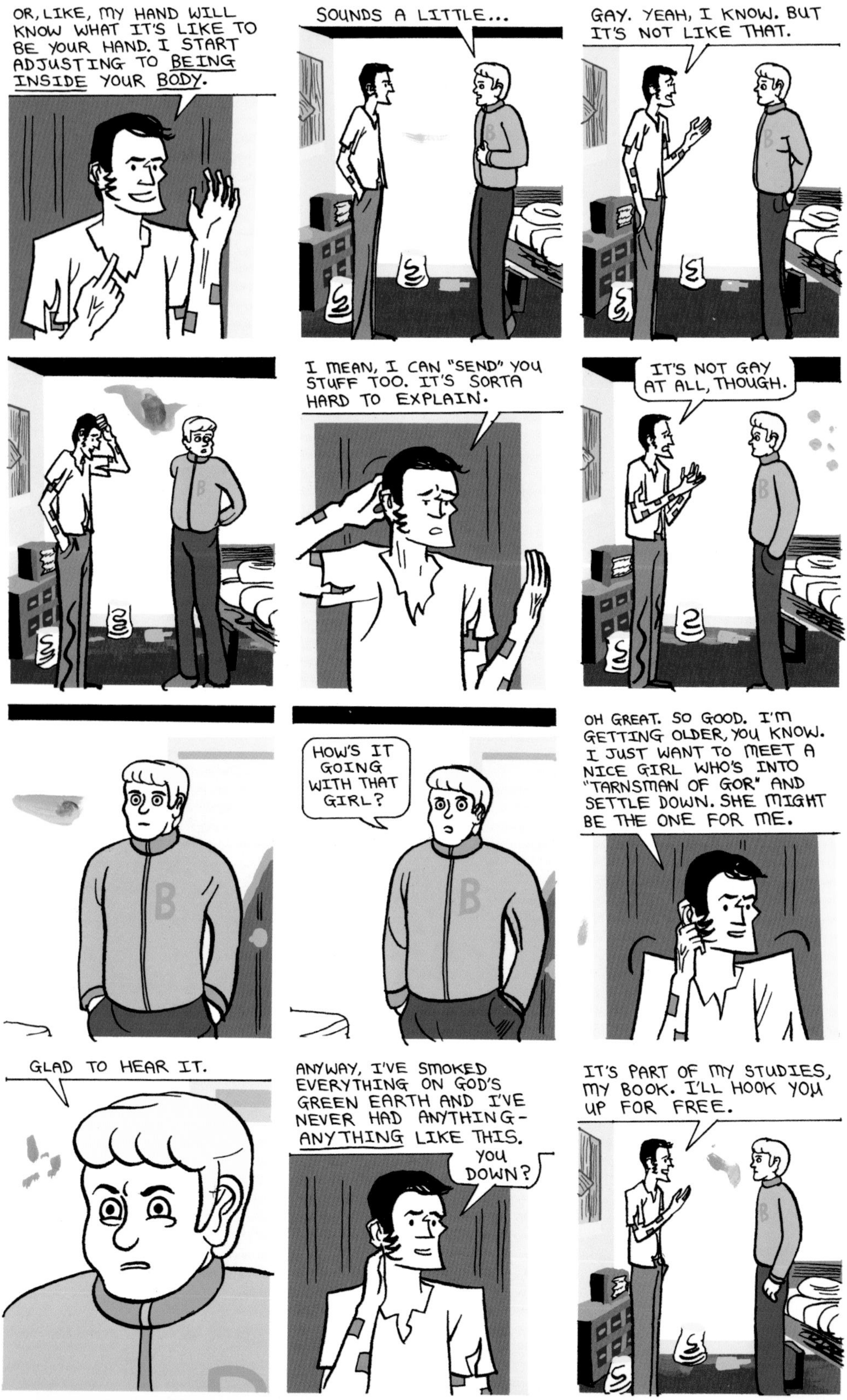
OR, LIKE, MY HAND WILL KNOW WHAT IT'S LIKE TO BE YOUR HAND. I START ADJUSTING TO BEING INSIDE YOUR BODY.
SOUNDS A LITTLE...
GAY. YEAH, I KNOW. BUT IT'S NOT LIKE THAT.
I MEAN, I CAN "SEND" YOU STUFF TOO. IT'S SORTA HARD TO EXPLAIN.
IT'S NOT GAY AT ALL, THOUGH.
HOW'S IT GOING WITH THAT GIRL?
OH GREAT. SO GOOD. I'M GETTING OLDER, YOU KNOW. I JUST WANT TO MEET A NICE GIRL WHO'S INTO "TARNSMAN OF GOR" AND SETTLE DOWN. SHE MIGHT BE THE ONE FOR ME.
GLAD TO HEAR IT.
ANYWAY, I'VE SMOKED EVERYTHING ON GOD'S GREEN EARTH AND I'VE NEVER HAD ANYTHING- ANYTHING LIKE THIS.
YOU DOWN?
IT'S PART OF MY STUDIES, MY BOOK. I'LL HOOK YOU UP FOR FREE.

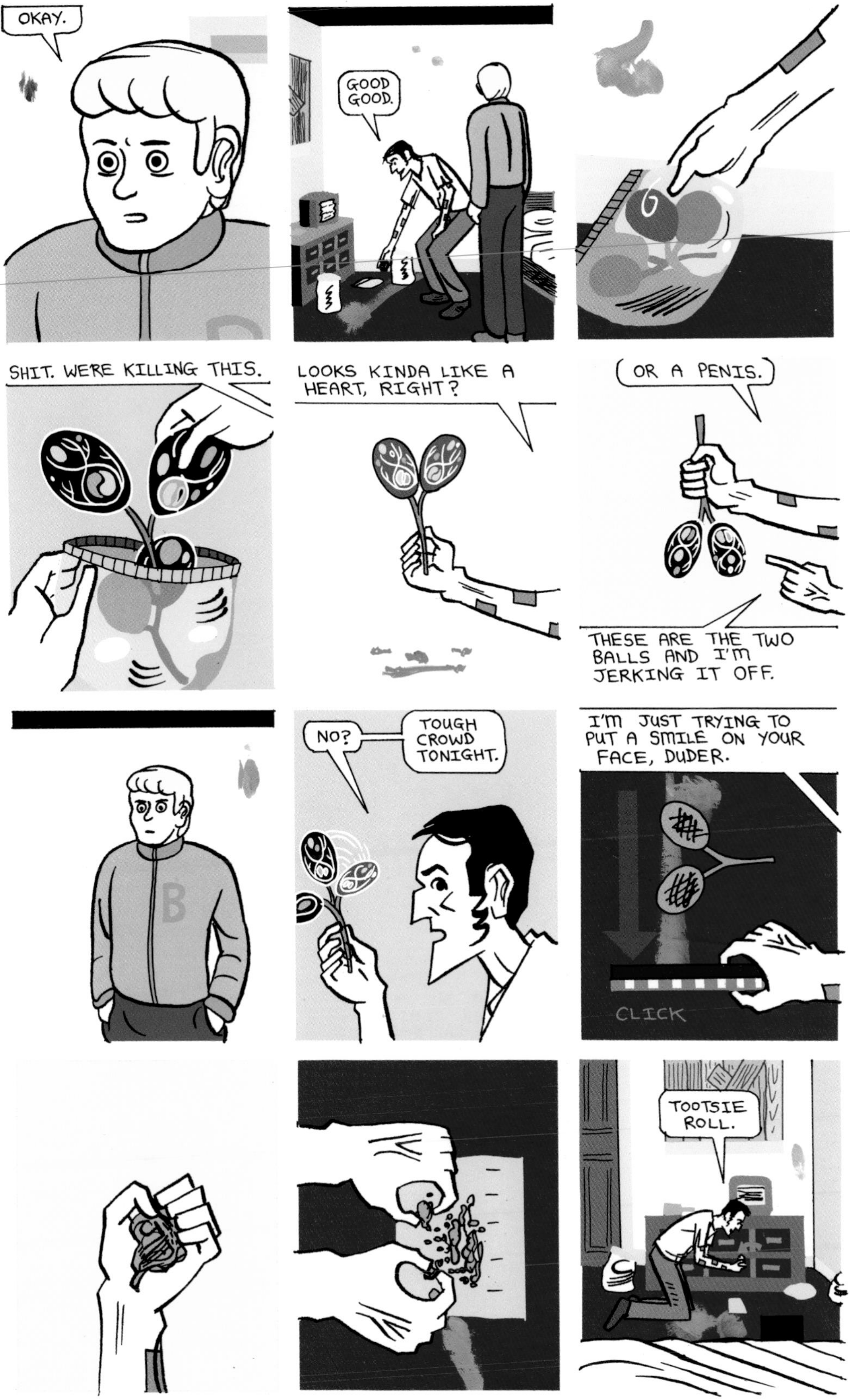
OKAY.
GOOD GOOD.
SHIT. WE'RE KILLING THIS.
LOOKS KINDA LIKE A HEART, RIGHT?
OR A PENIS.
THESE ARE THE TWO BALLS AND I'M JERKING IT OFF.
NO?
TOUGH CROWD TONIGHT.
I'M JUST TRYING TO PUT A SMILE ON YOUR FACE, DUDER.
CLICK
TOOTSIE ROLL.

OR A TWIX.
ONE FOR YOU, ONE FOR ME.

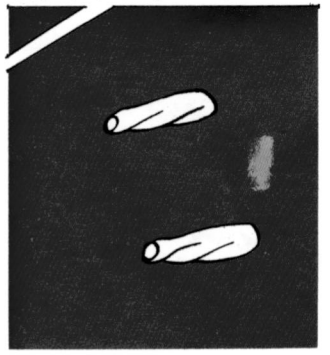

I LIKE TO PLAY
SOUNDSCAPES WHEN I'M
TESTING. HELPS "PAINT"
THE "SCENE." JUNGLE
SOUNDS, THE OCEAN.
STUFF LIKE THAT.

SO I ALWAYS DOWNLOAD
CRYSTALS FROM THAT
SECTION OF THE ONLINE
STORE. AND THEN ONE
DAY I COME ACROSS THIS.

IT'S CRAZY. IT'S GOT
EVERYTHING. IT'S CALLED
"AUTHENTIC SOUND EFFECTS
VOLUME SEVEN." I GUESS
MOVIE PEOPLE USE IT, OR
MOTHERS PLAY IT TO HELP
THEIR BABIES SLEEP.
I DONNO. BUT LISTEN TO
THESE TRACK TITLES:

TRACK ONE: BOTTLE DROPS.
TRACK EIGHT:
DRIPPING FAUCET. ooo.

TRACK ELEVEN:
GARBAGE DISPOSAL.

THAT'S A
GOOD ONE.

FOURTEEN: CAT MEOWING.
FIFTEEN: CAT PURRING.
NOT A CAT PERSON MY-
SELF (I LIKE MANATEES),
BUT THAT'S COOL. I DIG IT.

TWENTY: AMBULANCE
ARRIVES. THIRTY-ONE:
MAN'S HEAVY BREATHING.

SCRATCH

THIRTY-NINE: ZIPPER
ZIPPED UP. FORTY:
ZIPPER ZIPPED DOWN.

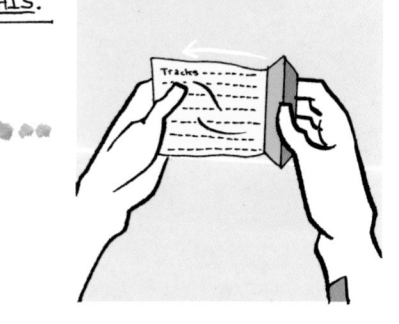

FORTY-TWO: PINBALL MACHINE.
FORTY-FIVE:
SHUFFLING CARDS.

SIXTY: ELECTRIC SAW.
SEVENTY: CAR DOOR CLOSES.
ONE THOUSAND AND ONE TRACKS!

I PRESS A BUTTON ON THIS TO RECORD OUR VOICES. IT TRANSFERS IT TO A WORD DOC AUTOMATICALLY.

YOU JUST SAY WHAT YOU'RE FEELING, EXPERIENCING, AND I'LL DO THE SAME.

AN EXPERIMENT. LIKE SCIENCE CLASS, RIGHT?

RIGHT.

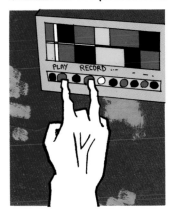

PLAY   RECORD ...

CRASH

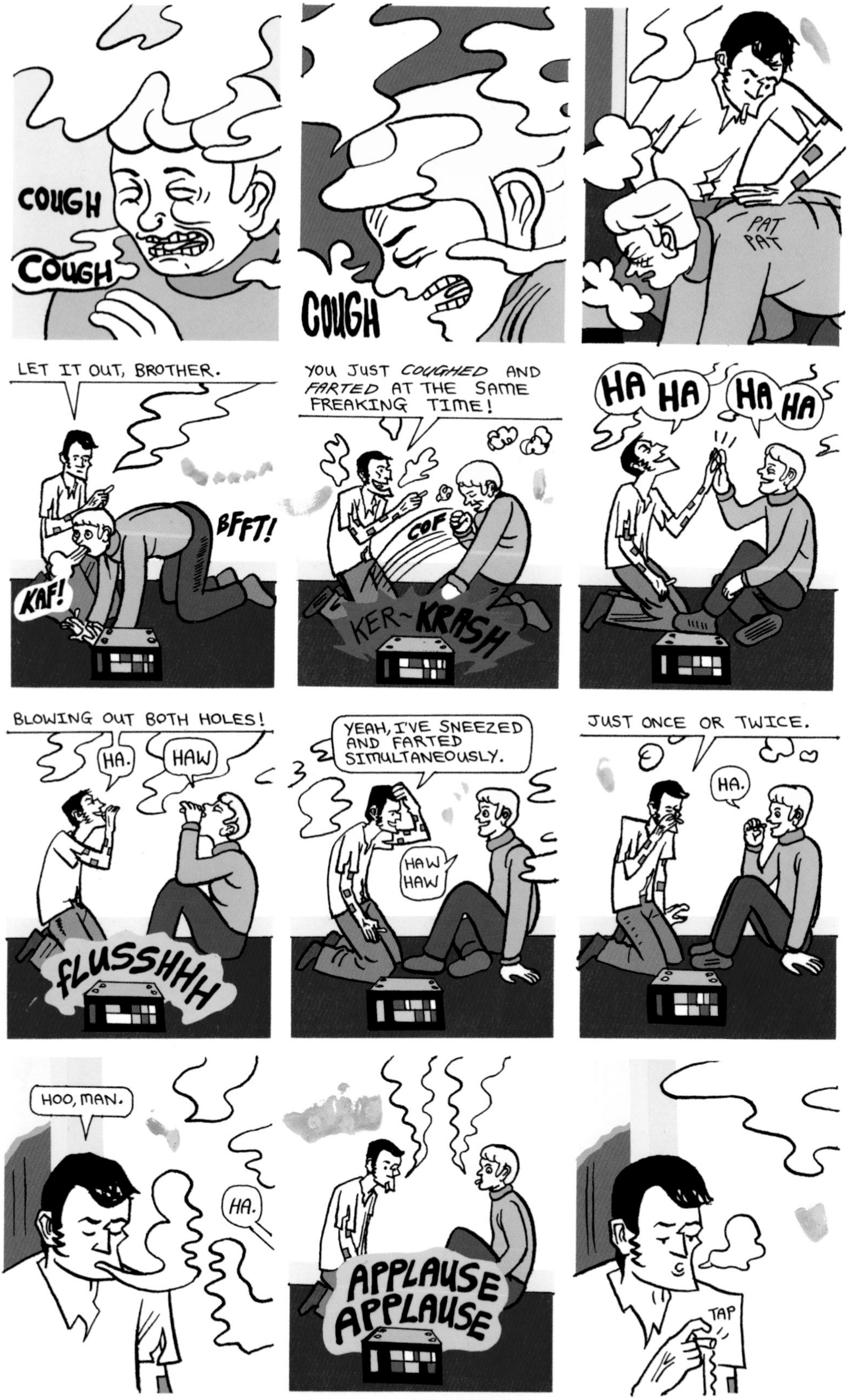
COUGH
COUGH
COUGH
PAT
PAT
LET IT OUT, BROTHER.
BFFT!
KAF!
YOU JUST COUGHED AND FARTED AT THE SAME FREAKING TIME!
COF
KER~KRASH
HA HA
HA HA
BLOWING OUT BOTH HOLES!
HA.
HAW
FLUSSHHH
YEAH, I'VE SNEEZED AND FARTED SIMULTANEOUSLY.
HAW HAW
JUST ONCE OR TWICE.
HA.
HOO, MAN.
HA.
APPLAUSE
APPLAUSE
TAP

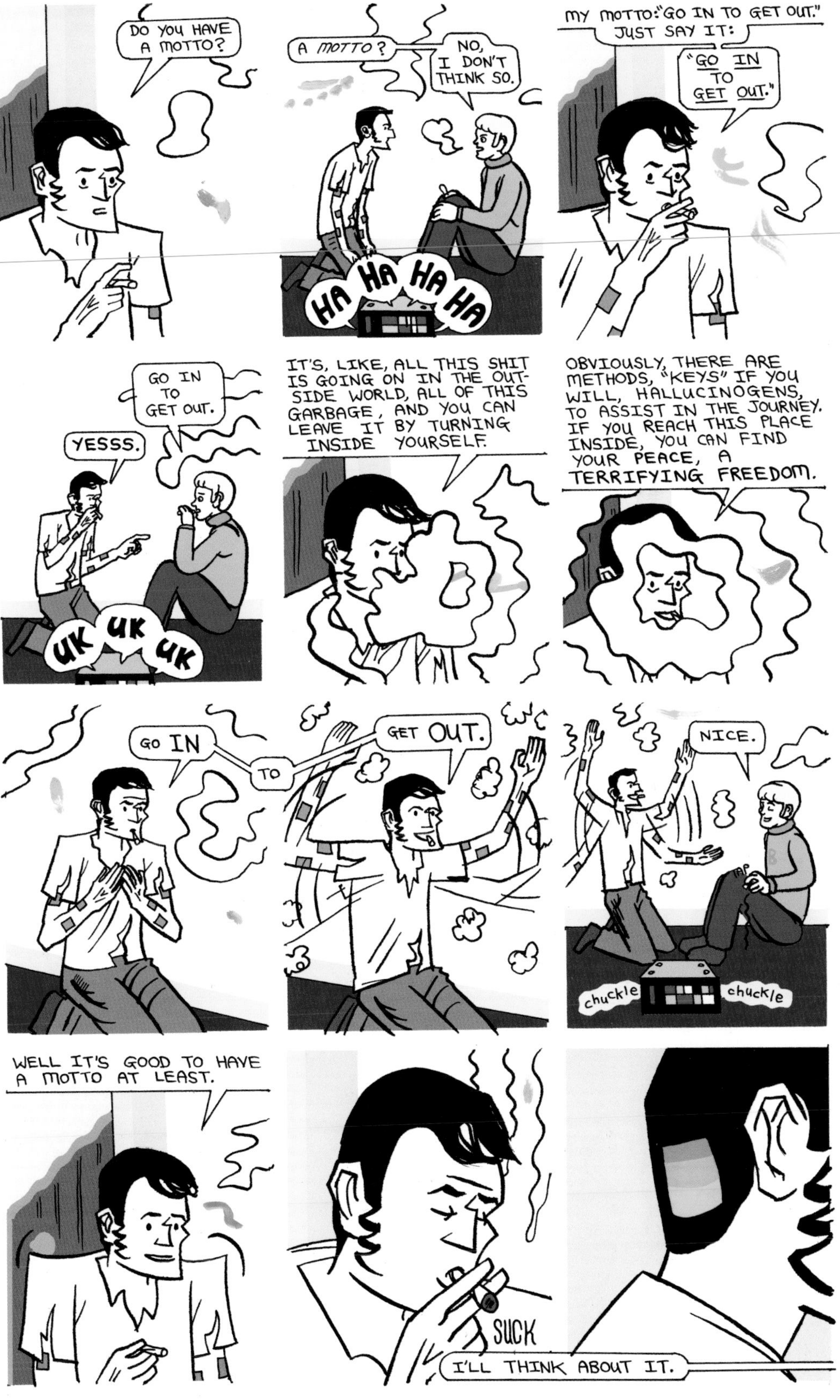
DO YOU HAVE A MOTTO?
A MOTTO?
NO, I DON'T THINK SO.
HA HA HA HA
MY MOTTO: "GO IN TO GET OUT." JUST SAY IT:
"GO IN TO GET OUT."
GO IN TO GET OUT.
YESSS.
UK UK UK
IT'S, LIKE, ALL THIS SHIT IS GOING ON IN THE OUTSIDE WORLD, ALL OF THIS GARBAGE, AND YOU CAN LEAVE IT BY TURNING INSIDE YOURSELF.
OBVIOUSLY, THERE ARE METHODS, "KEYS" IF YOU WILL, HALLUCINOGENS, TO ASSIST IN THE JOURNEY. IF YOU REACH THIS PLACE INSIDE, YOU CAN FIND YOUR PEACE, A TERRIFYING FREEDOM.
GO IN
TO
GET OUT.
NICE.
chuckle chuckle
WELL IT'S GOOD TO HAVE A MOTTO AT LEAST.
SUCK
I'LL THINK ABOUT IT.

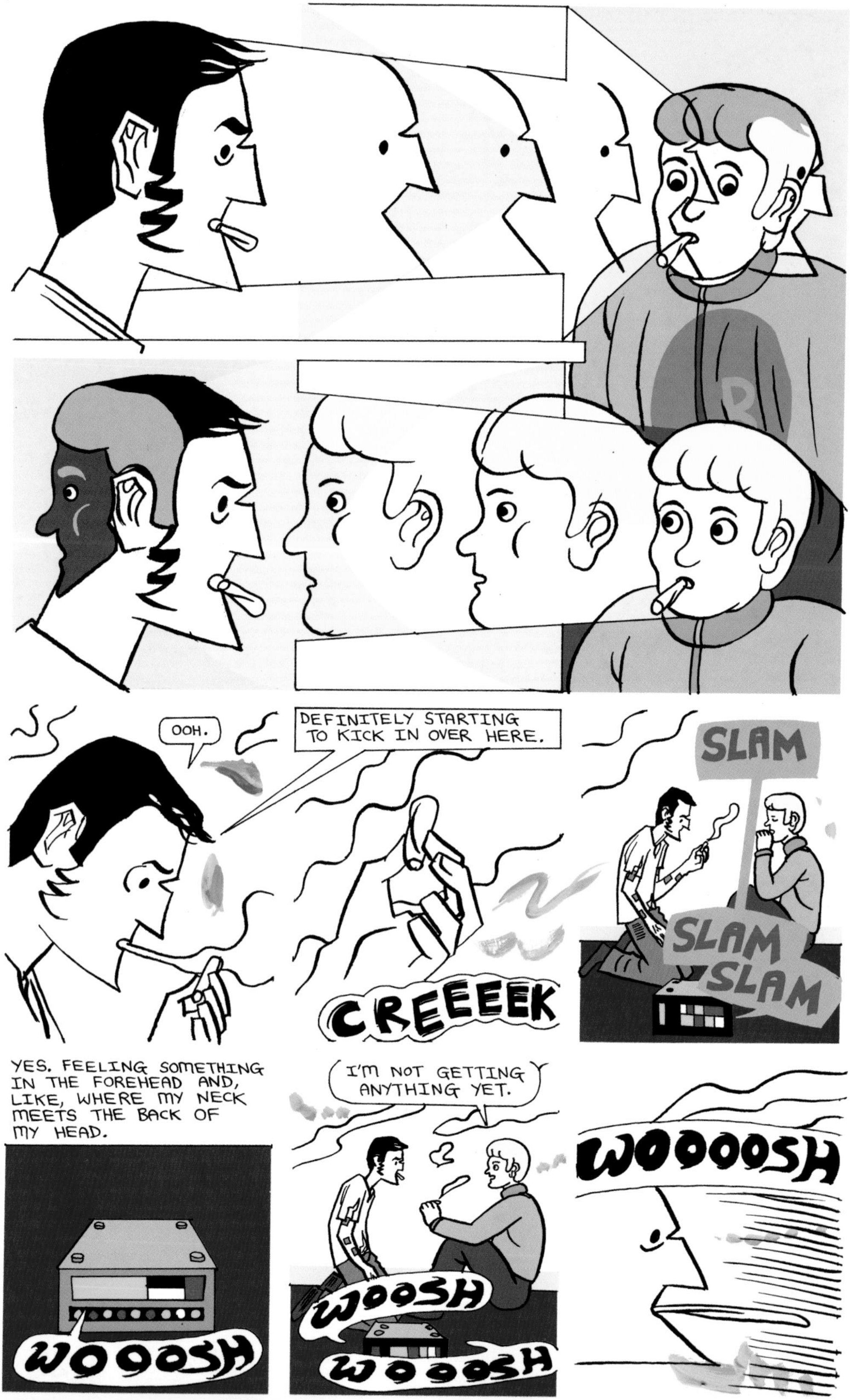
OOH.
DEFINITELY STARTING TO KICK IN OVER HERE.
CREEEEK
SLAM
SLAM
SLAM
YES. FEELING SOMETHING IN THE FOREHEAD AND, LIKE, WHERE MY NECK MEETS THE BACK OF MY HEAD.
WOOOSH
I'M NOT GETTING ANYTHING YET.
WOOSH
WOOOSH
WOOOOSH

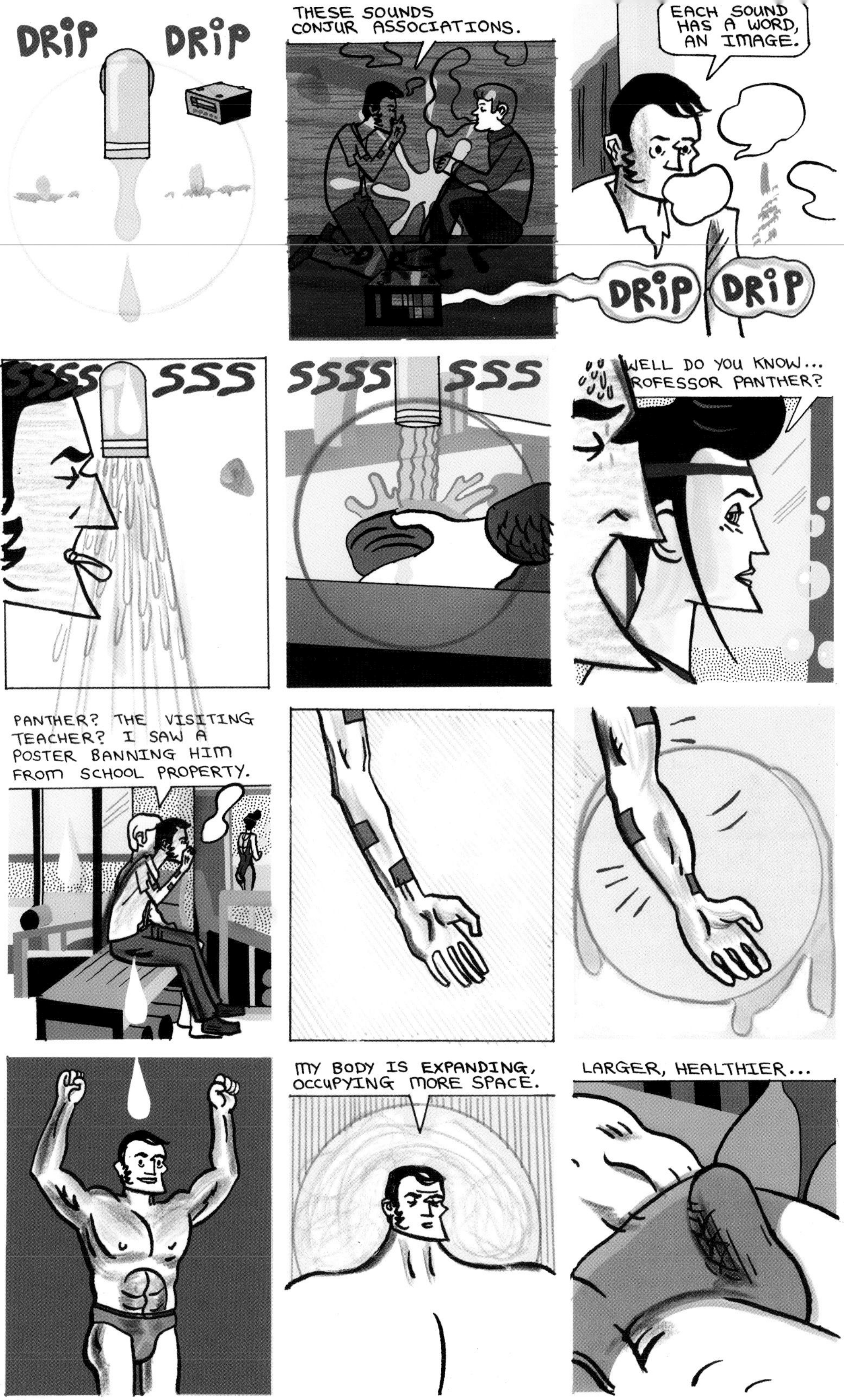
DRIP DRIP
THESE SOUNDS CONJUR ASSOCIATIONS.
EACH SOUND HAS A WORD, AN IMAGE.
DRIP DRIP
SSSS SSS
SSSS SSS
WELL DO YOU KNOW... ROFESSOR PANTHER?
PANTHER? THE VISITING TEACHER? I SAW A POSTER BANNING HIM FROM SCHOOL PROPERTY.
MY BODY IS EXPANDING, OCCUPYING MORE SPACE.
LARGER, HEALTHIER...

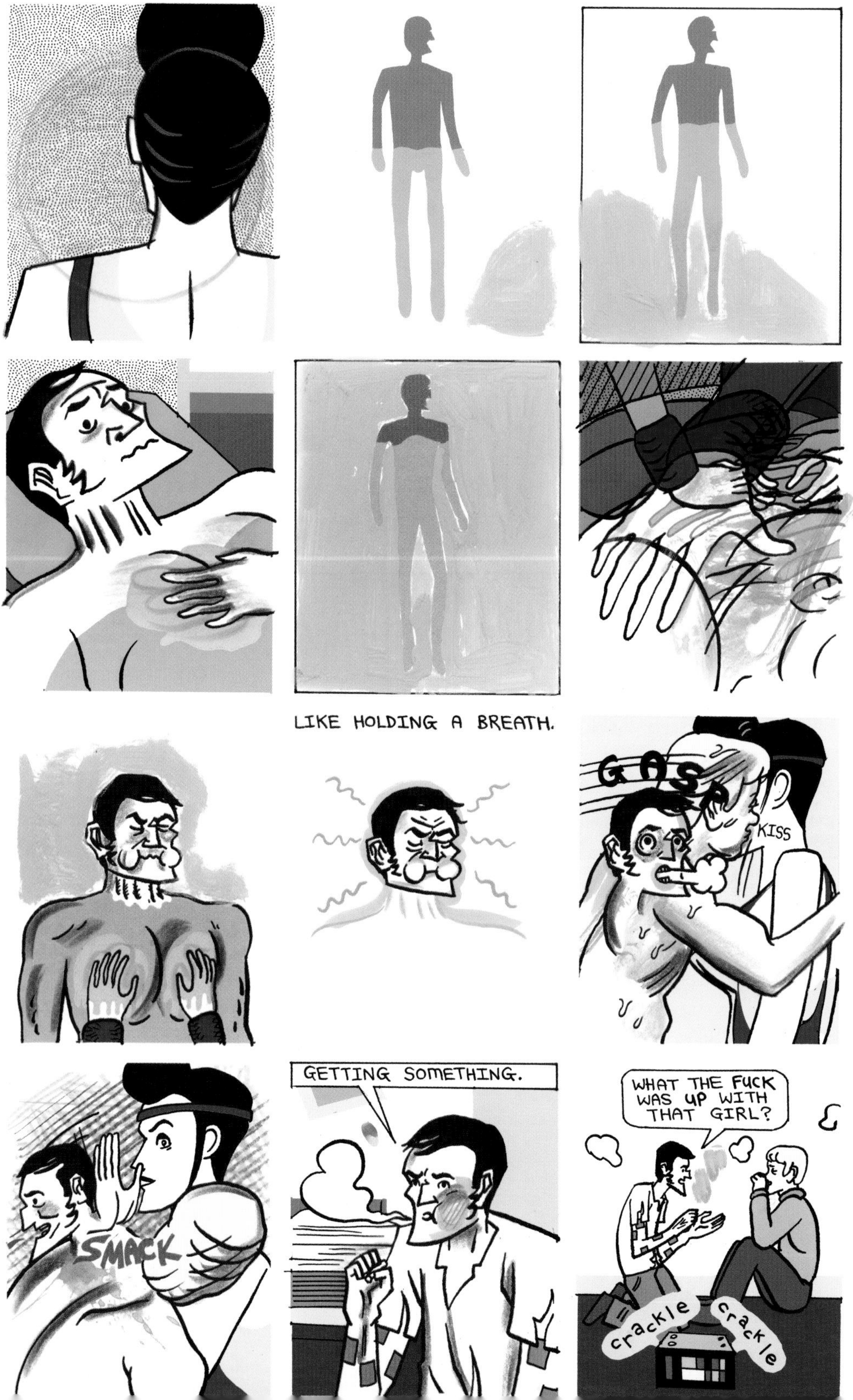
LIKE HOLDING A BREATH.
GASP
KISS
SMACK
GETTING SOMETHING.
WHAT THE FUCK WAS UP WITH THAT GIRL?
crackle
crackle

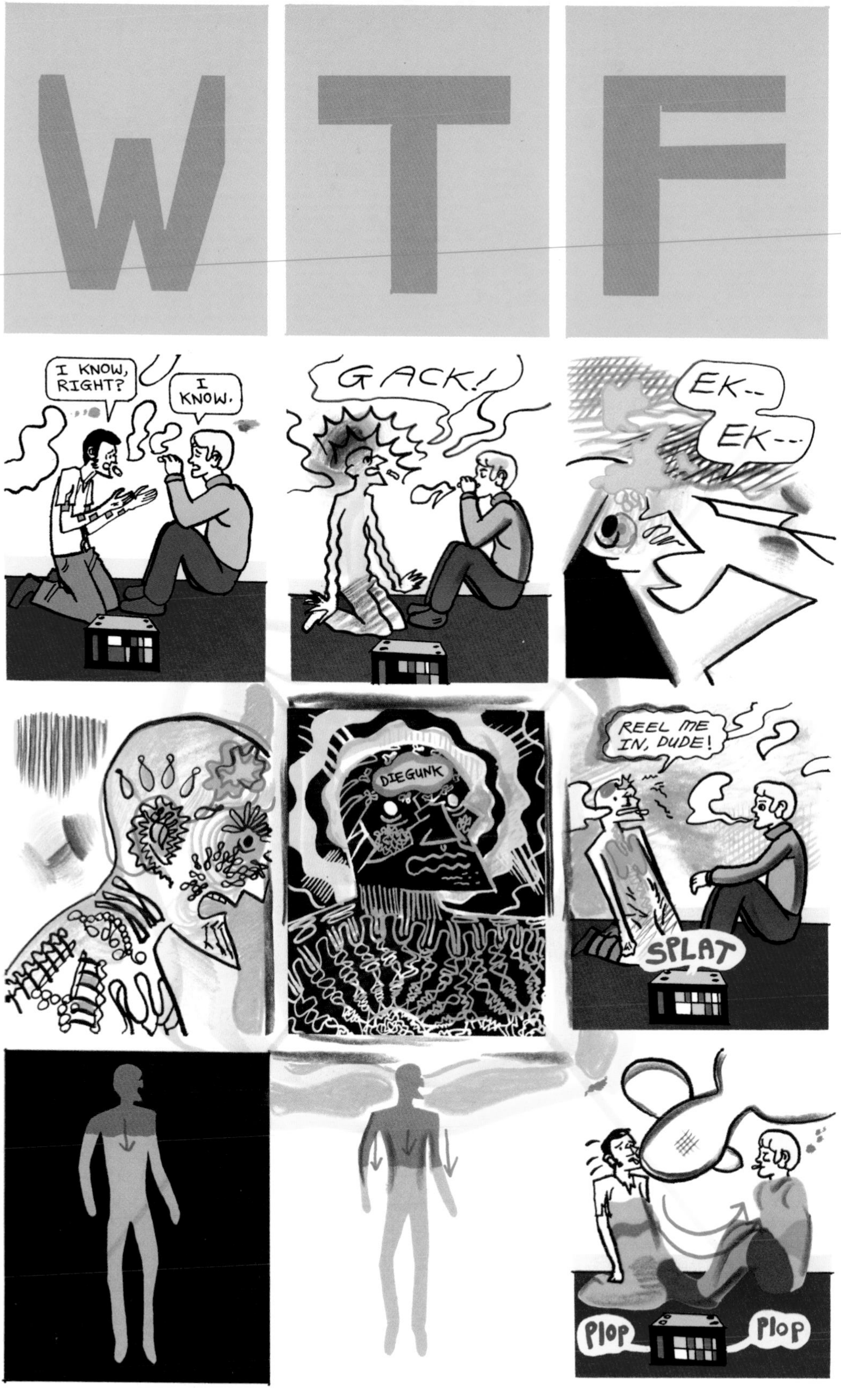

W
T
F
I KNOW, RIGHT?
I KNOW.
GACK!
EK--
EK--
DIEGUNK
REEL ME IN, DUDE!
SPLAT
PLOP
PLOP

STRETCHING OUT.

HA.

HA.

HA HA HA FEELS SO WEIRD.

HA HA
HA HA
HA HA
HA HA

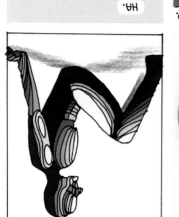

I'M GETTING SOMETHING.

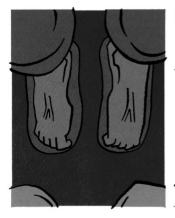

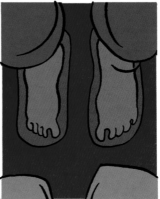

PA-TING

PA-TING

HOO.

BUTT SHRINKING. IT FEELS LIKE I'M SINKING DOWN.

MY STOMACH FEELS KINDA SICK AND EMPTY.

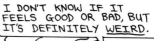

I DON'T KNOW IF IT FEELS GOOD OR BAD, BUT IT'S DEFINITELY WEIRD.

ROWF! ROWF!

AND... MY FACE...

LIKE I'M SUCKING IN MY CHEEKS...

AND I'M LOSING VISION. I SEE LESS.

WHAT?

MY VISION IS FINE!

CRASH

YOU WERE WITH HER TOO.

IN THIS ROOM.

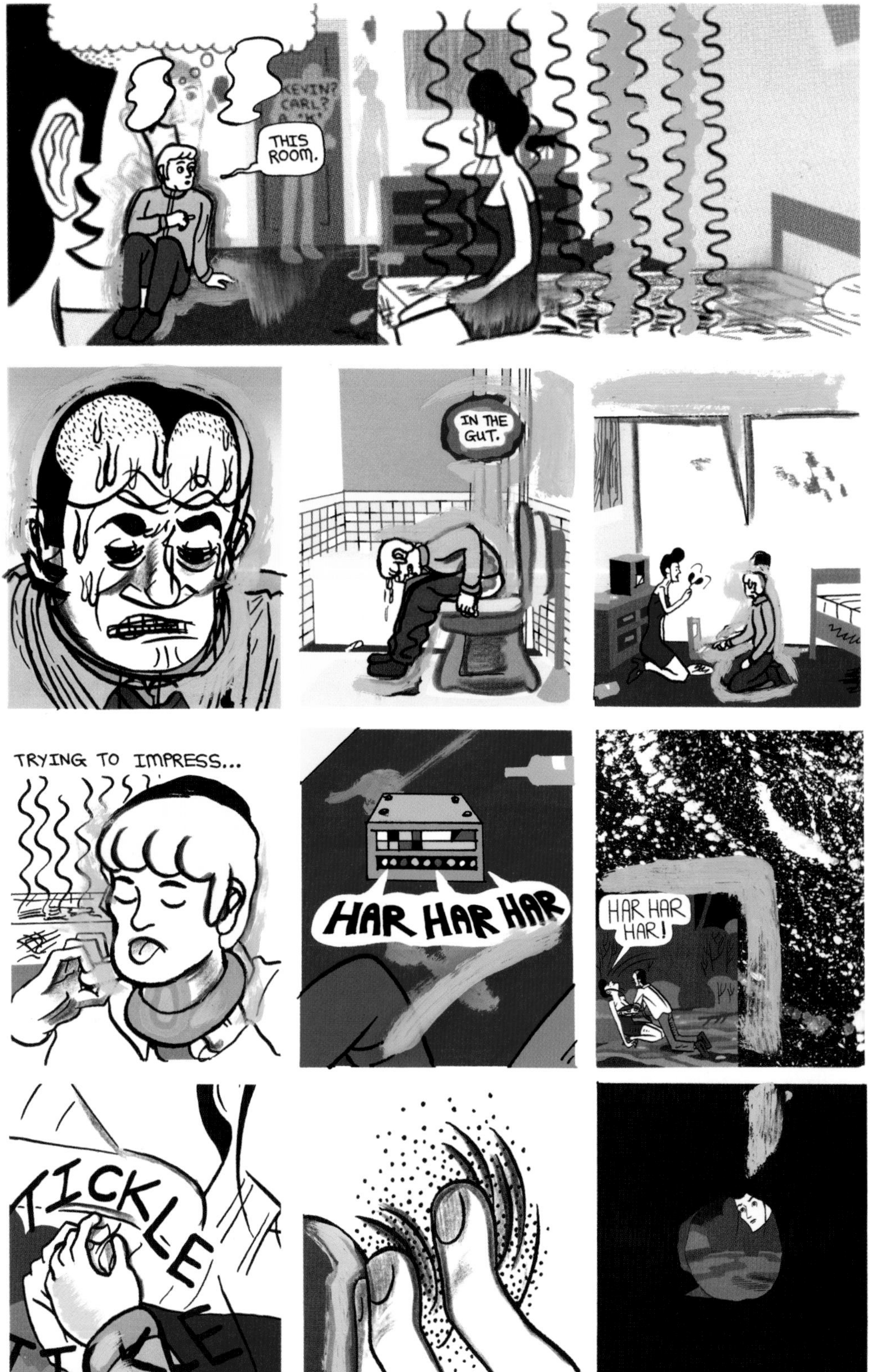
KEVIN?
CARL?
A "K"
THIS ROOM.
IN THE GUT.
TRYING TO IMPRESS...
HAR HAR HAR
HAR HAR HAR!
TICKLE
TICKLE

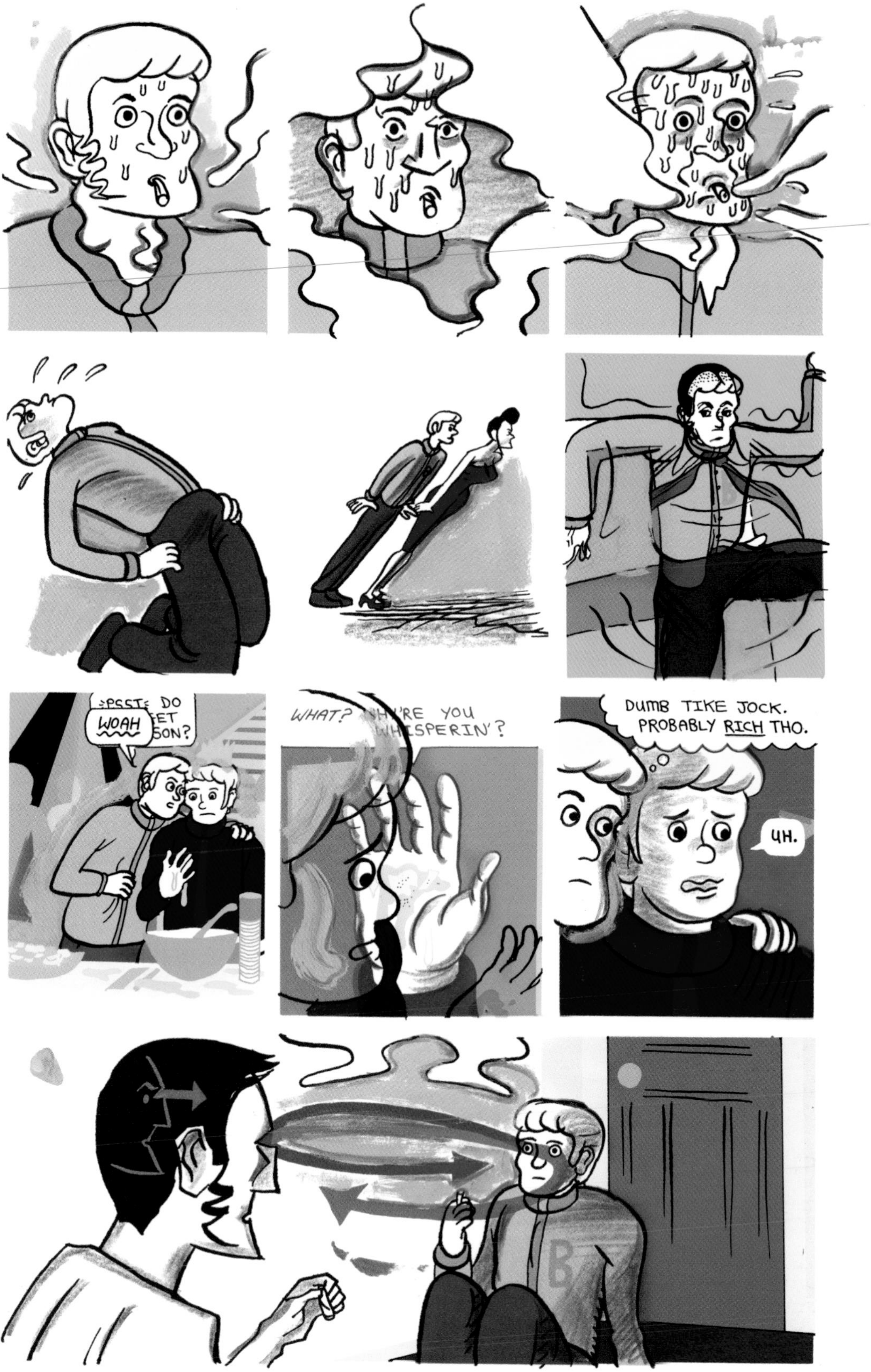

PSST DO
ET
SON?
WOAH
WHAT? WH'RE YOU WHISPERIN'?
DUMB TIKE JOCK. PROBABLY RICH THO.
UH.

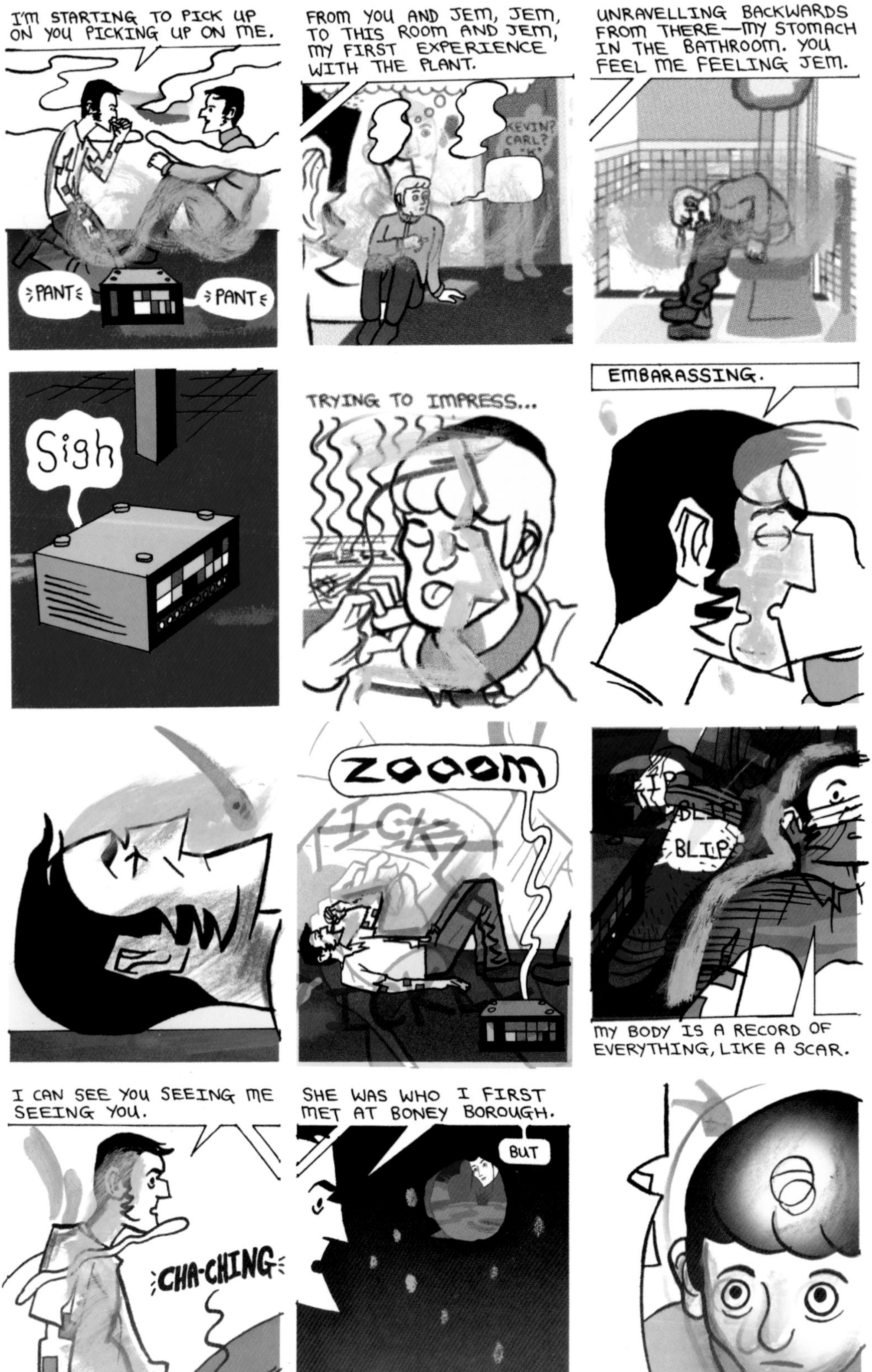

I'M STARTING TO PICK UP ON YOU PICKING UP ON ME.
PANT
PANT
FROM YOU AND JEM, JEM, TO THIS ROOM AND JEM, MY FIRST EXPERIENCE WITH THE PLANT.
KEVIN? CARL?
UNRAVELLING BACKWARDS FROM THERE—MY STOMACH IN THE BATHROOM. YOU FEEL ME FEELING JEM.
Sigh
TRYING TO IMPRESS...
EMBARASSING.
ZOOOM
BLIP
BLIP
MY BODY IS A RECORD OF EVERYTHING, LIKE A SCAR.
I CAN SEE YOU SEEING ME SEEING YOU.
CHA-CHING
SHE WAS WHO I FIRST MET AT BONEY BOROUGH.
BUT

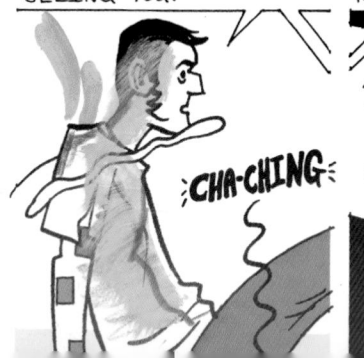

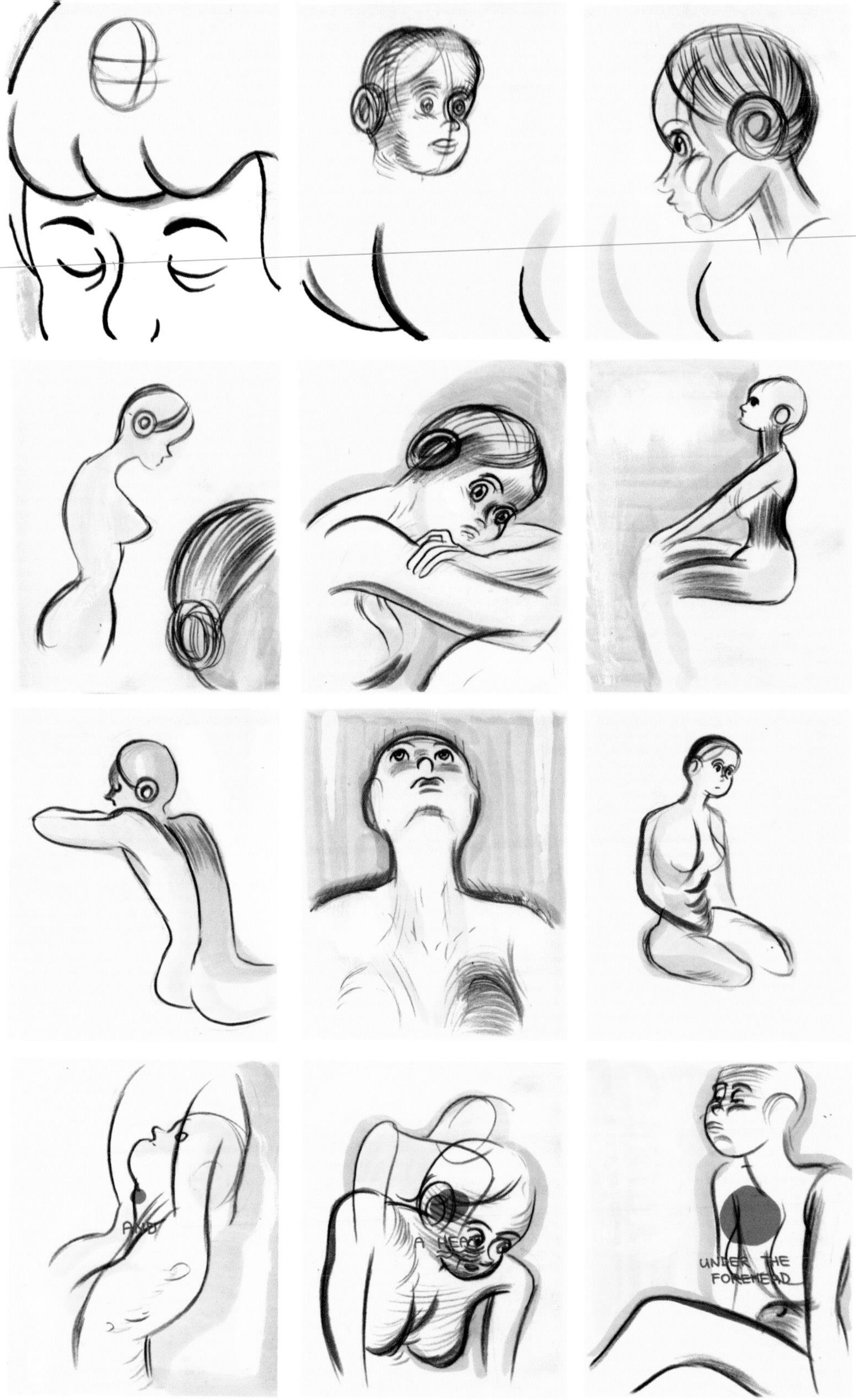
AND
A HEA
UNDER THE
FOREHEAD

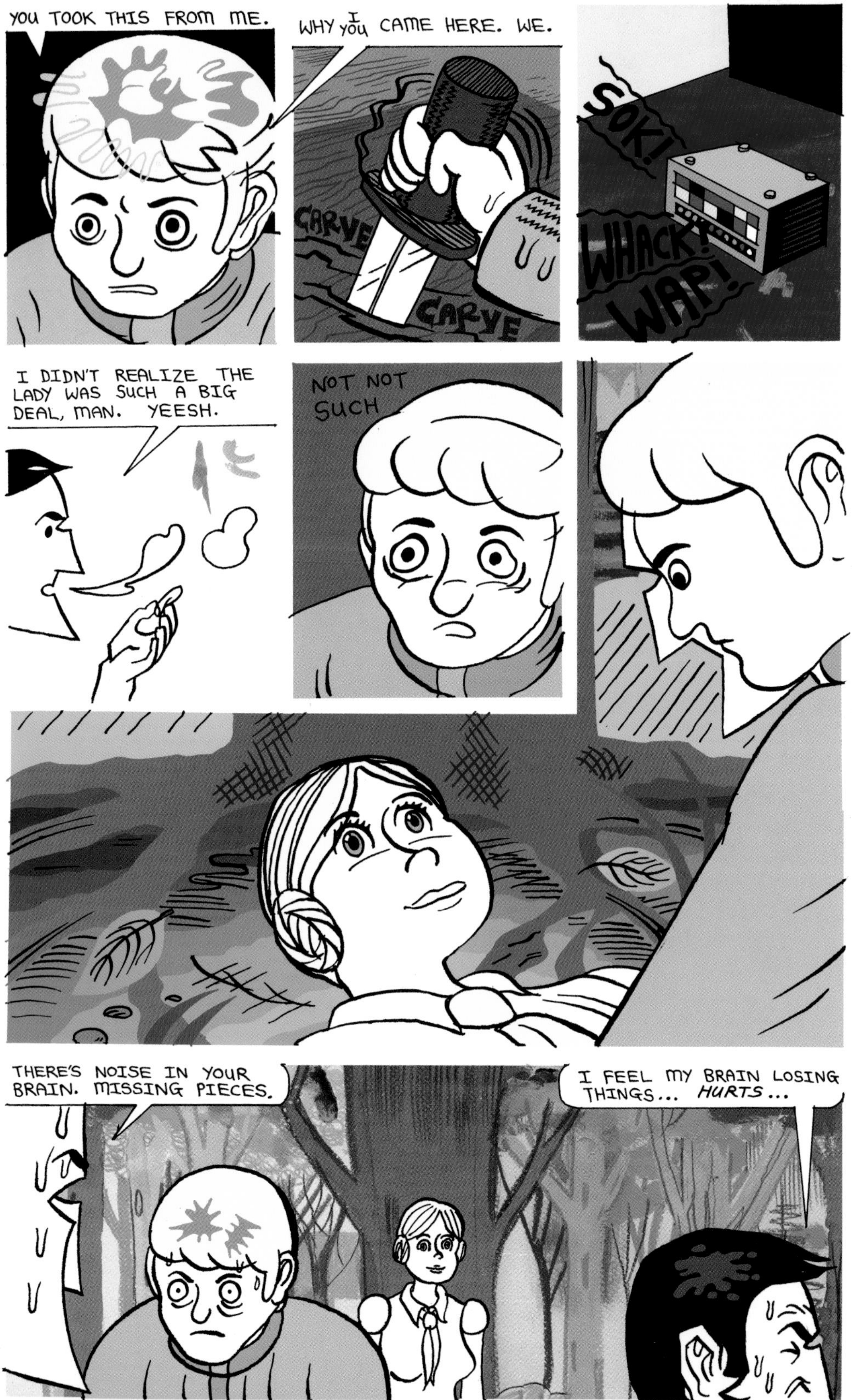
YOU TOOK THIS FROM ME.
WHY I you CAME HERE. WE.
CARVE
CARVE
SOK!
WHACK!
WAP!
I DIDN'T REALIZE THE LADY WAS SUCH A BIG DEAL, MAN. YEESH.
NOT NOT SUCH
THERE'S NOISE IN YOUR BRAIN. MISSING PIECES.
I FEEL MY BRAIN LOSING THINGS... *HURTS*...

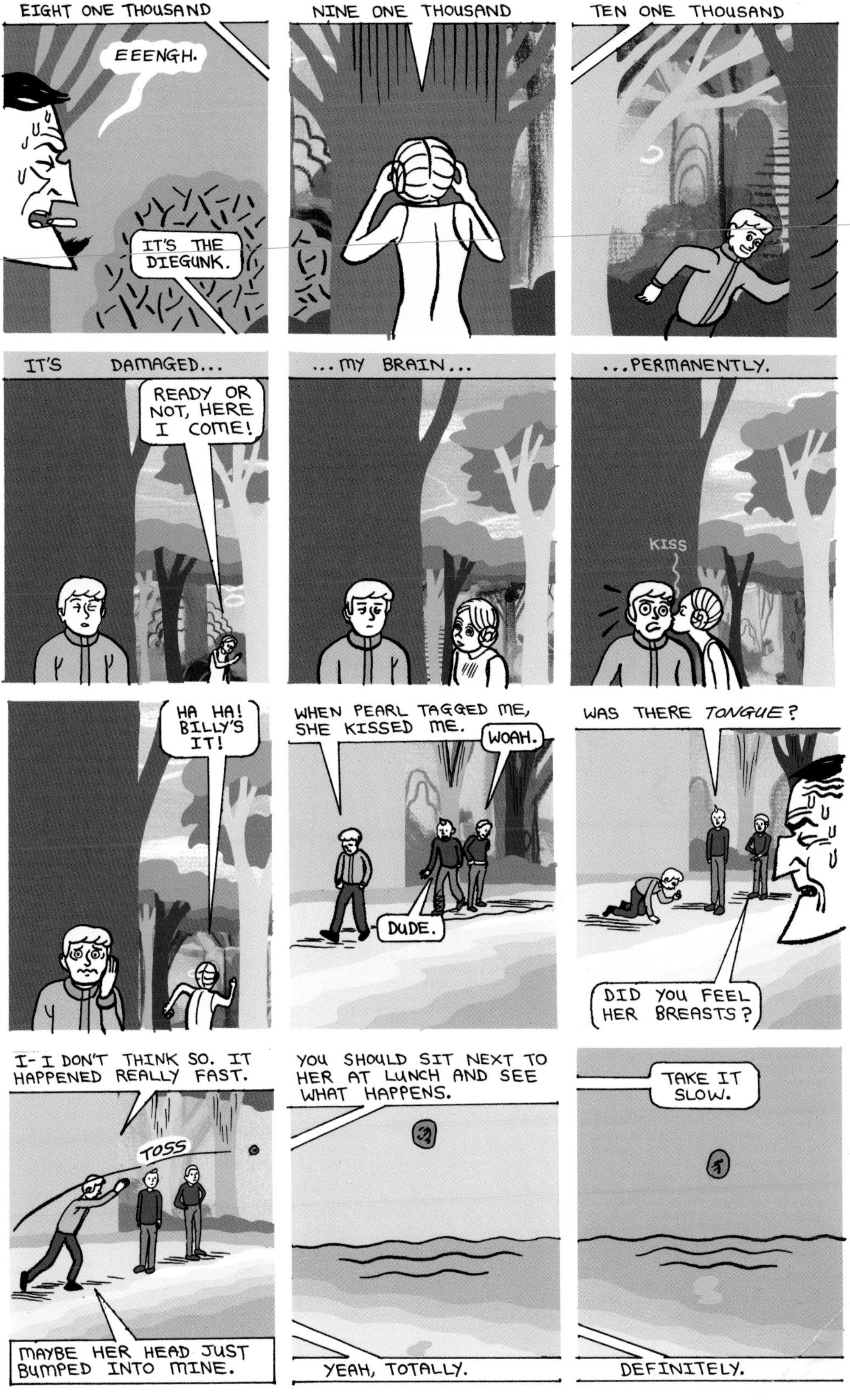
EIGHT ONE THOUSAND
EEENGH.
IT'S THE DIEGUNK.
NINE ONE THOUSAND
TEN ONE THOUSAND
IT'S DAMAGED...
READY OR NOT, HERE I COME!
...MY BRAIN...
...PERMANENTLY.
KISS
HA HA! BILLY'S IT!
WHEN PEARL TAGGED ME, SHE KISSED ME.
WOAH.
DUDE.
WAS THERE TONGUE?
DID YOU FEEL HER BREASTS?
I- I DON'T THINK SO. IT HAPPENED REALLY FAST.
TOSS
MAYBE HER HEAD JUST BUMPED INTO MINE.
YOU SHOULD SIT NEXT TO HER AT LUNCH AND SEE WHAT HAPPENS.
YEAH, TOTALLY.
TAKE IT SLOW.
DEFINITELY.

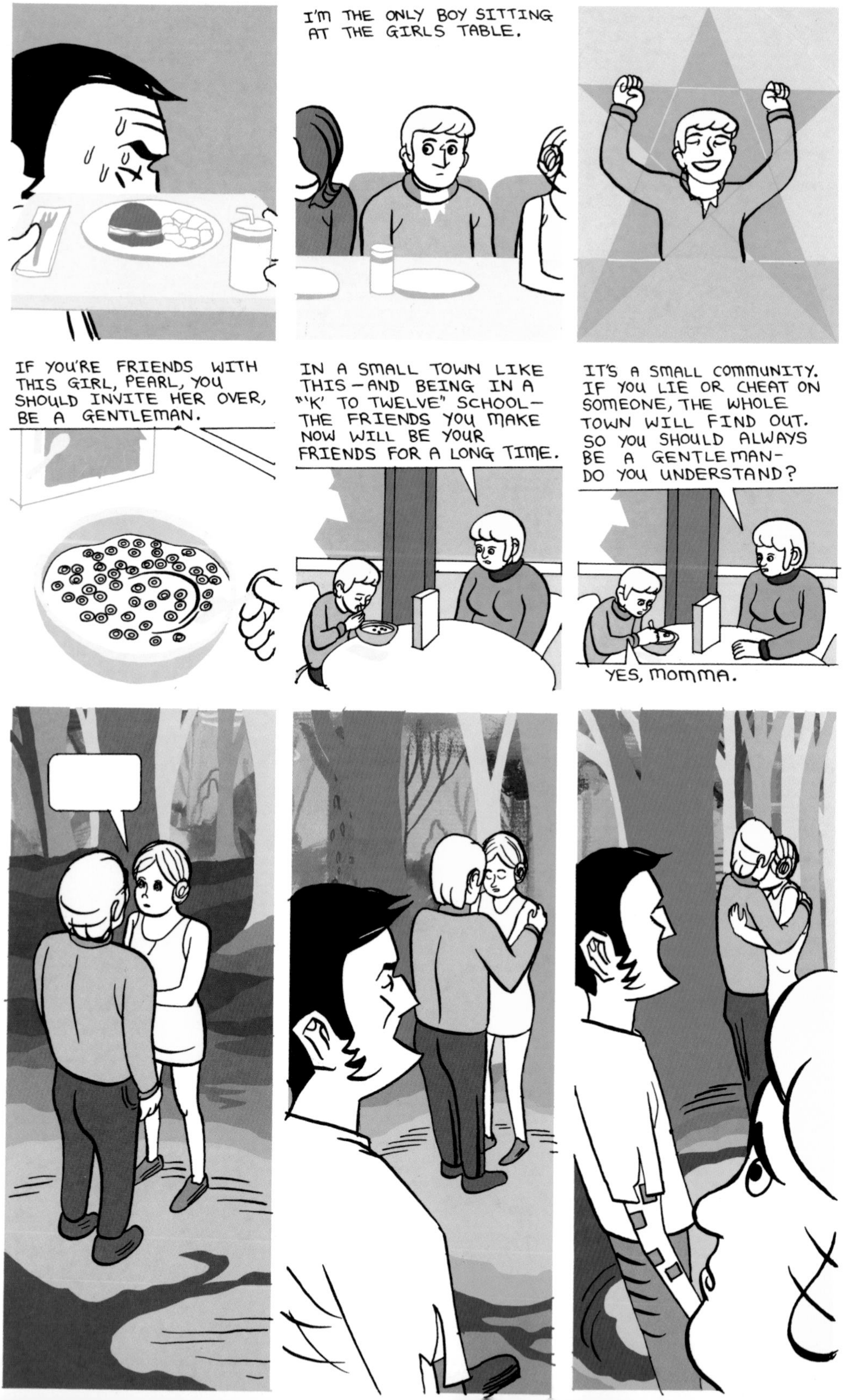
I'M THE ONLY BOY SITTING AT THE GIRLS TABLE.
IF YOU'RE FRIENDS WITH THIS GIRL, PEARL, YOU SHOULD INVITE HER OVER, BE A GENTLEMAN.
IN A SMALL TOWN LIKE THIS—AND BEING IN A "'K' TO TWELVE" SCHOOL—THE FRIENDS YOU MAKE NOW WILL BE YOUR FRIENDS FOR A LONG TIME.
IT'S A SMALL COMMUNITY. IF YOU LIE OR CHEAT ON SOMEONE, THE WHOLE TOWN WILL FIND OUT. SO YOU SHOULD ALWAYS BE A GENTLEMAN-DO YOU UNDERSTAND?
YES, MOMMA.

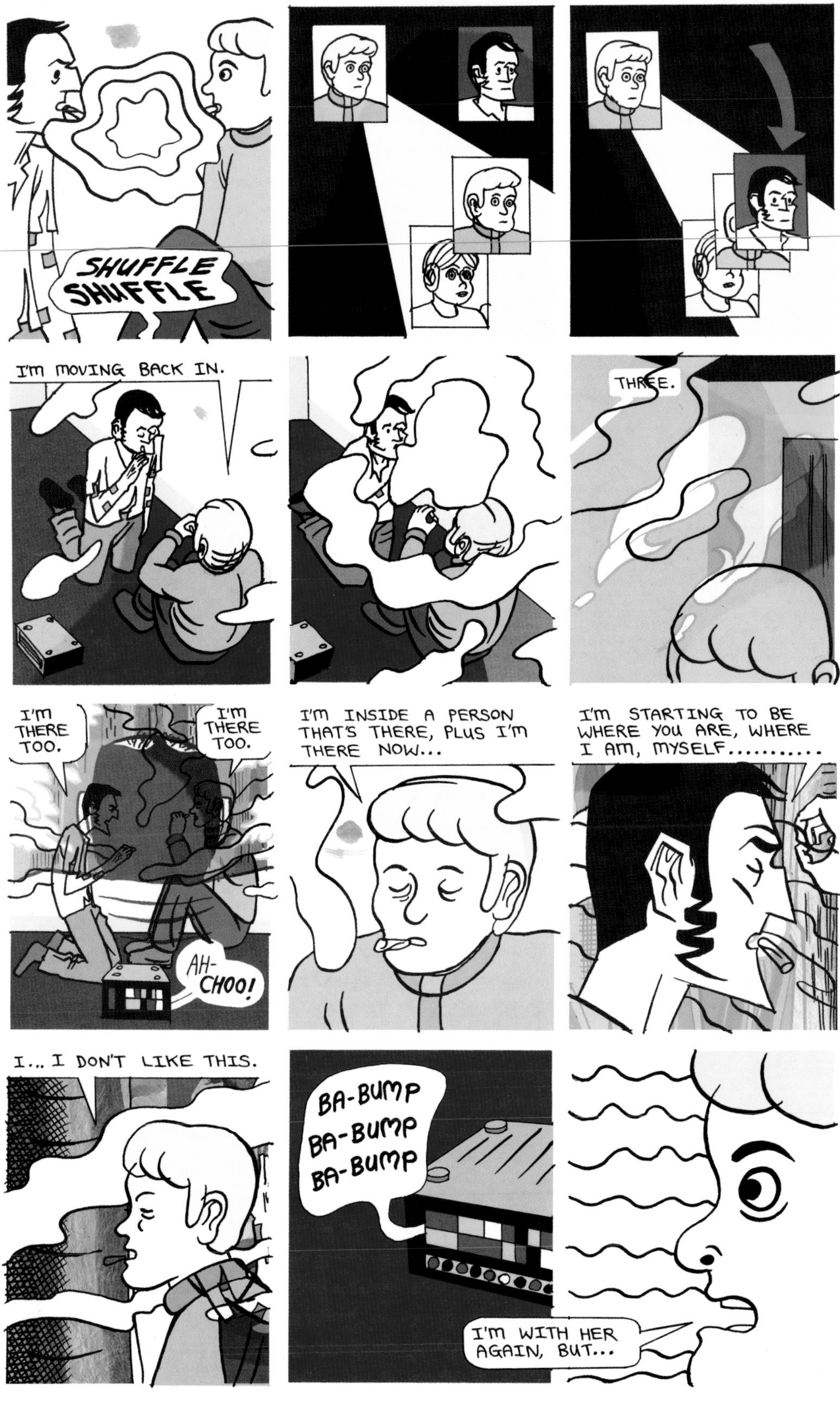
SHUFFLE
SHUFFLE
I'M MOVING BACK IN.
THREE.
I'M THERE TOO.
I'M THERE TOO.
AH-CHOO!
I'M INSIDE A PERSON THAT'S THERE, PLUS I'M THERE NOW...
I'M STARTING TO BE WHERE YOU ARE, WHERE I AM, MYSELF..........
I... I DON'T LIKE THIS.
BA-BUMP
BA-BUMP
BA-BUMP
I'M WITH HER AGAIN, BUT...

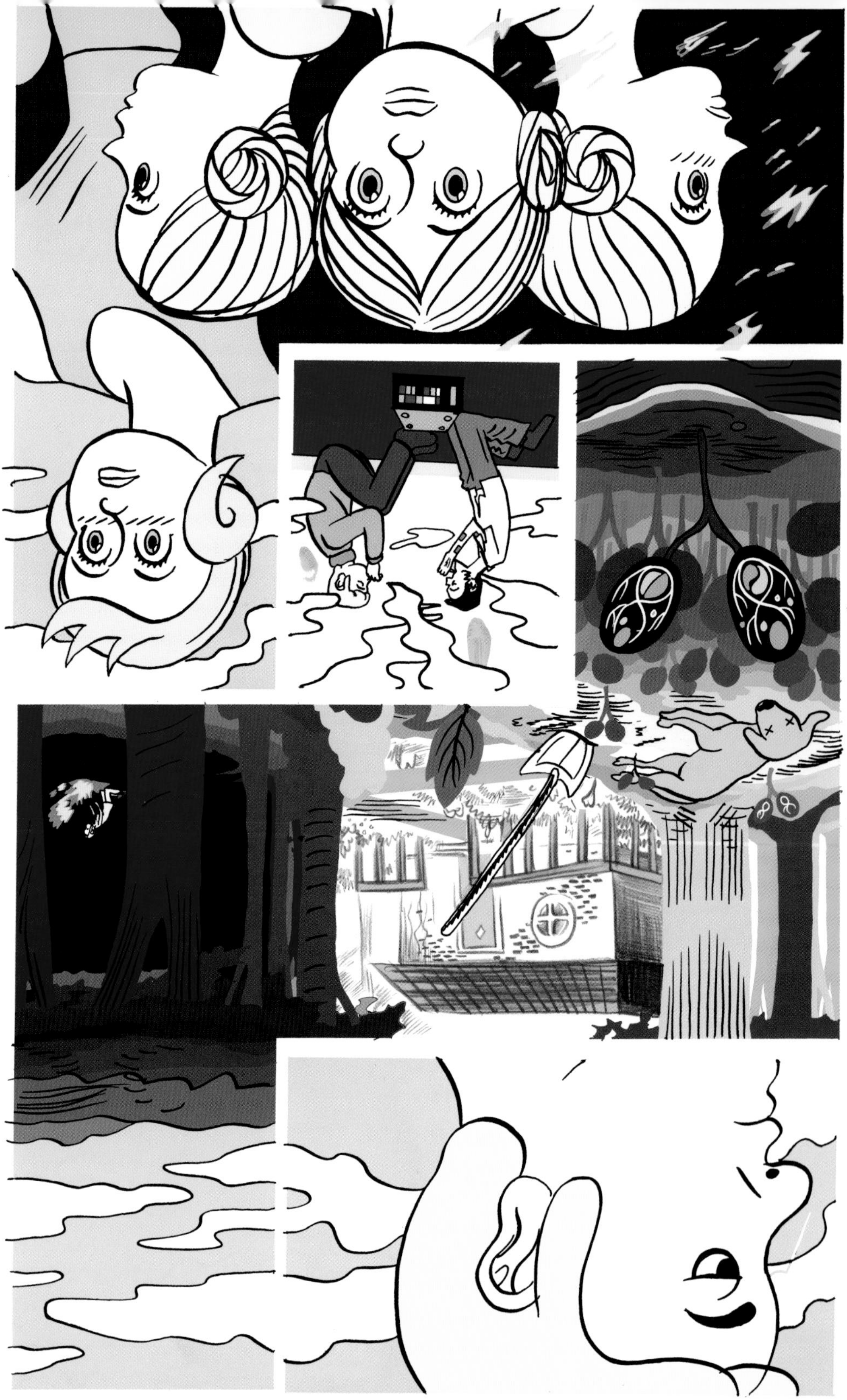

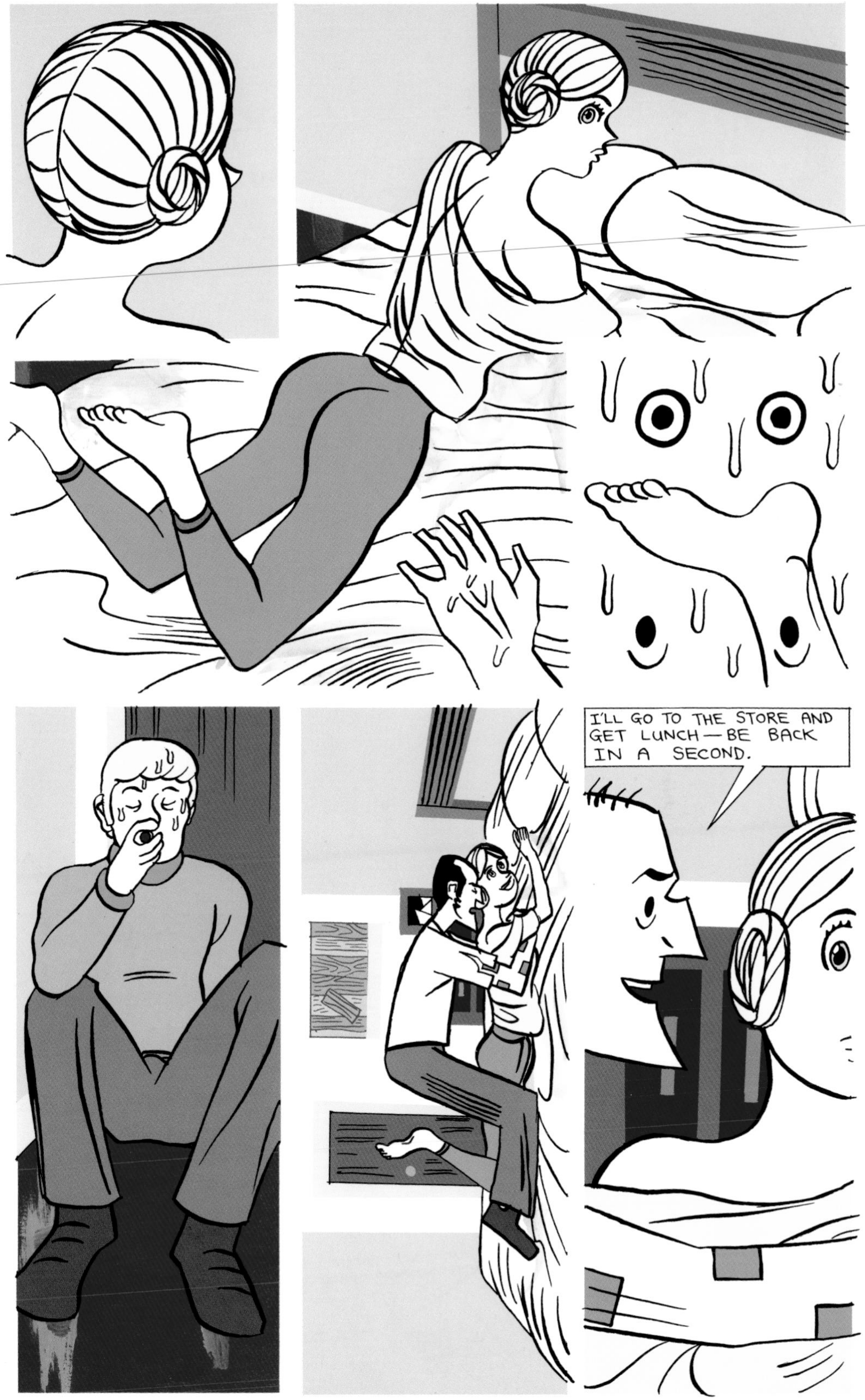
I'LL GO TO THE STORE AND GET LUNCH — BE BACK IN A SECOND.

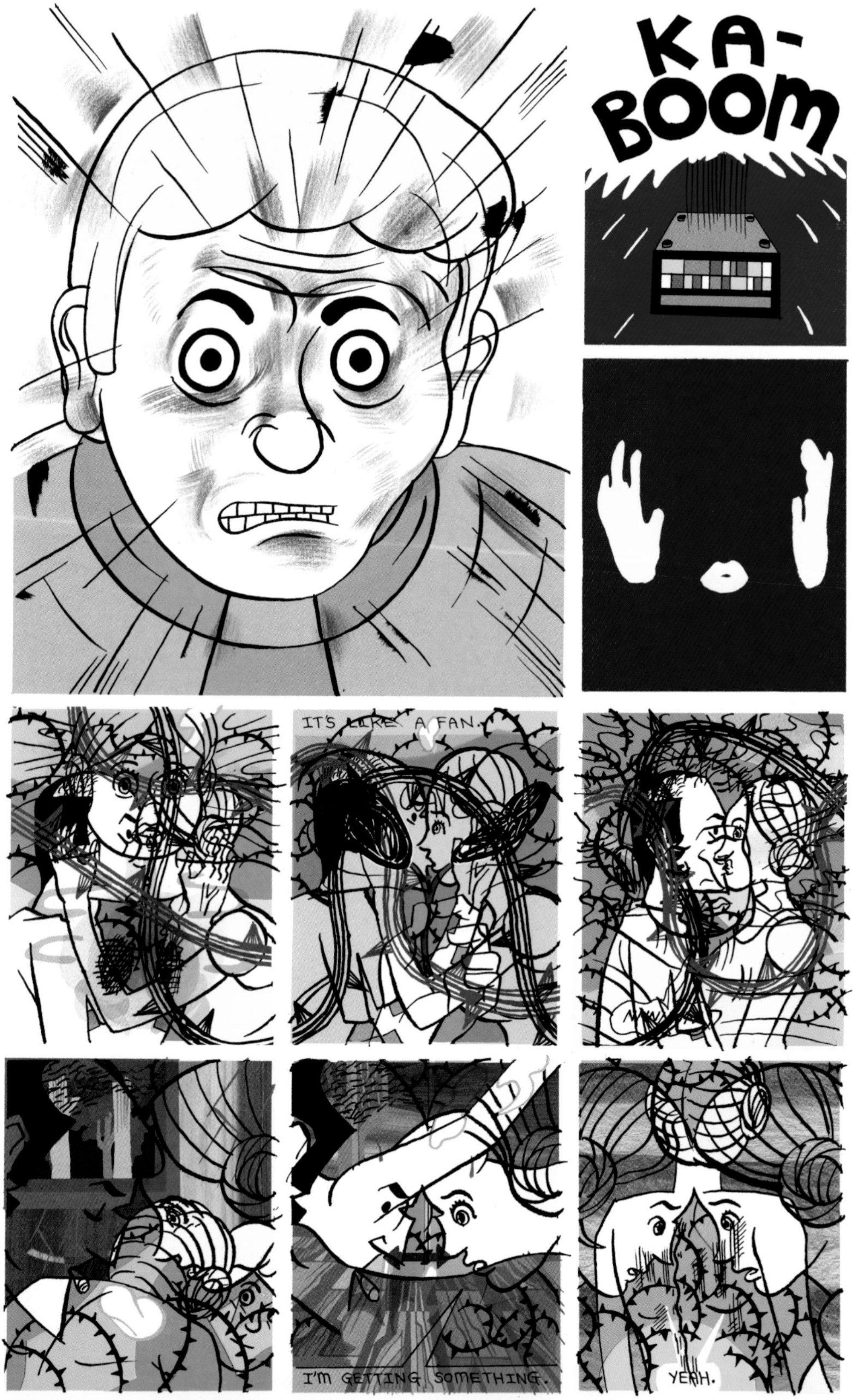
KA-BOOM
IT'S LIKE A FAN.
I'M GETTING SOMETHING.
YEAH.

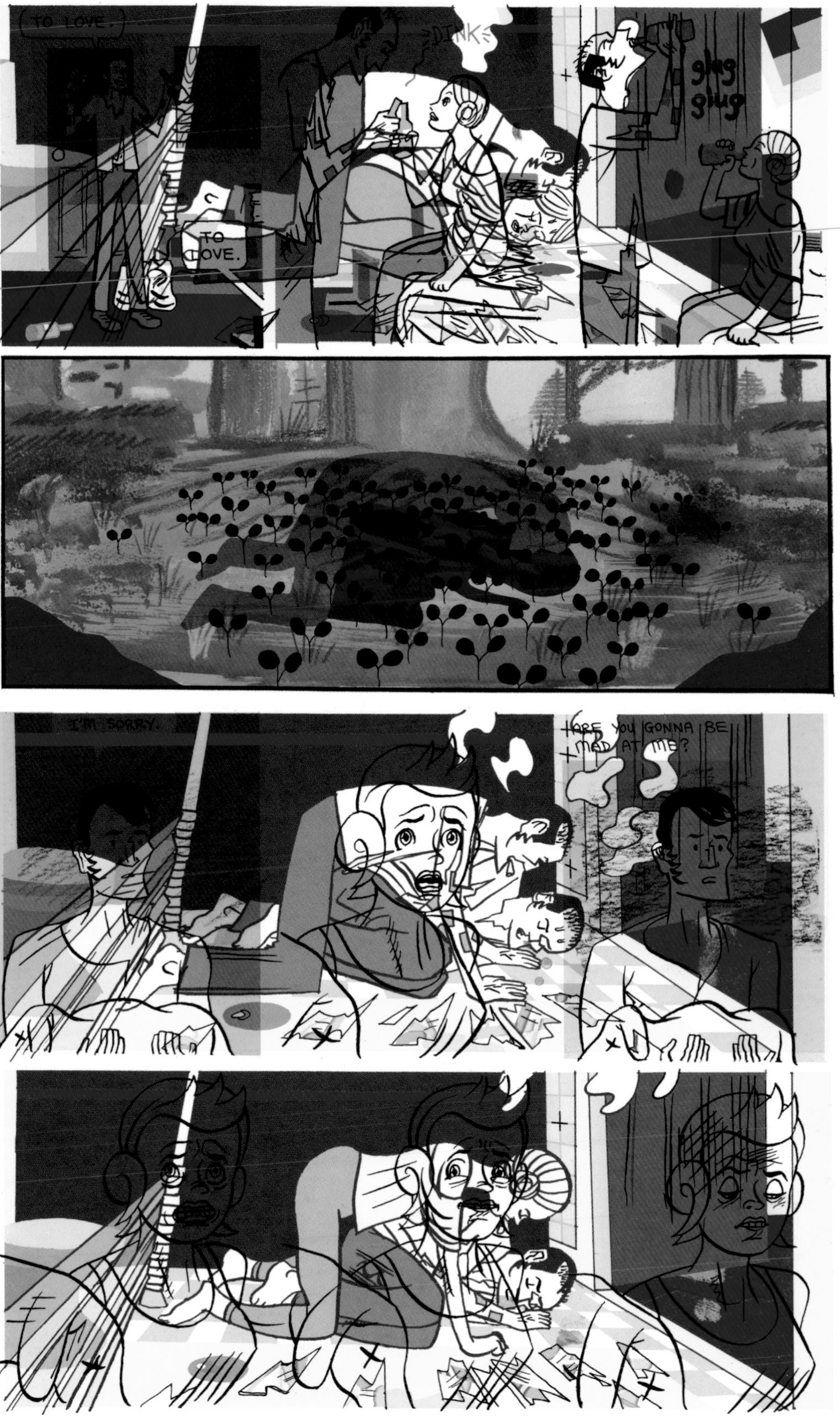
TO LOVE.
DINK
TO LOVE.
glug glug
I'M SORRY.
ARE YOU GONNA BE MAD AT ME?

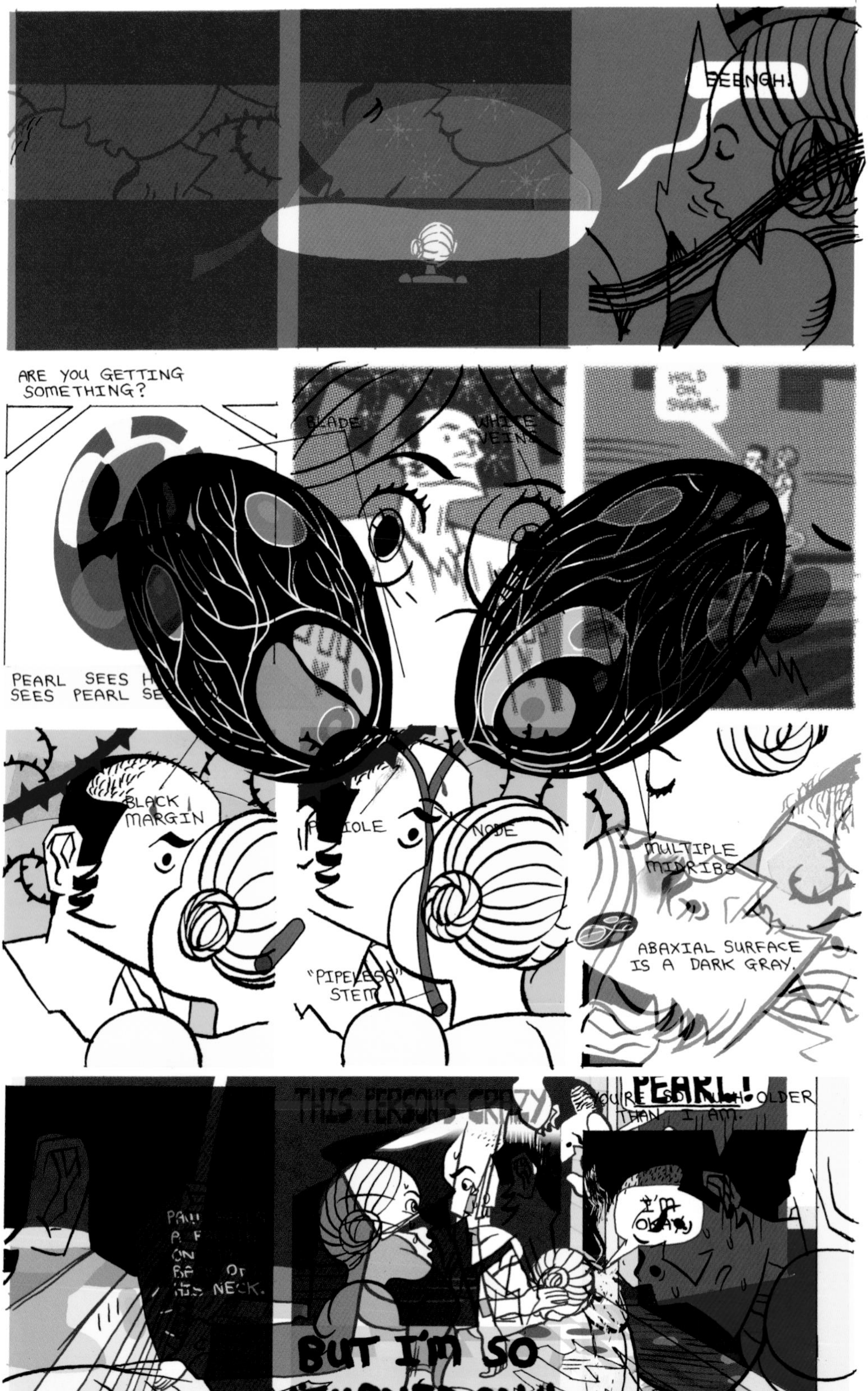
BEENGH!
ARE YOU GETTING SOMETHING?
BLADE
WHITE VEINS
PEARL SEES H
SEES PEARL SE
BLACK MARGIN
PETIOLE
NODE
"PIPELESS" STEM
MULTIPLE MIDRIBS
ABAXIAL SURFACE IS A DARK GRAY.
THIS PERSON'S CRAZY
PEARL!
YOU'RE SO MUCH OLDER THAN I AM.
I'M OKAY
BUT I'M SO "TURNED-ON."

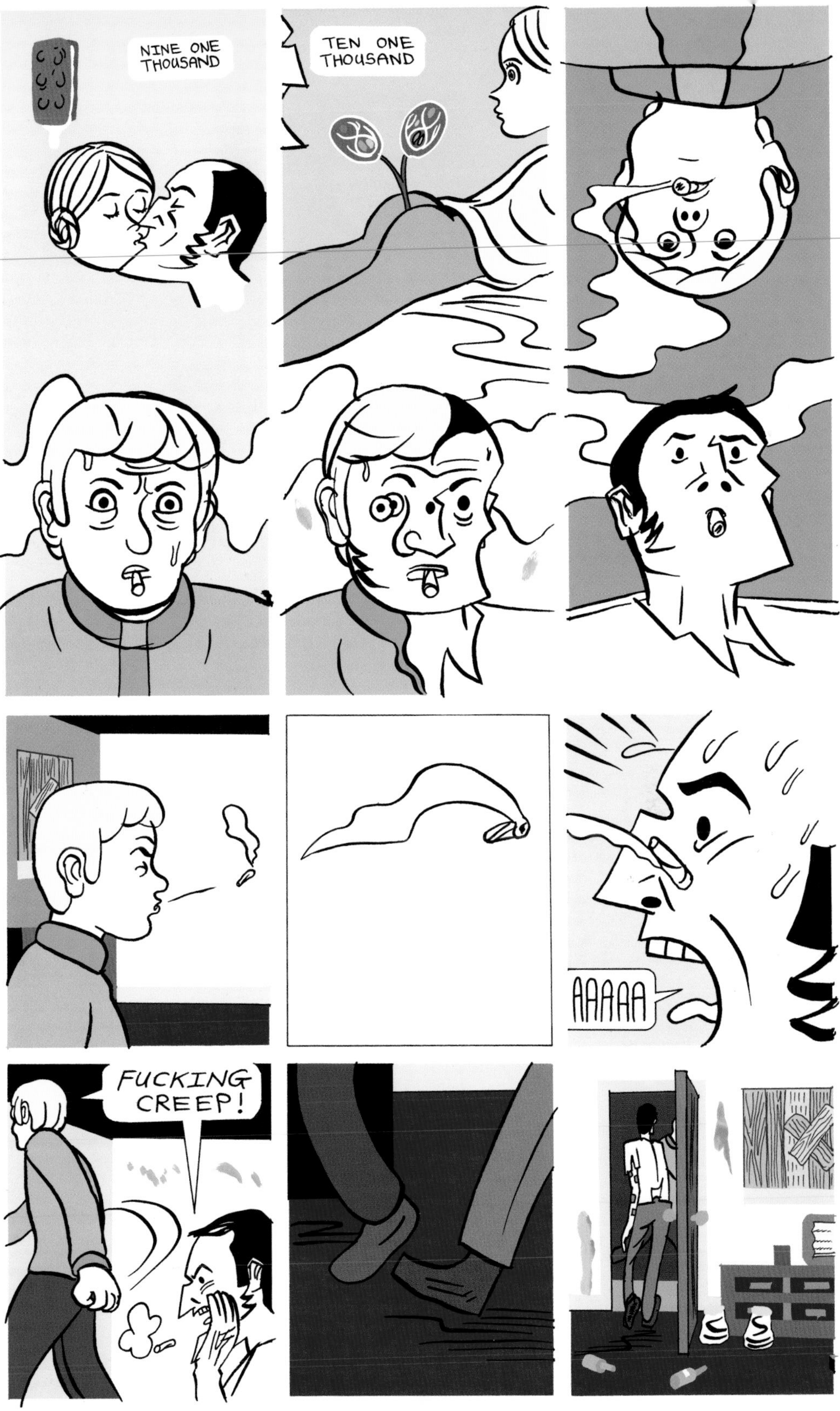
NINE ONE THOUSAND
TEN ONE THOUSAND
AAAAA
FUCKING CREEP!

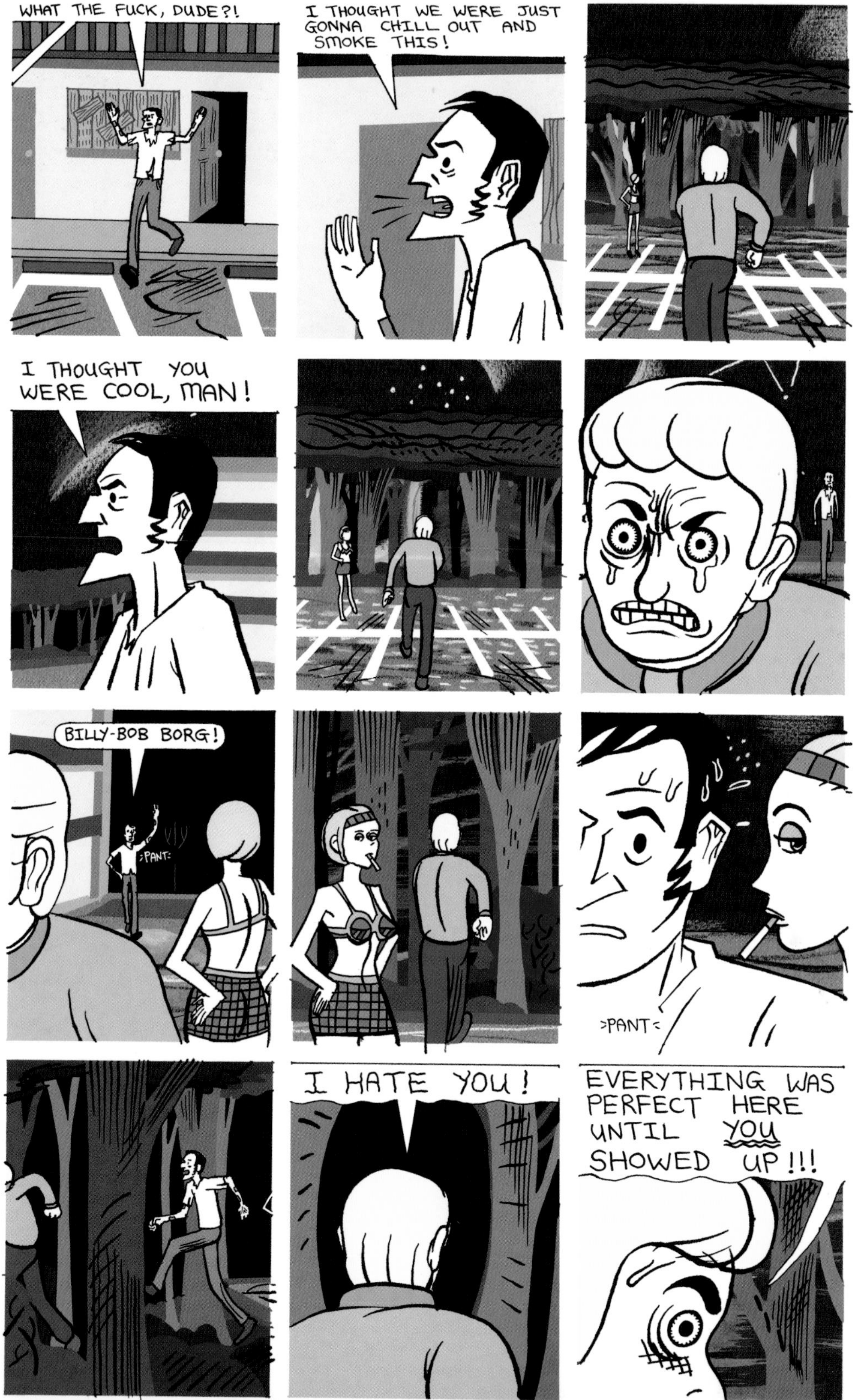
WHAT THE FUCK, DUDE?!
I THOUGHT WE WERE JUST GONNA CHILL OUT AND SMOKE THIS!
I THOUGHT YOU WERE COOL, MAN!
BILLY-BOB BORG!
>PANT<
>PANT<
I HATE YOU!
EVERYTHING WAS PERFECT HERE UNTIL YOU SHOWED UP!!!

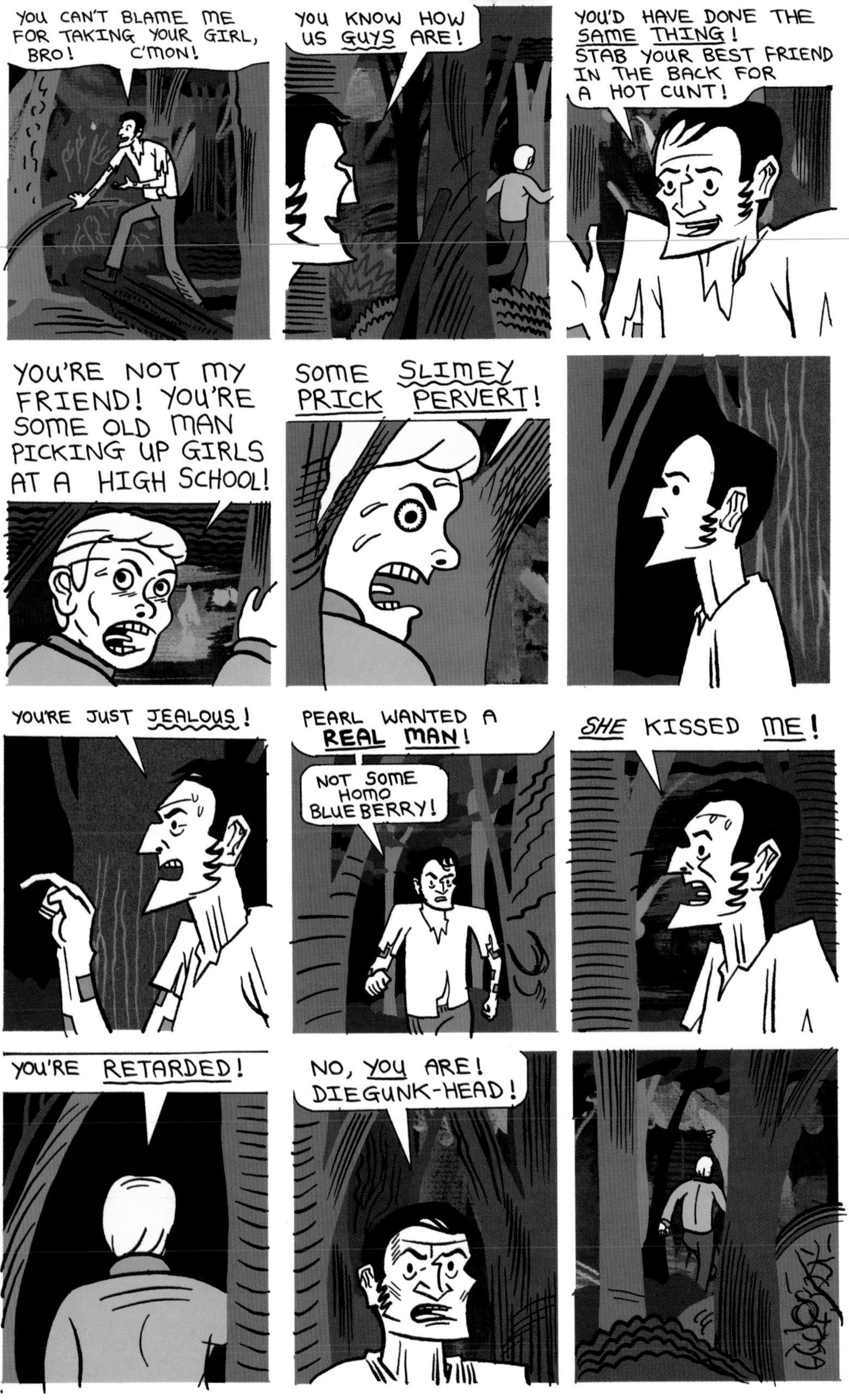
YOU CAN'T BLAME ME FOR TAKING YOUR GIRL, BRO! C'MON!
YOU KNOW HOW US GUYS ARE!
YOU'D HAVE DONE THE SAME THING! STAB YOUR BEST FRIEND IN THE BACK FOR A HOT CUNT!
YOU'RE NOT MY FRIEND! YOU'RE SOME OLD MAN PICKING UP GIRLS AT A HIGH SCHOOL!
SOME SLIMEY PRICK PERVERT!
YOU'RE JUST JEALOUS!
PEARL WANTED A REAL MAN!
NOT SOME HOMO BLUEBERRY!
SHE KISSED ME!
YOU'RE RETARDED!
NO, YOU ARE! DIEGUNK-HEAD!

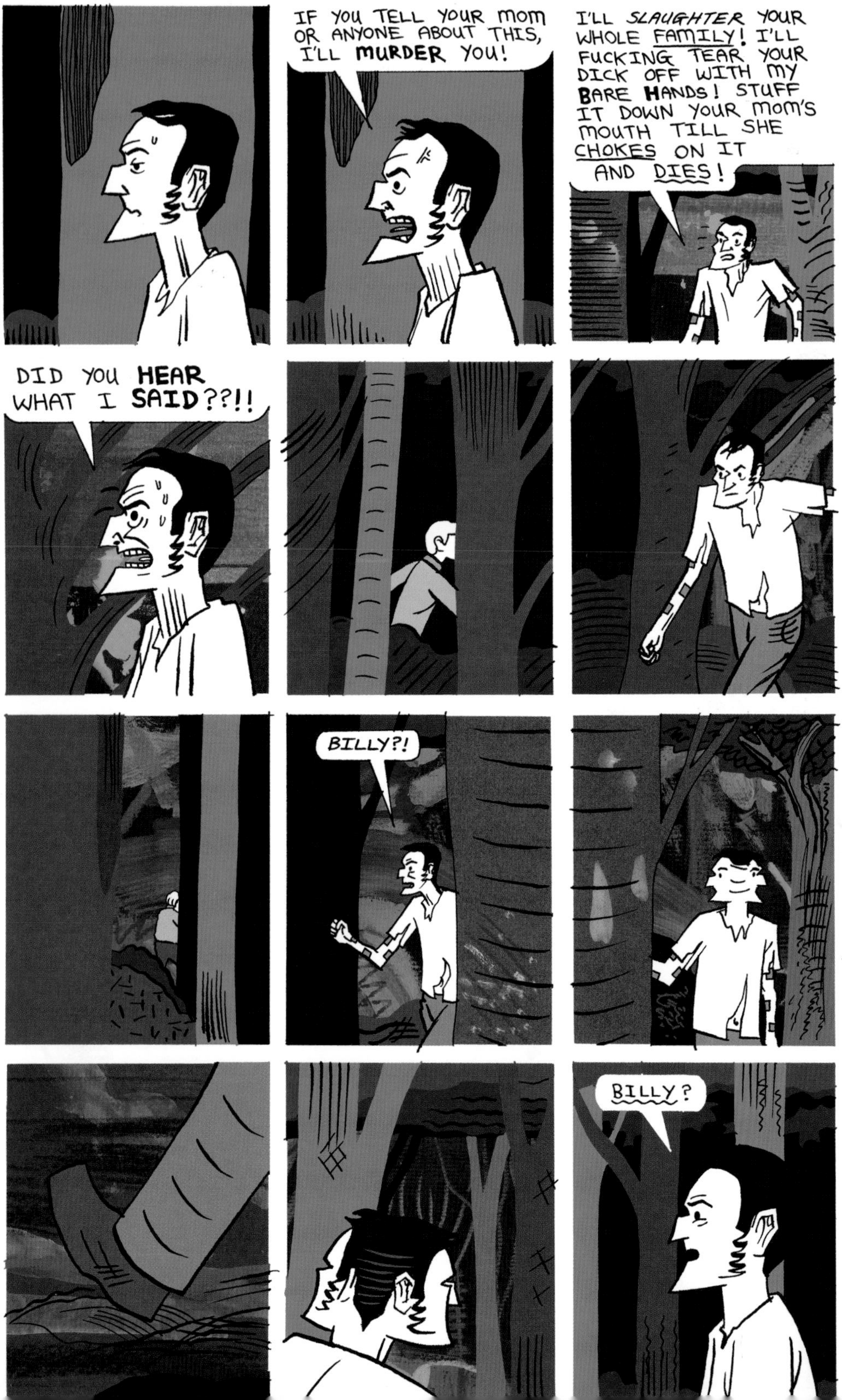
IF YOU TELL YOUR MOM OR ANYONE ABOUT THIS, I'LL **MURDER** YOU!
I'LL *SLAUGHTER* YOUR WHOLE FAMILY! I'LL FUCKING TEAR YOUR DICK OFF WITH MY **B**ARE **H**ANDS! STUFF IT DOWN YOUR MOM'S MOUTH TILL SHE CHOKES ON IT AND DIES!
DID YOU **HEAR** WHAT I **SAID**??!!
BILLY?!
BILLY?

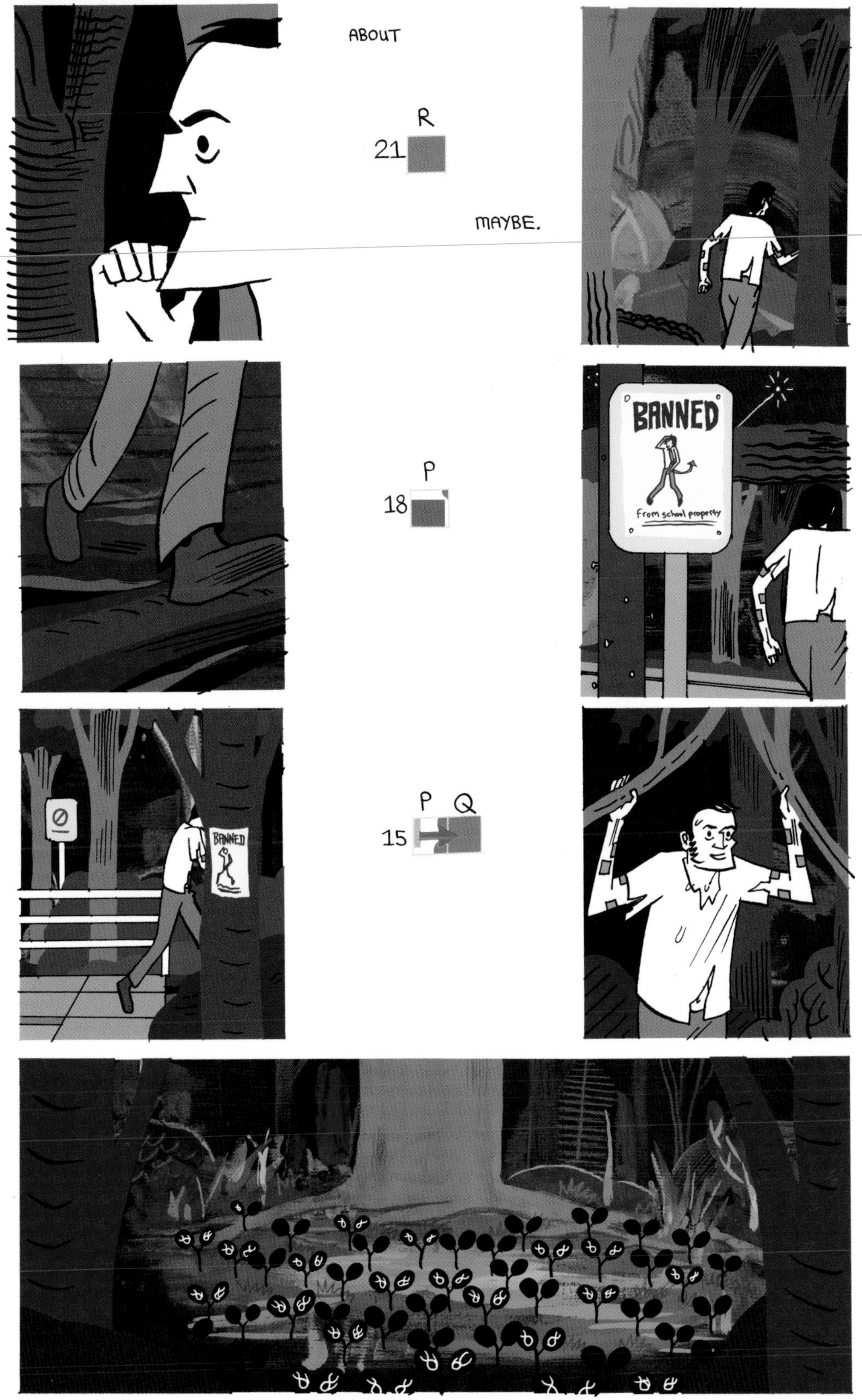
ABOUT
R
21
MAYBE.
P
18
BANNED
from school property
P Q
15
BANNED

PLUCK
PLUCK

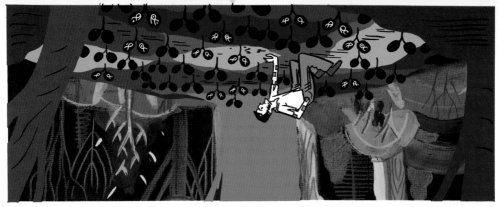

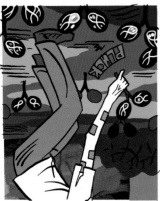

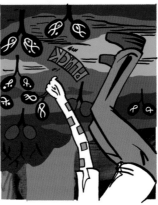

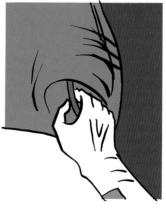

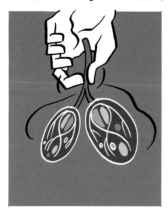

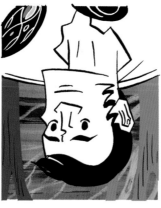

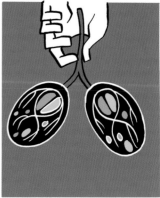

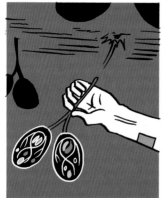

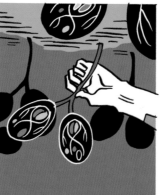

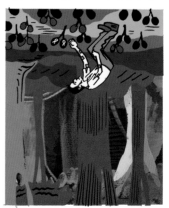

CRACK
shuffle
shuffle
shuffle

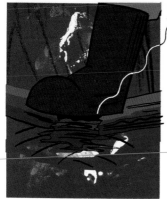

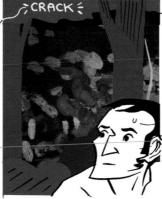

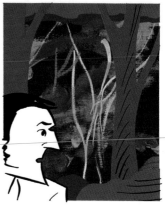

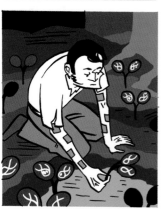

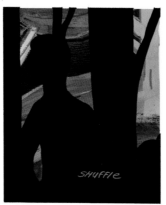

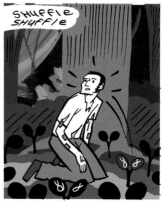

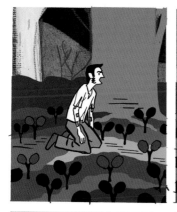

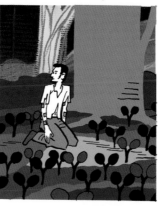

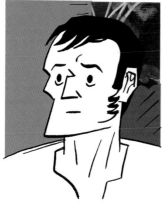

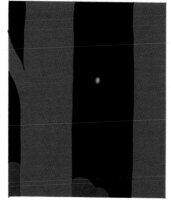

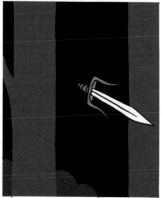

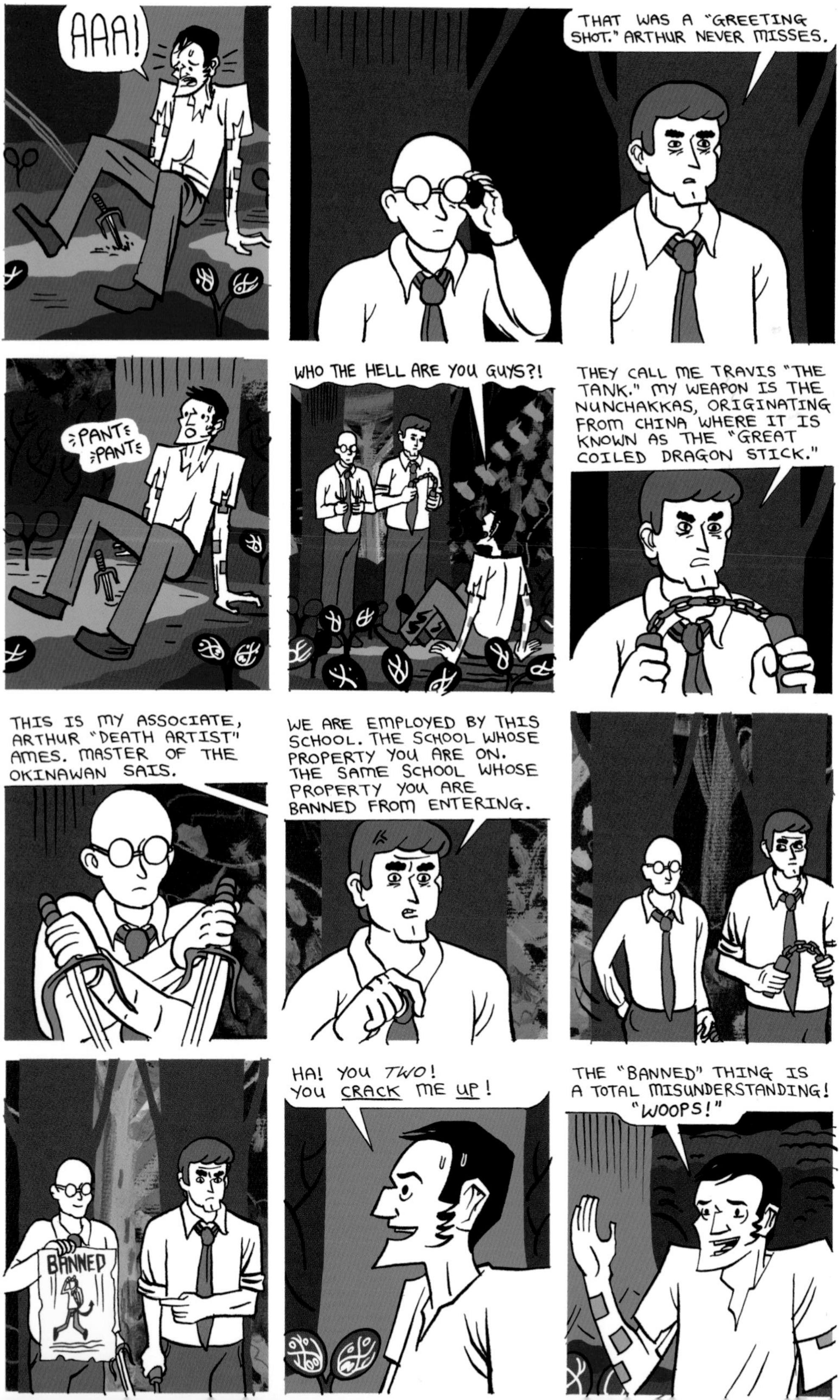
AAA!
THAT WAS A "GREETING SHOT." ARTHUR NEVER MISSES.
PANT PANT
WHO THE HELL ARE YOU GUYS?!
THEY CALL ME TRAVIS "THE TANK." MY WEAPON IS THE NUNCHAKKAS, ORIGINATING FROM CHINA WHERE IT IS KNOWN AS THE "GREAT COILED DRAGON STICK."
THIS IS MY ASSOCIATE, ARTHUR "DEATH ARTIST" AMES. MASTER OF THE OKINAWAN SAIS.
WE ARE EMPLOYED BY THIS SCHOOL. THE SCHOOL WHOSE PROPERTY YOU ARE ON. THE SAME SCHOOL WHOSE PROPERTY YOU ARE BANNED FROM ENTERING.
BANNED
HA! YOU *TWO*! YOU CRACK ME UP!
THE "BANNED" THING IS A TOTAL MISUNDERSTANDING! "WOOPS!"

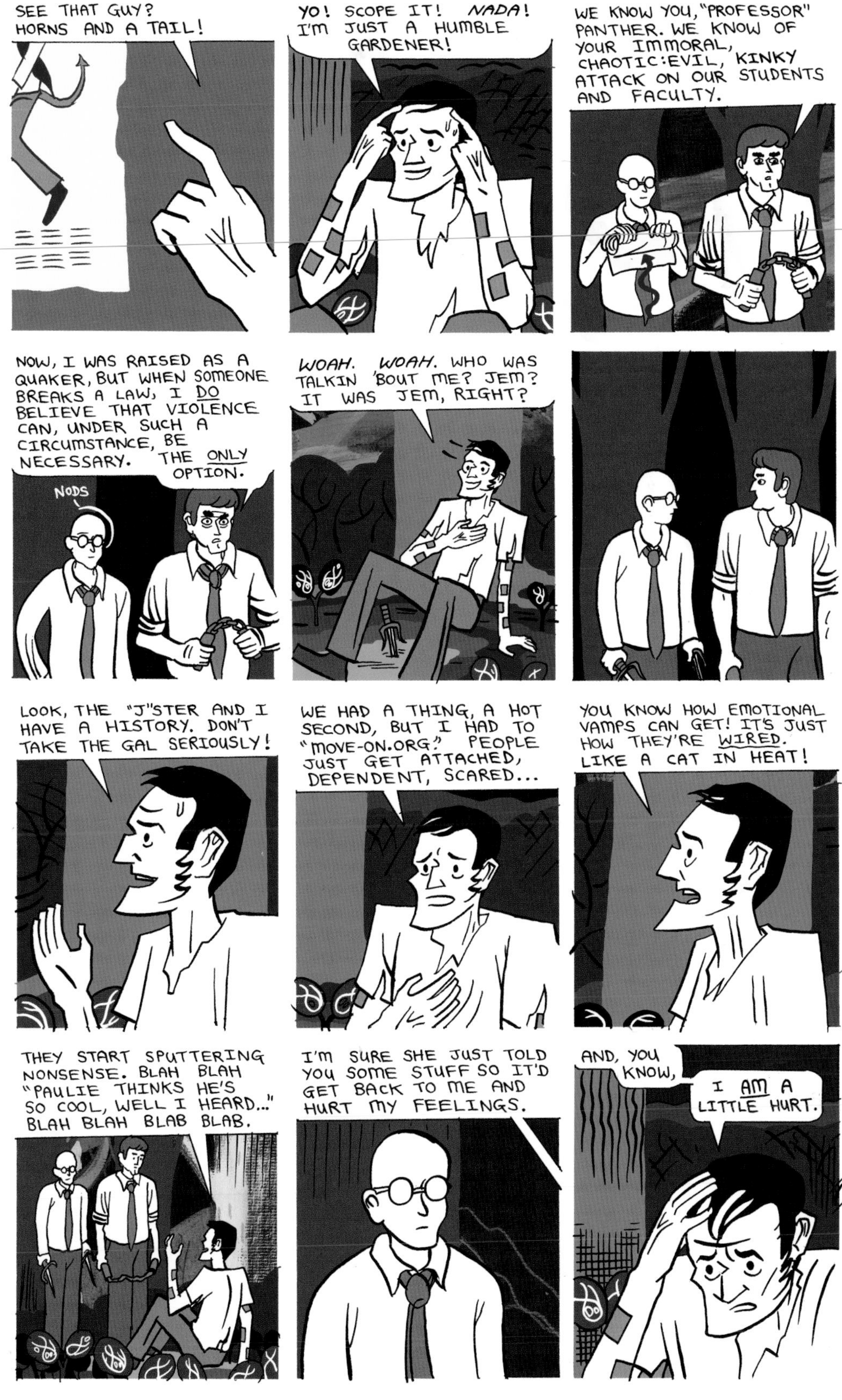
SEE THAT GUY? HORNS AND A TAIL!
YO! SCOPE IT! NADA! I'M JUST A HUMBLE GARDENER!
WE KNOW YOU, "PROFESSOR" PANTHER. WE KNOW OF YOUR IMMORAL, CHAOTIC:EVIL, KINKY ATTACK ON OUR STUDENTS AND FACULTY.
NOW, I WAS RAISED AS A QUAKER, BUT WHEN SOMEONE BREAKS A LAW, I DO BELIEVE THAT VIOLENCE CAN, UNDER SUCH A CIRCUMSTANCE, BE NECESSARY.
THE ONLY OPTION.
NODS
WOAH. WOAH. WHO WAS TALKIN 'BOUT ME? JEM? IT WAS JEM, RIGHT?
LOOK, THE "J"STER AND I HAVE A HISTORY. DON'T TAKE THE GAL SERIOUSLY!
WE HAD A THING, A HOT SECOND, BUT I HAD TO "MOVE-ON.ORG." PEOPLE JUST GET ATTACHED, DEPENDENT, SCARED...
YOU KNOW HOW EMOTIONAL VAMPS CAN GET! IT'S JUST HOW THEY'RE WIRED. LIKE A CAT IN HEAT!
THEY START SPUTTERING NONSENSE. BLAH BLAH "PAULIE THINKS HE'S SO COOL, WELL I HEARD..." BLAH BLAH BLAB BLAB.
I'M SURE SHE JUST TOLD YOU SOME STUFF SO IT'D GET BACK TO ME AND HURT MY FEELINGS.
AND, YOU KNOW,
I AM A LITTLE HURT.

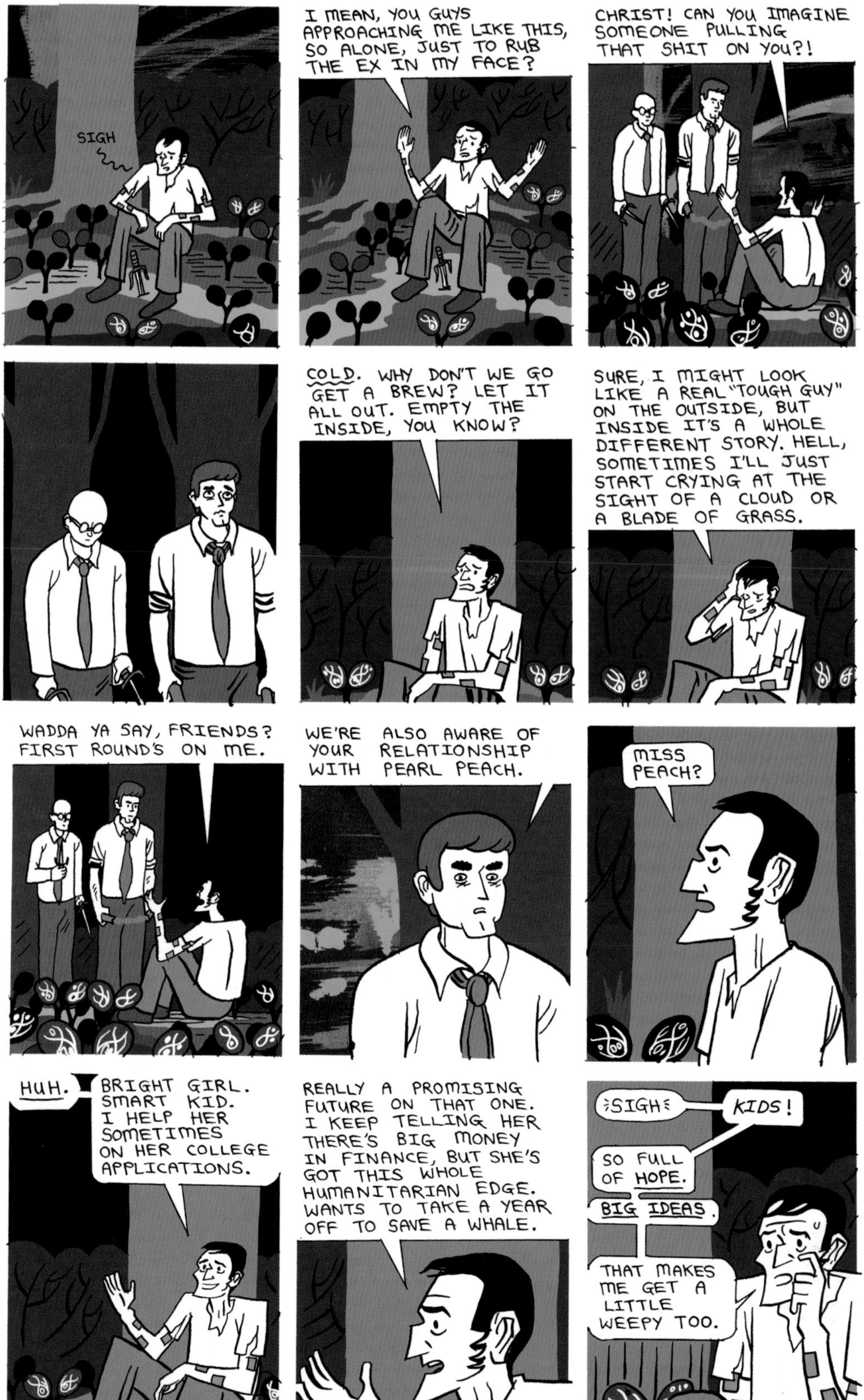
SIGH
I MEAN, YOU GUYS APPROACHING ME LIKE THIS, SO ALONE, JUST TO RUB THE EX IN MY FACE?
CHRIST! CAN YOU IMAGINE SOMEONE PULLING THAT SHIT ON YOU?!
COLD. WHY DON'T WE GO GET A BREW? LET IT ALL OUT. EMPTY THE INSIDE, YOU KNOW?
SURE, I MIGHT LOOK LIKE A REAL "TOUGH GUY" ON THE OUTSIDE, BUT INSIDE IT'S A WHOLE DIFFERENT STORY. HELL, SOMETIMES I'LL JUST START CRYING AT THE SIGHT OF A CLOUD OR A BLADE OF GRASS.
WADDA YA SAY, FRIENDS? FIRST ROUND'S ON ME.
WE'RE ALSO AWARE OF YOUR RELATIONSHIP WITH PEARL PEACH.
MISS PEACH?
HUH.
BRIGHT GIRL. SMART KID. I HELP HER SOMETIMES ON HER COLLEGE APPLICATIONS.
REALLY A PROMISING FUTURE ON THAT ONE. I KEEP TELLING HER THERE'S BIG MONEY IN FINANCE, BUT SHE'S GOT THIS WHOLE HUMANITARIAN EDGE. WANTS TO TAKE A YEAR OFF TO SAVE A WHALE.
SIGH
KIDS!
SO FULL OF HOPE.
BIG IDEAS.
THAT MAKES ME GET A LITTLE WEEPY TOO.

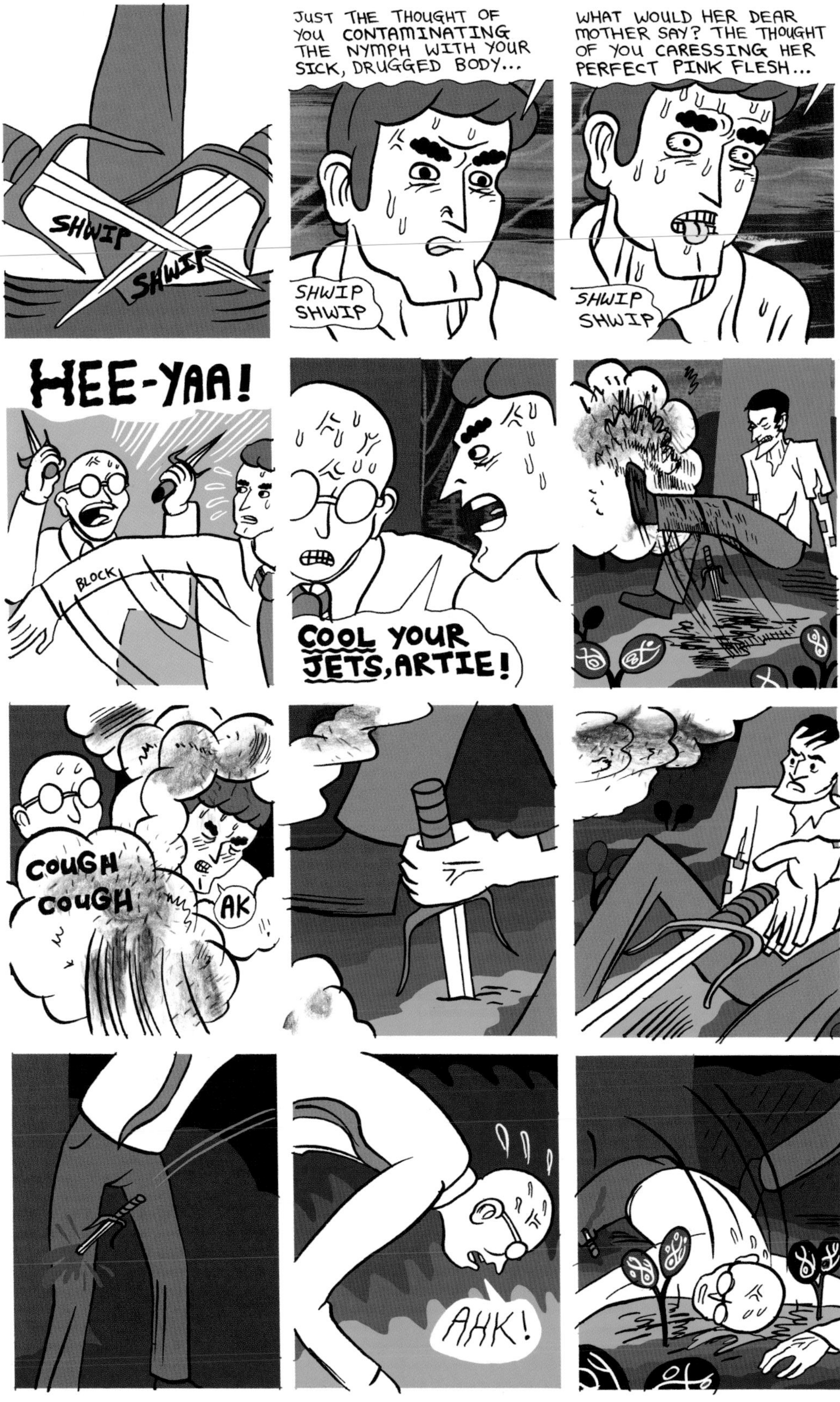
SHWIP
SHWIP
JUST THE THOUGHT OF YOU CONTAMINATING THE NYMPH WITH YOUR SICK, DRUGGED BODY...
SHWIP SHWIP
WHAT WOULD HER DEAR MOTHER SAY? THE THOUGHT OF YOU CARESSING HER PERFECT PINK FLESH...
SHWIP SHWIP
HEE-YAA!
BLOCK
COOL YOUR JETS, ARTIE!
COUGH COUGH
AK
AHK!

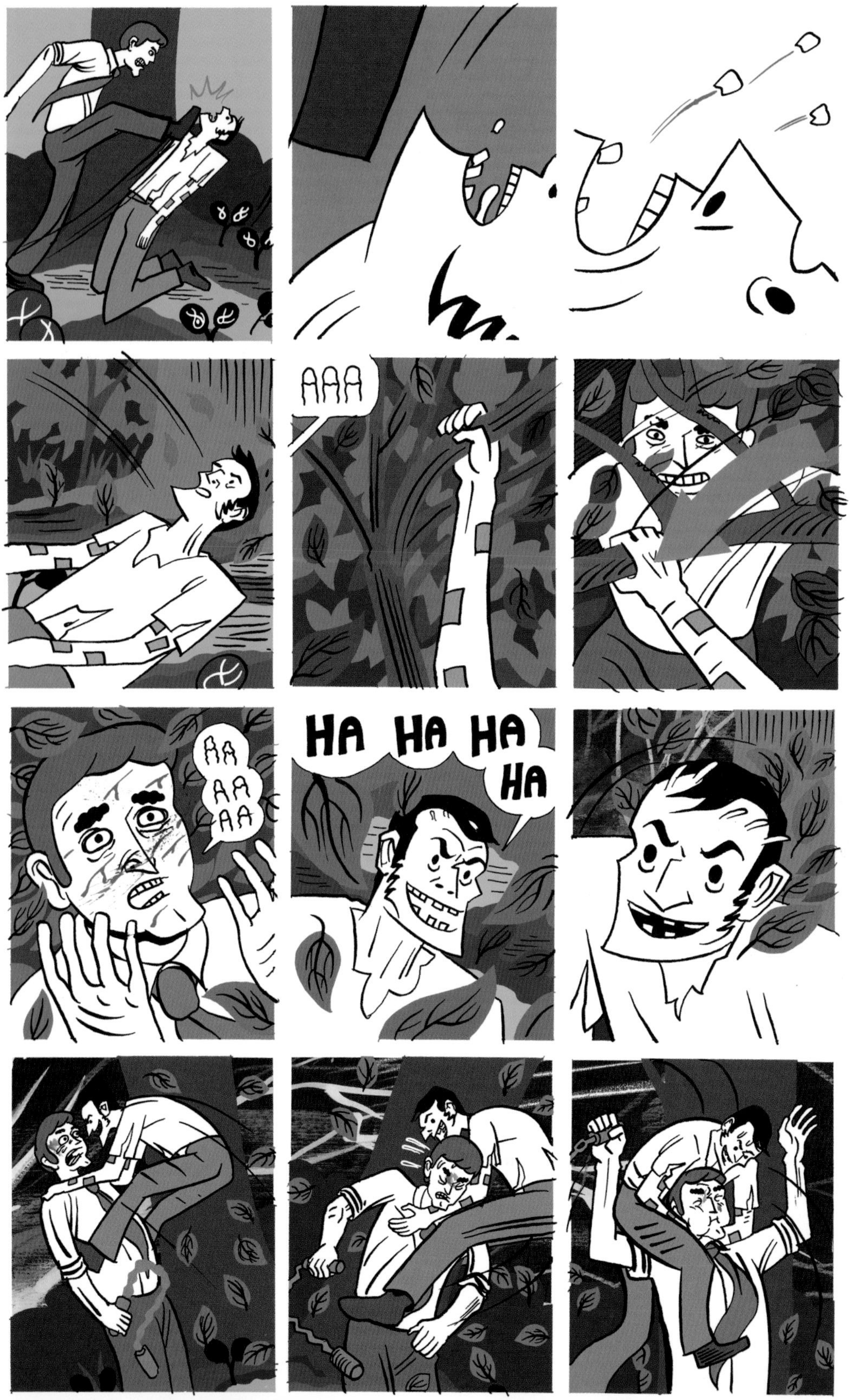
AAA
AA AA AA
HA HA HA HA

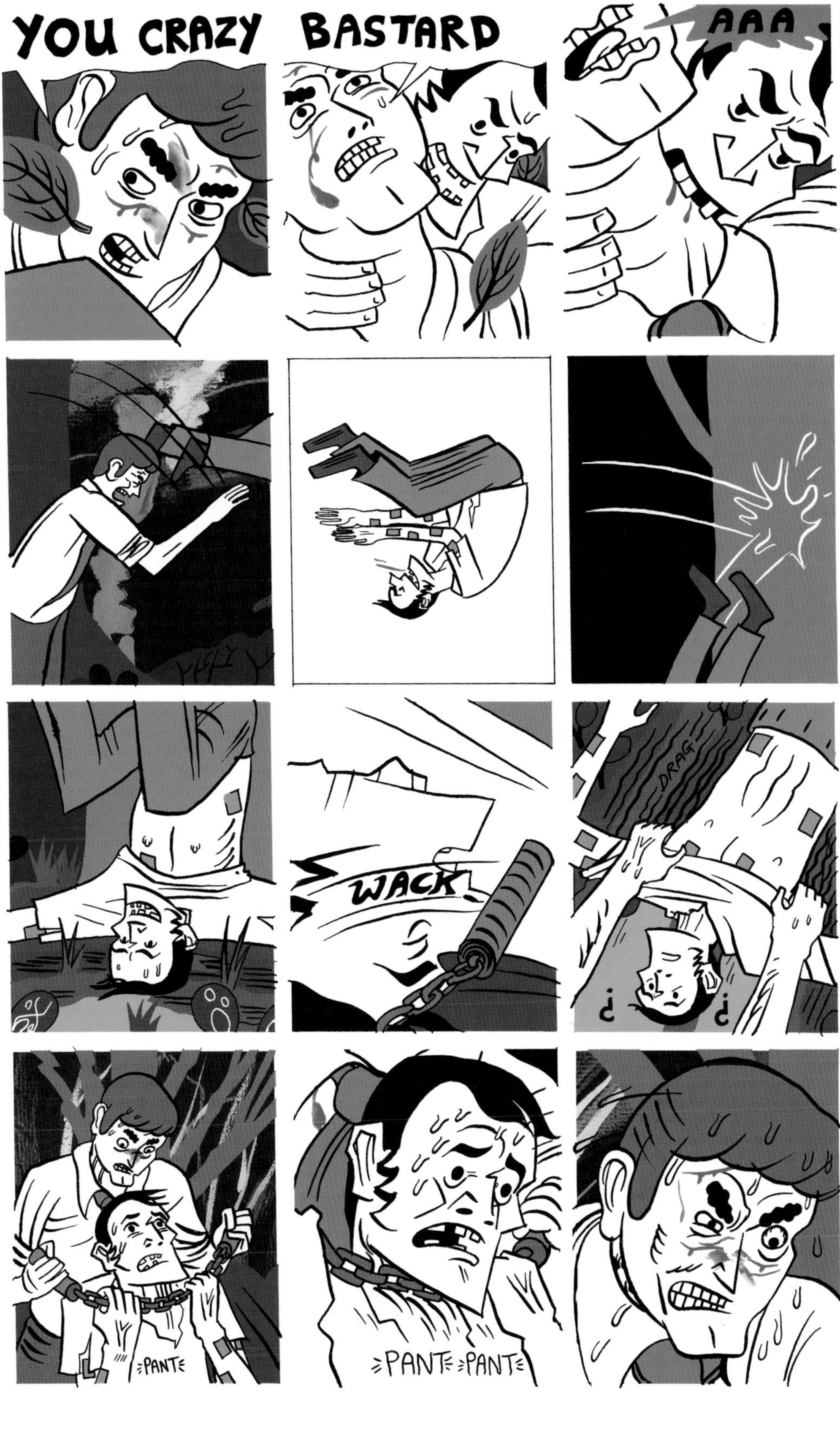
YOU CRAZY BASTARD
AAA
WACK
DRAG
¿ ¿
PANT
PANT PANT

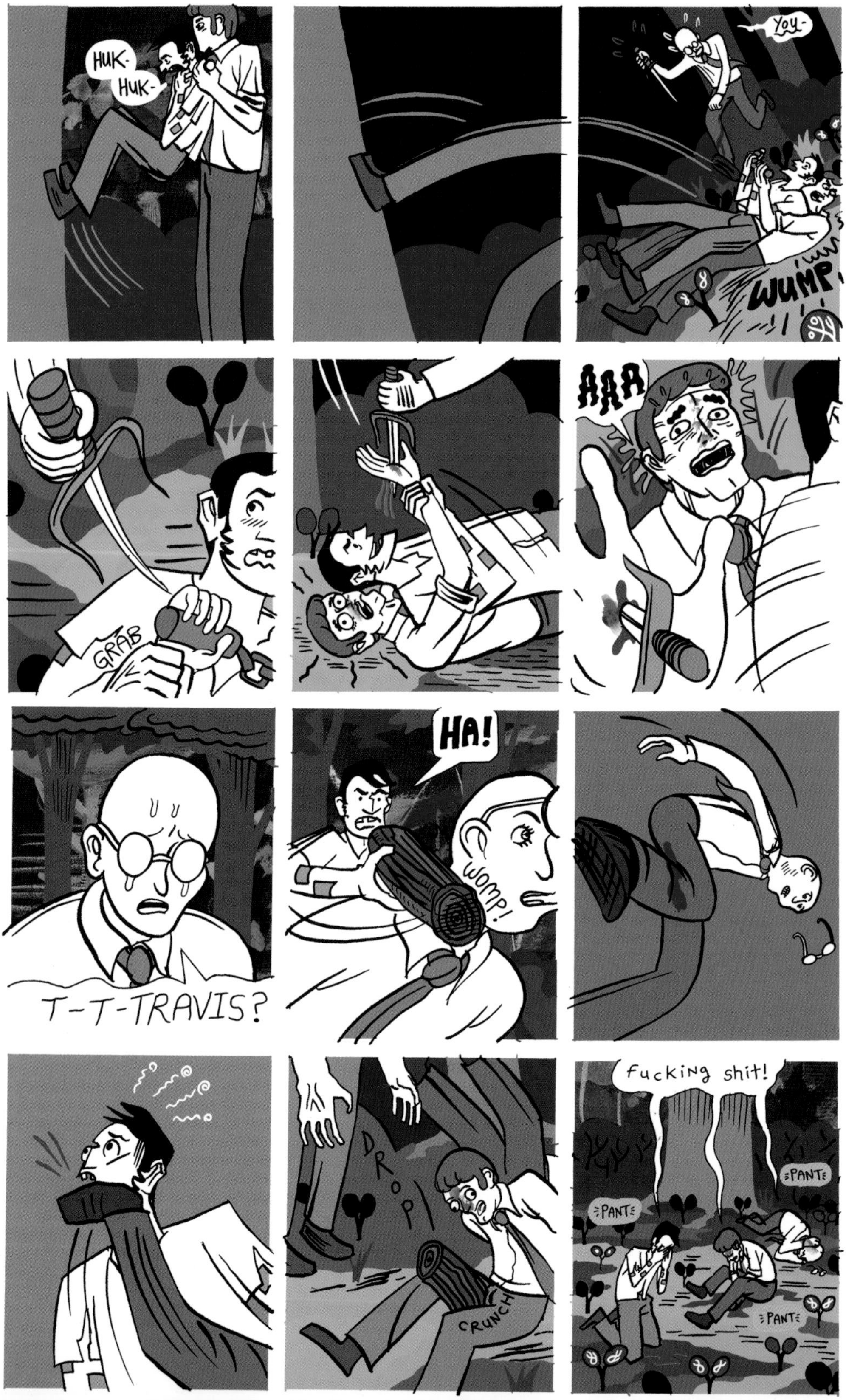
HUK-
HUK-
YOU-
WUMP
GRAB
AAA
T-T-TRAVIS?
HA!
WOMP!
DROP
CRUNCH
Fucking shit!
PANT
PANT
PANT

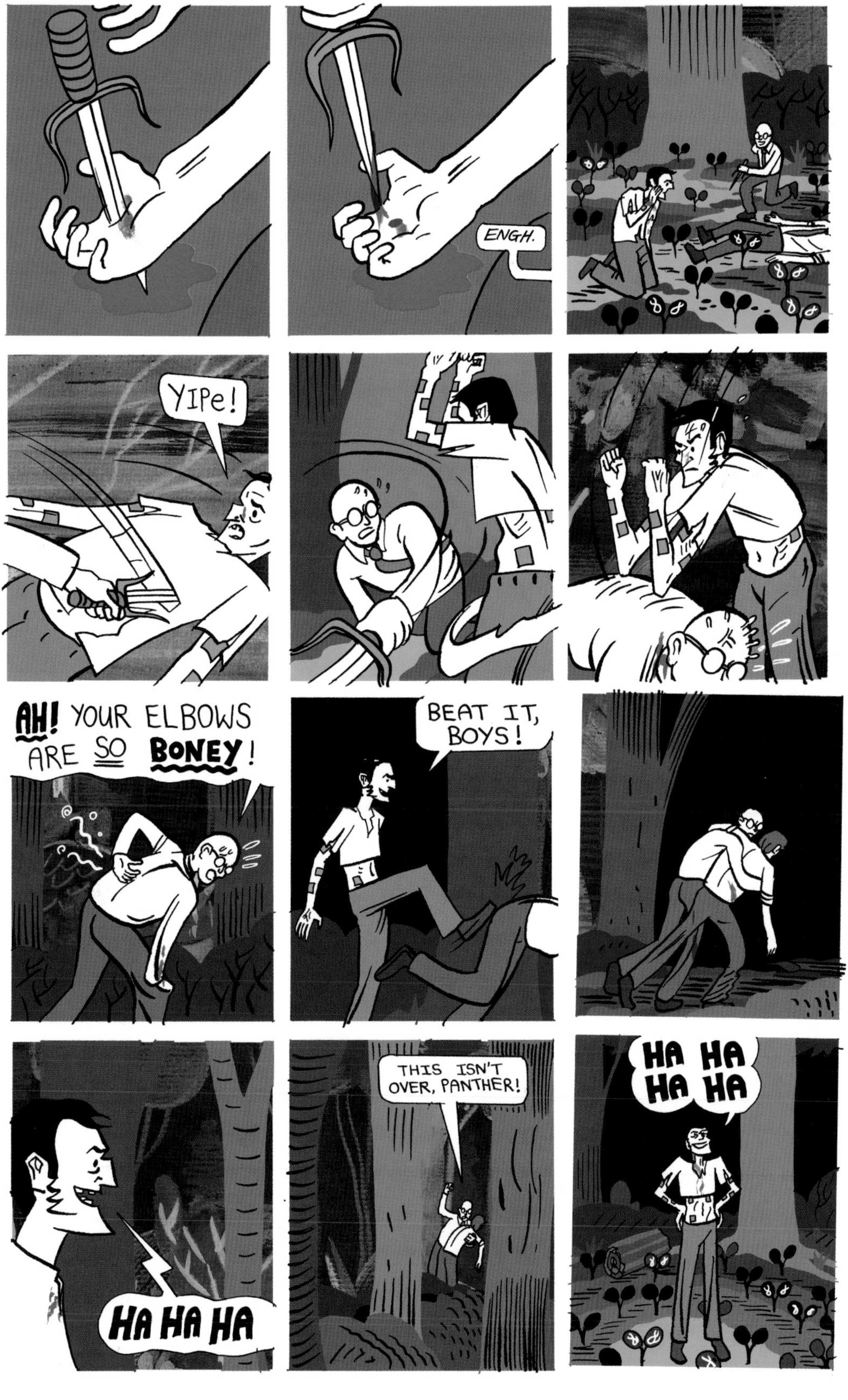
ENGH.
YIPE!
AH! YOUR ELBOWS ARE SO BONEY!
BEAT IT, BOYS!
HA HA HA
THIS ISN'T OVER, PANTHER!
HA HA HA HA

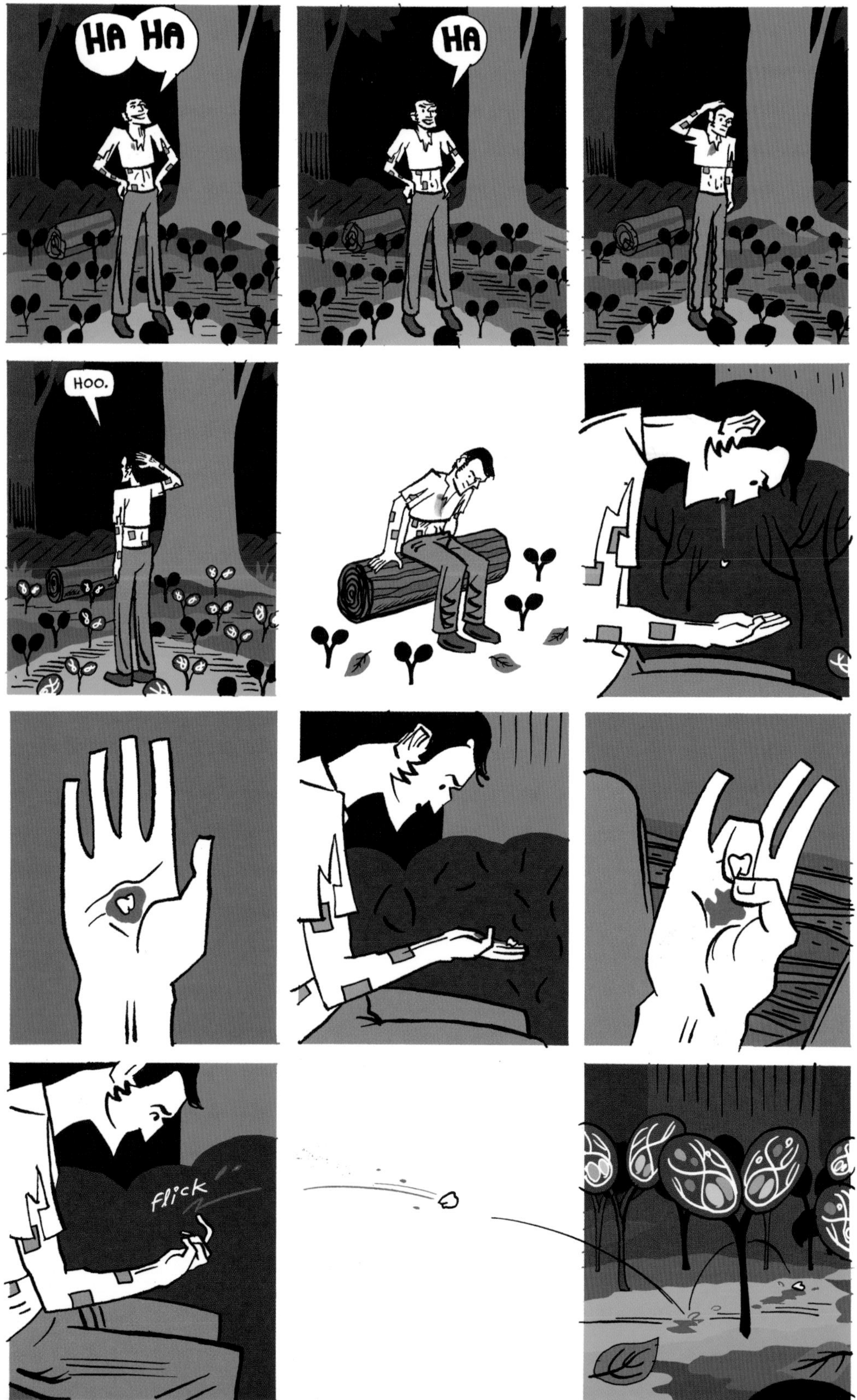
HA HA
HA
HOO.
flick

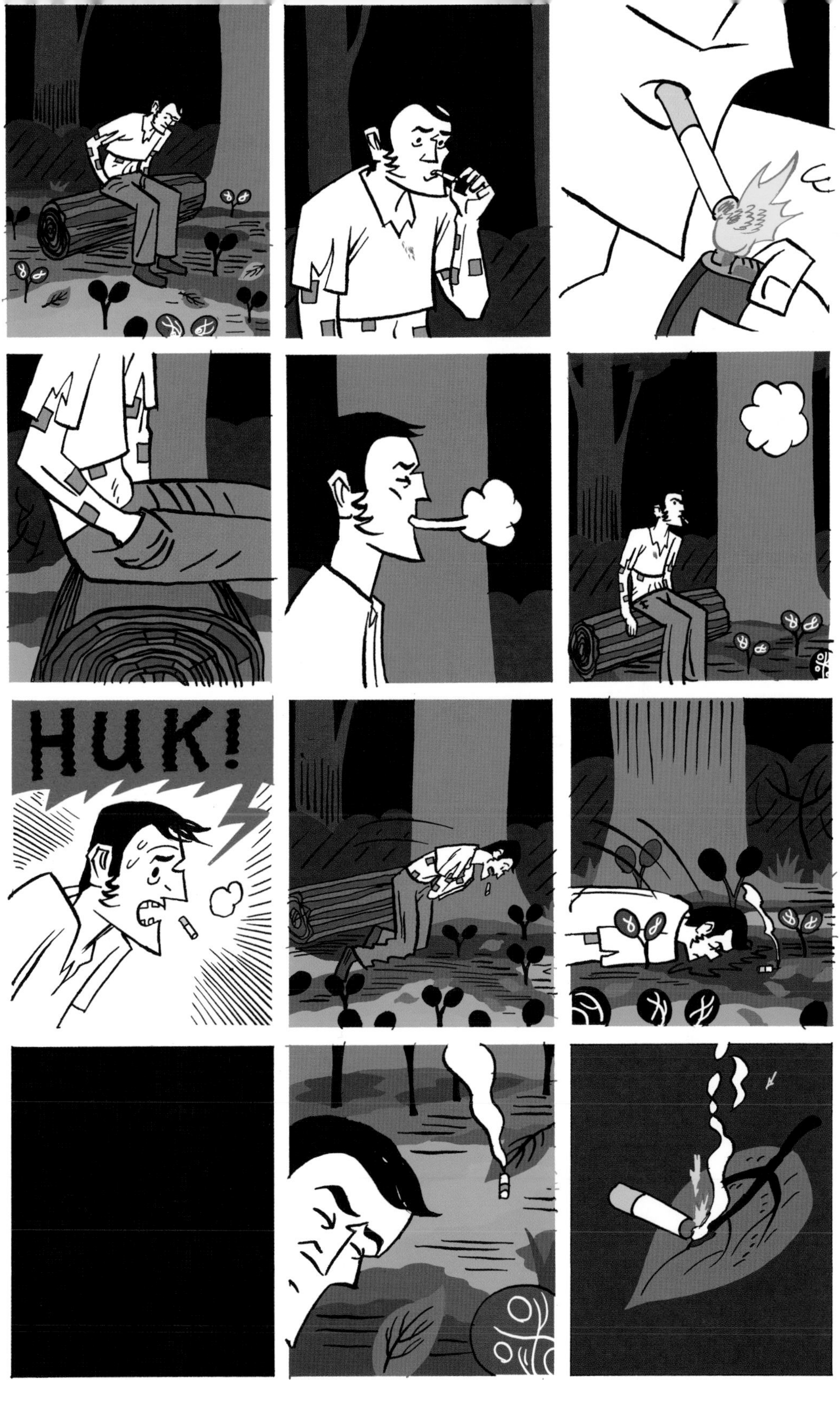
HUK!

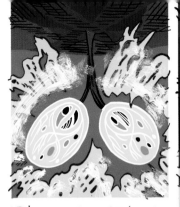

FWOOSH

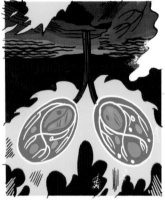

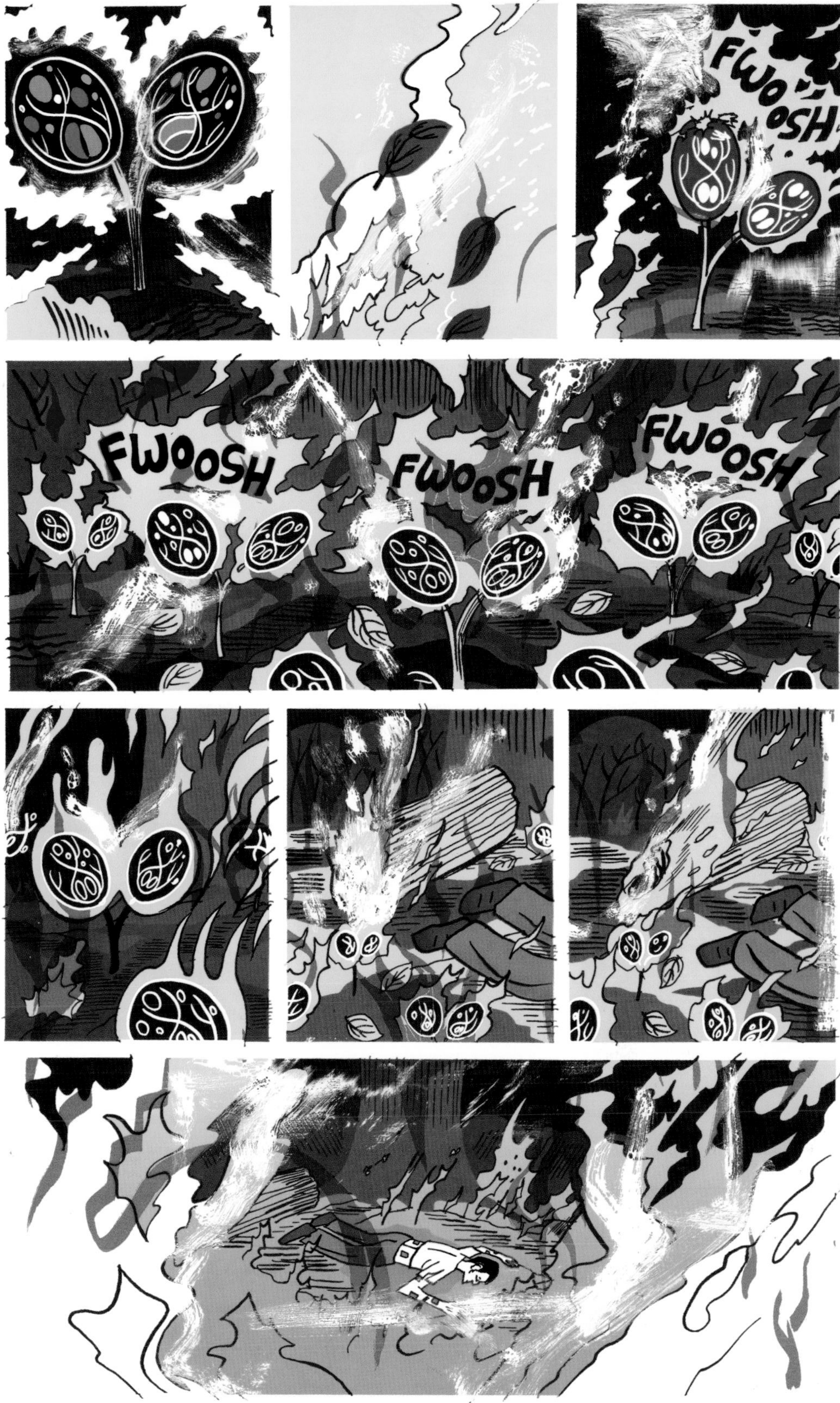
FWOOSH
FWOOSH
FWOOSH
FWOOSH

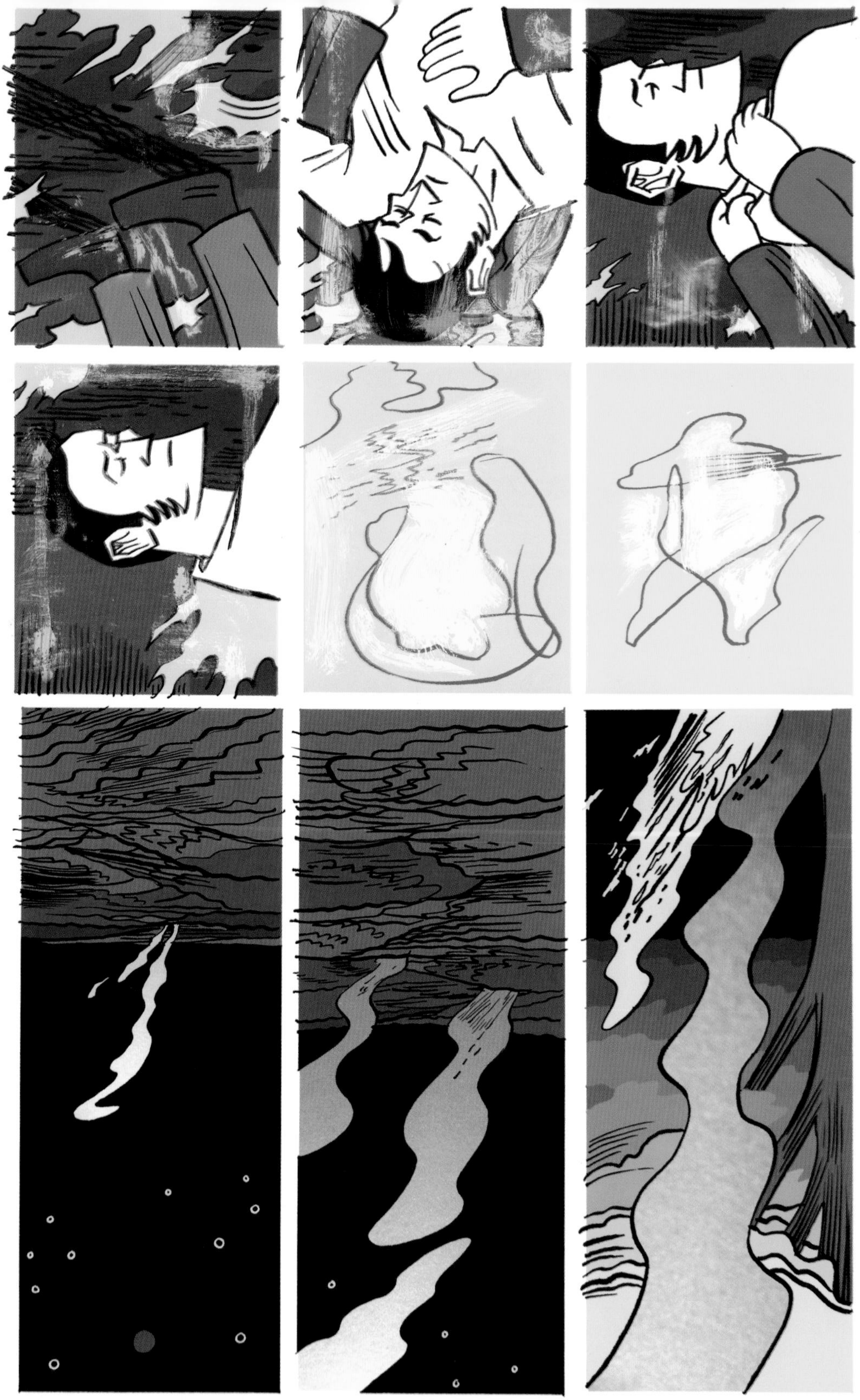

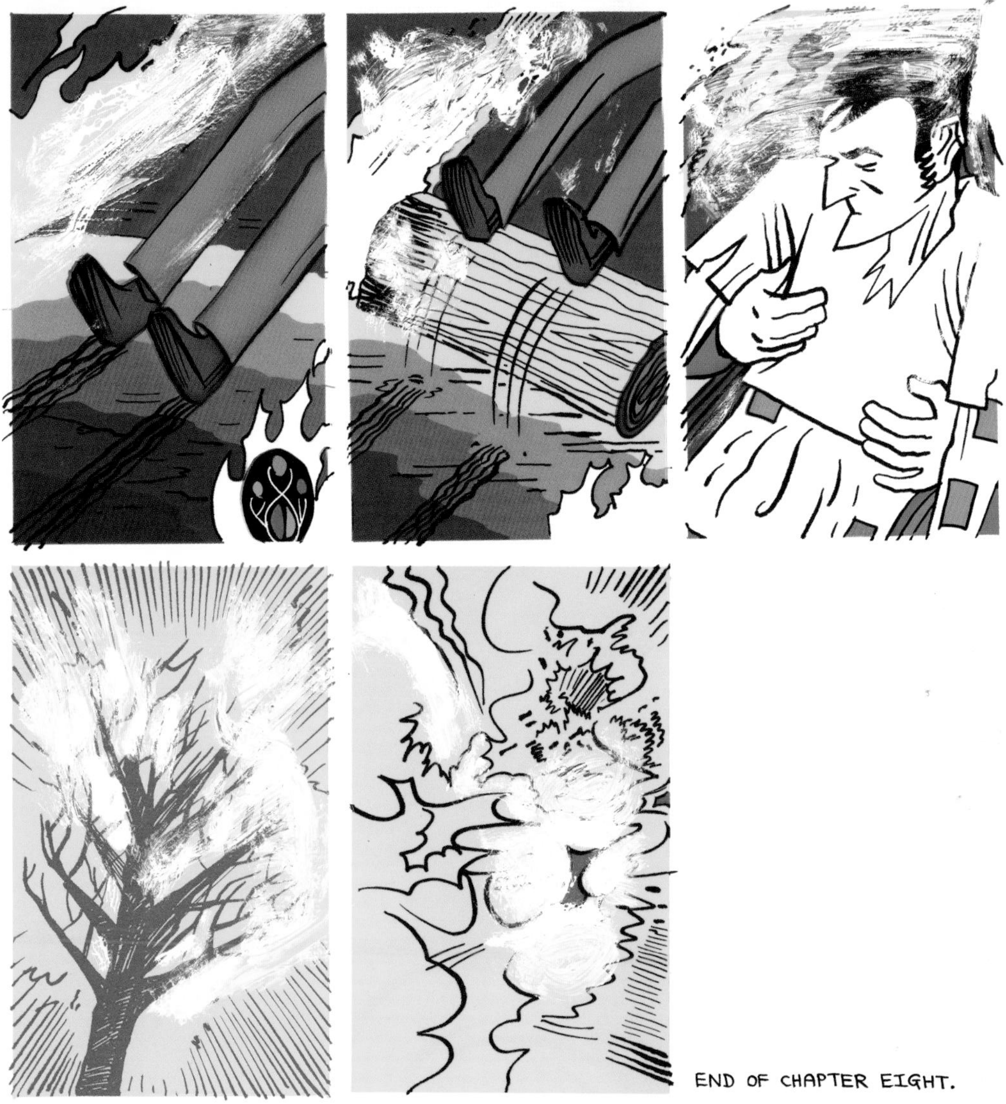

END OF CHAPTER EIGHT.

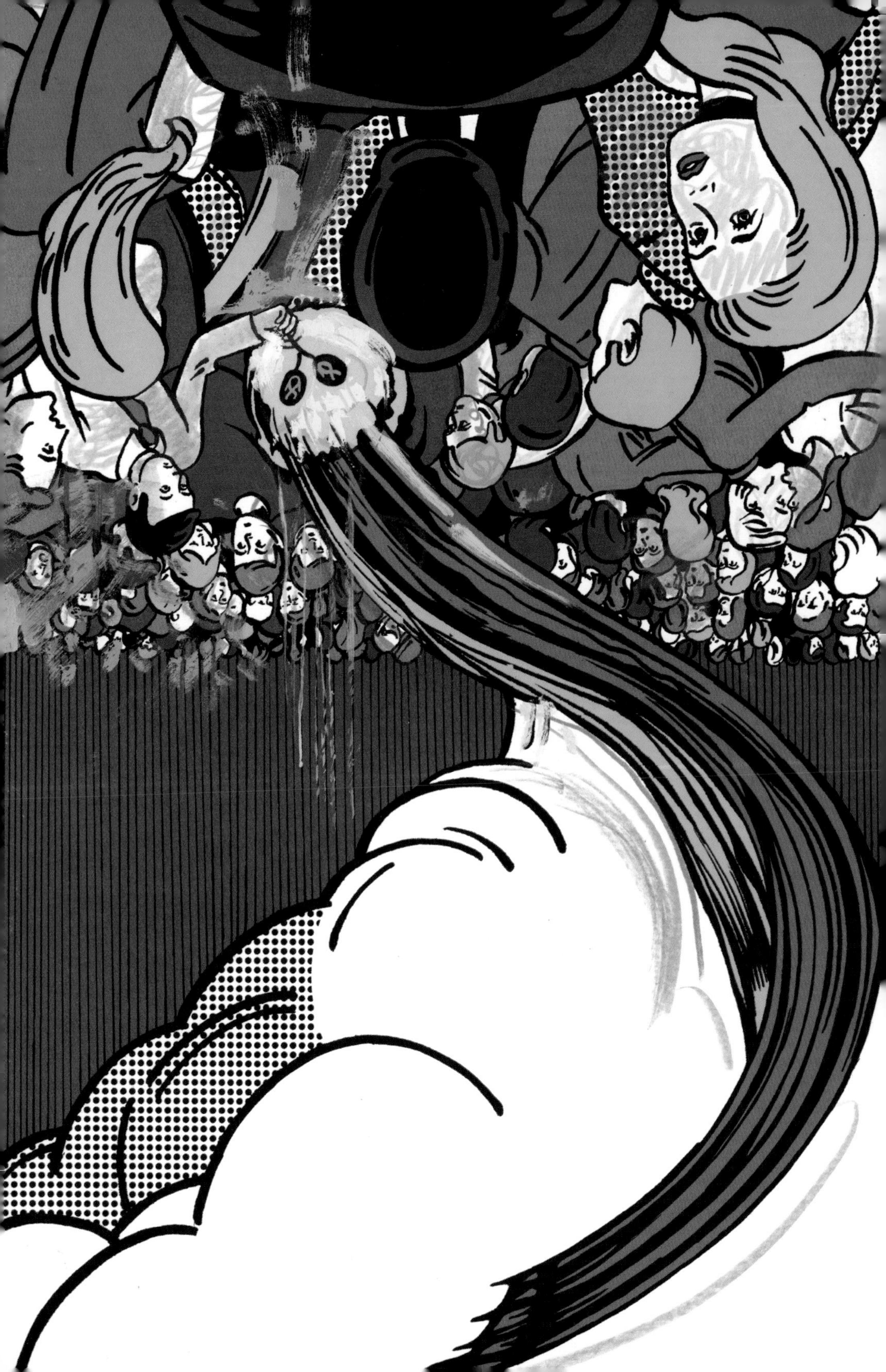

CHAPTER NINE

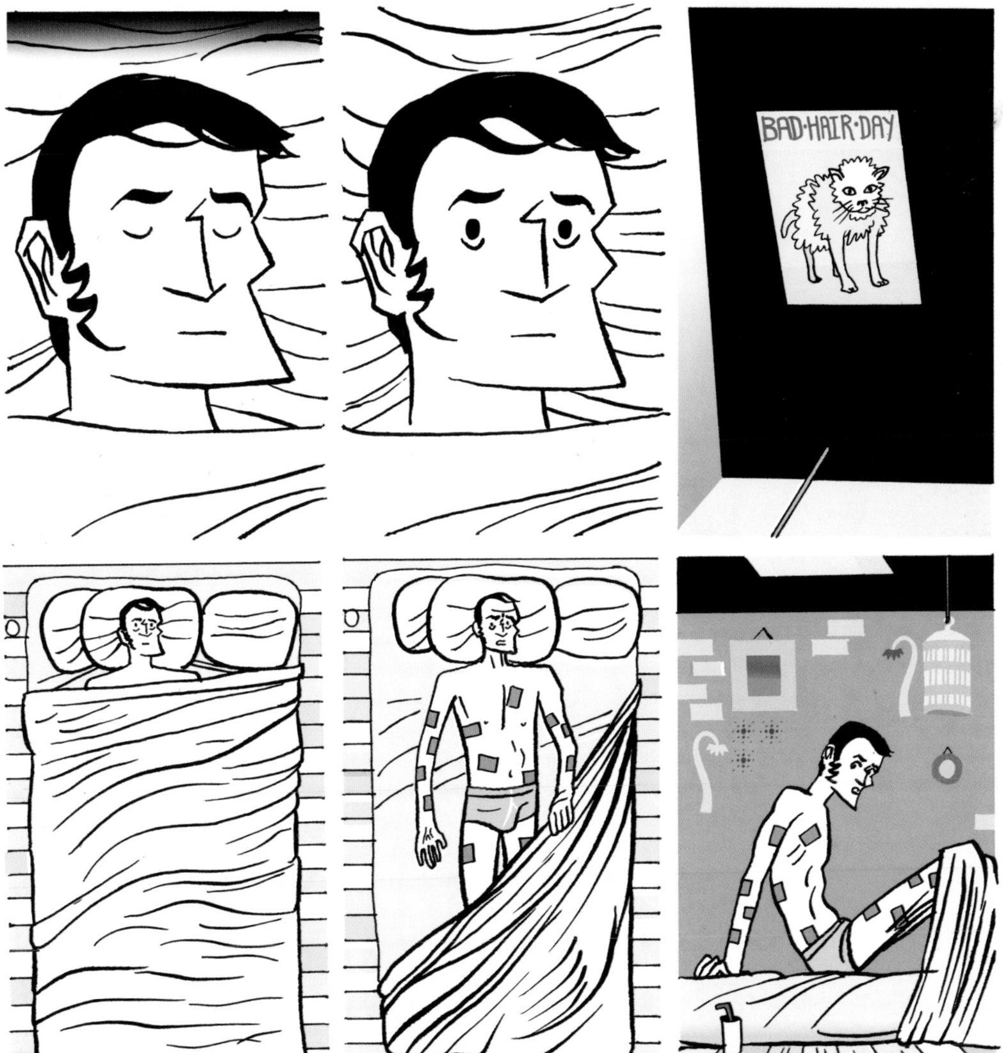
BAD·HAIR·DAY

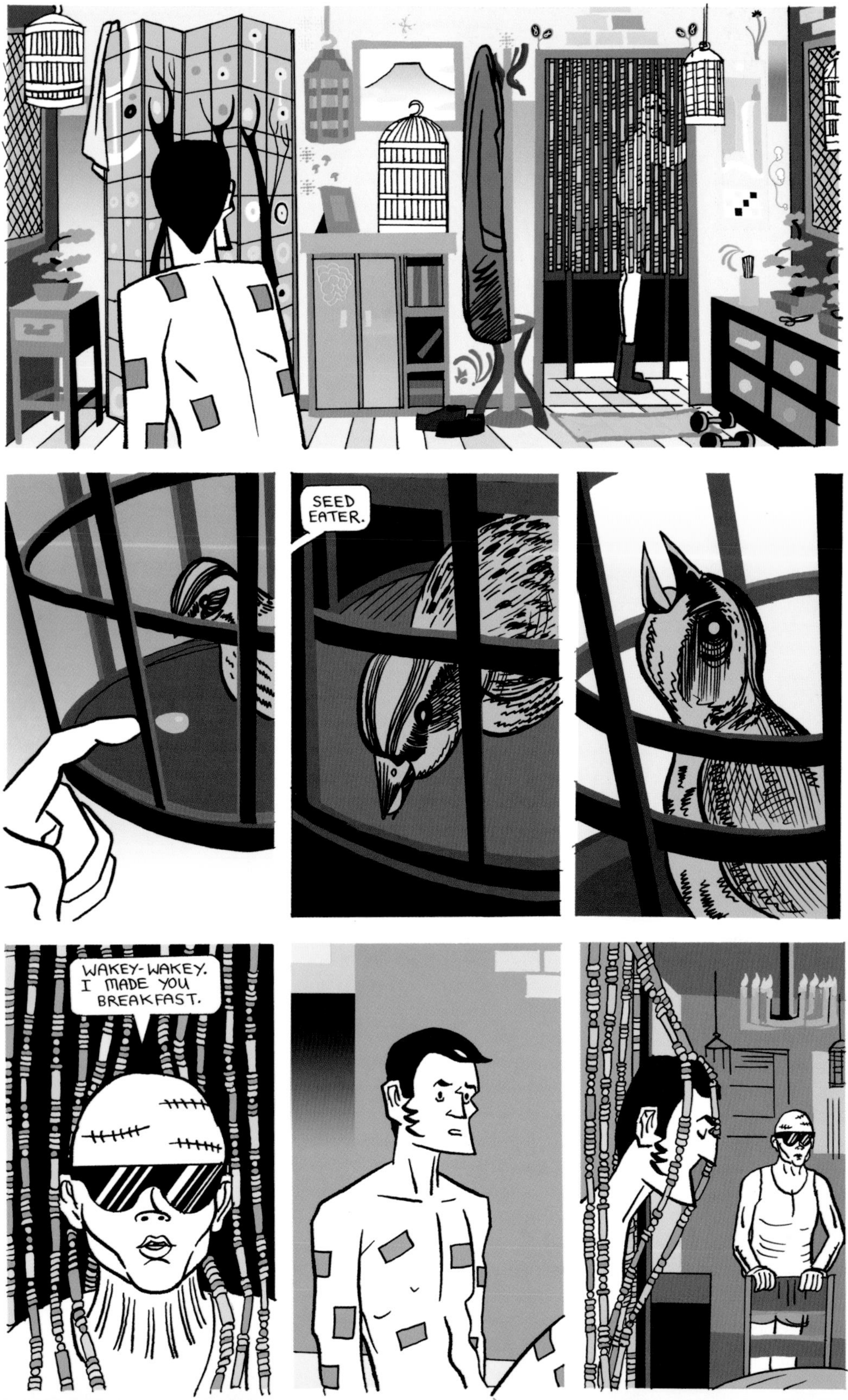
SEED EATER.
WAKEY-WAKEY. I MADE YOU BREAKFAST.

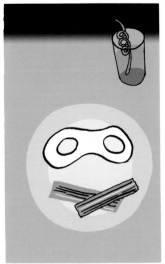

WHAT HAPPENED?

I PULLED YOU FROM THE CHAOS FLAMES, MENDED YOUR BATTLE WOUNDS.

THANKS, MAN.

I'M ACTUALLY MUCH LIKE YOU, PROFESSOR PANTHER.

I'M AN EXPERIMENTER. A RECORDER.

I, TOO, DOCUMENT THE EFFECTS OF A PLANT. HOWEVER, INSTEAD OF STUDYING ITS EFFECT ON A MIND OF ONE, I STUDY A CULTURE. A SOCIETY IS ONE MIND.

AND INSTEAD OF RECORDING THE EVENTS FOR FUTURE PUBLICATION, I HAVE PERSONAL CLIENTS, AN INTERESTED PARTY WHO GAVE ME THIS MISSION.

WHO ARE YOU?

YOU MAY CALL ME...

JOHNNY SCARHEAD.

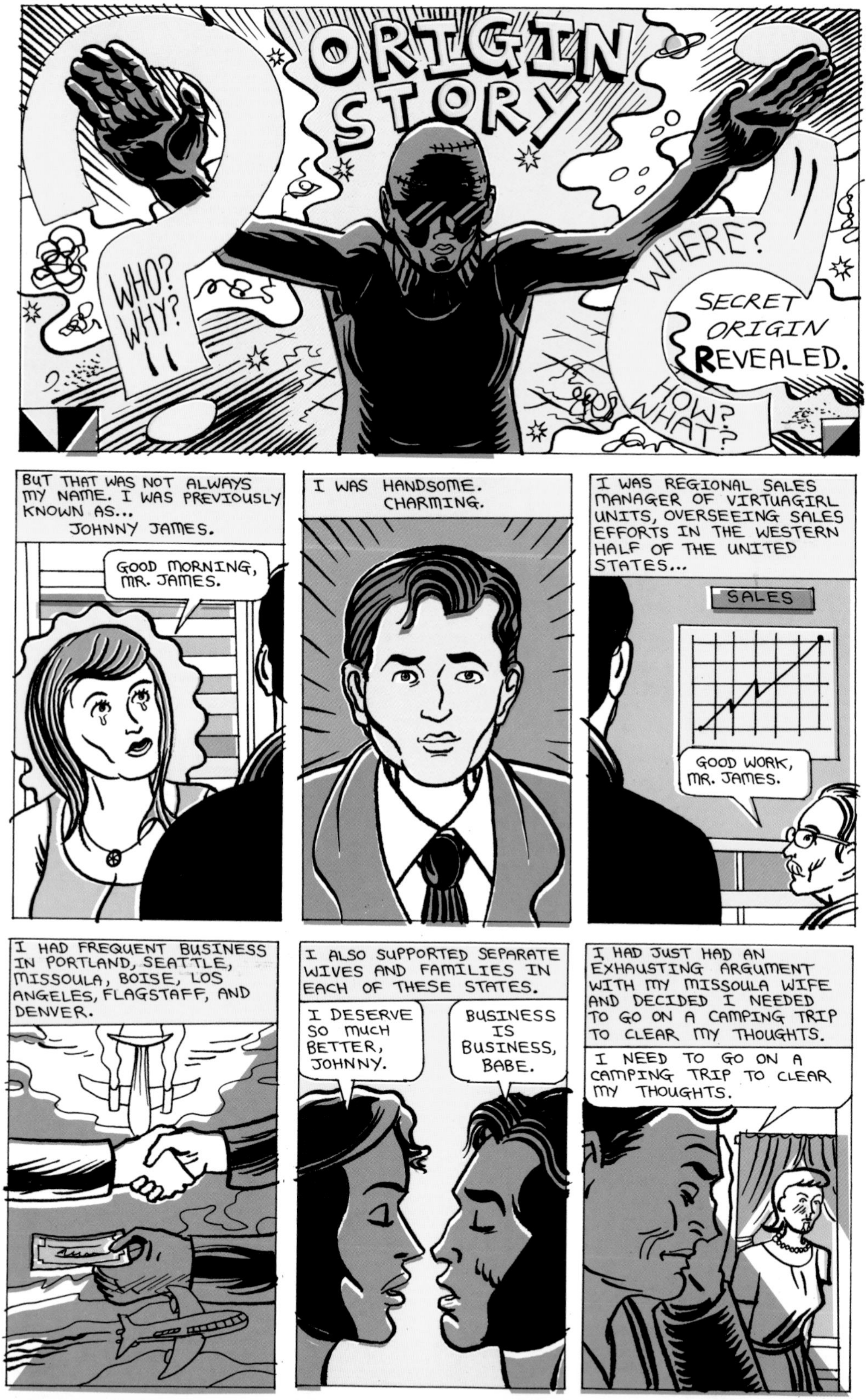
ORIGIN STORY
WHO? WHY?
WHERE?
SECRET ORIGIN REVEALED.
HOW? WHAT?
BUT THAT WAS NOT ALWAYS MY NAME. I WAS PREVIOUSLY KNOWN AS... JOHNNY JAMES.
GOOD MORNING, MR. JAMES.
I WAS HANDSOME. CHARMING.
I WAS REGIONAL SALES MANAGER OF VIRTUAGIRL UNITS, OVERSEEING SALES EFFORTS IN THE WESTERN HALF OF THE UNITED STATES...
SALES
GOOD WORK, MR. JAMES.
I HAD FREQUENT BUSINESS IN PORTLAND, SEATTLE, MISSOULA, BOISE, LOS ANGELES, FLAGSTAFF, AND DENVER.
I ALSO SUPPORTED SEPARATE WIVES AND FAMILIES IN EACH OF THESE STATES.
I DESERVE SO MUCH BETTER, JOHNNY.
BUSINESS IS BUSINESS, BABE.
I HAD JUST HAD AN EXHAUSTING ARGUMENT WITH MY MISSOULA WIFE AND DECIDED I NEEDED TO GO ON A CAMPING TRIP TO CLEAR MY THOUGHTS.
I NEED TO GO ON A CAMPING TRIP TO CLEAR MY THOUGHTS.

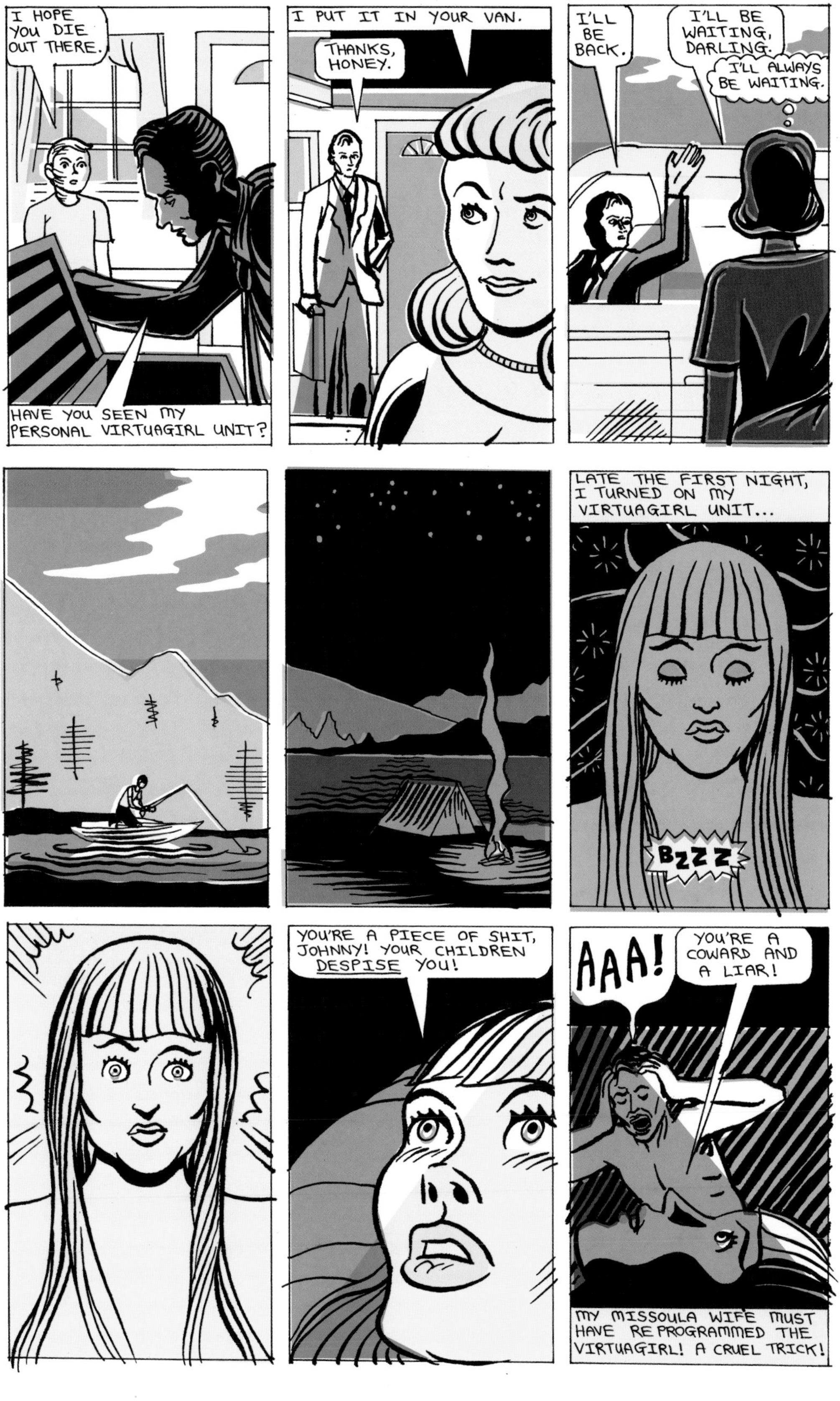
I HOPE YOU DIE OUT THERE.
HAVE YOU SEEN MY PERSONAL VIRTUAGIRL UNIT?
I PUT IT IN YOUR VAN.
THANKS, HONEY.
I'LL BE BACK.
I'LL BE WAITING, DARLING.
I'LL ALWAYS BE WAITING.
LATE THE FIRST NIGHT, I TURNED ON MY VIRTUAGIRL UNIT...
BZZZ
YOU'RE A PIECE OF SHIT, JOHNNY! YOUR CHILDREN DESPISE YOU!
AAA!
YOU'RE A COWARD AND A LIAR!
MY MISSOULA WIFE MUST HAVE REPROGRAMMED THE VIRTUAGIRL! A CRUEL TRICK!

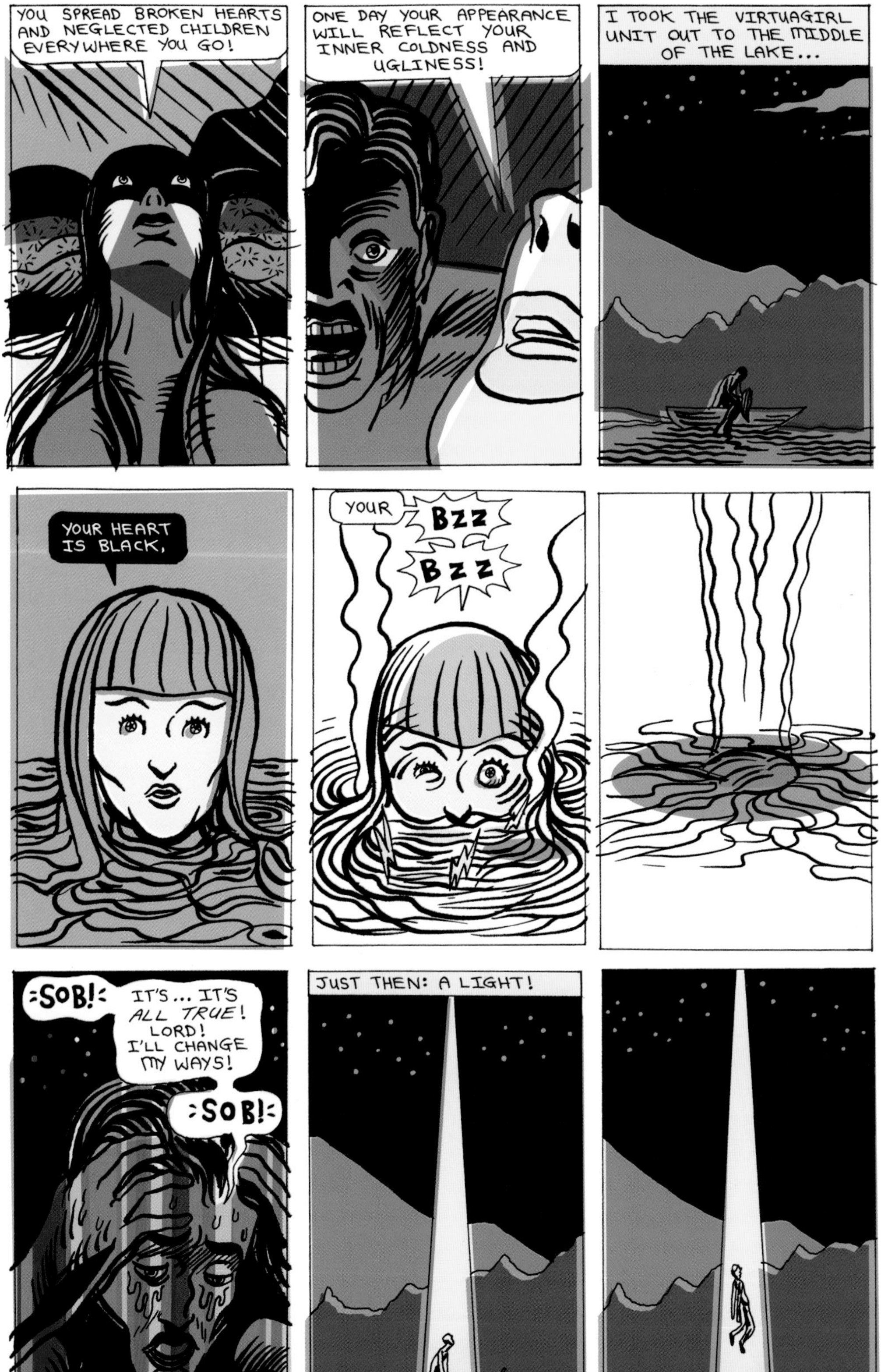
YOU SPREAD BROKEN HEARTS AND NEGLECTED CHILDREN EVERYWHERE YOU GO!
ONE DAY YOUR APPEARANCE WILL REFLECT YOUR INNER COLDNESS AND UGLINESS!
I TOOK THE VIRTUAGIRL UNIT OUT TO THE MIDDLE OF THE LAKE...
YOUR HEART IS BLACK,
YOUR
BZZ
BZZ
SOB!
IT'S... IT'S ALL TRUE! LORD! I'LL CHANGE MY WAYS!
SOB!
JUST THEN: A LIGHT!

THE MEMORIES FROM THIS TIME ARE SPOTTY AT BEST...

STRANGE SHAPES... WEIRD ENERGIES...

AN UNKNOWN LANGUAGE OF PICTURES INSTEAD OF SOUNDS.

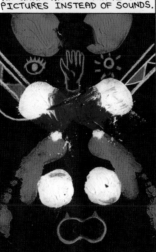

THE IMAGES FLICKERED ON THE ALIEN BODIES.

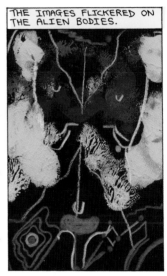

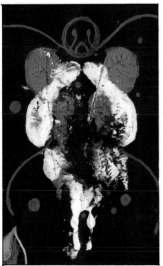

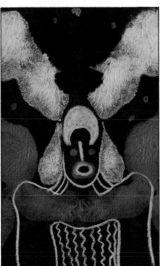

I THOUGHT I WAS GOING TO DIE...

BOISE WIFE! YOU WERE MY __TRUE__ LOVE!

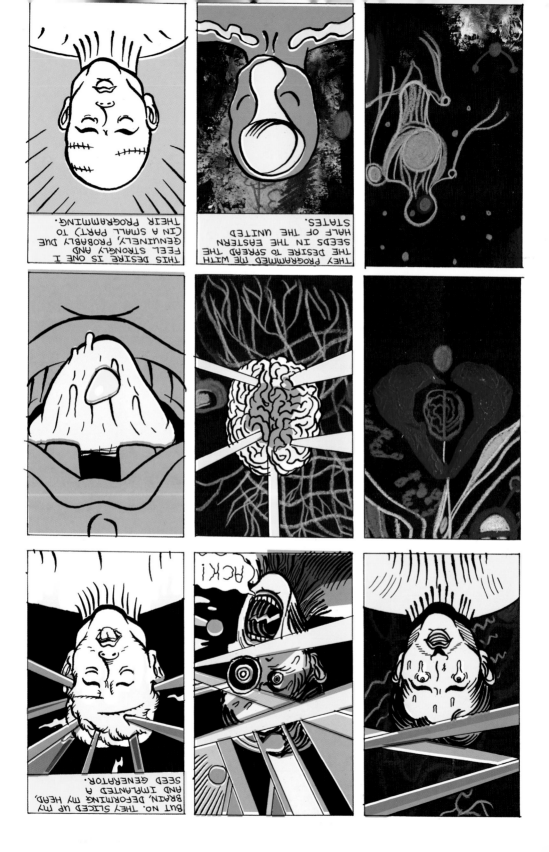

THIS DESIRE IS ONE I FEEL STRONGLY AND GENUINELY, PROBABLY DUE (IN A SMALL PART) TO THEIR PROGRAMMING.

THEY PROGRAMMED ME WITH THE DESIRE TO SPREAD THE SEEDS IN THE EASTERN HALF OF THE UNITED STATES.

BUT NO. THEY SLICED UP MY BRAIN, DEFORMING MY HEAD, AND IMPLANTED A SEED GENERATOR.

ACK!

REGARDLESS, IT'S A PERSONALLY REWARDING AND DEEPLY SATISFYING MISSION.

I WAS ALSO GIVEN "ALIEN EYES" TO RECORD THE AREA WHERE THE SEEDS ARE PLANTED. EVERYTHING I SEE IS SENT TO THE ALIEN FORCE FOR THEIR STUDY.

I SUSPECT THAT THIS ALIEN RACE IS INTERESTED IN HUMAN SOCIETY AND PSYCHOLOGY, ALTHOUGH THEY NEVER EXPLAINED ANYTHING TO ME DIRECTLY.

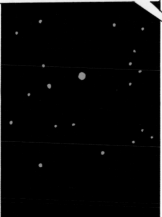

I'M AT PEACE NOW, WITH MY MISSION.

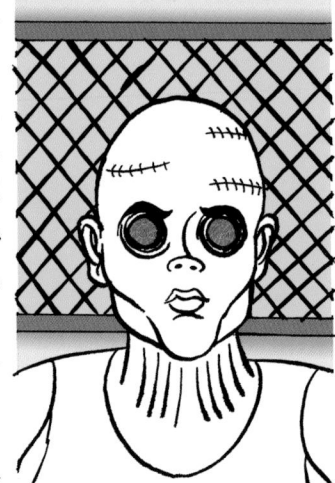

NOW *ALL* OF BONEY BOROUGH IS A TESTING GROUND!

IT'S ALREADY BEGUN! THERE'S NO STOPPING IT NOW!

THAT'S QUITE THE STORY.

WHERE ARE MY CLOTHES?

LOOK: I'D LOVE TO SIT AND CHAT WITH YOU ALL DAY, BUT YOU'RE SAYING SOME SERIOUSLY WACKED-OUT STUFF AND I JUST KIND OF WANT TO GET MY LOVED ONE AND SPLIT THIS PODUNK BOROUGH.

I'M NOT SAYING YOU'RE BONKERS OR INSANE OR "OFF YOUR ROCKER" OR A TOTAL FUCKING FREAK. HELL, YOU SEEM LIKE A NICE ENOUGH FELLAH. I KEEP AN OPEN MIND ABOUT THESE THINGS. I DON'T JUDGE.

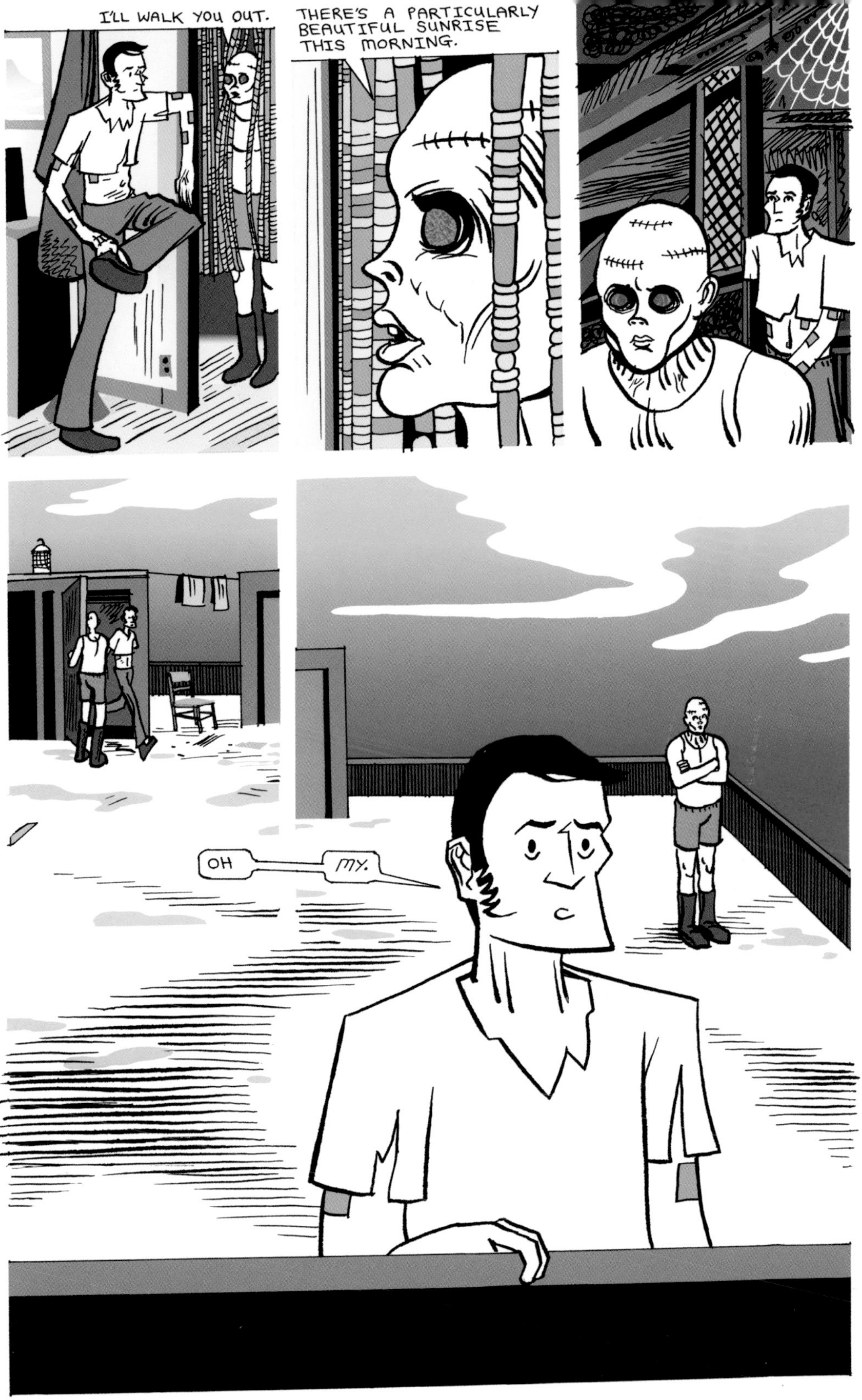
I'LL WALK YOU OUT.
THERE'S A PARTICULARLY BEAUTIFUL SUNRISE THIS MORNING.
OH
MY.

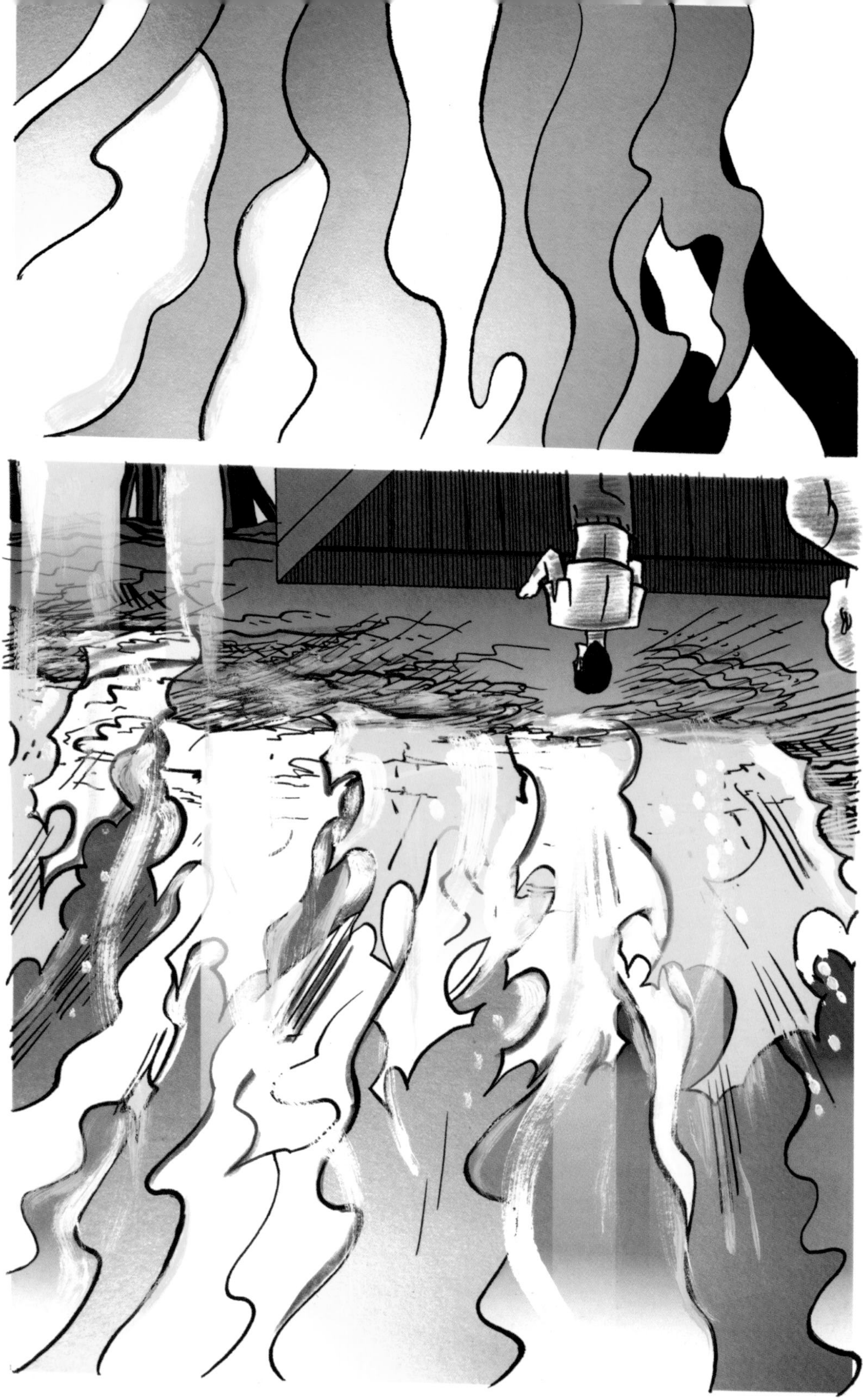

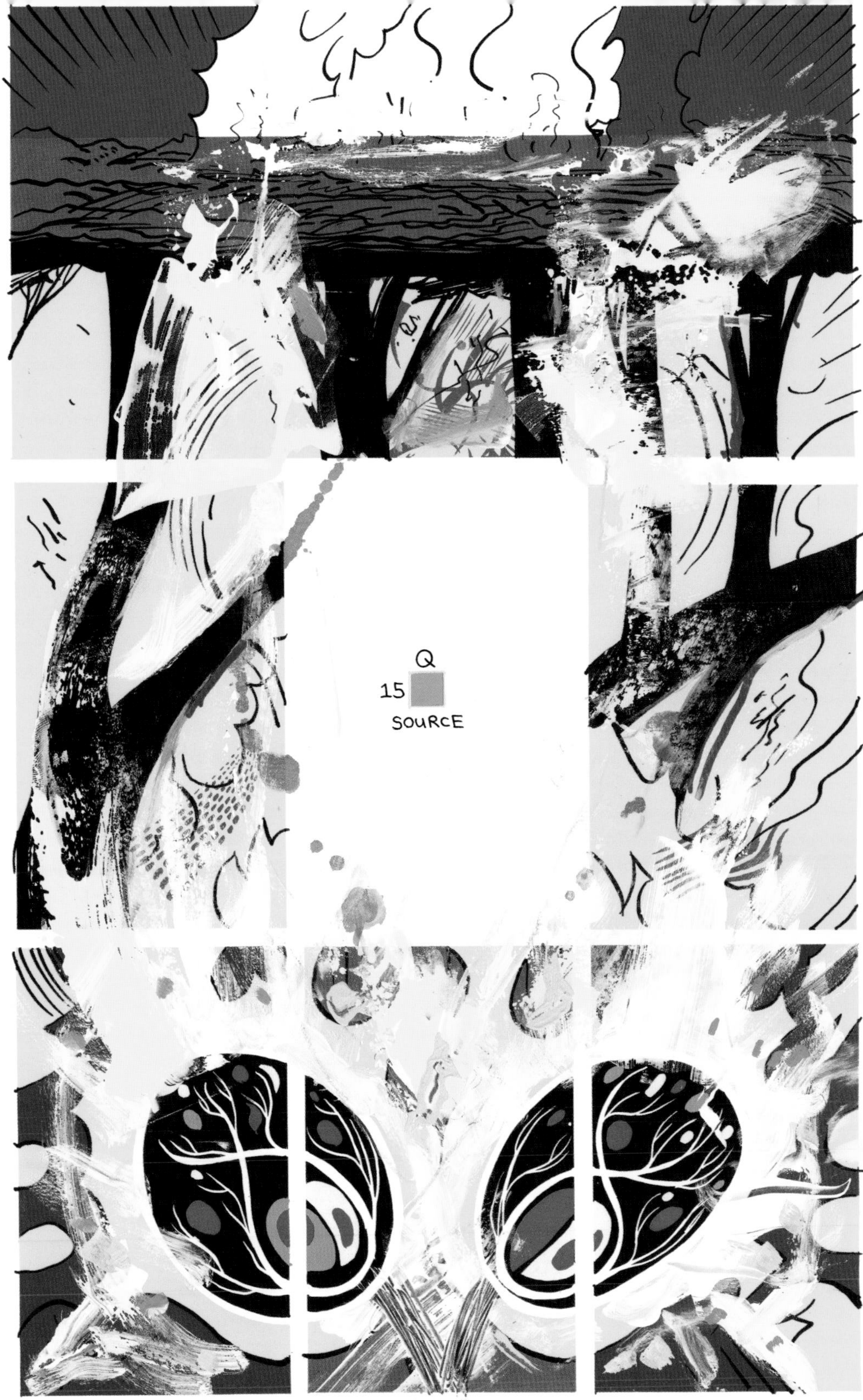
Q
15
SOURCE

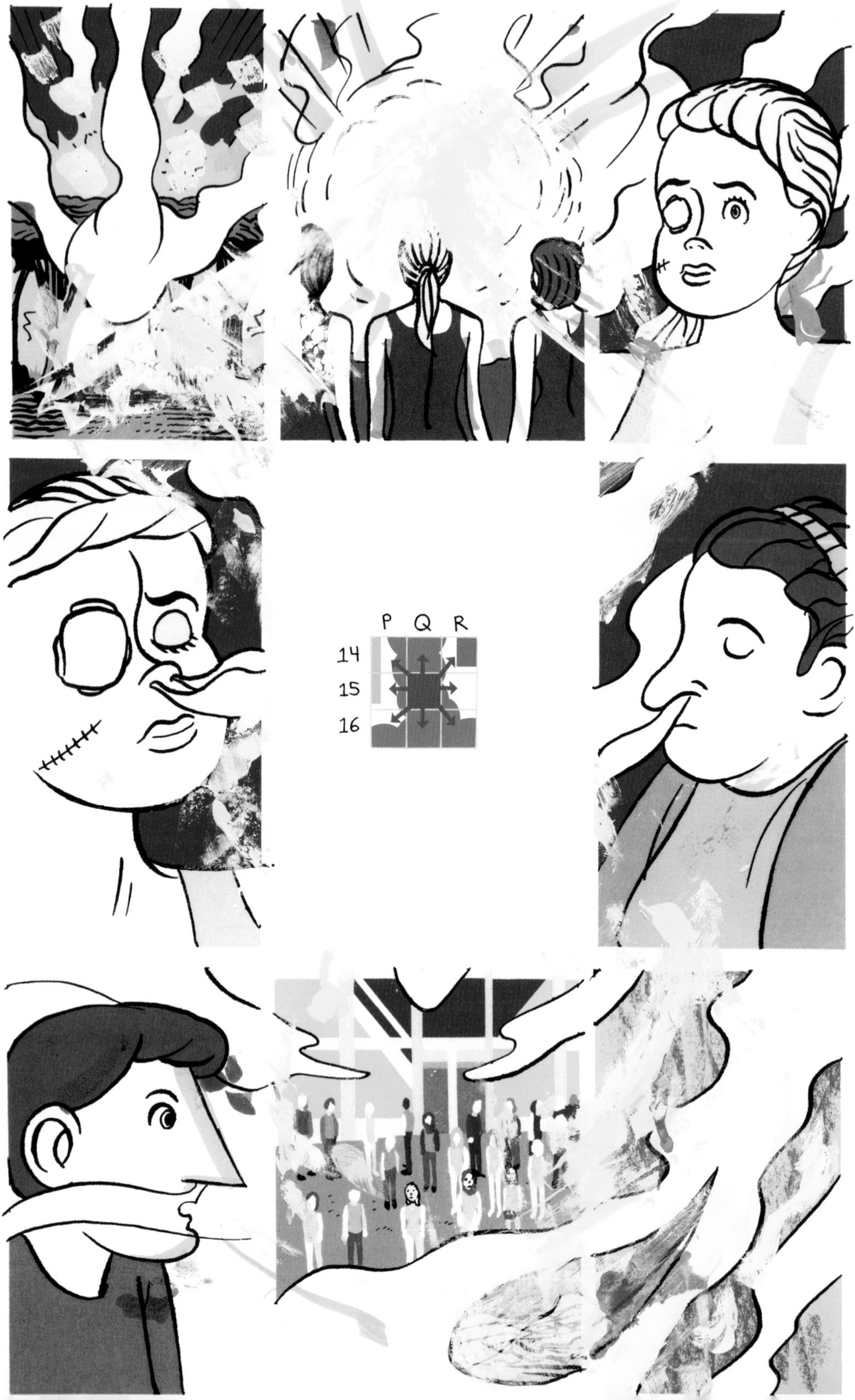
P Q R
14
15
16

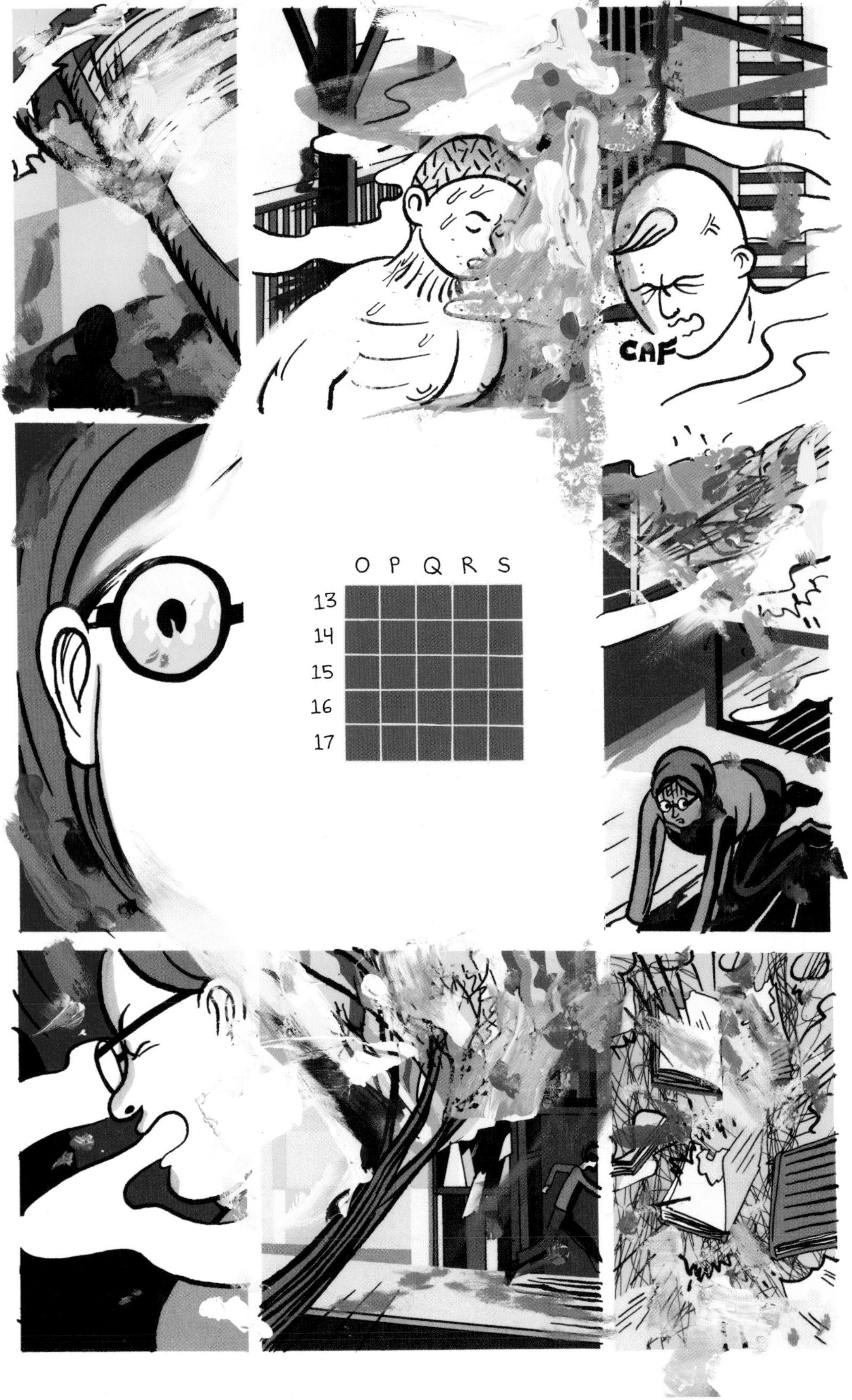
CAF
O P Q R S
13
14
15
16
17

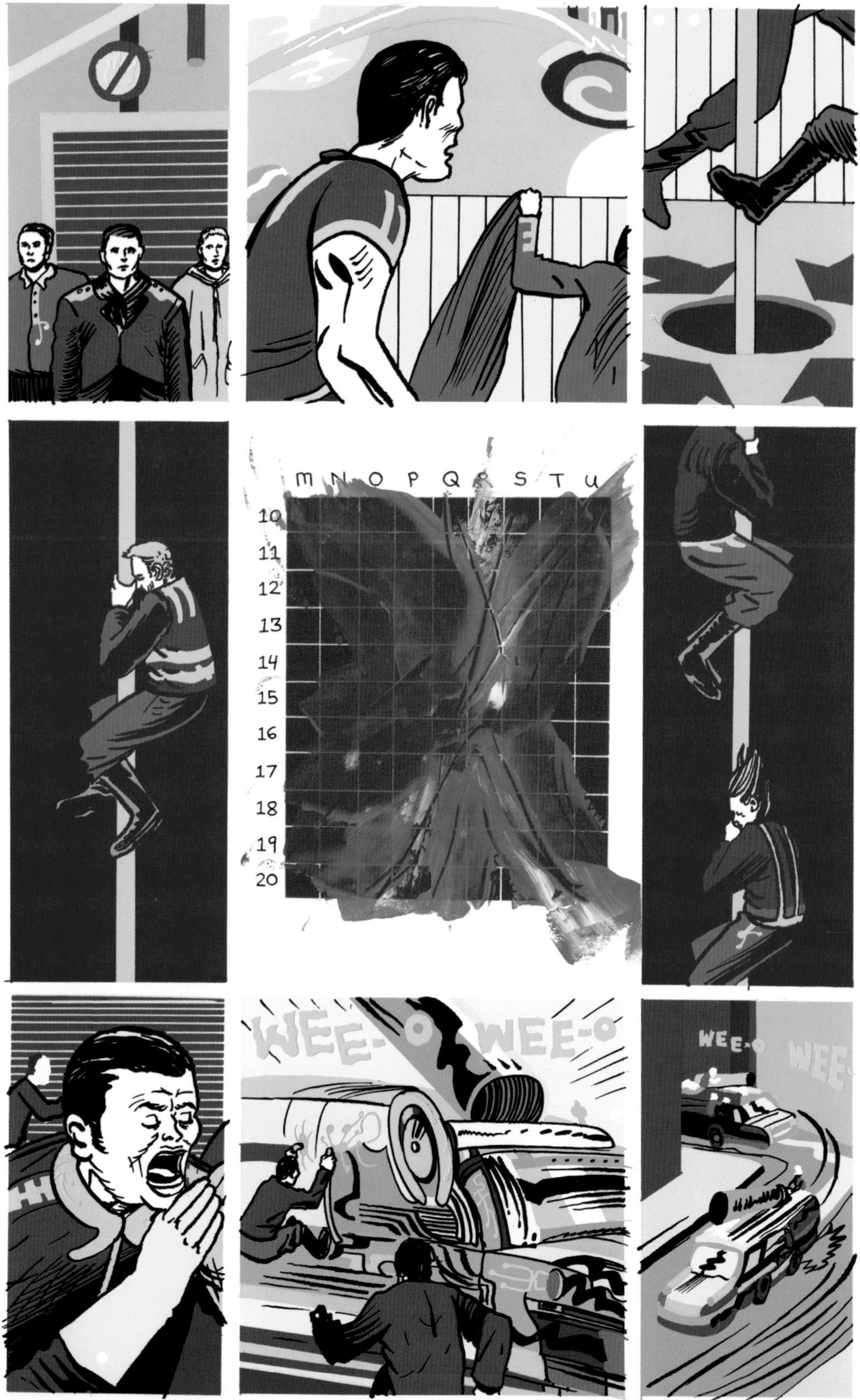
M N O P Q R S T U
10
11
12
13
14
15
16
17
18
19
20
WEE-O WEE-O
WEE-O WEE-

M N O P Q R S T U V
9
10
11
12
13
14
15
16
17
18
19
20
21
22

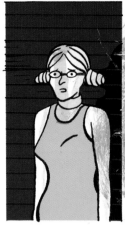

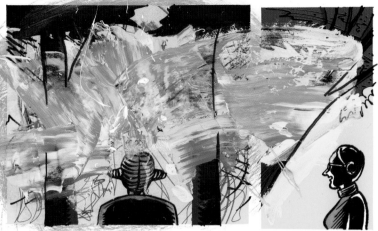

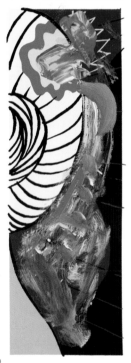

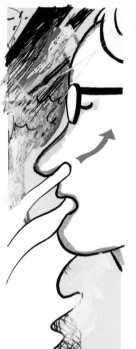

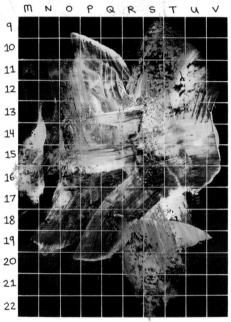

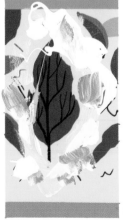

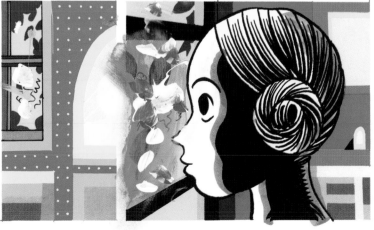

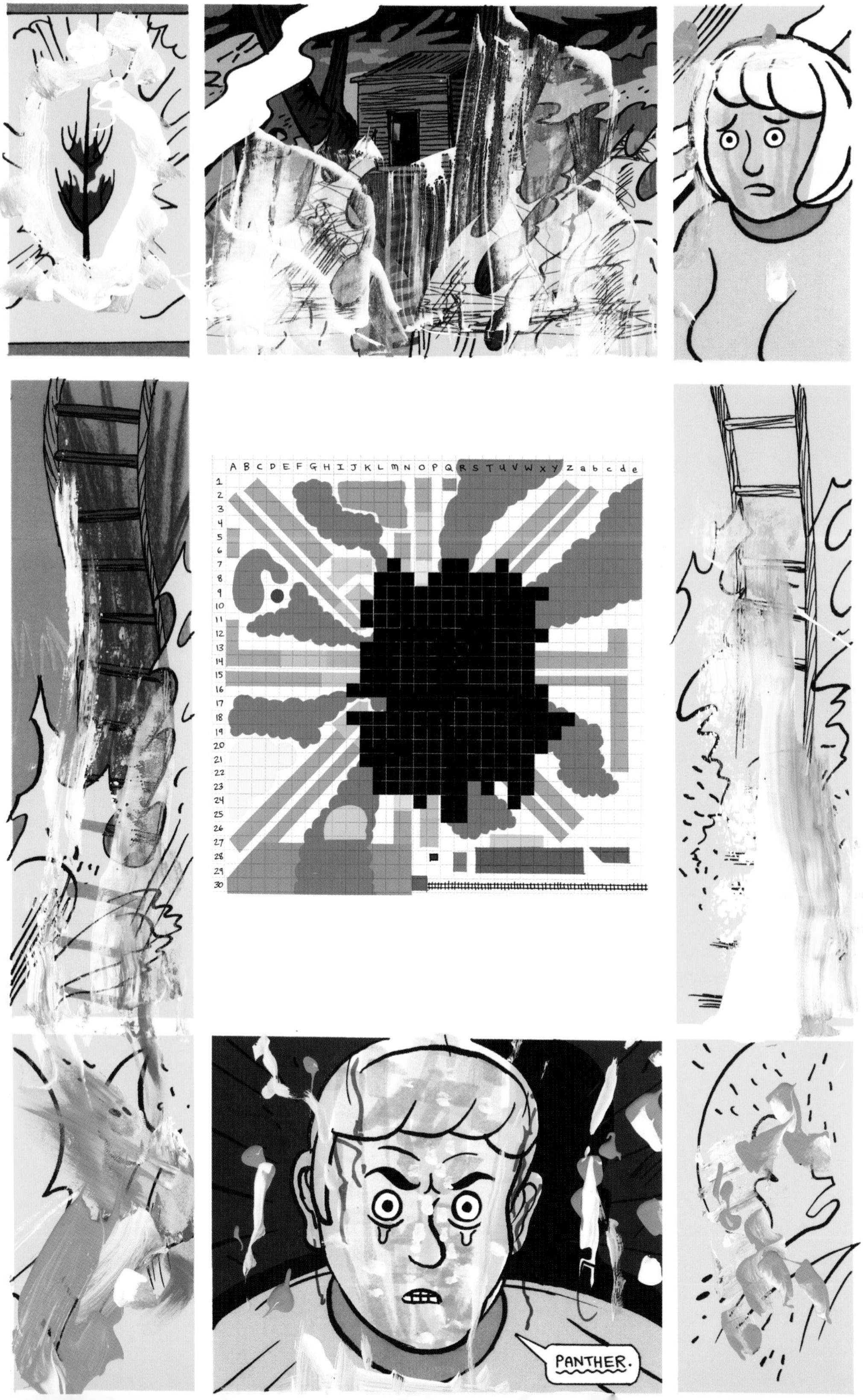
A B C D E F G H I J K L M N O P Q R S T U V W X Y Z a b c d e
1 2 3 4 5 6 7 8 9 10 11 12 13 14 15 16 17 18 19 20 21 22 23 24 25 26 27 28 29 30
PANTHER.

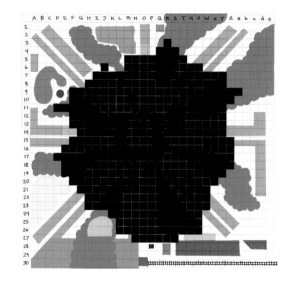

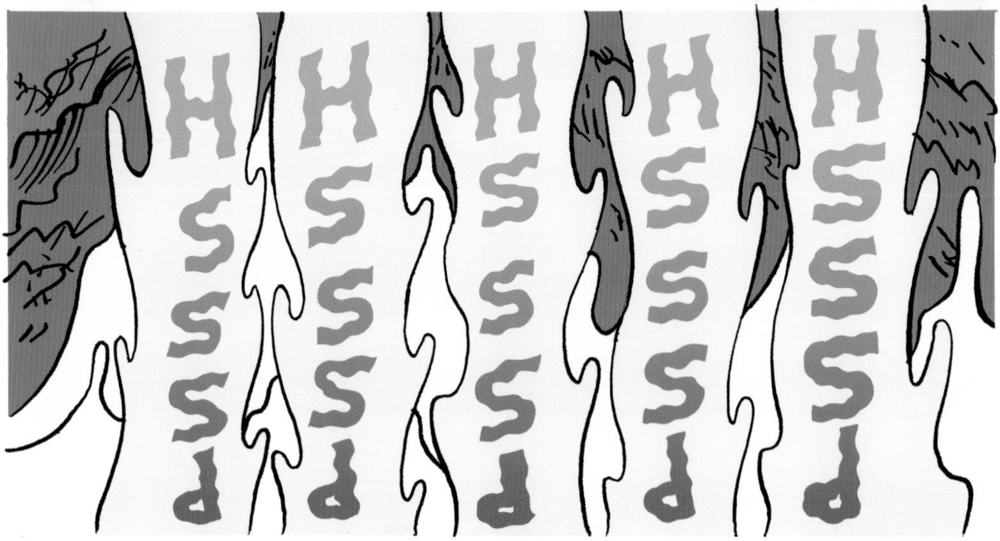
PSSSH
PSSSH
PSSSH
PSSSH
PSSSH

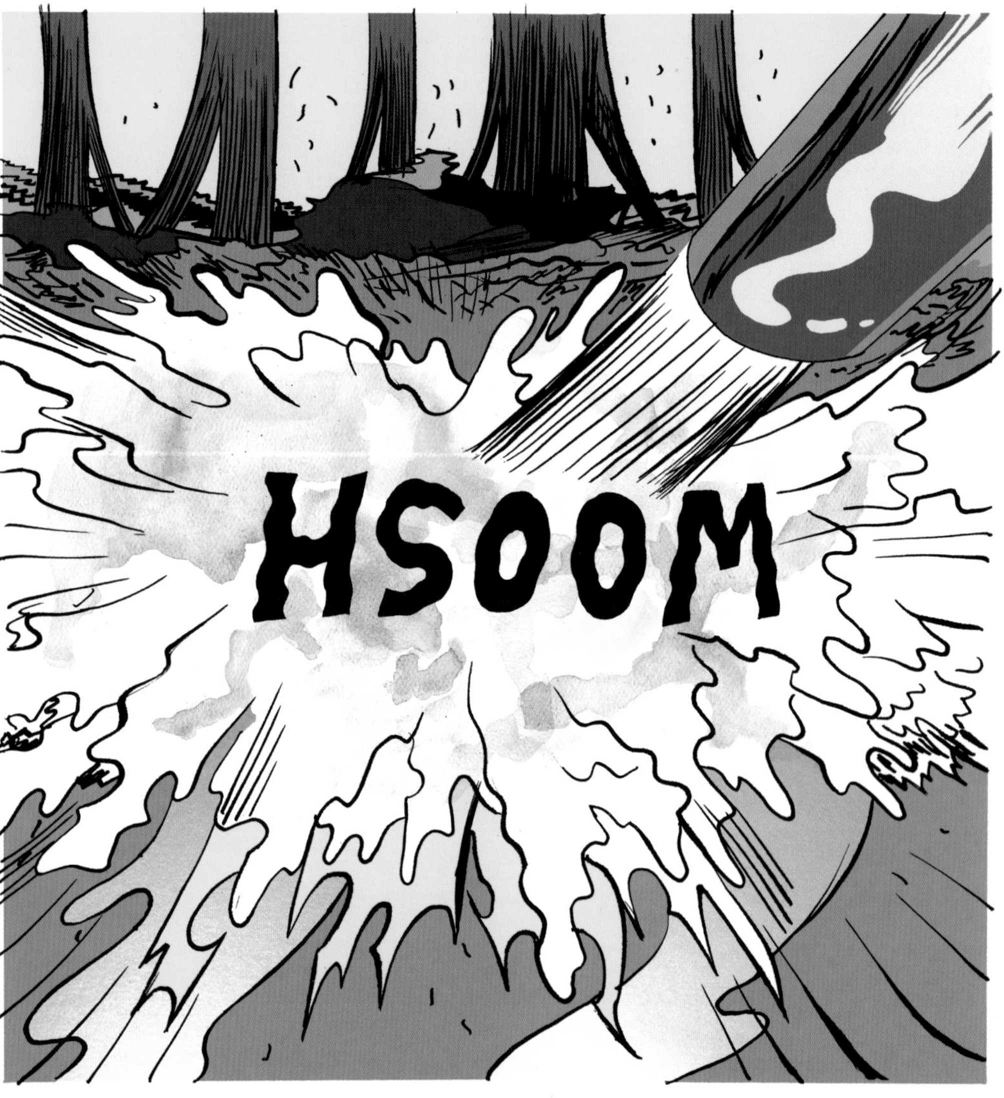
HSOOM

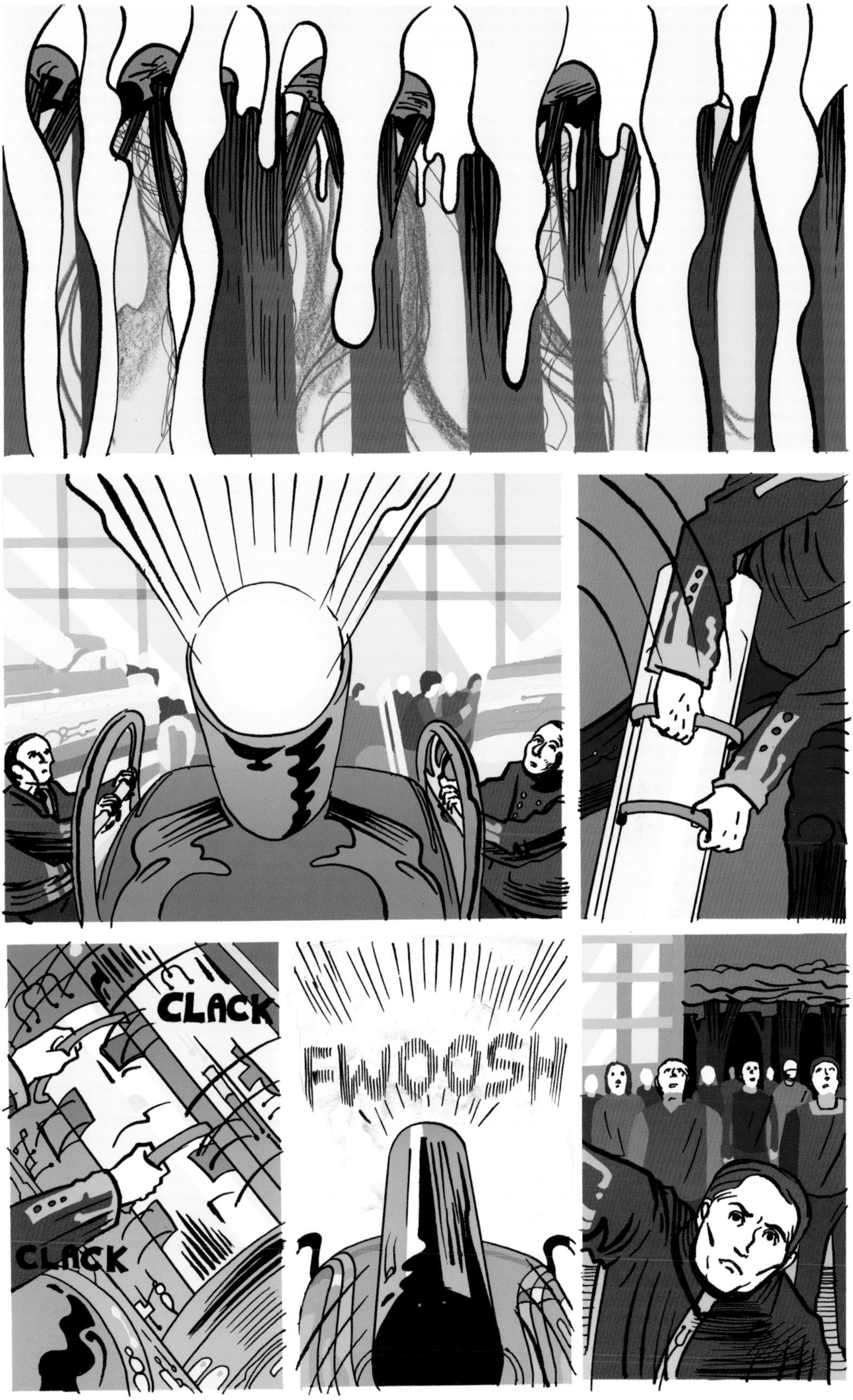
CLACK
CLACK
FWOOSH

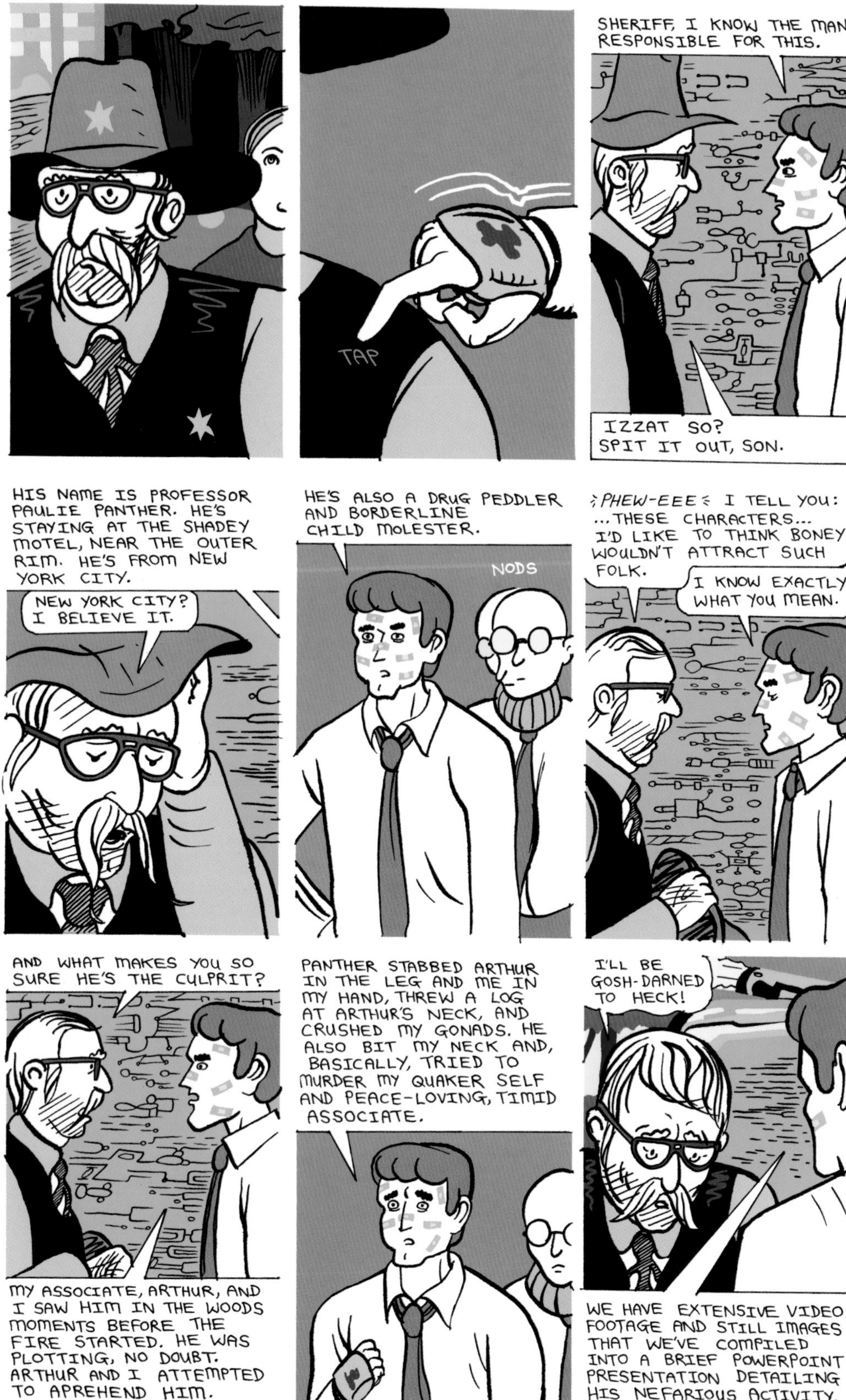
TAP
SHERIFF, I KNOW THE MAN RESPONSIBLE FOR THIS.
IZZAT SO? SPIT IT OUT, SON.
HIS NAME IS PROFESSOR PAULIE PANTHER. HE'S STAYING AT THE SHADEY MOTEL, NEAR THE OUTER RIM. HE'S FROM NEW YORK CITY.
NEW YORK CITY? I BELIEVE IT.
HE'S ALSO A DRUG PEDDLER AND BORDERLINE CHILD MOLESTER.
NODS
≶PHEW-EEE≶ I TELL YOU: ...THESE CHARACTERS... I'D LIKE TO THINK BONEY WOULDN'T ATTRACT SUCH FOLK.
I KNOW EXACTLY WHAT YOU MEAN.
AND WHAT MAKES YOU SO SURE HE'S THE CULPRIT?
MY ASSOCIATE, ARTHUR, AND I SAW HIM IN THE WOODS MOMENTS BEFORE THE FIRE STARTED. HE WAS PLOTTING, NO DOUBT. ARTHUR AND I ATTEMPTED TO APREHEND HIM.
PANTHER STABBED ARTHUR IN THE LEG AND ME IN MY HAND, THREW A LOG AT ARTHUR'S NECK, AND CRUSHED MY GONADS. HE ALSO BIT MY NECK AND, BASICALLY, TRIED TO MURDER MY QUAKER SELF AND PEACE-LOVING, TIMID ASSOCIATE.
I'LL BE GOSH-DARNED TO HECK!
WE HAVE EXTENSIVE VIDEO FOOTAGE AND STILL IMAGES THAT WE'VE COMPILED INTO A BRIEF POWERPOINT PRESENTATION DETAILING HIS NEFARIOUS ACTIVITY.

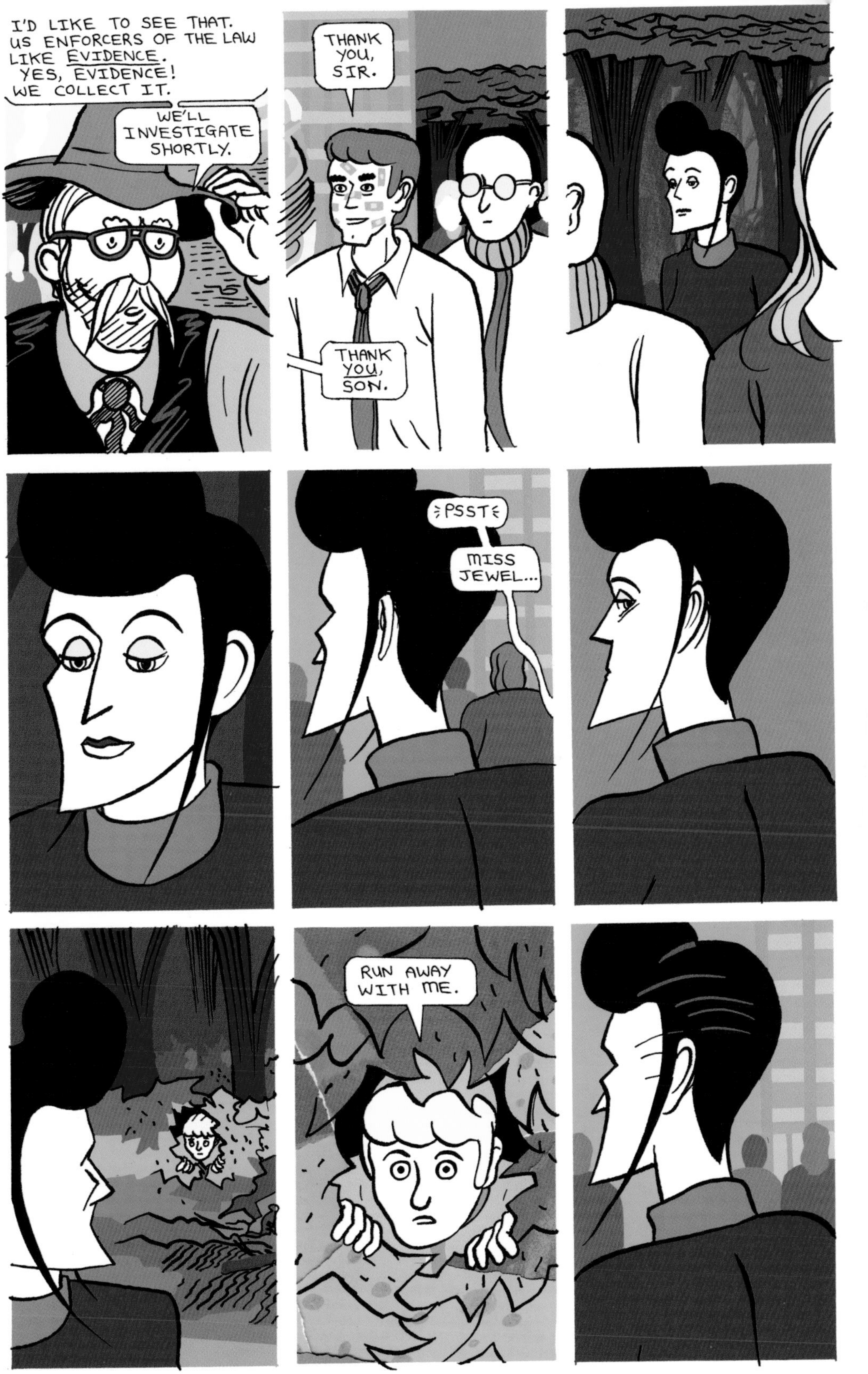
I'D LIKE TO SEE THAT. US ENFORCERS OF THE LAW LIKE EVIDENCE. YES, EVIDENCE! WE COLLECT IT.
WE'LL INVESTIGATE SHORTLY.
THANK YOU, SIR.
THANK YOU, SON.
PSST
MISS JEWEL...
RUN AWAY WITH ME.

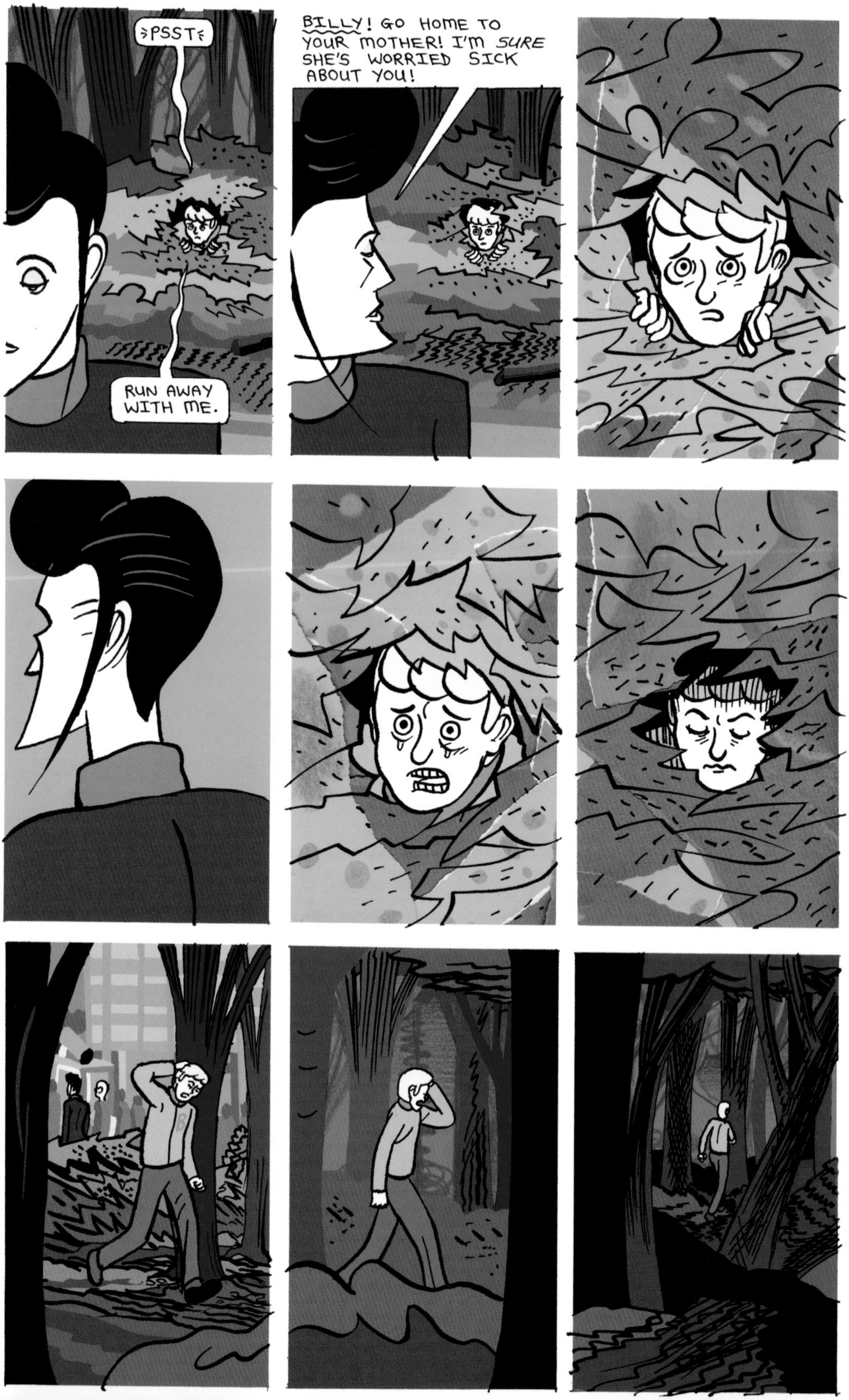
PSST
RUN AWAY WITH ME.
BILLY! GO HOME TO YOUR MOTHER! I'M SURE SHE'S WORRIED SICK ABOUT YOU!

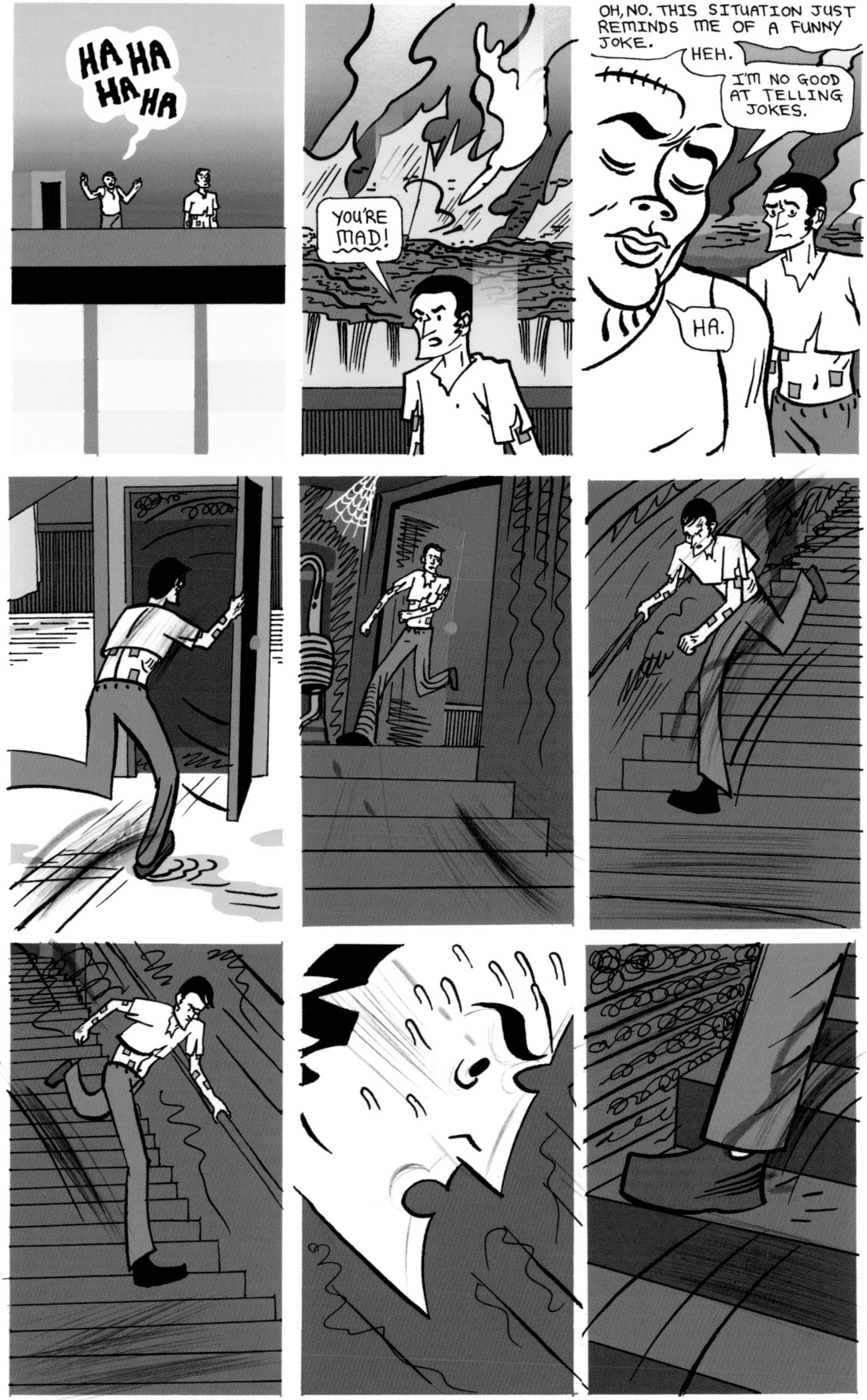
HA HA HA HA HA
YOU'RE MAD!
OH, NO. THIS SITUATION JUST REMINDS ME OF A FUNNY JOKE.
HEH.
I'M NO GOOD AT TELLING JOKES.
HA.

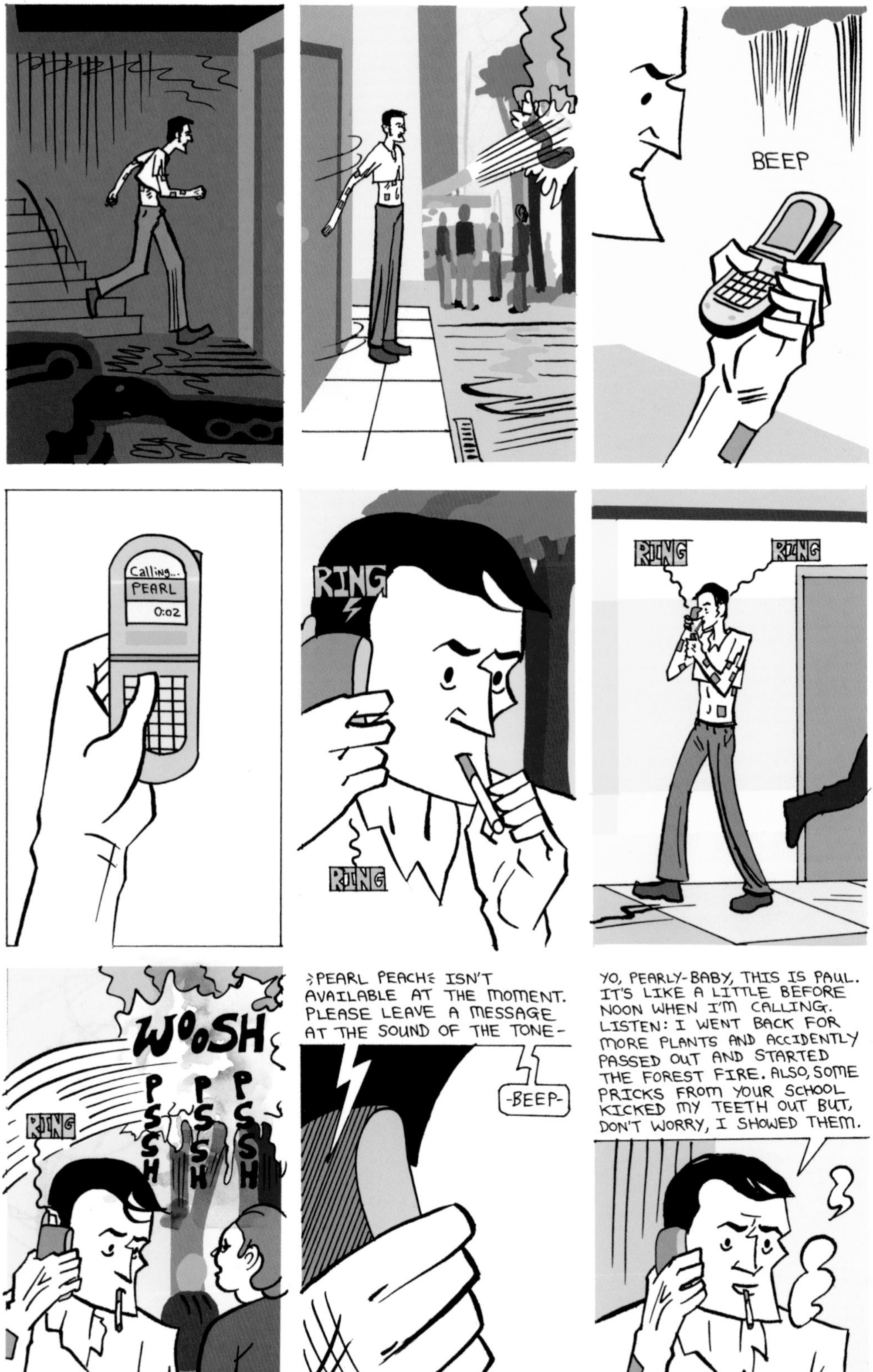
BEEP
Calling...
PEARL
0:02
RING
RING
RING
RING
WOOSH
PSSH
PSSH
PSSH
RING
⋟PEARL PEACH⋞ ISN'T AVAILABLE AT THE MOMENT. PLEASE LEAVE A MESSAGE AT THE SOUND OF THE TONE-
-BEEP-
YO, PEARLY-BABY, THIS IS PAUL. IT'S LIKE A LITTLE BEFORE NOON WHEN I'M CALLING. LISTEN: I WENT BACK FOR MORE PLANTS AND ACCIDENTLY PASSED OUT AND STARTED THE FOREST FIRE. ALSO, SOME PRICKS FROM YOUR SCHOOL KICKED MY TEETH OUT BUT, DON'T WORRY, I SHOWED THEM.

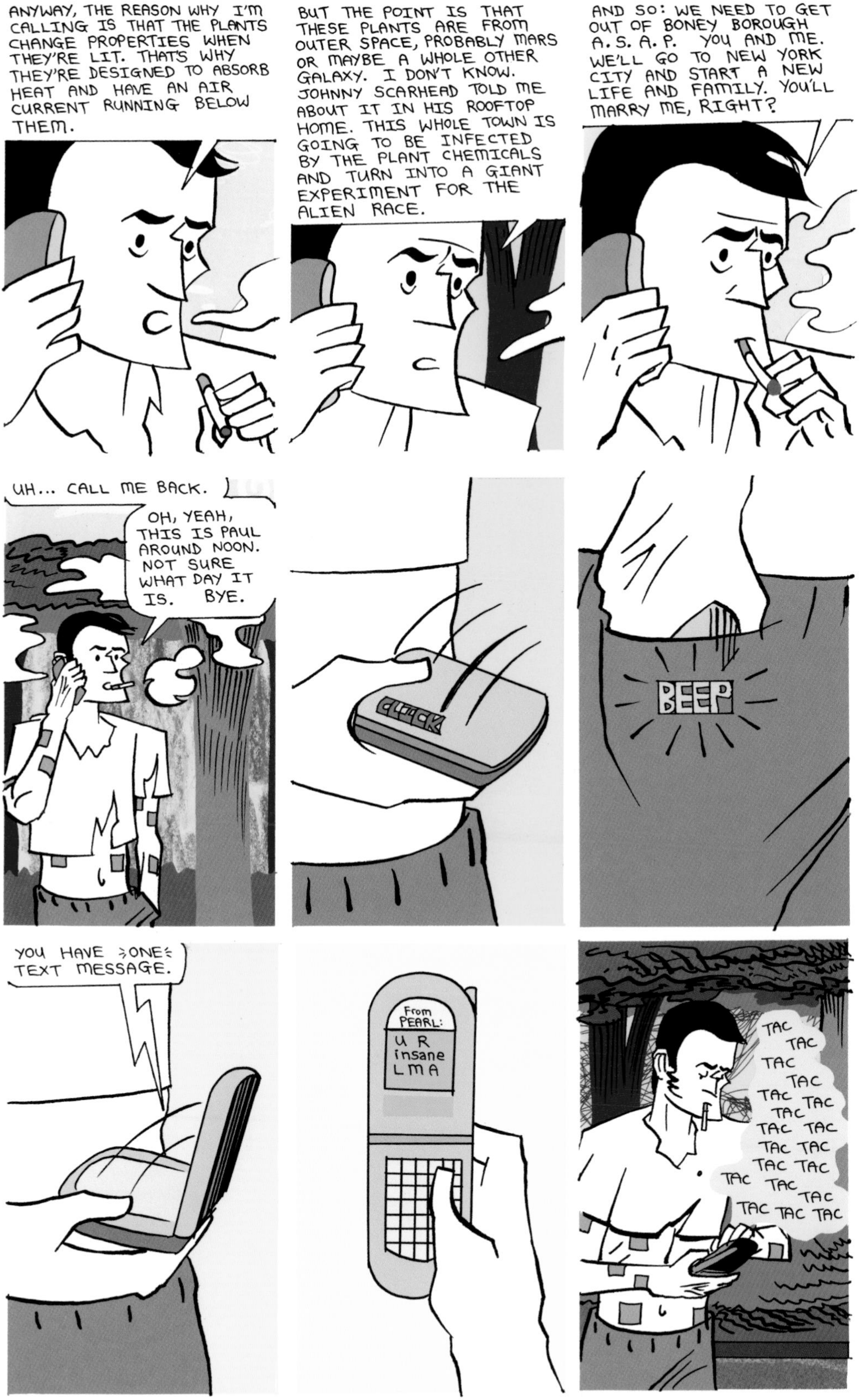

ANYWAY, THE REASON WHY I'M CALLING IS THAT THE PLANTS CHANGE PROPERTIES WHEN THEY'RE LIT. THAT'S WHY THEY'RE DESIGNED TO ABSORB HEAT AND HAVE AN AIR CURRENT RUNNING BELOW THEM.
BUT THE POINT IS THAT THESE PLANTS ARE FROM OUTER SPACE, PROBABLY MARS OR MAYBE A WHOLE OTHER GALAXY. I DON'T KNOW. JOHNNY SCARHEAD TOLD ME ABOUT IT IN HIS ROOFTOP HOME. THIS WHOLE TOWN IS GOING TO BE INFECTED BY THE PLANT CHEMICALS AND TURN INTO A GIANT EXPERIMENT FOR THE ALIEN RACE.
AND SO: WE NEED TO GET OUT OF BONEY BOROUGH A. S. A. P. YOU AND ME. WE'LL GO TO NEW YORK CITY AND START A NEW LIFE AND FAMILY. YOU'LL MARRY ME, RIGHT?
UH... CALL ME BACK.
OH, YEAH, THIS IS PAUL AROUND NOON. NOT SURE WHAT DAY IT IS. BYE.
CLICK
BEEP
YOU HAVE ONE TEXT MESSAGE.
From PEARL:
U R insane LMA
TAC TAC TAC TAC TAC TAC TAC TAC TAC TAC TAC TAC TAC TAC TAC TAC TAC TAC TAC TAC

What does "LMA" mean?
CLICK
BEEP
From PEARL: Leave Me Alone
TAC
TAC
Oh
CLICK

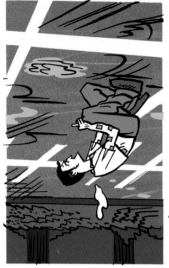

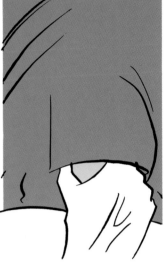

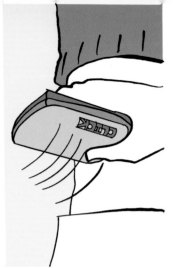

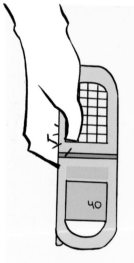

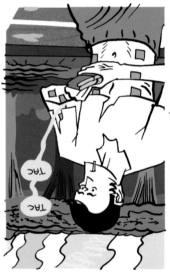

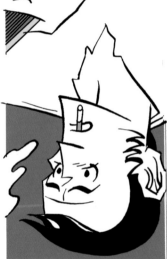

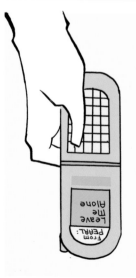

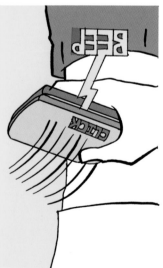

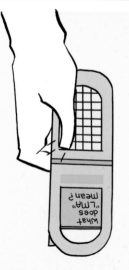

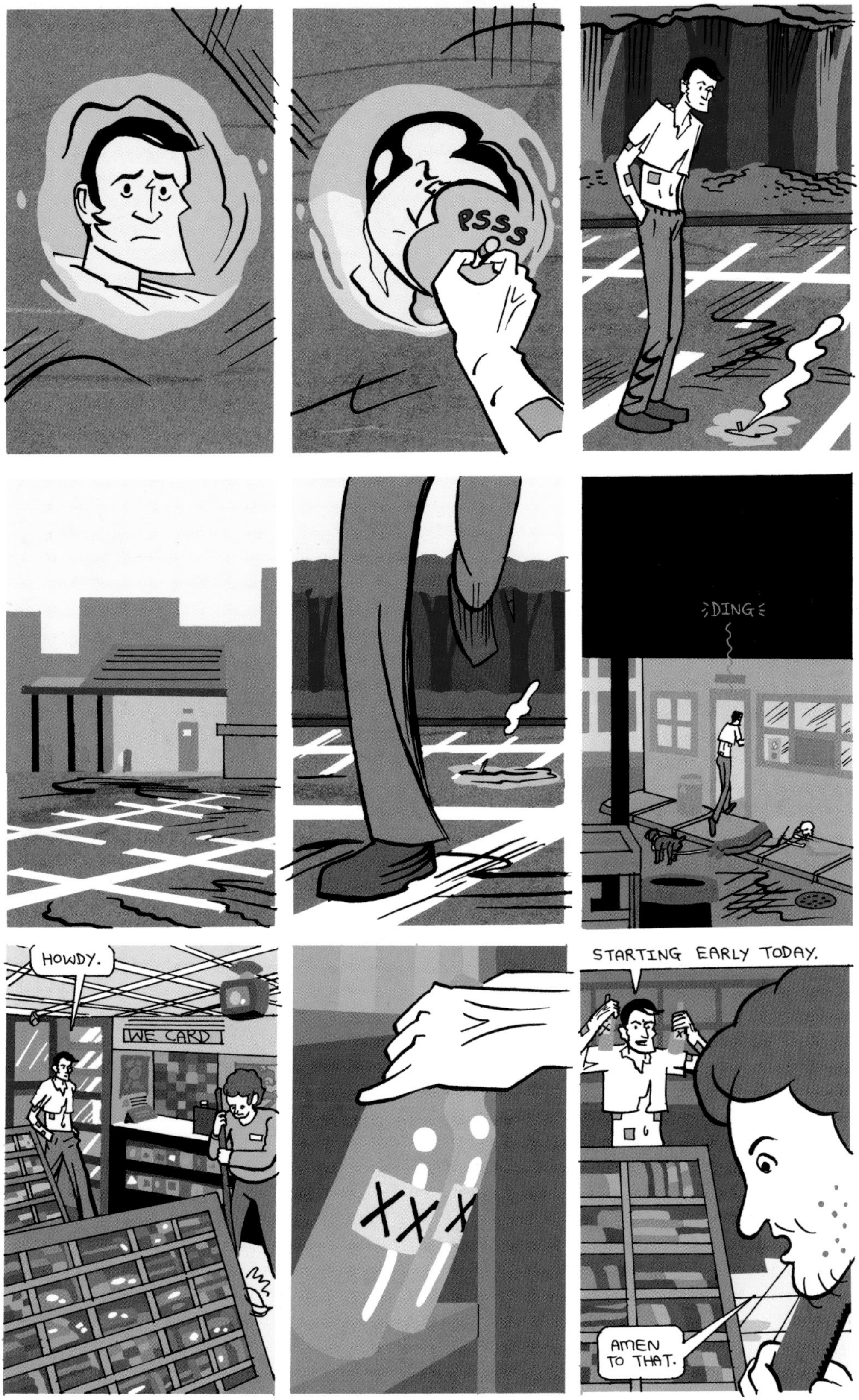
PSSS
DING
HOWDY.
WE CARD
STARTING EARLY TODAY.
AMEN TO THAT.

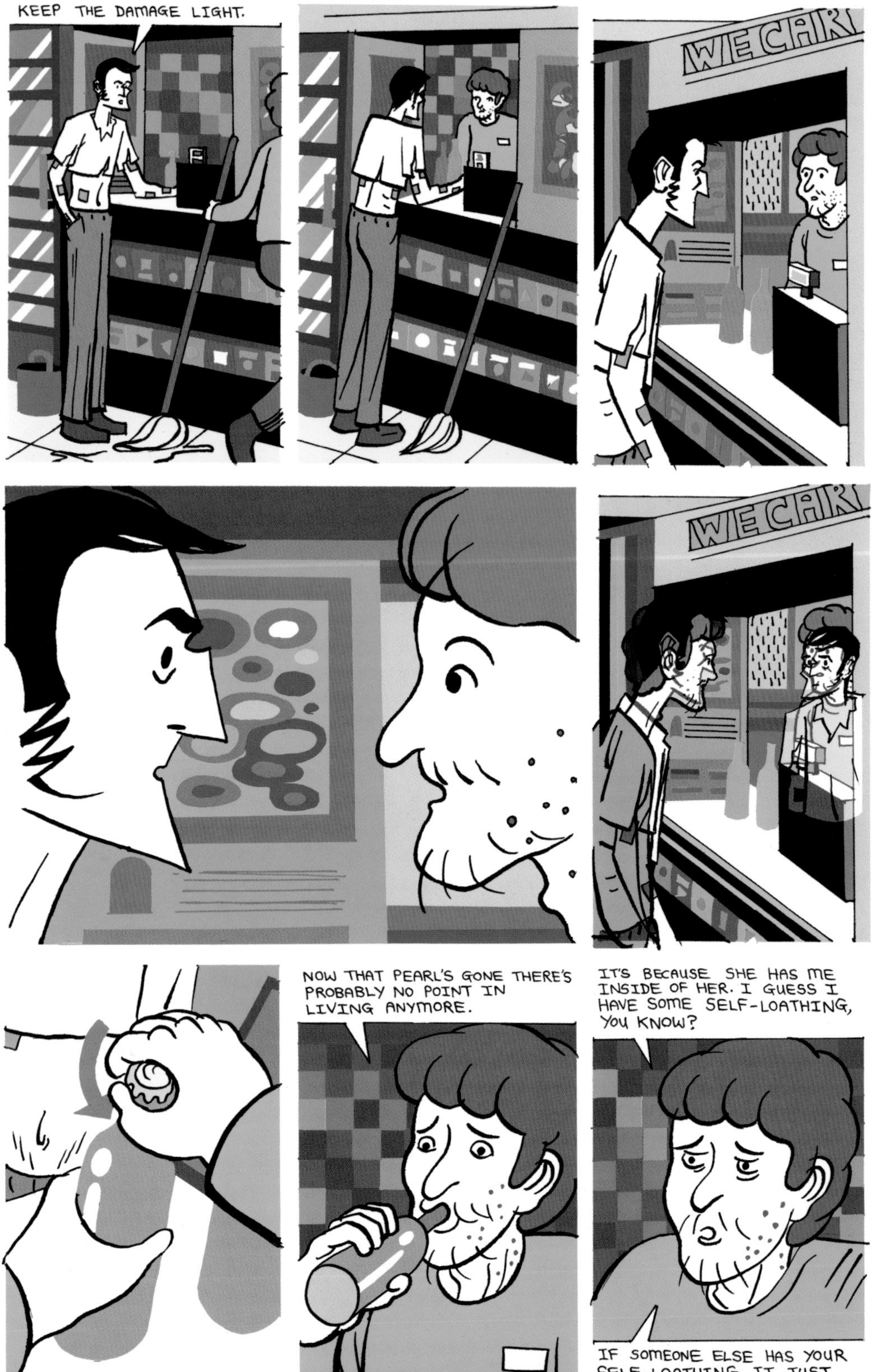
KEEP THE DAMAGE LIGHT.
WE CAR
WE CAR
NOW THAT PEARL'S GONE THERE'S PROBABLY NO POINT IN LIVING ANYMORE.
IT'S BECAUSE SHE HAS ME INSIDE OF HER. I GUESS I HAVE SOME SELF-LOATHING, YOU KNOW?
IF SOMEONE ELSE HAS YOUR SELF-LOATHING, IT JUST MEANS THAT THEY DON'T LIKE YOU. SHIT.

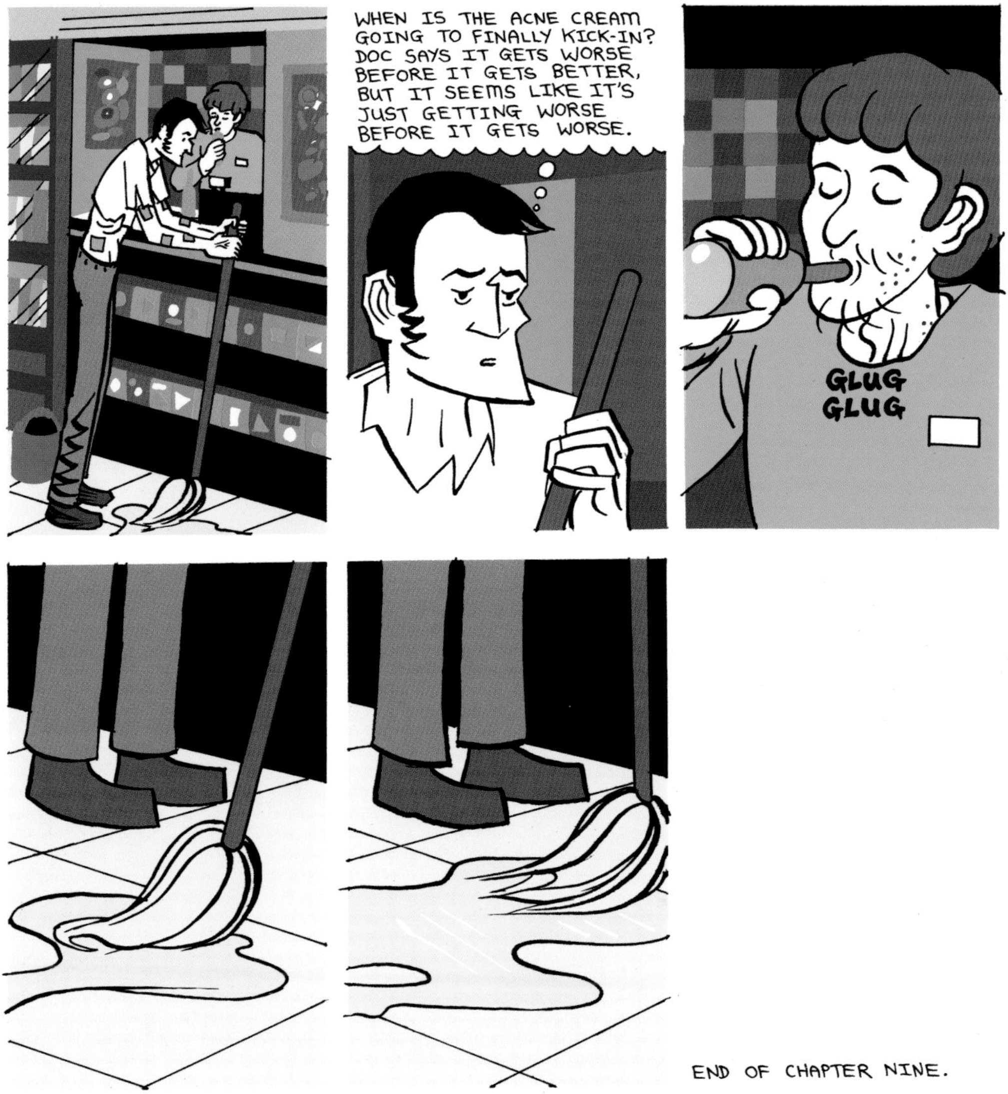
WHEN IS THE ACNE CREAM GOING TO FINALLY KICK-IN? DOC SAYS IT GETS WORSE BEFORE IT GETS BETTER, BUT IT SEEMS LIKE IT'S JUST GETTING WORSE BEFORE IT GETS WORSE.
GLUG GLUG

END OF CHAPTER NINE.

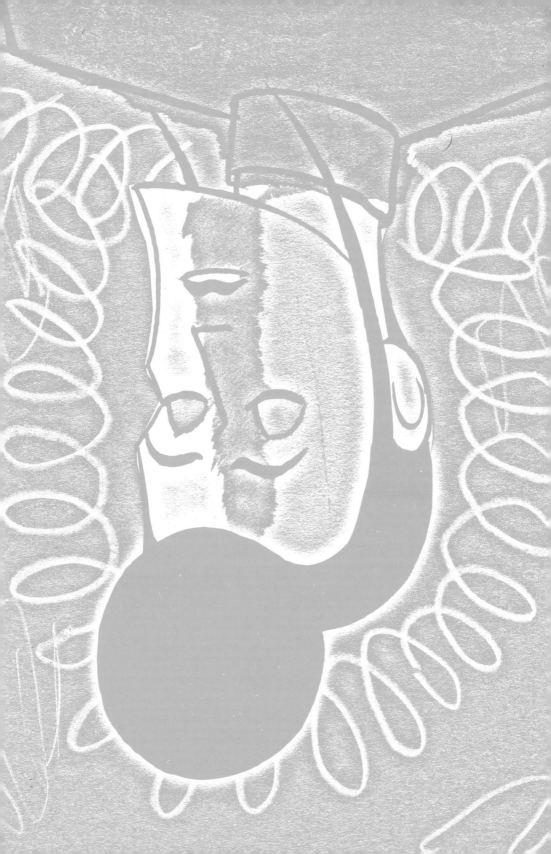

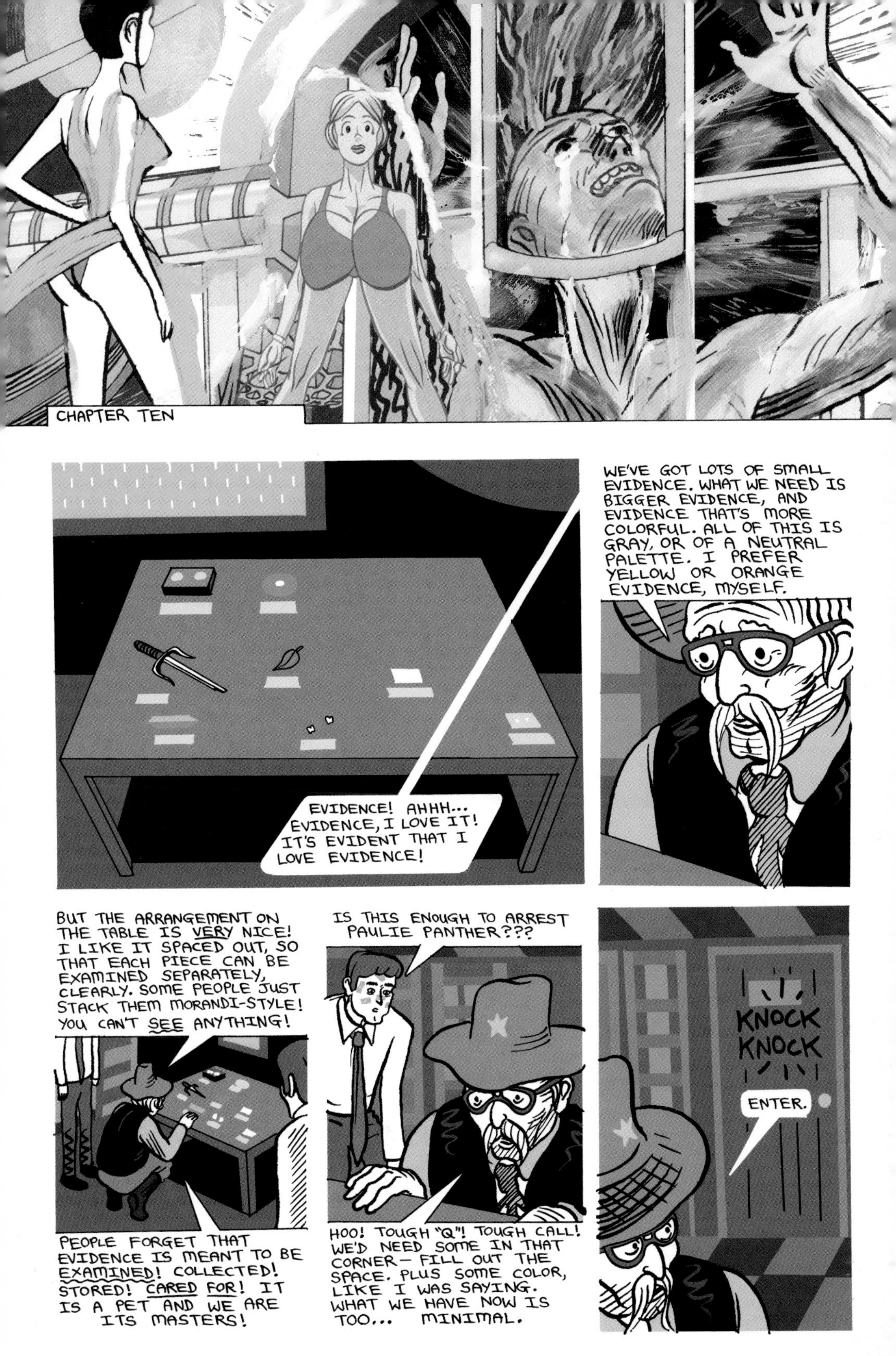
CHAPTER TEN
EVIDENCE! AHHH... EVIDENCE, I LOVE IT! IT'S EVIDENT THAT I LOVE EVIDENCE!
WE'VE GOT LOTS OF SMALL EVIDENCE. WHAT WE NEED IS BIGGER EVIDENCE, AND EVIDENCE THAT'S MORE COLORFUL. ALL OF THIS IS GRAY, OR OF A NEUTRAL PALETTE. I PREFER YELLOW OR ORANGE EVIDENCE, MYSELF.
BUT THE ARRANGEMENT ON THE TABLE IS VERY NICE! I LIKE IT SPACED OUT, SO THAT EACH PIECE CAN BE EXAMINED SEPARATELY, CLEARLY. SOME PEOPLE JUST STACK THEM MORANDI-STYLE! YOU CAN'T SEE ANYTHING!
PEOPLE FORGET THAT EVIDENCE IS MEANT TO BE EXAMINED! COLLECTED! STORED! CARED FOR! IT IS A PET AND WE ARE ITS MASTERS!
IS THIS ENOUGH TO ARREST PAULIE PANTHER???
HOO! TOUGH "Q"! TOUGH CALL! WE'D NEED SOME IN THAT CORNER— FILL OUT THE SPACE. PLUS SOME COLOR, LIKE I WAS SAYING. WHAT WE HAVE NOW IS TOO... MINIMAL.
KNOCK KNOCK
ENTER.

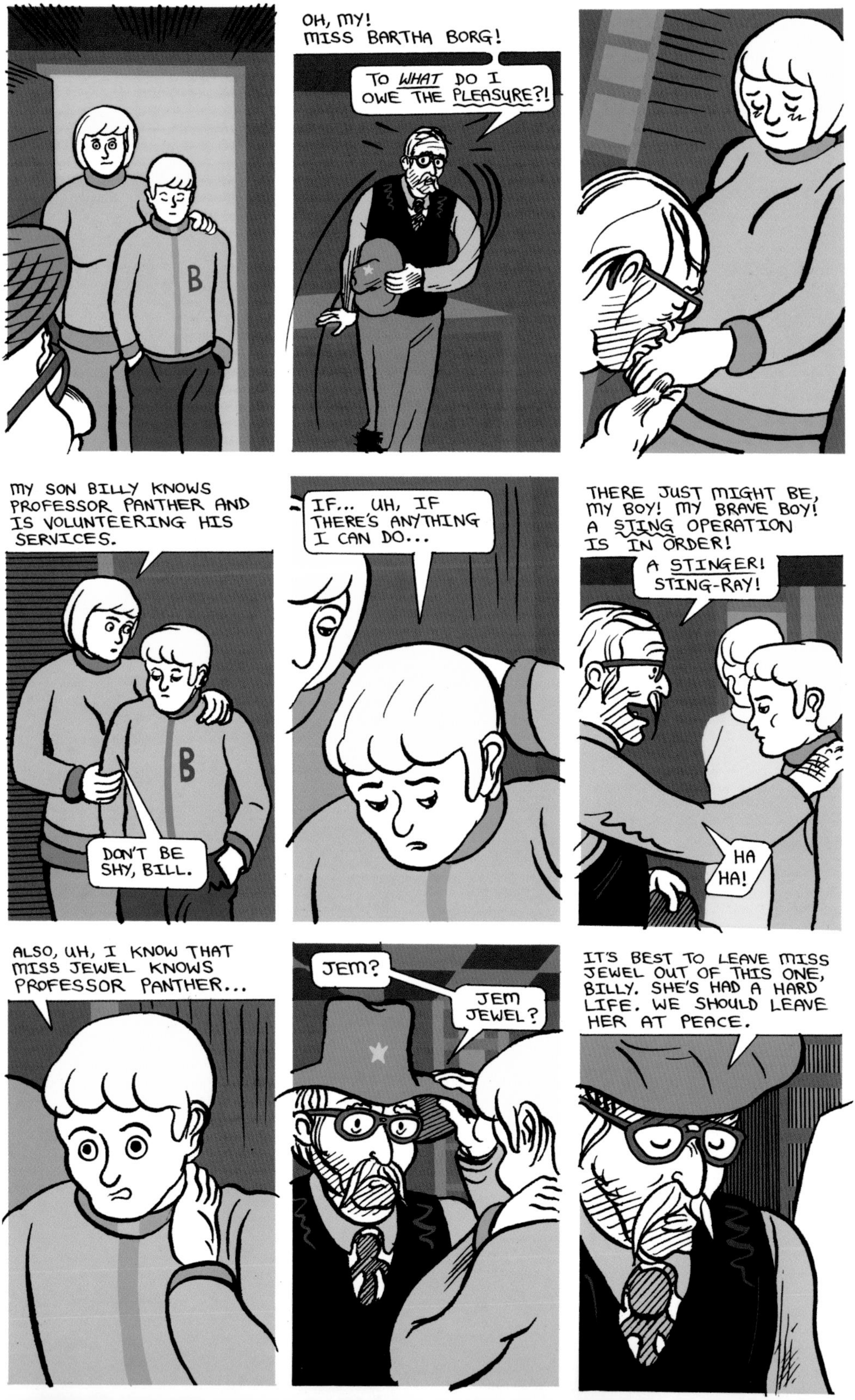
OH, MY!
MISS BARTHA BORG!
TO WHAT DO I OWE THE PLEASURE?!
MY SON BILLY KNOWS PROFESSOR PANTHER AND IS VOLUNTEERING HIS SERVICES.
DON'T BE SHY, BILL.
IF... UH, IF THERE'S ANYTHING I CAN DO...
THERE JUST MIGHT BE, MY BOY! MY BRAVE BOY! A STING OPERATION IS IN ORDER!
A STINGER! STING-RAY!
HA HA!
ALSO, UH, I KNOW THAT MISS JEWEL KNOWS PROFESSOR PANTHER...
JEM?
JEM JEWEL?
IT'S BEST TO LEAVE MISS JEWEL OUT OF THIS ONE, BILLY. SHE'S HAD A HARD LIFE. WE SHOULD LEAVE HER AT PEACE.

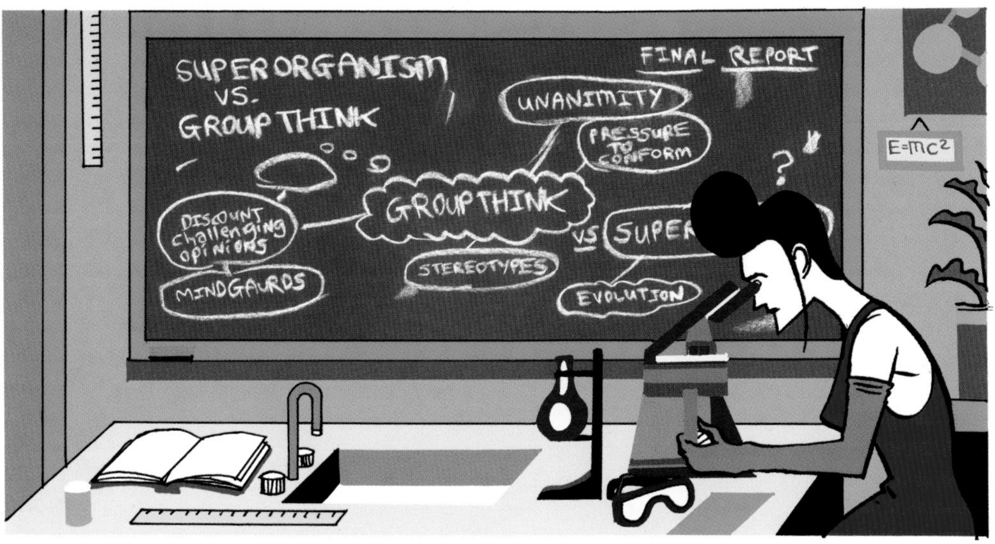
SUPERORGANISM
VS.
GROUPTHINK
FINAL REPORT
UNANIMITY
PRESSURE TO CONFORM
GROUPTHINK
DISCOUNT challenging opinions
MINDGAURDS
STEREOTYPES
VS
SUPER
EVOLUTION
E=mc²

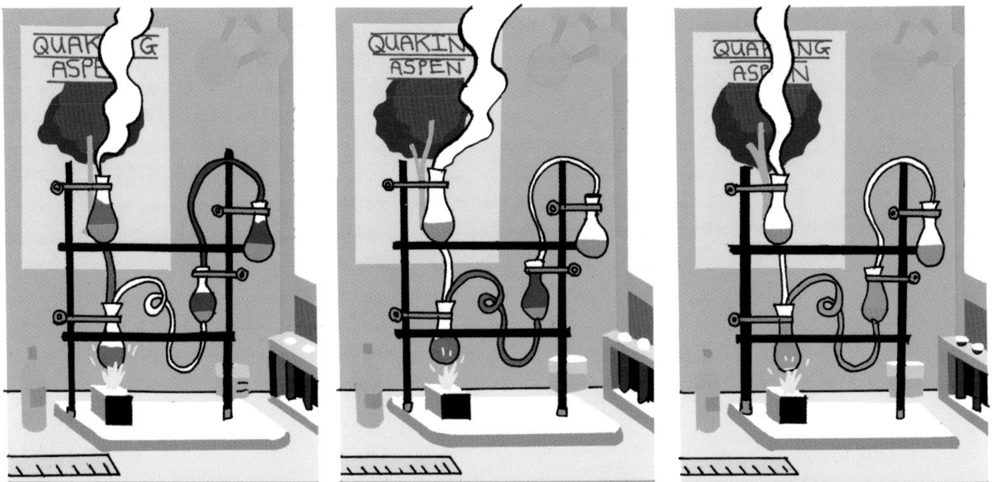
QUAK G
ASPE
QUAKIN
ASPEN
QUA ING
ASP N

KEEP UP THE GOOD WORK, FELLAS. I'LL BE SURE TO COMMENT ON ALL YOUR FACEBOOKS.

JUST, UH, ADMIRING THE MACHINERY. IT'S BEAUTIFULLY DESIGNED. NICE SCREWS.

WHAT ARE YOU DOING?

WATERING CAN.

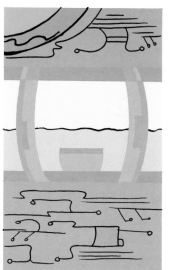

N
11

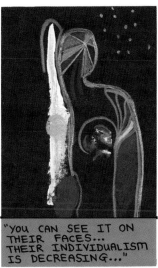

"YOU CAN SEE IT ON THEIR FACES... THEIR INDIVIDUALISM IS DECREASING..."

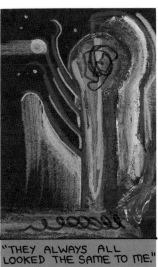

"THEY ALWAYS ALL LOOKED THE SAME TO ME."

"NO,  IS RIGHT. IT'S HAPPENING."

"WHEN THEY'RE ALL OF ONE BODYMIND, THEY'LL BE MUCH EASIER TO CONTROL."

[UNTRANSLATABLE IMAGES]

[LAUGHTER]

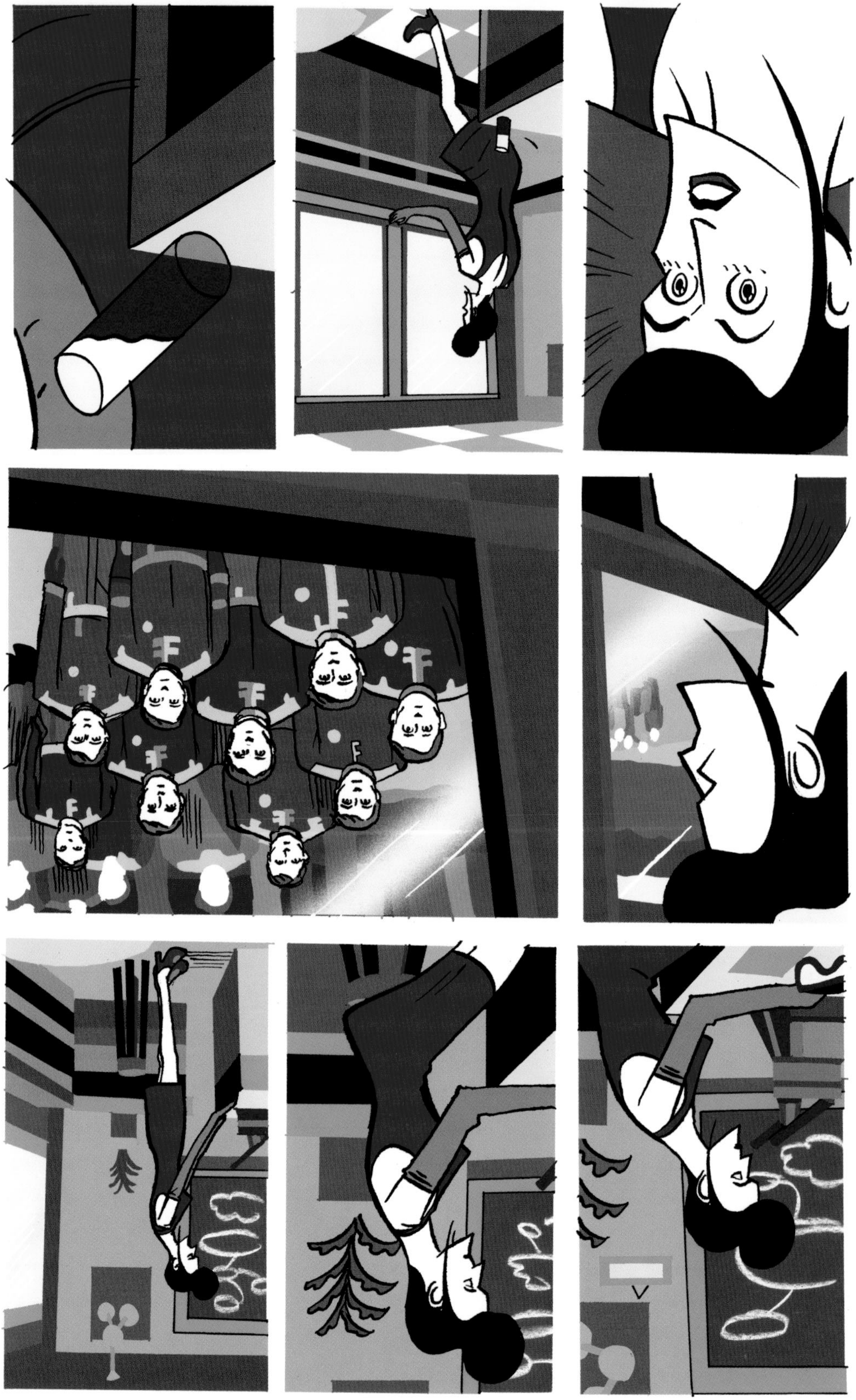

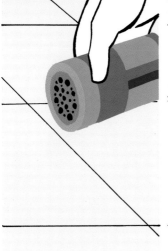

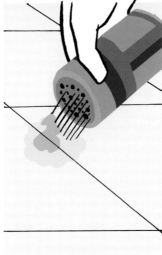

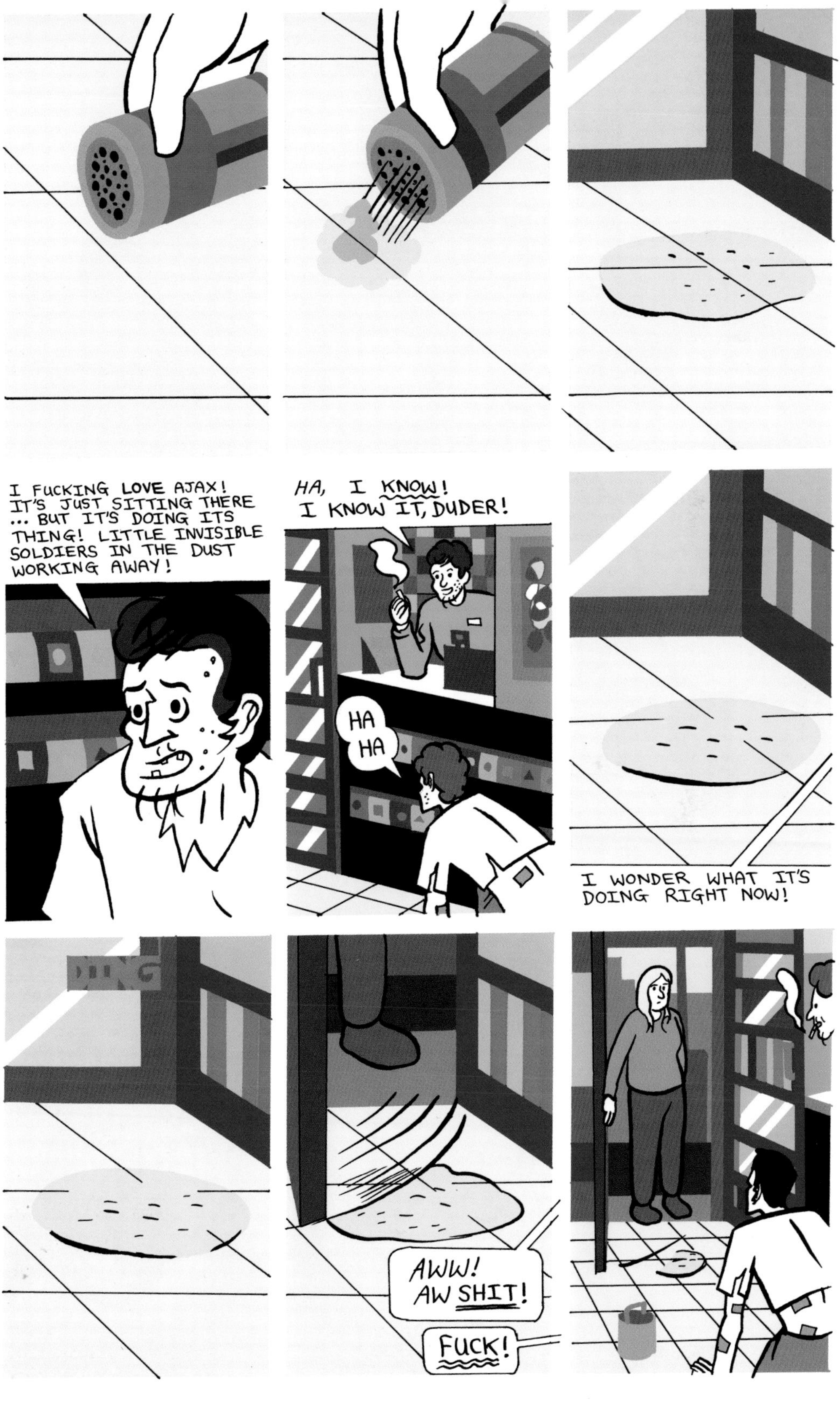

I FUCKING **LOVE** AJAX! IT'S JUST SITTING THERE ... BUT IT'S DOING ITS THING! LITTLE INVISIBLE SOLDIERS IN THE DUST WORKING AWAY!

HA, I KNOW! I KNOW IT, DUDER!

HA HA

I WONDER WHAT IT'S DOING RIGHT NOW!

AWW! AW **SHIT**!

FUCK!

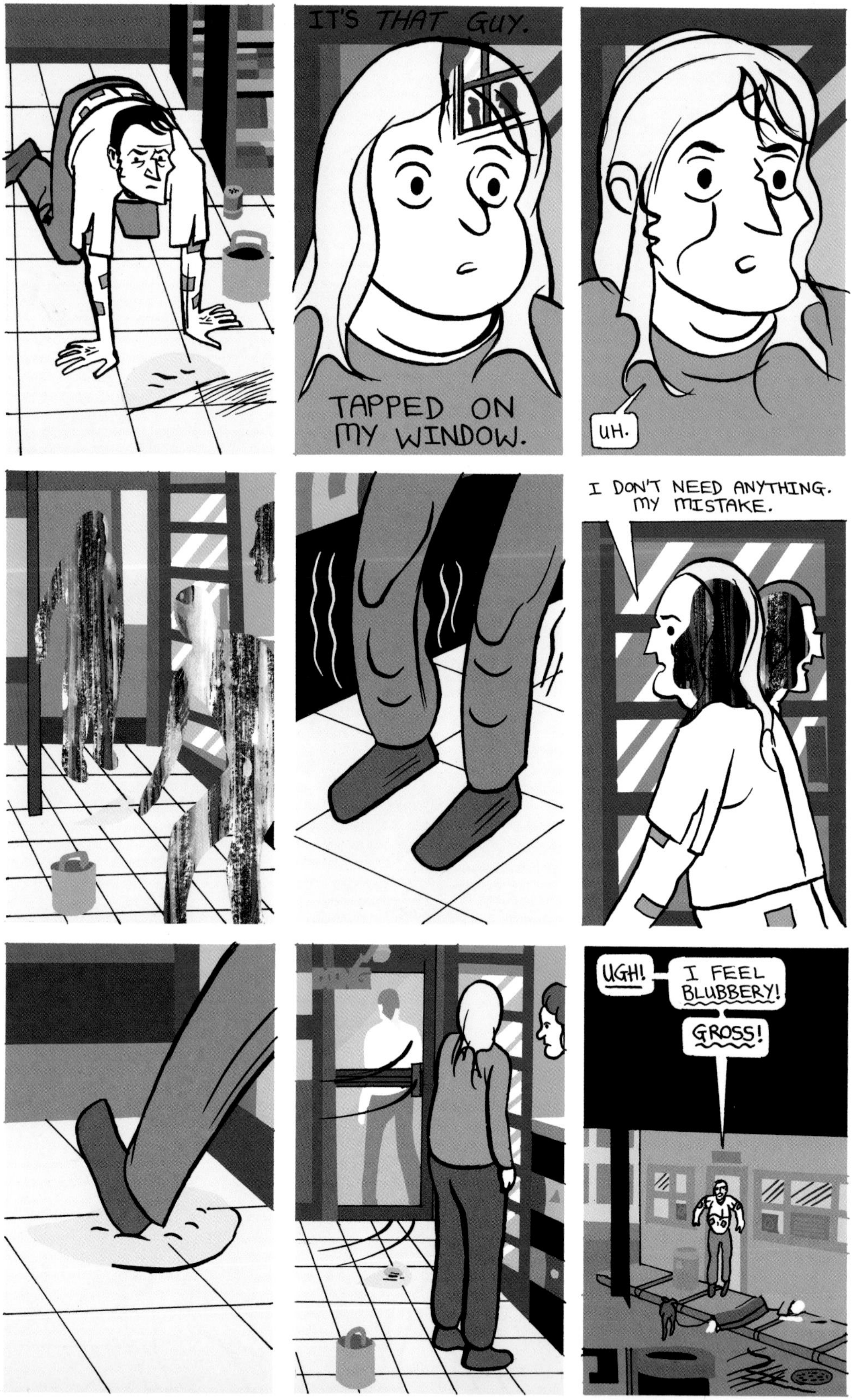
IT'S THAT GUY.
TAPPED ON MY WINDOW.
UH.
I DON'T NEED ANYTHING. MY MISTAKE.
UGH!
I FEEL BLUBBERY!
GROSS!

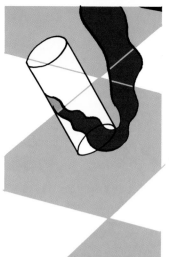

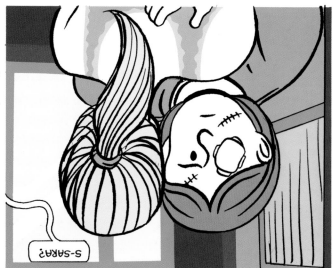

S-SARA?

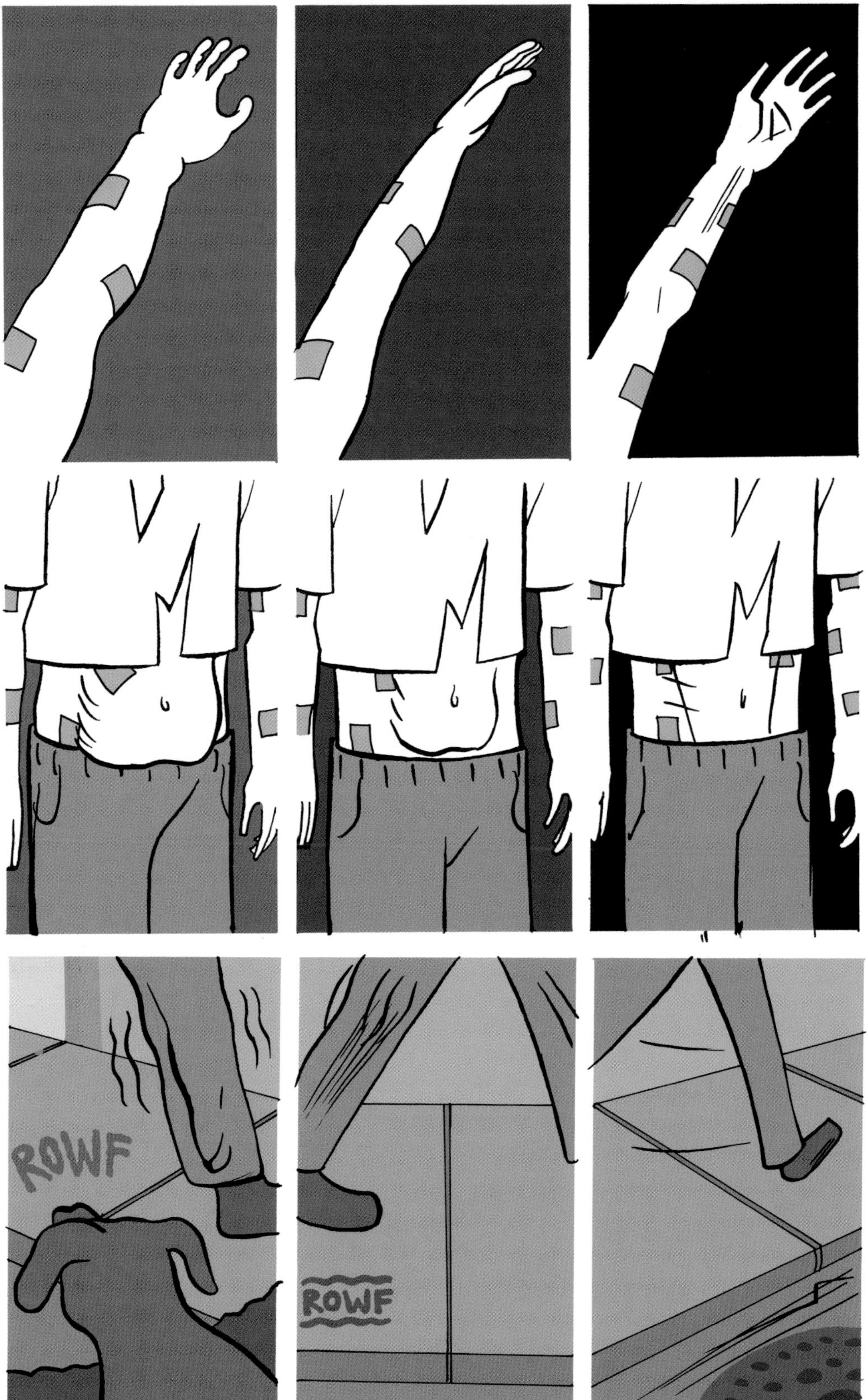
ROWF
ROWF

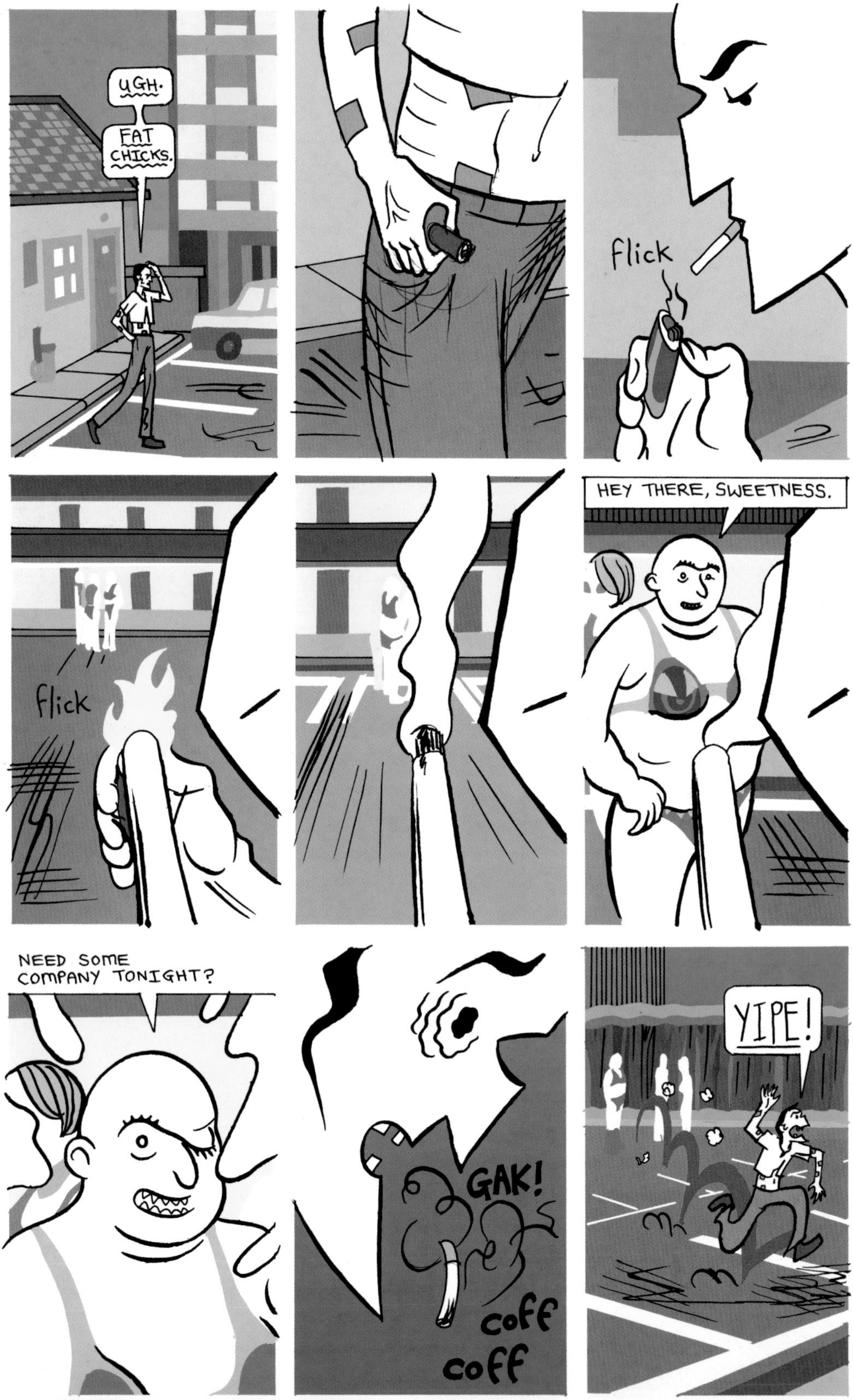
UGH.
FAT CHICKS.
flick
flick
HEY THERE, SWEETNESS.
NEED SOME COMPANY TONIGHT?
GAK!
coff
coff
YIPE!

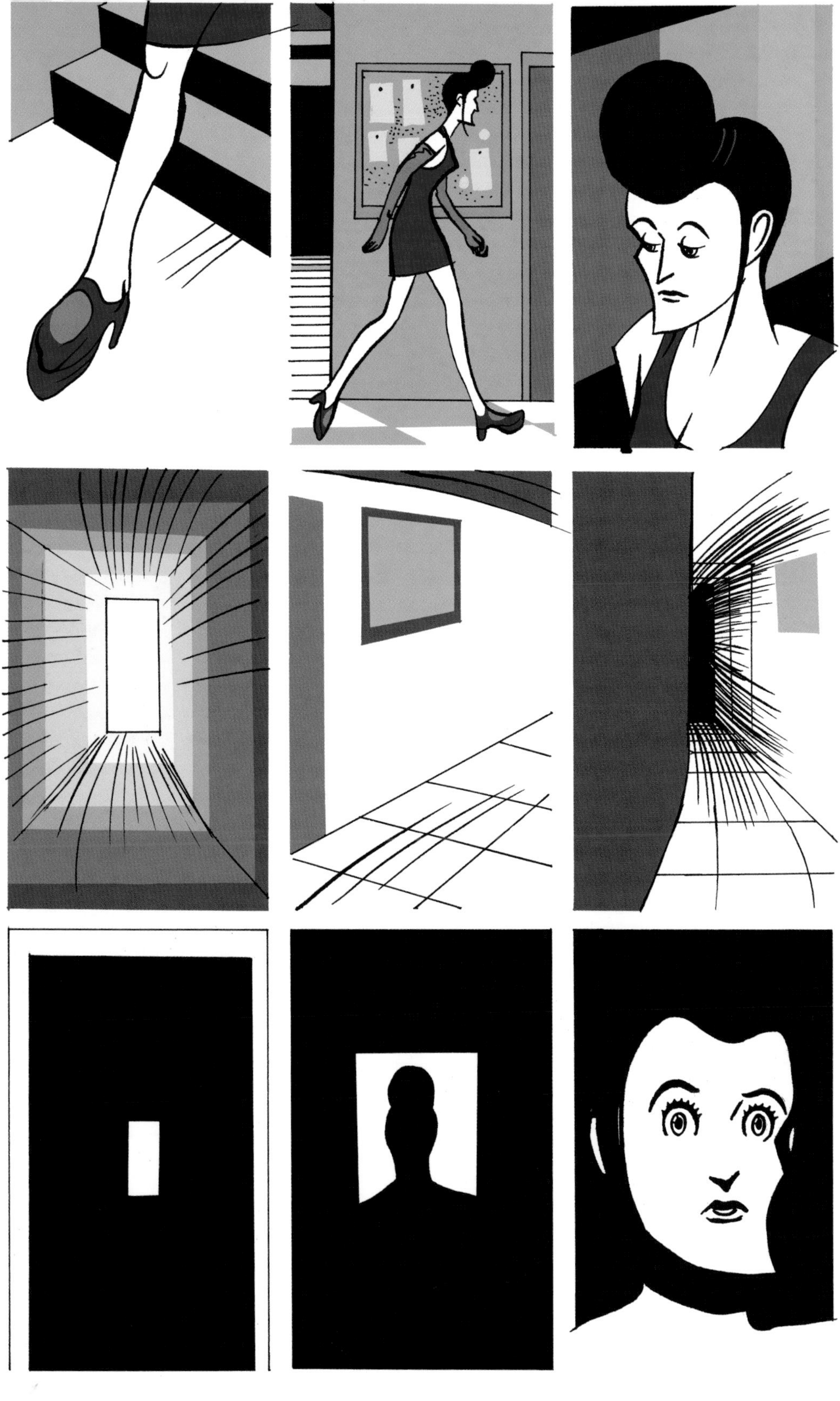

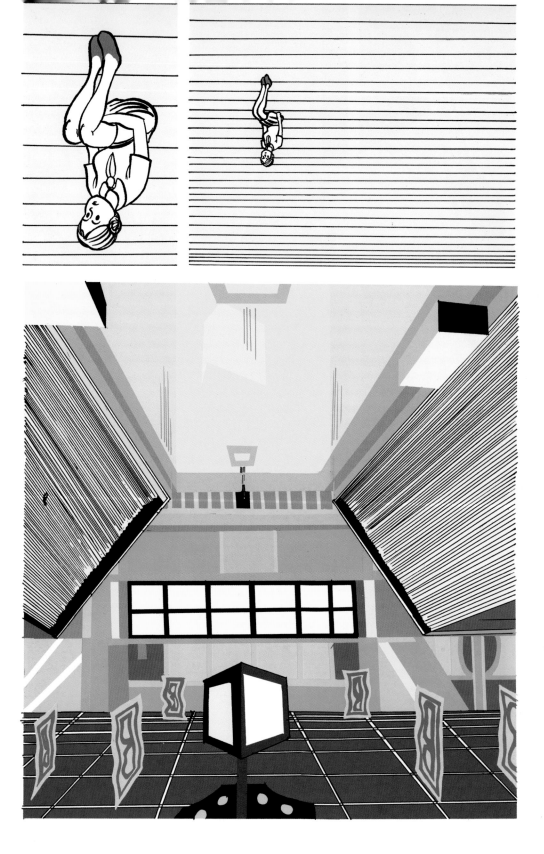

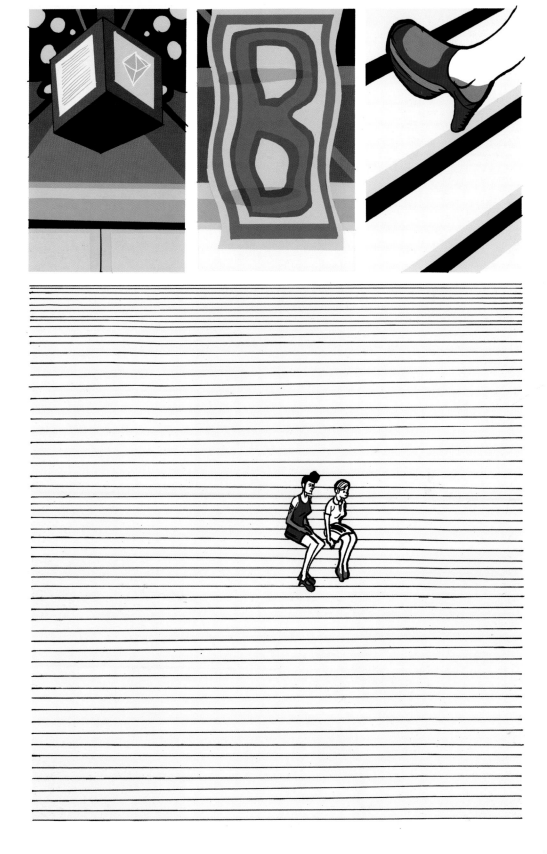

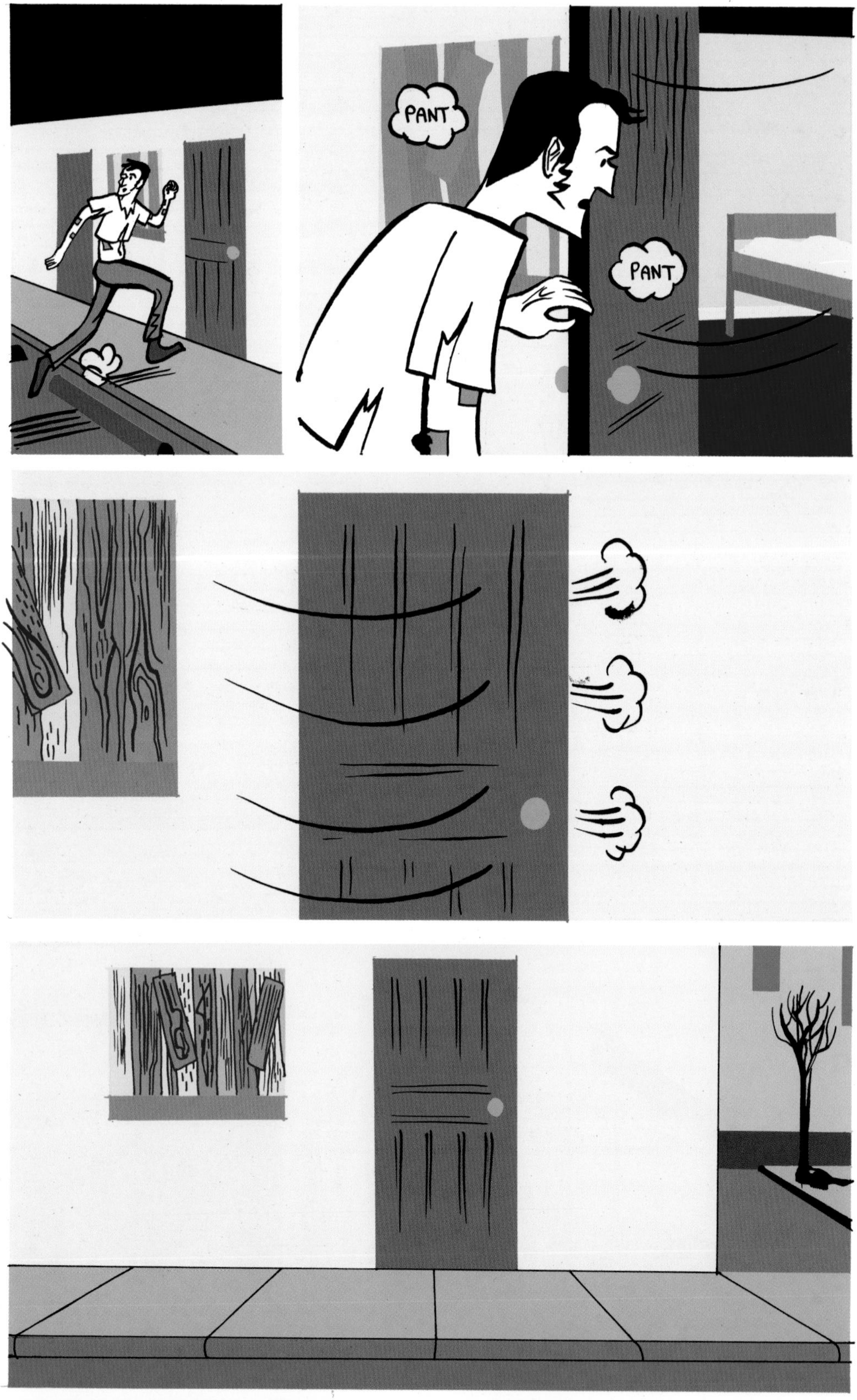
PANT
PANT

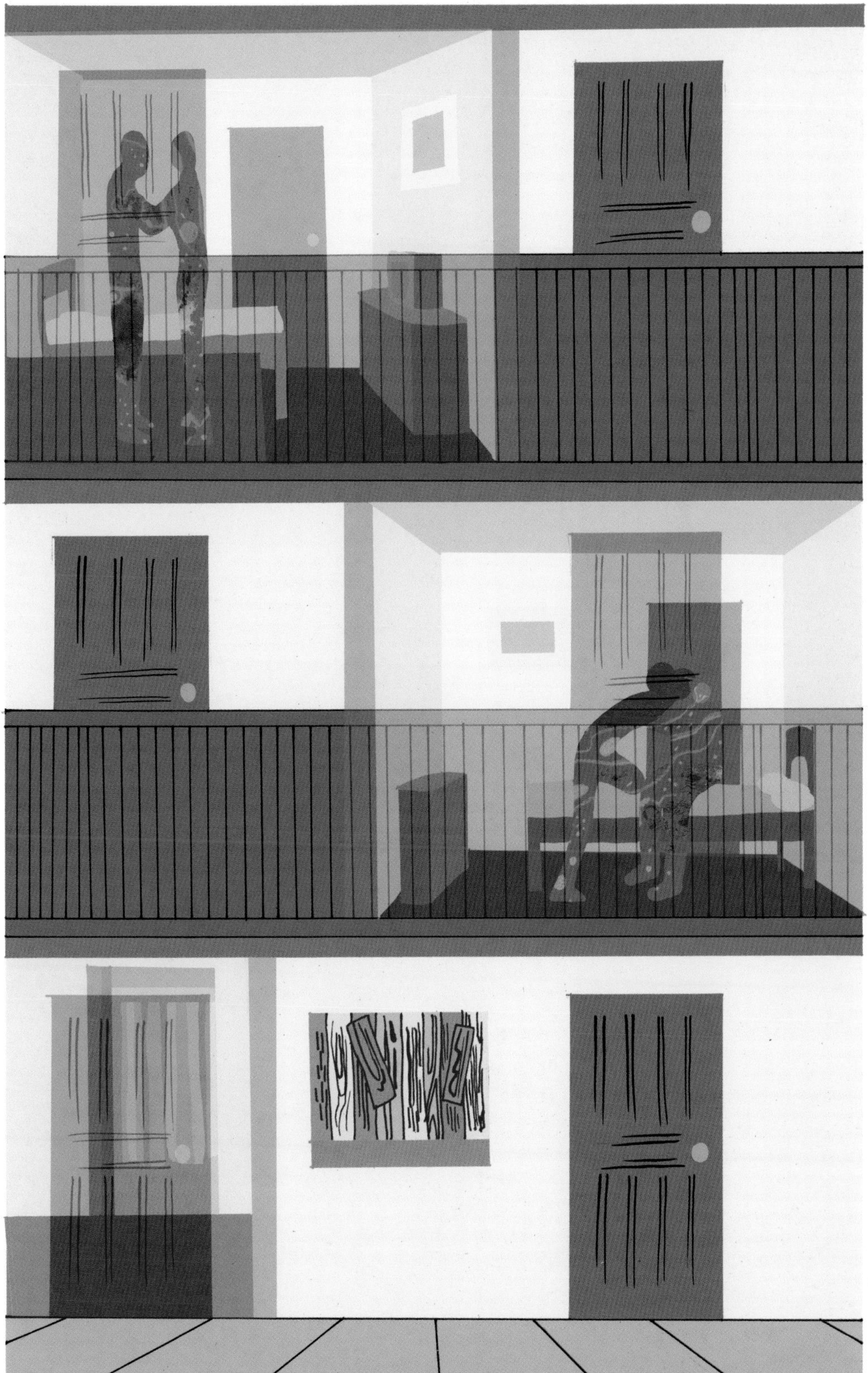

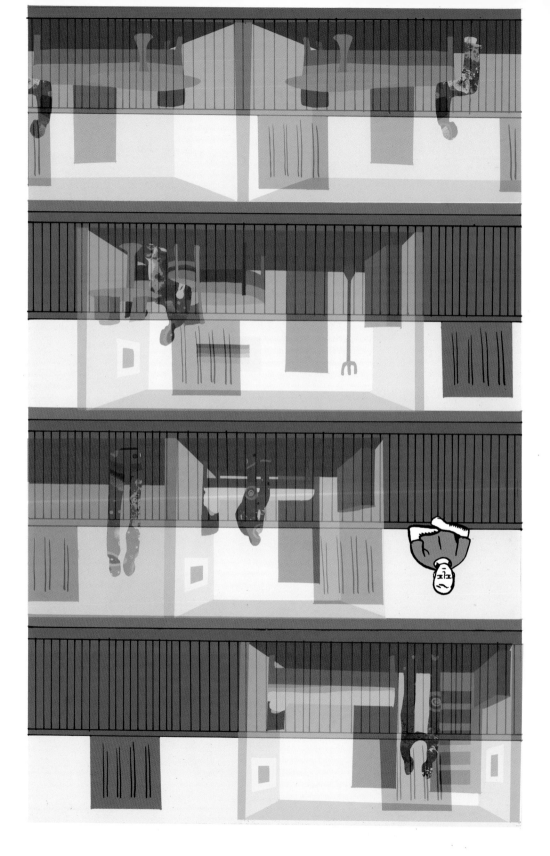

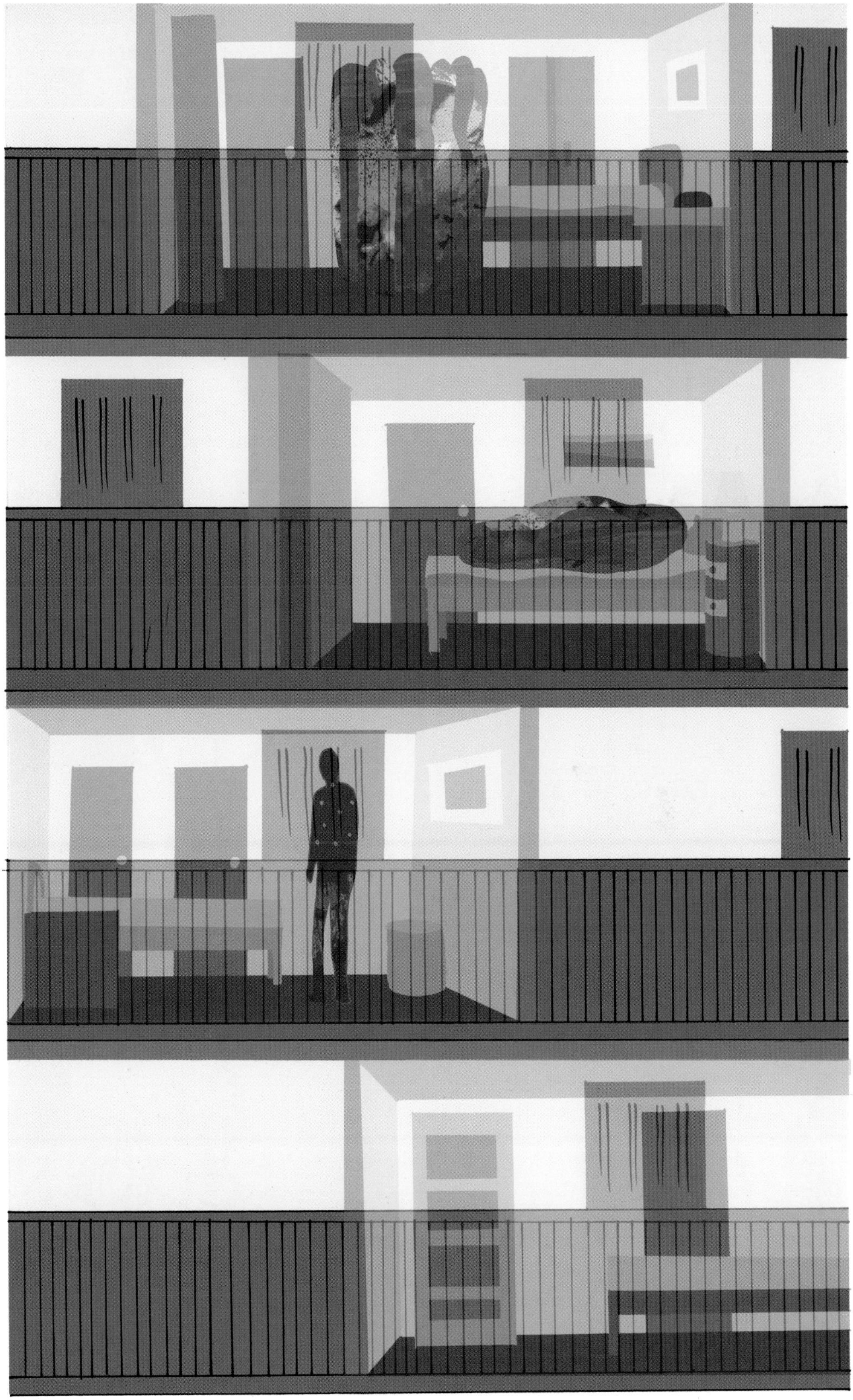

WHAT'RE YOU DOING HERE, PEARL? YOU NEVER LIKED THE GYMNASIUM.

HOW DID YOU KNOW THAT?

WHEN YOU'RE A TEACHER YOU NOTICE LOTS OF THINGS.

WHO'S FRIENDS WITH WHO. WHO DOESN'T LIKE WHO.

I WENT TO THIS SCHOOL TOO.

THE FRIENDS YOU HAVE IN ELEMENTARY SCHOOL, MIDDLE SCHOOL, HIGH SCHOOL... YOU'LL NEVER HAVE FRIENDS LIKE THAT AGAIN. I REMEMBER GETTING OFF THE BUS AND TALKING TO SOMEONE ALL DAY. THE ENTIRE DAY.

FOR MONTHS.

JUST SITTING AROUND IN THE WOODS, DOING NOTHING. WE'D KNOW EVERYTHING ABOUT EACH OTHER.

IT'S NOT LIKE THAT ANY-MORE. NOW EVERYONE HAS SECRETS, PASTS.

THERE'S SOMETHING ABOUT PEOPLE'S BRAINS IN HIGH SCHOOL. IT HITS YOU AT A POINT IN DEVELOP-MENT AND PERMANENTLY AFFECTS YOU.
IT'S STORED FOREVER.

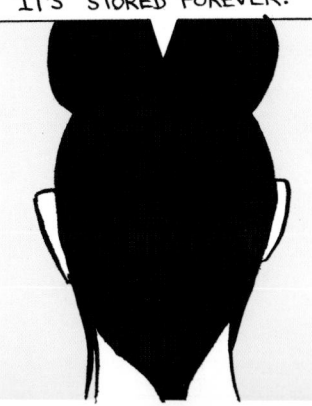

ALL OF MY DREAMS TAKE PLACE IN HIGH SCHOOL.

REALLY?!

THAT IS DEPRESSING.

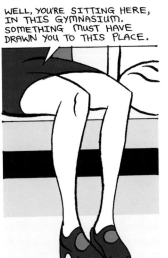

WELL, YOU'RE SITTING HERE, IN THIS GYMNASIUM. SOMETHING MUST HAVE DRAWN YOU TO THIS PLACE.

I JUST LIKE THAT IT'S FINALLY EMPTY.

WHEN'S THE LAST TIME YOU SAW... *PROFESSOR PANTHER* ?

PANTHER?

I SAW YOU TWO TOGETHER.

YOU DID.

RIGHT.

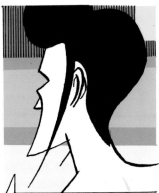

YOU REMIND ME OF MYSELF A BIT, PEARL. I'VE NEVER LEFT BONEY BOROUGH EITHER. WHEN I WAS YOUR AGE, I CONNECTED TO SOMEONE OLDER WHO I THOUGHT WOULD TAKE ME AWAY.

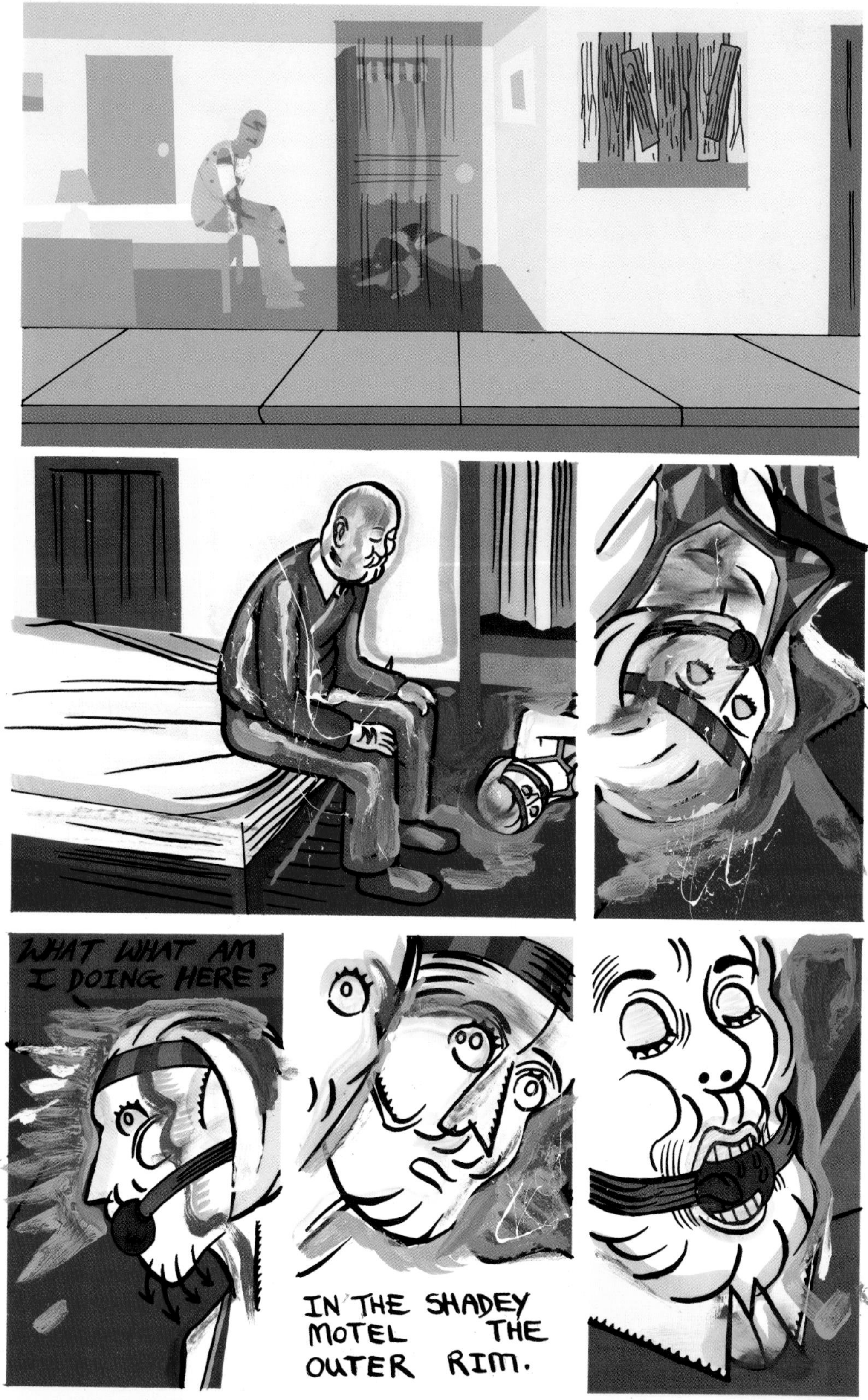
WHAT WHAT AM I DOING HERE?
IN THE SHADEY MOTEL THE OUTER RIM.

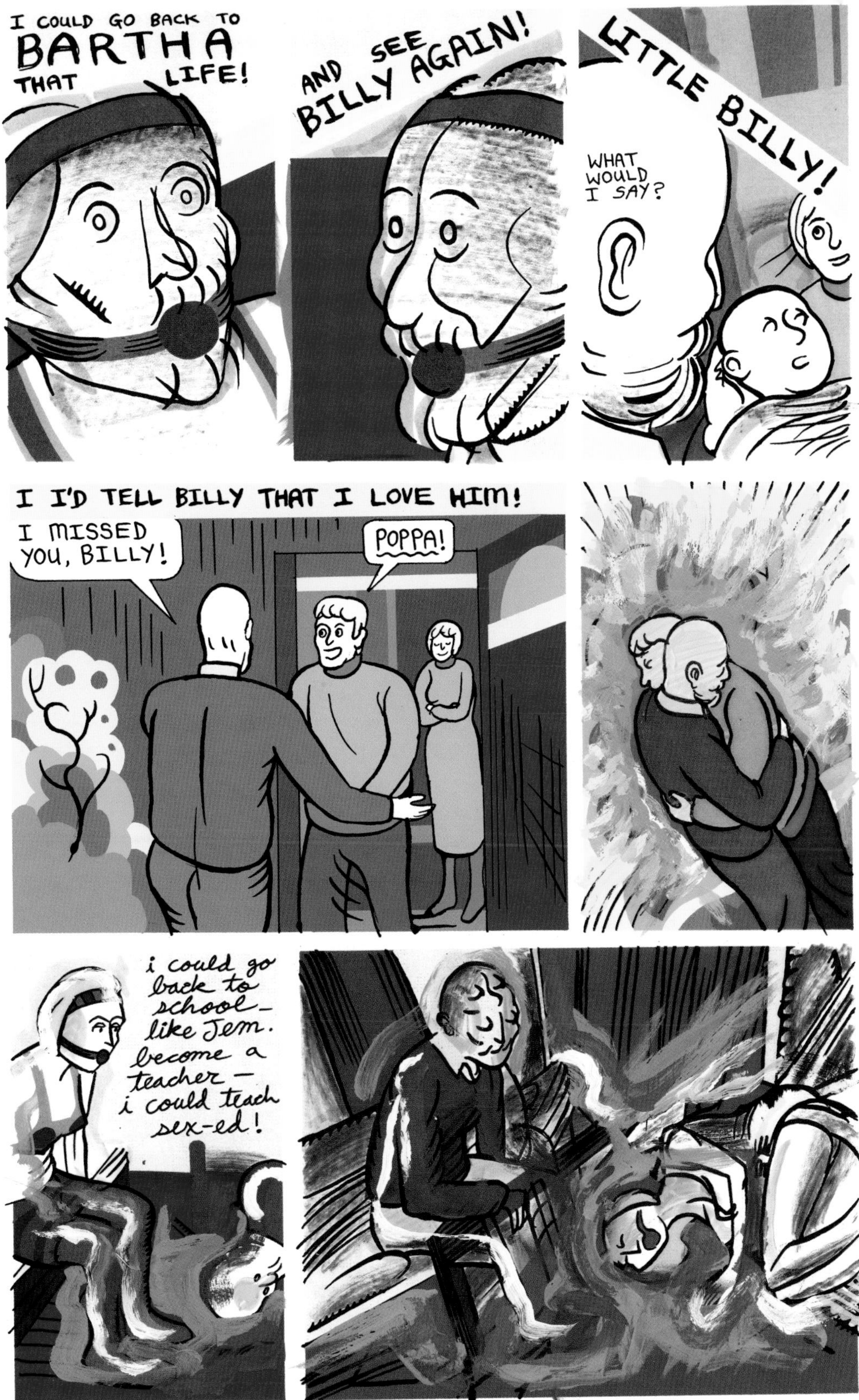
I COULD GO BACK TO BARTHA THAT LIFE!
AND SEE BILLY AGAIN!
LITTLE BILLY!
WHAT WOULD I SAY?
I I'D TELL BILLY THAT I LOVE HIM!
I MISSED YOU, BILLY!
POPPA!
i could go back to school— like Jem. become a teacher— i could teach sex-ed!

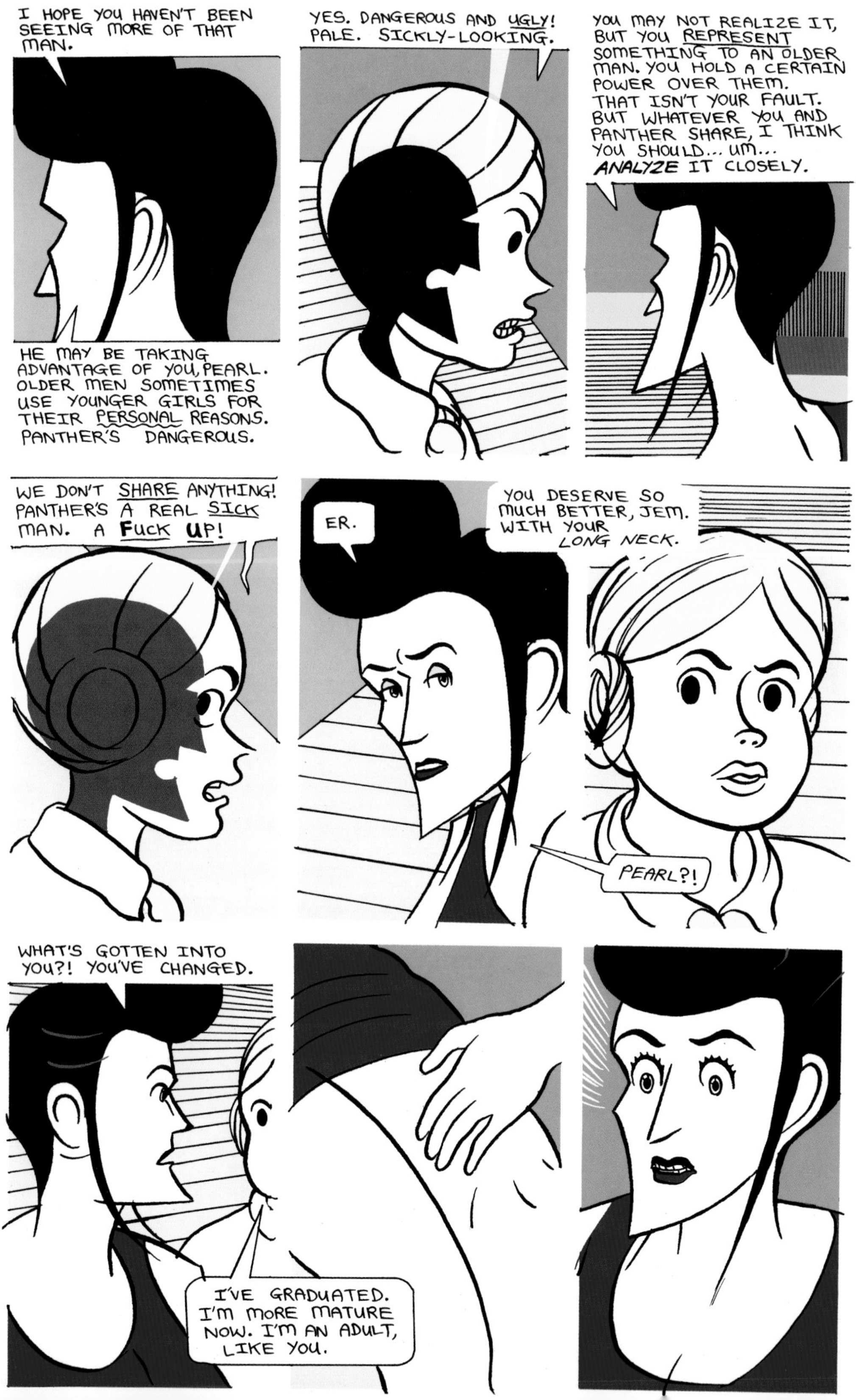
I HOPE YOU HAVEN'T BEEN SEEING MORE OF THAT MAN.
HE MAY BE TAKING ADVANTAGE OF YOU, PEARL. OLDER MEN SOMETIMES USE YOUNGER GIRLS FOR THEIR PERSONAL REASONS. PANTHER'S DANGEROUS.
YES. DANGEROUS AND UGLY! PALE. SICKLY-LOOKING.
YOU MAY NOT REALIZE IT, BUT YOU REPRESENT SOMETHING TO AN OLDER MAN. YOU HOLD A CERTAIN POWER OVER THEM. THAT ISN'T YOUR FAULT. BUT WHATEVER YOU AND PANTHER SHARE, I THINK YOU SHOULD... UM... ANALYZE IT CLOSELY.
WE DON'T SHARE ANYTHING! PANTHER'S A REAL SICK MAN. A FUCK UP!
ER.
YOU DESERVE SO MUCH BETTER, JEM. WITH YOUR LONG NECK.
PEARL?!
WHAT'S GOTTEN INTO YOU?! YOU'VE CHANGED.
I'VE GRADUATED. I'M MORE MATURE NOW. I'M AN ADULT, LIKE YOU.

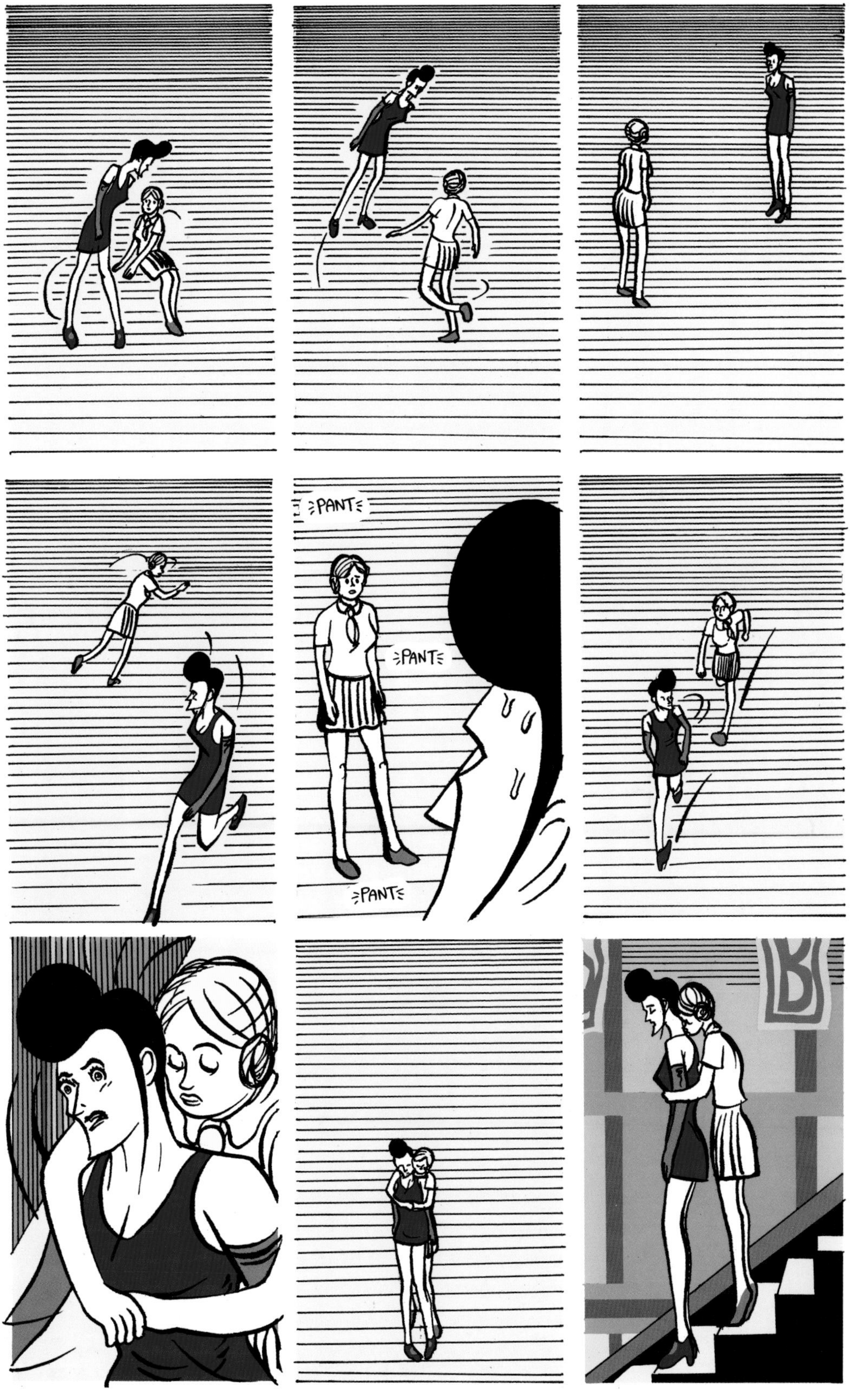
PANT
PANT
PANT

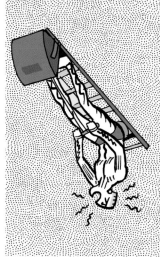

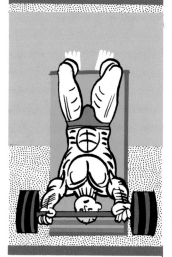
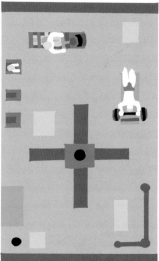
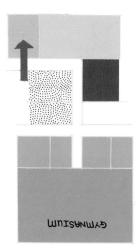

GYMNASIUM

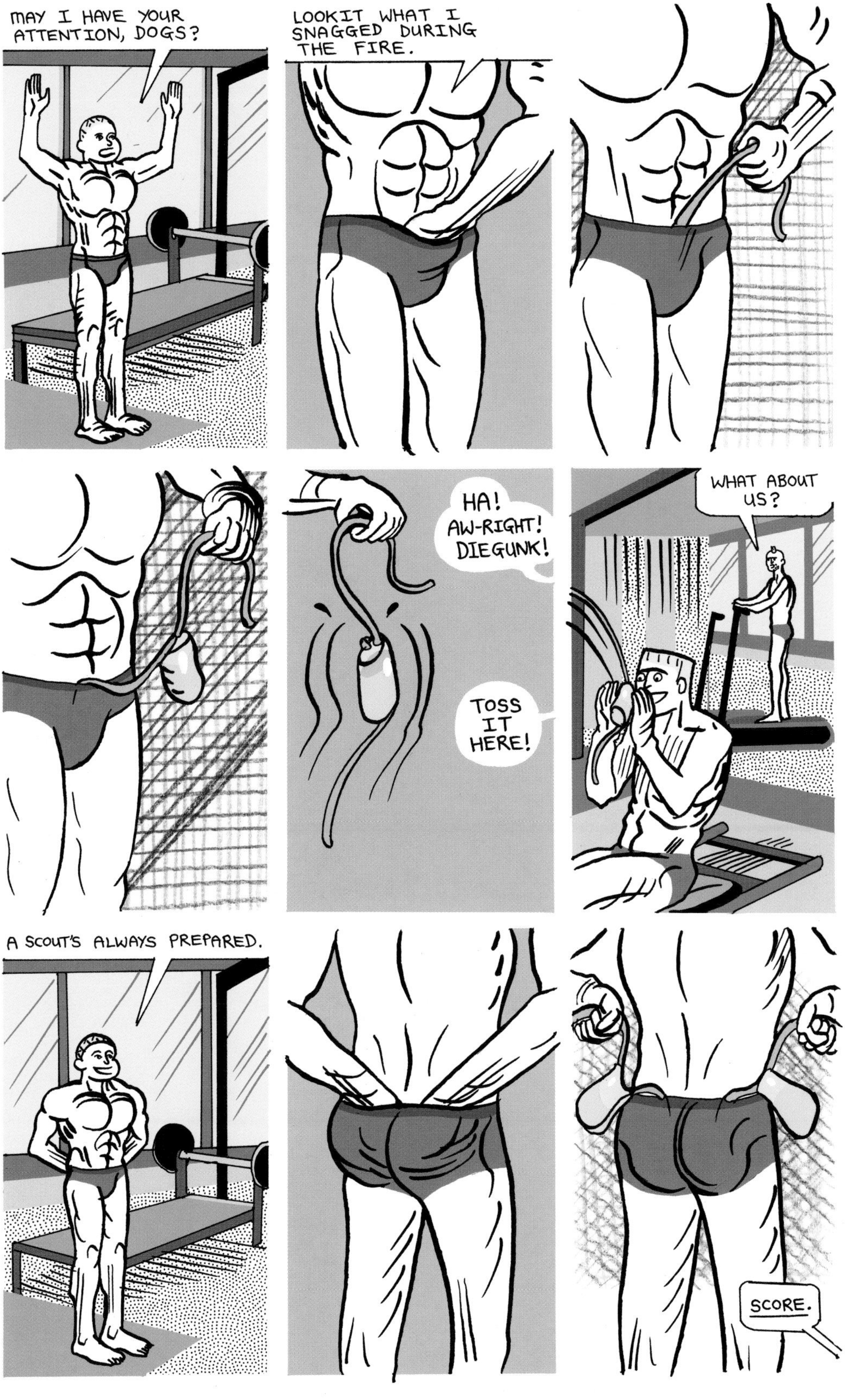
MAY I HAVE YOUR ATTENTION, DOGS?
LOOKIT WHAT I SNAGGED DURING THE FIRE.
HA! AW-RIGHT! DIEGUNK!
TOSS IT HERE!
WHAT ABOUT US?
A SCOUT'S ALWAYS PREPARED.
SCORE.

PANT
PANT
BREATH
BREATH

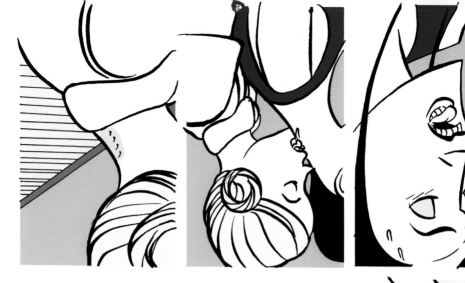

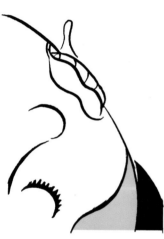

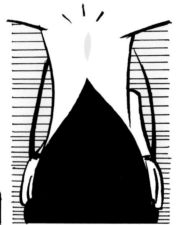

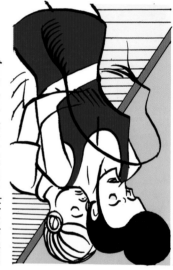

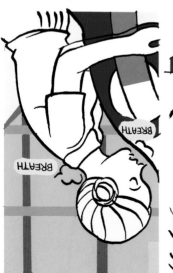

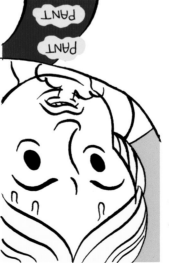

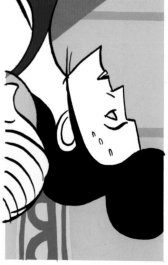

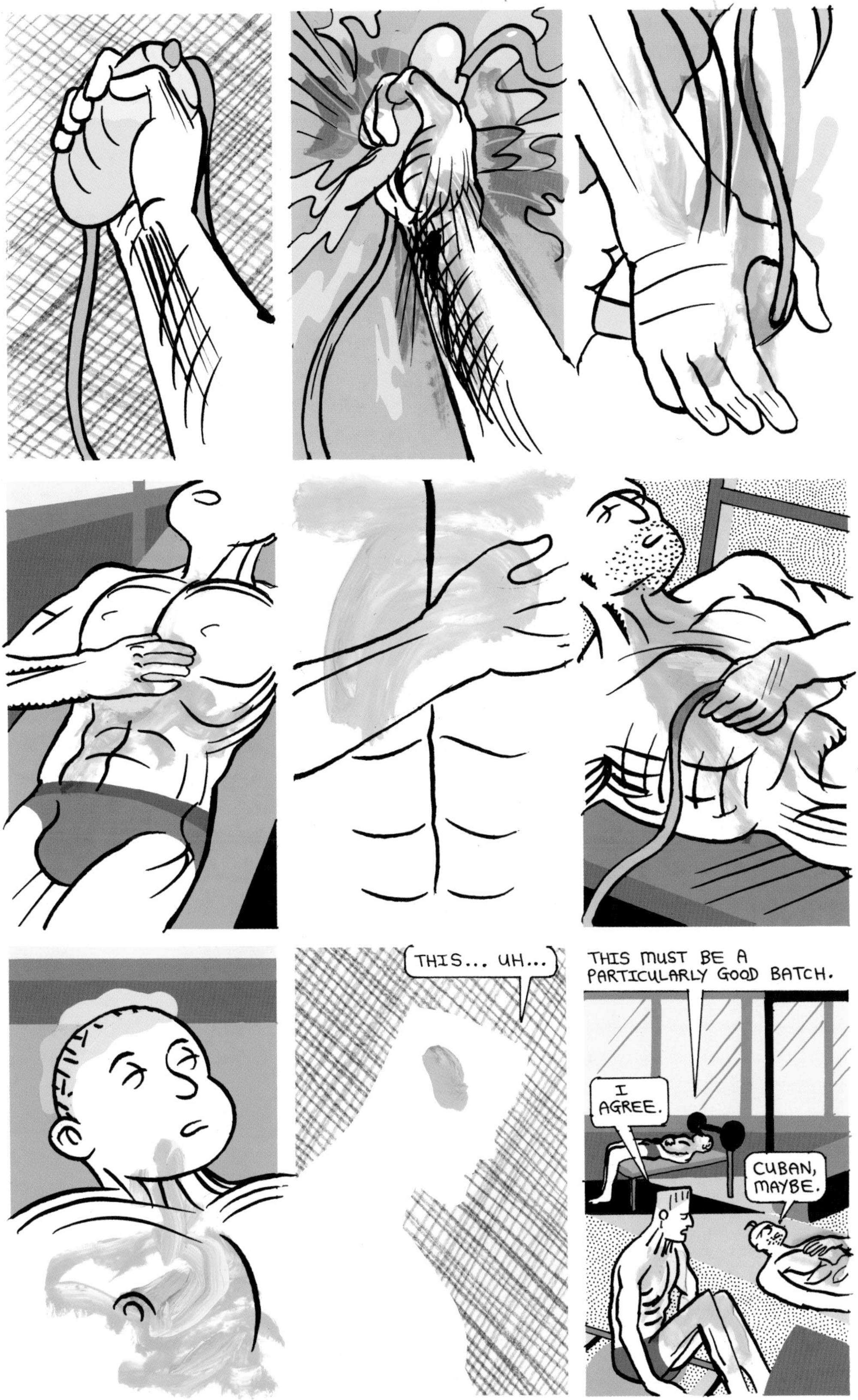
THIS... UH...
THIS MUST BE A PARTICULARLY GOOD BATCH.
I AGREE.
CUBAN, MAYBE.

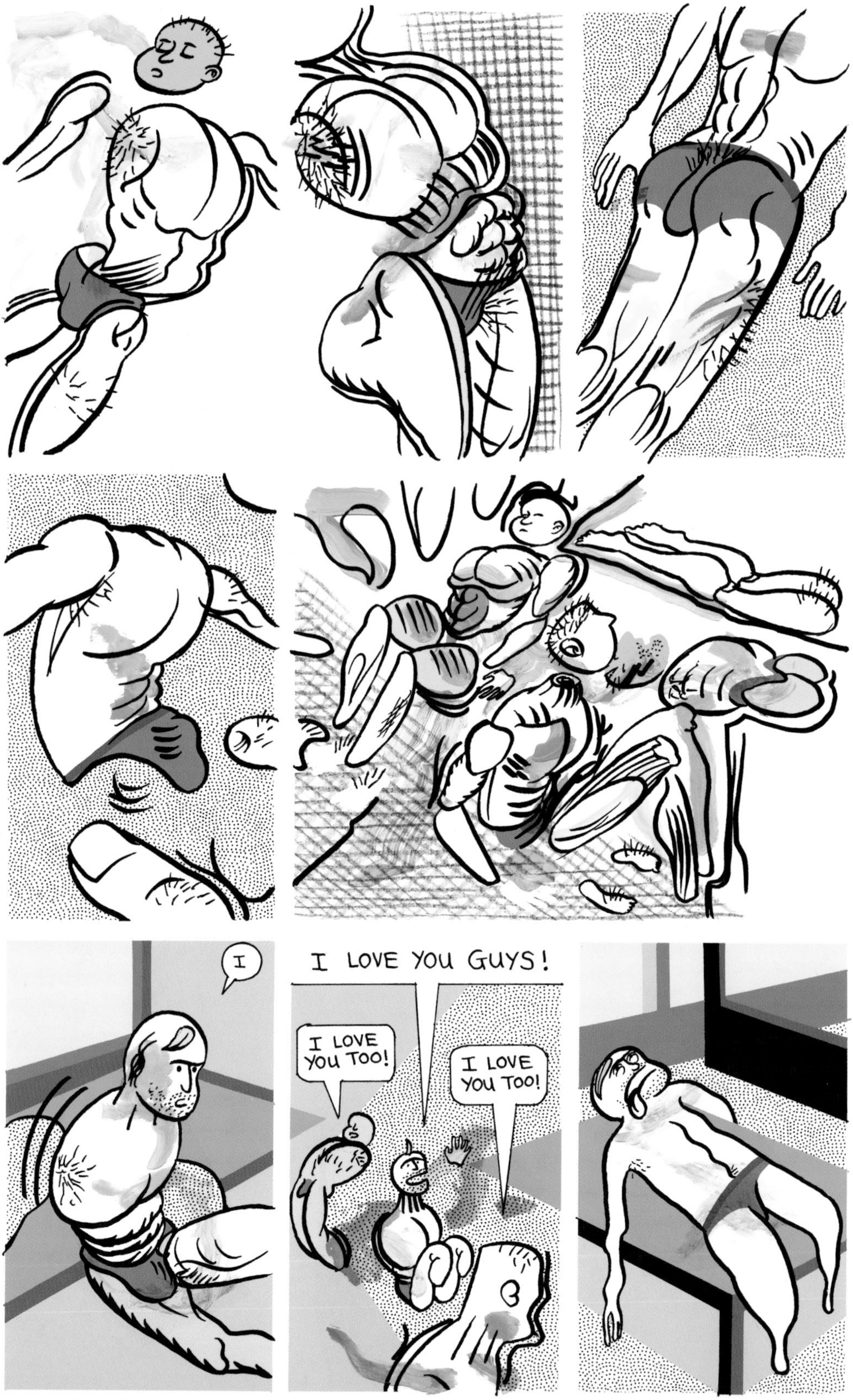
I
I LOVE YOU GUYS!
I LOVE YOU TOO!
I LOVE YOU TOO!

B

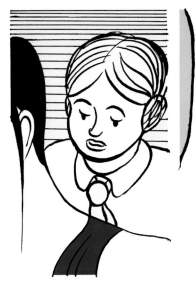

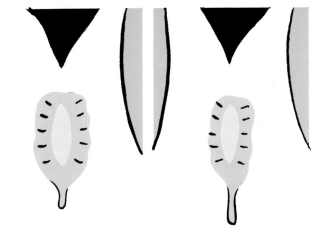

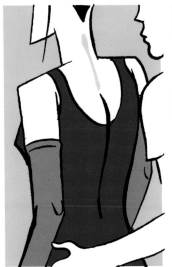

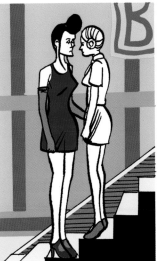

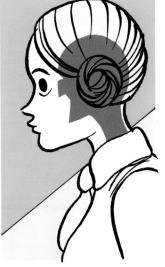

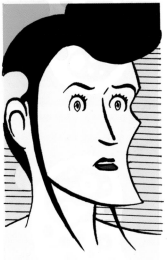

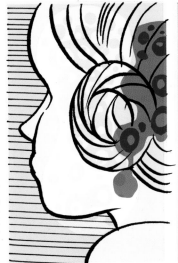

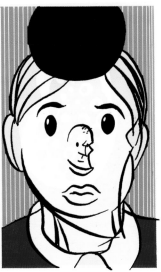

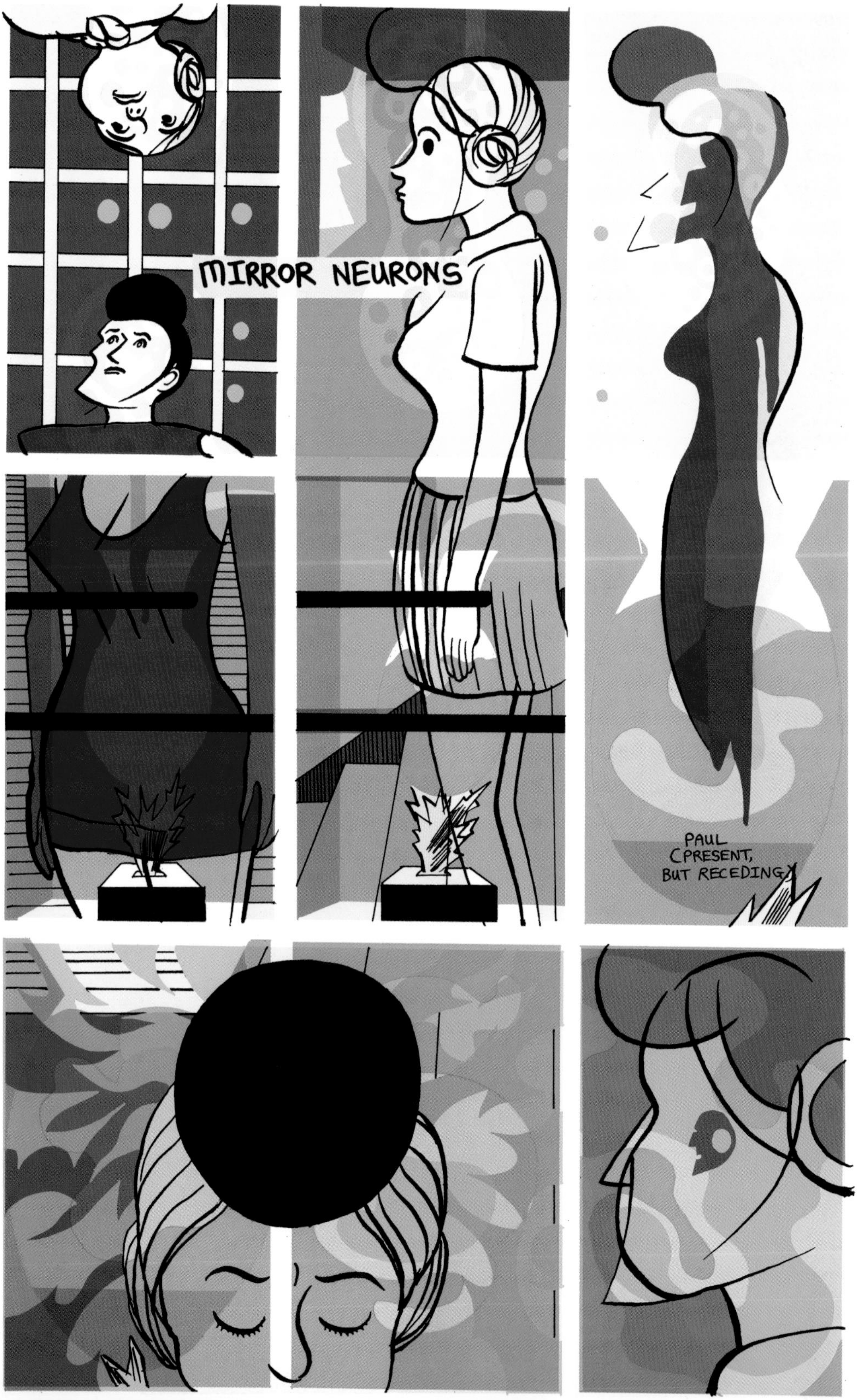
MIRROR NEURONS
PAUL
(PRESENT,
BUT RECEDING)

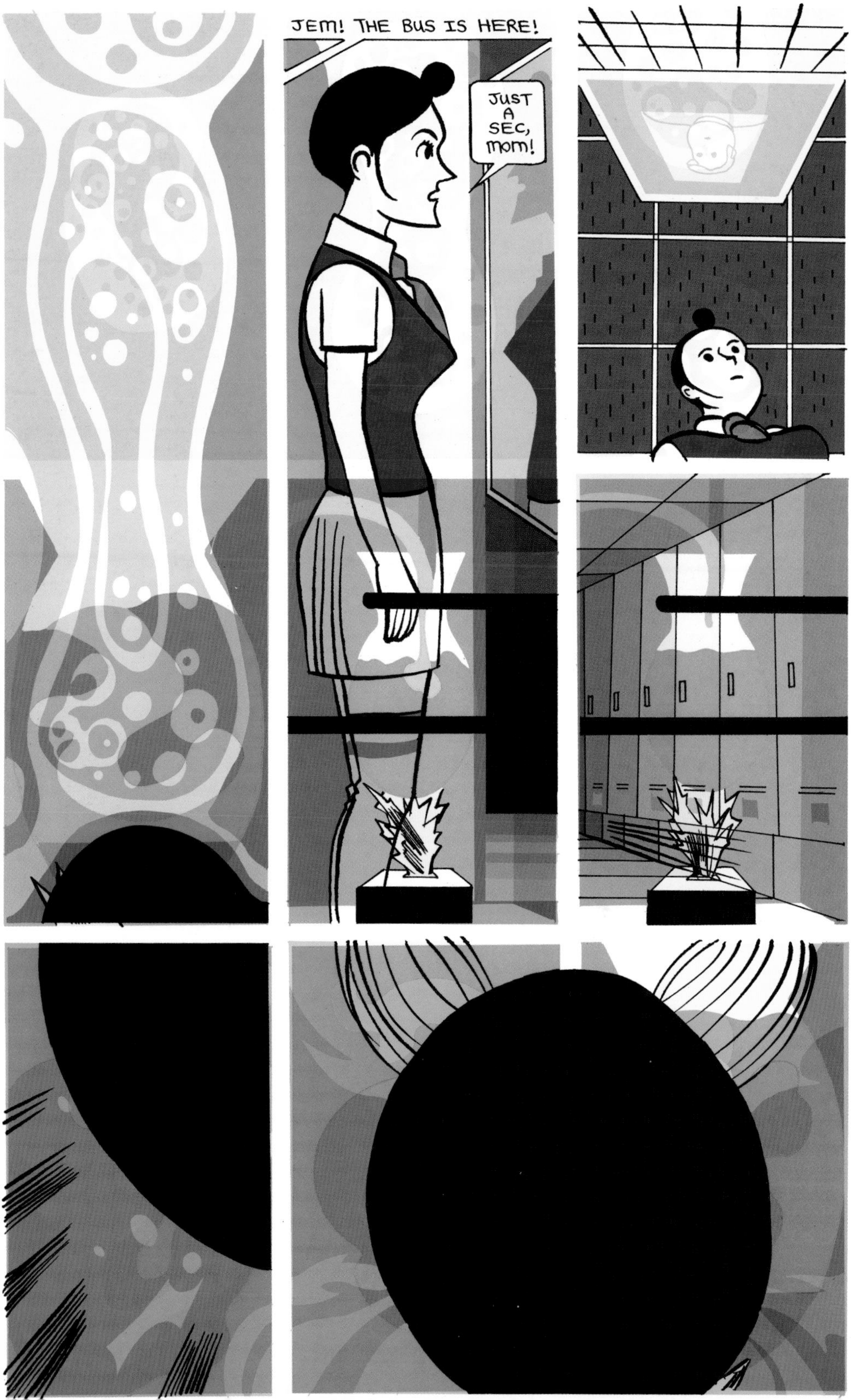
JEM! THE BUS IS HERE!
JUST A SEC, MOM!

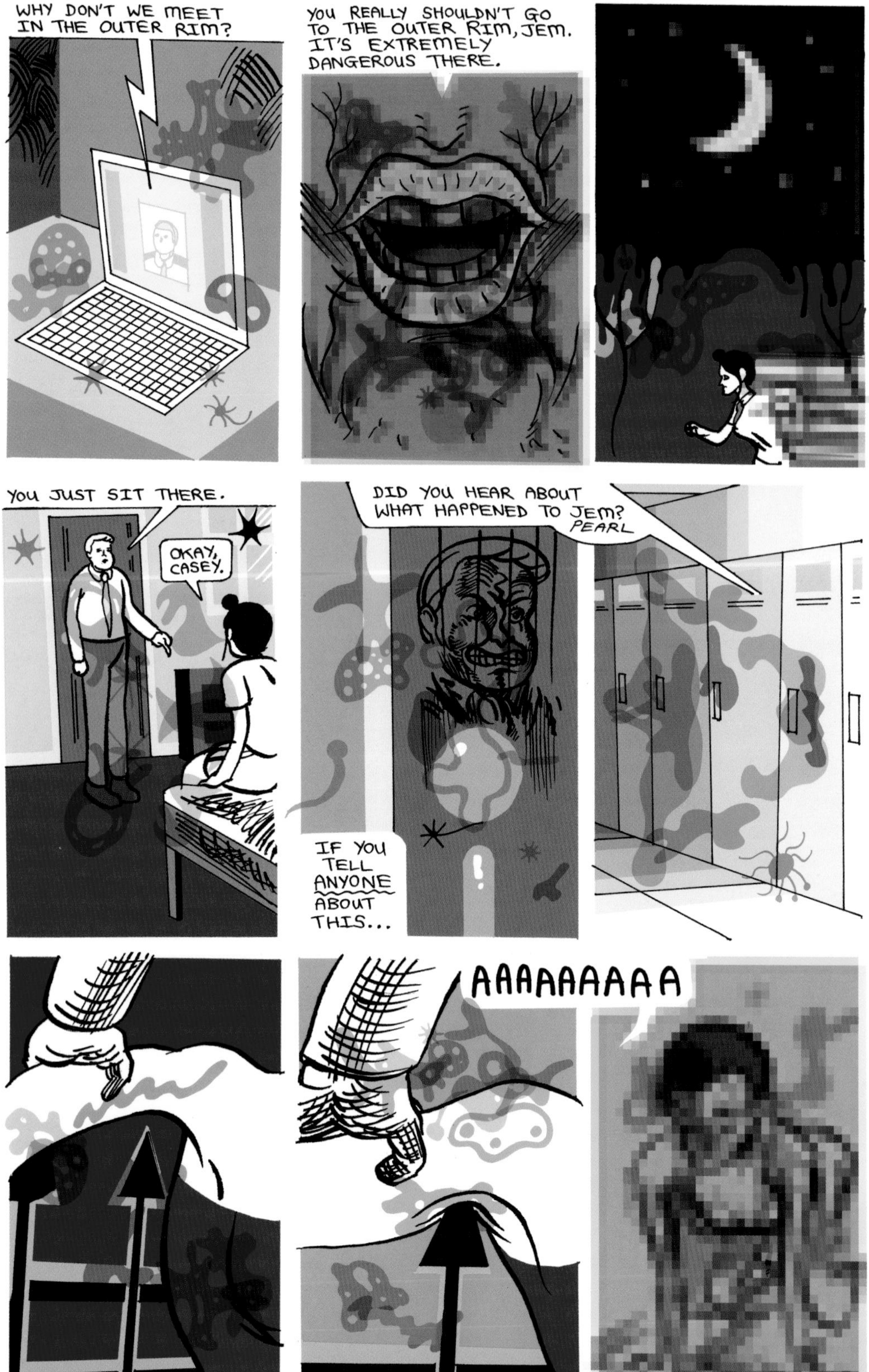
WHY DON'T WE MEET IN THE OUTER RIM?
YOU REALLY SHOULDN'T GO TO THE OUTER RIM, JEM. IT'S EXTREMELY DANGEROUS THERE.
YOU JUST SIT THERE.
OKAY, CASEY.
DID YOU HEAR ABOUT WHAT HAPPENED TO JEM? PEARL
IF YOU TELL ANYONE ABOUT THIS...
AAAAAAAAA

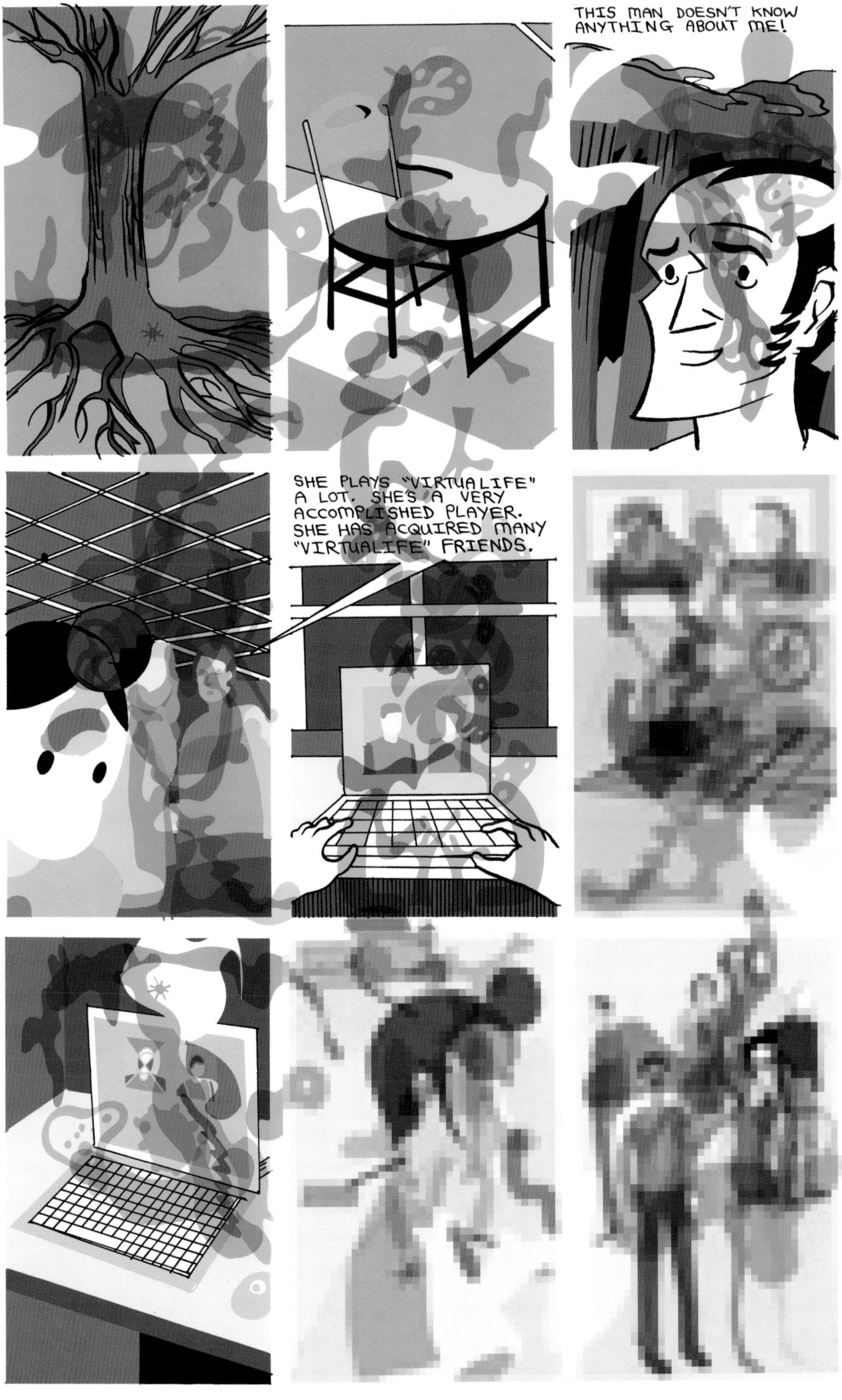

THIS MAN DOESN'T KNOW ANYTHING ABOUT ME!
SHE PLAYS "VIRTUALIFE" A LOT. SHE'S A VERY ACCOMPLISHED PLAYER. SHE HAS ACQUIRED MANY "VIRTUALIFE" FRIENDS.

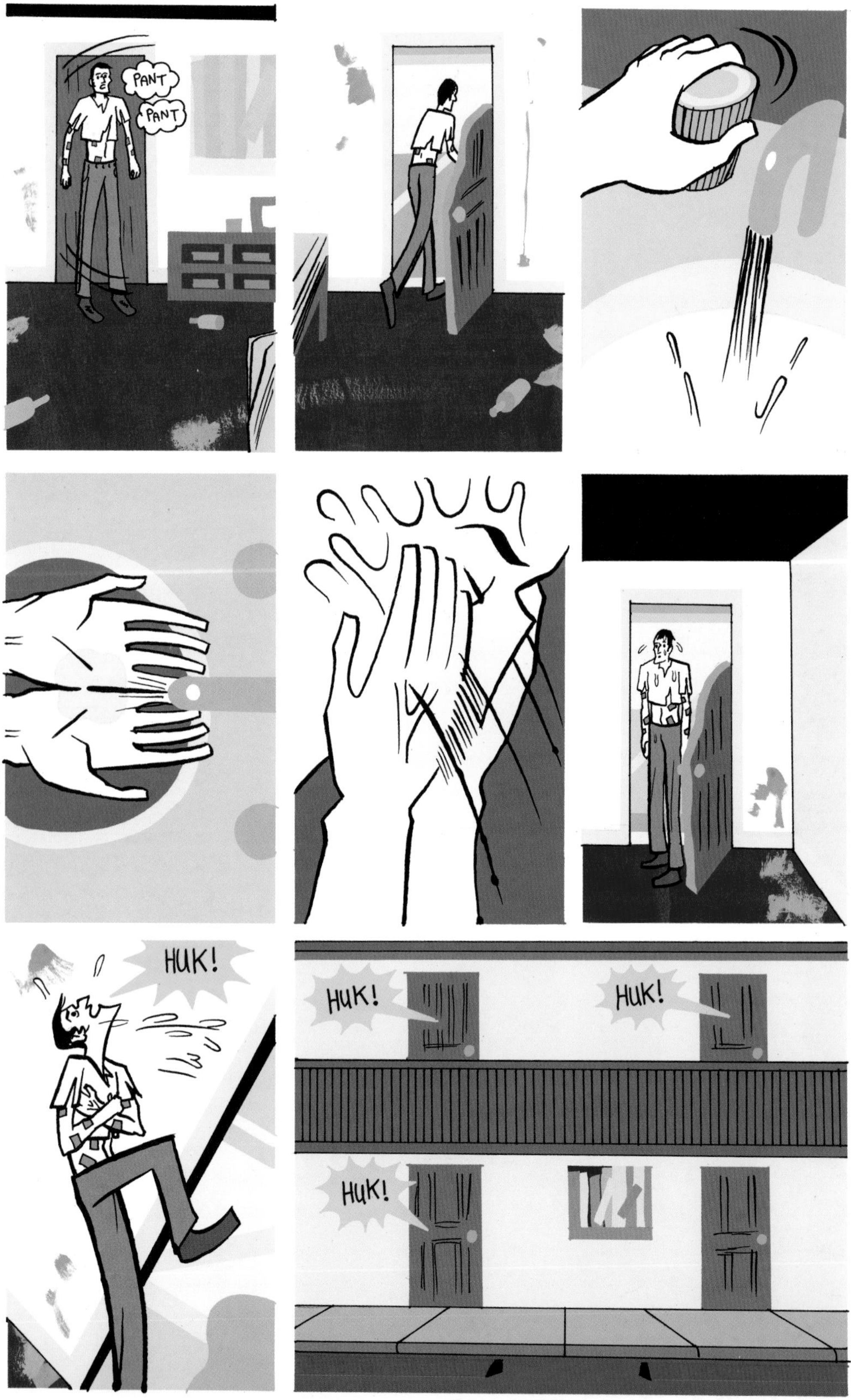
PANT
PANT
HUK!
HUK!
HUK!
HUK!

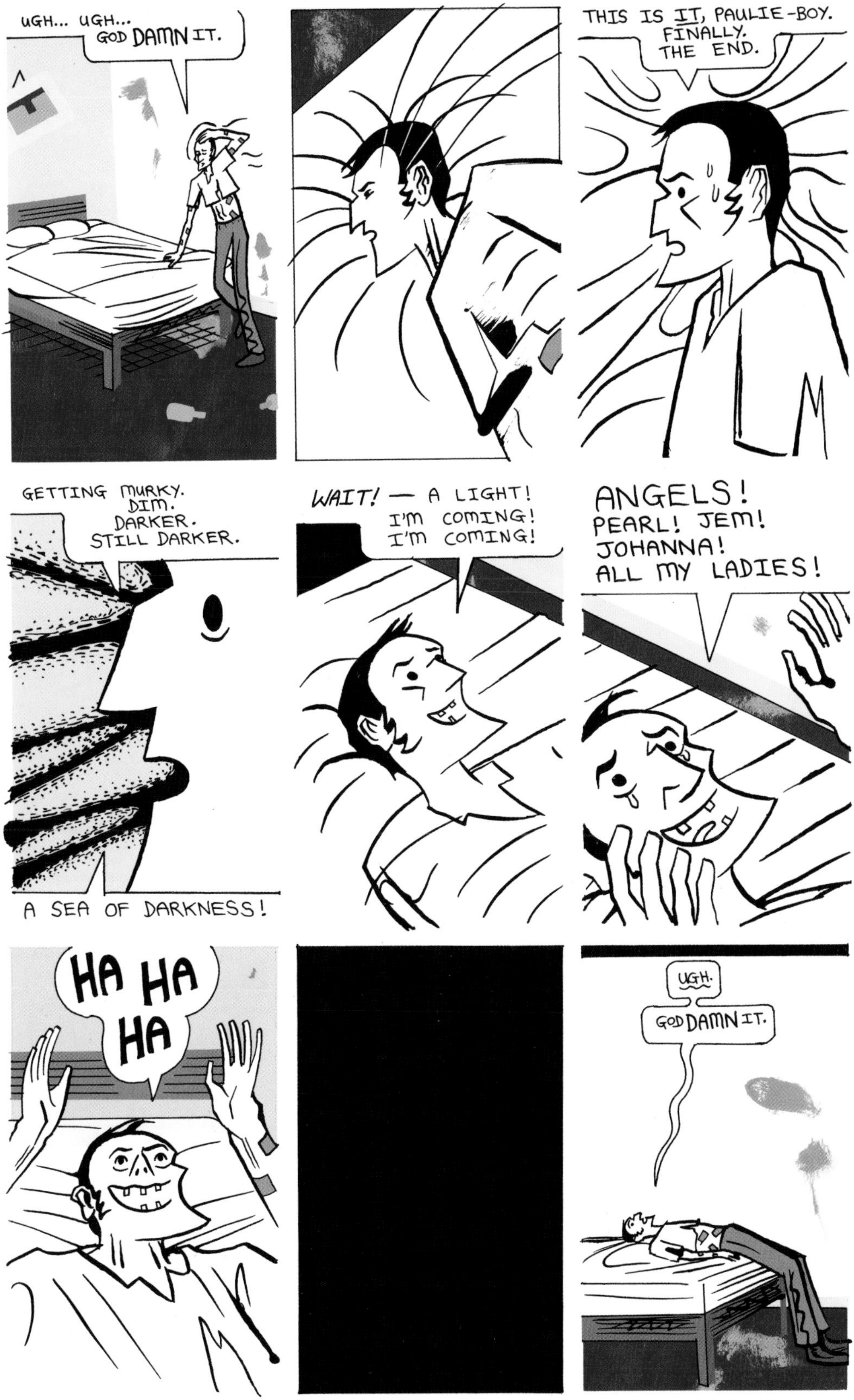
UGH... UGH...
GOD DAMN IT.
THIS IS IT, PAULIE-BOY. FINALLY. THE END.
GETTING MURKY. DIM. DARKER. STILL DARKER.
A SEA OF DARKNESS!
WAIT! — A LIGHT! I'M COMING! I'M COMING!
ANGELS! PEARL! JEM! JOHANNA! ALL MY LADIES!
HA HA HA HA
UGH.
GOD DAMN IT.

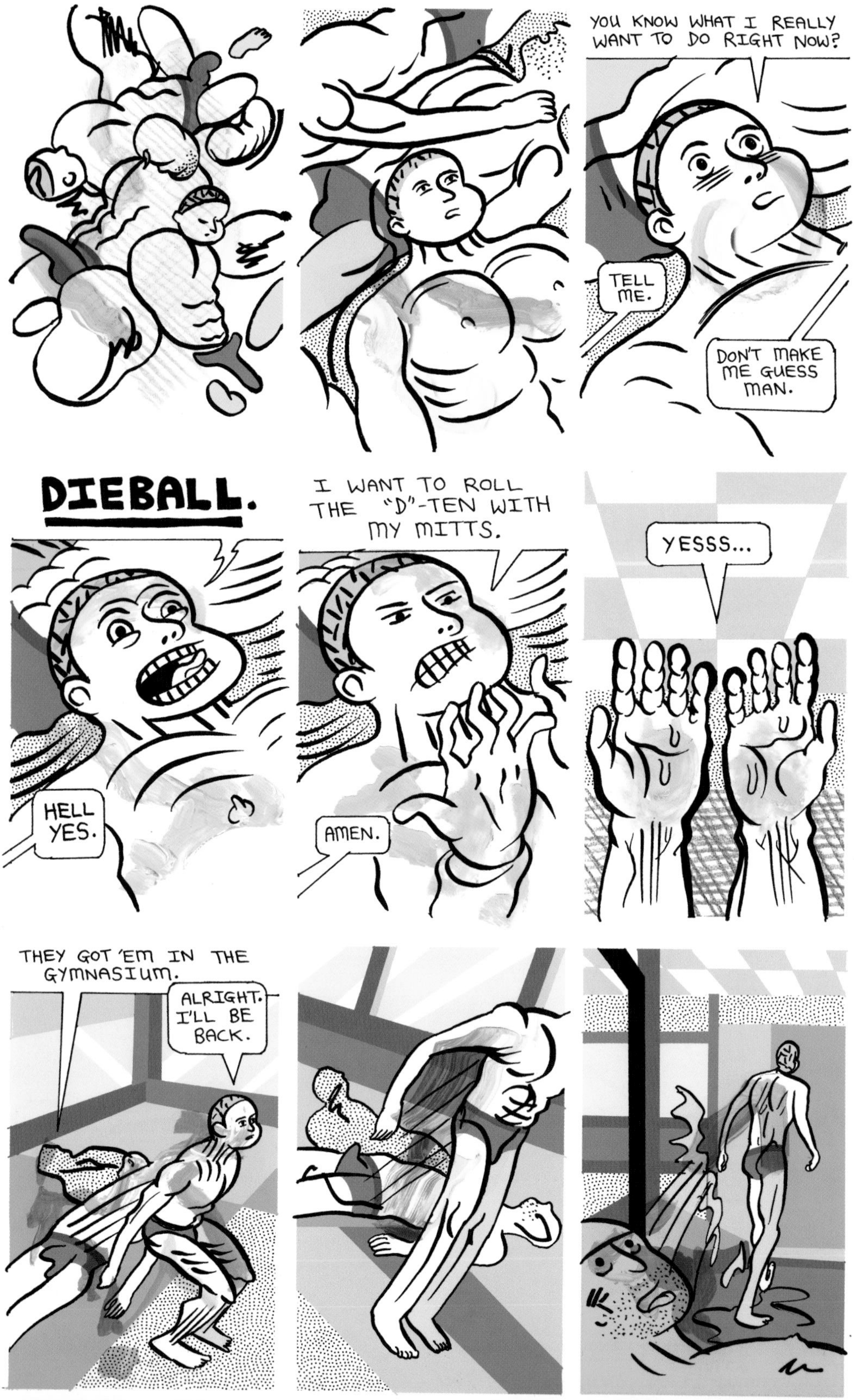
YOU KNOW WHAT I REALLY WANT TO DO RIGHT NOW?
TELL ME.
DON'T MAKE ME GUESS MAN.
DIEBALL.
HELL YES.
I WANT TO ROLL THE "D"-TEN WITH MY MITTS.
AMEN.
YESSS...
THEY GOT 'EM IN THE GYMNASIUM.
ALRIGHT. I'LL BE BACK.

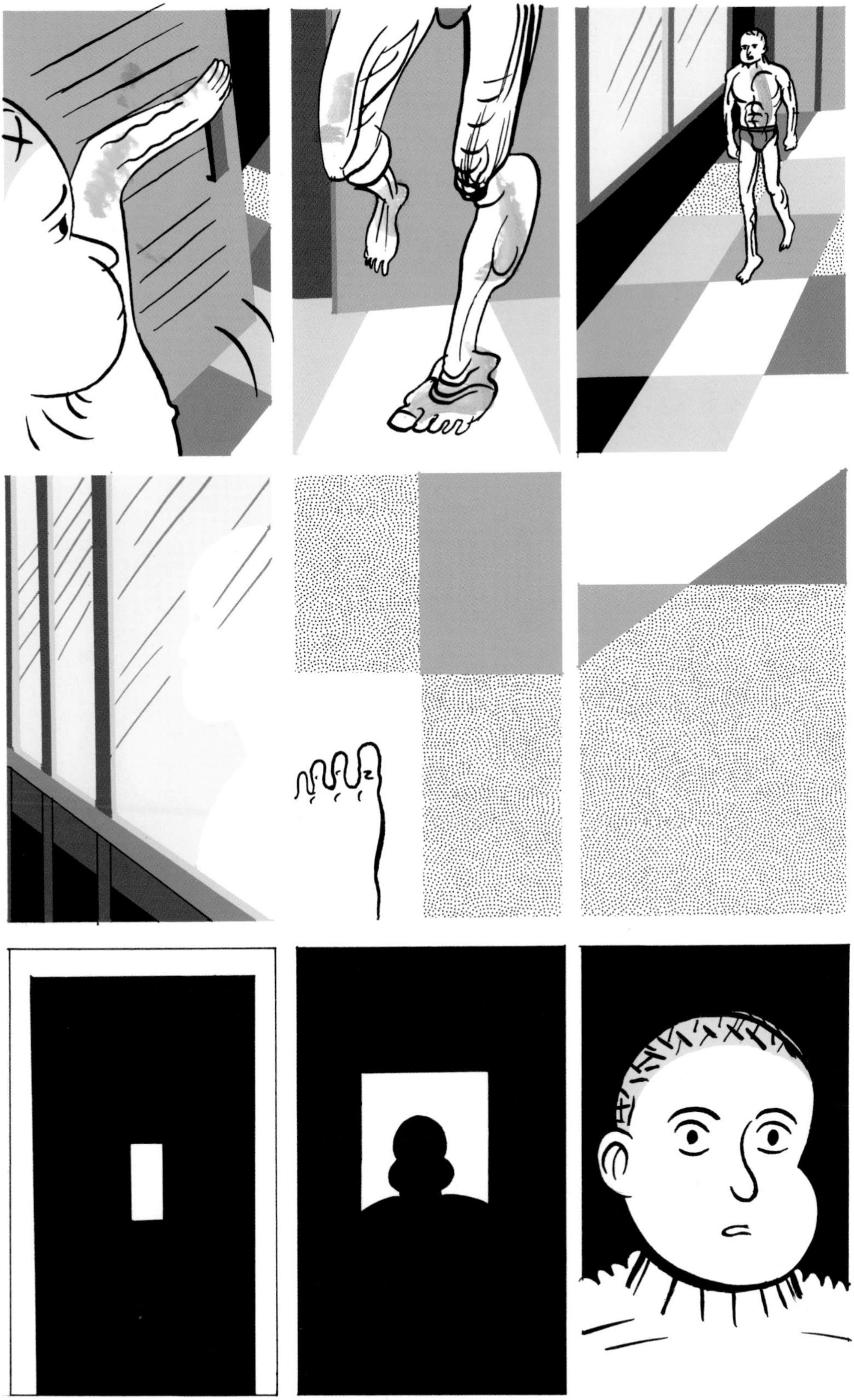

THEN MAYBE I WOULD BE FREED FROM THIS PLACE.

I WISH ALL OF BONEY BOROUGH HAD BURNED DOWN.

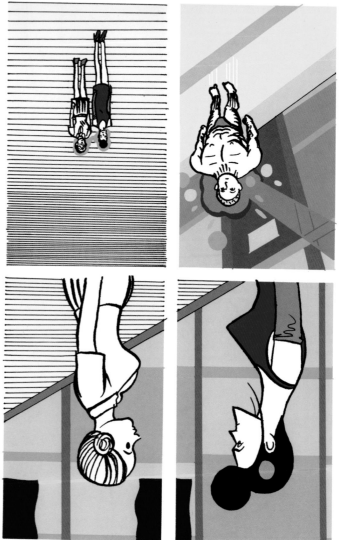

WHO'S GOING TO LOVE ME NOW?

I'M A WOMAN OVER THIRTY AND STILL IN HIGH SCHOOL.

END OF CHAPTER TEN.

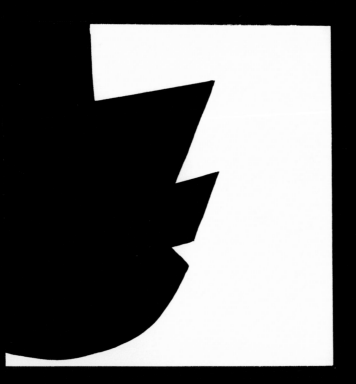

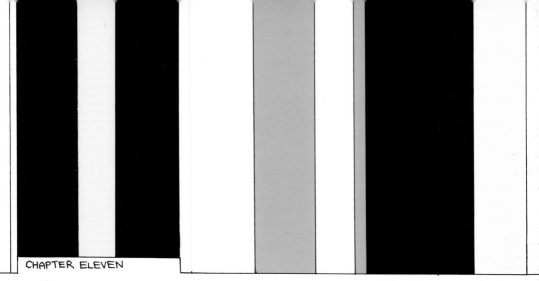

28 Q

RING

ENGH.

SHADEY MOTEL

RING

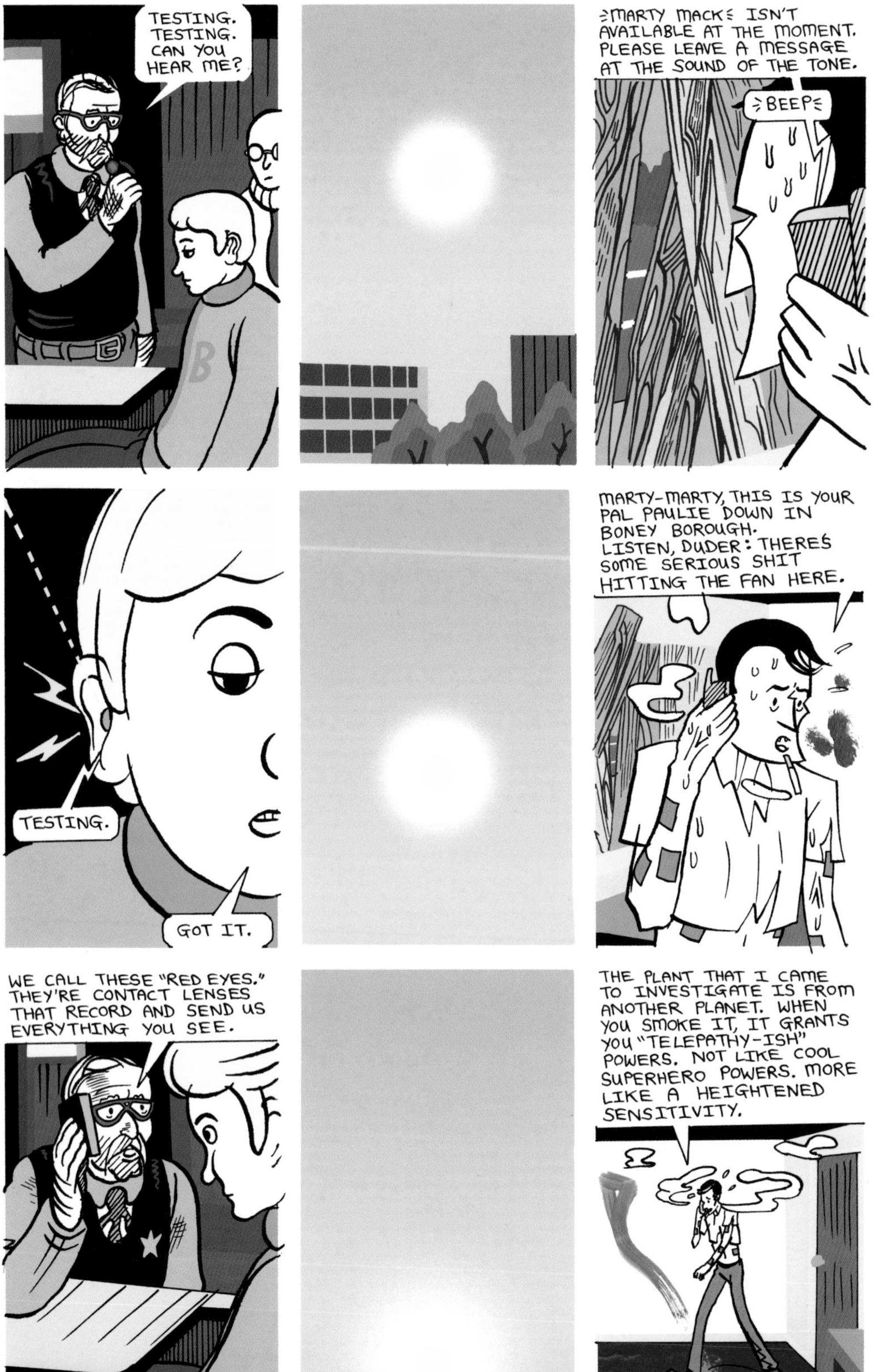
TESTING. TESTING. CAN YOU HEAR ME?
≡MARTY MACK≡ ISN'T AVAILABLE AT THE MOMENT. PLEASE LEAVE A MESSAGE AT THE SOUND OF THE TONE.
≡BEEP≡
TESTING.
GOT IT.
MARTY-MARTY, THIS IS YOUR PAL PAULIE DOWN IN BONEY BOROUGH. LISTEN, DUDER: THERE'S SOME SERIOUS SHIT HITTING THE FAN HERE.
WE CALL THESE "RED EYES." THEY'RE CONTACT LENSES THAT RECORD AND SEND US EVERYTHING YOU SEE.
THE PLANT THAT I CAME TO INVESTIGATE IS FROM ANOTHER PLANET. WHEN YOU SMOKE IT, IT GRANTS YOU "TELEPATHY-ISH" POWERS. NOT LIKE COOL SUPERHERO POWERS. MORE LIKE A HEIGHTENED SENSITIVITY.

THE ONLY PROBLEM WITH WEARING THEM IS THAT EVERYTHING YOU SEE IS RED.

UH. OKAY.

ALL OF THE PLANTS CAUGHT ON FIRE AND THE SUPER ABILITY SPREAD THROUGH THE TOWN IN THE SMOKE. *EVERYONE* TOOK A TOKE!

TRY TO RELAX.

A WHOLE TOWN INFECTED WITH A "TELEPATHY-ISH" VIRUS WOULD PROBABLY RESULT IN SOME KIND OF INSANE HIVE MIND OR UNPLEASANT ORGY. A GROSS ORGY BECAUSE, IF YOU THINK ABOUT IT, THE MAJORITY OF PEOPLE ARE UNATTRACTIVE.

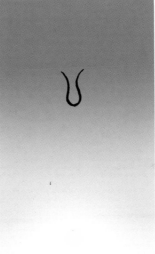

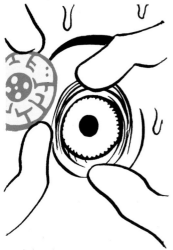

JUST NOW I WAS AT THE GAS STATION AND I "READ" THE CASHIER'S BODYMIND FOR ABOUT AN HOUR UNTIL SOMEONE ELSE CAME IN AND MY BODY "READ" HER FAT BODY'S DESIRE TO LEAVE. UGH. THE WHOLE EXPERIENCE LEFT A BAD TASTE IN MY MOUTH.

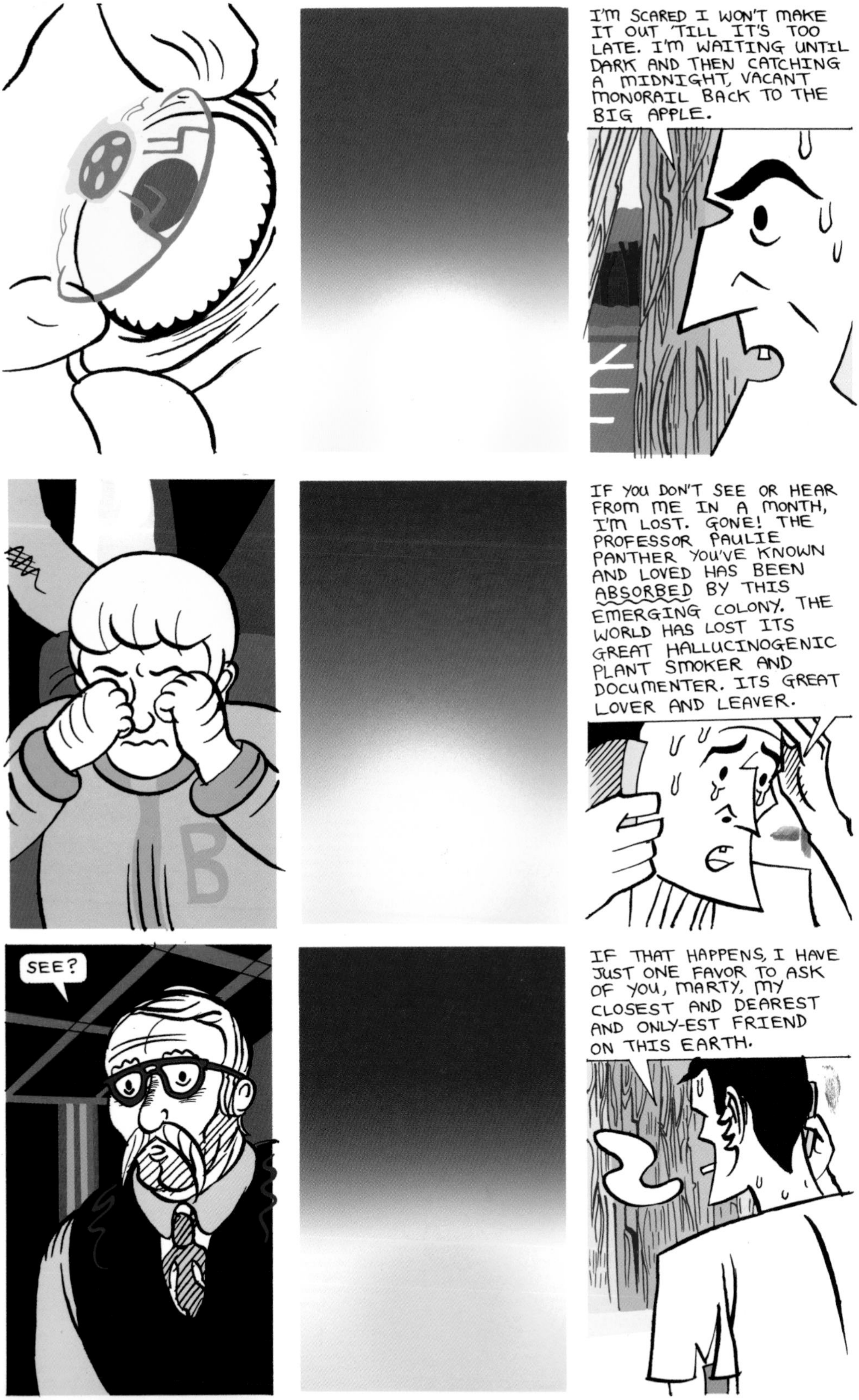
I'M SCARED I WON'T MAKE IT OUT 'TILL IT'S TOO LATE. I'M WAITING UNTIL DARK AND THEN CATCHING A MIDNIGHT, VACANT MONORAIL BACK TO THE BIG APPLE.
IF YOU DON'T SEE OR HEAR FROM ME IN A MONTH, I'M LOST. GONE! THE PROFESSOR PAULIE PANTHER YOU'VE KNOWN AND LOVED HAS BEEN ABSORBED BY THIS EMERGING COLONY. THE WORLD HAS LOST ITS GREAT HALLUCINOGENIC PLANT SMOKER AND DOCUMENTER. ITS GREAT LOVER AND LEAVER.
SEE?
IF THAT HAPPENS, I HAVE JUST ONE FAVOR TO ASK OF YOU, MARTY, MY CLOSEST AND DEAREST AND ONLY-EST FRIEND ON THIS EARTH.

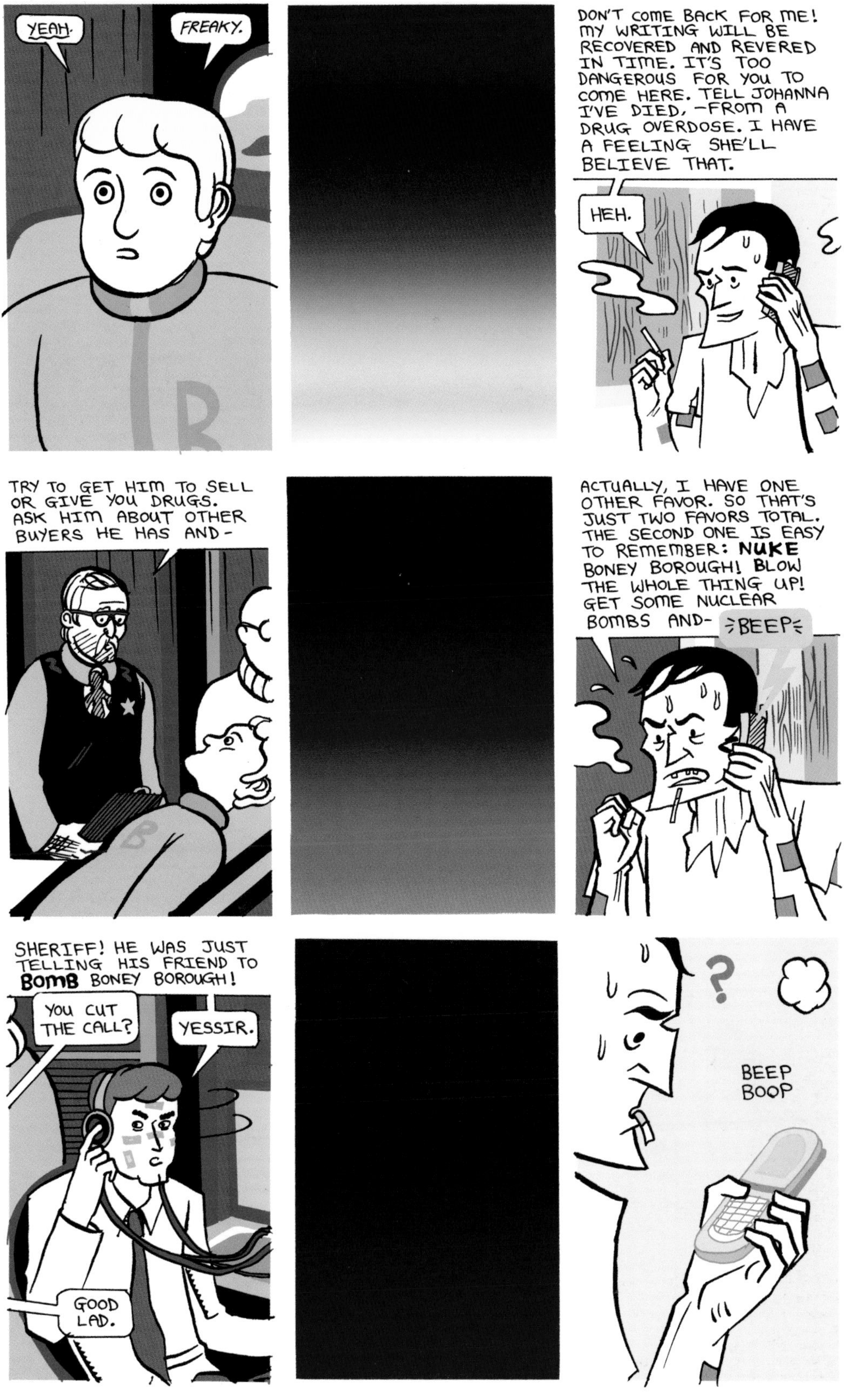
YEAH.
FREAKY.
DON'T COME BACK FOR ME! MY WRITING WILL BE RECOVERED AND REVERED IN TIME. IT'S TOO DANGEROUS FOR YOU TO COME HERE. TELL JOHANNA I'VE DIED, —FROM A DRUG OVERDOSE. I HAVE A FEELING SHE'LL BELIEVE THAT.
HEH.
TRY TO GET HIM TO SELL OR GIVE YOU DRUGS. ASK HIM ABOUT OTHER BUYERS HE HAS AND-
ACTUALLY, I HAVE ONE OTHER FAVOR. SO THAT'S JUST TWO FAVORS TOTAL. THE SECOND ONE IS EASY TO REMEMBER: NUKE BONEY BOROUGH! BLOW THE WHOLE THING UP! GET SOME NUCLEAR BOMBS AND-
BEEP
SHERIFF! HE WAS JUST TELLING HIS FRIEND TO BOMB BONEY BOROUGH!
YOU CUT THE CALL?
YESSIR.
GOOD LAD.
?
BEEP BOOP

UH. YOU SURE THIS ISN'T TOO DANGEROUS?
NAW! YOU'LL BE FINE! HE KNOWS YOU!
LAST TIME WE TALKED, IT DIDN'T END TOO GOOD. IT WAS SORT OF AN ARGUMENT.
Call... FAILED
PFF! A LITTLE SPAT! REMEMBER: YOU GOTTA MEND THE WOUNDS CUZ YOU NEED THE DRUGS! YOU'RE CRAZY FROM THE WITHDRAWAL. YOU'RE A DRUG-A-HOLIC!
I'M NOT GOOD AT LYING.
LYING'S JUST STORYTELLING, BILLY! LIKE A MOTHER TO HER SLEEPY CHILDREN!

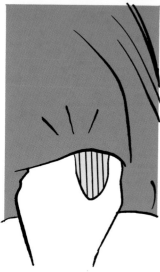

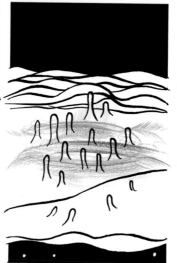

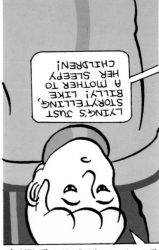

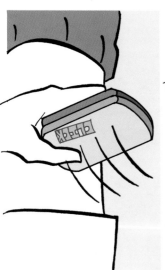

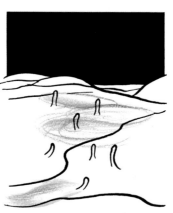

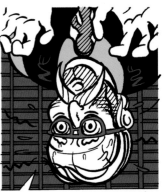

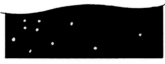

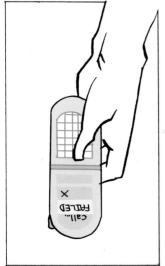

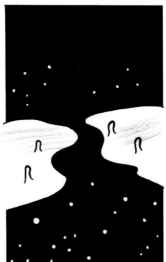

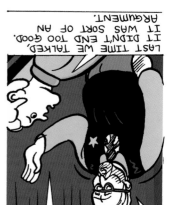

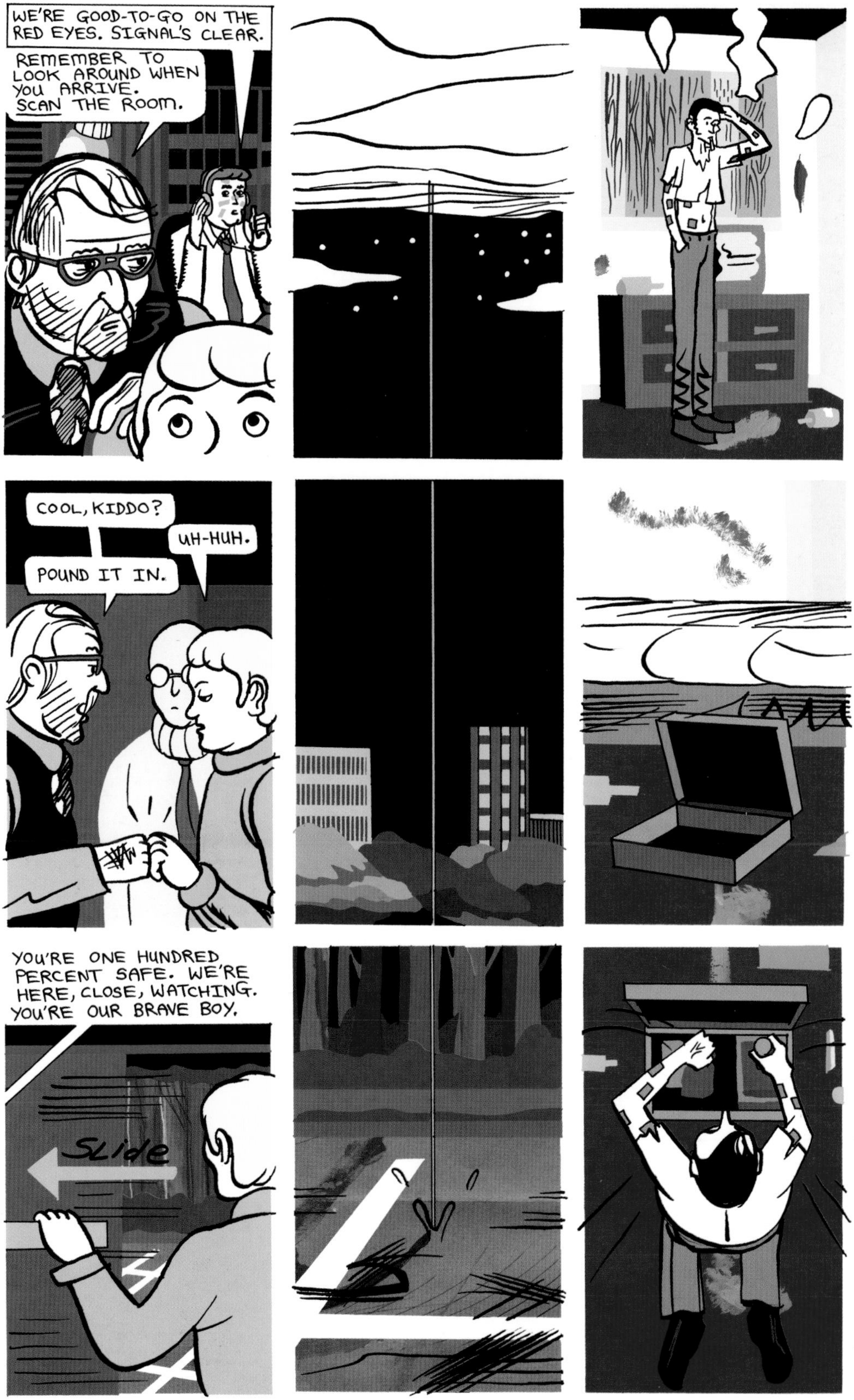
WE'RE GOOD-TO-GO ON THE RED EYES. SIGNAL'S CLEAR.
REMEMBER TO LOOK AROUND WHEN YOU ARRIVE. SCAN THE ROOM.
COOL, KIDDO?
UH-HUH.
POUND IT IN.
YOU'RE ONE HUNDRED PERCENT SAFE. WE'RE HERE, CLOSE, WATCHING. YOU'RE OUR BRAVE BOY.
SLIDE

RAIN HITTING PAVEMENT
SHUT
DRIP
DRIP
ROLL
SHADEY MOTEL
MOVING IN.
HE'S MOVING IN.
DRIP
DRIP

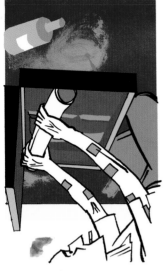

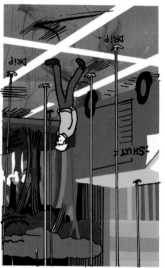

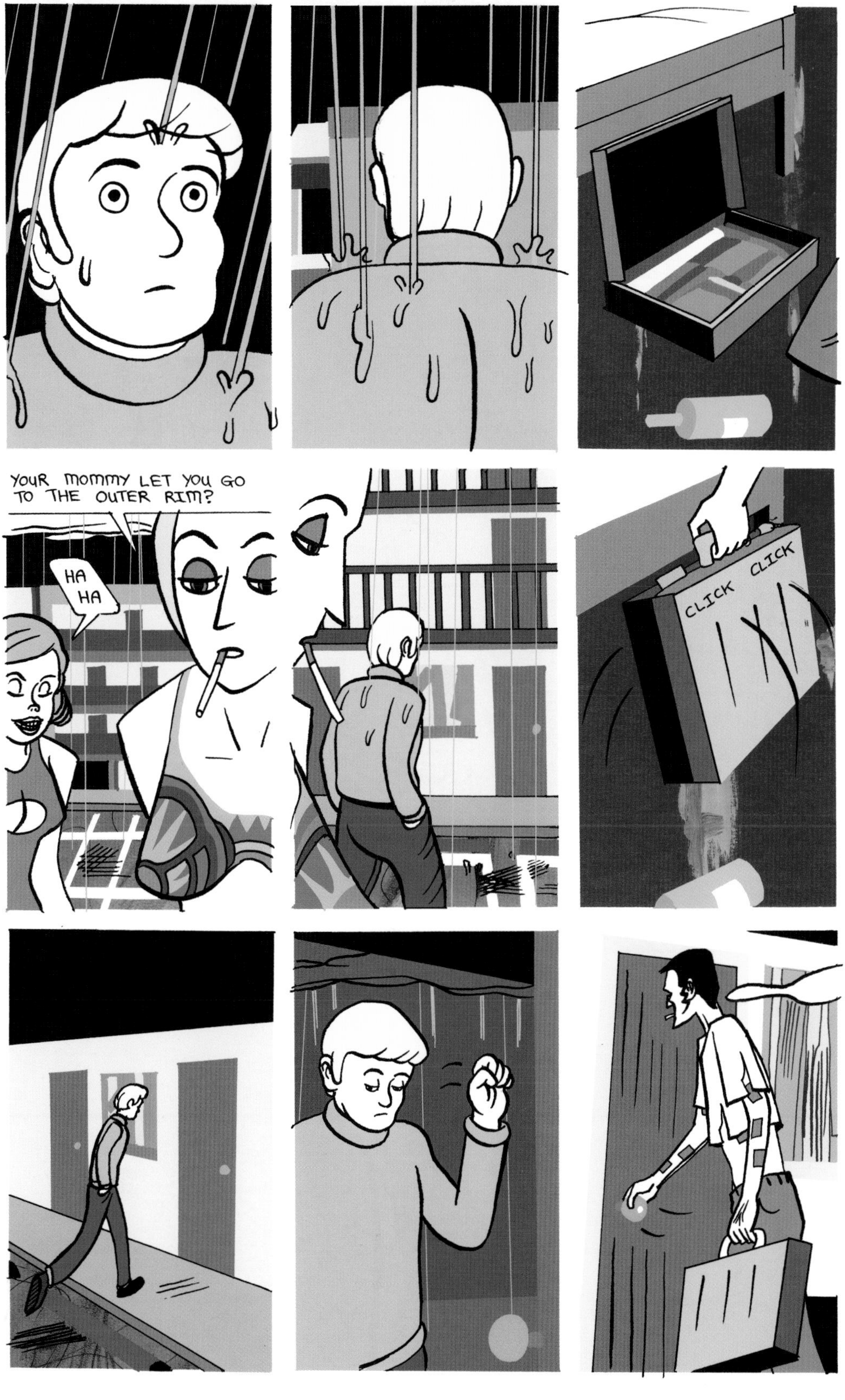
YOUR MOMMY LET YOU GO TO THE OUTER RIM?
HA HA
CLICK
CLICK

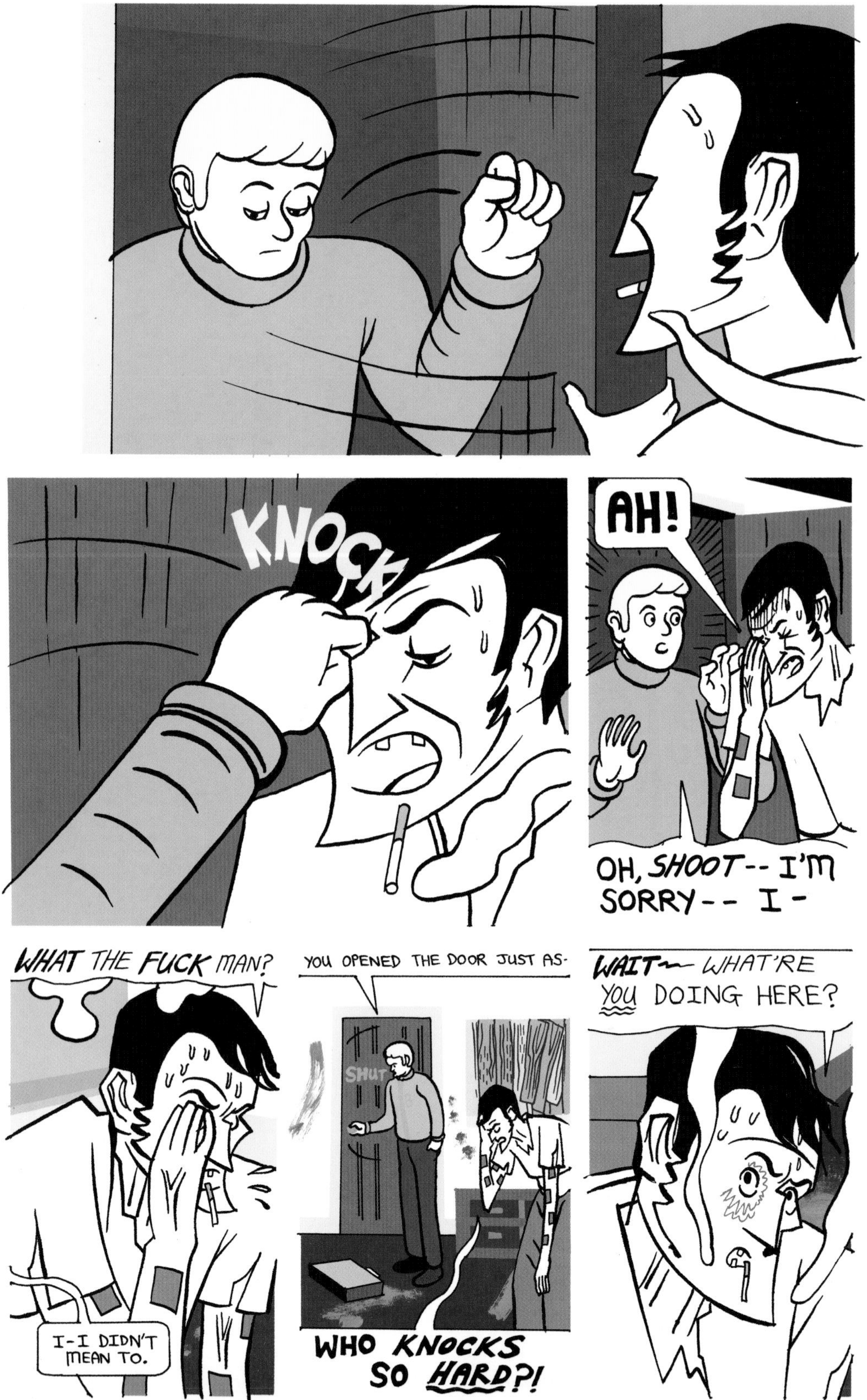
KNOCK
AH!
OH, SHOOT-- I'M SORRY-- I-
WHAT THE FUCK MAN?
I-I DIDN'T MEAN TO.
YOU OPENED THE DOOR JUST AS-
SHUT
WHO KNOCKS SO HARD?!
WAIT— WHAT'RE YOU DOING HERE?

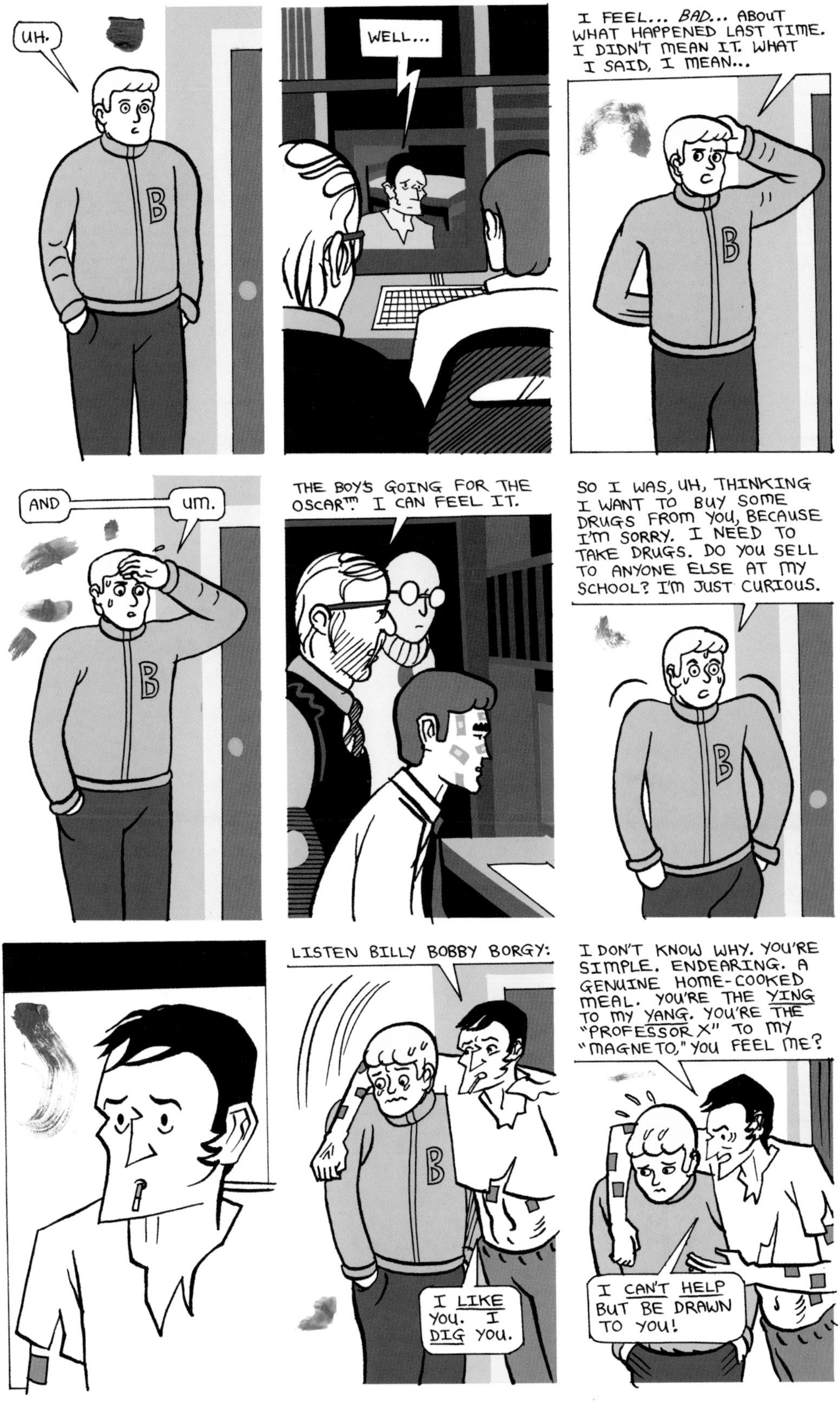
UH.
WELL...
I FEEL... BAD... ABOUT WHAT HAPPENED LAST TIME. I DIDN'T MEAN IT. WHAT I SAID, I MEAN...
AND
UM.
THE BOY'S GOING FOR THE OSCAR™. I CAN FEEL IT.
SO I WAS, UH, THINKING I WANT TO BUY SOME DRUGS FROM YOU, BECAUSE I'M SORRY. I NEED TO TAKE DRUGS. DO YOU SELL TO ANYONE ELSE AT MY SCHOOL? I'M JUST CURIOUS.
LISTEN BILLY BOBBY BORGY:
I LIKE YOU. I DIG YOU.
I DON'T KNOW WHY. YOU'RE SIMPLE. ENDEARING. A GENUINE HOME-COOKED MEAL. YOU'RE THE YING TO MY YANG. YOU'RE THE "PROFESSOR X" TO MY "MAGNETO," YOU FEEL ME?
I CAN'T HELP BUT BE DRAWN TO YOU!

WE COMPLETE EACH OTHER,

RIGHT?

UM

RIGHT.

SH-

SHIT-

UH. IS THERE SOME DRUGS I CAN BUY? OR SOME ALCOHOLIC DRINKS? I REALLY NEED THEM. I'M GOING CRAZY FOR THEM.

BLINK

BLINK

YOU MUST'VE PUNCHED ME REALLY HARD, DUDE.

MY VISION'S GOING RED.

MY HAND LOOKS LIKE IT'S COVERED IN BLOOD.

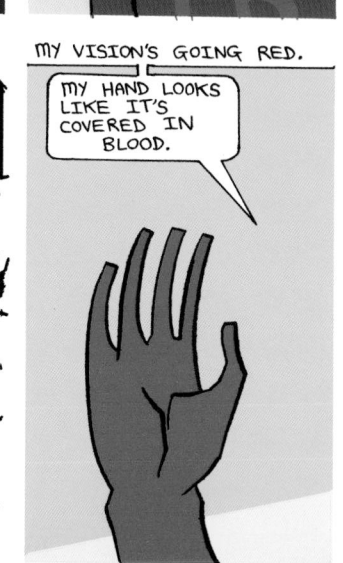

AM I *BLEEDING*?

NOT ANYWHERE THAT I CAN SEE.

MAYBE YOU'RE HALLUCINATING FROM GREAT DRUGS.

MY FACE FEELS LIKE IT'S... PUFFING UP.

I WANT TO HALLUCINATE TOO. CAN I HAVE SOME OF WHAT YOU'RE ON?

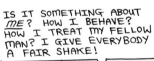

I'M "ON" *HEART* *ACHE*, BILLY.

DESPAIR.

THE HARD STUFF.

I DON'T THINK YOU COULD HANDLE WHAT I'M "ON."

JUST WHEN MY LIFE FINALLY FELT LIKE IT WAS COMING TOGETHER—A NEW GIRL, A NEW OUTLOOK—THE WHOLE FUCKING TOWN HAD TO TURN INTO AN ALIEN EXPERIMENT. *SHIT.*

WHY DOESN'T ANYTHING EVER WORK OUT FOR ME? WHY CAN'T I BE HAPPY?

IS IT SOMETHING ABOUT *ME*? HOW I BEHAVE? HOW I TREAT MY FELLOW MAN? I GIVE EVERYBODY A FAIR SHAKE!

HELL, YOU SPIT A LIT CIGARETTE AT MY FACE, BUT HERE WE ARE—PALS! CHATTING IT UP!

I DON'T KNOW WHY I DIDN'T THROW IN THE TOWEL YEARS AGO. LORD KNOWS I TRIED! YOU'D THINK I'D BE DEAD BY NOW, AT PEACE.

DON'T SAY THAT PROF. PANTHER.

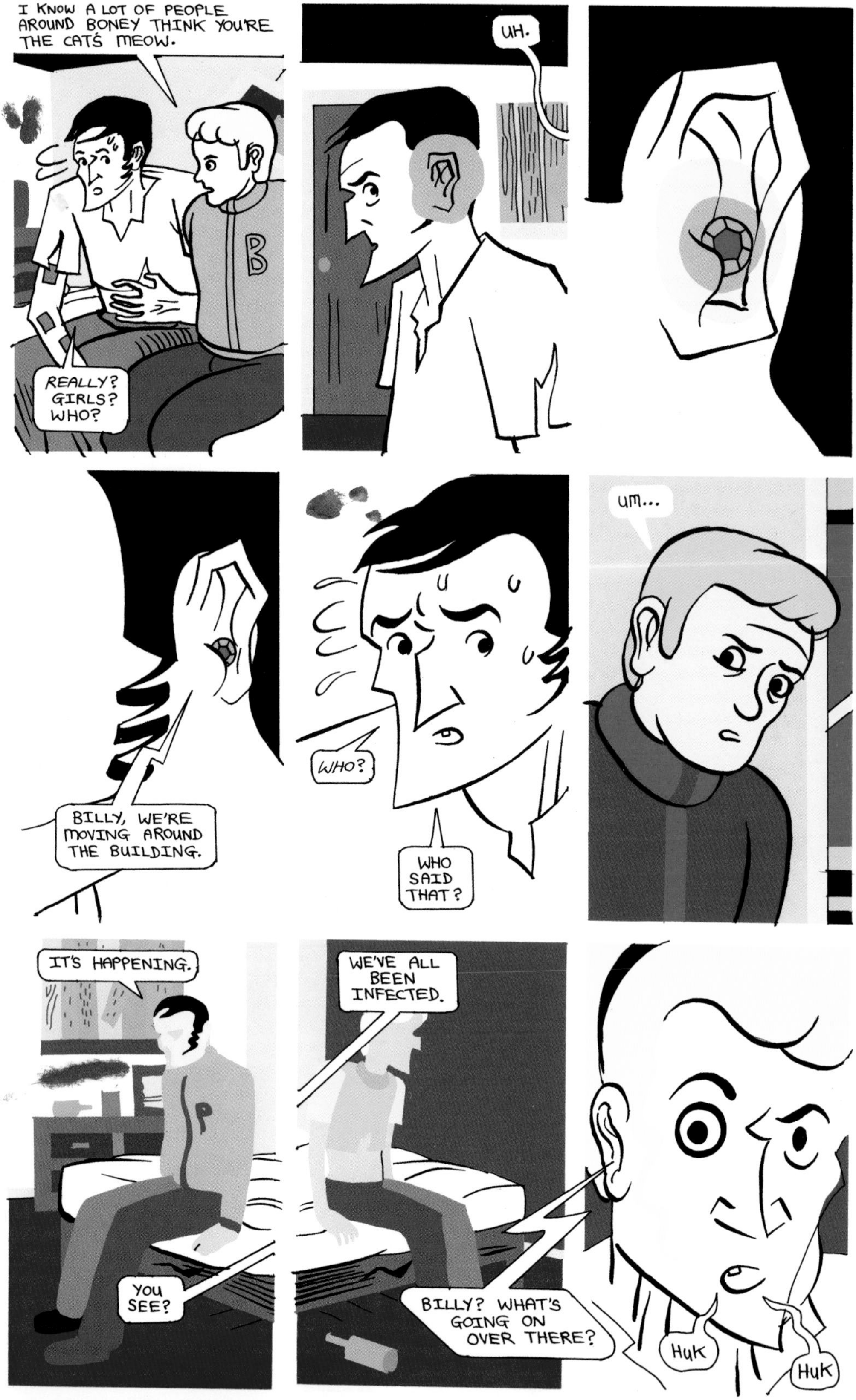
I KNOW A LOT OF PEOPLE AROUND BONEY THINK YOU'RE THE CAT'S MEOW.
REALLY? GIRLS? WHO?
UH.
BILLY, WE'RE MOVING AROUND THE BUILDING.
WHO?
WHO SAID THAT?
UM...
IT'S HAPPENING.
YOU SEE?
WE'VE ALL BEEN INFECTED.
BILLY? WHAT'S GOING ON OVER THERE?
HUK
HUK

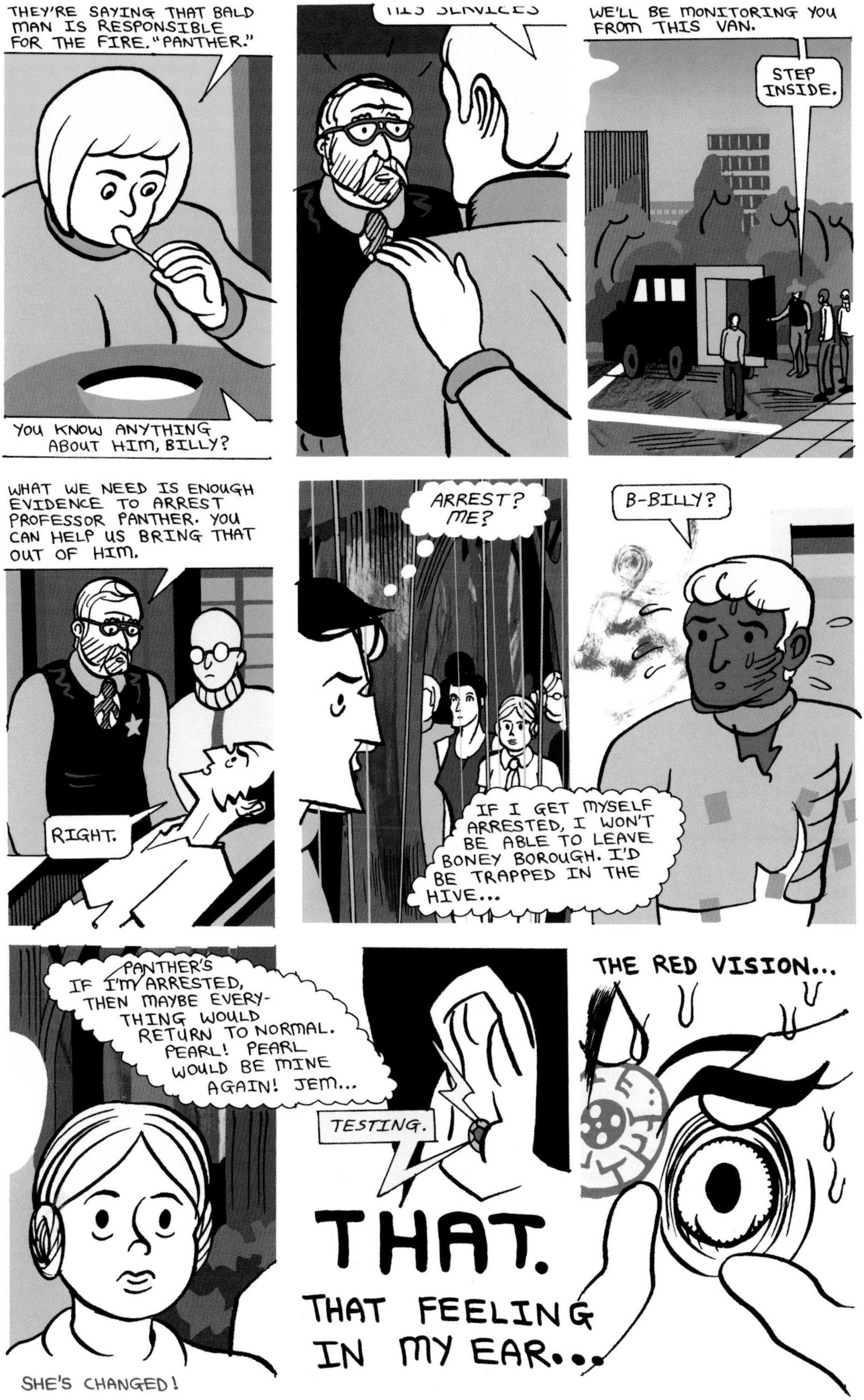
THEY'RE SAYING THAT BALD MAN IS RESPONSIBLE FOR THE FIRE. "PANTHER."
YOU KNOW ANYTHING ABOUT HIM, BILLY?
WE'LL BE MONITORING YOU FROM THIS VAN.
STEP INSIDE.
WHAT WE NEED IS ENOUGH EVIDENCE TO ARREST PROFESSOR PANTHER. YOU CAN HELP US BRING THAT OUT OF HIM.
RIGHT.
ARREST? ME?
IF I GET MYSELF ARRESTED, I WON'T BE ABLE TO LEAVE BONEY BOROUGH. I'D BE TRAPPED IN THE HIVE...
B-BILLY?
IF PANTHER'S ARRESTED, THEN MAYBE EVERYTHING WOULD RETURN TO NORMAL. PEARL! PEARL WOULD BE MINE AGAIN! JEM...
SHE'S CHANGED!
TESTING.
THAT.
THAT FEELING IN MY EAR...
THE RED VISION...

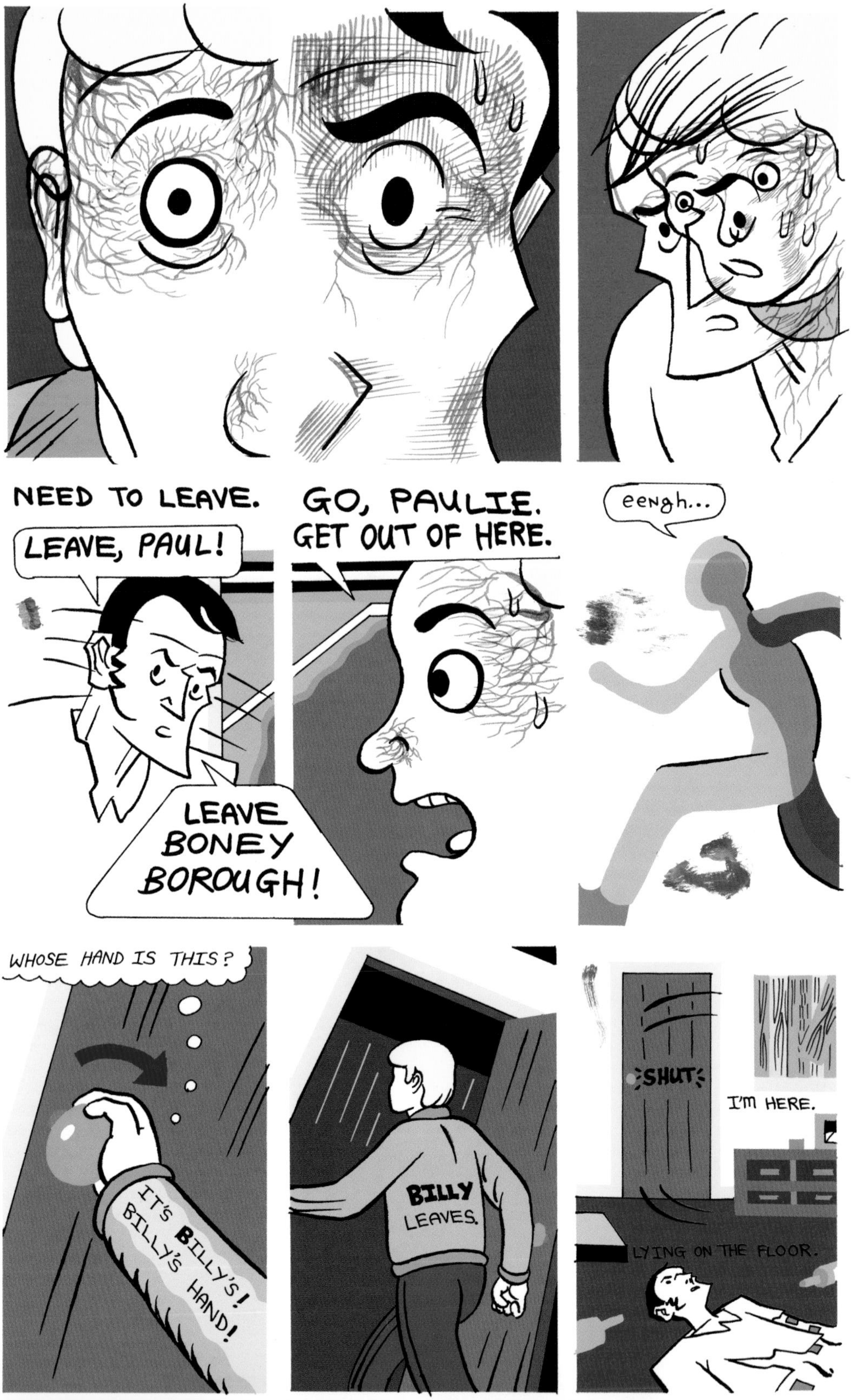
NEED TO LEAVE.
LEAVE, PAUL!
LEAVE BONEY BOROUGH!
GO, PAULIE. GET OUT OF HERE.
eengh...
WHOSE HAND IS THIS?
IT'S BILLY'S! BILLY'S HAND!
BILLY LEAVES.
SHUT
I'M HERE.
LYING ON THE FLOOR.

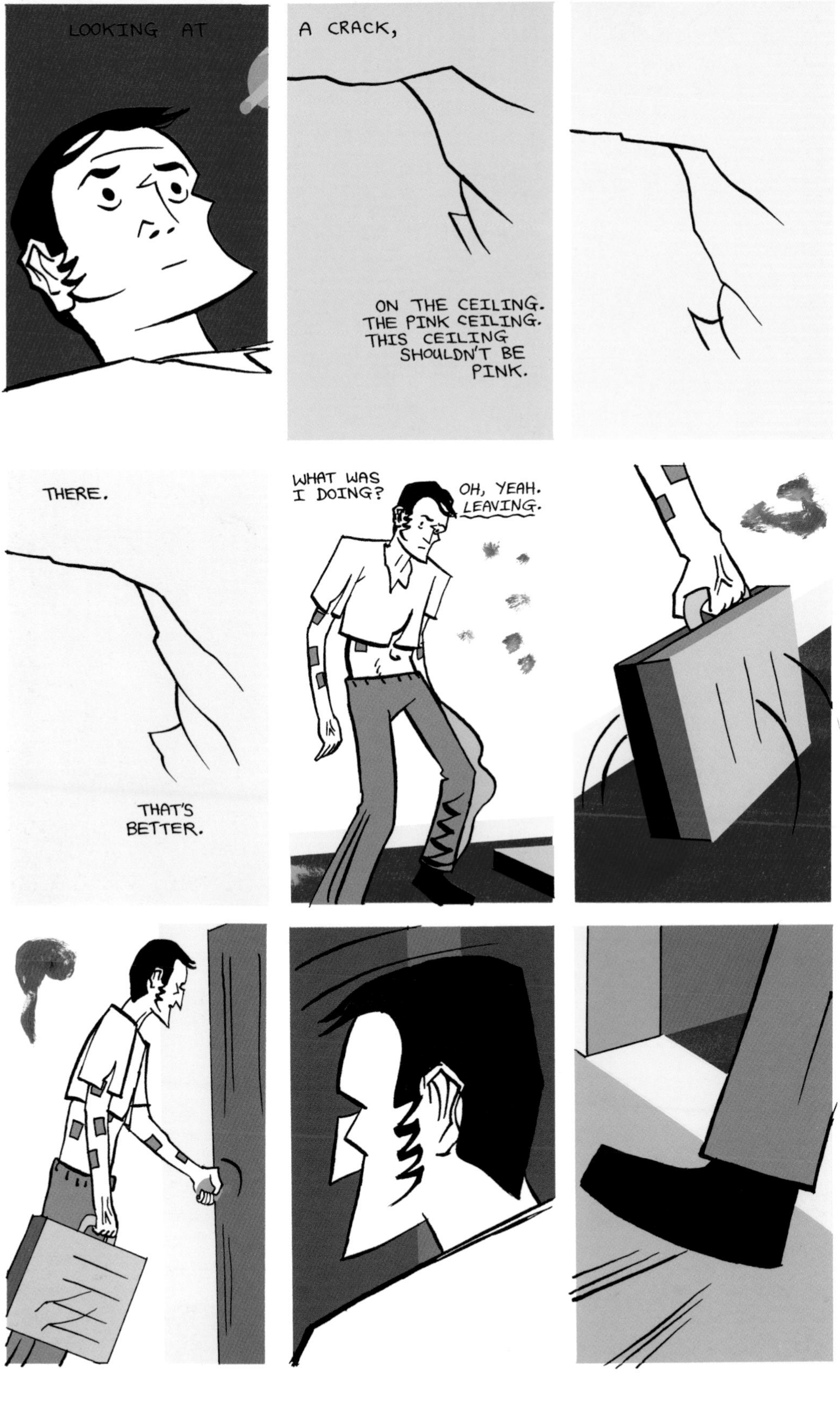
LOOKING AT
A CRACK,
ON THE CEILING. THE PINK CEILING. THIS CEILING SHOULDN'T BE PINK.
THERE.
THAT'S BETTER.
WHAT WAS I DOING?
OH, YEAH. LEAVING.

FREEZE PROFESSOR PANTHER!

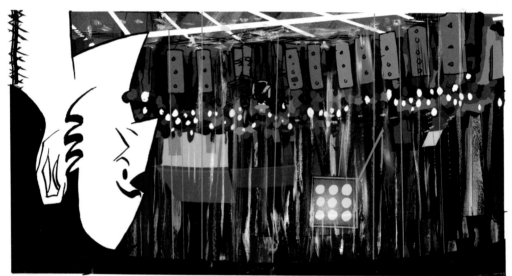

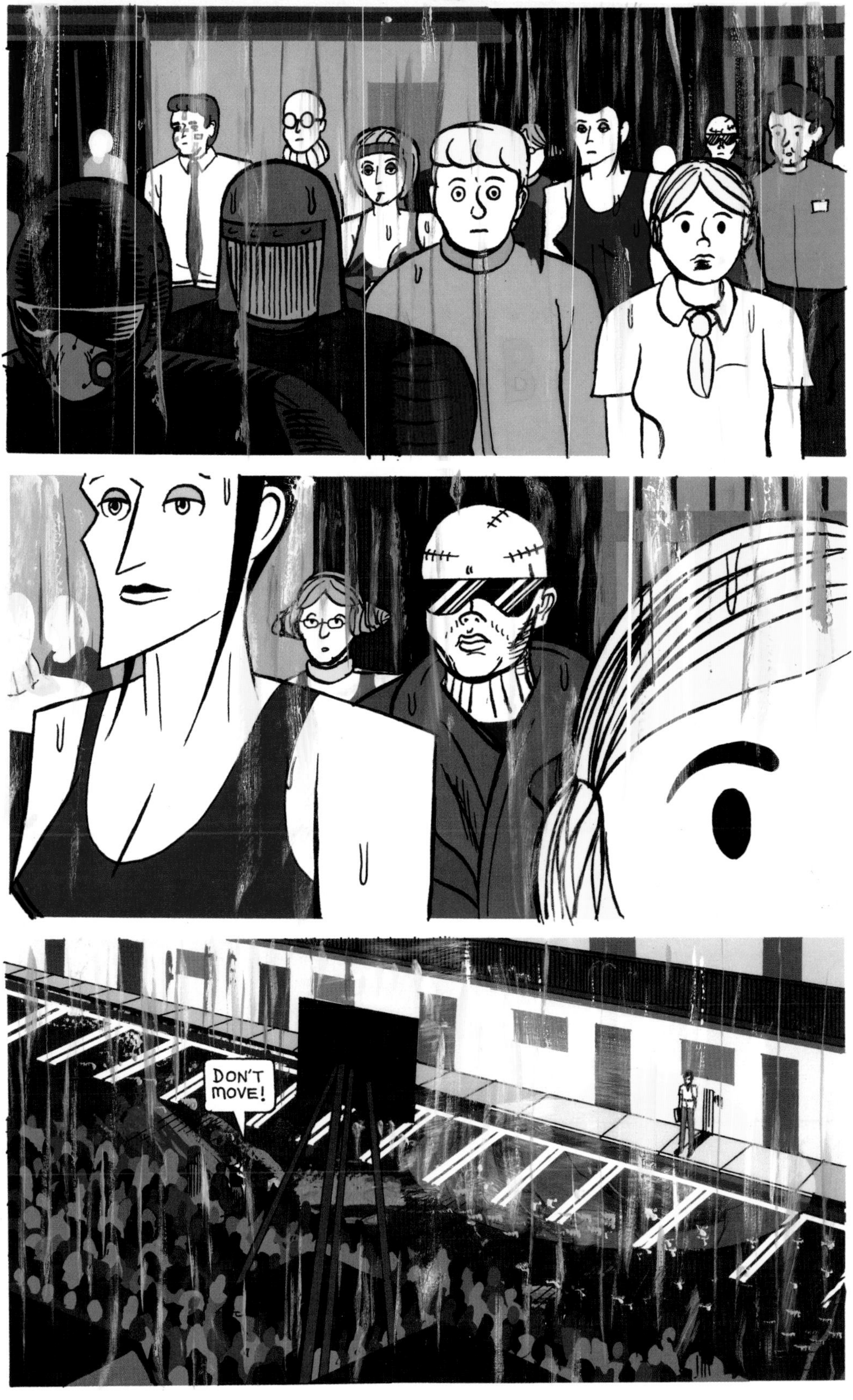
DON'T MOVE!

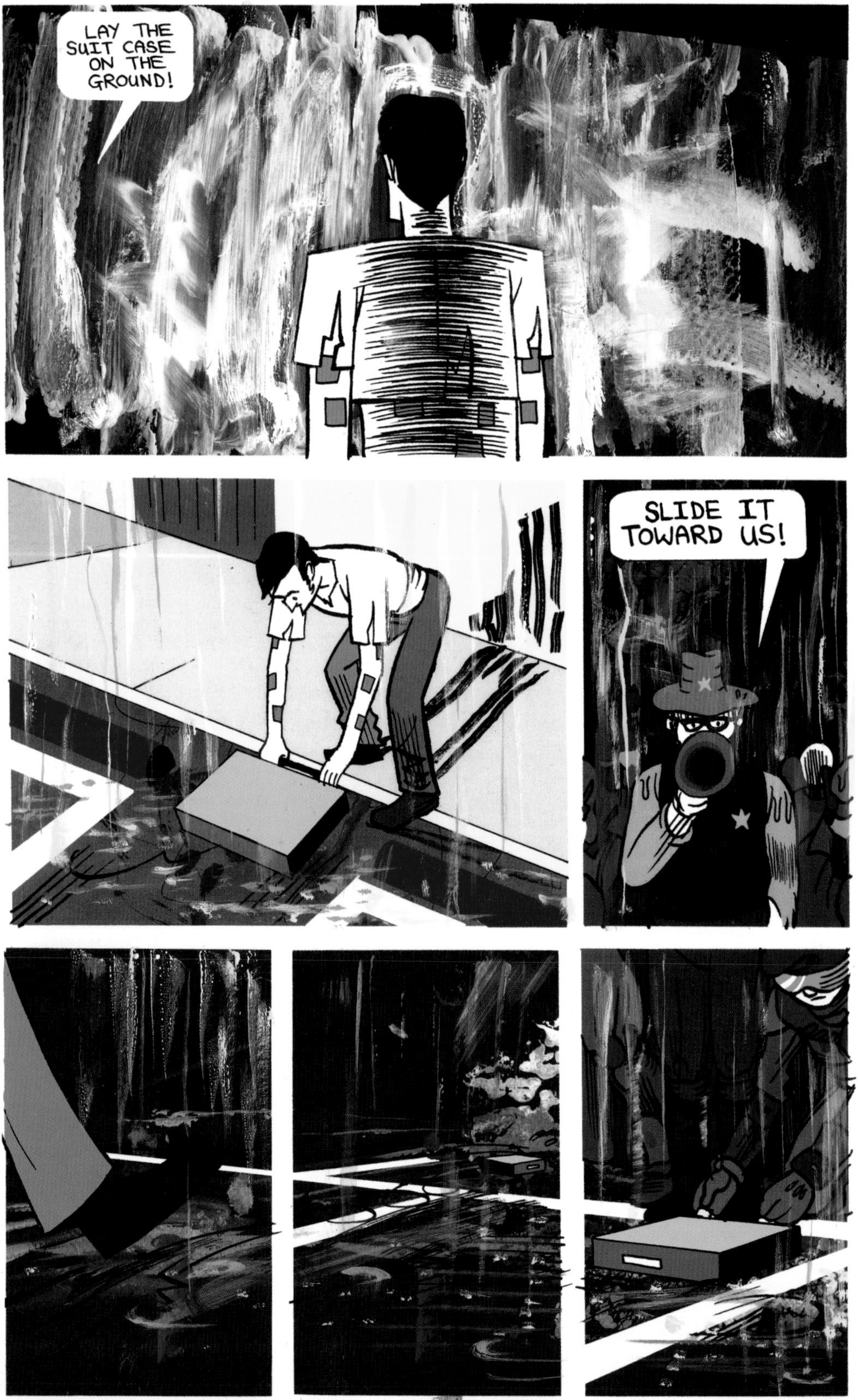
LAY THE SUIT CASE ON THE GROUND!
SLIDE IT TOWARD US!

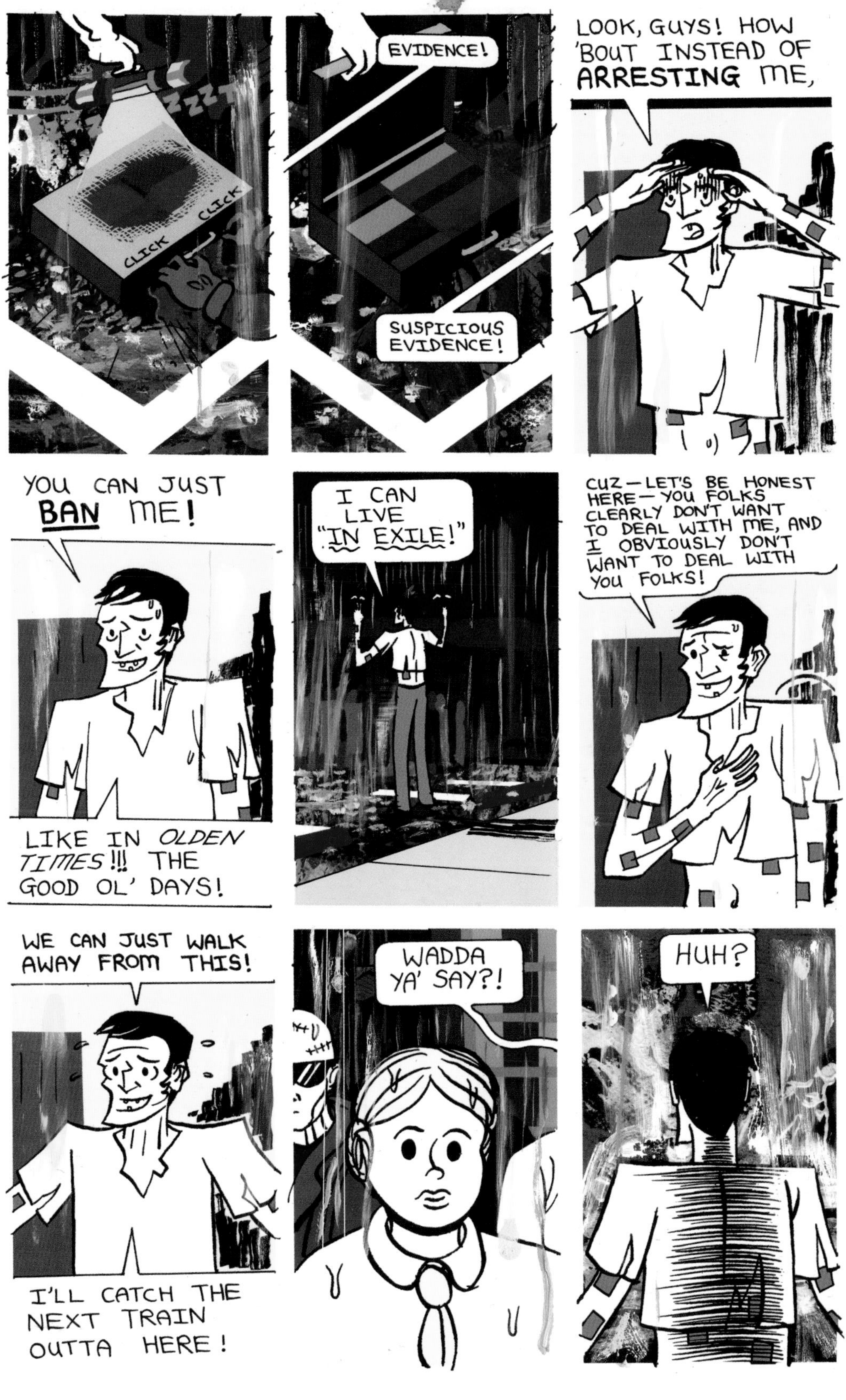
ZZZZ
CLICK
CLICK
EVIDENCE!
SUSPICIOUS EVIDENCE!
LOOK, GUYS! HOW 'BOUT INSTEAD OF ARRESTING ME,
YOU CAN JUST BAN ME!
LIKE IN OLDEN TIMES!!! THE GOOD OL' DAYS!
I CAN LIVE "IN EXILE!"
CUZ—LET'S BE HONEST HERE—YOU FOLKS CLEARLY DON'T WANT TO DEAL WITH ME, AND I OBVIOUSLY DON'T WANT TO DEAL WITH YOU FOLKS!
WE CAN JUST WALK AWAY FROM THIS!
I'LL CATCH THE NEXT TRAIN OUTTA HERE!
WADDA YA' SAY?!
HUH?

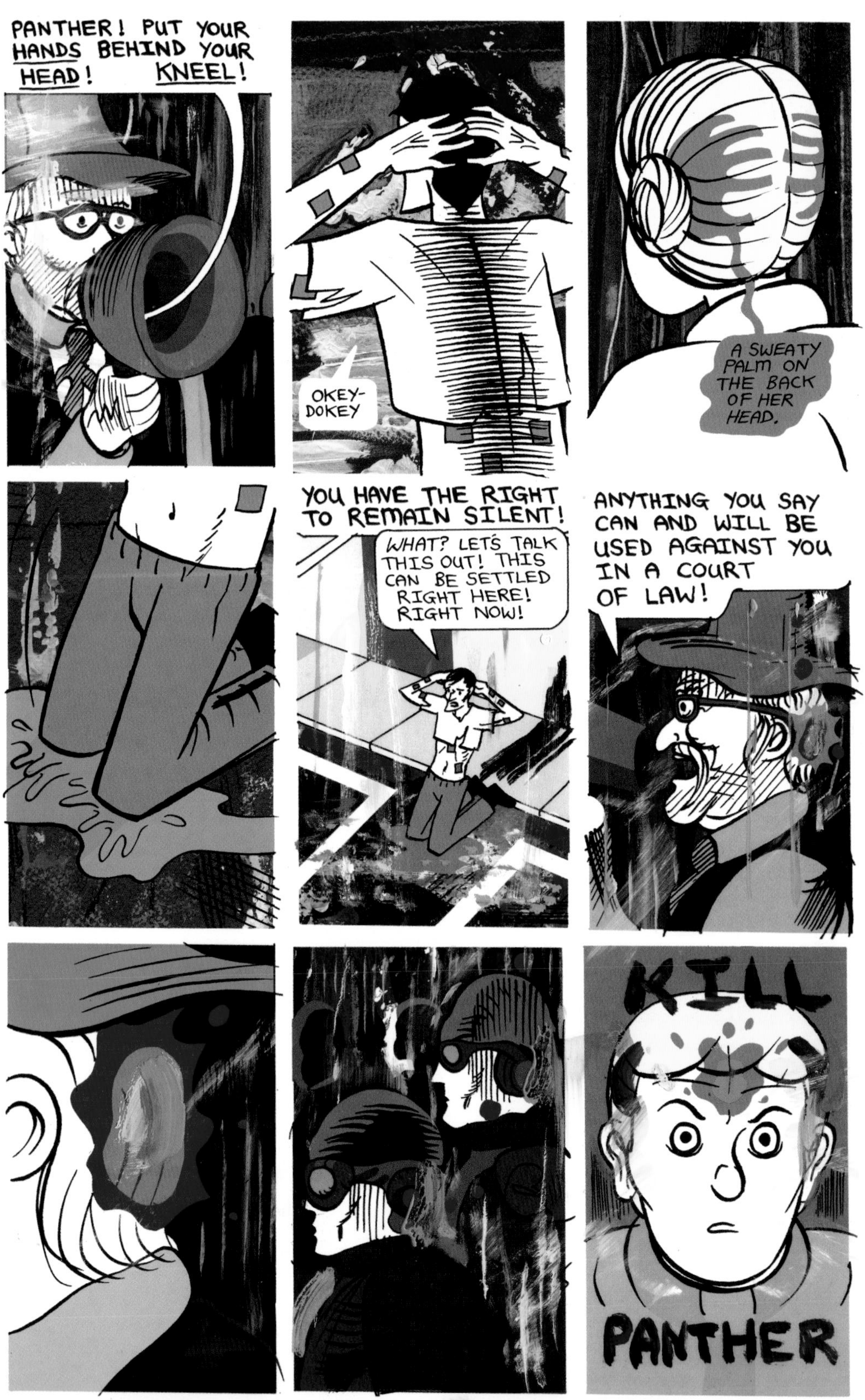
PANTHER! PUT YOUR HANDS BEHIND YOUR HEAD! KNEEL!
OKEY-DOKEY
A SWEATY PALM ON THE BACK OF HER HEAD.
YOU HAVE THE RIGHT TO REMAIN SILENT!
WHAT? LET'S TALK THIS OUT! THIS CAN BE SETTLED RIGHT HERE! RIGHT NOW!
ANYTHING YOU SAY CAN AND WILL BE USED AGAINST YOU IN A COURT OF LAW!
KILL
PANTHER

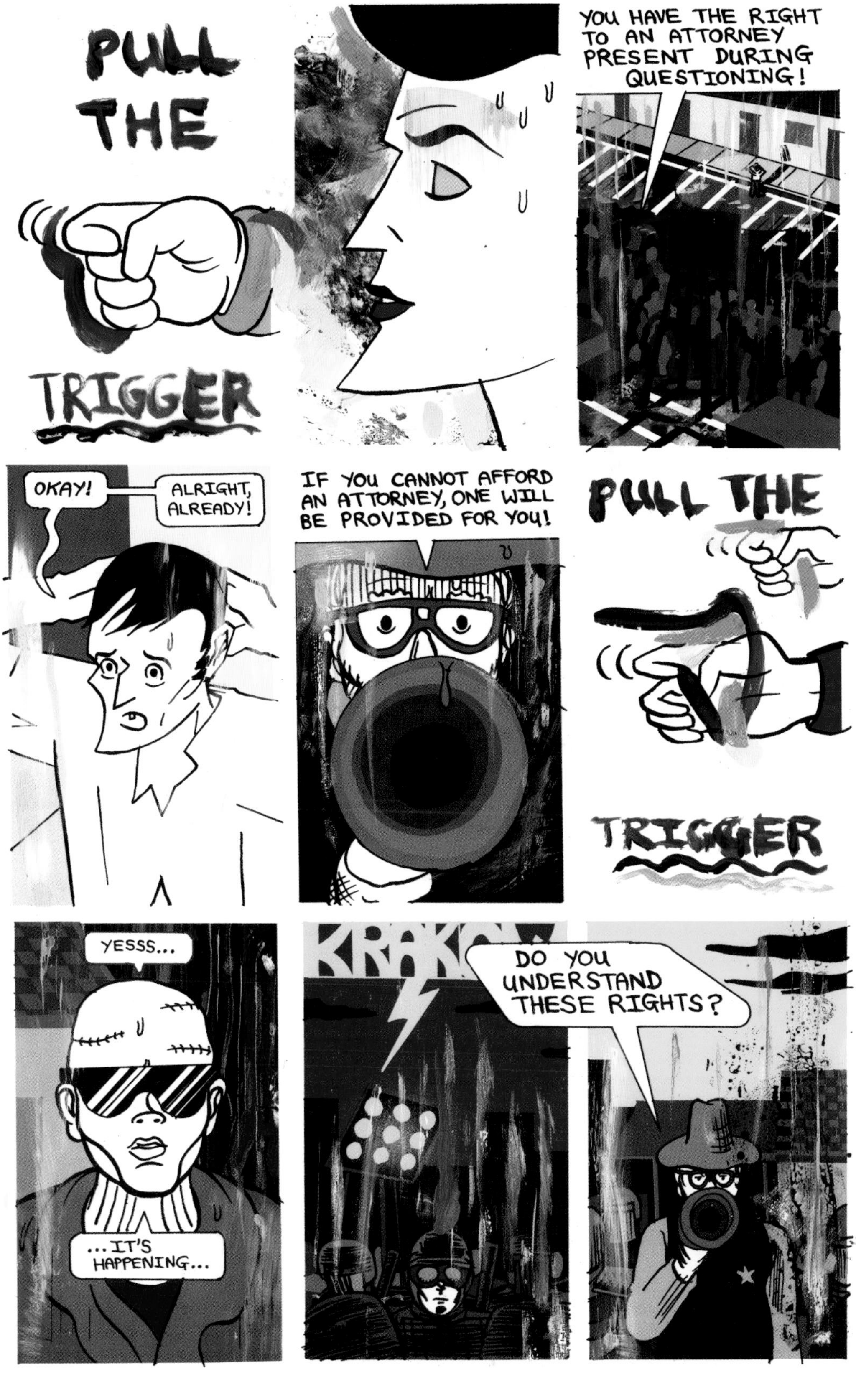
PULL THE
TRIGGER
YOU HAVE THE RIGHT TO AN ATTORNEY PRESENT DURING QUESTIONING!
OKAY!
ALRIGHT, ALREADY!
IF YOU CANNOT AFFORD AN ATTORNEY, ONE WILL BE PROVIDED FOR YOU!
PULL THE
TRIGGER
YESSS...
...IT'S HAPPENING...
DO YOU UNDERSTAND THESE RIGHTS?

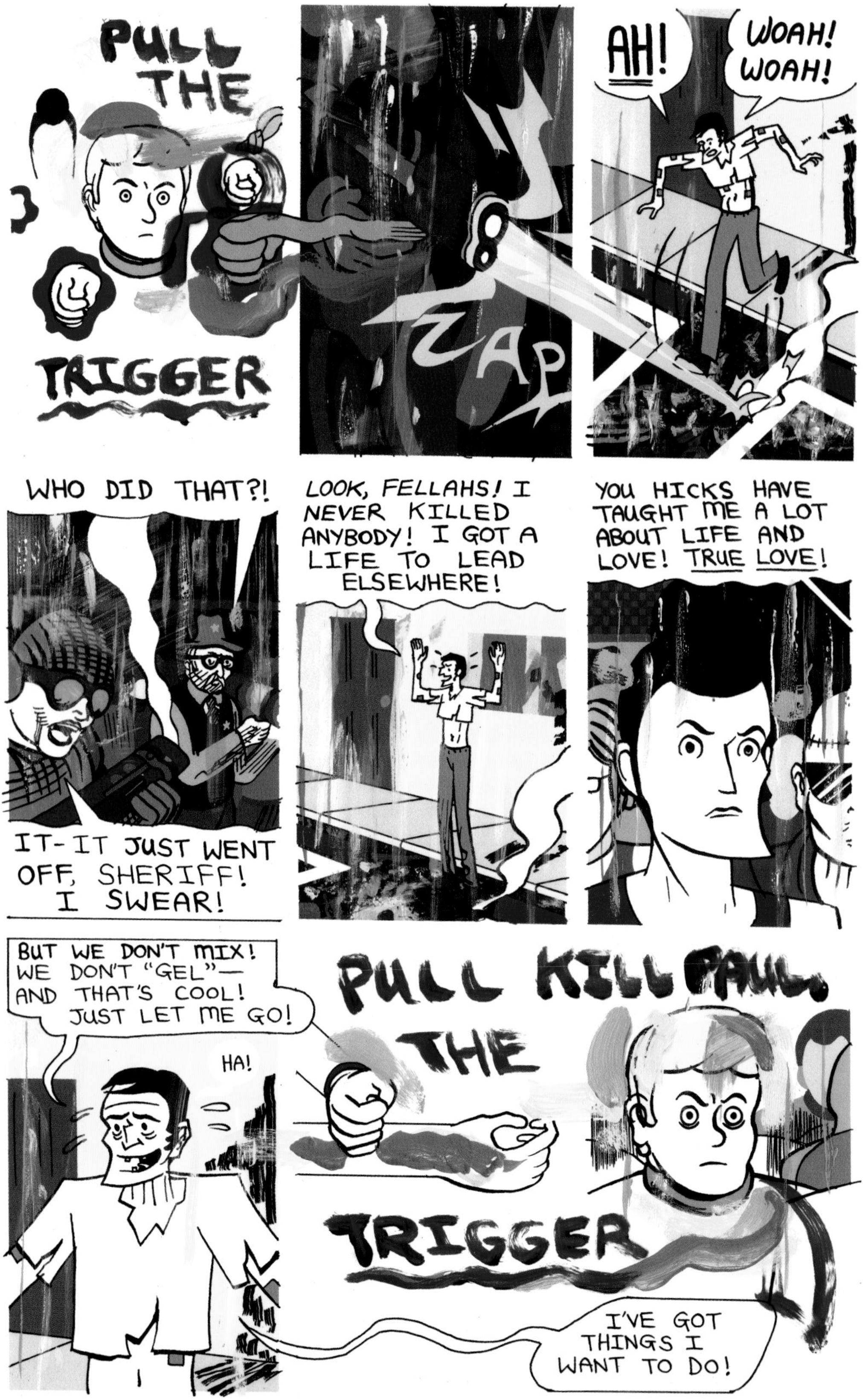
PULL THE TRIGGER
ZAP
AH!
WOAH! WOAH!
WHO DID THAT?!
IT-IT JUST WENT OFF, SHERIFF! I SWEAR!
LOOK, FELLAHS! I NEVER KILLED ANYBODY! I GOT A LIFE TO LEAD ELSEWHERE!
YOU HICKS HAVE TAUGHT ME A LOT ABOUT LIFE AND LOVE! TRUE LOVE!
BUT WE DON'T MIX! WE DON'T "GEL"— AND THAT'S COOL! JUST LET ME GO!
HA!
PULL KILL PAUL THE TRIGGER
I'VE GOT THINGS I WANT TO DO!

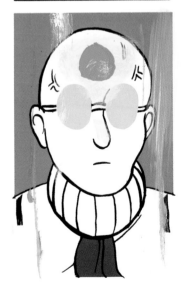

KRAKOW

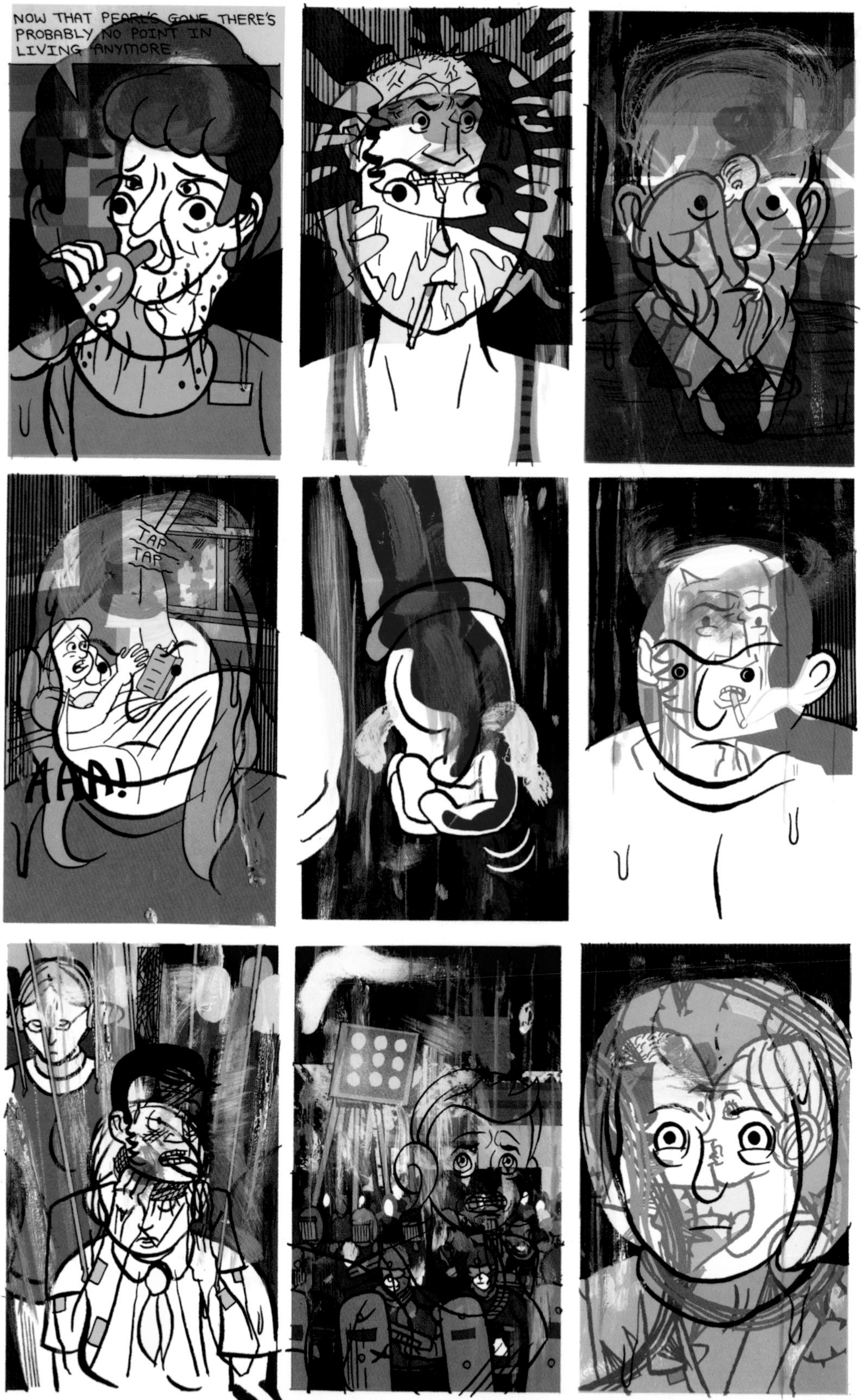
NOW THAT PEARL'S GONE THERE'S PROBABLY NO POINT IN LIVING ANYMORE.
TAP TAP
AAH!

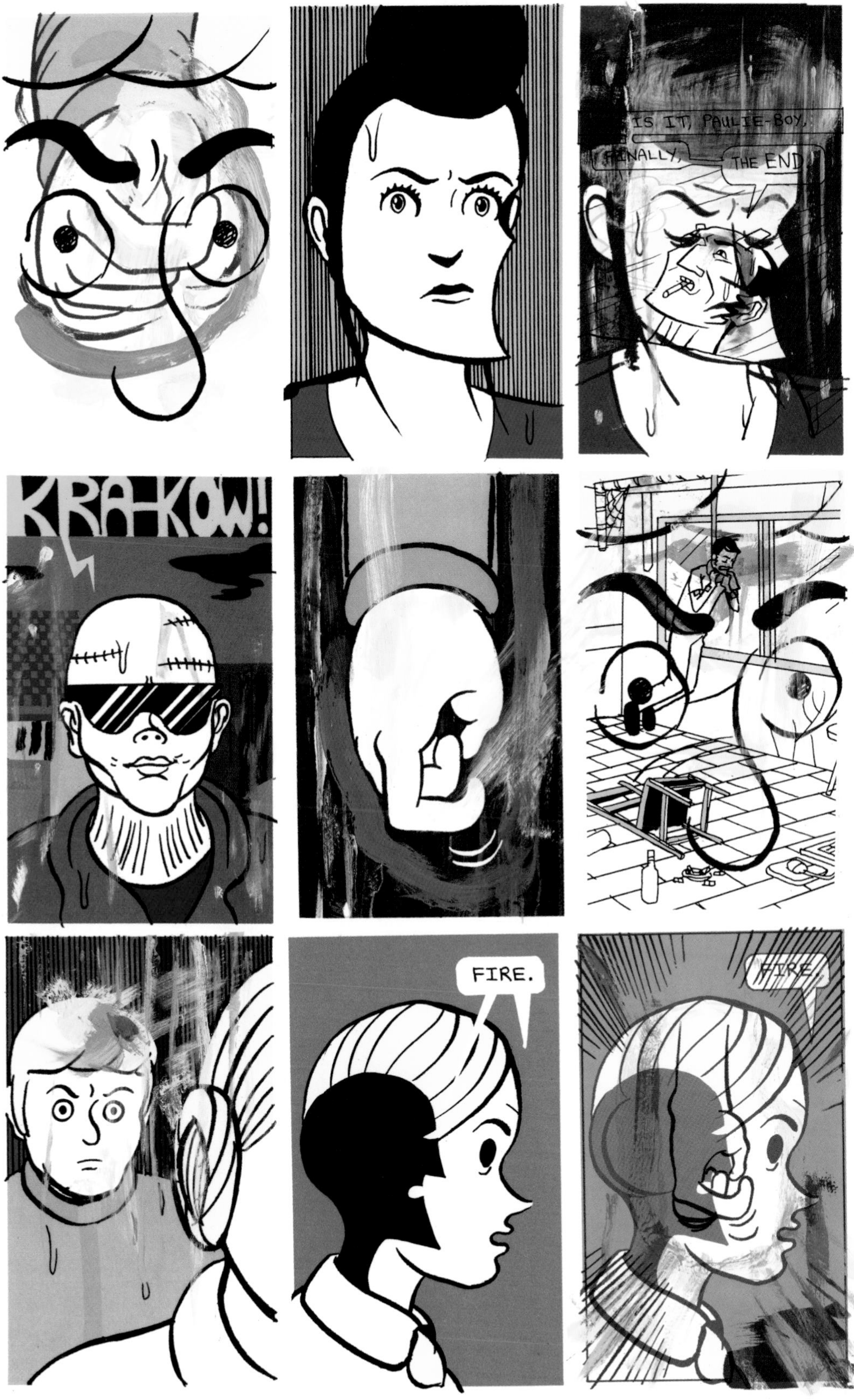

IS IT, PAULIE-BOY,
FINALLY,
THE END
KRA-KOW!!
FIRE.
FIRE.

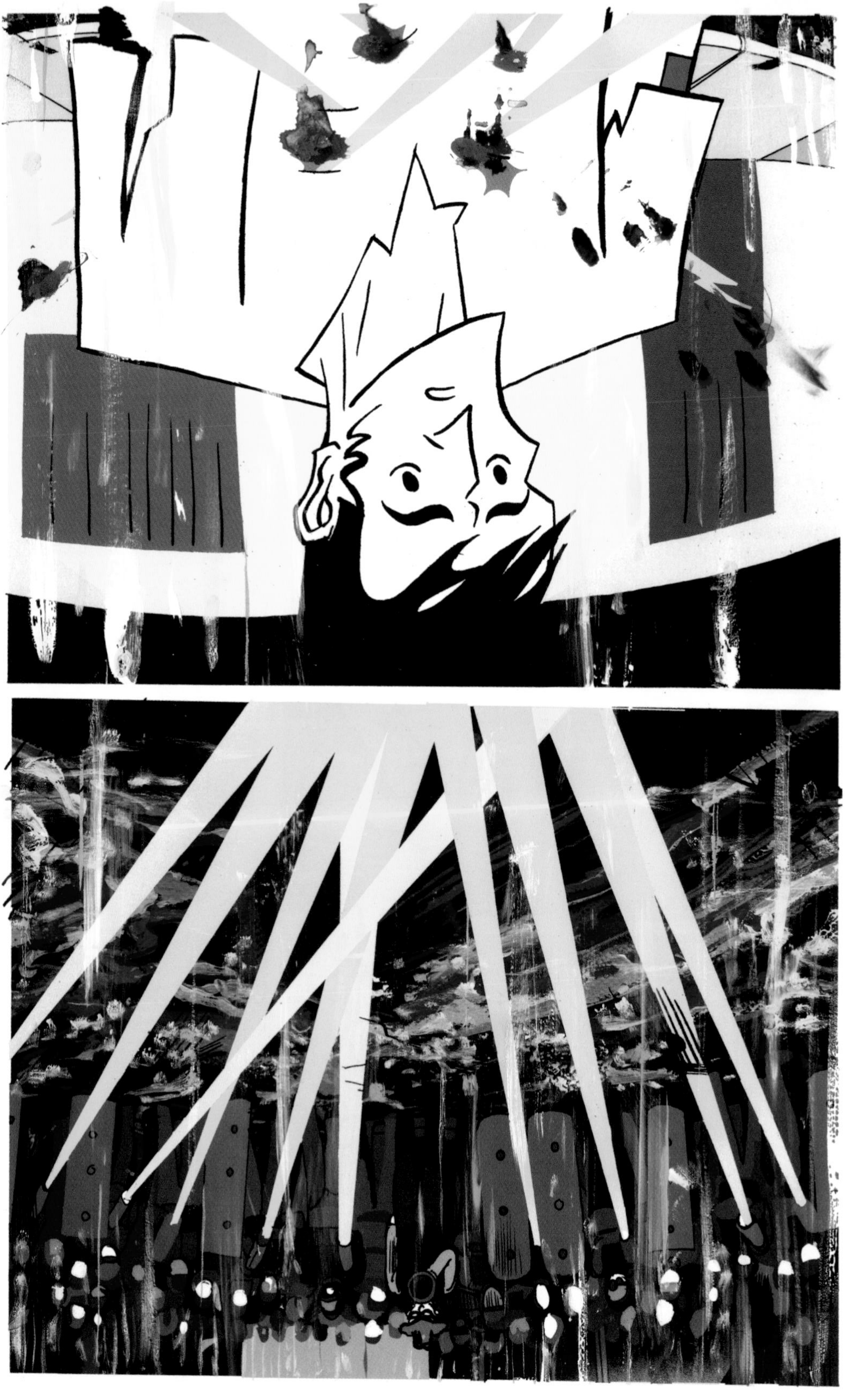

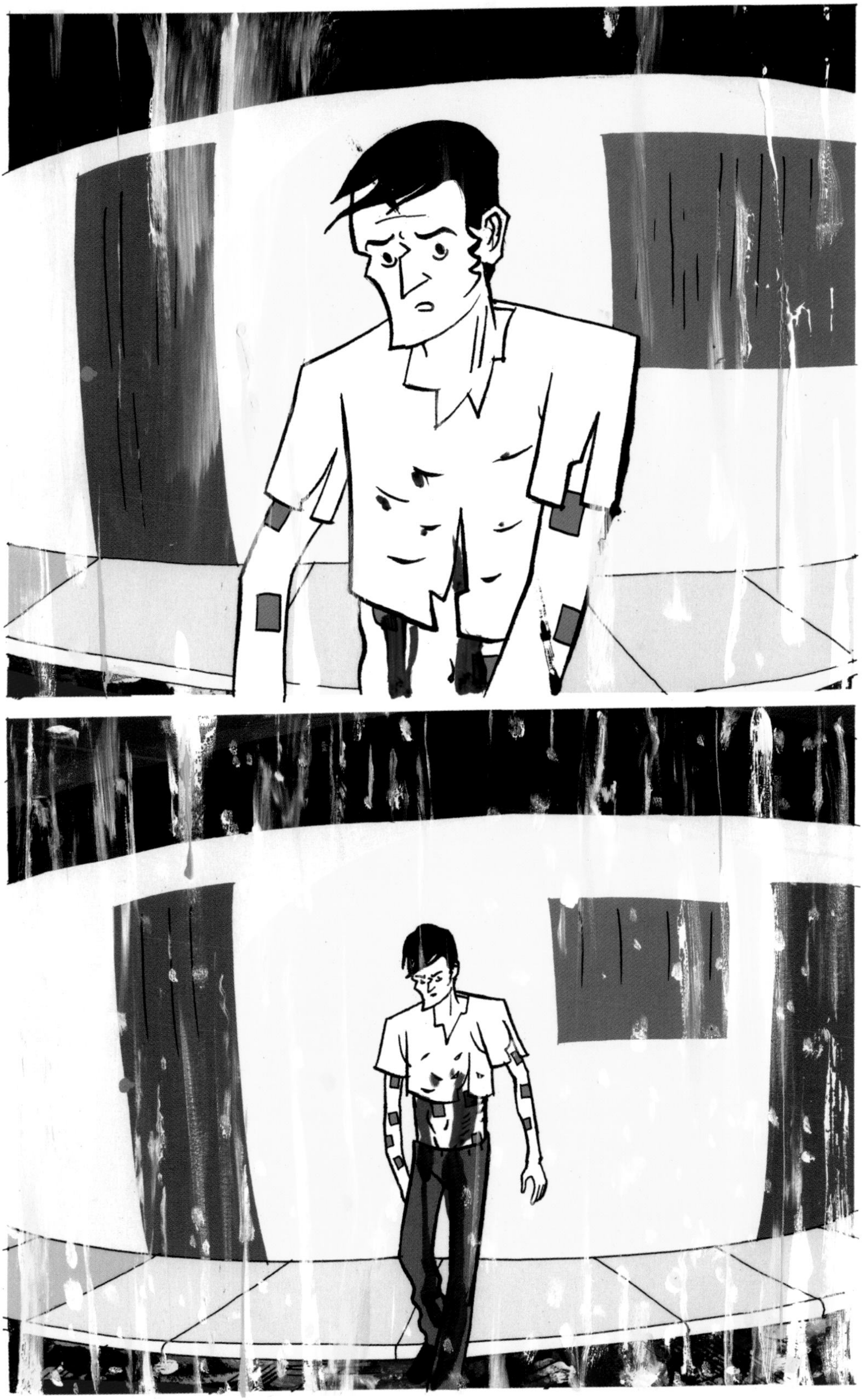

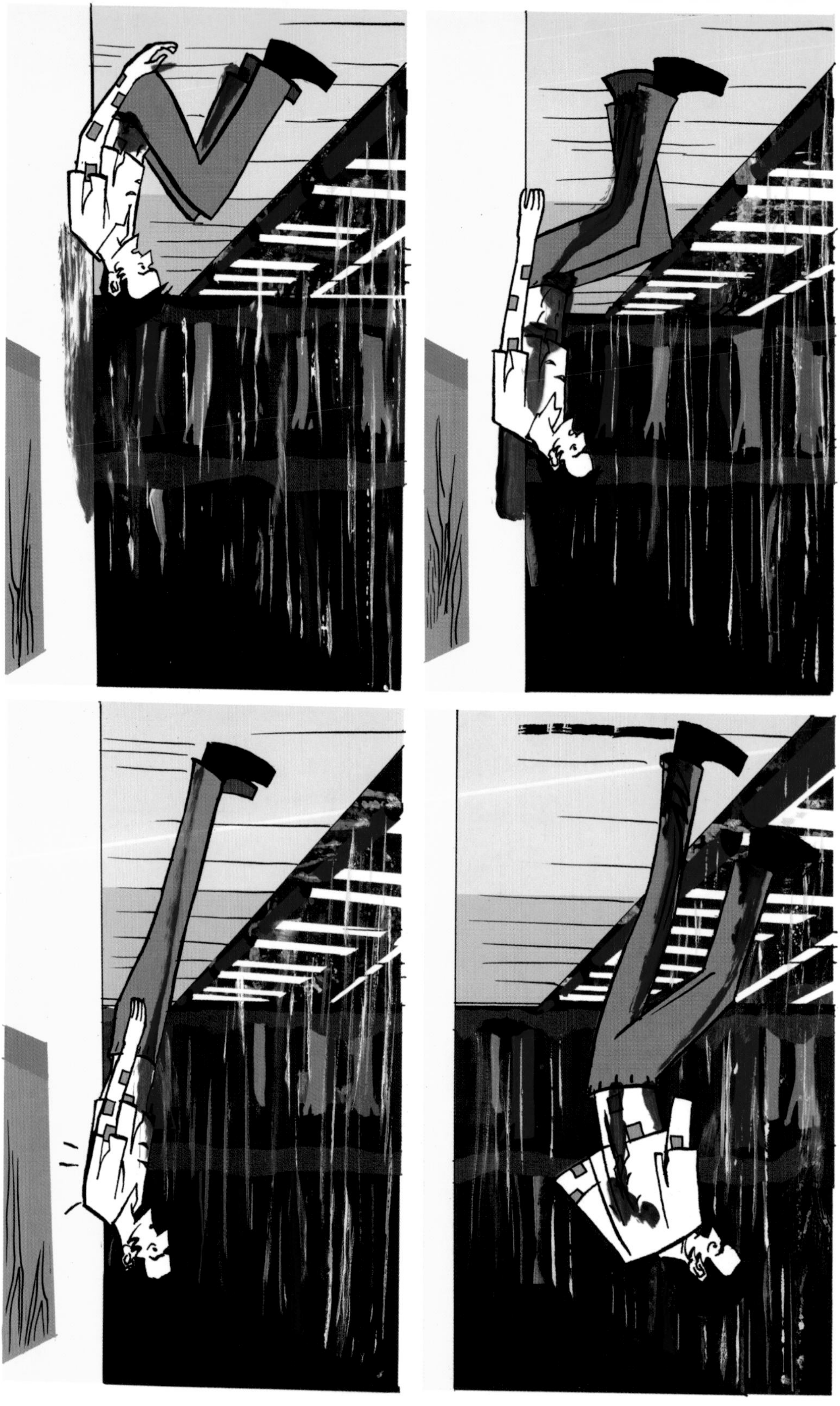

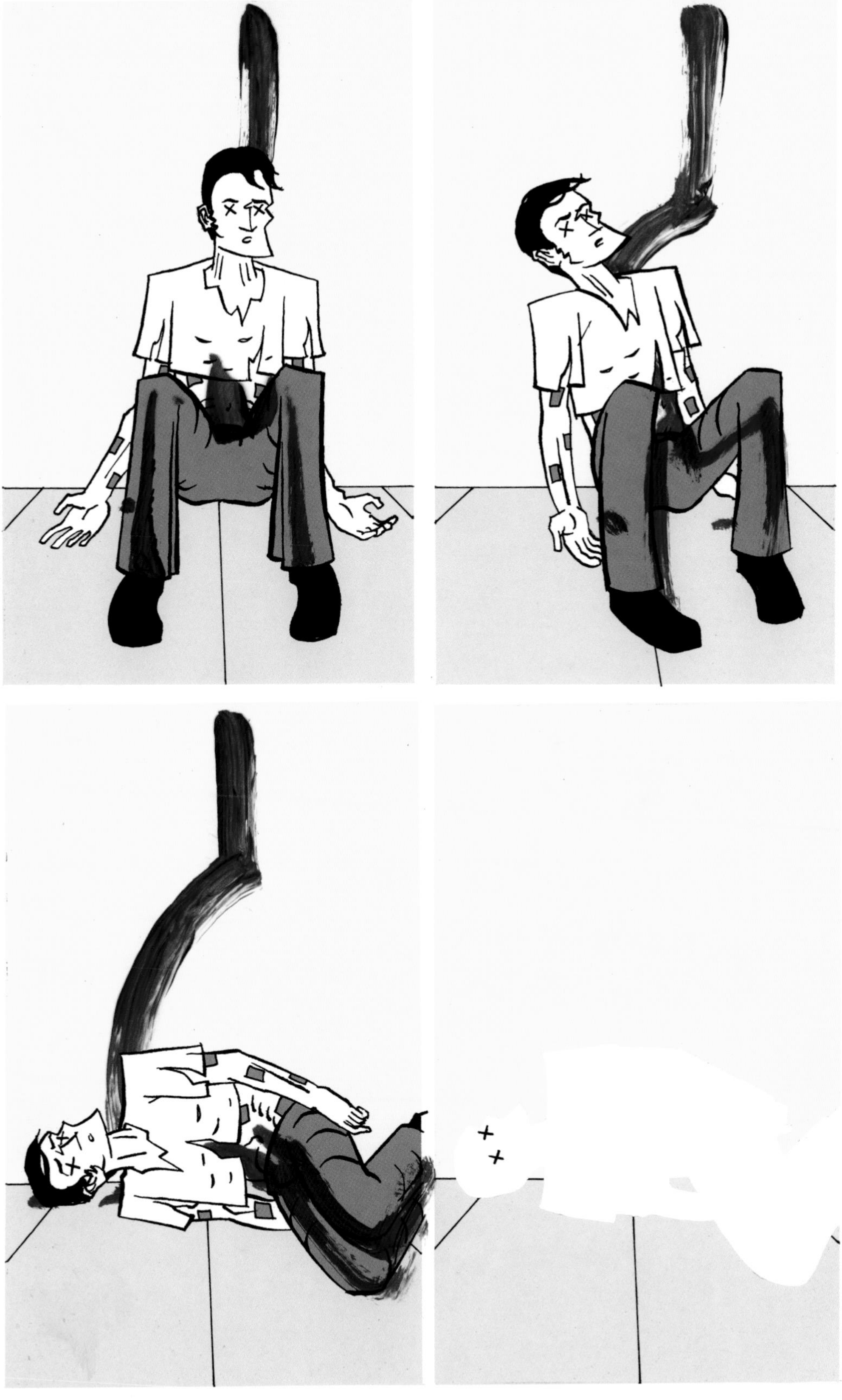

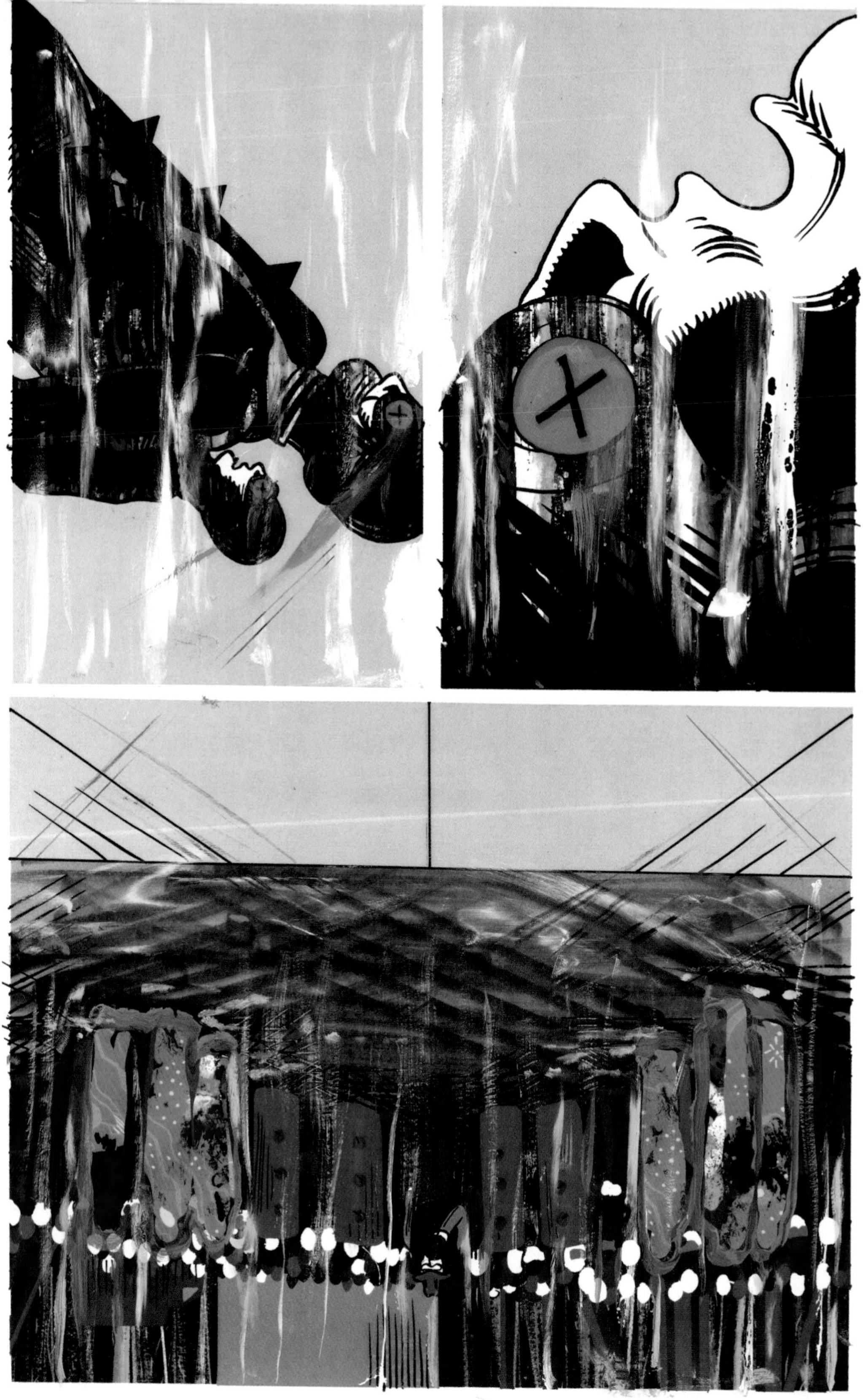

END OF CHAPTER ELEVEN.

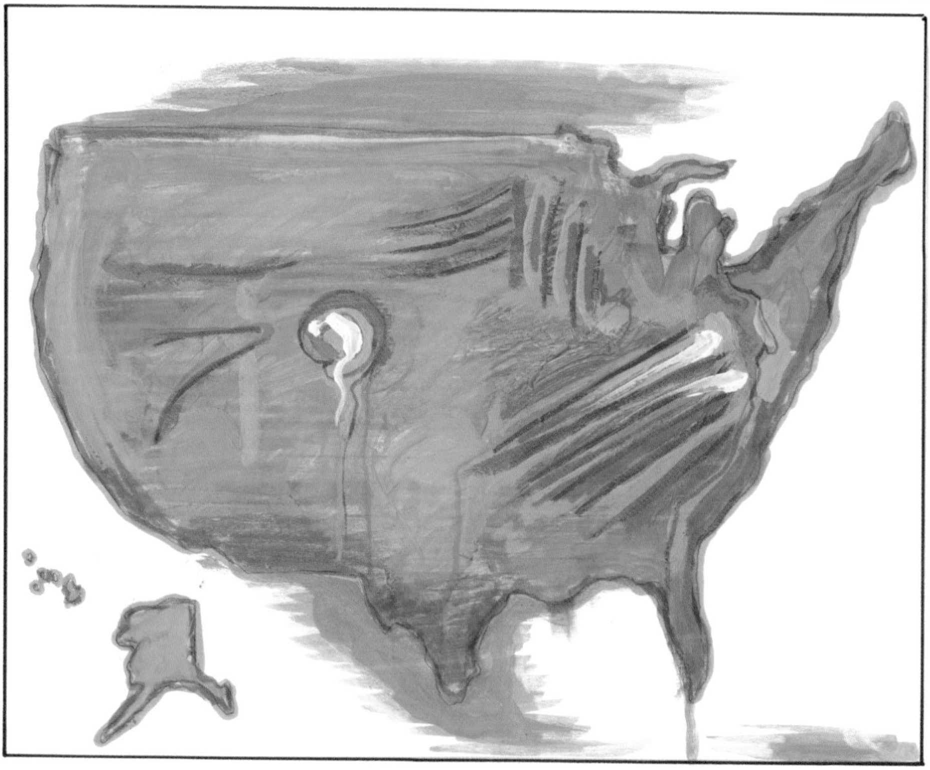

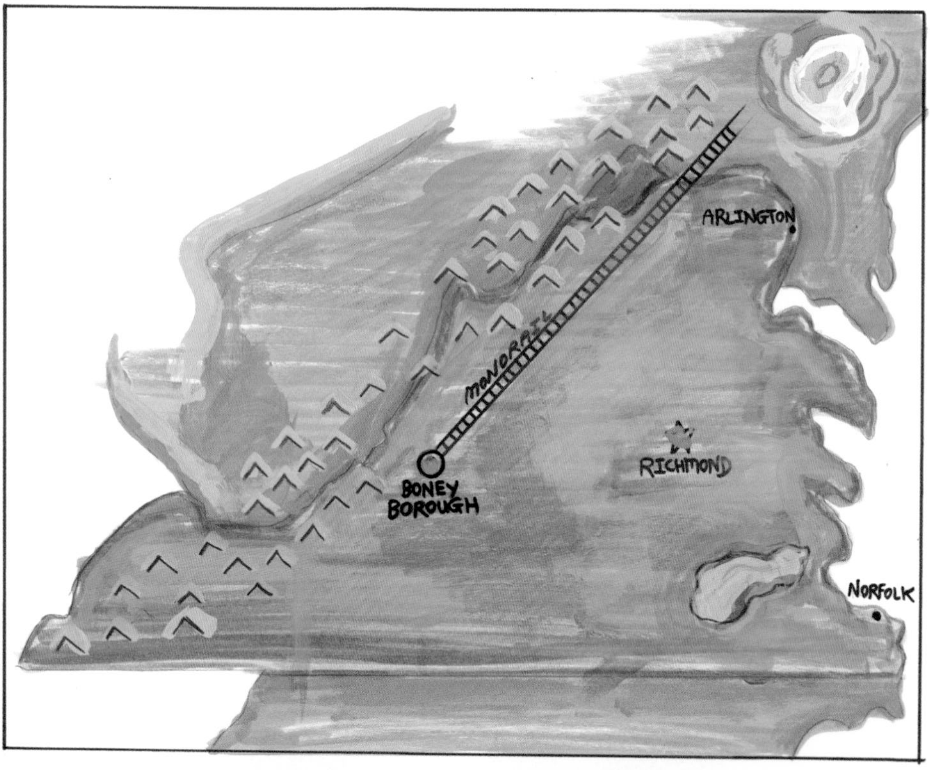
ARLINGTON
MONORAIL
BONEY BOROUGH
RICHMOND
NORFOLK

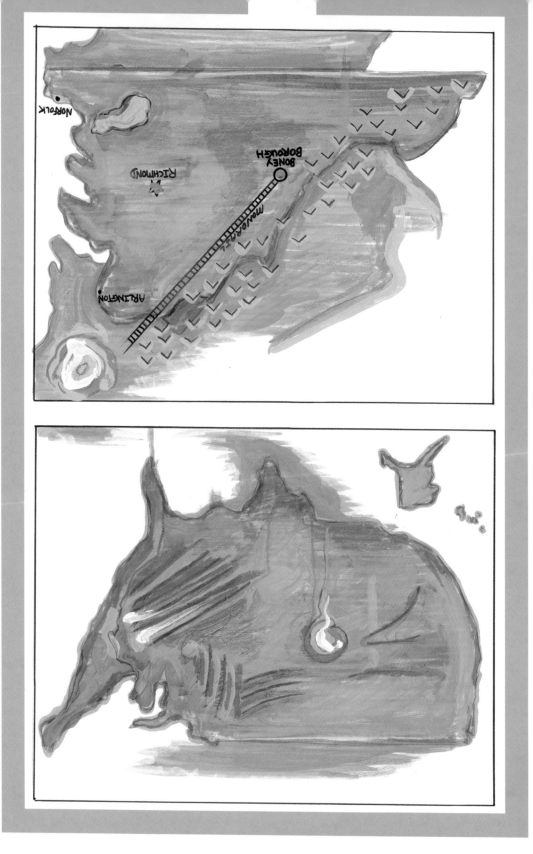

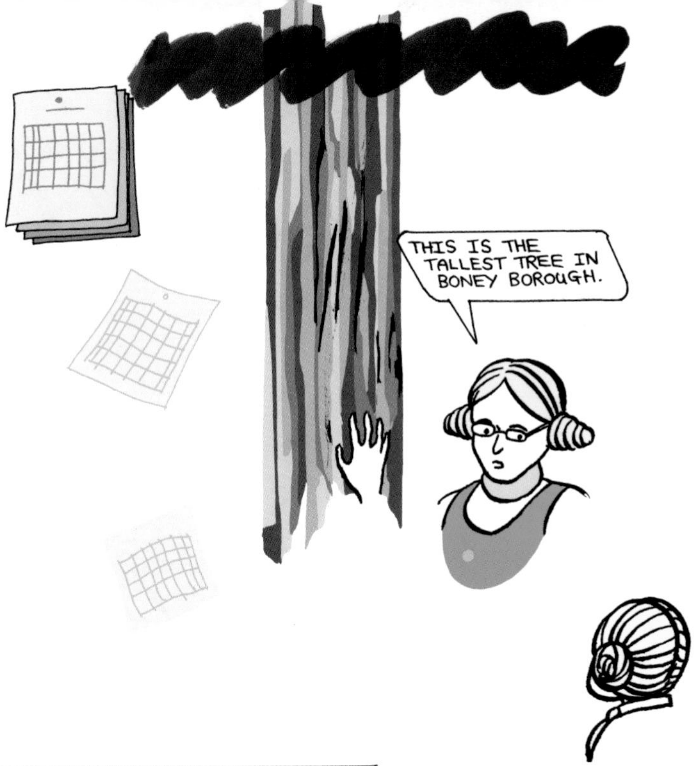
THIS IS THE TALLEST TREE IN BONEY BOROUGH.

CHAPTER TWELVE

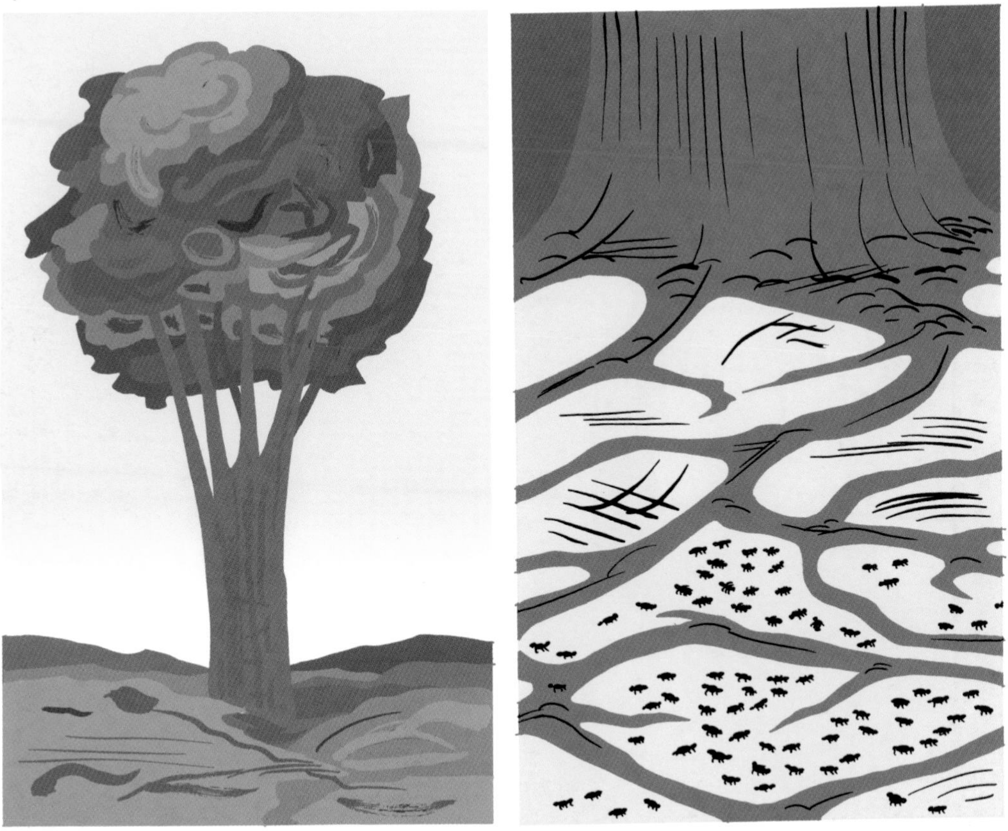

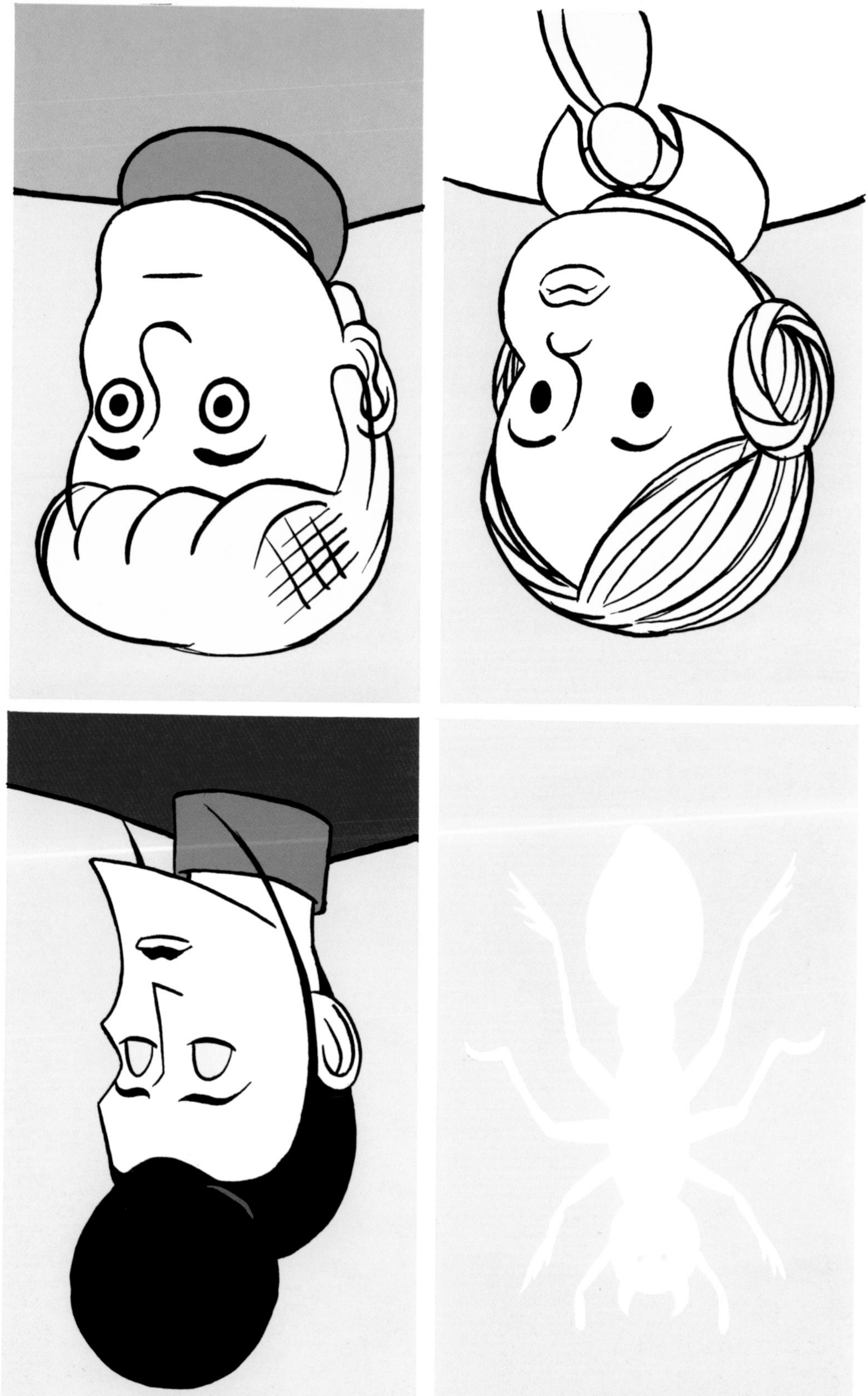

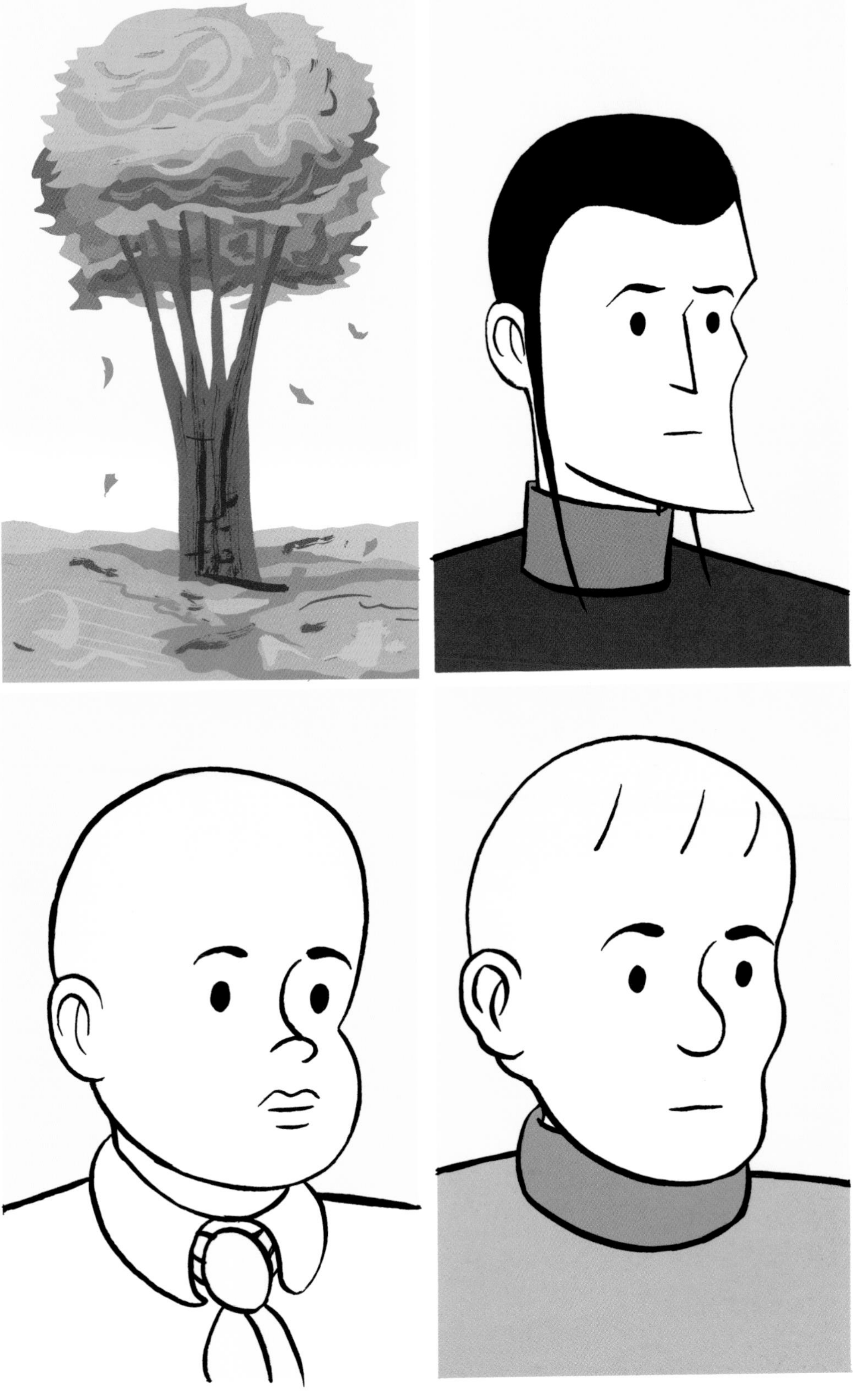

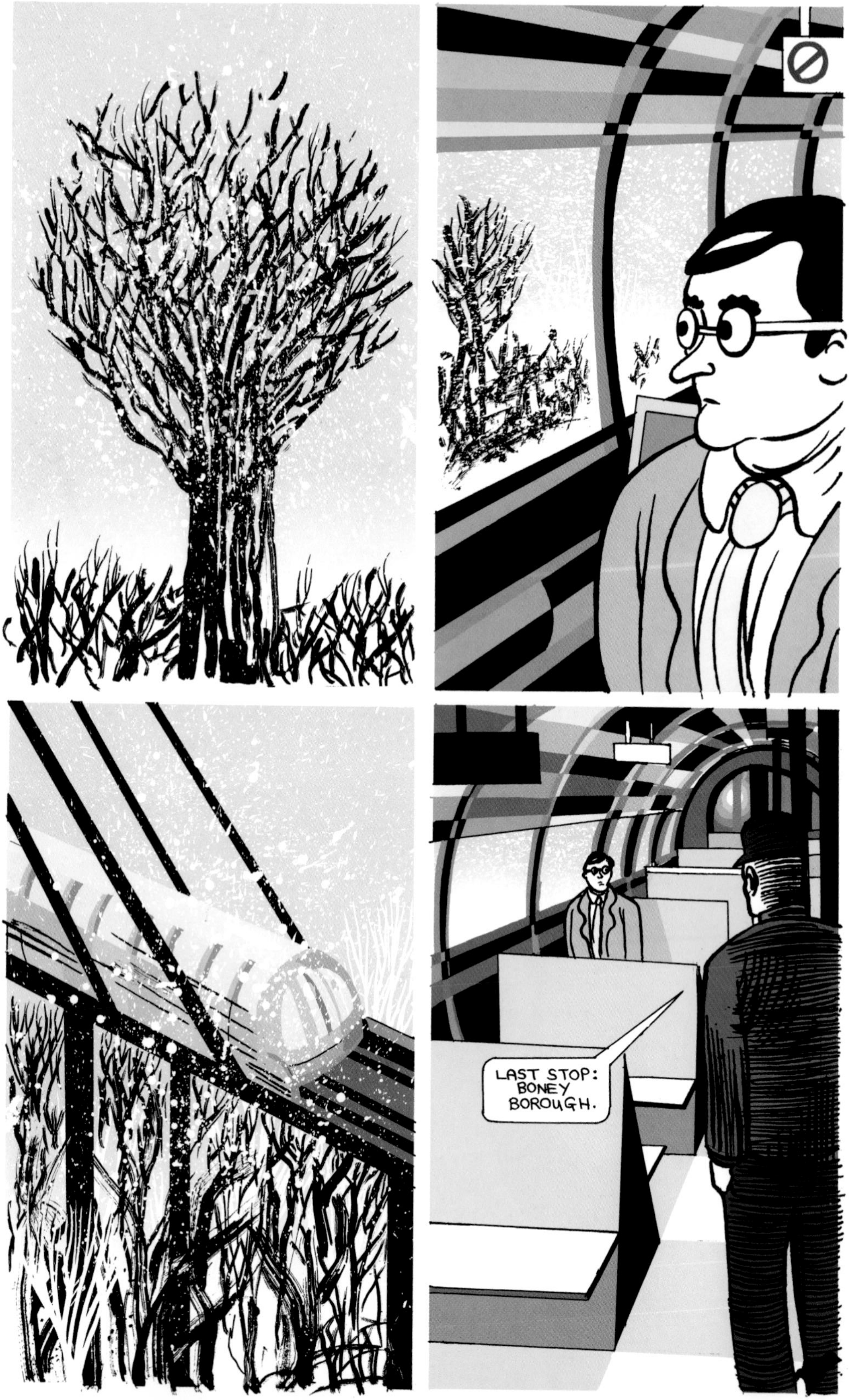
LAST STOP: BONEY BOROUGH.

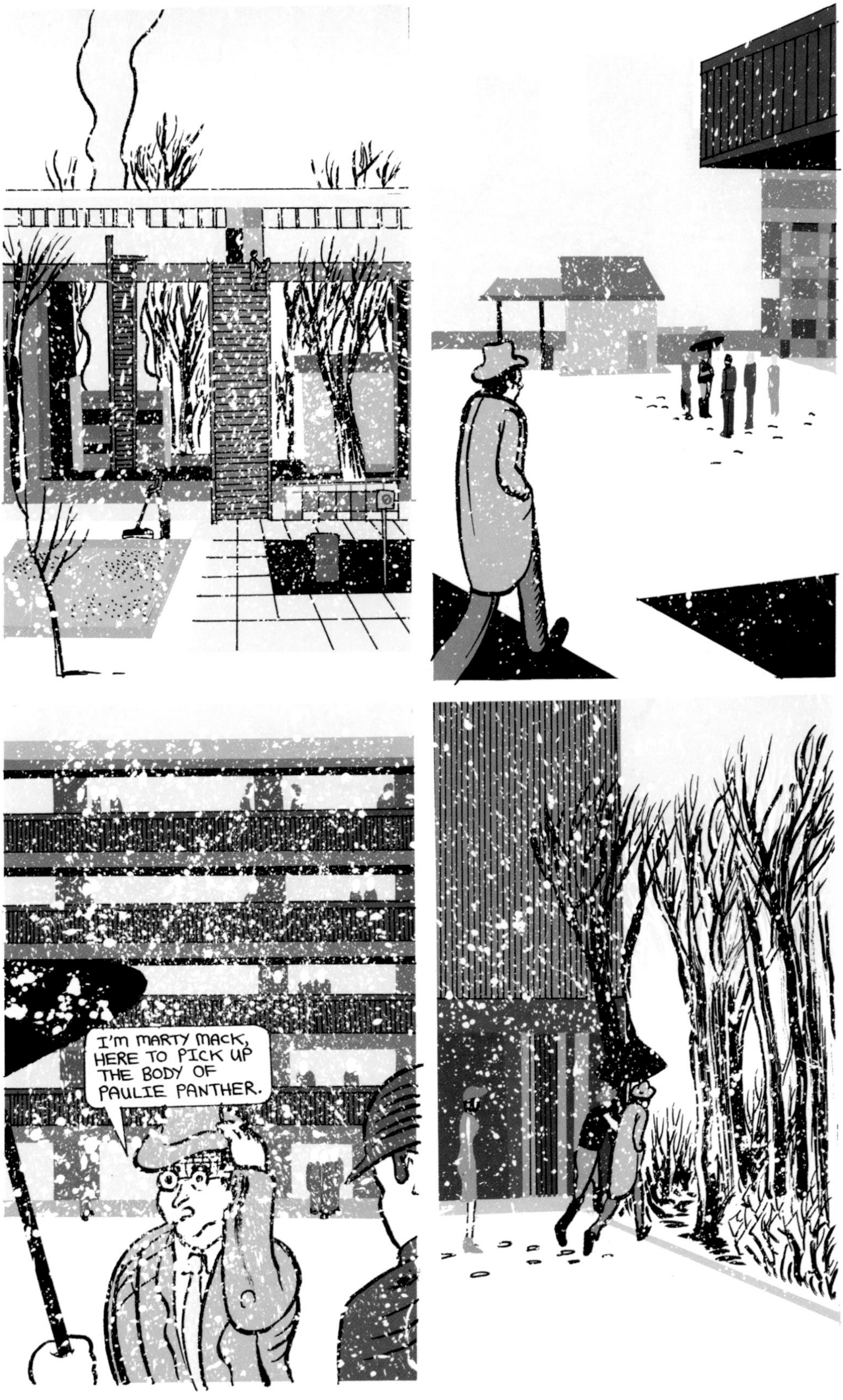
I'M MARTY MACK, HERE TO PICK UP THE BODY OF PAULIE PANTHER.

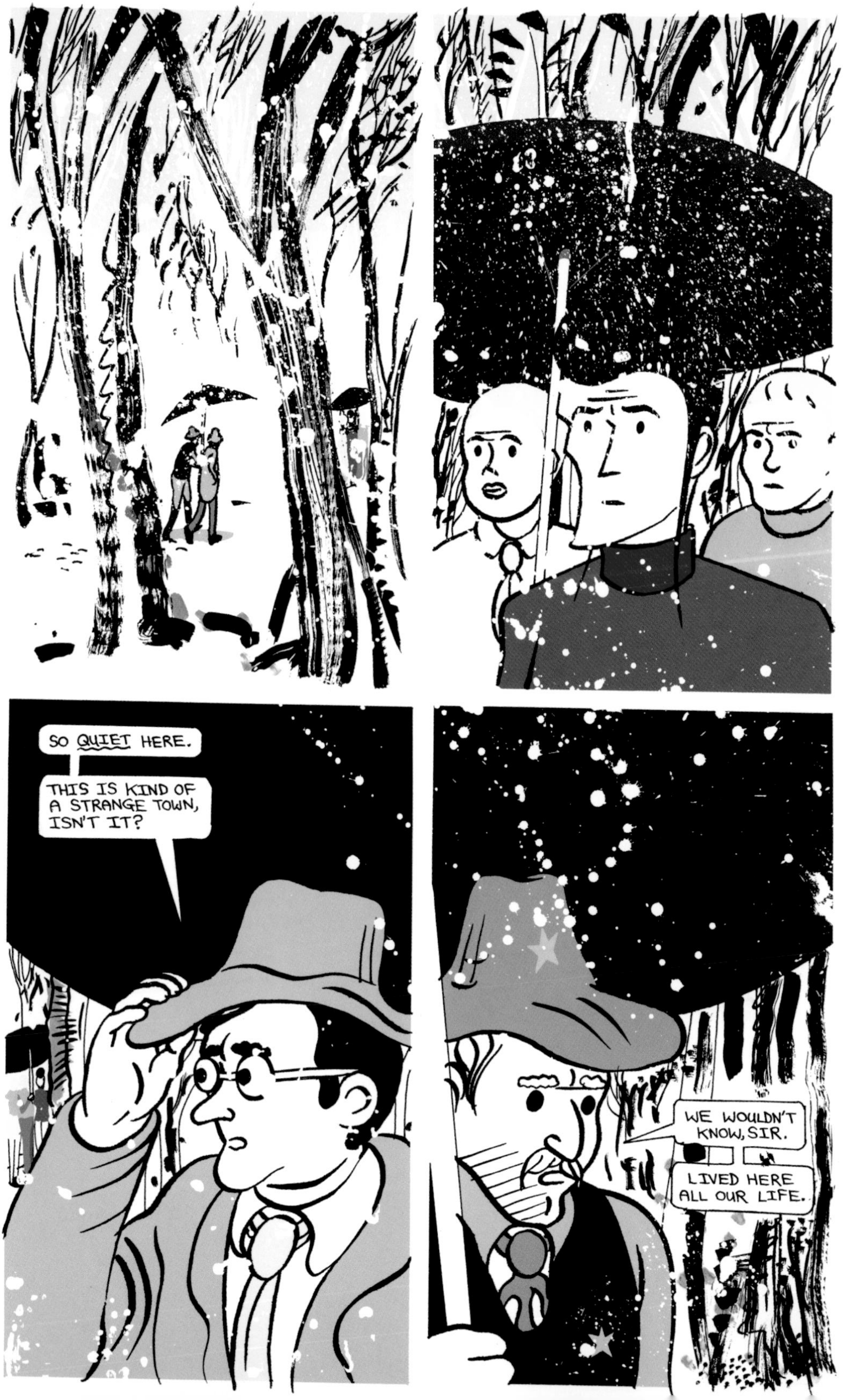
SO QUIET HERE.
THIS IS KIND OF A STRANGE TOWN, ISN'T IT?
WE WOULDN'T KNOW, SIR.
LIVED HERE ALL OUR LIFE.

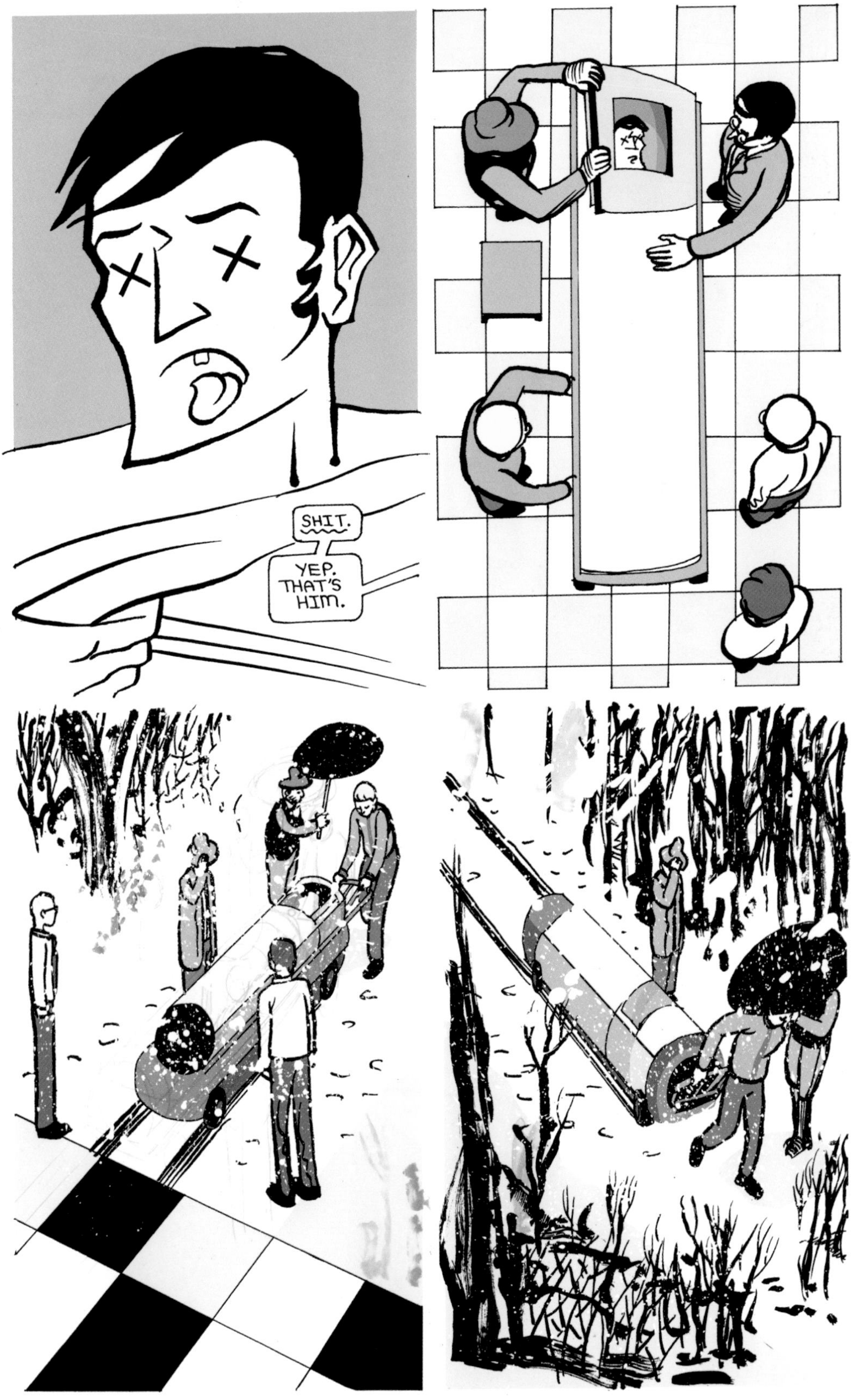
SHIT.
YEP. THAT'S HIM.

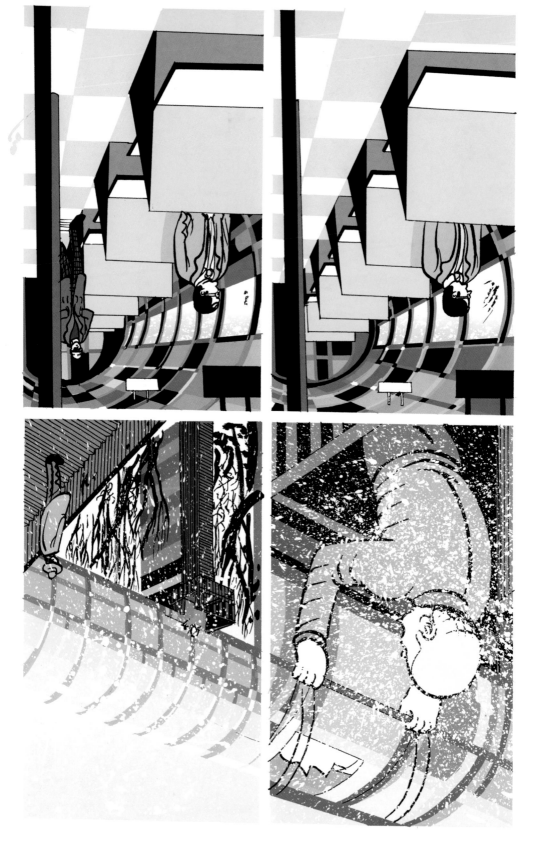

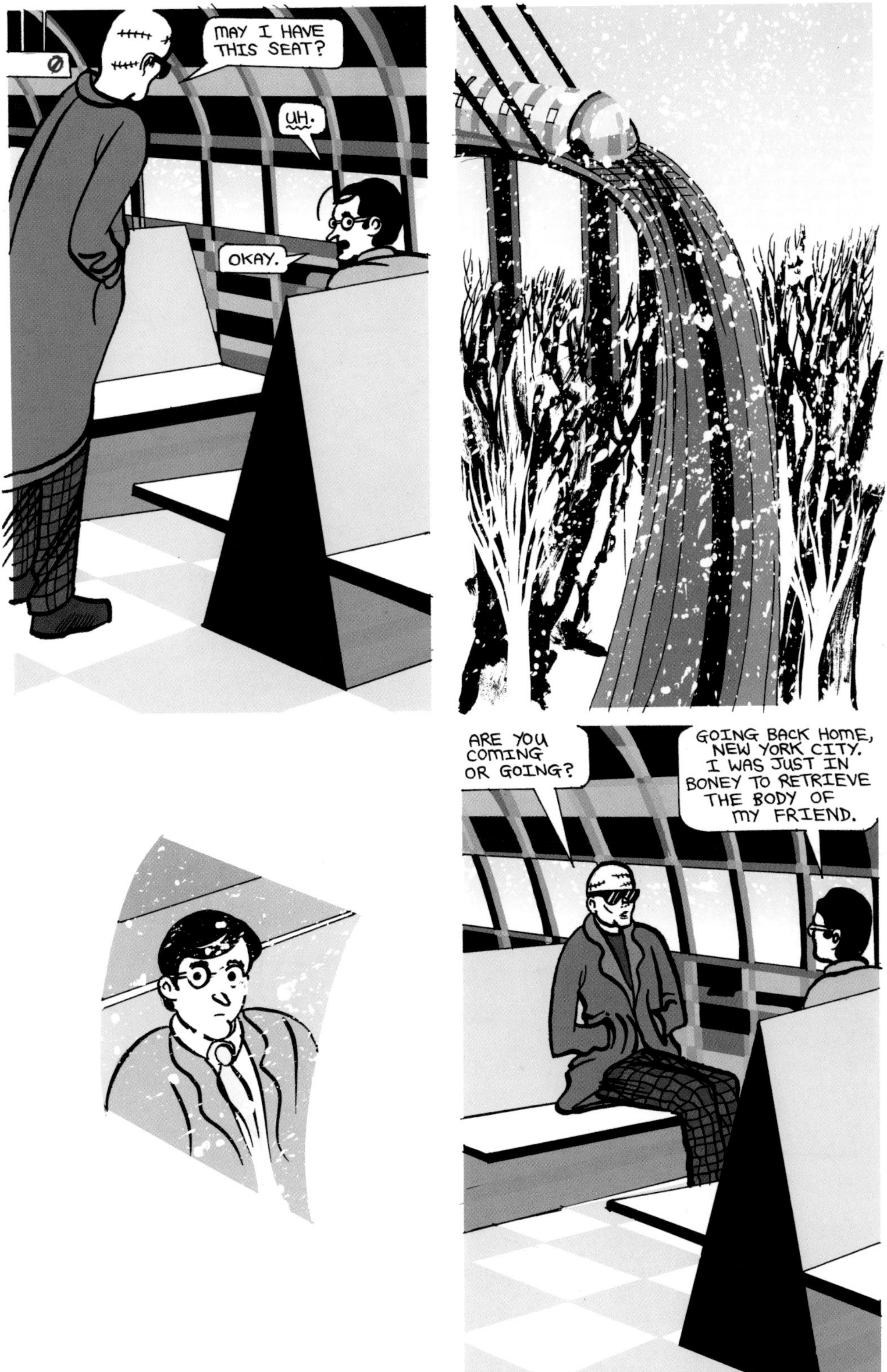
MAY I HAVE THIS SEAT?
UH.
OKAY.
ARE YOU COMING OR GOING?
GOING BACK HOME, NEW YORK CITY. I WAS JUST IN BONEY TO RETRIEVE THE BODY OF MY FRIEND.

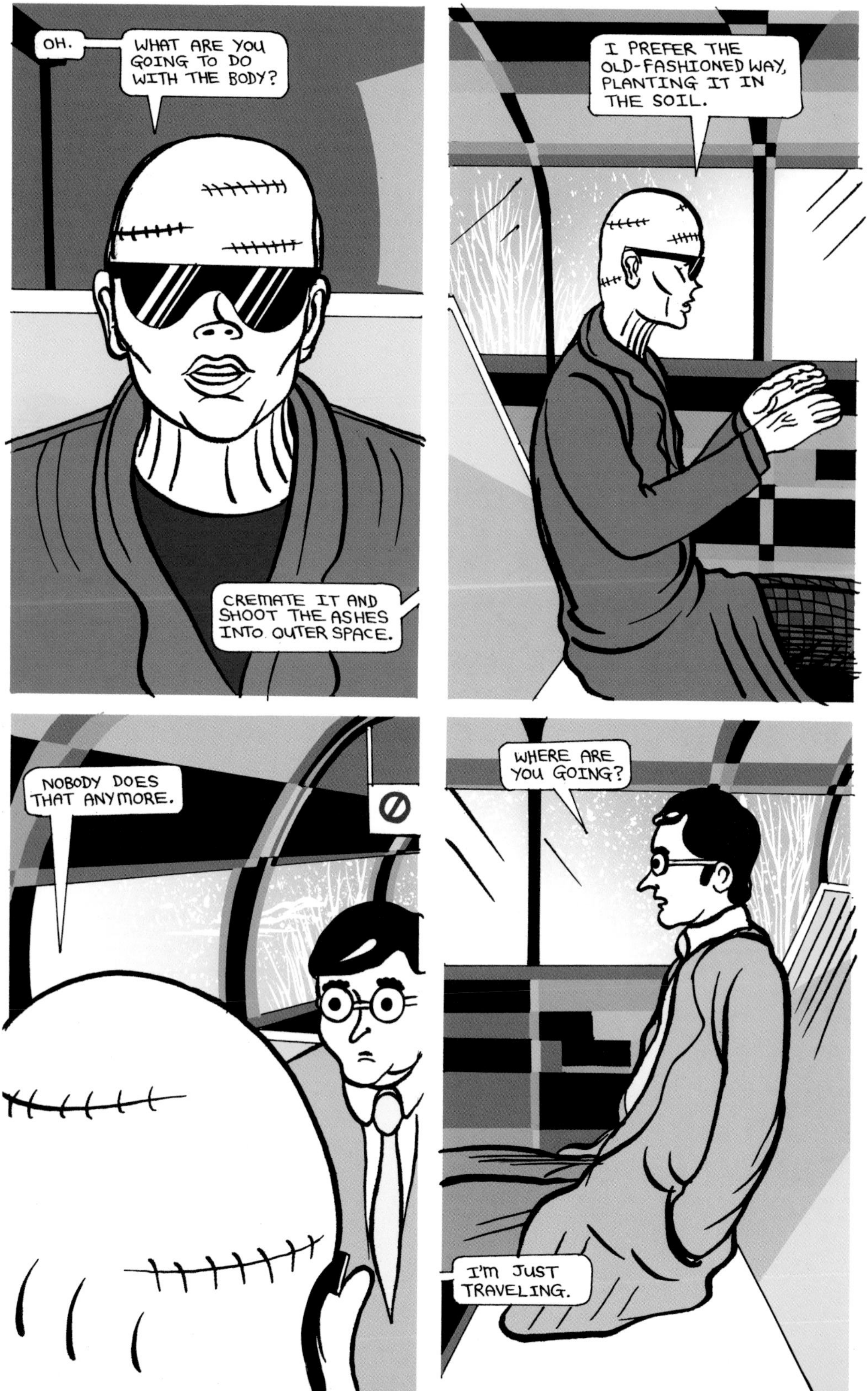
OH.
WHAT ARE YOU GOING TO DO WITH THE BODY?
CREMATE IT AND SHOOT THE ASHES INTO OUTER SPACE.
I PREFER THE OLD-FASHIONED WAY, PLANTING IT IN THE SOIL.
NOBODY DOES THAT ANYMORE.
WHERE ARE YOU GOING?
I'M JUST TRAVELING.

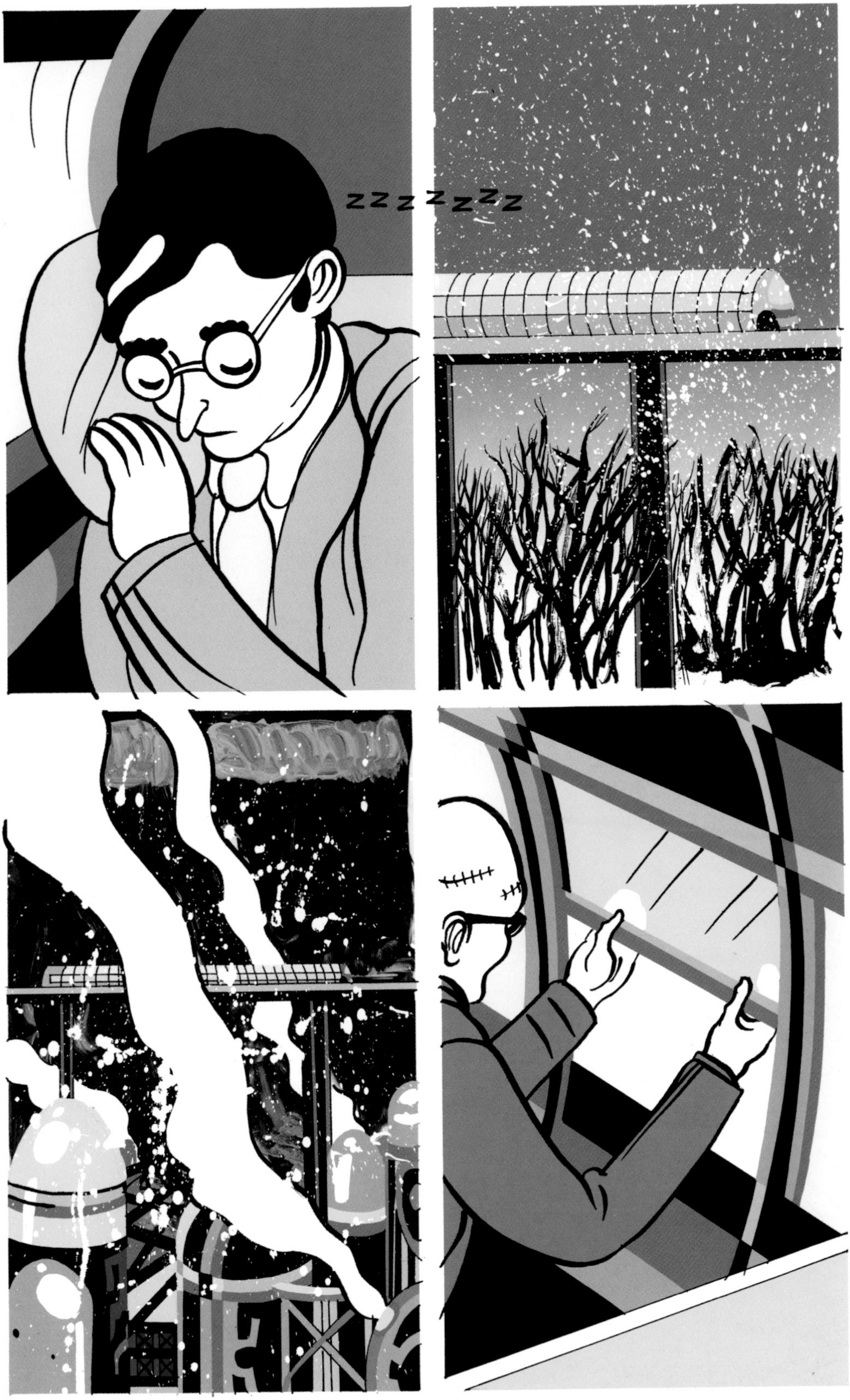
ZZZZZZZZ

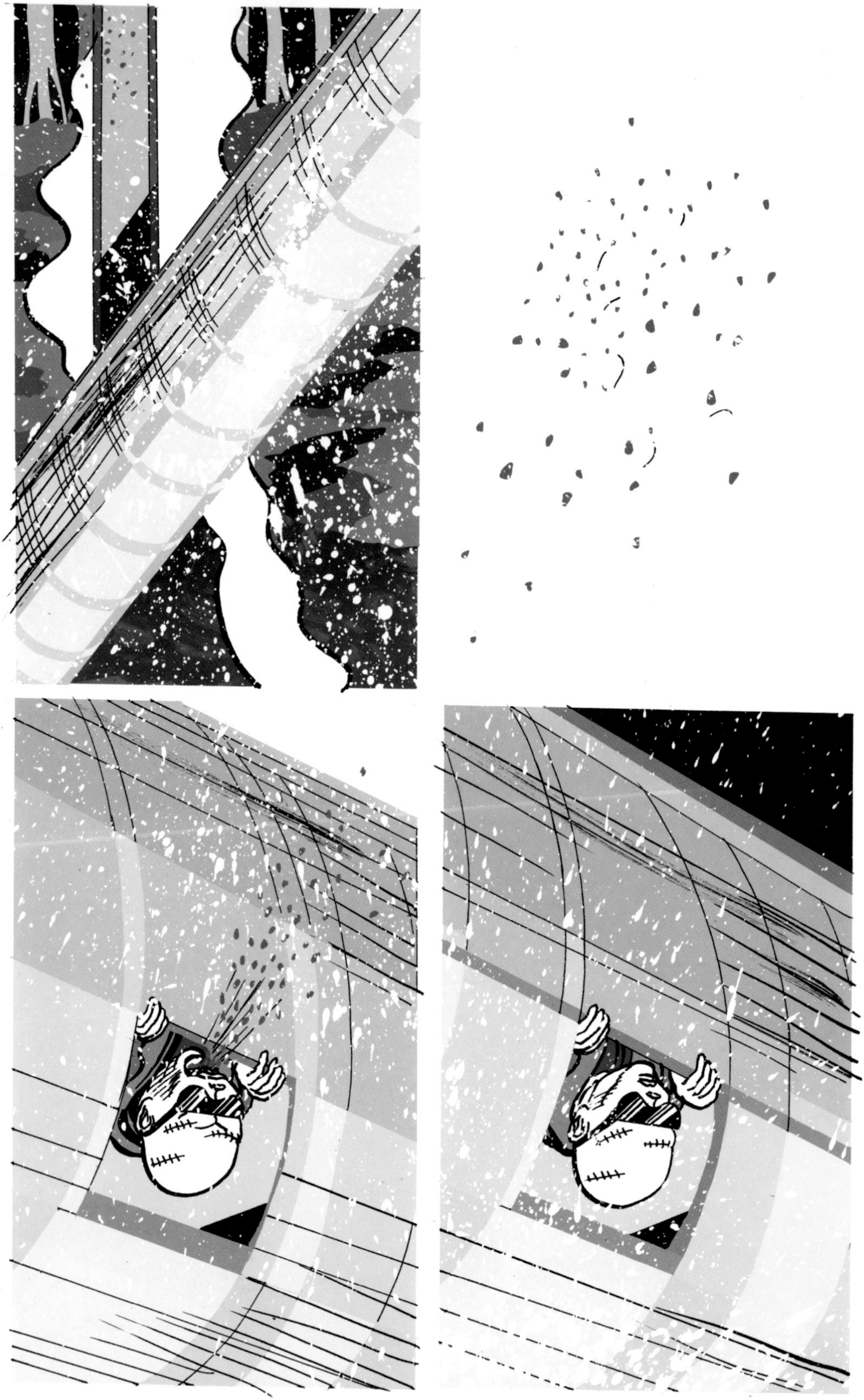

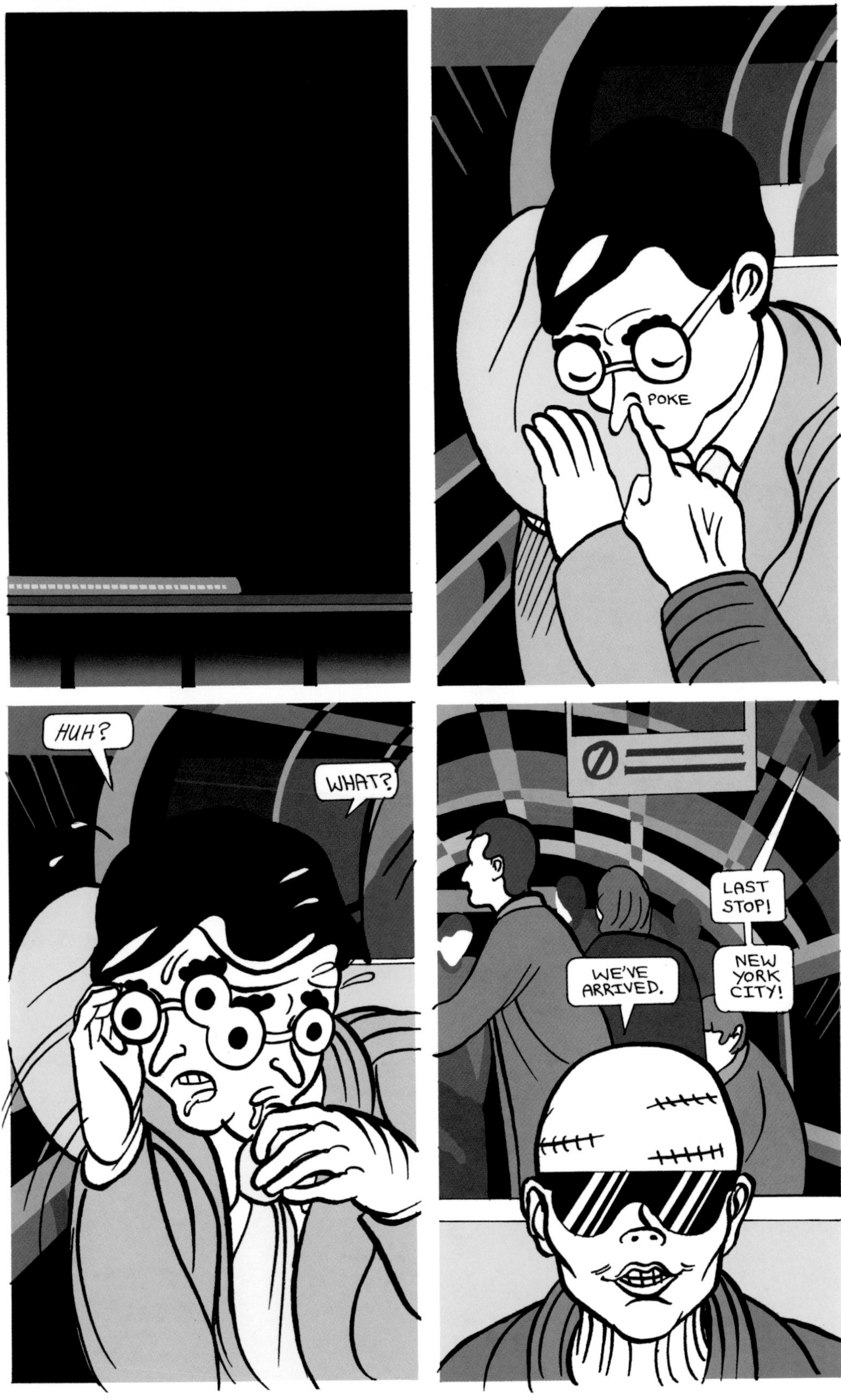
POKE
HUH?
WHAT?
LAST STOP!
NEW YORK CITY!
WE'VE ARRIVED.

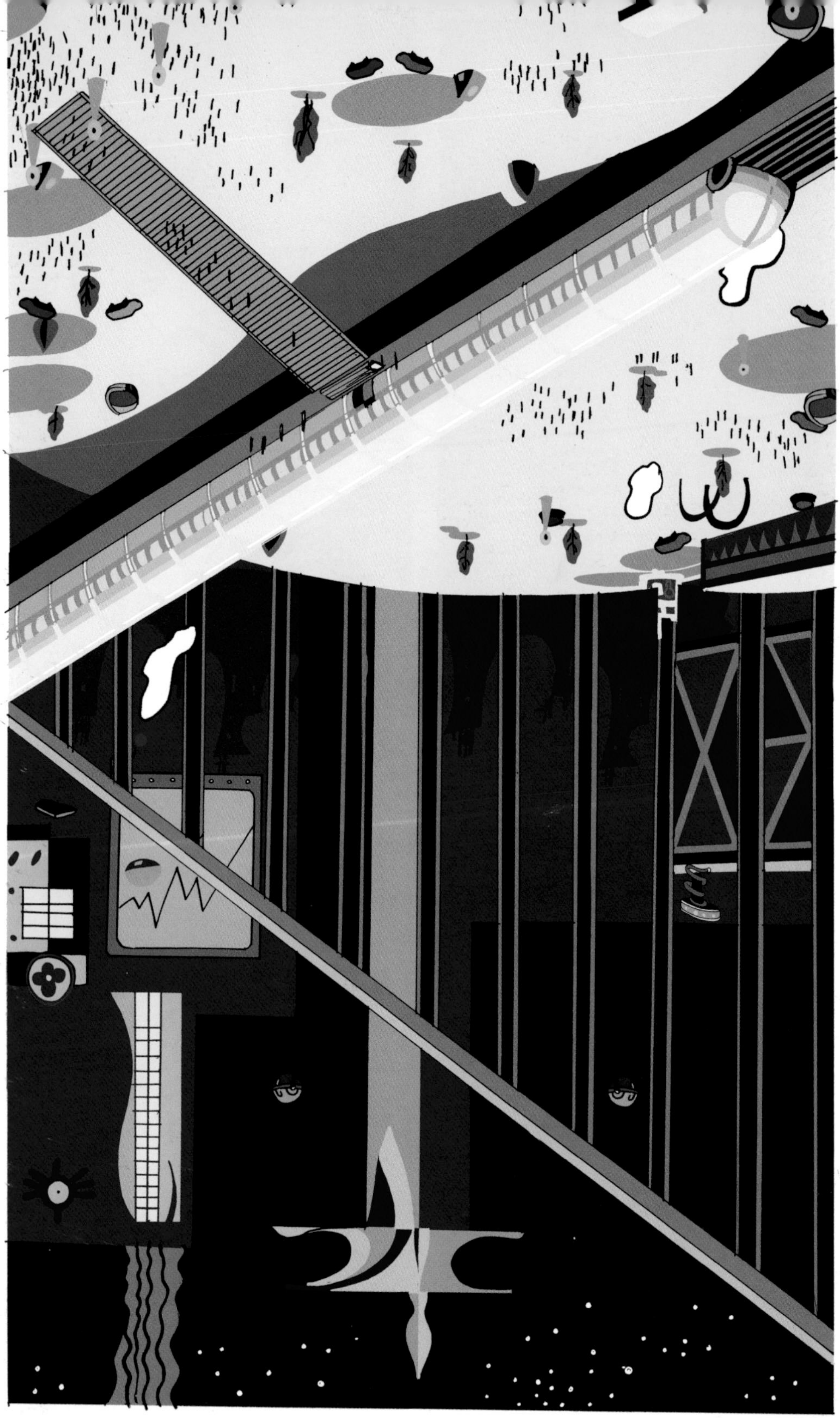

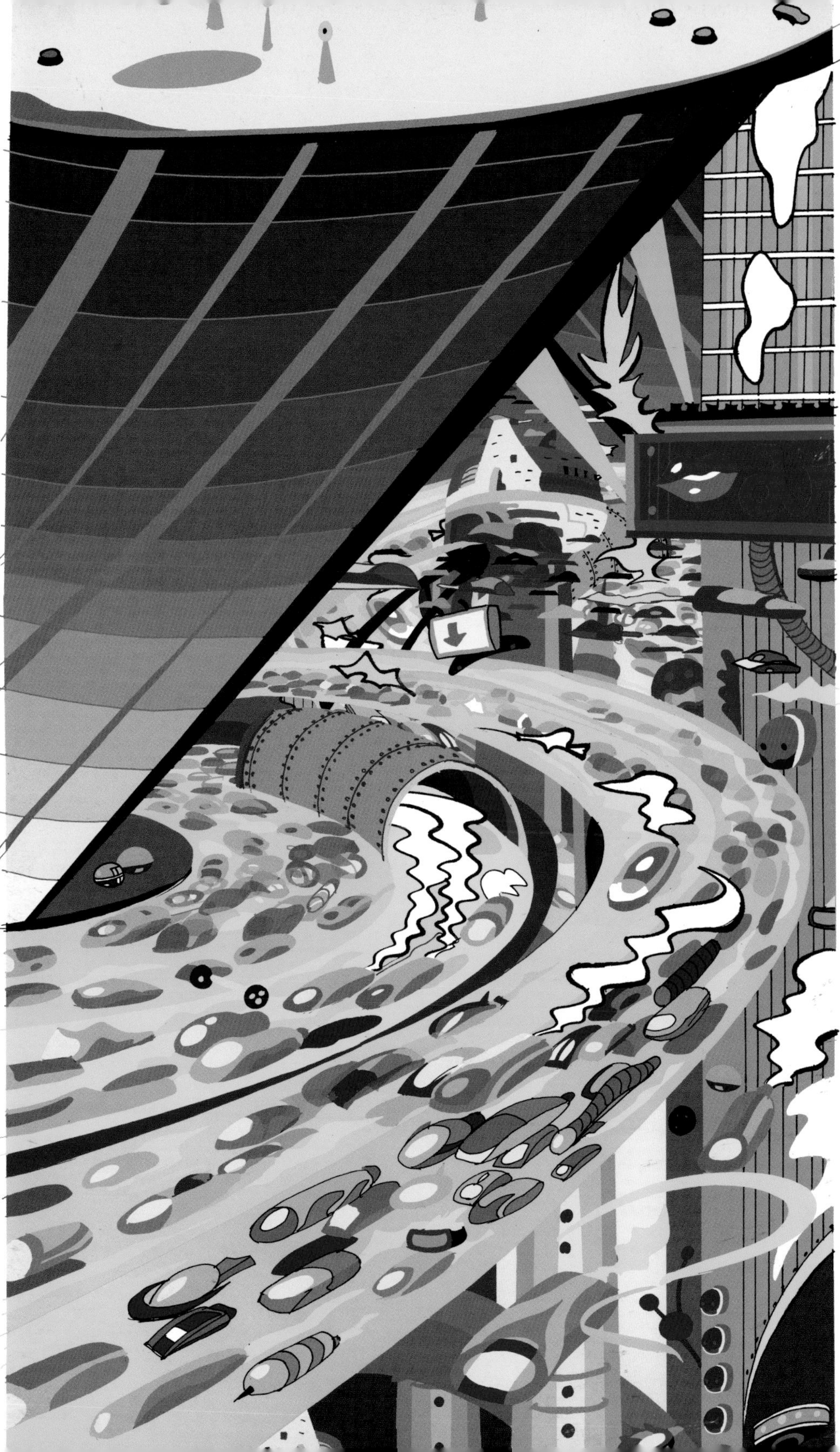

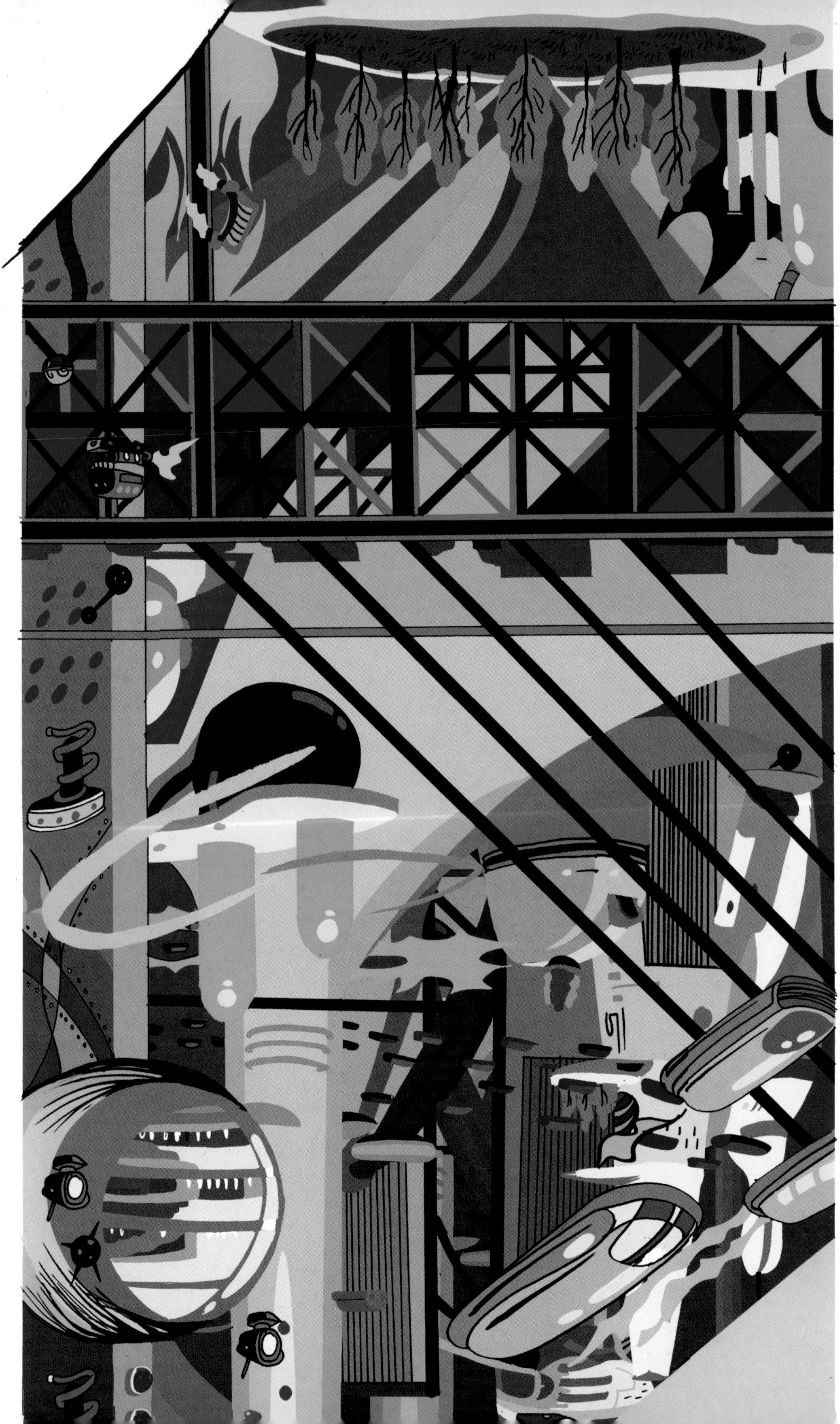

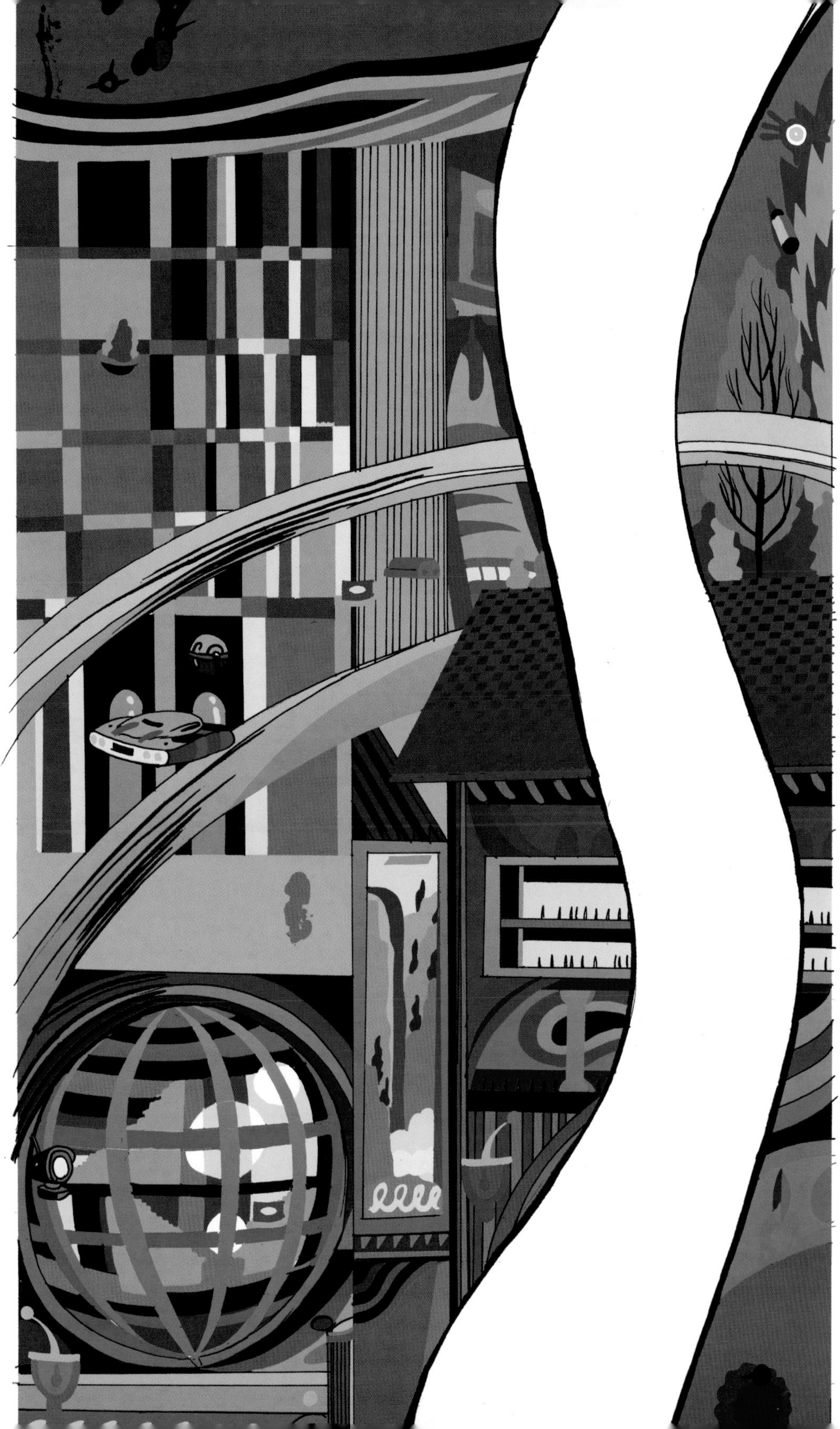

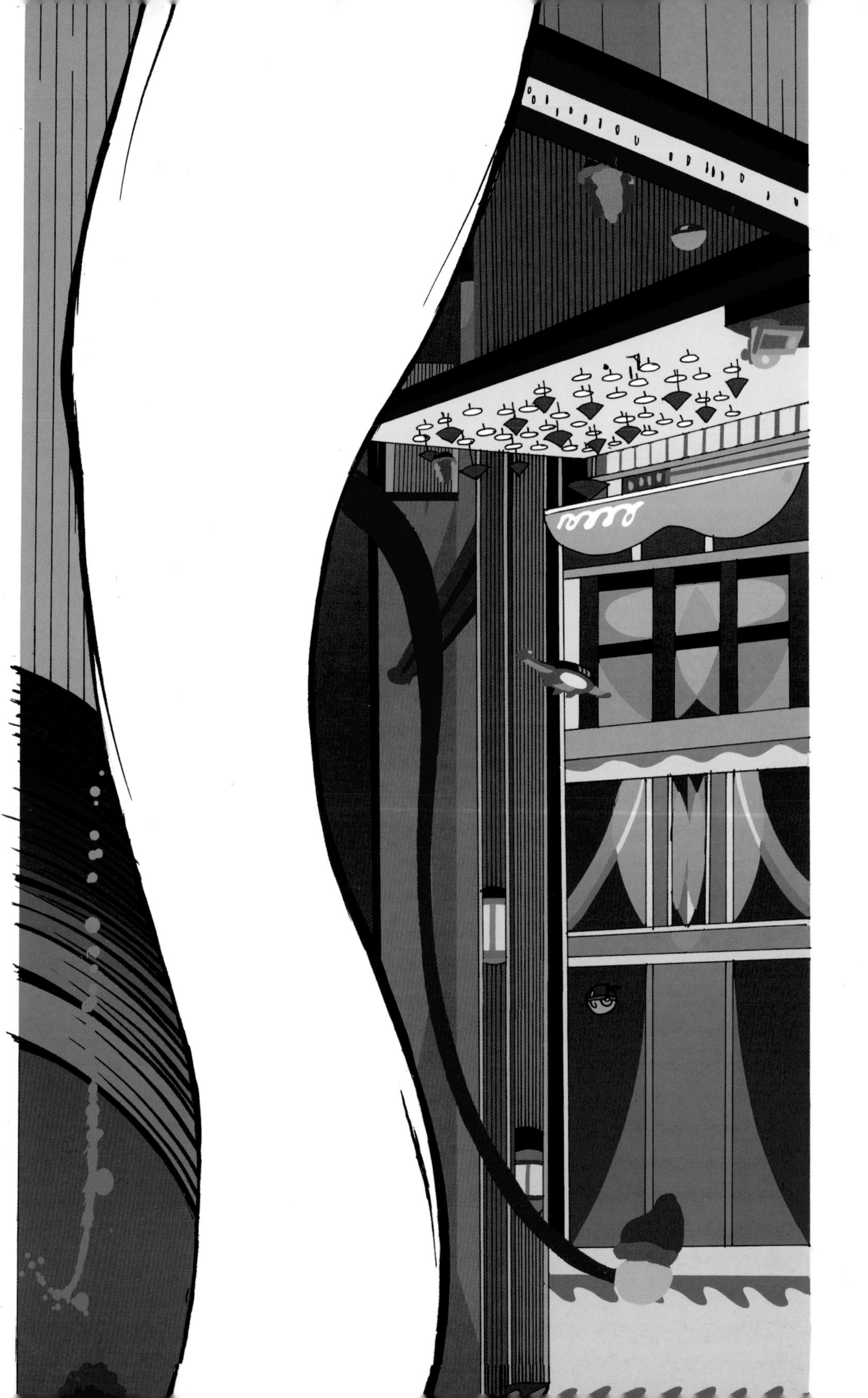

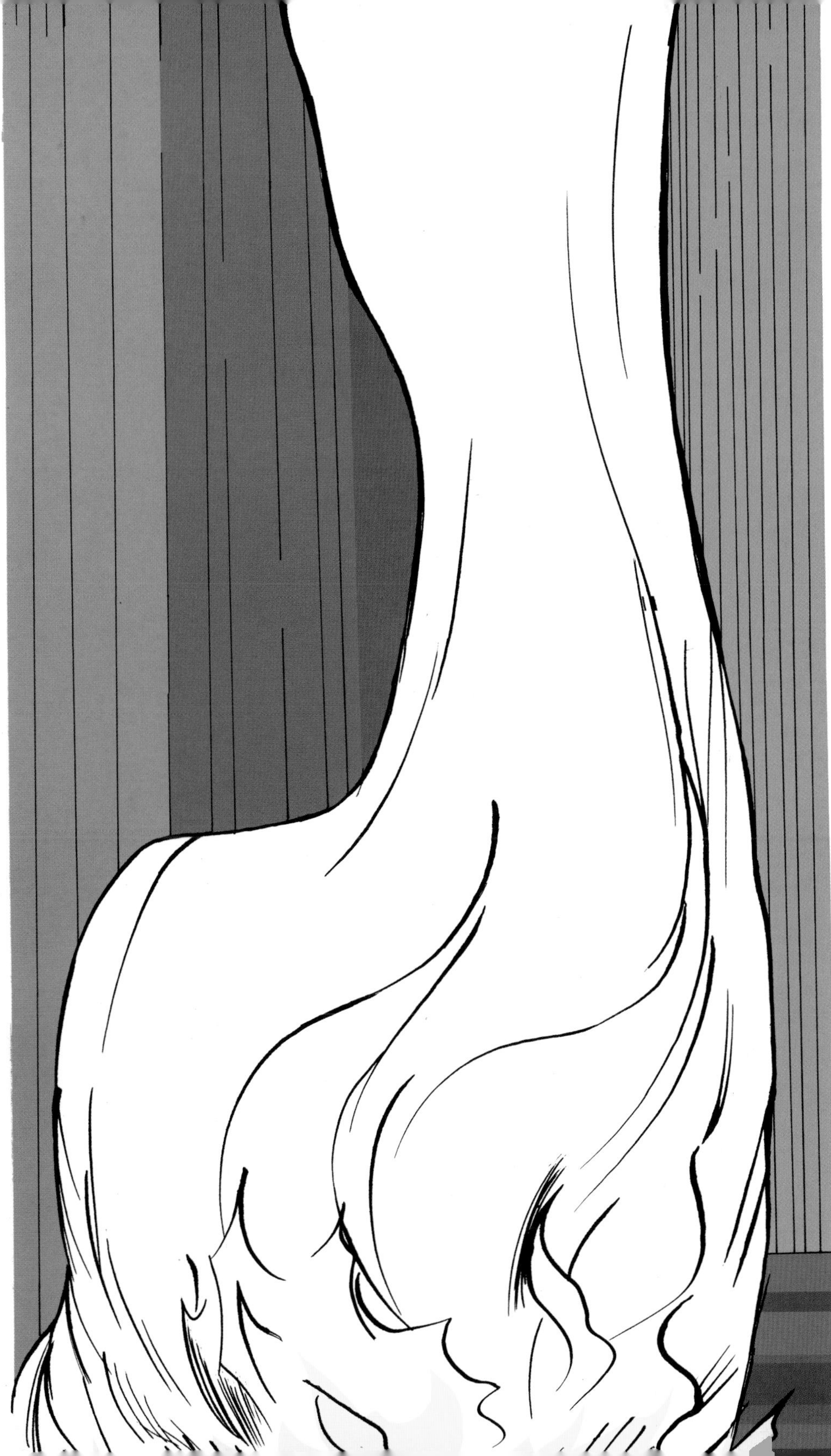

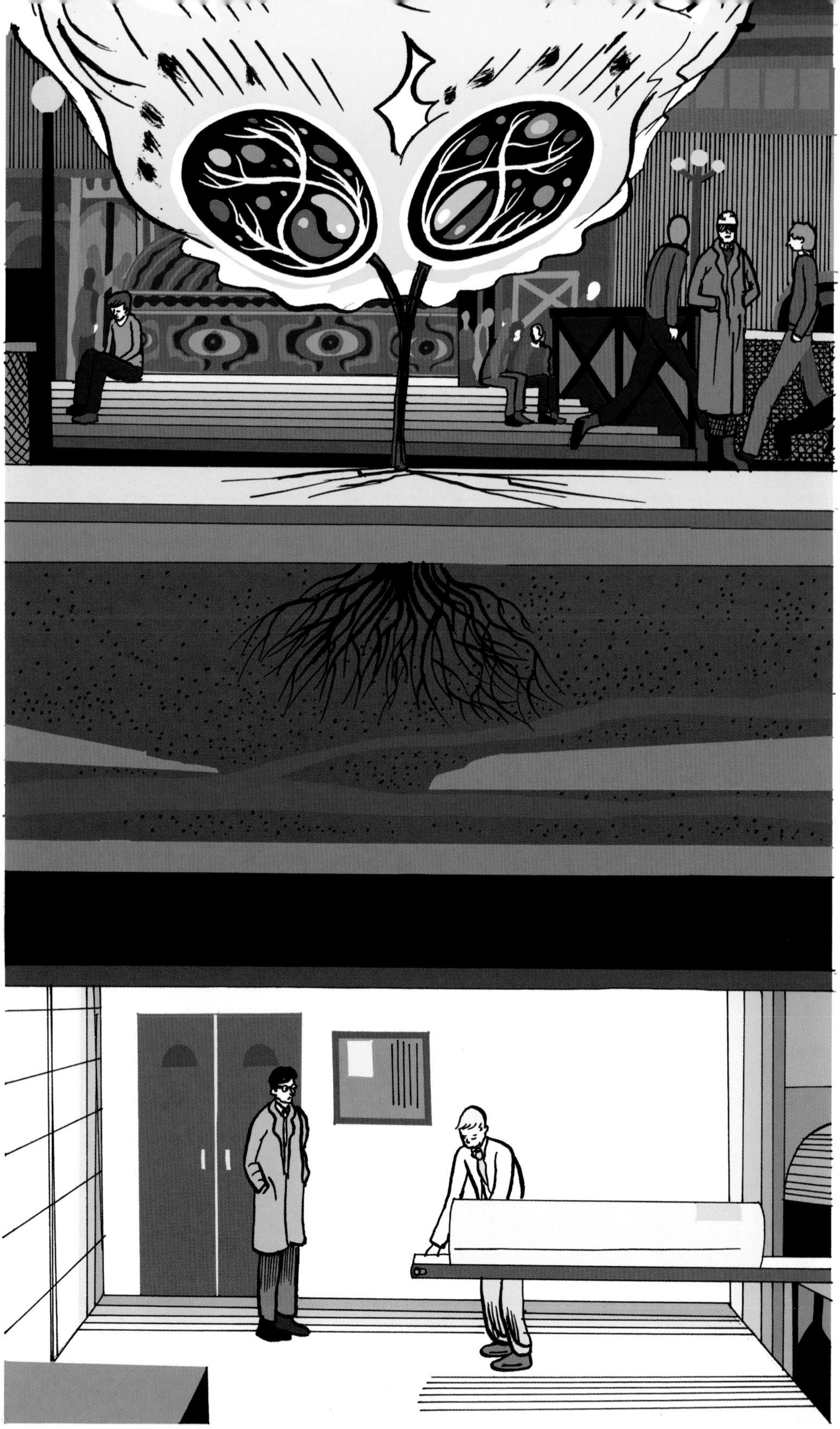

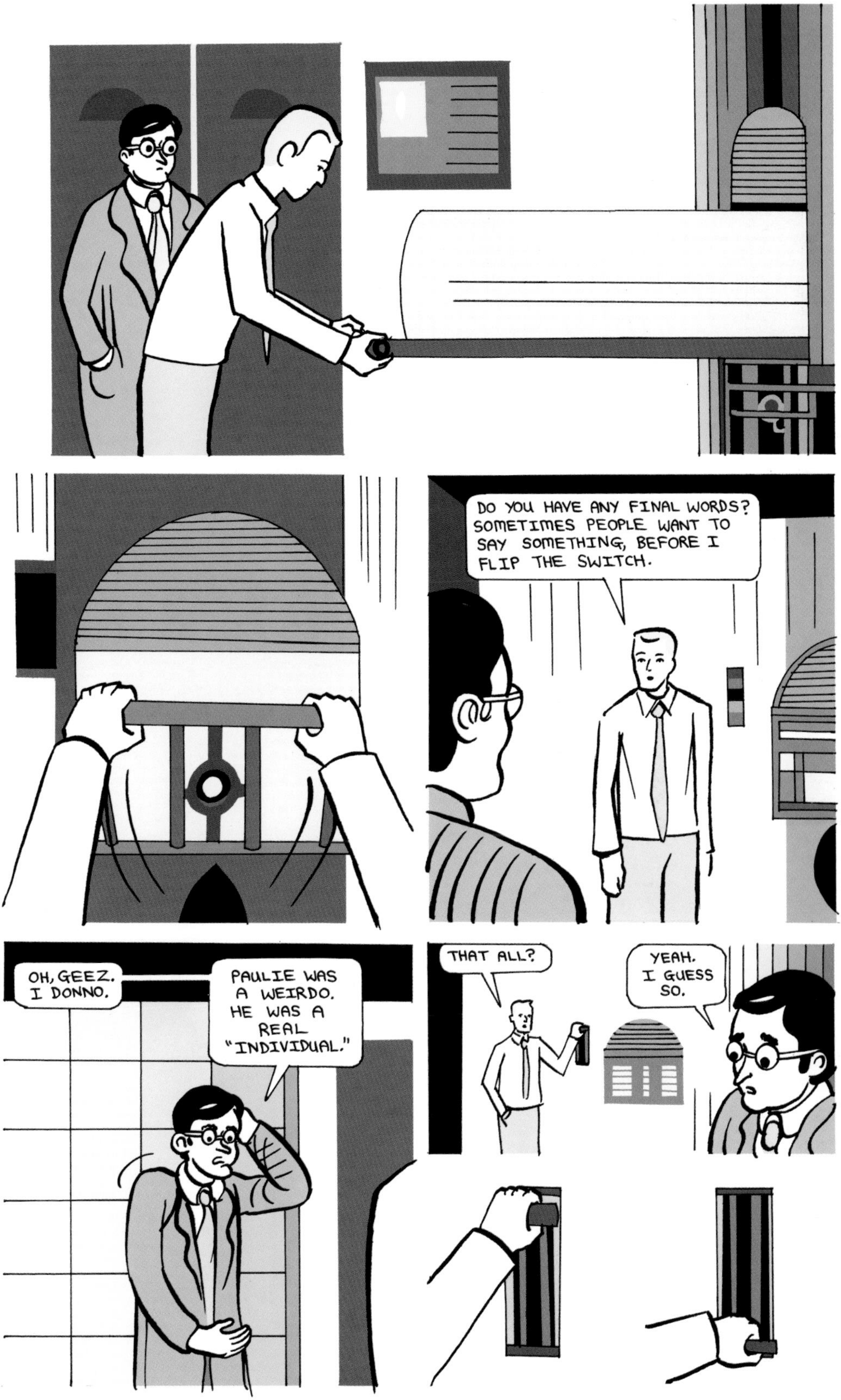
DO YOU HAVE ANY FINAL WORDS? SOMETIMES PEOPLE WANT TO SAY SOMETHING, BEFORE I FLIP THE SWITCH.
OH, GEEZ. I DONNO.
PAULIE WAS A WEIRDO. HE WAS A REAL "INDIVIDUAL."
THAT ALL?
YEAH. I GUESS SO.

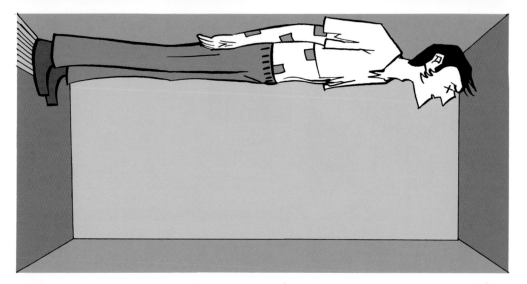

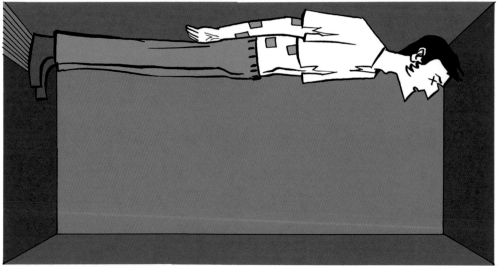

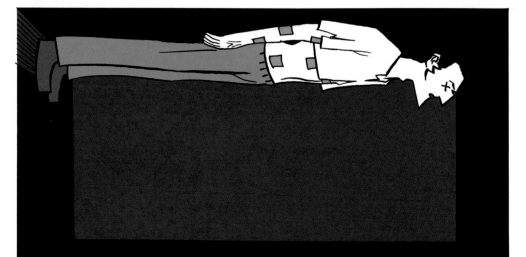

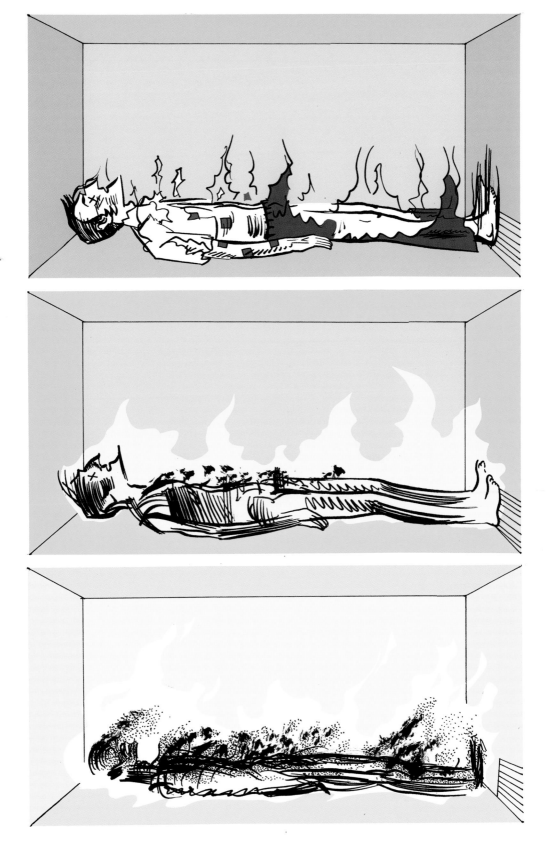

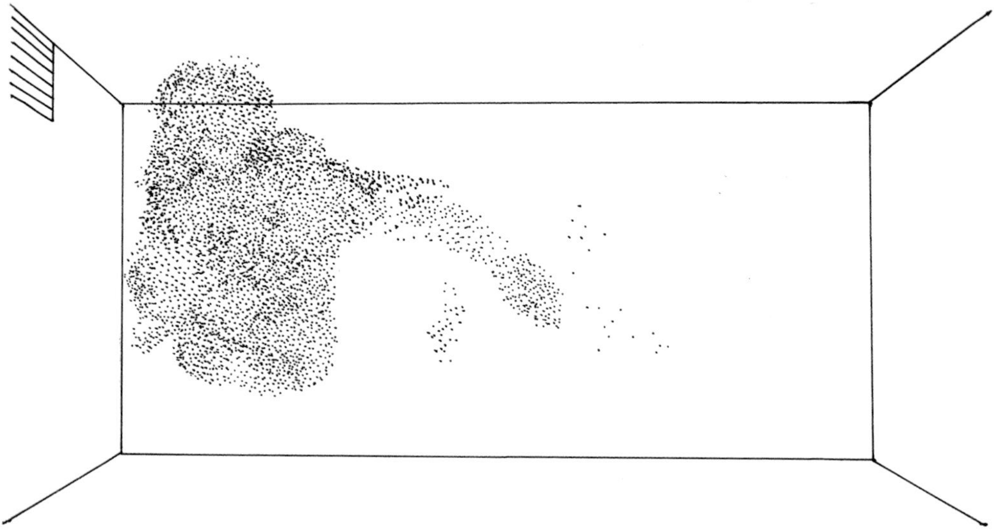

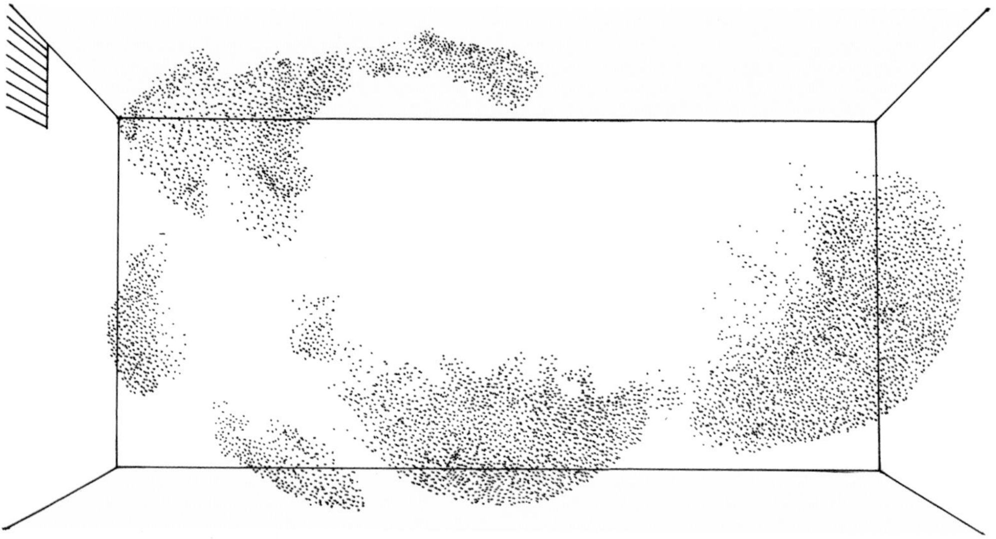

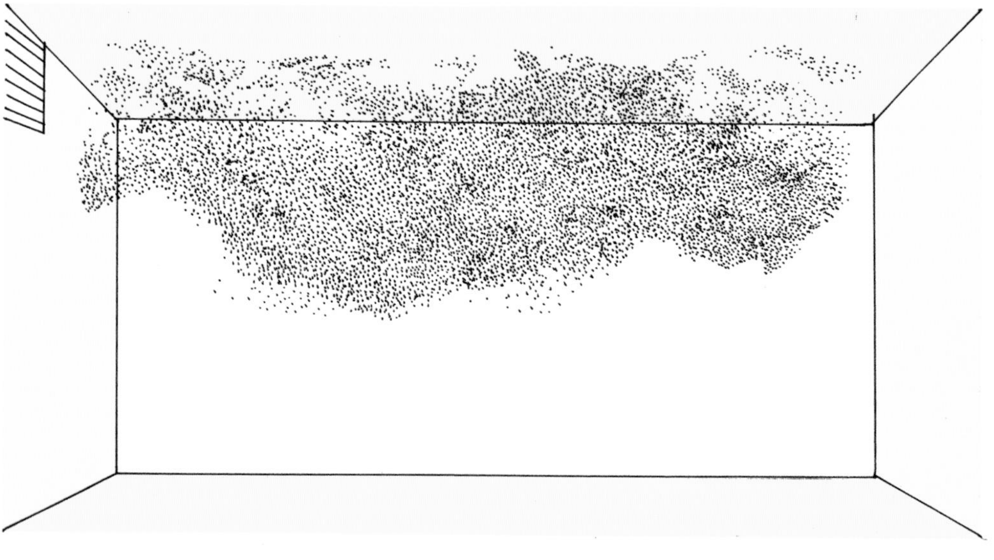

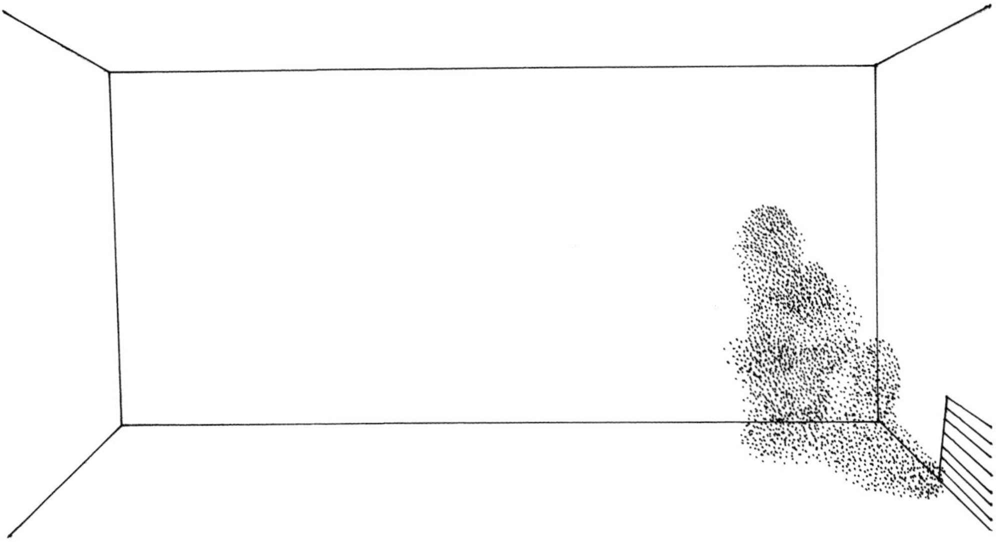

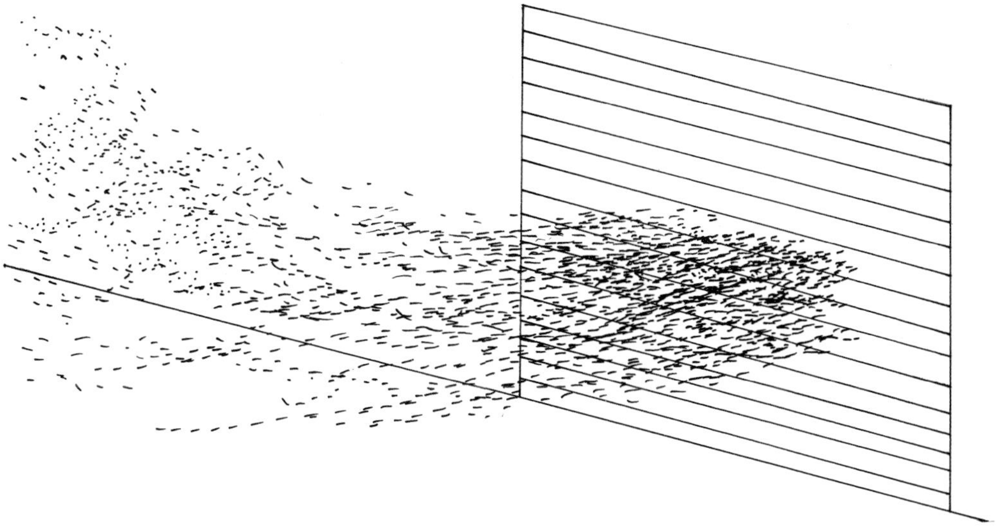

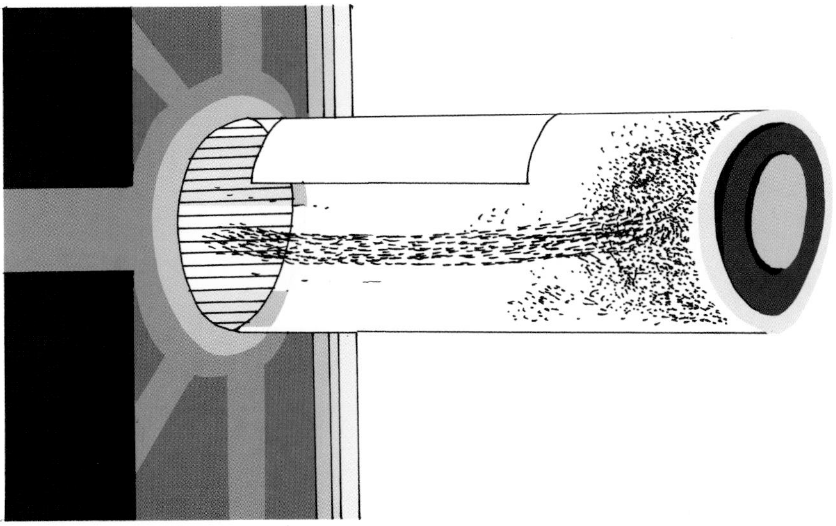

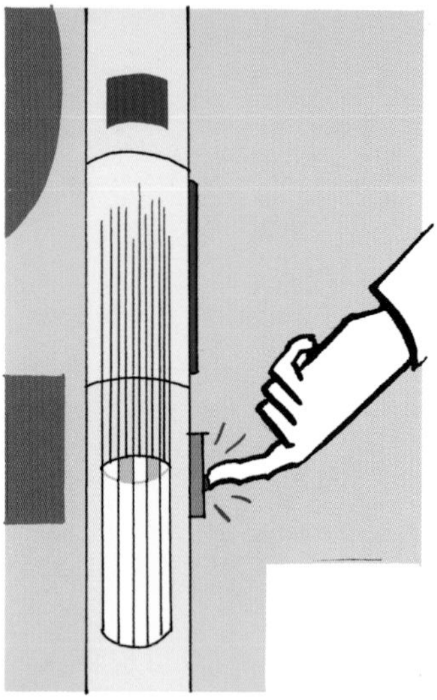

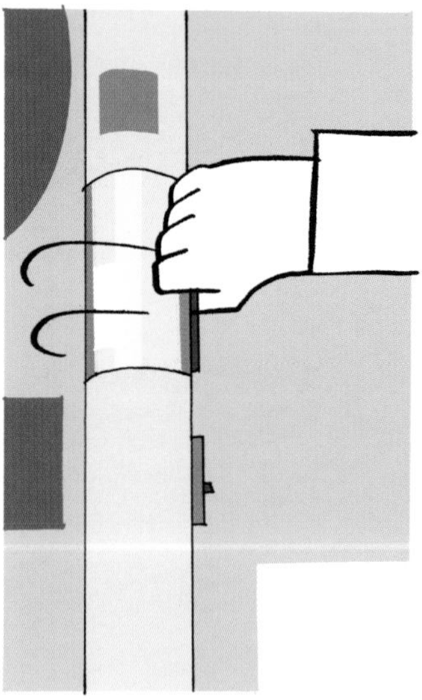

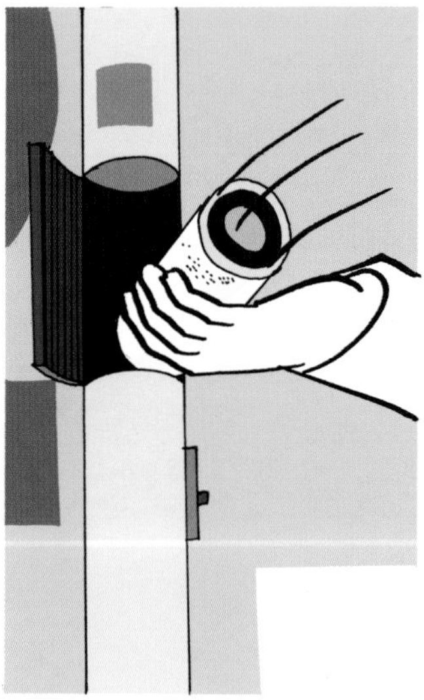

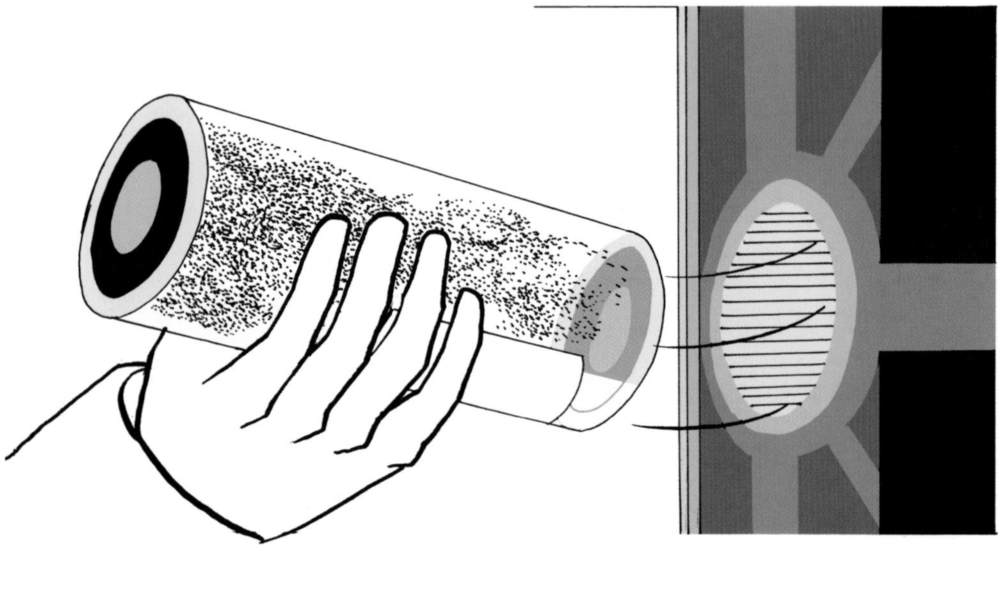

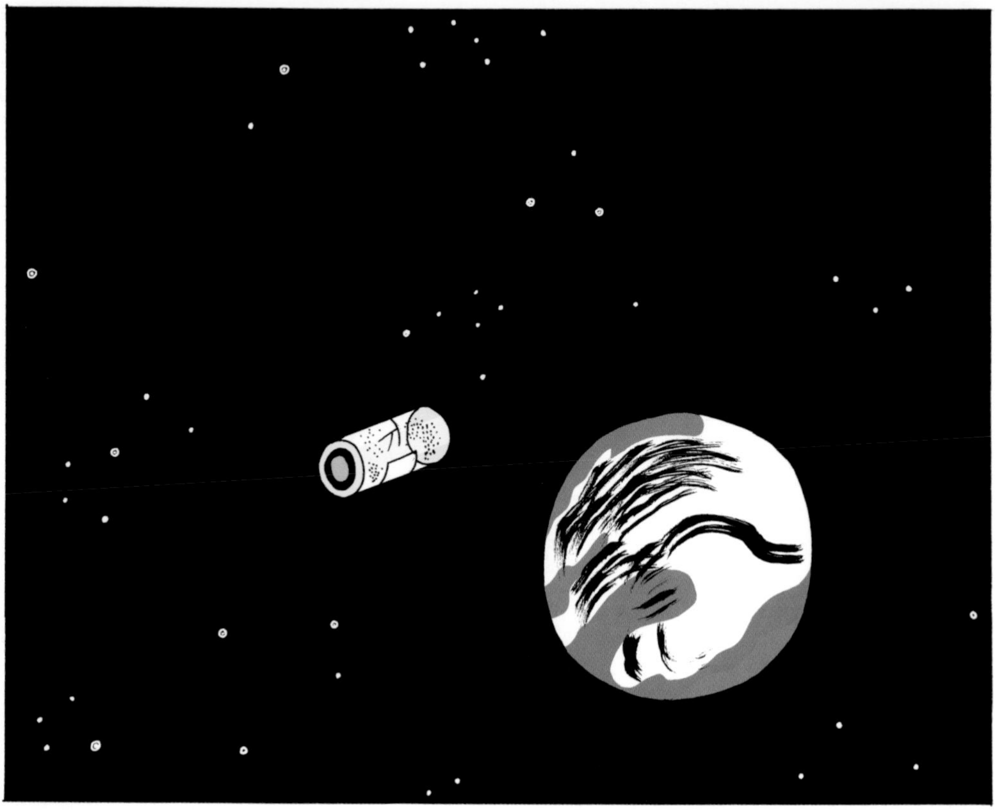
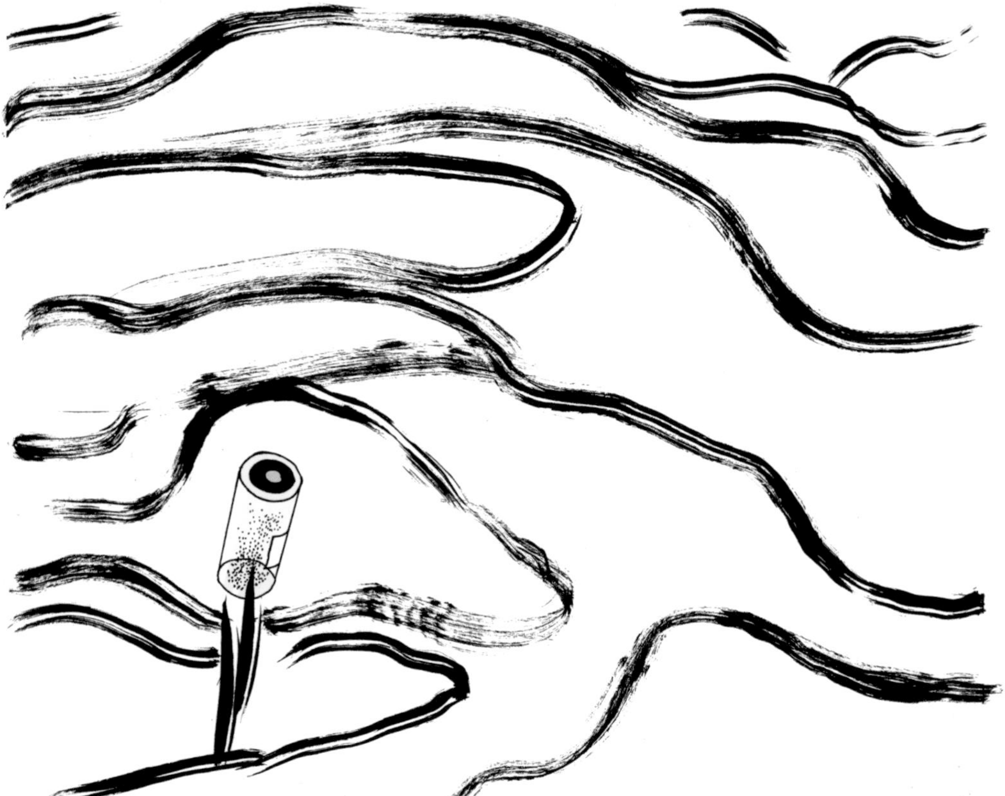

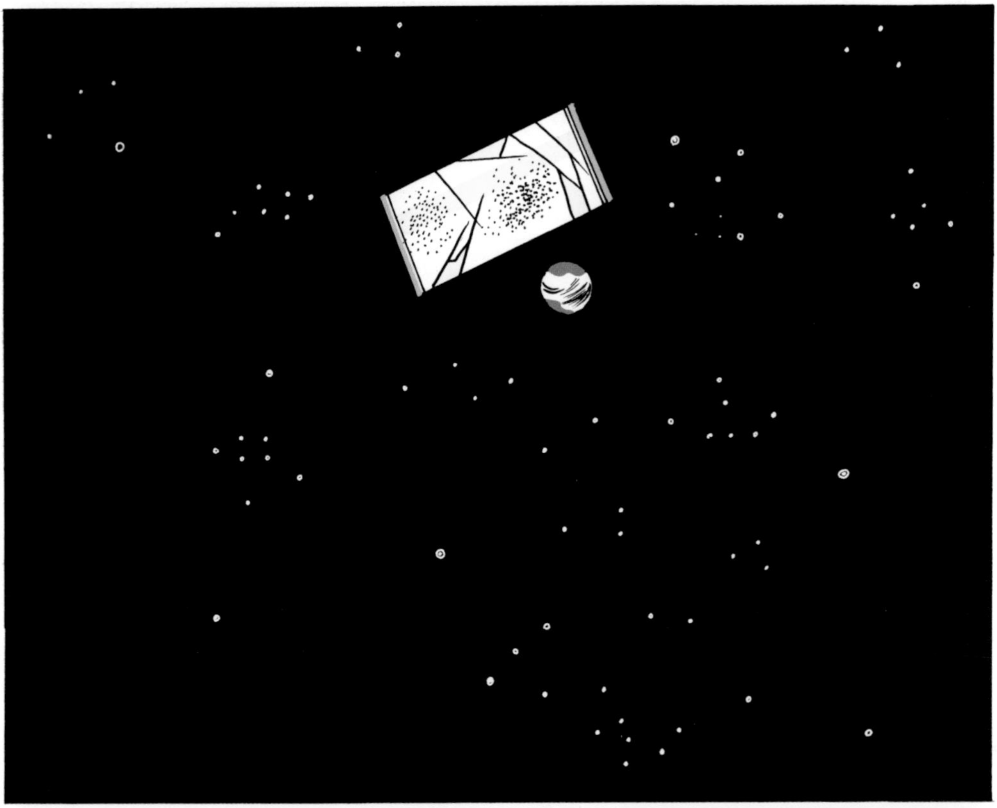

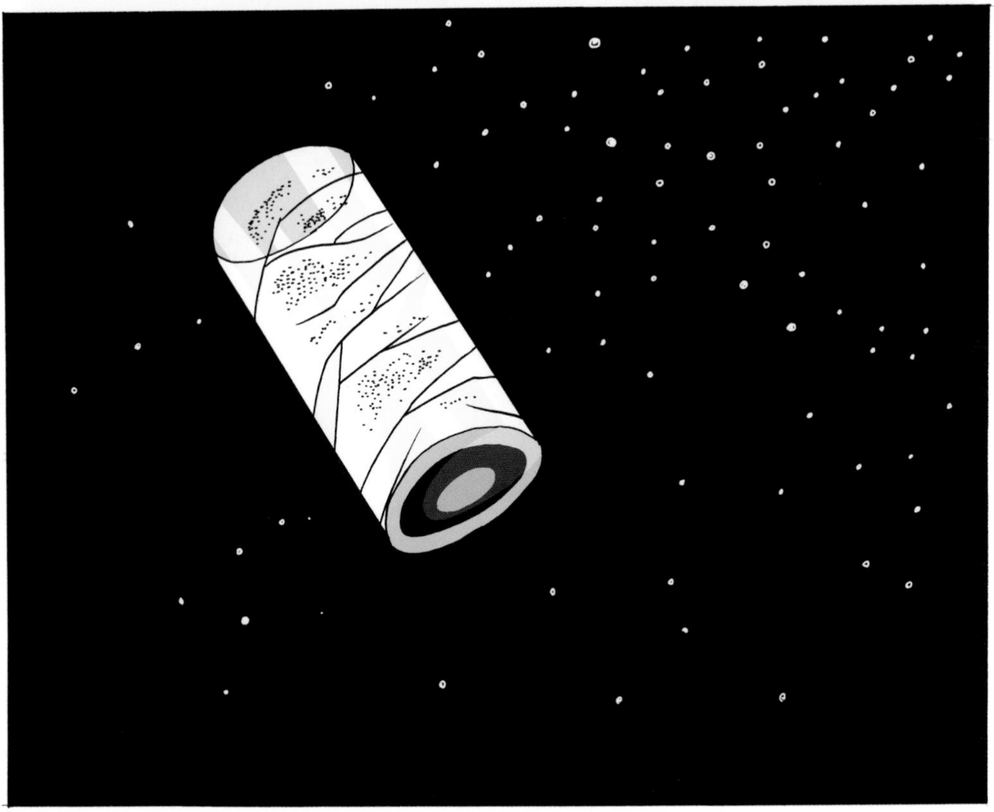

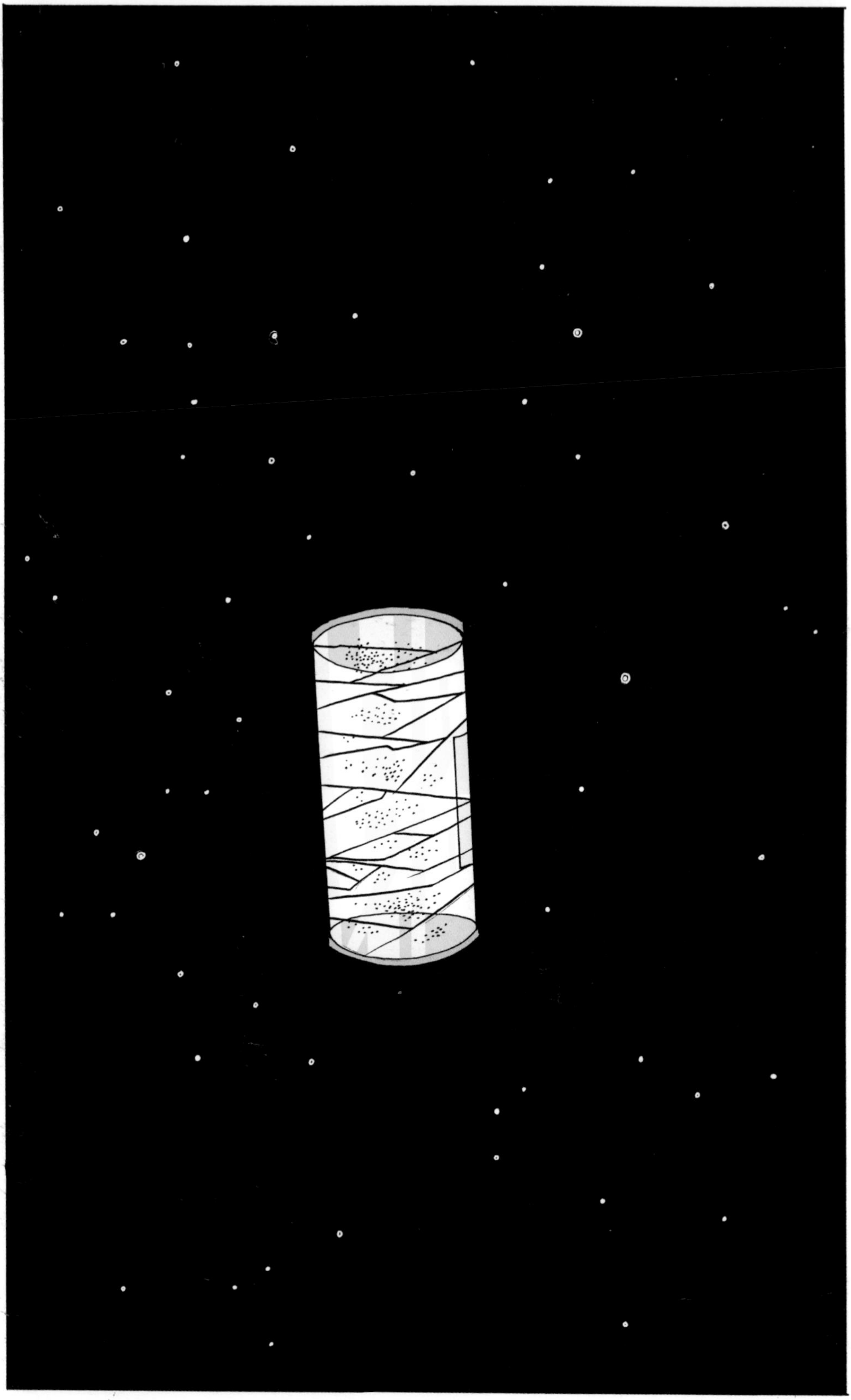

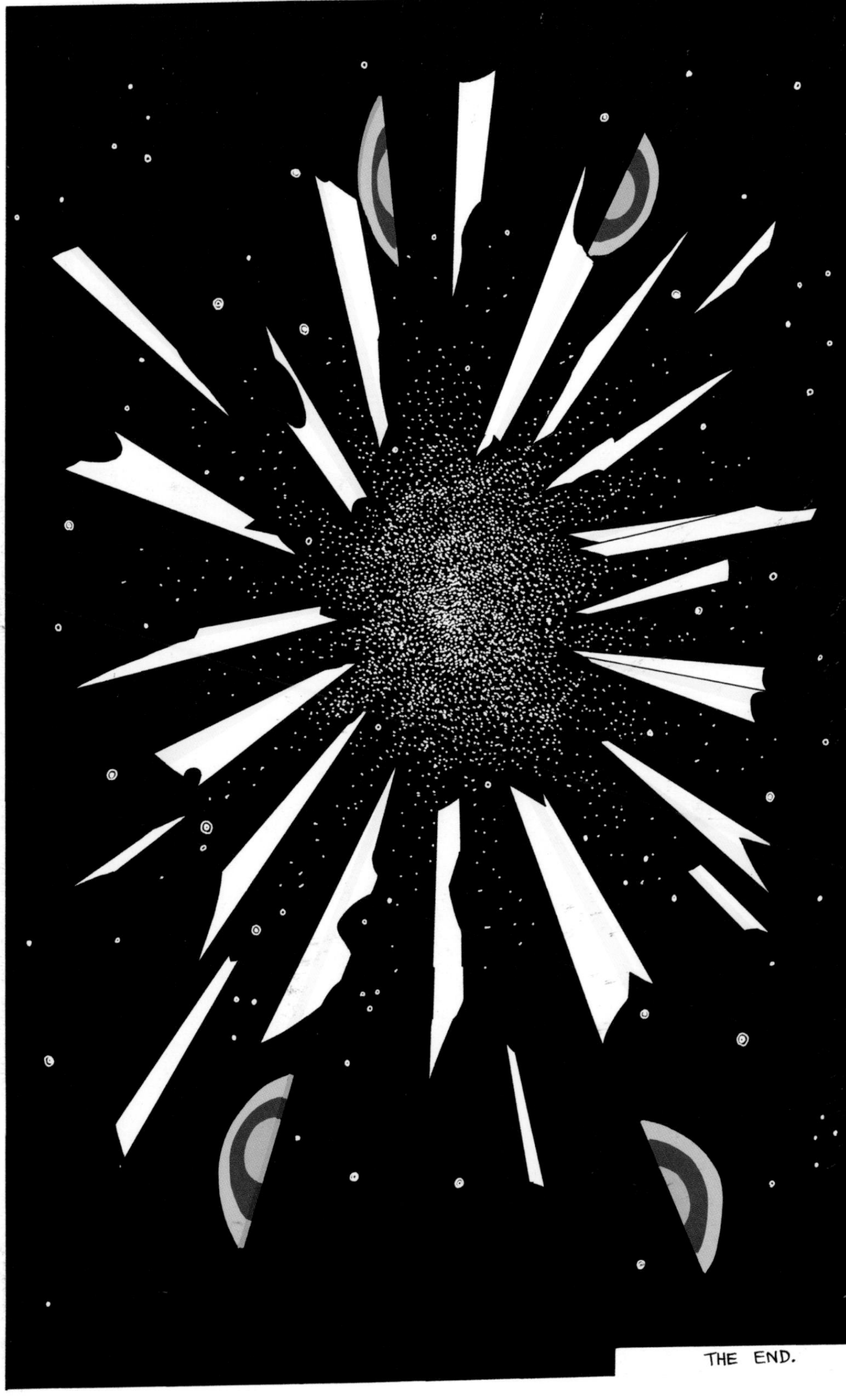
THE END.

DEDICATED TO: JAMES

THANKS TO:

D CORTEZ, S EWENCZYK, S FISHER, D FRANK,
G GROTH, A HUGHES, D KARP, A KARPER,
C KIDD, P MATTOO, D MAZZUCCHELLI,
J McMULLAN, B MCCOY, JC MITCHELL,
C MOORE, G PANTER, T RAGON,
J SAMBORSKI, F SANTORO, D&M SHAW,
B STILLER, Z WAGMAN

VISIT:

WWW.DASHSHAW.COM FOR COMICS/CARTOONS.

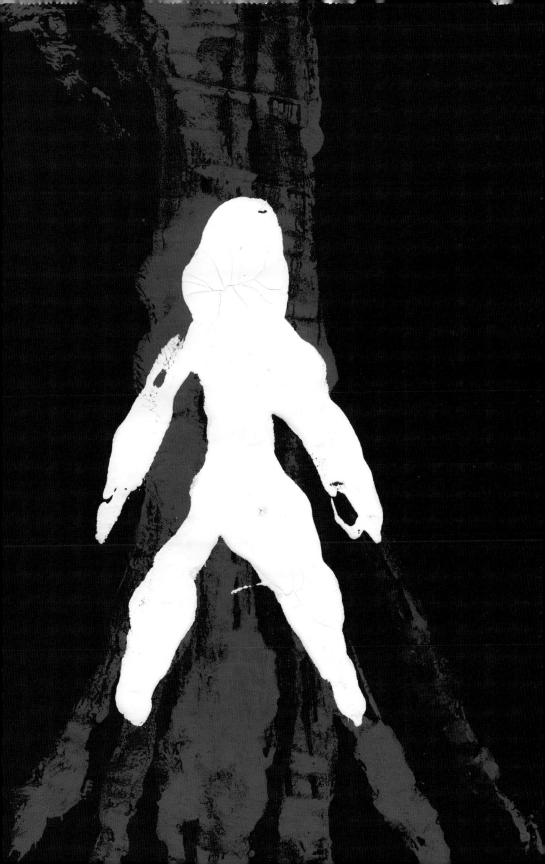

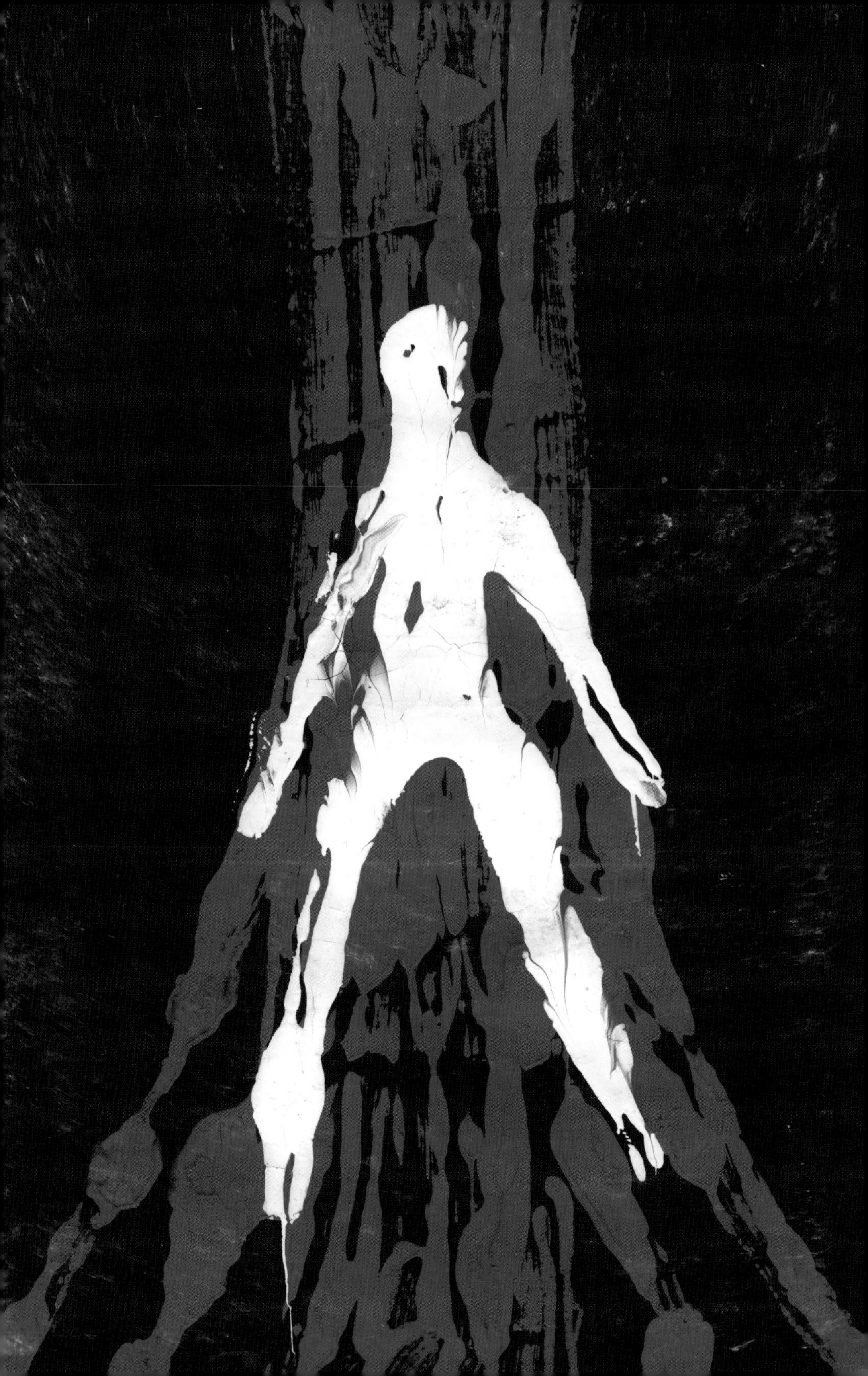